D1795758

THE PROTECTION OF GEOGRAPHICAL INDICATIONS

ELGAR INTELLECTUAL PROPERTY LAW AND PRACTICE

Series Editors: Trevor Cook, *Partner, WilmerHale* and Johanna Gibson, *Herchel Smith Professor of Intellectual Property Law, Queen Mary University of London*

The Elgar Intellectual Property Law and Practice series is a library of works by leading practitioners and scholars covering discrete areas of law in the field of intellectual property. Each title will describe the law in detail, but will also be deeply analytical, highlighting and unpicking the legal issues that are most critical and relevant to practice. Designed to be detailed, focused reference works, the books in this series aim to offer an authoritative statement on the law and practice in key topics within the field, from *Trade Marks* to *Pharmaceuticals*, from *Patent Standards* to *Trade Secrecy* and from *IP Licensing* to *IP Valuation*.

Titles in this series include:

Patent Law in Greater China
Edited by Stefan Luginbuehl and Peter Ganea

Trade Secrecy and International Transactions
Law and Practice
Elizabeth A. Rowe and Sharon K. Sandeen

The Law and Practice of Trademark Transactions
A Global and Local Outlook
Edited by Irene Calboli and Jacques de Werra

Certification and Collective Marks
Law and Practice
Jeffrey Belson

Intellectual Property Jurisdiction Strategies
Where to Litigate Unitary Rights vs National Rights in the EU
Torsten Bjørn Larsen

Cross-Border Copyright Licensing
Law and Practice
Edited by Carlo Scollo Lavizzari and René Viljoen

Copyright in the Information Society
A Guide to National Implementation of the European Directive, Second Edition
Edited by Brigitte Lindner and Ted Shapiro

The Protection of Geographical Indications
Law and Practice, Second Edition
Michael Blakeney

THE PROTECTION OF GEOGRAPHICAL INDICATIONS

Law and Practice, Second Edition

MICHAEL BLAKENEY

Winthrop Professor, The University of Western Australia and Letizia Gianformaggio Chair in Law, University of Ferrara, Italy

ELGAR INTELLECTUAL PROPERTY LAW AND PRACTICE

Edward Elgar
PUBLISHING

Cheltenham, UK • Northampton, MA, USA

© Michael Blakeney 2019

All rights reserved. No part of this publication may be reproduced, stored in a retrieval system or transmitted in any form or by any means, electronic, mechanical or photocopying, recording, or otherwise without the prior permission of the publisher.

Published by
Edward Elgar Publishing Limited
The Lypiatts
15 Lansdown Road
Cheltenham
Glos GL50 2JA
UK

Edward Elgar Publishing, Inc.
William Pratt House
9 Dewey Court
Northampton
Massachusetts 01060
USA

A catalogue record for this book
is available from the British Library

Library of Congress Control Number: 2019951581

This book is available electronically in the **Elgar**online
Law subject collection
DOI 10.4337/9781788975414

ISBN 978 1 78897 540 7 (cased)
ISBN 978 1 78897 541 4 (eBook)

Typeset by Columns Design XML Ltd, Reading

Printed and bound by CPI Group (UK) Ltd, Croydon, CR0 4YY

CONTENTS

EXTENDED TABLE OF CONTENTS

ABBREVIATIONS

ACTA	Anti-counterfeiting Trade Agreement
AO	appellations of origin
AoA	Agreement on Agriculture
AoC	controlled appellation of origin
AUSFTA	Australia-US Free Trade Agreement
BNIC	Bureau National Interprofessionnel du Cognac
CA	Court of Appeal
CAP	Common agricultural policy
CBD	Convention on Biological Diversity
ccTLD	country code top level domain
CEN	European Committee for Standardization
CIS	Customs Information System
CJEU	Court of Justice of the European Union
CMLRev	*Common Market Law Review*
CN	combined nomenclature
DCFTA	Deep and Comprehensive Free Trade Area
DNS	Domain Name System
DSB	Dispute Settlement Body
DSU	Understanding on Rules and Procedures Governing the Settlement of Disputes
EAFRD	European Agricultural Fund for Rural Development
EAGGF	European Agricultural Guidance and Guarantee Fund
EBA	Extended Board of Appeals of the European Patent Organisation
EC	European Community
ECJ	European Court of Justice
ECR	European Court Reports
EEA	European Economic Area
EFOW	European Federation of Origin Wines
EPO	European Patent Office

ETMR	*European Trade Mark Reports*
EU	European Union
FSR	*Fleet Street Reports*
FTAs	Free Trade Agreements
GAC	Government Advisory Committee to the ICANN Board
GATT	General Agreement on Tariffs and Trade
GIs	geographical indications
GRUR	Gewerblicher Rechtsschutz und Urheberrecht: Internationaler Teil
gTLD	generic Top Level Domains
IBPGR	International Board for Plant Genetic Resources
ICAAN	Internet Corporation for Assigned Names and Numbers
ICC	International Chamber of Commerce
IIC	*International Review of Intellectual Property and Competition Law*
INAO	Institut national des appellations d'origine
INTA	The International Trademark Association
Int.T.L.R.	International Trade Law & Regulation
IP	intellectual property
IPQ	*Intellectual Property Quarterly*
IPR	intellectual property right
ISO	International Organization for Standardization
JIPP	*Journal of Intellectual Property Law & Practice*
MATRIC	Midwest Agribusiness Trade Research and Information Center
MFN	Most-favoured-nation
OHIM	Office for Harmonization in the Internal Market
OIV	International Vine and Wine Office/ *Office International de la Vigne et du Vin*
OJ	*Official Journal of the European Communities*
oriGIn	Organization for an International Geographical Indications Network
PBRs	plant breeders' rights
PDO	Protected designations of origin
PGI	Protected geographical indications
psr	produced in a specific region
QWPSR	quality wines produced in specified regions
RAO	Recognised Appellation of Origin
RGI	Recognised Geographical Indication
RPC	*Reports of Patent, Design and Trade Mark Cases*

SCT WIPO	Standing Committee on the Law of Trademarks, Industrial Designs and Geographical Indications
SMEs	small- and medium-sized businesses
SWA	Scotch Whisky Association
TJWIP	*The Journal of World Intellectual Property*
TMR	*Trademark Reporter*
TRIPS Agreement	WTO Agreement on Trade Related Aspects of Intellectual Property Rights
TSG	Traditional Specialities Guaranteed
UDRP	Uniform Domain Name Dispute Resolution Policy
UPOV	Union for the Protection of Plant Varieties
URS	Uniform Rapid Suspension
USC	United States Code
USPTO	United States Patents and Trademarks Office
WIPO	World Intellectual Property Organization
WTO	World Trade Organization

TABLE OF CASES

European Cases

The Office for Harmonization in the Internal Market (OHIM)

World Intellectual Property Organization (WIPO)

World Trade Organization

NATIONAL CASES

Australia

United States of America

TABLE OF LEGISLATION

EU Directives

CONVENTIONS AND OTHER INTERNATIONAL INSTRUMENTS

AGREEMENTS AND FTAS

1

INTRODUCTION

A study undertaken for the European Commission by Chever et al[1] and **1.01** published in October 2012 estimated the worldwide sales value of products sold under geographical indications (GIs) registered in the EU at €54.3 billion in 2010 and had increased by 12 per cent between 2005 and 2010. Over that period wines accounted for 56 per cent of total sales (€30.4 billion), agricultural products and foodstuffs for 29 per cent (€15.8 billion), spirit drinks for 15 per cent (€8.1 billion) and aromatised wines for 0.1 per cent (€31.3 million). Domestic EU sales were the main markets for these products (60 per cent), intra-EU trade accounted for 20 per cent and extra-EU trade accounted for 19 per cent. Over the period, extra-EU trade increased by 29 per cent.

The leading Member State was France (€20.9 billion including 75 per cent for **1.02** wines, 15 per cent for agricultural products and foodstuffs and 10 per cent for spirits), the second was Italy with a balance between the GIs registered in the different schemes (€11.8 billion including 51 per cent for agricultural products and foodstuffs, 48 per cent for wines and 1 per cent for spirits). The next two Member States were Germany (€5.7 billion including 59 per cent for agricultural products and foodstuffs, 40 per cent for wines and 1 per cent for spirits) and the United Kingdom (€5.5 billion including 81 per cent for spirits and 19 per cent for agricultural products and foodstuffs).

This valuable trade is worth protecting and this book examines the detail of **1.03** that protection.

---

1   Chever et al, 2012, 4.

A. SCOPE OF THE BOOK

1.04 The book examines the European laws concerning the protection of GIs and geographical trade marks and looks at the application of those laws in the UK. This introductory chapter reviews the history of GIs and grapples with definitional issues. Chapter 2 looks at the international context, in particular the GIs provisions of the WTO Agreement on Trade Related Aspects of Intellectual Property Rights (TRIPS Agreement), which is increasingly influencing the jurisprudence of the Court of Justice of the European Union (CJEU) on this subject. Chapter 3 examines the European legislation concerned with the protection of GIs and designations of origin for agricultural products and foodstuffs. This is based on the legal framework provided by EU Regulation No 1151/2012 of the European Parliament and of the Council of 21 November 2012 on quality schemes for agricultural products and foodstuffs and Regulation (EU) No 1308/2013 of the European Parliament and of the Council of 17 December 2013 establishing a common organisation of the markets in agricultural products.

1.05 Chapter 4 surveys the European legislation concerning wines, focusing upon Council Regulation No 479/2008 of 29 April 2008 on the common organisation of the market in wine as updated by Commission Regulation (EC) No 607/2009 of 14 July 2009 and by Commission Regulation (EC) No 114/2009 of 6 February 2009. Chapter 5 deals with the protection of GIs and designations of origin for spirits in Europe and looks at the regime inaugurated by Regulation (EC) No 110/2008 of 15 January 2008 of the European Parliament and of the Council of 15 January 2008 on the definition, description, presentation, labelling and the protection of geographical indications of spirit drinks. This chapter also examines Commission Implementing Regulation (EU) No 716/2013 of 25 July 2013, which contains rules dealing in particular with the use of compound terms, allusions, sales denominations and GIs for the presentation of spirit drinks and the application and objections process for GIs.

1.06 Chapter 6 is taken up with the protection of GIs by European trade marks, collective marks and certification marks legislation. It looks at the proposed amendments to the Community Trade Mark Regulation to provide for the registration of certification marks. The common law remedy in passing off is examined in its application to geographical marks and the chapter concludes with an examination of the World Intellectual Property Organization's (WIPO) Uniform Domain Name Dispute Resolution Policy.

Chapter 7 looks at the enforcement of GIs in Europe. This entails a detailed **1.07** consideration of the Civil Enforcement Directive (Directive 2004/48/EC of the European Parliament and of the Council of 29 April 2004 on the enforcement of intellectual property rights) and Regulation (EU) No 608/2013 of the European Parliament and of the Council of 12 June 2013 concerning customs enforcement of intellectual property.

Chapter 8 looks at the protection of EU geographical indications outside **1.08** Europe, both by registration and by Free Trade Agreements (FTAs).

Chapter 9 looks at the impact of Brexit on the protection of British geograph- **1.09** ical indications.

Despite this significant recent European legislative activism on the subject of **1.10** GIs, it is to be expected that further legislation is in prospect, particularly in relation to the protection of GIs for products outside the existing schemes. The EU is currently engaged in trade negotiations with countries which have laws which protect all GIs products. These countries, such as Brazil, India and Thailand, have a significant interest in the protection of their non-agricultural GI products at the EU level beyond the community trade mark system. It is perceived that the lack of a legal framework to protect these products could hamper the ability of the EU to secure protection of EU agricultural and wine and spirits products in these countries. At the same time, the EU is a leading advocate of the extension of the additional protection in Art 23 of the TRIPS Agreement for wines and spirits to agricultural products and handicrafts. This extension debate is examined in Chapter 2. An indication of the EU's thoughts for the future is the publication by the European Commission in 2009 of a study on the protection of GIs for products other than wines, spirits, agricultural products or foodstuffs. The Study analysed 28 non-agricultural products enjoying protection in certain EU Member States and in non-EU countries. It compared the protection systems available to these products and analysed the strengths and weaknesses of the protection systems identified. On 22 March 2013 the Commission published an updated version of this study, which was expected to 'feed into the Commission's on-going analysis of whether action at EU level is required in this area'.[2]

On 15 July 2014 the European Parliament issued a Green Paper, *Making the* **1.11** *most out of Europe's traditional know-how: a possible extension of geographical indication protection of the European Union to non-agricultural products*.[3] This

---

2 Insight Consulting, 2013.
3 COM/2014/0469 final.

was issued as an aid to consultation with all on whether there is a need, in the EU, to increase GI protection for non-agricultural products, and, if so, what approach should be taken.[4] On 6 October 2015 the European Parliament passed a resolution in support of the establishment of:

> a protection instrument ... at European level, as part of a broader strategy for promoting high-quality EU products, based on a stronger commitment from the EU institutions to treat manufacturing and craft industries as a driving force for growth and the completion of the single market, thus enhancing the prestige of locally based manufacturing and handicraft production, supporting local economic development and employment in the areas concerned, boosting tourism, and strengthening consumer confidence.[5]

1.12 The resolution called on the Commission 'to propose without delay a legislative proposal with the aim of establishing a single European system of protection of geographical indications for non-agricultural products' taking account of 'the effects of the new system on producers, their competitors, consumers and Member States'.

B. HISTORY

1.13 The association between the unique qualities of goods and the geographical place of their production explains the genesis of GIs as a vehicle for trade. The international reputation of Toledo steel, Korean Celadon ware, Bruges lace and Burgundy wines secured the access of those products to markets well beyond their place of production. To take advantage of the commercial attractiveness of these local reputations, merchants branded their goods with marks which designated the place of origin of these products. These brands utilised depictions of local animals (panda beer), land marks (Mt Fuji sake), buildings (Pisa silk), heraldic signs (*fleur de lys* butter) or well-known local personalities (Napoleon brandy, Mozart chocolates). In a preliterate society these signs indicating the geographical origins of goods could be regarded as the earliest types of trade mark as these brands were tantamount to a warranty of the quality of goods.

1.14 To protect the commercial reputation of these goods, local legislators passed laws to prevent the adulteration of local produce by the addition of inferior introduced goods or ingredients. These laws punished the adulteration of goods and established systems of marking approved local goods with marks

---

4 Ibid., at 5.
5 2015/2053(INI) at cl.2.

certifying their quality (eg wool marks for cloth, hallmarks for goods made from precious metals). Where the reputation of local goods was attributable to the skills and technology of local artisans, associations or guilds of master workers grew up. The taxing authorities saw an advantage in preserving the skills and revenue-earning capacities of these guilds and conferred upon them a monopoly of manufacture. To regulate this monopoly, the guilds developed service marks, or heraldic-type designs, which were placed upon goods produced by guild members.

Prior to the Industrial Revolution in Britain, which commenced in the **1.15** eighteenth century, industrial production was on a small scale. The corporate form of industrial organisation did not yet exist. Until this time, the principal products that entered international trade were primary products, such as minerals and agricultural produce, and simple manufactured goods, such as pottery and woven fabrics. In the competition to earn revenues from the international trade that was developing at that time, it became apparent that the products of particular regions were more saleable than comparable products from other regions, because of their superior quality. This superior quality resulted either from natural geographic advantages, such as climate and geology (eg Seville oranges, Kentish hops, Roquefort cheese); recipes and food processing techniques local to a region (eg Kyoto bean cakes, Malmesbury mead, Frankfurter sausages) or indigenous manufacturing skills (eg Delft ceramic ware, Bohemian crystal ware).

The historical origins of GIs laws are usually traced back to the mediaeval **1.16** French laws which conferred a number of advantages upon Bordeaux wine producers.[6] Principal among these were the *privilège de la descente* and the *privilège de la barrique*. The former excluded non-Bordeaux wines from the Bordeaux wine market until 11 November of each year. The effect of this was to give Bordeaux wines an advantage in dealings with the lucrative English and Dutch markets as end-of-year dealings were vulnerable to the icing-up of northern ports. Non-Bordeaux wines were marked as such and sequestered in designated wine cellars in the city. This had the effect of developing administrative arrangements for identifying the geographic origins of wines.

The *privilège de la barrique* reinforced the commercial advantage of Bordeaux **1.17** wines as the only wines entitled to a barrel made of superior wood and of specified dimensions, which gave them an advantage for transportation in the merchant vessels of the time. In 1764 the *Arret de la Cour du Parlement concernant la police des vins* obliged each wine grower to identify, by way of a

---

6   See van Caenegem, 2003.

red brand on the bottom of each barrique, his name and that of the parish from which the wine originated to prevent the illicit use of the Bordeaux barrique.

1.18 As with contemporary GIs, this distinctive marking actually provided an opportunity for unscrupulous traders to pass off inferior wines as having a Bordeaux provenance, and within Bordeaux wine from the lower quality parishes was mixed with or passed off as wine from parishes of higher repute.

1.19 The privileges which Bordeaux enjoyed were swept away by the legislation of the National Constituent Assembly, which abolished feudalism and revoked the privileges of towns, provinces, companies and cities throughout France.[7] In seeking to preserve its privileges Bordeaux argued that as the land of the province was unsuitable for any other crops viticulture merited encouragement and protection. This foreshadowed the modern debate around *sui generis* GIs systems where they are justified for the purposes of rural development and the maintenance of rural populations.

1.20 A number of commentators have pointed out that the French appellations system has a much more modern origin than suggested by the mediaeval *privileges* and point to the opening of the railway between Bordeaux and Paris in the mid-nineteenth century as a significant development.[8] Others point to the development of concern for consumers arising from wine adulteration, fraud and falsification.[9] Stanziani points out that the establishment of the French AOC system to protect wines was the outcome of a long process in which the trade mark system was utilised with limited success in a series of nineteenth century cases concerning deceptive designations.[10] This necessitated remedial legislation. The Law of 6 May 1919 concerning *appellations d'origine* was enacted as part of a package of legislation concerning the elimination of fraudulent and misleading designations for wines and food-stuffs. This law sought to provide a methodology for designating wine regions. This was reinforced by the establishment in 1935 of AOCs, under the supervision of a Committee which, from 1947, became the INAO (Institut National des Appellations d'Origine).

1.21 Hughes[11] points out that of the more than 35 protected appellations for cheese in France, only 11 are more than 30 years old and that even Chianti did not

---

7   Decree of 4 August 1789, discussed in Jennings, 2011 at 29.
8   Olszak, 2001 at 6; Hughes, 2006 at 306–7.
9   Stanziani, 2004.
10 Stanziani, 2009.
11 Hughes, 2006, 350.

become a protected *denominazione* in Italy until 1967. He suggests that the European enthusiasm for protecting GIs is more a reflection of contemporary agricultural policy than a desire to preserve historic institutions.

The development of large-scale industrial production, which was a feature of **1.22** the Industrial Revolution, led to demands for the legal protection of the brands of individual producers as indications of the source of their goods. Large-scale production made it possible for manufacturers to produce goods of a consistent quality and their brands became a warranty of the quality of their goods. Unlike GIs which referred to the geographical place of production, manufacturers demanded a system for the protection of their reputation either as producers of goods, or later on, as standing behind the quality of the goods produced in their name. The passing off action was developed by the English courts as a means for manufacturers to protect the indicia of their commercial reputations from misappropriation by those seeking to have a free ride on those reputations. These indicia included names, marks and symbols. To secure protection under the tort of passing off, plaintiffs had first to establish the existence of a commercial reputation in the jurisdiction. A protectable commercial reputation was typically established on the basis of the evidence of others in the trade and of consumers. This tended to take up a considerable amount of court time and as a consequence the registered trade marks system was developed under which possession of a valid trade mark registration certificate replaced the necessity to prove a commercial reputation. Under the registered trade marks system individual traders could enforce the exclusive right to their marks as a private proprietary right.

The evolution of the private trade mark system did not result in the disappear- **1.23** ance of geographical marks. Particularly in Europe, substantial processed foods markets and markets for alcoholic beverages remained dependent upon the continued recognition of geographical marks. Indeed, for European negotiators, the inclusion of these marks in the TRIPS Agreement was a significant achievement of the Uruguay Round of the General Agreement on Tariffs and Trade (GATT).

C. DEFINITIONS

A number of commentators on the law of GIs note a considerable diversity in **1.24** the terminology concerning GIs. Norma Dawson[12] among others[13] suggests

---

12 Dawson, 2000, 591–2.
13 See eg, Conrad, 1996, 13–14.

that this terminological diversity might result from the various international agreements that have attempted to deal with GIs. The Paris Convention 1883 in Art 10 provided for the seizure of imports of goods bearing 'false indications of the source of goods'. This expression was repeated in the Madrid Agreement for the Repression of False or Deceptive Indications of Source of Goods 1891. The International Convention on the Use of Appellations of Origin and Denominations of Cheeses ('Stresa Convention') 1951 borrowed the term *appellations d'origine* from the French AOC legislation. This in turn was repeated in the Lisbon Agreement for the Protection of Appellations of Origin and their Registration, 1958. Article 2 of the Lisbon Agreement defined 'appellation of origin' to mean:

> the geographical name of a country, region, or locality, which serves to designate a product originating therein, the quality and characteristics of which are due exclusively or essentially to the geographical environment, including natural and human factors.

1.25 Article 22 of the TRIPS Agreement defines geographical indications as:

> indications which identify a good as originating in the territory of a Member, or a region or locality in that territory, where a given quality, reputation or other characteristic of the good is essentially attributable to its geographical origin.

1.26 This definition expands the Lisbon Agreement concept of appellation of origin to protect goods which merely derive a reputation from their place of origin without possessing a given quality or other characteristics which are due to that place. Also, under the TRIPS Agreement, to be protected, a GI has to be an indication, but not necessarily the name of a geographical place on earth.

1.27 The WTO Secretariat in a survey of national laws identified 23 different terms and as a consequence adopted the term 'indications of geographical origin' to designate the different expressions used by WTO Members to protect geographical origin of products.[14]

1.28 Dev Gangjee[15] suggests that the terminological diversity in this area may be attributable to the various policies to be served by GIs, such as agricultural marketing, rural development, the preservation of traditional knowledge and cultural heritage.

---

14 Note by the WTO Secretariat IP/C/W/253, dated April 2001, in 'Review under Article 24.2 of the application of the provisions of the section of the TRIPS Agreement on geographical indications. Summary of the responses to the checklist of questions (IP/C/13 and Add.1)'. For a more recent global survey of GIs legislation see O'Connor et al, 2007.

15 Gangjee, 2012, 2–18.

It should be noted that as early as the Madrid Agreement for the Repression **1.29** of False or Deceptive Indications of Source on Goods 1891, most laws embrace indirect GIs. The Madrid Agreement in Art 1(1) provides for the seizure on importation of '[a]ll goods bearing a false or deceptive indication by which one of the countries to which this Agreement applies, or a place situated therein, is directly or indirectly indicated as being the country or place of origin'. An example of such an indirect indication mentioned during the 1934 London Revision Conference was the wax from the carnauba fan palm tree which, although not an actual place name, was 'indissolubly linked' to its origins in the north-eastern savannahs of Brazil.[16] A more modern illustration is 'Basmati' as indicative of the Indian sub-continent.[17]

Advocate General Colomer, in *Budějovický Budvar, národní podnik v Rudolf* **1.30** *Ammersin GmbH*[18] had to consider whether the trade mark 'BUD' was an indirect indication of the Bohemian town Česke Budějovice (formerly Budweis). He explained:

> 68. Geographical indications and even designations of origin do not always consist of geographical names. They are called 'direct' when they do and 'indirect' when they do not, provided the indication or designation at least informs consumers that the foodstuff to which it relates comes from a specific place, region or country.
>
> ...
>
> 71. Regardless of whether the Czech public can guess where 'Bud beer' comes from, it must be ascertained whether the expression 'Bud' is sufficiently clear to evoke a product, beer, and its origin, the town of Česke Budějovice.
>
> 72. In the same way that the words 'cava' or 'grappa' call to mind the Spanish and Italian birthplaces of a sparkling wine and of a liqueur respectively and that 'feta' identifies a Greek cheese were it to be found that 'Bud' represents a geographical indication, Czech consumers would have to associate the expression with a precise place and with the brewing of beer.

Another example of an indirect GI in European litigation is the *Bocksbeutel* **1.31** bottle, which has a characteristic bulbous shape and is used for the marketing of wine in Franconia, Baden-Franconia parts of Central Baden.[19]

---

16 See Gangjee, 2012, 66.
17 See Blakeney and Lightbourne, 2005.
18 [2003] ECR I-13617.
19 *Criminal proceedings against Karl Prantl*, Case 16/83 [1984] ECR 01299.

2

INTERNATIONAL GEOGRAPHICAL INDICATIONS REGIMES

A. PRECURSORS TO TRIPS

2.01 The GIs provisions of the TRIPS Agreement were anticipated as early as the 1883 Paris Convention on Industrial Property, which, as will be seen below imposed merely general obligations in relation to 'indications of source or appellations of origin' which were undefined terms. The Madrid Agreement for the Repression of False or Deceptive Indications of Source of Goods 1891, which was enacted as a special treaty under the Paris Convention, contained more specific obligations, but it was not until the Lisbon Agreement on the Protection of Appellations of Origin and their International Registration 1958 that at least appellations of origin were defined and elements of this definition were carried forward into the definition of GIs in the TRIPS Agreement.

Prior to the Lisbon Agreement, the 1951 Stresa Convention proposed a **2.02** system for the protection of appellations of origin and designations for cheeses contained in an annex to the Convention. The Lisbon Agreement, by way of contrast, envisaged protection of appellations of origin by their registration. The TRIPS Agreement did not prescribe a preferred method for the protection of GIs but leaves this to signatories to decide. The possible establishment of a system for the registration of GIs was left to subsequent negotiation and as will be seen below, after more than 15 years of deliberations, the TRIPS signatories have yet to reach agreement on this subject.

1. Paris Convention for the Protection of Industrial Property 1883[1]

(a) Scope

The first multilateral agreement, which included 'indications of source or **2.03** appellations of origin' as objects for protection by national industrial property laws, was the Paris Convention. According to Article 2(2) the objects of protection of industrial property include 'indications of source or appellations of origin'. However, the Paris Convention does not define these terms and does not expressly require Member States to provide for protection of indications of source and appellations of origin.

Article 2(3) of the Paris Convention provides that 'industrial property shall be **2.04** understood in the broadest sense and shall apply not only to industry and commerce proper, but likewise to agricultural and extractive industries and to all manufactured or natural products, for example, wines, grain, tobacco leaf, fruit, cattle, minerals, mineral waters, beer, flowers, and flour'.

(b) Seizure of goods bearing a false indication of source

Article 9(1) of the Paris Convention provides for the seizure upon importation **2.05** of all goods unlawfully bearing a legally protected 'trademark or trade name'. Article 9(3) provides that 'seizure shall take place at the request of the public prosecutor, or any other competent authority, or any interested party, whether

---

1   The Paris Convention was agreed in 1883 and complemented by the Madrid Protocol of 1891. It was revised at Brussels (1900), Washington (1911), The Hague (1925), London (1934), Lisbon (1958) and Stockholm (1967), and amended in 1979. The Paris Convention as of September 2013 had 175 contracting parties.

a natural person or a legal entity, in conformity with the domestic legislation of each country'.

2.06 Article 10(1) provides for the application of the provisions of Art 9 'in cases of direct or indirect use of a false indication of the source of the goods or the identity of the producer, manufacturer or merchant'. Unlike Art 9(1), which catches misleading indications, Art 10(1) requires that the indications be factually false and not misleading. Although the provision only speaks of 'indications of source', it is understood that it includes 'appellations of origin', as referred to in Art 1(2).[2] As Art 10(1) refers to any direct or indirect use, the false indication does not have to be expressed in words and appear on the product. It would include also the use of a false indication in advertising or on business documents.

2.07 The only sanction referred to in Art 10(1) is seizure of the goods concerned but no further civil or criminal sanctions are envisaged. Also the obligation to seize goods on importation only applies to the extent that such a measure has been adopted under national law.

2.08 Under Art 10(2), any:

> producer, manufacturer, or merchant whether a natural person or legal entity, engaged in the production or manufacture of or trade in such goods and established either in the locality falsely indicated as the source, or in the region where such locality is situated, or in the country falsely indicated, or in the country where the false indication of source is used, shall in any case be deemed an interested party.

(c) Repression of unfair competition

2.09 Article 10*bis* also affords protection against false or misleading indications of source as a means of repressing unfair competition. Article 10*bis* (2) defines as an act of unfair competition 'any act of competition contrary to honest practices in industrial or commercial matters'.

2.10 The ECJ, in its various trade marks determinations, has observed that the requirement to act in accordance with honest practices in industrial or commercial matters 'constitutes in substance the expression of a duty to act fairly in relation to the legitimate interests of the trade mark proprietor'.[3]

---

2 Pflüger, 2011, 274.

3 See Case C-63/97 *Bayerische Motorenwerke AG v Deenik* [1999] ECR I-905 at [61], Case C-100/02 *Gerolsteiner Brunnen GmbH & Co v Putsch GmbH* [2004] ECR I-691 at [24], Case C-245/02 *Anheuser–Busch Inc v Budejovicky Budvar np* [2004] I-10989 at [82], Case 228/03 *Gillette Co v LA-Laboratories Ltd Oy* [2005] ECR I-2337 at [41] and Case C-17/06 *Céline SARL v Céline SA* [2007] ECR I-7041 at [33].

2. Madrid Agreement for the Repression of False or Deceptive Indications of Source of Goods 1891[4]

(a) Seizure of goods bearing a false or misleading indication

The original form of the Paris Convention prohibited the use of false GIs. A **2.11** number of signatory nations proposed a more comprehensive form of regulation for what was considered to be a significant intellectual property abuse. The 1891 Madrid Agreement concerning the protection of geographical indications was their response. Article 1(1) provided that all goods 'bearing a false or misleading indication' to a signatory country, or to a place in that country 'shall be seized on importation'. Article 1(2) provided for seizure also 'in the country where the false or deceptive indication of source has been applied, or into which the goods bearing the false or deceptive indication have been imported'. Where the laws of a country do not permit seizure upon importation Art 1(3) provides that such seizure shall be replaced by prohibition of importation. In the absence of any special sanctions ensuring the repression of false or deceptive indications of source, Art 1(5) provides that 'the sanctions provided by the corresponding provisions of the laws relating to marks or trade names shall be applicable'.

Article 2(1) provides that seizure shall take place at the instance of the customs **2.12** authorities, who shall immediately inform the interested party, whether an individual person or a legal entity, in order that such party may, if it so desires, take appropriate steps in connection with the seizure effected as a conservatory measure. However, the public prosecutor or any other competent authority may demand seizure either at the request of the injured party or *ex officio*; the procedure shall then follow its normal course. Excluded from seizure by Art 2(2) are goods in transit.

(b) Prohibited use of deceptive indications in advertising, etc

Article 3*bis* provides that signatory countries undertake to prohibit the use, in **2.13** connection with the sale or display or offering for sale of any goods, of all indications in the nature of publicity capable of deceiving the public as to the source of the goods, and appearing on signs, advertisements, invoices, wine lists, business letters or papers, or any other commercial communication.

---

4 The Madrid Agreement was adopted in 1891 and revised at Washington (1911), The Hague (1925), London (1934), and Lisbon (1958). It was supplemented by the Additional Act of Stockholm (1967), and as of September 2013 had 36 contracting parties.

(c) Exception of indications of name and address

2.14 Article 3 provides that the Madrid provisions shall not prevent the vendor from indicating his name or address upon goods coming from a country other than that in which the sale takes place; but in such case the address or the name must be accompanied by an exact indication in clear characters of the country or place of manufacture or production, or by some other indication sufficient to avoid any error as to the true source of the wares.

(d) Generic indications

2.15 Article 4 permitted the courts of each signatory to decide what appellations, on account of their generic character, do not fall within the provisions of the Agreement. However, this article excluded from this reservation regional appellations concerning the source of products of the vine. This provision apparently explained why this Agreement failed to attract the accession of significant trading nations such as the USA, Germany and Italy.

3. International Convention on the Use of Appellations of Origin and Denominations of Cheeses ('Stresa Convention') 1951

2.16 The parties to the Stresa Convention, which are some of the cheese-producing countries of Europe,[5] 'pledge themselves to prohibit and repress within their respective territorial confines the use, in the language of the state or in a foreign language, of the "appellations d'origine"', denominations and designations of cheeses contrary to the principles stated in Arts 2–9 inclusive. The Convention, which entered into force on 1 September 1953, applies to all specifications which constitute false information as to the origin, variety, nature or specific qualities of cheeses, which are stated on products which might be confused with cheese. The term 'cheese', according to Art 2.1 of the Convention, is reserved for 'fresh and matured products obtained by draining after the coagulation of milk, cream, skimmed or partially skimmed milk or a combination of these', or by 'products obtained by the partial concentration of whey, or of buttermilk, but excluding the addition of any fatty matter to milk'.

2.17 Article 3 provides that the appellations of origin of those cheeses 'manufactured or matured in traditional regions, by virtue of local, loyal and uninterrupted usages', which are listed in Annex A, are exclusively reserved to those cheeses 'whether they are used alone or accompanied by a qualifying or even corrective term such as "type", "kind", "imitation" or other term'. Annex A

---

5 The Stresa Convention was ratified by Austria (12 June 1953); Denmark (2 August 1953); France (20 May 1952); the Netherlands (29 October 1955); Norway (31 August 1951); Sweden (27 January 1951) and Switzerland (5 June 1951).

lists: Gorgonzola, Parmigiana Romano, Pecorino Romano and Roquefort. Annex B lists a number of designations for cheese that are prohibited by Art 4.2 for products which do not meet the requirements provided by Contracting Parties in relation to 'shape, weight, size, type and colour of the rind and curd, as well as the fat content of the cheese'. Listed in Annex B are Asiago, Camembert, Cambozola, Danablu, Edam, Emmental, Esrom, Fiore Sardo, Fontina, Gruyère, Pinnzgauer Berkäse, Samsöe and Svecia.

The Stresa Convention came into force prior to the EEC Treaty and its **2.18** regime providing for the free movement of goods.

In the *Deserbais* case[6] the Court had to construe Art 234 (now Art 307) of the **2.19** EC Treaty which provided that the application of the Treaty did not affect the duty of the EC Member State in respect the rights of non-Member countries under a prior international agreement. The Stresa Convention had been signed before the EEC Treaty entered into force and only Denmark, France, Italy and the Netherlands were parties to it. The Court found on the facts that in this case, the rights of non-Member countries were not involved, and therefore, a Member State could not rely on the provisions of a pre-existing international agreement to justify restrictions on the marketing of products coming from another Member State, where the marketing was otherwise lawful by virtue of the free movement of goods provided for by the Treaty.

Similarly, in the *Cambozola* case[7] the ECJ ruled that the free movement of **2.20** goods principle was subordinated to the Stresa Convention and Council Regulation (EEC) No 2081/92 permitting the registration and enforcement of rights in relation to designations of origin.

4. Lisbon Agreement for the Protection of Appellations of Origin and their Registration 1958[8]

(a) Introduction

The Lisbon Agreement established an international system of registration and **2.21** protection of appellations of origin (AO) among members of the Lisbon Union, which comprised signatory states. Article 1(2) obliged parties to the Agreement to protect on their territories 'the appellations of origin of products' of signatory countries, 'recognized and protected as such in the

---

6 [1988] ECR-4907, 22 September 1988.
7 [1999] ECR-1, 4 March 1999.
8 This agreement was concluded in Lisbon on 31 October 1958. It was revised in Stockholm in 1967 and amended in 1979. As of September 2013 there were 28 contracting parties.

country of origin' and registered at the International Bureau of WIPO. Article 4 of the Agreement provides that the Agreement does not exclude the protection already granted to appellations of origin in each of the countries of the Lisbon Union by virtue of other international instruments, such as the Paris and the Madrid Agreement for the Repression of False or Deceptive Indications of Source on Goods, 'or by virtue of national legislation or court decisions'.

2.22 The Lisbon Agreement failed to attract support from more than a few nations (only 28 signatories by September 2013[9]). Gervais[10] observed from an examination of all current appellations on the Lisbon register that 11 countries hold 97.5 per cent of all entries, with the top three holding over 78 per cent, of which France holds 62.5 per cent (almost 90 per cent of which was for wines and spirits). One problem was that accession was confined to those nations which protected appellations of origin 'as such'. Thus, states which protected this form of intellectual property under trade mark, unfair competition or consumer protection laws were locked out. Also, the Agreement did not make an exception for GIs, which had already become generic in Member States.

(b) Protected indications

2.23 Article 2(1) of the Agreement defined 'appellation of origin' to mean 'the geographical name of a country, region, or locality, which serves to designate a product originating therein, the quality and characteristics of which are due exclusively or essentially to the geographical environment, including natural and human factors'. The country of origin is defined in Art 2(2) as 'the country whose name, or the country in which is situated the region or locality whose name, constitutes the appellation of origin which has given the product its reputation'.

(c) Breadth of protection

2.24 Article 3 of the Lisbon Agreement requires that '[p]rotection shall be ensured against any usurpation or imitation, even if the true origin of the product is indicated or if the appellation is used in translated form or accompanied by terms such as "kind," "type," "make," "imitation," or the like'. As will be seen below, this language was included in Art 23 of the TRIPS Agreement, to provide for additional protection for wines and spirits. The Acts of the Lisbon

---

9   Algeria, Bosnia and Herzegovina, Bulgaria, Burkina Faso, Congo, Costa Rica, Cuba, Czech Republic, Democratic People's Republic of Korea, France, Gabon, Georgia, Hungary, Islamic Republic of Iran, Israel, Italy, Mexico, Montenegro, Nicaragua, Peru, Portugal, Republic of Moldova, Serbia, Slovakia, the former Yugoslav Republic of Macedonia, Togo, Tunisia.

10   Gervais, 2010 at 79.

Conference define usurpation as the 'illicit adoption' or counterfeiting of an appellation.[11]

(d) Registration

Article 5(1) provided for the registration of AO at the International Bureau of **2.25** WIPO, at the request of the IP offices of the countries of the Lisbon Union, 'in the name of any natural persons or legal entities, public or private, having, according to their national legislation, a right to use such appellations'. Thus, international protection is based upon the existence of a national registration.

Article 5(2) requires the International Bureau, without delay, to notify the **2.26** relevant offices of the various countries of the Lisbon Union of such registrations and for these to be published in a periodical.

Article 5(3) provides for an IP office of a Member country to 'declare that it **2.27** cannot ensure the protection of an AO whose registration has been notified to it' provided that this is notified to the International Bureau of WIPO, together with an indication of the grounds therefor, within a period of one year from the receipt of the notification of registration and 'provided that such declaration is not detrimental, in the country concerned, to the other forms of protection of the appellation which the owner thereof may be entitled to claim under Article 4'. Article 5(4) provides that such declaration may not be opposed by the Offices of the countries of the Union after the expiration of the period of one year from receipt of the notification. Article 5(5) requires the International Bureau of WIPO, as soon as possible, to notify the office of the country of origin of any declaration made under Art 5(3) by the office of another country. Article 5(5) provides that 'the interested party', when informed by the national office of the declaration made by another country, 'may resort, in that other country, to all the judicial and administrative remedies open to the nationals of that country'. The Lisbon Agreement does not define what is meant by 'interested party', although Art 8 envisages that legal action required for ensuring the protection of appellations of origin may be taken in each of the countries of the Lisbon Union 'by any interested party, whether a natural person or a legal entity, whether public or private'.

Where an appellation which has been granted protection in a given country **2.28** pursuant to notification of its international registration has already been used by third parties in that country from a date prior to such notification, Art 5(6) provides that the competent office of that country 'shall have the right to grant

---

11 *Actes de la conférence reunie A Lisbonne du 6 au 31 octobre 1958* BIRPI, Geneva, 1963.

to such third parties a period not exceeding two years to terminate such use', on condition that it advises the International Bureau accordingly during the three months following the expiration of the period of one year provided for in Art 5(3).

(e) Duration of protection

2.29 The Lisbon Agreement makes an unclear reference to the duration of protection of a registered AO. Article 7, which is sub-headed 'Period of Validity', provides: '(1) Registration effected at the International Bureau in conformity with Article 5 shall ensure, without renewal, protection for the whole of the period referred to in the foregoing Article.' Article 5 makes no specific reference to a time period for protection; its only reference to time periods relates to the process of declaring that certain appellations cannot be protected. However, since Art 7(1) refers to an absence of renewals, the assumption is that an appellation is protected for as long as it remains an appellation in the relevant country of origin.

(f) Generic appellations

2.30 Article 6 provides that an appellation which has been granted protection in one of the countries of the Lisbon Union pursuant to the procedure under Art 5 cannot, in that country, be deemed to have become generic, as long as it is protected as an appellation of origin in the country of origin.

(g) Enforcement

2.31 Article 8 of the Lisbon Agreement provides that legal action required for ensuring the protection of AO may be taken in each of the countries of the Lisbon Union under the provisions of national legislation:

1. at the instance of the competent Office or at the request of the public prosecutor;
2. by any interested party, whether a natural person or a legal entity, whether public or private.

5. The International Wine Organization

2.32 The idea for an international organisation to represent the interests of the wine industry were prompted by the nineteenth century phylloxera epidemic. In 1922 the French Society for Encouraging Agriculture suggested the establishment of the International Wine Organization. International conferences were held in Genoa in 1923 and in Paris in 1924, and on 29 November 1924 Spain, Tunisia, France, Portugal, Hungary, Luxembourg, Greece and Italy signed an agreement establishing the 'International Office of Vine and

Wine' (OIV) in Paris. The OIV came into existence on 3 December 1927 after ratification of the agreement by five countries. According to its constituent instrument of 1924, the OIV was responsible for ensuring the protection of appellations of origin. In 1947 it adopted an initial definition of appellation of origin.

On 4 September 1958 the organisation's name was changed to the International Vine and Wine Office (*Office International de la Vigne et du Vin*) (OIV). **2.33**

In 1992, the OIV adopted two definitions 'Recognised Geographical Indication (RGI)' and 'Recognised Appellation of Origin (RAO)'.[12] In 1994 the OIV adopted a resolution on the relationship between RAO and RGI and the brands, which provides for an equal level of protection for brands, recognised appellations of origin, recognised GIs and recognised traditional names. This protection is determined by priority (of recognition, registration or usage depending on the type of distinctive brand) while taking into account the distinctive character and reputation. **2.34**

During its General Assembly in Germany, the OIV added to its recommendations through the section on homonyms and a resolution on principles regarding GIs and the Internet. **2.35**

Following a 35-nation agreement on 3 April 2001, which came into effect on 1 January 2004, the International Vine and Wine Office was replaced by the International Organisation of Vine and Wine. The responsibility to protect appellations of origin was included in the Agreement of 3 April 2001 establishing the International Organisation of Vine and Wine. The 2012 International Standard for the Labelling of Wines represents the deliberations of the Member States between 1983 and 2011 and concerns 'the compulsory information which appears on the labelling of pre-packed wines in view of their sale to the consumer, as well as optional information left to the discretion of manufacturers or Member States'.[13] The chapter on compulsory information includes the following standards on denominations: **2.36**

2.   COMPULSORY INFORMATION

2.1.   The denomination of the product

2.1.1   The use of the word 'wine'.

---

12   http://www.oiv.int/oiv/info/entableaucomparatifs.
13   www.oiv.int/../OIV%20Wine%20Labelling%20Standard%20EN_2012.

The use of the word 'wine' or, (without prejudice to article 2.1.2.2) other substitutive recognised indication, is obligatory in the labelling of the product which respects the definition quoted in article 1.2.1. It may be completed by mentioning its type or particular classification. Subject to the provisions which the Member States make compulsory for their own production, no opposition can be made to the release onto the market of the product which respects this definition and which is presented under the single name 'wine'.

Without prejudice to the particular provisions made for certain products which bear in their name the word 'wine' alongside complementary information, the word 'wine' used alone can only apply to the product defined in article 1.2.1.

2.1.2.   Recognised appellation of origin or recognised geographic indication

2.1.2.1 Definitions

Recognised Geographic Indication

It is the name of the country, the region or the place used in the designation of a product originating from this country, region, place or area defined to this end under this name and recognised by the competent authorities of the country concerned.

As far as wine is concerned, the recognition of this name:

* is linked to a quality and/or to a characteristic of the product attributed to the geographic milieu including natural or human factors; and
* is subordinate to the grapes being harvested in the country, region, place or defined area.

As far as spirits of a vitivinicultural origin are concerned, the recognition of this name:

* is linked to a quality and/or a characteristic that the product acquires as a result of a decisive phase of its production; and
* is subordinate to this decisive phase being carried out in the country, region, place or defined area.

Recognised Appellation of Origin

It is the name of the country, region or the place used in the designation of a product originating from this country, region, place or area as defined to this end, under this name and recognised by the competent authorities of the country concerned.

As far as wine and spirit beverages from a vitivinicultural origin are concerned, the recognised appellation of origin

* refers to a product whose quality or characteristics are due exclusively or essentially to the geographic milieu, including natural and human factors, and
* is subordinate to the harvest as well as its transformation in the country, region, place or defined area.

2.1.2.2 When a wine benefits from a recognised appellation of origin or from a recognised geographic indication such as defined above, and figures on a list published by the International Organisation of Vine and Wine, the use of this recognised appellation of origin or the recognised geographic indication on the label, conforming to the laws of the producer country, is obligatory.

In this case the recognised appellation of origin or the recognised geographic indication can constitute the denomination of the product and take the place of the word 'wine'.

To avoid confusion with other designations it is recommended that the use of a complementary mention characterising the product, such as 'Appellation of Origin ...' is made compulsory.

The OIV Extraordinary General Assembly approved the 2009–2012 Strategic **2.37** Plan at its meeting in October 2008. Point M of the Strategic Plan (Designation and labelling), states in Action M.6 to 'draw up an inventory for wines and spirits of viticultural origin, on the Denomination of Origin and Geographic Indications in OIV Member States including their respective national legislations'. This list is a compilation of the names of vitivinicultural GIs or appellations of origin which are legally protected and recognised. The list provides information based on notifications by the relevant authorities in each state. The list carries no rights or legal obligations.

The OIV resolution on geographical indications and homonyms[14] defines the **2.38** homonymy of a geographic indicator as used to designate a wine or spirit beverage of viticultural origin as used in several countries with a common spelling and/or identical pronunciation and recommends that Member States of the OIV should, when setting differentiation rules for these homonymous names:

- consider the official recognition used in the country of origin,
- consider the length of time the name has been in use,
- consider whether the usage is in good faith,
- consider the importance of presenting the homonymous labels to marketing,
- encourage mentioning sufficient distinguishing information to avoid confusion of consumers.

B. THE WTO TRIPS AGREEMENT

The protection of GIs was a key demand of European negotiators at the **2.39** Uruguay Round of the GATT. The competing positions were those of

---

14   Resolution ECO 3/99 at http://www.oiv.int/oiv/info/enresolution.

the EU and Switzerland, which proposed a French style of protection, and the USA, which favoured the protection of GIs through a certification mark system. In the result, section 3 of Part VII of the TRIPS Agreement covers four main topics: (a) protection of GIs; (b) GIs and trade marks; (c) additional protection for GIs for wines and spirits; and (d) review of section 3. These topics are examined below together with an account of GIs disputes under the TRIPS Agreement.

1. Protection of geographical indications

(a) Definition

2.40 Article 22.1 of the TRIPS Agreement defines geographical indications for the purposes of the Agreement as 'indications which identify a good as originating in the territory of a Member, or a region or locality in that territory, where a given quality, reputation or other characteristic of the good is essentially attributable to its geographical origin'. This definition expands the Lisbon Agreement concept of appellation of origin to protect goods which merely derive a reputation from their place of origin without possessing a given quality or other characteristics which is due to that place.

2.41 In its only determinations to date on GIs under the TRIPS Agreement the WTO Dispute Panel ruled that a 'designation of origin' and 'geographical indication' as defined in EC legislation in different terms were a subset of geographical indications as defined in Art 22.1.[15]

2.42 Under the TRIPS Agreement a GI to be protected has to be an indication, but not necessarily the name of a geographical place on earth. Thus, for example, 'Basmati' is taken to be an indication for rice coming from the Indian subcontinent, although it is not a place name as such. The indication has to identify goods as originating in the territory of a Member, a region or a locality of that territory. This definition also indicates that goods to be protected should originate in the territory, region or locality to which they are associated. This suggests that licences for the use of GIs cannot be protected under the TRIPS Agreement.

---

15 European Communities – Protection of Trademarks and Geographical Indications for Agricultural Products and Foodstuffs, Complaint by the United States, Report of the Panel (hereinafter '*Panel Report, EC – Trademarks and Geographical Indications (US)*'), WT/DS174/R, 15 March 2005, para 7.738; European Communities – Protection of Trademarks and Geographical Indications for Agricultural Products and Foodstuffs, Complaint by Australia, Report of the Panel (hereinafter '*Panel Report, EC – Trademarks and Geographical Indications (Australia)*'), WT/DS290/R 15 March 2005, para 7.711.

The TRIPS definition permits Members to protect the GIs of goods where **2.43** the quality, reputation or other characteristic of goods are attributable to their geographical origin.

(b) Permitted methods for the protection of geographical indications

Article 22.2 of the TRIPS Agreement requires that 'in respect of geographical **2.44** indications', Members of the WTO shall provide the 'legal means' for 'interested parties' to prevent:

(a) the use of any means in the designation or presentation of a good that indicates or suggests that the good in question originates in a geographical area other than the true place of origin in a manner which misleads the public as to the geographical origin of the good;

(b) any use which constitutes an act of unfair competition within the meaning of Article 10*bis* of the Paris Convention (1967).

i. 'In respect of'

In *EC – Trademarks and Geographical Indications (Australia)* the Panel inter- **2.45** preted the obligation to provide certain legal means 'in respect of' GIs as an obligation to provide for the protection of GIs and rejected a claim concerning situations where geographical indications might have an impact upon trade mark protection.[16]

ii. 'Legal means'

In relation to (a) Art 22.2 does not specify the legal means to protect GIs. This **2.46** is left for Members to decide. Thus GIs could be protected under consumer protection laws or as an aspect of trade marks laws, such as by a certification or collective mark. In relation to (b) GIs could be protected under unfair competition laws or under actions such as passing off.

iii. 'Interested parties'

In *EC – Trademarks and Geographical Indications (US)* the Panel explained that **2.47** the obligation in Art 22.2 is to provide certain legal means to 'interested parties' who are nationals of other Members in accordance with the criteria referred to in Art 1.3. The interested parties must qualify as 'nationals of other Members' in accordance with the criteria referred to in Art 1.3. The Panel pointed out that these persons can be private parties, which is reflected in the fourth Recital of the preamble to the agreement, which reads '*[r]ecognizing that intellectual property rights are private rights*'.[17]

---

16 Panel Report, *EC – Trademarks and Geographical Indications (Australia)*, para 7.714.
17 Panel Report, *EC – Trademarks and Geographical Indications (US)*, paras 7.742–7.743.

2.48 Although the term 'interested party' is also used in Art 10(2) of the Paris Convention (1967) as incorporated in the TRIPS Agreement, by Art 2(1) of the TRIPS Agreement, in *EC – Trademarks and Geographical Indications (US)*, the Panel observed that Art 10(2) of the Paris Convention (1967) did not set out a criterion for eligibility for protection for the purposes of the TRIPS Agreement although it may provide guidance on the interpretation of Arts 22 and 23 of the TRIPS Agreement.[18]

(c) Non-protection of expired geographical indications

2.49 Article 24.9 provides that there is no obligation under the TRIPS Agreement to protect GIs 'which are not or cease to be protected in their country of origin, or which have fallen into disuse in that country'.

(d) Non-diminution of geographical indications protection

2.50 Article 24.3 of the TRIPS Agreement requires that in implementing the GIs provisions a WTO Member shall not diminish the protection of GIs that existed in that Member immediately prior to the date of entry into force of the WTO Agreement.

2.51 In *EC – Trademarks and Geographical Indications* the Panel found that the scope of Art 24.3 was limited to the implementation of section 3 of Part II of the TRIPS Agreement on geographical indications, and did not apply to the implementation of section 2 of Part II on trade marks.[19]

2.52 The Panel interpreted the phrase 'the protection of geographical indications that existed in that Member immediately prior to the date of entry into force of the WTO Agreement' to mean the state of protection of individual GIs immediately prior to 1 January 1995.[20]

2. Geographical indications and trade marks

2.53 Given the novelty of GIs protection for some countries, compared with their more long-standing protection of registered trade marks, the GIs provisions of the TRIPS Agreement seek to reconcile the two systems of protection. In *EC – Trademarks and Geographical Indications* the Panel recognised that the rights provided for in Art 22.2 and Art 16.1, concerned with trade mark protection,

---

18 Panel Report in *EC – Trademarks and Geographical Indications (US)*, para 7.170.
19 Panel Reports, *EC – Trademarks and Geographical Indications (US)*, paras 7.631–7.632, and *(Australia)*, paras 7.631–7.632.
20 Panel Reports, *EC – Trademarks and Geographical Indications (US)*, para 7.636, and *(Australia)*, para 7.636.

could lead to a conflict between private parties but it considered that the treaty provisions themselves did not conflict.[21]

(a) Refusal or invalidation of the registration of a trade mark comprising a geographical indication

Article 22.3 of the TRIPS Agreement provides for *ex officio* action by a WTO **2.54** Member or, if its legislation permits or at the request of an interested party, refusal or invalidation of the registration of a trade mark which contains or consists of a GI with respect to goods not originating in the territory indicated, if use of the indication in the trade mark for such goods in that Member is of such a nature as to mislead the public as to the true place of origin. In *EC – Trademarks and Geographical Indications* the Panel confined Art 22.3 to the resolution of conflicts between GIs and later trade marks, but not prior trade marks.[22]

(b) Refusal or invalidation of a trade mark containing a false representation of origin

Additionally, Art 22.4 provides that the protection under paras 1, 2 and 3 of **2.55** Art 22 shall be applicable against a geographical indication which, although literally true as to the territory, region or locality in which the goods originate, falsely represents to the public that the goods originate in another territory.

(c) Exemption of trade marks applied for or registered in good faith

Cognisant of the fact that for most countries the protection of GIs will be an **2.56** innovation, Art 24.4 exempts from this form of protection trademarks which have been 'applied for or registered in good faith' or where the rights to the trade mark 'have been acquired through use in good faith' either before the implementation of the TRIPS provisions, or before the geographical indication is protected in its country of origin.

Article 24.5 provides that in a situation where a trade mark has been applied **2.57** for or registered in good faith, or where rights to a trade mark have been acquired through use in good faith either:

(a) before the date of application of these provisions in that Member as defined in Part VI; or
(b) before the geographical indication is protected in its country of origin

---

21 Panel Reports, *EC – Trademarks and Geographical Indications (US)*, paras 7.623–7.624, and *(Australia)*, paras 7.623–7.624.
22 Panel Reports, *EC – Trademarks and Geographical Indications (US)*, para 7.622, and *(Australia)*, para 7.622.

measures adopted to implement the GIs provisions contained in section 3 of the TRIPS Agreement shall not prejudice eligibility for or the validity of the registration of a trade mark, or the right to use a trade mark, 'on the basis that such a trade mark is identical with, or similar to, a geographical indication'.

2.58 In *EC – Trademarks and Geographical Indications* the Panel interpreted Art 24.5 as an exception to GIs protection, and rejected arguments that it impliedly limited trade mark rights or impliedly preserved any trade mark rights that it does not specifically mention.[23]

2.59 Article 24.7 provides that a Member may provide that any request made under the section in connection with the use or registration of a trade mark must be presented within five years after the adverse use of the protected indication has become generally known in that Member, or after the date of registration of that trade mark, provided the registration has been published and 'provided that the geographical indication is not used or registered in bad faith'.

2.60 Similar to the analogous provision in most trade mark laws, Art 24.7 preserves 'the right of a person to use, in the course of trade, that person's name or the name of that person's predecessor in business, except where such name is used in such a manner as to mislead the public'.

(d) Use of terms common in the trade

2.61 Article 24.6 provides that nothing contained in section 3 of the TRIPS Agreement containing the GIs provisions shall require a WTO Member to apply its provisions in respect of a geographical indication of any other Member with respect to goods or services for which the relevant indication is identical with the term customary in common language as the common name for such goods or services in the territory of that Member.

(e) Use of person's name

2.62 Article 24.8 of the TRIPS Agreement provides that section 3 of the TRIPS Agreement containing the GIs provisions shall in no way prejudice the right of any person to use, in the course of trade, that person's name or the name of that person's predecessor in business, except where such name is used in such a manner as to mislead the public. The equivalent provision in trade marks law requires the use of a person's name to be in good faith. Article 24.8, instead of focusing upon motive, addresses the effect of the use of the name. It requires the public to be misled, rather than the narrower focus of consumer protection legislation, which typically prohibits the misleading of consumers or potential

---

23   Panel Reports, *EC – Trademarks and Geographical Indications (US)*, para 7.609, and *(Australia)*, para 7.609.

consumers. The relevant focus will have a bearing on the standard of credulity which a court may impose. The name of a person known to consumers of a particular product, might not be known to the public at large. Of course, to fall within this provision the relevant name would have to indicate a geographical origin.

3. Additional protection for geographical indications for wines and spirits

In addition to the general protection for GIs for wines and spirits within the **2.63** general context for the protection of GIs contained in Art 22, additional protection is accorded GIs for wines and spirits by Art 23.

(a) False indications

Article 23.1 provides that: **2.64**

> Each Member shall provide the legal means for interested parties to prevent use of a geographical indication identifying wines for wines not originating in the place indicated by the geographical indication in question or identifying spirits for spirits not originating in the place indicated by the geographical indication in question, even where the true origin of the goods is indicated or the geographical indication is used in translation or accompanied by expressions such as 'kind', 'type', 'style', 'imitation' or the like.

This provision is footnoted to provide that Members may, with respect to these obligations, provide for enforcement by administrative action.

Article 23.2 provides that the registration of a trade mark for wines or spirits **2.65** which contains or consists of a geographical indication 'shall be refused or invalidated, *ex officio* if a Member's legislation so permits or at the request of an interested party, with respect to such wines or spirits not having this origin'.

In *EC – Trademarks and Geographical Indications* the Panel found that Art 23.2 **2.66** can resolve conflicts between GIs and later trade marks, but not prior trade marks.[24]

(b) Homonymous indications

Article 23.3 provides that in the case of homonymous GIs for wines, **2.67** protection shall be accorded to each indication, subject to the provisions of para 4 of Art 22, concerning false representations. The scope of this provision

---

24 Panel Reports, *EC – Trademarks and Geographical Indications (US)*, para 7.622, and *(Australia)*, para 7.622.

is limited to homonymous GIs only for wines. Each Member is permitted by Art 23.3 to 'determine the practical conditions under which the homonymous indications in question will be differentiated from each other, taking into account the need to ensure equitable treatment of the producers concerned and that consumers are not misled'.

2.68 Homonymous indications are those that are spelled and pronounced alike, but which are different in meaning and which are used to designate the geographical origin of products stemming from different countries. For example, 'Rioja' is the name of a region in Spain and in Argentina and the expression applies for wines produced in both countries.

2.69 Conflicts typically arise where products on which homonymous GIs are used are sold into the same market. The problem is accentuated where the homonymous GIs in question are used on identical products. Honest use of such GIs should be possible, because the indications designate the true geographical origin of the products on which they are used. However, concurrent use of homonymous GIs in the same territory may be problematic where the products on which a GI is used have specific qualities and characteristics which are absent from the products on which the homonym of that GI is used. In this case, the use of the homonymous GI would be misleading, since expectations concerning the quality of the products on which the homonymous GI is used are not met.

2.70 The WIPO Standing Committee on The Law of Trademarks, Industrial Designs and Geographical Indications recommended that the extension of this principle to geographical indications, regardless of the kind of products for which they are used, be considered.[25]

(c) Use of terms common in the wine trade

2.71 Article 24.6 provides that nothing contained in section 3 of the TRIPS Agreement containing the GIs provisions shall require a WTO Member to apply its provisions in respect of a GI of any other Member with respect to products of the vine for which the relevant indication is identical with the customary name of a grape variety existing in the territory of that Member as of the date of entry into force of the WTO Agreement.

---

25 WIPO Standing Committee On The Law Of Trademarks, Industrial Designs And Geographical Indications, 'Possible Solutions For Conflicts Between Trademarks and Geographical Indications and for Conflicts Between Homonymous Geographical Indications', WIPO Doc, Sct/5/3, 8 June 2000.

(d) Pre-existing use

Article 24.4 of the TRIPS Agreement provides that nothing in its GIs **2.72** provisions shall require a WTO Member

> to prevent continued and similar use of a particular geographical indication of another Member identifying wines or spirits in connection with goods or services by any of its nationals or domiciliaries who have used that geographical indication in a continuous manner with regard to the same or related goods or services in the territory of that Member either (*a*) for at least 10 years preceding 15 April 1994 or (*b*) in good faith preceding that date.

(e) Multilateral system

Article 23.4 provides that in order to facilitate the protection of GIs for wines, **2.73** negotiations shall be undertaken in the Council for TRIPS concerning the establishment of a multilateral system of notification and registration of GIs for wines eligible for protection in those Members participating in the system. Preliminary work was initiated at the Council's meeting in February 1997.[26] Paragraph 18 of the Doha Ministerial Declaration, adopted on 14 November 2001, provided that:

> [w]ith a view to completing the work started in the Council for Trade-Related Aspects of Intellectual Property Rights (Council for TRIPS) on the implementation of Art 23.4, we agree to negotiate the establishment of a multilateral system of notification and registration of geographical indications for wines and spirits by the Fifth Session of the Ministerial Conference.[27]

Article 24.1 of the TRIPS Agreement provides that WTO Members 'agree to **2.74** enter into negotiations aimed at increasing the protection of individual geographical indications under Article 23'. In addition Art 24.2 contains a general obligation for the Council for TRIPS to keep under review the application of the provisions of section 3 of the TRIPS Agreement, which contains its GIs chapter and that 'the first such review shall take place within two years of the entry into force of the WTO Agreement'.

As will be seen below, there has occasionally been confusion between the **2.75** negotiations for a multilateral system for wines and spirits and the general review of the GIs provisions, including the possibility of extending the protection conferred upon wines and spirits to other products as well as extending the multilateral system to these other products.

---

26 Council for Trade-Related Aspects of Intellectual Property Rights – Minutes of Meeting – Held in the Centre William Rappard on 27 February 1997, WTO Doc, IP/C/M/12.

27 The text of the Declaration can be found in WTO Doc WT/MIN(01)/DEC/1 20 November 2001.

2.76 On 1 February 2002 the Trade Negotiations Committee of the WTO established the Special Session of the Council for TRIPS to conduct the negotiations. On 1 August 2004 the General Council adopted a decision on the 'Doha Work Programme'. In its paragraph 1.f, the General Council reaffirmed Members' commitment to progress in this area of negotiations in line with the Doha mandates.[28] In para 29 of the Hong Kong Ministerial Declaration adopted on 18 December 2005, Ministers 'agree[d] to intensify these negotiations in order to complete them within the overall time-frame for the conclusion of the negotiations that were foreseen in the Doha Ministerial Declaration'.[29]

2.77 In June 2005 the EC submitted a proposal to amend the TRIPS Agreement to provide global protection for GIs in a multilateral system of registration. This proposal sought to bring international protection for GIs into conformity with the European Union. The EC submission set out provisions for a centralised register that would be compulsory and have legal effect.[30] The EC proposal aimed at preserving each WTO Member's prerogative to determine whether a certain sign, indication or geographical name met the TRIPS definition of a GI.[31] Opponents of the EC proposal, the US, Australia, Argentina, Australia, Canada, Chile, Ecuador, El Salvador and New Zealand, opposed the extension of GIs protection, taking the position that the international protection of GIs was adequate as it stands and that such a drastic development would only serve to undermine future gains in market access for non-European food and agricultural products.[32] Concern has also been expressed about the additional costs and administrative burdens of implementing a distinct system of GI protection in addition to the TRIPS obligations. They advocated a system of voluntary notification and registration with no obligation to protect registered GIs. A revised Communication from Argentina, Australia, Canada, Chile, Costa Rica, Dominican Republic, Ecuador, El Salvador, Guatemala, Honduras, Japan, Korea, Mexico, New Zealand, Nicaragua, Paraguay, Chinese Taipei, South Africa and the US proposed that the TRIPS Council should set up a voluntary system where notified GIs would be registered in a database.

---

28 Doha Work Programme – Decision Adopted by the General Council on 1 August 2004, WTO Doc WT/L/579.

29 See WTO Doc, WT/MIN/(05)/DEC.

30 Communication from the European Communities. The communication, dated, is being circulated to the General Council, to the TNC and to the Special Session of the Council for TRIPS at the request of the Delegation of the European Commission (TN/IP/W/11) of 13 June 2005. This new proposal maintains the level of ambition of the EC as regards both 'extension' and the multilateral register of GIs, as contained in its earlier proposals in documents IP/C/W/107/Rev.1 (on the GI register) and IP/C/W/353 (on 'extension').

31 Para 3.2(a).

32 See Communication from Argentina, Australia, Canada, Chile, Ecuador, El Salvador, New Zealand and the United States, TN/IP/W/9, 13 April 2004.

Those governments choosing to participate in the system would have to consult the database when taking decisions on protection in their own countries. Non-participating members would be 'encouraged' but 'not obliged' to consult the database.[33]

Hong Kong and China proposed a compromise under which a registered term **2.78** would enjoy a more limited 'presumption' than under the EU proposal, and only in those countries choosing to participate in the system.[34]

In July 2008 a group of WTO Members called for a 'procedural decision' to **2.79** negotiate three intellectual property issues in parallel: these two GIs issues and a proposal to require patent applicants to disclose the origin of genetic resources or traditional knowledge used in their inventions.[35] In relation to the GIs Register the proposed text was that:

1. Members agree to establish a register open to geographical indications for wines and spirits protected by any of the WTO Members as per TRIPS. Following receipt of a notification of a geographical indication, the WTO Secretariat shall register the notified geographical indication on the register. The elements of the notification will be agreed.
2. Each WTO Member shall provide that domestic authorities will consult the Register and take its information into account when making decisions regarding registration and protection of trademarks and geographical indications in accordance with its domestic procedures. In the framework of these procedures, and in the absence of proof to the contrary in the course of these, the Register shall be considered as a *prima facie* evidence that, in that Member, the registered geographical indication meets the definition of 'geographical indication' laid down in TRIPS Article 22.1. In the framework of these procedures, domestic authorities shall consider assertions on the genericness exception laid down in TRIPS Article 24.6 only if these are substantiated.
3. Text based negotiations shall be intensified, in Special Sessions of the TRIPS Council and as an integral part of the Single Undertaking, to amend the TRIPS Agreement in order to establish the Register accordingly.

To date WTO Members remain divided over the proposal to negotiate the **2.80** three subjects in parallel, with opponents arguing that the only mandate for the TRIPS Council is to negotiate the multilateral register. Under the Chairmanship of Ambassador Trevor C. Clarke (Barbados) during 2008–09,

---

33 TN/IP/W/10/Rev.2, 24 July 2008.
34 TN/IP/W/8, 23 April 2003.
35 Communication from Albania, Brazil, China, Colombia, Ecuador, the European Communities, Iceland, India, Indonesia, the Kyrgyz Republic, Liechtenstein, the Former Yugoslav Republic of Macedonia, Pakistan, Peru, Sri Lanka, Switzerland, Thailand, Turkey, the ACP Group and the African Group, TN/C/W/52 of 19 July 2008.

the Special Session of the TRIPS Council considered the various proposals which had been made and the Chairman identified as 'crucial' the two issues of participation and consequences/legal effects of registration.[36]

2.81 ⸱With respect to the issue of whether participation in the system should be voluntary or mandatory, some WTO Members interpreted the reference in the mandate concerning 'a multilateral system' to mean that the system should apply to all Members. Other Members argued that the words 'those Members participating in the system' mean that not all Members are expected to participate. Ambassador Clarke encouraged Members 'to continue searching for an acceptable solution that would determine a participation of Members in the Register that renders it a useful and meaningful tool in line with its purpose to facilitate protection'.[37] With respect to the consequences/legal effects of registration, all Members seem to accept an obligation to consult the information on the Register and to take the information on the Register into account when making decisions regarding registration and protection of trade marks and GIs under their national procedures. However, views differ significantly as to how such information should be taken into account, what weight and significance should be given to it, and whether there should be a specific legal obligation to take the information into account.

2.82 Ambassador Clarke's successor as Chairman of the Special Session of the Council for TRIPS, Ambassador Darlington Mwape (Zambia) announced, upon assuming this office, that the specific negotiating mandate of the Special Session was limited to the negotiations of a Register of GIs for wines and spirits.[38] Ambassador Mwape circulated a work programme suggesting a list of 'Possible Elements for Developing Texts' for the future Register.[39] Applying this structure a drafting group developed a single draft composite text on the Register.[40] Ambassador Mwape reported that despite the fact that this text reflects the current state of negotiations in this negotiating group and represents significant progress, views differ on whether or not it could be forwarded to the Trade Negotiations Committee by Easter 2011, the deadline set by Pascal Lamy, the Director General of the WTO, for the conclusion of the Doha Round of negotiations.[41]

---

36 Multilateral System of Notification and Registration of Geographical Indications for Wines and Spirits, Report by the Chairman, Ambassador C. Trevor Clarke (Barbados), TN/IP/19, 25 November 2009, para 10.

37 Ibid, para 11.

38 Multilateral System of Notification and Registration of Geographical Indications for Wines and Spirits, Report by the Chairman, Ambassador Darlington Mwape (Zambia), TN/IP/20, 22 March 2010, para 4.

39 See WTO Doc TN/IP/21, 21 April 2011.

40 That was circulated as JOB/IP/3 on 11 April 2011.

41 WTO Doc TN/IP/21, 21 April 2011, para 16.

Ambassador Mwape explained that: **2.83**

> I have made strenuous attempts to resolve this and have offered to use my prerogative
> as Chair to improve textual compliance with the Special Session of the Council for
> TRIPS mandate. However, Members have been unable to engage constructively on
> this question and have instead insisted that the purely bottom-up and Member-driven
> nature of the text be scrupulously respected at this time.[42]

4. TRIPS revision

Article 24.1 of the TRIPS Agreement provides that WTO Members 'agree to **2.84**
enter into negotiations aimed at increasing the protection of individual
geographical indications under Article 23'. It also provides that the provisions
of paras 4–8 of Art 24 'shall not be used by a Member to refuse to conduct
negotiations or to conclude bilateral or multilateral agreements'. It concludes
with the observation that in the context of such negotiations, 'Members
shall be willing to consider the continued applicability of these provisions
to individual geographical indications whose use was the subject of such
negotiations.'

Article 24.2 requires the Council for TRIPS to keep under review the **2.85**
application of the provisions of section 3 containing the GIs provisions and
that the first such review shall take place within two years of the entry into
force of the WTO Agreement.

A submission by Turkey of 9 July 1999, prior to the Seattle Ministerial, **2.86**
proposed the extension of the multilateral register to products other than
wines and spirits. This proposal was endorsed by the African group of
countries. In a document of 6 August 1999 Kenya, on behalf of the African
Group, noted that at the Singapore Ministerial that the Art 23.4 negotiations
concerning a multilateral register for wines had been extended to include
spirits and that:

> Considering that Ministers made no distinction between the two above-mentioned
> products, the African Group is of the view that the negotiations envisaged under
> Article 23.4 should be extended to other categories, and requests, in this regard, that
> the scope of the system of notification and registration be expanded to other products
> recognizable by their geographical origins (handicrafts, agro-food products).[43]

---

42 Ibid.
43 *Preparations for the 1999 Ministerial Conference the TRIPS Agreement Communication from Kenya on Behalf of
the African Group*, WTO Doc. WT/GC/W/302, 6 August 1999, paras 26–7.

2.87 At the TRIPS Council meetings in 2000 some misgivings were expressed by some delegations about the extension of Art 23.1 protection and the multilateral register beyond wines and spirits. The Chair of the TRIPS Council sought to separate the discussion of Art 23.2 from that of Art 24.2 to avoid confusion. A response to this suggestion was a proposal in October 2001 from Bulgaria, the Czech Republic, Egypt, Iceland, India, Kenya, Liechtenstein, Pakistan, Slovenia, Sri Lanka, Switzerland and Turkey that the extension of GIs to products other than wines and spirits be included as an extension of the built-in agenda.[44]

2.88 Paragraph 18 of the Doha Ministerial Declaration adopted on 14 November 2001 noted 'that issues related to the extension of the protection of geographical indications provided for in Article 23 to products other than wines and spirits will be addressed in the Council for TRIPS pursuant to paragraph 12 of this declaration'.[45] In para 39 of the Hong Kong Ministerial Declaration, Ministers inter alia '[took] note of the work undertaken by the Director-General in his consultative process on all outstanding implementation issues under paragraph 12(b) of the Doha Ministerial Declaration, including on issues related to the extension of the protection of geographical indications provided for in Art 23 to products other than wines'.

2.89 In opposition to the proposals for an extension of the protection of GIs for wines and spirits under TRIPS to all products, on 29 June 2001 a joint communication was sent to the TRIPS Council by Argentina, Australia, Canada, Chile, Guatemala, New Zealand, Paraguay and the United States (Joint Communication).[46] The Communication argued that the advantages of Art 23 protection were overstated and, relevantly for the current project, that the proposals for the extension of the TRIPS wines and spirits provisions to all products had insufficiently addressed the costs and burdens of this extension. It stated that '[t]hese new costs and burdens include administration costs, trade implications for producers, increased potential for consumer confusion, potential producer conflicts within the WTO Members and a heightened risk of WTO disputes'.[47]

2.90 As was mentioned in the preceding section, in July 2008 a group of WTO Members called for a 'procedural decision' to negotiate the multilateral register and the extension of Art 23 in parallel, together with a proposal to require

---

44   WTO Doc IP/C/W/204/Rev.1, 2 October 2000.
45   WTO Doc WT/MIN(01)/DEC/1, 20 November 2001.
46   WTO Doc IP/C/W/289.
47   Ibid., Attachment at para 13.

patent applicants to disclose the origin of genetic resources or traditional knowledge used in their inventions.

In relation to GI-Extension the proposed text was that: **2.91**

1. Members agree to the extension of the protection of Article 23 of the TRIPS Agreement to geographical indications for all products, including the extension of the Register.
2. Text based negotiations shall be undertaken, in Special Sessions of the TRIPS Council and as an integral part of the Single Undertaking, to amend the TRIPS Agreement in order to extend the protection of Article 23 of the TRIPS Agreement to geographical indications for all products as well as to apply to these the exceptions provided in Article 24 of the TRIPS Agreement *mutatis mutandis*.

On 19 April 2011 a Communication from Albania, China, Croatia, the **2.92** European Union, Georgia, Guinea, Jamaica, Kenya, Liechtenstein, Madagascar, Sri Lanka, Thailand, Turkey and Switzerland proposed that section 3 of TRIPS be amended by removing the reference to Wines and Spirits in the heading of Art 23 and by deleting all the references to wines and spirits in that Article, thereby rendering that Article applicable to all goods.[48]

On 21 April 2011 WTO Director-General Pascal Lamy circulated a report on **2.93** his consultations on GIs extension and proposals dealing with the relationship between the TRIPS Agreement and the Convention on Biological Diversity. In relation to extension he described the 'state of play' as characterised by 'divergent views' and 'with no convergence evident on the specific question of extension of Art 23 coverage: some Members continued to argue for extension of Art 23 protection to all products; others maintained that this was undesirable and created unreasonable burdens'.[49] Confirming that trade mark systems were legitimate forms of protecting GIs in line with the general principle that Members are entitled to choose their own means of implementing their TRIPS obligations, he reported that extension proponents sought guarantees that the trade mark system could and would protect their GIs at the higher level for all goods.[50]

---

48 Draft Decision to Amend Section 3 of Part II of The TRIPS Agreement', WTO Doc TN/C/W/6, 19 April 2011.
49 Issues related to the extension of the protection of geographical indications provided for in Article 23 of the TRIPS Agreement to products other than wines and spirits and those related to the relationship between the TRIPS Agreement and the Convention On Biological Diversity', Report by the Director-General, WTO Doc WT/GC/W/633, TN/C/W/61, 21 April 2011, para 17.
50 Ibid.

5. The TRIPS GIs disputes

2.94 A number of WTO Members had argued that the EU scheme for the protection of GIs was TRIPS-deficient in a number of areas. For example, the statement of the US to the WTO on the WTO trade policy review of the EU expressed the concern that 'foreign persons wishing to obtain protection for their GIs in the EU itself face a non-transparent process that appears to come into some conflict with the EU's TRIPS obligations' and that 'EU rulemaking processes are often perceived by third countries as exclusionary, allowing no meaningful opportunity for non-EU parties to influence the outcome of regulatory decisions'.[51] On 1 June 1999 the US requested consultations with the European Communities (EC) pursuant to Art 4 of the *Understanding on Rules and Procedures Governing the Settlement of Disputes* (DSU) and Art 64 of the TRIPS Agreement regarding EC Council Regulation (EEC) No 2081/92 of 14 July 1992 on the protection of geographical indications and designations of origin for agricultural products and foodstuffs. The US and the EC held consultations on 9 July 1999, and thereafter, but these and following consultations failed to resolve the dispute.

2.95 On 18 August 2003 the US and Australia requested the establishment of a WTO dispute settlement panel to review the consistency of EU Regulation 2081/92 with the rules of the TRIPS and GATT Agreements. The US and Australia argued that the EC Regulation was discriminatory and in violation of the national treatment obligations and the most-favoured-nation obligations in Arts 3 and 4 of the TRIPS Agreement and Arts I and III of the GATT 1994. The US and Australia argued that: (i) Regulation 2081/92 did not provide the same treatment to other nationals and products originating outside the EC that it provided to the EC's own nationals and products; (ii) the EU did not accord immediately and unconditionally to the nationals and products of each WTO Member any advantage, favour, privilege or immunity granted to the nationals and products of other WTO Members; (iii) the EU diminished the legal protection for trade marks; (iv) the EU did not provide legal means for interested parties to prevent the misleading use of a GI; (v) it did not define a GI in a manner that was consistent with the definition provided in the TRIPS Agreement; (vi) the EU was not sufficiently transparent in its registration procedures; and (vii) it did not provide adequate enforcement procedures.

---

51 WTO Trade Policy Review of the European Union, Statement by the United States to the WTO, 24 July 2002.

The US and Australia claimed that the EU Regulation imposed two require- **2.96** ments which contravened the national treatment principle contained in Art 2(2) of the Paris Convention as incorporated by Art 2.1 of the TRIPS Agreement: (i) the requirement that enterprises seeking to register GIs possessed a commercial establishment in the EU; and (ii) the requirement that GIs located in the territory of a WTO Member outside the EU could only be registered if that Member had adopted a system for GI protection that was equivalent to that in the EC and provided reciprocal protection to products from the EC.

The Panel Report in the dispute was adopted at a meeting of the Dispute **2.97** Settlement Body on 20 April 2005. Concerning the discriminatory conditions regarding the registration of foreign GIs and the requirement for reciprocity of protection, the Panel decided in favour of the US and Australia. Pursuant to Art 19.1 of the DSU, the Panel recommended that:

(a) the European Communities bring the Regulation into conformity with the TRIPS Agreement and GATT 1994;
(b) the European Communities could implement the above recommendation with respect to the equivalence and reciprocity conditions, by amending the Regulation so as for those conditions not to apply to the procedures for registration of GIs located in other WTO Members.

In an affirmation of the GI as intellectual property, the Panel endorsed the **2.98** European principle of its coexistence with all but the most famous of prior trade marks. The Panel found that Art 14(2) of the Regulation was a 'limited exception' permitted by Art 17 of TRIPS because it only allows use by those producers who are established in the geographical area of products that comply with the specification.

On the critical issue of whether the nationals of other WTO Members were **2.99** accorded less favourable treatment than the ECs' own nationals, the Panel ruled that the conditions in the Regulations modified the effective equality of opportunities to obtain protection with respect to intellectual property in two ways. First, GI protection was not available in respect of geographical areas located in third countries which the Commission had not recognised. It was confirmed that the European Commission had not recognised any third countries. Second, GI protection under the Regulation could become available if the third country in which the GI is located entered into an international agreement with the EU. For the Panel, both of those requirements represented a significant 'extra hurdle' in obtaining GI protection which did not apply to geographical areas located in the EC. The significance of the hurdle was taken to be reflected in the fact that currently no third country had entered into such an agreement or satisfied those conditions. Accordingly, the Panel found that the equivalence and reciprocity conditions modified the effective equality of opportunities with respect to the availability of protection to persons wishing to obtain GI protection under the EU legislation, to the detriment of those wishing to obtain protection in respect of geographical areas located in third countries, including WTO Members. This was held to be less favourable treatment.

2.100 The Panel noted that whilst the Regulation did not prevent a foreign national from producing goods within the territory of the EC, the different procedures which applied to foreign nationals compared with those of the EU, were perceived as disadvantageous to the nationals of other Members.

6. TRIPS enforcement

(a) Introduction

2.101 Article 41.1 of the TRIPS Agreement imposes upon Members of the WTO the general obligation to make available the enforcement procedures listed in the Agreement 'so as to permit effective action against any act of infringement of intellectual property rights' covered by the Agreement. These procedures are required also to include 'expeditious remedies to prevent infringements and remedies which constitute a deterrent to further infringements'. Consistent with the general trade liberalisation objectives of the WTO, these procedures are required to be 'applied in a manner as to avoid the creation of barriers to legitimate trade and to provide for safeguards against their abuse'.

2.102 In amplification of the latter qualifications, Art 41.2 requires that '[p]rocedures concerning the enforcement of intellectual property rights shall be fair and equitable'. More specifically, the paragraph requires that procedures 'shall not be unnecessarily complicated or costly, or entail unreasonable time-limits or unwarranted delays'. Article 41.3 requires that '[d]ecisions on the merits of a case shall preferably be in writing and reasoned' and that they 'shall be made available at least to the parties to the proceeding without undue delay'. Due process is also required by the paragraph which insists that '[d]ecisions on the merits of a case shall be based only on evidence in respect of which parties were offered the opportunity to be heard'.

2.103 An opportunity for judicial review of final administrative decisions and 'the legal aspects of initial judicial decisions on the merits of a case' is required by Art 41.4. However, para 4 provides that there is 'no obligation to provide an opportunity for review of acquittals in criminal cases'.

(b) Civil procedures

In relation to the intellectual property rights covered by the TRIPS Agreement, Art 42 requires Members to make available civil judicial procedures for the enforcement of those rights to rights holders, including federations and associations having legal standing to assert such rights. This will be important for those GIs which are held or supervised by consortia. **2.104**

Article 42 requires that these procedures are fair and equitable in that **2.105** defendants are entitled to 'written notice which is timely and contains sufficient detail, including the basis of the claims'.

Representation by independent legal counsel is also required by Art 42. All **2.106** parties to such procedures 'shall be duly entitled to substantiate their claim and to present all relevant evidence', without the procedures imposing 'overly burdensome requirements concerning mandatory personal appearances'.

Finally, Art 42 provides that the procedure 'shall provide a means to identify **2.107** and protect confidential information, unless this would be contrary to existing constitutional requirements'.

i. Discovery and interrogatories

As is conventional in civil proceedings in most jurisdictions, Art 43.1 provides **2.108** for procedures in the nature of discovery and the administration of interrogatories, once a party has 'presented reasonably available evidence to support its claims and has specified evidence relevant to substantiation of its claims which lies in the control of the opposing party'. A concern which is particularly acute in patent actions is that these pre-trial procedures may result in trade secrets being revealed. Article 43.1 provides that the production of evidence may be compelled, 'subject in appropriate cases to conditions which ensure the protection of confidential information'. In the UK a plaintiff is required in these circumstances to show that there are 'formidable grounds' for suspicion that the defendant is infringing a plaintiff's rights.[52] Where there are concerns about the disclosure of trade secrets to a commercial rival the court may require the inspection of discovered evidence to be by an independent expert.

In the event that a party to a proceeding 'voluntarily and without good reason **2.109** refuses access to, or otherwise does not provide necessary information within a reasonable period, or significantly impedes a procedure relating to an enforcement action', Art 43.2 permits Members to accord the judicial authorities 'the

---

52   *Wahl & Anor v Buhler-Miag (England) Ltd* [1979] FSR 183.

authority to make preliminary and final determinations, affirmative or negative on the basis of the information presented to them'. This will include 'the complaint or the allegation presented by the party adversely affected by the denial of access to information'. Article 43.2 does, however, provide the opportunity for the parties to be heard on the allegations or evidence.

ii. Seizure orders

2.110 Compelling a defendant to respond to interrogatories or requests for discovery presupposes the sort of defendant who may not be typical of the worst sort of infringer of intellectual property rights. In cases where the defendant is conducting clandestine infringement activities on a large scale the defendant will not usually remain available to answer interrogatories or to discover documents. Indeed, on detection, relevant evidence will immediately be removed or destroyed. To deal with this situation the English Court of Appeal in *Anton Piller v Manufacturing Processes*[53] approved a procedure whereby on an *ex parte* application in camera, an order would be granted to an applicant that the defendant, advised by his legal representative, grant access to the applicant to inspect the defendant's premises to seize, copy or photograph material which may be used as evidence of the alleged infringement. The defendant may be obliged to deliver up infringing goods and tooling and may also be obliged to provide information about sources of supply and about the destination of infringing products.

2.111 Because of the exceptional nature of an *Anton Piller* order in its impact upon an individual's civil rights, after the demonstration that there is a very strong prima facie case of infringement, the courts have insisted upon proof that there is a strong possibility that evidence in the possession of a defendant is likely to be destroyed before an application inter partes can be made. Additionally, the British courts have insisted upon the safeguards of the attendance upon a search, conducted in business hours, by both parties' legal representatives, sometimes with a neutral supervising solicitor who has experience in the execution of these orders. Refusal to comply with an *Anton Piller* order will be a contempt of court. On the other hand, the use of the order for abusive purposes may result in the grant of substantial compensation to a defendant.

2.112 In the *Anton Piller* case itself the Court of Appeal predicted that such orders would be extremely rare,[54] however with the burgeoning of the large-scale copyright piracy and trade-mark counterfeiting which precipitated the adoption of trade-related intellectual property rights as a matter for GATT, the use

---

53   [1976] RPC 719.
54   Ibid., at 725, per Ormrod, LJ.

of this procedure has become increasingly common. Infringement of GIs rights has not yet attracted the use of *Anton Piller* orders but with the increase, in particular, of wine-label counterfeiting, this may be a remedy for the future.

The *Anton Piller* order is adopted in the scheme which is provided in Art 50 of **2.113** the TRIPS Agreement for the making of 'provisional measures' by the judicial authorities. Article 50.1 provides that the judicial authorities shall have the authority 'to order prompt and effective provisional measures: ... (b) to preserve relevant evidence in regard to the alleged infringement'.

As with the *Anton Piller* order, Art 50.2 permits the judicial authorities 'to **2.114** adopt provisional measures *inaudita altera parte* where appropriate, ... where there is a demonstrable risk of evidence being destroyed'. Also the judicial authorities may have authority pursuant to Art 50.3 'to require the applicant to provide any reasonably available evidence in order to satisfy them with a sufficient degree of certainty that the applicant is the right holder' and that an infringement has occurred or is imminent. Additionally, Art 50.5 provides that to assist the authority which will enforce the provisional measure, 'the applicant may be required to supply other information necessary for the identification of the goods concerned'.

As measures to prevent abuse and to protect a defendant's rights, Art 50.3 **2.115** provides for an applicant to be ordered 'to provide a security or equivalent assurance' and Art 50.4 provides that where provisional measures have been adopted *inaudita altera parte*, notice must be provided to the affected parties 'without delay after the execution of the measures at the latest'. Paragraph 4 also provides for 'a review, including a right to be heard' upon the request of the defendant 'with a view to deciding, within a reasonable period of notification of the measures' whether they should be 'modified, revoked or confirmed'. Additionally, if proceedings leading to a decision on the merits of the case have not been initiated within a reasonable period, Art 50.6 permits the defendant to request the revocation of the provisional measures or for a determination that they cease to have effect.

Similar to the safeguards which have been developed in relation to the *Anton* **2.116** *Piller* procedure, Art 50.7 provides for the compensation of a defendant where 'the provisional measures are revoked or where they lapse due to any act or omission by the applicant, or where it is found subsequently that there has been no infringement or threat of infringement of an intellectual property right'.

iii. Injunctions

2.117 A civil remedy which is important for the preservation of intellectual property rights is injunctive relief. This is particularly the case where infringement may damage or undermine the establishment of a commercial reputation immediately upon the launching of a new product; similarly, where the widespread counterfeiting of a trademarked product may have the effect of destroying the distinctiveness of a proprietor's mark, thereby rendering the trade mark registration voidable. Article 44 permits the conferral upon the judicial authorities of the power 'to order a party to desist from an infringement, inter alia, to prevent the entry into channels of commerce in their jurisdiction of imported goods that involve the infringement of intellectual property rights'.

2.118 The injunctions which may be granted under Art 44 are grounded upon infringing conduct. Where proof of consumer deception is the central feature of the infringement, the remedy proffered by Art 44 may be rendered nugatory where a sufficient time is required to provide an opportunity for consumers to become deceived. After this has occurred, it might be futile to hope that this deception can be undone. In this circumstance the provision of interlocutory relief is essential.

Interlocutory injunctions

2.119 Article 50.1 provides that the judicial authorities 'shall have the authority to order prompt and effective provisional measures … (a) to prevent an infringement of any intellectual property right from occurring'. The trade-related context of this remedy is emphasised by the supplementary particularisation in sub-paragraph (a) that provisional measures may be taken 'to prevent the entry into the channels of commerce in their jurisdiction of goods including imported goods immediately after customs clearance'.

2.120 As mentioned above, a provisional order of particular utility in an intellectual property context will be the grant of interlocutory injunctions for the purpose of freezing the status quo until a trial of the merits can take place.

2.121 As a matter of practice the interlocutory injunction, although it is only intended to have a preservative effect, will actually be the basis of the final determination of parties' rights, as it is very seldom that after the interlocutory hearing, the defeated party will proceed to the determination of final relief. If an appeal is to be taken, it will usually be on the issue of interlocutory relief. Provision is made in Art 50.6 for a defendant to request that provisional measures be revoked 'if proceedings leading to a decision on the merits of the case are not initiated within a reasonable period, to be determined by the judicial authority'. Where such a period is not determined, Art 50.6 prescribes 20 working days or 31 calendar days, whichever is the longer.

A provisional order, or interlocutory or interim injunction are of particular **2.122** utility in an intellectual property rights (IPRs) enforcement context to freeze the status quo until a trial of the merits can take place. As a matter of practice, although these orders are intended to have a preservative effect, for the purpose of avoiding the infliction of uncompensable damage upon a right holder, until the merits can be decided, in most cases the provisional measures will actually be the basis of the final determination of parties' rights. In cases of egregious counterfeiting or piracy the defendant is not likely to appear to oppose the grant of a provisional order. Even in contested IPR enforcement actions it is very seldom that after the interlocutory hearing, the defeated party will proceed to the determination of final relief.

In the US to obtain a preliminary injunction the applicant must establish **2.123** '(1) irreparable harm and (2) either (a) a likelihood of success on the merits, or (b) sufficiently serious questions going to the merits of its claims to make them fair ground for litigation, plus a balance of the hardships tipping decidedly in [its favour].'[55]

In the UK, until the 1975 decision of the House of Lords in the patent case **2.124** *American Cyanamid Co v Ethicon Ltd*,[56] an applicant for interlocutory relief had to establish a prima facie case and the balance of convenience lay in favour of restraining the defendant until the trial. Following this decision the courts in British and Commonwealth countries have ascertained merely whether there is a 'serious question to be tried'.[57] This standard was considered to fall short of requiring proof of a prima facie case and to be more in the nature of not being 'hopelessly optimistic'.[58] Greater significance under the American Cyanamid standard is placed upon issues of convenience. Where the damage claimed will easily be compensable by way of damages, the court may lean against the grant of injunctive relief. This will particularly be the case where the grant of an interlocutory injunction will have a significant impact upon the business of the defendant. On the other hand, where the claimed infringement may be likely to have a significantly deleterious impact upon the business of

---

55 *Monserrate v NY State Senate*, 599 F.3d 148, 154 (2d Cir. 2010). Applied most recently in *Louboutin v Yves Saint Laurent America, Inc.*, No. 11 Civ. 2381 (VM), United States District Court, S.D. New York, 10 August, 2011.

56 [1975] RPC 513.

57 Eg in Australia, *Beecham Group Ltd v Bristol Laboratories Pty Ltd* (1968) 118 CLR 618 at 622–3 applied most recently in *Apple Inc v Samsung Electronics Co Ltd* [2011] FCA 1164.

58 *Mothercare Ltd v Robson Books Ltd* [1979] FSR 466.

the applicant, the court may consider the inconvenience to the respondent to be accommodated by an undertaking by the applicant or by the payment by it of monies into court in anticipation of compensation or costs being granted to the respondent.

2.125 Grant of all injunctive relief in common law countries is discretionary. A factor that is taken into account in disqualifying relief is the conduct of the defendant and even a small delay, without reasonable grounds, in seeking the freezing of the status quo may debar an applicant from relief.

Final injunctions

2.126 As mentioned above, it will be usual that allegedly infringing conduct will be restrained by interlocutory relief. Although the courts are only obliged to ascertain whether there is a serious question to be tried, in practice these cases have begun to approximate final deliberations on the merits. Article 44 permits the judicial authorities 'to order a party to desist from infringement, inter alia, to prevent the entry into channels of commerce in their jurisdiction of imported goods that involve the infringement of an intellectual property right'.

2.127 The remedy of injunction is usually granted on a discretionary basis. Among the factors considered are whether: (a) damages provides an adequate remedy; (b) the order will require constant supervision by the court; (c) the applicant has engaged in some disentitling conduct, such as its own infringing activity; and (d) the applicant has delayed in seeking its remedy or has acquiesced in the respondent's conduct.

2.128 Another discretionary ground which is contained in Art 44 is that Members are not obliged to accord the remedy of injunction 'in respect of protected subject matter acquired or ordered by a person prior to knowing or having reasonable grounds to know that dealing in such subject matter would entail the infringement of an intellectual property right'. It is difficult to see the justification for this qualification and how it will operate in practice. Article 50 permits the grant of provisional measures to prevent an infringement occurring on the application of a single party, where appropriate. A respondent may at that time discover that the products which it has purchased are infringing, but it cannot be enjoined from selling those products under Art 44, since it acquired the knowledge of infringement after the date of the contract of acquisition. Some sense may be made of this qualification by virtue of the fact that the respondent would still be liable to pay damages if it persisted in distributing infringing products.

iv. Damages

Article 45.1 provides that the judicial authorities shall have the authority to **2.129** order 'the infringer to pay the rights holder damages adequate to compensate for the injury ... suffered because of an infringement of that person's intellectual property right by an infringer who knowingly, or with reasonable grounds to know, engaged in infringing activity'.

Similarly to Art 13(1) of the Enforcement Directive,[59] Art 45.1 provides that **2.130** the obligation to pay damages may be imposed only on infringers 'who knowingly or with reasonable grounds to know' engaged in an infringing activity.

The general principles of damages computation in an IPR infringement action **2.131** are usefully summarised by Kitchin J in *Ultraframe (UK) Ltd v Eurocell Building Plastics Ltd & Anor*,[60] a patent infringement case, but which could equally apply to the infringement of a GI. However, it should be noted that the practice of awarding damages in IPR cases varies between countries. For example, the European Observatory on Counterfeiting and Piracy found varying standards in EU Member States for the award of damages in IPR cases.[61] It noted that in some countries right holders often cannot recover in full the compensation appropriate to an infringement, or the full costs that the right holder has borne to redress the infringement. Different methods were also found to be used to calculate lost profits. To deal with variations in damages calculations, it recommended that Member States 'should provide that lump-sum damages, reflecting all negative economic consequences that the right holder has been reasonably found to have suffered, are available at the right holder's discretion at least as an alternative to any lost profits that can be proved'.[62]

v. Knowledge

Article 45.1 provides for compensation orders against infringers 'who know- **2.132** ingly, or with reasonable grounds to know, engaged in infringing activity'. A general standard of reasonableness is usually applied to the question of guilty knowledge. The courts have taken the view, for example, that a person who copies a new product ought to have enquired whether it was patented.[63]

---

59   Directive 2004/48/EC of 29 April 2004 on the enforcement of intellectual property rights.
60   [2006] EWHC 1344 (Pat).
61   European Observatory on Counterfeiting and Piracy, Damages in Intellectual Property Rights, (2010), accessed at http://ec.europa.eu/internal_market/iprenforcement/docs/damages_en.pdf.
62   Ibid., at 5.
63   *Lancer Boss Ltd v Henley Fork Lift Co Ltd* [1975] RPC 301.

Conventionally, the existence of relevant knowledge is sought to be established by the delivery of a cease and desist letter to an infringer. A continuation of infringing activity after receipt of such a letter is evidence of guilty knowledge.

2.133 Article 45.2 permits Members to authorise the judicial authorities 'to order the recovery of profits and/or payment of pre-established damages even where the infringer did not knowingly, or with reasonable grounds to know, engage in infringing activity'. This sort of remedy is usually ordered in cases of unfair competition or passing off.

vi. Costs

2.134 Article 45.2 permits judicial authorities 'to order the infringer to pay the rights holder expenses, which may include appropriate attorney's fees'.

vii. Other remedies

2.135 Article 46, under the justification of creating an effective deterrent to infringement, allows Members to empower the judicial authorities 'to order that the goods which they have found to be infringing be, without compensation of any sort, disposed of outside the channels of commerce in such a manner as to avoid any harm caused to the rights holder'. Alternatively, where existing constitutional requirements so permit, the infringing goods may be destroyed. A constitutional obstacle which exists in some jurisdictions is the obligation to provide 'just terms' for any goods which are compulsorily acquired.

2.136 A supplementary power which is conferred upon the judicial authorities is the power 'to order that materials and implements, the predominant use of which has been in the creation of the infringing goods' be similarly disposed of outside the channels of commerce in such a manner as 'to minimise the risks of further infringements'.

2.137 In considering requests for orders to dispose of or destroy infringing goods and equipment used to produce such goods, the judicial authorities are required to take into account 'the need for proportionality between the seriousness of the infringement and the remedies ordered as well as the interests of third parties'. In the case of counterfeit trade mark goods, Art 46 indicates that 'the simple removal of the trade mark unlawfully affixed shall not be sufficient, other than in exceptional cases, to permit the release of goods into the channels of commerce'.

2.138 The language of Art 46 was addressed by the WTO Dispute Panel in *China – Measures Affecting the Protection and Enforcement of Intellectual Property*

Rights.[64] One question which arose was whether the reference to the judicial authorities having 'the authority' to order the destruction of goods and implements meant that they had to exercise that authority. The Dispute Panel ruled that the obligation is to 'have' authority, not an obligation to 'exercise' authority.[65] The Panel also took the view that the phrase 'shall have the authority' did not require Members to take any action in the absence of an application or request.[66] This was considered to be consistent with the nature of IPRs as private rights.

This determination mainly addressed the question of the disposal of goods, **2.139** rather than materials and implements outside the channels of commerce. The Panel observed that it was not disputed that donations (ie gifts) to social welfare bodies for their own use or for charitable distribution was outside the channels of commerce, unless those recipients later sold goods (or presumably materials and implements) donated to them for charitable distribution, in which case they would not in fact be disposed of outside the channels of commerce but into the channels of commerce.[67] On the other hand the Panel observed that if the social welfare bodies charitably distribute goods donated to them by customs but the goods later found their way back into the channels of commerce, this did not alter the fact that the goods were disposed of outside the channels of commerce, in the ordinary sense of 'disposal'.[68]

The Panel noted that the passive voice in the expression that goods 'be **2.140** disposed of' meant that there was no obligation that the relevant authorities carry out the disposal themselves but rather they may entrust the actual disposal to another body.[69] Finally, the disposal in Art 46 is qualified by the principle that the disposal shall be 'so as to' avoid any harm to the right holder. This is phrased in terms of purpose, not result.

viii.   *Right of information*

A particularly useful innovation is the authority which is conferred by Art 47 **2.141** 'to order the infringer to inform the right holder of the identity of third persons involved in the production and distribution of the infringing goods or services and of their channels of distribution'. Article 47 counsels the exercise of this power where it is not 'out of all proportion to the seriousness of the infringement'. No guidance is provided as to how seriousness is to be evaluated

---

64   Report of the Panel, WT/DS362/R, 26 January 2009.
65   Ibid., para 7.236.
66   Ibid., para 7.247.
67   Ibid., para 7.279.
68   Ibid.
69   Ibid., para 7.280.

nor whether the touchstone of seriousness is damage to the party seeking the information, or whether from the perspective of the public interest in suppressing wrongful acts. For example, the large-scale counterfeiting of low-quality trade marked goods may be of minimal concern to a trader producing high-quality products which are not likely to be confused with the counterfeiter's products. However, there may be a public interest in the protection of consumers from the poorer-quality goods. There may also be a more fundamental public interest in inculcating an ethos of commercial morality.

2.142 A limiting condition in Art 47 is that information will not be provided if it is out of proportion to the seriousness of the infringement, although no guidance is provided as to the test of proportionality.

2.143 TRIPS Art 47 provides that the information which may be provided to a right holder is 'the identity of third persons involved in the production and distribution of the infringing goods or services and of their channels of distribution'. Article 8(1) of the EU's Enforcement Directive is even more broadly drawn. Although it commences with the qualification of justification and proportionality, it provides that the competent judicial authorities may order that information on the origin and distribution networks of the goods or services which infringe an intellectual property right be provided not only by the infringer, but also by any other person who:

(a) was found in possession of the infringing goods on a commercial scale;
(b) was found to be using the infringing services on a commercial scale;
(c) was found to be providing on a commercial scale services used in infringing activities; or
(d) was indicated by the person referred to in point (a), (b) or (c) as being involved in the production, manufacture or distribution of the goods or the provision of the services.

2.144 Article 8(2) of the Enforcement Directive then itemises the type of information which may be provided, including:

(a) the names and addresses of the producers, manufacturers, distributors, suppliers and other previous holders of the goods or services, as well as the intended wholesalers and retailers;
(b) information on the quantities produced, manufactured, delivered, received or ordered, as well as the price obtained for the goods or services in question.

2.145 The general qualification to the information which may be provided under laws implementing the Directive is that the information applies in respect of acts carried out on 'a commercial scale'. This term is not defined in the substantive part of the Directive but in Recital (14), which states that acts carried out on a commercial scale 'are those carried out for direct or indirect economic or commercial advantage; this would normally exclude acts carried out by end consumers acting in good faith'.

In the UK, responding to complaints from right holders that for the purposes **2.146** of civil litigation, they were unable to obtain information from the Trading Standards Service, which, among other things, conducts investigations into counterfeiting, changes were made to Part 9 of the Enterprise Act 2002. Section 241A of that Act enables public authorities subject to competition law concerns to disclose information where the information is to be used for civil proceedings 'relating to or arising out of the infringement of an intellectual property right or relating to or arising out of passing off or the misuse of a trade secret'.[70]

ix. Indemnification of the defendant

Where 'enforcement measures have been abused' Art 48.1 provides that the **2.147** judicial authorities shall have the authority to order a party 'at whose request enforcement measures were taken' to provide 'adequate compensation for the injury suffered because of such abuse' to a person wrongfully enjoined or restrained. Article 48.1 also provides for the applicant to be ordered to pay the defendant's 'appropriate attorney's fees'.

(c) Criminal sanctions

i. Overview

Article 61 provides that Members shall provide for criminal procedures and **2.148** penalties 'to be applied at least in cases of wilful trademark counterfeiting or copyright piracy on a commercial scale'. The expression 'at least' leaves it open for criminal penalties to be imposed in cases concerning other IPR offences, such as where a law might criminalise GI infringements. Among the criminal sanctions which are listed in the Article are: 'imprisonment, and/or monetary fines sufficient to provide a deterrent, consistently with the level of penalties applied for fines of a corresponding gravity'. Also in appropriate cases, Art 61 provides for 'the seizure, forfeiture and destruction of the infringing goods and any materials and implements the predominant use of which has been in the commission of the offence'.

---

70 Department for Business Enterprise and Regulatory Reform, 'A Guidance Note on Information Disclosure to Consumers and Intellectual Property Rights Holders for Civil Proceedings', March, 2008, accessed at http://www.bis.gov.uk/files/file41381.pdf.

2.149 Article 61 also provides for criminal procedures and penalties to be applied in other cases of infringement of intellectual property rights, 'in particular where they are committed wilfully and on a commercial scale'.

(d) Border measures

i. Introduction

2.150 A key feature of the TRIPS Agreement was the obligation of Members to introduce border measures for the protection of IPRs. It is obviously more effective to seize a single shipment of infringing products at the border than to await their distribution in the market. The stratagem of utilising border seizure to control the trade in infringing goods was foreshadowed in the Paris Convention, which in Art 9(1) provides that 'all goods unlawfully bearing a trade mark or trade name shall be seized on importation into those countries of the Union where such mark or trade name is entitled to protection'. It was envisaged in Art 9(3) that this seizure would take place at the request of 'the public prosecutor, or any other competent authority, or any interested party'. The Paris Convention contains no provisions providing for the seizure upon importation of other intellectual property infringements.

ii. Suspension of release of goods by customs authorities

2.151 The key border control provision of the TRIPS Agreement is Art 51, which requires Members to adopt procedures to enable a right holder, who has valid grounds for suspecting that the importation of counterfeit trade mark or pirated copyright goods may take place, to lodge an application with competent authorities, administrative or judicial, for the suspension by the customs authorities of the release into free circulation of such goods.

2.152 As a footnote to this provision, the term 'counterfeit trademark goods' is defined to mean:

> any goods, including packaging, bearing without authorization a trademark which is identical to the trademark validly registered in respect of such goods, or which cannot be distinguished in its essential aspects from such a trademark, and which thereby infringes the rights of the owner of the trademark in question under the law of the country of importation.

The term 'pirated copyright goods' is defined to mean:

> any goods which are copies made without consent of the rights holder in the country of production and which are made directly or indirectly from any article where the making of that copy would have constituted an infringement of a copyright or a related right under the law of the country of importation.

In addition to the suspension of release of goods involving a suspected **2.153** counterfeit trade mark, or which are pirated copyright goods, Art 51 also provides that an application for suspension may also be made in respect of other intellectual property rights infringements, such as carrying ornamentation which infringes a registered design or involving production in breach of a patented process.

The Article also provides that the procedures for the suspension of imported **2.154** goods also apply to the 'release of infringing goods destined for exportation from their territories'. On its wording this provision could permit the seizure of goods originating within the country served by the customs authority, as well as goods which are in transit, having originated in another country. As a matter of practice, the customs authorities are not particularly well suited to dealing with goods which are being shipped from the hinterland as the perspective of the customs authorities tends to be outward facing. However, there is no reason why they cannot scrutinise goods passing in both directions.

The Article does not apply to a Member of the WTO which 'has dismantled **2.155** substantially all controls over movement of goods across its border with another Member with which it forms part of a customs union'. For example, the EU provides in its statutes for the free movement of goods between Member countries.

iii. Goods in transit

Footnote 13 to Art 51 of the TRIPS Agreement provides that WTO **2.156** Members have no obligations to apply border measures to goods which are 'in transit'. Within the EU, customs control of goods in transit has been urged because once goods are in transit through the territory of the EU it has been very easy to change their status from 'goods in transit' to 'Community goods'. In some countries, where customs posts are distant from points of entry, there is the possibility of tampering with shipments en route to those posts.

iv. Application process

Article 52 provides that: **2.157**

> Any right holder initiating the procedures under Article 51 shall be required to provide adequate evidence to satisfy the competent authorities that, under the laws of the country of importation, there is prima facie an infringement of the right holder's intellectual property right and to supply a sufficiently detailed description of the goods to make them readily recognizable by the customs authorities.

In relation to those intellectual property rights which are obtained by registration, such as trade marks, registered designs and patents, it would be reasonable for a customs authority to require submission of documentary proof of ownership of that right, such as a copy of the relevant registration certificate, by an applicant for suspension. Particular problems will arise in relation to those rights which do not arise from registration in the jurisdiction. In practice, the most important of these will be well-known trade marks and copyrighted works.

2.158 Following receipt of an application for suspension, the competent authorities are required by Art 52 to inform the applicant 'within a reasonable period whether they have accepted the application' and, where it has been determined, the period within which action will be taken by the competent authorities.

v. Security or equivalent assurance

2.159 To protect persons who are the subject of an application for suspension, and also the competent authorities, from abuse, Art 53.1 empowers the competent authorities to require the provision of 'a security or equivalent assurance to protect the defendant and the competent authorities'. However, Art 53.1 provides that the requirement of a security or equivalent assurance shall not unreasonably deter recourse to these procedures.

2.160 In certain limited circumstances, Art 53.2 provides for the release of suspended goods upon the payment by a defendant of an amount sufficient to protect the right holder for any infringement as security. This procedure applies (a) where there has been a suspension of goods involving industrial designs, patents, layout designs or undisclosed information by customs authorities on the basis of an administrative decision which has not been reviewed by a judicial or independent authority; (b) the period prescribed by Art 55 for notification to the customs authorities of commencement of proceedings to determine the merits has expired; and (c) all other conditions for importation have been complied with.

2.161 Article 53.2 provides that the payment of such security shall not prejudice any other remedy available to the right holder and that the security shall be released if the right holder fails to pursue the right of action within a reasonable period of time.

vi. Notice of suspension

2.162 Article 54 provides for the prompt notification of both the importer and the applicant of the suspension of the release of goods under Art 51.

vii. Duration of suspension

Article 55 provides for the release of suspended goods by the customs **2.163** authorities, provided that all other conditions for importation or export have been complied with, if

> within a period not exceeding 10 working days after the applicant has been served notice of the suspension, the customs authorities have not been informed that proceedings leading to a decision on the merits of the case have been initiated by a party other than the defendant, or that the duly empowered authority has taken provisional measures prolonging the suspension of the release of the goods.

The Article provides for an extension of the time-limit by another ten working days in 'appropriate cases'.

Where proceedings leading to a decision on the merits of a case have been **2.164** initiated, the defendant is permitted by Art 55 to request a 'review, including a right to be heard' with a view to deciding, within a reasonable period, 'whether these measures should be modified, revoked or confirmed'.

Finally Art 55 provides that where the suspension of the release of goods is **2.165** carried out or continued in accordance with a provisional judicial measure, Art 50.6 shall apply to require that the suspension shall be revoked or cease to have effect if proceedings leading to a decision on the merits of the case are not initiated within a reasonable period, to be determined by the judicial authority, or, in the absence of such a determination, within 20 working days or 31 calendar days, whichever is the longer.

viii. Indemnification of the importer and of the owner of goods

Where the importer, consignee and the owner of goods suffer injury through **2.166** the wrongful detention of goods, or through the detention of goods released under Art 55, Art 56 empowers the relevant authorities to order the applicant to pay those persons 'appropriate compensation'.

ix. Right of inspection and information

A particularly useful innovation effected by the border control provisions of **2.167** the TRIPS Agreement is the authority conferred by Art 57 empowering Members to provide the competent authorities, where a positive determination has been made on the merits of a case, with the authority to inform the right holder 'of the names and addresses of the consignor, the importer and the consignee and of the quantity of the goods in question'. This will obviously assist a right holder in its further investigation of other persons involved in the counterfeiting or piracy of goods.

2.168 The right holder is inevitably in the best position to assist in the identification of infringing goods. Article 57 permits Members to provide the competent authorities with the authority to provide the right holder with 'sufficient opportunity to have any goods detained by the customs authorities inspected in order to substantiate the right holder's claims'. Similarly, the competent authorities are also to be provided with the authority to give the importer an equivalent opportunity to have the goods inspected.

x. Ex officio *action*

2.169 Article 58 envisages that Members may permit the competent authorities to act upon their own initiative in suspending the release of goods where they have prima facie evidence that an intellectual property right is being infringed. In these circumstances the Article permits the competent authorities to 'seek from the right holder any information that may assist them to exercise these powers'.

2.170 Article 58(b) requires that both the importer and right holder shall be promptly notified of the suspension and that where the importer has lodged an appeal against the suspension with the competent authorities, the suspension shall be subject to the conditions, *mutatis mutandis*, set out in Art 55.

2.171 An exemption is provided by Art 58(c) to both public authorities and officials 'from liability to appropriate remedial measures where actions are taken or intended in good faith'.

xi. *Remedies*

2.172 Without prejudice to the infringement actions which may be brought by a right holder, and subject to the right of a defendant to seek review by a judicial authority, Art 59 provides that the competent authorities shall have the authority to 'order the destruction or disposal of infringing goods' in accordance with the principles set out in Art 46. Article 46 requires any disposal of goods to be outside the channels of commerce 'in such a way as to avoid any harm caused to a right holder'. In deciding upon destruction, the competent authorities will take into account the seriousness of the infringement and the interest of third parties. In regard to counterfeit goods, Art 46 provides that 'the simple removal of a trademark, unlawfully affixed shall not be sufficient, other than in exceptional cases to permit the release of the goods into the channels of commerce'. Similarly, Art 59 provides, in relation to counterfeit goods, that the authorities 'shall not allow the re-exportation of the infringing goods in an unaltered state or subject them to a different customs procedure, other than in exceptional circumstances'.

The scope of Art 59 was addressed by the WTO Dispute Panel in *China –* **2.173** *Measures Affecting the Protection and Enforcement of Intellectual Property Rights.*[71] This determination addressed, inter alia, whether China's Regulations on Customs Protection of Intellectual Property Rights, 2003 complied with Art 59. The Regulations permitted confiscated goods which infringed IPRs to be used by public welfare bodies in social public welfare undertakings. Where the goods concerned could not be disposed of in this way, but the infringing features could be eradicated, they could, according to the Regulation, be auctioned off after eradicating the infringing features. Where the distinguishing features could not be eradicated the goods had to be destroyed. The US claimed that as the Chinese customs authorities were required first to donate seized goods to social welfare bodies, they lacked the discretion to order the destruction or disposal of infringing goods required by Art 59 of the TRIPS Agreement. The response of China was that this donation constituted disposal outside the channels of commerce in such a way as to avoid harm to the right holder.[72]

In interpreting the meaning of 'infringing goods' in Art 59 the Panel read **2.174** down the meaning of these words, by reference to their context, which included the first sentence of Art 51, which provided for the relevant procedures to apply, as a minimum, to 'the importation' of 'counterfeit trademark or pirated copyright goods'.[73] The Panel noted that the IPR infringements covered by the Chinese Customs Regulations included not only counterfeit trade mark goods and pirated copyright goods, but certain other infringements such as other trade mark-infringing goods, other copyright-infringing goods, and patent-infringing goods. Thus China's border measures provided a level of protection higher than the minimum standard required by the TRIPS Agreement.

The obligation in the first sentence of Art 59 of the TRIPS Agreement is that **2.175** competent authorities 'shall have the authority' to order certain types of remedies with respect to infringing goods. The Panel noted that the word 'authority' can be defined as 'power or right to enforce obedience; moral or legal supremacy; right to command or give a final decision'. The obligation is to 'have' authority, not an obligation to 'exercise' authority.[74] The Panel concluded that the obligation that competent authorities 'shall have the

---

71   Report of the Panel, WT/DS362/R, 26 January 2009.
72   Ibid., paras 7.197–7.198.
73   Ibid., para 7.221.
74   Ibid., para 7.236.

authority' to make certain orders 'is not an obligation that competent authorities shall exercise that authority in a particular way, unless otherwise specified'.[75] The Panel recognised that the obligation that competent authorities
'shall have the authority' to order certain types of remedies left Members free
to provide that competent authorities may have authority to order other
remedies not required by Art 59, which requires authority to order 'destruction
or disposal'.

2.176 The Panel observed that it was not disputed that where competent authorities
have authority in any given situation within the scope of Art 59 to order either
destruction or disposal (in accordance with applicable principles), this was
sufficient to implement the obligation in the first sentence of Art 59.
Therefore, a condition that precluded the authority to order one remedy
(eg destruction) could be consistent with Art 59 as long as competent
authorities still had the authority to order the other remedy (in this example,
disposal).[76]

2.177 The 'authority' required by Art 59 concerns two types of remedies, namely
'destruction or disposal'. The meaning of 'destruction' did not require definition by the Panel as its meaning is uncontroversial. As for 'disposal', the Panel
noted that the English text of Art 59 did not qualify this word so that it could,
in accordance with its ordinary meaning, refer both to disposal outside the
channels of commerce as well as to release into the channels of commerce.
This ambiguity did not occur in the French and Spanish texts. The French
text of Art 59 refers to authority to order 'la mise hors circuit', which is a
reference to the authority to order that infringing goods be 'écartées des
circuits commerciaux' in Art 46. The Spanish text of Art 59 refers to authority
to order 'eliminación', which, read in its context as an alternative to 'destruc-
ción', is evidently a reference to the authority to order that infringing goods be
'apartadas de los circuitos comerciales' in Art 46.

2.178 The US argued that the possibility that goods donated to social welfare bodies
might later be sold by them did not constitute disposal 'outside the channels of
commerce in such a manner as to avoid any harm caused to the right holder'.
The Panel agreed that if the social welfare bodies sold goods donated to them
by customs for charitable distribution, even to raise money for charitable aims,
the goods were disposed of 'into the channels of commerce'.[77]

---

75   Ibid., para 7.238.
76   Ibid., para 7.246.
77   Ibid., para 7.246.

The critical issue was whether such disposal would harm the right holder. The **2.179** US argued that the donation of 'shoddy counterfeit goods', if they fail to perform properly and especially if defective or dangerous, would damage the right holder's reputation or even expose it to claims for compensation.[78] However, the US did not allege that any sub-standard, defective or dangerous goods had actually been donated by Chinese customs to social welfare bodies and thus the Panel found that it had not been demonstrated that customs lacked authority to donate goods to social welfare bodies in such a manner as to avoid any harm to the right holder caused by defective or dangerous goods.[79] The US submitted that counterfeit and pirated goods that were usable but of lower quality could easily harm the right holder's reputation, but again the Panel indicated that evidence of actual harm caused to the right holder by the manner of disposal was required.[80]

The Panel noted that although under ordinary circumstances, consumers may **2.180** be misled as to the origin of counterfeit and pirated goods, and counterfeit goods with quality problems may harm right holders' reputations, nothing in the measures at issue in the determination obliged customs or the social welfare bodies receiving seized goods to remove counterfeit trademarks.[81] The Panel noted that goods donated by customs to the Red Cross were not distributed in ordinary circumstances. The distribution of donated goods by the Red Cross, including in disaster relief projects, was outside the channels of commerce, thus it could not simply be assumed that the recipients were misled as to the origin of the goods. The recipients did not choose the goods in the way that ordinary consumers did, nor could it be assumed that the recipients were potential consumers of the genuine goods.

xii.   De minimis exports

Article 60 permits Members to exclude 'small quantities of goods of a **2.181** non-commercial nature contained in travellers' personal luggage or sent in small consignments' from the border control provisions of the TRIPS Agreement.

xiii.   Parallel importation

Article 6 of the TRIPS Agreement explicitly states that '[f]or the purposes of **2.182** dispute settlement under this Agreement, subject to the provisions of Articles 3 and 4 nothing in this Agreement shall be used to address the issue

---

78   Ibid., para 7.288.
79   Ibid., para 7.291.
80   Ibid., paras 7.294–7.298.
81   Ibid., paras 7.294–7.296.

of the exhaustion of intellectual property rights'. The reference to 'dispute settlement under this Agreement' raises the possibility that exhaustion of IPRs might be raised in other areas of WTO regulation. For example, the use of trademarks or GIs on agricultural products might be regulated by the Agreement on Agriculture (AoA). The plain language of Art 6 suggests that rules of TRIPS might be used to address an exhaustion of IPRs issues in dispute settlement under the AoA. An IPR may have the same effects as a quota, thus there is a possibility for a Member to assert that a rule of national exhaustion that permitted IPRs holders to block importation of goods is inconsistent with Art XI.1 of GATT 1994. Thus the language of Art 6 might permit a GATT panel to evaluate an IPR as a measure with the equivalent effect of a quota. On the other hand, the view has been taken that TRIPS constitutes a *lex specialis* or self-contained set of rules applicable to IPRs and trade regulation, and that the exhaustion question could not be examined by a GATT panel in a non-TRIPS dispute.[82] In any event, Art 6 of TRIPS is confined in its operation to WTO disputes and leaves open the subject of exhaustion for national litigation.

7. TRIPS rights under European law

2.183 Probably because of the recent history of the EU before a WTO Dispute Panel, interpreting the GIs and trade marks provisions of the TRIPS Agreement, the ECJ has taken account of the WTO TRIPS Agreement in its interpretation of the language of its legislation. In Case C-245/02 *Anheuser-Busch Inc. v Budějovický Budvar*[83] the ECJ said that since the Community is a party to the TRIPS Agreement, 'it is indeed under an obligation to interpret its trade-mark legislation, as far as possible, in the light of the wording and purpose of that agreement'.[84] It observed that:

> when called upon to apply national rules with a view to ordering measures for the protection of rights in a field to which the TRIPS Agreement applies and in which the Community has already legislated, as is the case with the field of trade marks, the national courts are required under Community law to do so, as far as possible, in the light of the wording and purpose of the relevant provisions of the TRIPS Agreement.[85]

---

82   Bronckers, 1998.
83   [2005] ETMR 286.
84   Ibid., at para 42.
85   Ibid., at para 55.

In *Anheuser–Busch Inc. v Budĕjovický Budvar*[86] the Court held that applying **2.184** Art 70(2) of the TRIPS Agreement, obligations arising from that agreement apply in respect of 'all subject-matter existing … and which is protected' on the date of application of that Agreement to a Member of the WTO so that, 'from that date, such a member is required to fulfil all the obligations arising from that agreement in respect of that existing subject-matter'.[87]

Furthermore, the Court pointed out that Art 70(4) of the TRIPS Agreement **2.185** applied to acts in respect of specific objects embodying protected subject matter, which become infringing under the terms of legislation in conformity with that Agreement, and which were commenced, or in respect of which a significant investment was made, before the date of acceptance of the WTO Agreement. In such a situation, Art 70(4) allows the Members to provide for limitations of the remedies available to the holder of the right against continued performance of such acts after the date of application of the TRIPS Agreement to the WTO Member concerned.[88] Thus in the case before it the acts which the defendant was alleged to have committed had occurred before the date of application of the TRIPS Agreement but continued after that date, so the Court ruled that the TRIPS Agreement applied to that situation.[89]

In referring to the specific issues raised by the case the ECJ concluded that a **2.186** trade name which is not registered or established by use in the Member State in which the trade mark is registered and in which protection against the trade name in question is sought may be regarded as an existing prior right within the meaning of the third sentence of Art 16(1) of the TRIPS Agreement if the proprietor of the trade name has a right falling within the substantive and temporal scope of that Agreement which arose prior to the trade mark with which it is alleged to conflict and which entitles him to use a sign identical or similar to that trade mark.[90]

In Case T-237/08 *Abadía Retuerta, SA v OHIM*,[91] which concerned an **2.187** application for a geographical trade mark under the Community Trade Mark Regulation, the ECJ pointed out that although the provisions of TRIPS do

---

86 [2005] ETMR 286.
87 Ibid., at para 49.
88 Ibid., at para 50.
89 Ibid., at para 52.
90 Ibid., at para 100.
91 Judgment 11 May 2010.

not have direct effect, trade mark legislation, including Art 7(1)(j) of Regulation No 40/94 on the Community trade mark, must, as far as possible, be interpreted in the light of the wording and purpose of that agreement.[92]

2.188 The Court recited that it is settled case law that a provision of an agreement entered into by the Community with non-Member countries must be regarded as being directly applicable when, 'regard being had to the wording, purpose and nature of the agreement', it may be concluded that 'the provision contains a clear, precise and unconditional obligation which is not subject, in its implementation or effects, to the adoption of any subsequent measure'.[93]

2.189 The Court noted that it has already held that, first, having regard to their nature and structure, the WTO Agreement and the annexes thereto are not in principle among the rules in the light of which the Court is to review measures of the Community institutions in the context of an action for annulment and the provisions of the TRIPS Agreement are not such as to create rights upon which individuals may rely directly before the courts by virtue of Community law.[94] However, it observed that although the provisions of the TRIPS Agreement do not have direct effect, Art 7(1)(j) of Regulation No 40/94 must, as far as possible, be interpreted in the light of the wording and purpose of that agreement.[95]

2.190 The Court observed that the:

> concept of a geographical indication identifying wines ... must be read in the light of the relevant provisions of Community law on determining and protecting geographical indications relating to wines. Consequently, it is necessary to refer to Regulation No 1493/1999, which is also intended to ensure that Community law is consistent with the provisions of the TRIPS Agreement, as is apparent from recitals 56 and 80 in the preamble to that regulation.[96]

---

92 Ibid., at para 64 applying Case C-245/02 *Anheuser-Busch Inc. v Budějovický Budvar* at para 42.
93 Ibid., at para 65, citing Joined Cases C-300/98 and C-392/98 *Dior and Others* [2000] ECR I-11307, para 42.
94 Ibid., at para 66.
95 Ibid., at para 67.
96 Ibid., at para 74.

C. GENEVA ACT OF THE LISBON AGREEMENT 2015

1. Introduction

As was noted above, the Lisbon Agreement 1958 failed to secure much **2.191** support beyond the countries of the Mediterranean. The failure of the negotiations in the TRIPS Council to settle the operating principles as well as the details for a multilateral system for the registration of GIs has led to an examination of the possibility that the Lisbon Agreement might be modified to allow registration. Gervais[97] suggested a protocol to the Lisbon Agreement as a means of achieving this result under which the Lisbon Agreement would apply to GIs as defined in TRIPS with no substantive protection norms and leaving it to the WTO dispute system to deal with conflicts.[98] In September 2008 the Assembly of the Lisbon Union established a Working Group on the Development of the Lisbon System to explore possible improvements to the procedures under the Lisbon System to make it more attractive for users and prospective new Members. Since 2009, the Working Group has engaged in a full review of the Lisbon International Registration System involving its possible extension to GIs in addition to appellations of origin. Various sessions of the Working Group considered drafts of proposed changes to the Lisbon System, culminating at its sixth session, in December 2012, in the Working Group on the Development of the Lisbon System (Appellations of Origin) requesting the International Bureau of WIPO to prepare a Draft Revised Lisbon Agreement that would take the form of a single instrument covering both appellations of origin and GIs and providing for a high and single level of protection for both, while maintaining separate definitions, on the understanding that the same substantive provisions would apply to both appellations of origin and GIs.[99] A Draft Agreement and associated Regulations were presented to the Seventh Session of the Working Group, which was held from 29 April to 3 May 2013.[100] This Draft Agreement was adopted as the Geneva Act of the Lisbon Agreement, together with accompanying Regulations on 20 May 2015.

2. Subject matter

Article 2(1) of the Geneva Act provides that it applies in respect of: **2.192**

---

97 Gervais, 2010.
98 Ibid., at 123.
99 WIPO Secretariat, 'Draft Revised Lisbon Agreement on Appellations of Origin and Geographical Indications', WIPO Doc, LI/WG/DEV/6/2, 28 September 2012.
100 WIPO Secretariat, 'Draft Revised Lisbon Agreement on Appellations of Origin and Geographical Indications', WIPO Doc, LI/WG/DEV/7/2, 22 March 2013.

(i) any denomination protected in the Contracting Party of Origin consisting of or containing the name of a geographical area situated in that Contracting Party, or another denomination known as referring to such area, which serves to designate a good as originating in that geographical area, where the quality or characteristics of the good are due exclusively or essentially to the geographical environment, including natural and human factors, and which has given the good its reputation; …

Art 1(vi) defines this denomination to be an appellation of origin (AO).

(ii) any indication protected in the Contracting Party of Origin which identifies a good as originating in a geographical area situated in that Contracting Party, where the quality, reputation or other characteristic of the good is essentially attributable to its geographical origin.

Art 1(vii) defines this denomination to be a geographical indication (GI).

2.193 Article 2(2) provides that a geographical area of origin as described in para (1):

may consist of the entire territory of the Contracting Party of Origin or a region, locality or place in the Contracting Party of Origin. This does not exclude the application of this Act in respect of a geographical area of origin, as described in paragraph (1), consisting of a trans-border geographical area, or a part thereof.

3. Competent Authority

2.194 Article 3 requires each Contracting Party to designate an entity which shall be responsible for the administration of this Act in its territory and for communications with the International Bureau of WIPO under the Act and the Regulations. The details of the Competent Authority have to be notified to the International Bureau. Rule 4(1) of the Regulations stipulates that the Competent Authority shall make available information on the applicable procedures in the Contracting Party for the enforcement of rights in AOs and GIs.

4. Registration

2.195 Article 4 establishes an International Register to be maintained by the International Bureau, recording international registrations of AOs and GIs effected under this Act or under the Lisbon Agreement and data relating to the status of such international registrations. Article 5(1) requires these applications to be filed with the International Bureau.

Article 5(2) provides that such applications may be filed in the name of: (i) the natural and legal persons entitled, under the law of the Contracting Party of Origin, to use the appellation of origin or the GI; or (ii) a legal entity which has legal standing to assert the rights of such beneficiaries or other rights in the AO or the GI.

Article 5(3) envisages the direct filing of an application by the beneficiaries or **2.196** by a natural person or legal entity referred to in para (2)(ii), if the legislation of the Contracting Party of Origin permits. A declaration to this effect is required from the Contracting Party at the time of deposit of its instrument of ratification or accession or at any later time.

The mandatory contents of an application are prescribed in Rule 5(2)(a) of the **2.197** Regulations requiring the application to indicate:

(i)   the Contracting Party of Origin;
(ii) the Competent Authority presenting the application or, in the case of Art 5(3), details identifying the beneficiaries or the natural person or legal entity referred to in Art 5(2)(ii);
(iii) the beneficiaries, designated collectively or, where collective designation is not possible, by name, or the natural person or legal entity having legal standing under the law of the Contracting Party of Origin to assert the rights of the beneficiaries or other rights in the AO or the GI;
(iv) the AO or the GI for which registration is sought, in the official language of the Contracting Party of Origin or, where the Contracting Party of Origin has more than one official language, in the official language or languages in which the appellation of (v) the good or goods to which the AO, or the GI, applies, as precisely as possible;
...
(vi) the geographical area of origin or the geographical area of production of the good or goods;
(vii) the identifying details, including the date of the registration, the legislative or administrative act, or the judicial or administrative decision, by virtue of which protection is granted to the AO, or to the GI, in the Contracting Party of Origin.

Where the denomination is not in Latin characters, Rule 5(2)(b) requires the **2.198** application to include a transliteration of the names of the beneficiaries or the natural person or legal entity referred to in Art 5(2)(ii), of the geographical area of origin, and of the AO or the GI for which registration is sought. The transliteration shall use the phonetics of the language of the application.

Where a Contracting Party requires that, for the protection of a registered AO **2.199** or GI in its territory, that the application further indicate particulars concerning, in the case of an AO, the quality or characteristics of the good and its connection with the geographical environment of the geographical area of production, and, in the case of a GI, the quality, reputation or other characteristic of the good and its connection with the geographical area of origin, Rule 5(3) requires it to notify that requirement to the Director General. Similarly Rule 5(4) requires the Director-General to be notified where an application has to be signed by a person having legal standing to assert the rights conferred by such protection and where the application has to be accompanied by a declaration of intention to use the registered AO or GI.

2.200 The optional contents of an application listed in Rule 5(6) are:

    (i)   the addresses of the beneficiaries;
   (ii)   a declaration that protection is renounced in one or more Contracting Parties;
  (iii)   a copy in the original language of the registration, the legislative or administrative act, or the judicial or administrative decision, by virtue of which protection is granted to the AO or the GI in the Contracting Party of Origin;
  (iv)   a statement to the effect that protection is not claimed for certain elements, other than those referred to in paragraph (5), of the AO or the GI.

2.201 Rule 5(5) requires the application to indicate whether or not, to the best knowledge of the applicant, the registration, the legislative or administrative act, or the judicial or administrative decision, by virtue of which protection is granted to the AO or the GI in the Contracting Party of Origin, specifies that protection is not granted for certain elements of the AO or the GI. Any such elements shall be indicated in the application in a working language.

2.202 Article 5(4) provides that in the case of a geographical area of origin consisting of a trans-border geographical area, the adjacent Contracting Parties may, in accordance with their agreement, file an application jointly through a commonly designated Competent Authority.

2.203 Where the International Bureau finds that an application does not satisfy the conditions set out in Rule 3(1) or Rule 5, Rule 6 requires it to defer registration and invite the Competent Authority or, in the case of Art 5(3), the beneficiaries or the natural person or legal entity referred to in Art 5(2)(ii), to remedy the irregularity found within a period of three months from the date on which the invitation was sent.

2.204 Article 6(1) provides for an examination by the International Bureau that formalities have been complied with and Art 6(2) provides that the date of the international registration shall be the date on which the application was received by the International Bureau. However, where the application does not contain particulars of the competent authority in the Contracting Party responsible for the administration of the Agreement; the applicant or applicants and, where applicable, the legal entity referred to in Art 5(2)(ii); the AO, or the GI for which international registration is sought; or the good to which the AO, or the GI applies, Art 6(3) provides that the date of the international registration shall be the date on which the last of the missing particulars is received by the International Bureau.

Article 6(4) requires the International Bureau, without delay, to publish each **2.205** international registration and notify the Competent Authority of each Contracting Party of the international registration.

Article 6(5)(a) provides that subject to subpara (b), a registered AO or GI **2.206** shall, in each Contracting Party that has not refused protection in accordance with Art 15, or that has sent to the International Bureau a notification of grant of protection in accordance with Art 18, be protected from the date of the international registration.

Article 6(5)(b) permits a Contracting Party by a declaration, to notify the **2.207** Director General that, in accordance with its national or regional legislation, a registered appellation of origin or GI is protected from a date that is mentioned in the declaration, which date shall however not be later than the date of expiry of the time limit for refusal specified in the Regulations in accordance with Art 15(1)(a).

5. Fees

Article 5(1) provides for the payment of fees to be specified in the Regulations **2.208** for the international registration of each AO and each GI. Reduced fees are permitted by Art 5(3) in respect of certain international registrations particularly those in respect of which the Contracting Party of Origin is a developing country or a least-developed country.

Article 5(4)(a) allows any Contracting Party by a declaration, to notify the **2.209** Director General that the protection resulting from international registration shall extend to it only if a fee is paid to cover its cost of substantive examination of the international registration.

Article 5(4)(b) provides that the non-payment of an individual fee shall, in **2.210** accordance with the Regulations, have the effect that protection is renounced in respect of the Contracting Party requiring the fee.

2.211 Rule 8(1) provides that he International Bureau shall collect the following fees, payable in Swiss francs:

    (i)   fee for international registration;

    (ii) fee for each modification of an international registration;

    (iii) fee for providing an extract from the International Register;

    (iv) fee for providing an attestation or any other written information concerning the contents of the International Register;

    (v) individual fees as referred to in para (2) of Rule 8, which is a fee which might be declared by a Contracting Party.

6. The Register

2.212 Rule 7(1) of the Regulations requires the International Bureau, where it finds that the application satisfies the conditions set out in Rules 3(1) and 5 have been met, to enter the AO or the GI in the International Register.

2.213 The contents of the international registration are set out in Rule 7(b) to include:

    (i)   all the particulars given in the application;

    (ii) the language in which the International Bureau received the application;

    (iii) the number of the international registration;

    (iv) the date of the international registration.

2.214 Rule 7(3) requires the International Bureau to send a certificate of international registration to the Competent Authority of the Contracting Party of Origin or, in the case of Art 5(3), to the beneficiaries or the natural person or legal entity referred to in Art 5(2)(ii) that requested the registration and notify the international registration to the Competent Authority of each Contracting Party.

2.215 Rule 12(1) permits a Contracting Party, within the time limit referred to in Rule 9(1), to send to the International Bureau a statement confirming that protection is granted to the AO or the GI that is the subject of an international registration.

2.216 Article 20 of the Geneva Act requires the procedures for the modification of international registrations and other entries in the International Register to be specified in the Regulations.

2.217 Permissible modifications are listed in Rule15(1), including:

(i)   the addition or deletion of a beneficiary or some beneficiaries;

(ii)   a modification of the names or addresses of the beneficiaries;

(iii) a modification of the limits of the geographical area of origin of the good or goods to which the AO, or the GI, applies;

(iv)   a modification relating to the legislative or administrative act, the judicial or administrative decision, or the registration referred to in Rule 5(2)(a)(vii);

(v)   a modification relating to the Contracting Party of Origin that does not affect the geographical area of origin of the good or goods to which the AO or the GI applies;

(vi)   a modification under Rule 16.

The procedure for modification is set out in Rule 15(2). It requires a request **2.218** for entry of a modification to be presented to the International Bureau by the Competent Authority of the Contracting Party of Origin or, in the case of Art 5(3), the beneficiaries or the natural person or legal entity referred to in Art 5(2)(ii), and shall be accompanied by the fee specified in Rule 8. A request for entry of a modification referred to in para (1) shall, where it concerns a newly established trans-border geographical area of origin, be presented to the International Bureau by the commonly designated Competent Authority.

Rule 15(3) requires the International Bureau to enter in the International **2.219** Register any modification requested in accordance with paras (1) and (2) together with the date of receipt of the request by the International Bureau, confirm the entry to the Competent Authority that requested the modification, and communicate such modification to the Competent Authorities of the other Contracting Parties.

7.   Period of validity of international registrations

Article 8(1) provides that international registrations shall be valid indefinitely, **2.220** on the understanding that the protection of a registered AO or GI shall no longer be required if the denomination constituting the AO, or the indication constituting the GI is no longer protected in the Contracting Party of Origin.

8.   Protection

Article 9 requires each Contracting Party to protect registered AOs and GIs **2.221** on their territory, within their own legal system and practice but in accordance with the terms of this Act, subject to any refusal, renunciation, invalidation or cancellation that may become effective with respect to its territory. It is understood that Contracting Parties which do not distinguish in their national or regional legislation as between AOs and GIs shall not be required to introduce such a distinction into their national or regional legislation.

2.222 Article 10(1) provides that each Contracting Party shall be free to choose the type of legislation under which it establishes the protection stipulated in the Geneva Act, provided that such legislation meets the substantive requirements of this Act. Further Art 10(2) provides that the provisions of the Geneva Act shall not in any way affect any other protection a Contracting Party may accord in respect of registered appellations of origin or registered GIs under its national or regional legislation, or under other international instruments and Art 10(3) provides that nothing in this Act shall derogate from any obligations that Contracting Parties have to each other under any other international instruments, nor shall it prejudice any rights that a Contracting Party has under any other international instruments.

9. Protection in respect of registered AOs and GIs

2.223 Article 11(1) provides that subject to the provisions of the Geneva Act, in respect of a registered AO or a registered GI, each Contracting Party shall provide the legal means to prevent:

(a) use of the AO or the GI:
   (i) in respect of goods of the same kind as those to which the AO or the GI applies, not originating in the geographical area of origin or not complying with any other applicable requirements for using the AO or the GI;
   (ii) in respect of goods that are not of the same kind as those to which the AO or GI applies or services, if such use would indicate or suggest a connection between those goods or services and the beneficiaries of the AO or the GI, and would be likely to damage their interests, or, where applicable, because of the reputation of the AO or GI in the Contracting Party concerned, such use would be likely to impair or dilute in an unfair manner, or take unfair advantage of, that reputation;
(b) any other practice liable to mislead consumers as to the true origin, provenance or nature of the goods. Article 11(2) provides that para (1)(a) shall also apply to use of the AO or GI amounting to its imitation, even if the true origin of the goods is indicated, or if the AO or the GI is used in translated form or is accompanied by terms such as 'style', 'kind', 'type', 'make', 'imitation', 'method', 'as produced in', 'like', 'similar', or the like any other practice liable to mislead the consumer as to the true origin, provenance.

2.224 Article 11(3) provides that without prejudice to Art 13(1), a Contracting Party shall, *ex officio* if its legislation so permits or at the request of an interested party, refuse or invalidate the registration of a later trade mark if use of the trade mark would result in one of the situations covered by para (1).

10. Renunciation of protection

Rule 16(1) provides for the Competent Authority of the Contracting Party of **2.225** Origin, or, in the case of Art 5(3), the beneficiaries or the natural person or legal entity referred to in Art 5(2)(ii) or the Competent Authority of the Contracting Party of Origin, may at any time notify the International Bureau that protection of the AO, or the GI, is renounced, in whole or in part, in respect of one or some of the Contracting Parties. The notification of renunciation of protection shall state the number of the international registration concerned, preferably accompanied by other information enabling the identity of the international registration to be confirmed, such as the denomination constituting the AO, or the indication constituting the GI.

Rule 16(2) permits the withdrawal in whole or in part of any renunciation, **2.226** including a renunciation under Rule 6(1)(d), at any time by the Competent Authority or, in the case of Art 5(3), the beneficiaries or the natural person or legal entity referred to in Art 5(2)(ii) or the Competent Authority of the Contracting Party of Origin, subject to payment of the fee for a modification and, in the case of a renunciation under Rule 6(1)(d), the correction of the irregularity.

Rule 16(3) requires the International Bureau to enter in the International **2.227** Register any renunciation of protection referred to in para (1), or any withdrawal of a renunciation referred to in para (2), confirm the entry to the Competent Authority of the Contracting Party of Origin and, in the case of Art 5(3), the beneficiaries or the natural person or legal entity, while also informing the Competent Authority of the Contracting Party of Origin, and shall communicate the entry of such modification in the International Register to the Competent Authorities of each Contracting Party to which the renunciation, or the withdrawal of the renunciation relates.

Where the Competent Authority of a Contracting Party receives a notification **2.228** of the withdrawal of a renunciation, Rule 16(4) provides that it may notify the International Bureau of the refusal of the effects of the international registration in its territory. The declaration shall be addressed to the International Bureau by such Competent Authority within a period of one year from the date of receipt of the notification by the International Bureau of the withdrawal of the renunciation. Rules 9 to 12 shall apply *mutatis mutandis*.

11. Genericity

2.229 Article 12 provides that, subject to the provisions of this Act, registered AOs and registered GIs cannot be considered to have become generic[101] in a Contracting Party.

12. Safeguards in respect of trade marks and business names

2.230 Article 13(1) provides that the provisions of this Act shall not prejudice a prior trade mark applied for or registered in good faith, or acquired through use in good faith, in a Contracting Party. Where the law of a Contracting Party provides a limited exception to the rights conferred by a trade mark to the effect that such a prior trade mark in certain circumstances may not entitle its owner to prevent a registered AO or GI from being granted protection or used in that Contracting Party, protection of the registered AO or GI shall not limit the rights conferred by that trade mark in any other way.

2.231 In relation to business names, Art 13(2) provides that the provisions of this Act shall not prejudice the right of any person to use, in the course of trade, that person's name or the name of that person's predecessor in business, except where such name is used in such a manner as to mislead the public.

13. Safeguards in respect of plant variety or animal breed denominations

2.232 Article 13(3) provides that the provisions of this Act shall not prejudice the right of any person to use a plant variety or animal breed denomination in the course of trade, except where such plant variety or animal breed denomination is used in such a manner as to mislead the public.

14. Enforcement, procedures and remedies

2.233 Article 14 requires each Contracting Party to make available effective legal remedies for the protection of registered AOs and registered GIs and provide that legal proceedings for ensuring their protection may be brought by a public

---

101 An Agreed Statement to this Article provides that for the purposes of this Act, it is understood that Art 12 is without prejudice to the application of the provisions of this Act concerning prior use, as, prior to international registration, the denomination or indication constituting the appellation of origin or geographical indication may already, in whole or in part, be generic in a Contracting Party other than the Contracting Party of Origin, eg, because the denomination or indication, or part of it, is identical with a term customary in common language as the common name of a good or service in such Contracting Party, or is identical with the customary name of a grape variety in such Contracting Party.

authority or by any interested party, whether a natural person or a legal entity and whether public or private, depending on its legal system and practice.

15. Refusal of registration

Article 15(1)(a) provides that within the time limit specified in the Regu- **2.234** lations,[102] the Competent Authority of a Contracting Party may notify the International Bureau of the refusal of the effects of an international registration in its territory. The notification of refusal may be made by the Competent Authority *ex officio*, if its legislation so permits, or at the request of an interested party. Article 15(1)(b) requires the notification of refusal shall set out the grounds on which the refusal is based.

Article 15(2) provides that the notification of a refusal shall not be detrimental **2.235** to any other protection that may be available, in accordance with Art 10(2), to the denomination or indication concerned in the Contracting Party to which the refusal relates.

Article 15(3) requires each Contracting Party to provide a reasonable oppor- **2.236** tunity, for anyone whose interests would be affected by an international registration, to request the Competent Authority to notify a refusal in respect of the international registration.

The contents of a refusal are set out in Rule 9(2), requiring an indication of: **2.237**

(i) the Competent Authority notifying the refusal;
(ii) the number of the relevant international registration, preferably accompanied by further information enabling the identity of the international registration to be confirmed, such as the denomination constituting the AO or GI;
(iii) the grounds on which the refusal is based;
(iv) where the refusal is based on the existence of a prior right, as referred to in Art 13, the essential particulars of that prior right and, in particular, if it is constituted by a national, regional or international trademark application or registration, the date and number of such application or registration, the priority date (where appropriate), the name and address of the holder, a reproduction of the trade mark, together with the list of relevant goods and services given in the trade mark application or registration, it being understood that the list may be submitted in the language of the said application or registration;

---

102 Rule 9(1) prescribes one year from the receipt of the notification of international registration under Art 6(4) and that in the case of Art 29(4), this time limit may be extended by another year.

    (v)   where the refusal concerns only certain elements of the AO or the GI, an indication of the elements that it concerns;

    (vi) the judicial or administrative remedies available to contest the refusal, together with the applicable time limits.

2.238   The International Bureau is required by Art 15(4) to record the refusal and the grounds for the refusal in the International Register and to publish the refusal and the grounds for the refusal and communicate the notification of refusal to the Competent Authority of the Contracting Party of Origin or, where the application has been filed directly in accordance with Art 5(3), to the beneficiaries or the natural person or legal entity referred to in Art 5(2)(ii) as well as the Competent Authority of the Contracting Party of Origin.

2.239   Rule 9(3) requires the International Bureau to enter in the International Register any refusal, together with the date on which the notification of refusal was sent to the International Bureau, and shall communicate a copy of the notification of refusal to the Competent Authority of the Contracting Party of Origin or, in the case of Art 5(3), the beneficiaries or the natural person or legal entity referred to in Art 5(2)(ii) as well as the Competent Authority of the Contracting Party of Origin.

2.240   National Treatment is required by Art 15(5) which requires each Contracting Party to make available to interested parties affected by a refusal the same judicial and administrative remedies that are available to its own nationals in respect of the refusal of protection for an AO or a GI.

2.241   Article 16 allows a refusal to be withdrawn in accordance with the procedures specified in the Regulations. Rule 11(1) provides that a refusal may be withdrawn, in part or in whole, at any time by the Competent Authority that notified it. The withdrawal of a refusal shall be notified to the International Bureau by the relevant Competent Authority and shall be signed by such authority.

2.242   Rule 11(2) requires the notification of withdrawal of a refusal to indicate:

    (i)   the number of the international registration concerned, preferably accompanied by other information enabling the identity of the international registration to be confirmed, such as the denomination constituting the AO or the indication constituting the GI;

    (ii) the reason for the withdrawal and, in case of a partial withdrawal, the particulars referred to in Rule 9(2)(v);

    (iii) the date on which the refusal was withdrawn.

Rule 11(3) requires the International Bureau to enter in the International **2.243** Register any withdrawal referred to in para (1) and to communicate a copy of the notification of withdrawal to the Competent Authority of the Contracting Party of Origin or, in the case of Art 5(3), the beneficiaries or the natural person or legal entity referred to in Art 5(2)(ii) as well as the Competent Authority of the Contracting Party of Origin.

16. Prior use

Article 17(1) provides that without prejudice to Art 13, where a Contracting **2.244** Party has not refused the effects of an international registration on the ground of prior use by a third party or has withdrawn such refusal or has notified a grant of protection, it may, if its legislation so permits, grant a defined period as specified in the Regulations, for terminating such use.

The Contracting Party is required by Art 17(2) to notify the International **2.245** Bureau of any such period, in accordance with the procedures specified in the Regulations. Rule 14(1) of the Regulations provides that where a third party has been granted a defined period of time in which to terminate the use of a registered AO, or a registered GI, in a Contracting Party, in accordance with Art 17(1), the Competent Authority of that Contracting Party shall notify the International Bureau accordingly. The notification shall indicate:

(i) the number of the international registration concerned, preferably accompanied by other information enabling the identity of the international registration to be confirmed, such as the denomination constituting the AO, or the indication constituting the GI;

(ii) the identity of the third party concerned;

(iii) the period granted to the third party, preferably accompanied by information about the scope of the use during the transitional period;

(iv) the date from which the defined period begins, it being understood that the date may not be later than one year and three months from the receipt of the notification of international registration under Art 6(4) or, in the case of Art 29(4), no later than two years and three months from such receipt.

Rule 14(2) provides that the duration of the period granted to a third party **2.246** shall not be longer than 15 years, it being understood that the period may depend on the specific situation of each case and that a period longer than ten years would be exceptional.

2.247   Rule 14(3) provides that subject to the notification referred to in para (1) being sent by the Competent Authority to the International Bureau before the date referred to in para (1)(iv), the International Bureau shall enter such notification in the International Register together with the particulars shown therein and shall communicate a copy of the notification to the Competent Authority of the Contracting Party of Origin or, in the case of Art 5(3), the beneficiaries or the natural person or legal entity referred to in Art 5(2)(ii) as well as the Competent Authority of the Contracting Party of Origin.

17.   Notification of grant of protection

2.248   Article 18 provides that the Competent Authority of a Contracting Party may notify the International Bureau of the grant of protection to a registered AO or GI. The International Bureau is required to record any such notification in the International Register and publish it.

18.   Safeguards in the case of notification of withdrawal of refusal or a grant of protection

2.249   Article 13(4) provides that where a Contracting Party that has refused the effects of an international registration under Art 15 on the ground of use under a prior trade mark or other right, as referred to in this Article, notifies the withdrawal of that refusal under Art 16 or a grant of protection under Art 18, the resulting protection of the AO or GI shall not prejudice that right or its use, unless the protection was granted following the cancellation, non-renewal, revocation or invalidation of the right.

19.   Invalidation

2.250   Article 19(1) provides that the invalidation of the effects, in part or in whole, of an international registration in the territory of a Contracting Party may be pronounced only after having given the beneficiaries an opportunity to defend their rights. Such opportunity shall also be given to the natural person or legal entity referred to in Art 5(2)(ii).

2.251   Article 19(2) requires the Contracting Party to notify the invalidation of the effects of an international registration to the International Bureau, which shall record the invalidation in the International Register and publish it.

2.252   Rule 13(1) provides that where the effects of an international registration are invalidated in a Contracting Party, in whole or in part, and the invalidation is no longer subject to appeal, the Competent Authority of the concerned

Contracting Party shall transmit to the International Bureau a notification of invalidation. The notification shall indicate or contain:

(i) the number of the international registration concerned, preferably accompanied by other information enabling the identity of the international registration to be confirmed, such as the denomination constituting the AO, or the indication constituting the GI;

(ii) the authority that pronounced the invalidation;

(iii) the date on which the invalidation was pronounced;

(iv) where the invalidation is partial, the particulars referred to in Rule 9(2)(v);

(v) the grounds on the basis of which the invalidation was pronounced;

(vi) a copy of the decision that invalidated the effects of the international registration.

Rule 13(2) requires the International Bureau to enter the invalidation in the **2.253** International Register together with the particulars referred to in items (i)–(v) of para (1) and shall communicate a copy of the notification to the Competent Authority of the Contracting Party of Origin or, in the case of Art 5(3), the beneficiaries or the natural person or legal entity referred to in Art 5(2)(ii) as well as the Competent Authority of the Contracting Party of Origin.

Article 19(3) provides that invalidation shall not be detrimental to any other **2.254** protection that may be available, in accordance with Art 10(2), to the denomination or indication concerned in the Contracting Party that invalidated the effects of the international registration.

20. Cancellation

Article 8(1) of the Geneva Act provides that the Competent Authority of the **2.255** Contracting Party of Origin, or, in the case of Art 5(3), the beneficiaries or the natural person or legal entity referred to in Art 5(2)(ii) or the Competent Authority of the Contracting Party of Origin, under Art 8(2) may at any time request the International Bureau to cancel the international registration concerned. In case the denomination constituting a registered AO or the indication constituting a registered GI is no longer protected in the Contracting Party of Origin, the Competent Authority of the Contracting Party of Origin shall request cancellation of the international registration.

Rule 17(1) requires the request for cancellation to state the number of the **2.256** international registration concerned, preferably accompanied by other information enabling the identity of the international registration to be confirmed, such as the denomination constituting the appellation of origin or the indication constituting the geographical indication.

2.257 Upon cancellation Rule 17(2) requires the International Bureau to enter in the International Register any cancellation together with the particulars given in the request, confirm the entry to the Competent Authority of the Contracting Party of Origin or, in the case of Art 5(3), the beneficiaries or the natural person or legal entity referred to in Art 5(2)(ii), while also informing the Competent Authority of the Contracting Party of Origin, and shall communicate the cancellation to the Competent Authorities of the other Contracting Parties.

21. Corrections

2.258 Rule 18(1) provides that the International Bureau, acting *ex officio* or at the request of the Competent Authority of the Contracting Party of Origin, if it finds that the International Register contains an error with respect to an international registration, it shall correct the Register accordingly.

2.259 In the case of Art 5(3), Rule 18(2) provides that a request under para (1) can also be submitted by the beneficiaries or by the natural person or legal entity referred to in Art 5(2)(ii) and that the beneficiaries or the natural person or legal entity shall be notified by the International Bureau of any correction concerning the international registration.

2.260 Article 18(3) requires the International Bureau to notify any correction of the International Register to the Competent Authorities of all Contracting Parties as well as, in the case of Art 5(3), the beneficiaries or the natural person or legal entity referred to in Art 5(2)(ii).

D. BILATERAL AND PLURILATERAL AGREEMENTS

2.261 Parallel to, but distinct from, the TRIPS Agreement have been a number of bilateral and plurilateral (including regional) agreements, which contain provisions modifying the TRIPS provisions dealing with GIs. These are discussed in Chapter 8.

3

PROTECTION OF GEOGRAPHICAL INDICATIONS AND DESIGNATIONS OF ORIGIN FOR AGRICULTURAL PRODUCTS AND FOODSTUFFS IN EUROPE

A. INTRODUCTION

The first agricultural product quality policy measures, which incidentally dealt **3.01** with GIs and designations of origin, were laid down in Council Regulation (EEC) No 1601/91 of 10 June 1991 laying down general rules on the definition, description and presentation of aromatised wines, aromatised wine-based drinks and aromatised wine-product cocktails;[1] Council Directive 2001/110/EC of 20 December 2001 relating to honey;[2] Council Regulation (EC) No 247/2006 of 30 January 2006 laying down specific measures for agriculture in the outermost regions of the Union;[3] Council Regulation (EC) No 509/2006 of 20 March 2006 on agricultural products and foodstuffs as traditional specialities guaranteed;[4] Council Regulation (EC) No 510/2006 of 20 March 2006 on the protection of geographical indications and designations of origin for agricultural products and foodstuffs;[5] Council Regulation (EC) No 1234/2007 of 22 October 2007 establishing a common organisation of agricultural markets and on specific provisions for certain agricultural products (Single CMO Regulation);[6] Council Regulation (EC) No 834/2007 of 28 June 2007 on organic production and labelling of organic products;[7] and Regulation (EC) No 110/2008 of the European Parliament and of the

---

1 OJ L 149, 14.6.1991, p. 1.
2 OJ L 10, 12.1.2002, p. 47.
3 OJ L 42, 14.2.2006, p. 1.
4 OJ L 93, 31.3.2006, p. 1.
5 OJ L 93, 31.3.2006, p. 12.
6 OJ L 299, 16.11.2007, p. 1.
7 OJ L 189, 20.7.2007, p. 1.

Council of 15 January 2008 on the definition, description, presentation, labelling and the protection of geographical indications of spirit drinks.[8]

3.02 In addition to legislation dealing with agricultural quality, GIs and designations of origin were mentioned in a series of instruments concerned with the labelling of agricultural products and foodstuffs. Principal among these are the general rules laid down in Directive 2000/13/EC of the European Parliament and of the Council of 20 March 2000 on the approximation of the laws of the Member States relating to the labelling, presentation and advertising of foodstuffs[9] and Regulation (EU) No 1169/2011 of the European Parliament and of the Council of 25 October 2011 on the provision of food information to consumers.[10]

3.03 The first comprehensive European legislation for the registration of geographical indications and designations of origin was Council Regulation 2081/92 on the protection of GIs and designations for agricultural products and foodstuffs[11] and Council Regulation 2082/92 on certificates of specific character for agricultural products and foodstuffs.[12] Council Regulation 2081/92 was considered by a WTO Dispute Panel to be in breach of the TRIPS Agreement and this regulation was repealed and replaced by Council Regulation (EC) No 510/2006 of 20 March 2006.[13]

3.04 In 2006 the European Commission announced a policy review of the Community system for the protection of GIs, expressing its concern with growing global competition for agricultural commodities.[14] One of the chief topics identified for review was the use of the trade mark system as an alternative instrument for the protection of GIs.[15] Subsequently, in the 'Green Paper on Agricultural Product Quality' of 2008[16] and the 'Impact Assessment Report

---

8 OJ L 109, 6.5.2000, p. 29.
9 Ibid.
10 OJ L 304, 22.11.2011, pp. 18–63.
11 OJ L 208, 24 July 1992, p. 1, as amended by 535/97 of 17 March 1997, OJ L 83, 25 March 1997, p. 3.
12 Ibid., p. 9.
13 Regulation (EU) No 1151/2012 of the European Parliament and of the Council of 21 November 2012 on quality schemes for agricultural products and foodstuffs, OJ L 93, 31 March 2006, pp. 12–25.
14 See 'Opinion of the European Economic and Social Committee on Geographical Indications and Designations', OJ 2008, C 204/57 at para 1.2.2.
15 Review of Regulation (EC) no 510/2006 cited in DG Agriculture, 'Background Paper to the Green Paper on Agricultural Product Quality', 2008, 12.
16 European Commission, Green Paper on Agricultural Product Quality: Product Standards, Farming Requirements and Quality Schemes, Brussels, 2008, 13.

on Agricultural Product Quality Policy' of 2009,[17] the Commission affirmed the value of identifying the complementarities between the trade mark and GI systems.

A supervening concern for the EU was the impact of the global financial crisis **3.05** of 2007/08 on economic growth. Its major response was the announcement of the Europe 2020 policy as the EU's growth strategy for the decade from 2010 to 2020. A central feature of this policy was the prioritisation of innovation. In this area agricultural product quality policy was identified to 'provide producers with the right tools to better identify and promote those of their products that have specific characteristics while protecting those producers against unfair practices'.[18] Responding to this priority on 21 November 2012 the European Parliament and the Council promulgated Regulation (EU) No 1151/2012 on quality schemes for agricultural products and foodstuffs.[19]

On 29 July 2013 the EU notified the WTO of a Commission Delegated **3.06** Regulation, together with the Commission Implementing Regulation laying down rules for the application of Regulation (EU) No 1151/2012.[20] The two Commission Regulations replace the Commission Regulation (EC) No 1898/ 2006 of 14 December 2006 laying down detailed rules of implementation of Council Regulation (EC) No 510/2006[21] and Commission Regulation (EC) No 1216/2007 of 18 October 2007 laying down detailed rules for the implementation of Council Regulation (EC) No 509/2006.[22]

The provisions of Council Regulation (EC) No 1151/2012 are detailed below, **3.07** together with the Commission Implementing Regulation laying down rules for the application of Regulation (EU) No 1151/2012 and relevant judicial determinations. References to 'the Regulation' are to Council Regulation (EC) No 1151/2012.

---

17 European Commission of Agricultural Product Quality Policy: Impact Assessment Agricultural Product Quality Policy: Impact Assessment, Part B, Geographical Indications pp. 4–5.
18 Recital (5) Regulation (EU) No 1151/2012 of the European Parliament and of the Council of 21 November 2012 on quality schemes for agricultural products and foodstuffs, OJ L 343, 14.12.2012, p. 1.
19 Ibid.
20 Commission Delegated Regulation (EU) No … /.of XXX supplementing Regulation (EU) No 1151/2012 of the European Parliament and of the Council with regard to the establishment of the Union symbols for protected designations of origin, protected geographical indications and traditional specialities guaranteed and with regard to certain rules on sourcing, certain procedural rules and certain additional transitional rules, WTO Doc., G/TBT/N/EU/139 (hereinafter 'Draft Delegated Regulation').
21 OJ L 369, 23.12.2006, p. 1.
22 OJ L 275, 19.10.2007, p. 3.

B. POLICY UNDERPINNING THE REGULATION

1. Promotion of agricultural diversity

3.08 The Recitals to the Regulation identify a number of policy concerns in addition to the role of agricultural product quality as an ingredient in the Europe 2010 policy. Recital (1) refers to the quality and diversity of the EU's agricultural, fisheries and aquaculture production as one of its important strengths, giving a competitive advantage to the EU's producers and making a major contribution to its living cultural and gastronomic heritage. This is attributed to the capacities of EU farmers and producers 'to maintain their traditions while taking into account the developments of new production methods and material'.

2. Consumer demands

3.09 At the same time Recital (2) observes that EU consumers 'increasingly demand quality as well as traditional products' and are also concerned to maintain the diversity of the agricultural production, which 'generates a demand for agricultural products or foodstuffs with identifiable specific characteristics, in particular those linked to their geographical origin'.

3. Fair competition

3.10 Recital (3) explains that this diversity can only be maintained if producers are rewarded fairly for their effort, which requires that they are able to communicate to buyers and consumers the characteristics of their product under conditions of fair competition and to be able to correctly identify their products on the market place.

4. Rural development

3.11 Recital (4) suggests that operating quality schemes for producers which reward them for their efforts to produce a diverse range of quality products can benefit the rural economy, particularly in less-favoured areas, in mountain areas and in the most remote regions, where the farming sector accounts for a significant part of the economy and production costs are high. Thus Recital (4) suggests that quality schemes are able to contribute to and complement rural development policy as well as market and income support policies of the common agricultural policy (CAP).

5. Legislative coherence

With the plethora of European legislation on agricultural policy and foodstuffs **3.12** labelling, as well as on GIs and designations of origin, Recital (9) identifies the achievement of a greater overall coherence and consistency of agricultural product quality policy as a priority for geographical indications schemes for agricultural products and foodstuffs and traditional specialities.

At the same time Recital (11) points out that as the EU has been pursuing the **3.13** simplification of the regulatory framework of the CAP, this approach should also be applied to regulations in the field of agricultural product quality policy, without, in so doing, calling into question the specific characteristics of those products.

Given these considerations Recital (13) proposes the amalgamation into a **3.14** single legal framework of Regulations (EC) No 509/2006 and (EC) No 510/2006 by the repeal of those regulations and their replacement by Council Regulation (EC) No 1151/2012. This repeal is effected by Art 58 of the Regulation.

6. External influences

Recital (20) to the Regulation explains that it reflects the requirement to make **3.15** provision for the development of designations of origin and GIs at the EU level and for promoting the creation of mechanisms for their protection in third countries in the framework of the WTO or multilateral and bilateral agreements and Recital (21) refers to the experience gained from the implementation of Council Regulation (EEC) No 2081/92 as identifying 'a need to address certain issues, to clarify and simplify some rules and to streamline the procedures of this scheme'. An objective identified in Recital (22) is that in the light of existing practice, the two different instruments for identifying the link between the product and its geographical origin, namely the protected designation of origin (PDO) and the protected geographical indication (PGI), should be further defined and maintained. Without changing the concept of those instruments, 'some modifications to the definitions should be adopted in order to better take into account the definition of GIs laid down in the TRIPS Agreement and to make them simpler and clearer for operators to understand'.

7. Coordination of name protection

3.16 Recital (19) states that '[e]nsuring uniform respect throughout the Union for the intellectual property rights related to names protected in the Union is a priority that can be achieved more effectively at Union level'. This may well underrate the significance of the Trade Marks Directive, which envisages a horizontal approach to the protection of names registered as trade marks.

3.17 Recital (24) maintains that to qualify for protection in the territories of Member States, designations of origin and GIs should be registered only at Union level.

C. OBJECTIVES

1. Communication of product characteristics and farming attributes

3.18 The objectives of the Regulation are identified in Art 1(1) as aiming to help producers of agricultural products and foodstuffs to communicate the product characteristics and farming attributes of those products and foodstuffs to buyers and consumers, thereby ensuring:

    (a) fair competition for farmers and producers of agricultural products and foodstuffs having value-adding characteristics and attributes;
    (b) the availability to consumers of reliable information pertaining to such products;
    (c) respect for intellectual property rights; and
    (d) the integrity of the internal market.

3.19 Evans[23] and Bramley and Bienabe[24] explain that GIs provide mechanisms that facilitate the creation of territorially differentiated niche markets. In Europe there are some empirically based suggestions that consumers and producers both have expectations about the quality of origin products in the European market.[25] Geographical indications are also identified in the scholarship as providing a means for the legal regulation of the use of origin product designations as a means of avoiding the deception of consumers as to the true origin of products, production methods and as to the specific quality of products.[26]

---

23   Evans, 2006.
24   Bramley and Bienabe, 2012.
25   See Teuber, 2011 and Stasi et al, 2011.
26   See O'Connor, 2004; van Caenegem, 2004; Tregear and Giraud, 2011; Barjolle et al, 2011.

2. Rural development

Article 1(1) explains that the measures set out in the Regulation 'are intended **3.20** to support agricultural and processing activities and the farming systems associated with high quality products, thereby contributing to the achievement of rural development policy objectives'.

There is a significant corpus of scholarship on the theory of the contribution **3.21** of origin products to rural development[27] and this is supported by a number of case studies.[28] Sylvander[29] observes that the importance of GIs for sustainable rural development should be assessed by keeping in mind its 'multifactorial' nature, which extends beyond market-related benefits to include also positive social and environmental externalities within the region.

3. Identification of product attributes

Article 1(2) explains that the Regulation establishes quality schemes which **3.22** provide the basis for the identification and, where appropriate, protection of names and terms that, in particular, indicate or describe agricultural products with:

(a) value-adding characteristics; or
(b) value-adding attributes as a result of the farming or processing methods used in their production, or of the place of their production or marketing.

Ittersum et al[30] have made the point that although origin-based marketing has **3.23** a long history, its contemporary relevance is increasing, partly as a reaction to globalisation as local producers need to be able to distinguish their product in the eyes of consumers from generic competition. A number of researchers have identified the capacity of origin labelling to differentiate otherwise homogeneous commodities as the basis for charging premium prices.[31]

---

27 See Ray, 1998; Banks and Marsden, 2000; Marsden et al, 2000; Ilbery and Kneafsey, 2000a and 2000b; Pacciani et al, 2001; Beletti and Marescotti, 2002; Treagear, 2003; Rangnekar, 2004; Réviron and Paus, 2006; Tregear et al, 2007; Blakeney and Mengistie, 2010.

28 See Morgan et al, 2006; Williams, 2007; Blakeney et al, 2012.

29 Sylvander, 2004.

30 Ittersum et al, 2003.

31 Babcock (2003) reports that Bresse poultry in France receives quadruple the commodity price for poultry meat; Italian 'Toscano' oil gains a 20% premium above commodity oil. Gerz and Dupont (2006) conclude that French farmers receive an average of 14% more for milk destined for Comté cheese and that dairy farms in the Comté area have become more profitable since 1990. O'Connor and Company (2005) refer to the protection of 'Lentilles vertes du Puy' which is said to have increased the production of lentils from 13,600 quintals in 1990 to 34,000 quintals in 1996 and 49,776 quintals in 2002. See also the studies by Agarwal and Barone, 2005; Marette, 2005; Williams, 2007; Réviron et al, 2009; Teuber, 2010.

D. SCOPE

1. Agricultural products intended for human consumption

3.24 Recital (15) to the Regulation states that its scope should be limited to the agricultural products intended for human consumption listed in Annex I to the Treaty and to a list of products outside the scope of that Annex that are closely linked to agricultural production or to the rural economy. This is sought to be achieved by Art 2(1) which provides that the Regulation covers agricultural products intended for human consumption listed in Annex I to the Treaty and other agricultural products and foodstuffs listed in Annex I to this Regulation.[32]

3.25 Recital (17) proposes that the scope for designations of origin and GIs should be limited to products for which an intrinsic link exists between product or foodstuff characteristics and geographical origin. It maintains that the inclusion in the current scheme of only certain types of chocolate as confectionery products is an anomaly that should be corrected.

3.26 Annex I under the heading 'Designations of Origin and Geographical Indications' lists beer, chocolate and derived products, bread, pastry, cakes, confectionery, biscuits and other baker's wares, beverages made from plant extracts, pasta, salt, mustard paste, cochineal. Under the heading 'Traditional specialities guaranteed' Annex II lists prepared meals, beer, chocolate and derived products, bread, pastry, cakes, confectionery, biscuits and other baker's wares, beverages made from plant extracts, pasta, salt.

3.27 Annex I of the EU Treaty includes basic foods intended for human consumption such as meat, dairy and fish products, honey, fruits and vegetables. The Regulation does not currently include condiments and sauces, soups, ice cream, sorbet and products containing cocoa. Mention has been made of the unregistrability under the previous Regulation of the fish sauce 'Phu Quoc', one of few GIs registered in Vietnam.[33] This would seem to remain the case.

3.28 Under the Regulation, the coverage of agricultural products is broader than applications to foods, For example, listed in Annex I under the heading 'Designations of Origin and Geographical Indications' are natural gums and

---

32 Art 2(1) envisages that in order to 'take into account international commitments or new production methods or material', the Commission shall be empowered to adopt delegated acts, in accordance with Art 56, supplementing the list of products set out in Annex I to this Regulation. Such products shall be closely linked to agricultural products or to the rural economy.

33 Evans, 2010, 660.

resins, hay, essential oils, cork, flowers and ornamental plants, cotton, wool, wicker, scutched flax, leather, fur and feather.

2. Excluded products

Recital (16) states that the rules provided for in the Regulation should apply **3.29** without affecting existing Union legislation on wines, aromatised wines, spirit drinks, product of organic farming, or outermost regions.

Consequently, Art 2(2) excludes from the Regulation 'spirit drinks, aroma- **3.30** tised wines or grapevine products as defined in Annex XIb to Regulation (EC) No 1234/2007, with the exception of wine-vinegars'.

3. Related provisions

Article 2(3) provides that the Regulation 'shall apply without prejudice to **3.31** other specific Union provisions relating to the placing of products on the market and, in particular, to the single common organisation of the markets, and to food labelling'.

4. Excluded provisions

Article 2(4) of Directive 98/34/EC of the European Parliament and of the **3.32** Council of 22 June 1998 laying down a procedure for the provision of information in the field of technical standards and regulations and of rules on Information Society services[34] shall not apply to the quality schemes established by this Regulation.

E. DEFINITIONS

Article 3 provides that for the purposes of this Regulation the following **3.33** definitions shall apply:

(1) 'quality schemes' means the schemes established under Titles II, III and IV;
(2) 'group' means any association, irrespective of its legal form, mainly composed of producers or processors working with the same product;
(3) 'traditional' means proven usage on the domestic market for a period that allows transmission between generations; this period is to be at least 30 years;

---

34 OJ L 204, 21.7.1998, p. 37.

    (4) 'labelling' means any words, particulars, trade marks, brand name, pictorial matter or symbol relating to a foodstuff and placed on any packaging, document, notice, label, ring or collar accompanying or referring to such foodstuff;

    (5) 'specific character' in relation to a product means the characteristic production attributes which distinguish a product clearly from other similar products of the same category;

    (6) 'generic terms ' means the names of products which, although relating to the place, region or country where the product was originally produced or marketed, have become the common name of a product in the Union;

    (7) 'production step' means production, processing or preparation;

    (8) 'processed products' means foodstuffs resulting from the processing of unprocessed products. Processed products may contain ingredients that are necessary for their manufacture or to give them specific characteristics.

F. PROTECTED DESIGNATIONS OF ORIGIN AND PROTECTED GEOGRAPHICAL INDICATIONS

3.34 Title II of the Regulation contains the provisions for PDOs and PGIs.

1. Objective

3.35 The specific objectives of protecting designations of origin and GIs are securing a fair return for farmers and producers for the qualities and characteristics of a given product, or of its mode of production, and providing clear information on products with specific characteristics linked to geographical origin, thereby enabling consumers to make more informed purchasing choices.

3.36 Article 4 of the Regulation identifies the objective of these provisions to establish a scheme for PDOs and PGIs in order to help producers of products linked to a geographical area by:

    (a) securing fair returns for the qualities of their products;

    (b) ensuring uniform protection of the names as an intellectual property right in the territory of the Union;

    (c) providing clear information on the value-adding attributes of the product to consumers.

This objective is explained by Recital (18) to the Regulation which notes the specific objectives of protecting designations of origin and GIs to be aimed at 'securing a fair return for farmers and producers for the qualities and characteristics of a given product, or of its mode of production, and providing clear information on products with specific characteristics linked to geographical origin, thereby enabling consumers to make more informed purchasing choices'.

2. Requirements for protecting designations of origin and geographical indications

(a) Introduction

There is no equivalent bifurcation for designations of origin and GIs in the **3.37** TRIPS Agreement, or other national bodies of legislation not based upon the EU regulations. As will be seen below, to qualify for a PDO, the product must be produced within a specified geographical area, and the product's quality or characteristics must be 'essentially due to that area'. By comparison, to qualify for a PGI the product has to be produced, processed or prepared in the geographical area, and the quality, reputation or other characteristics must be generally 'attributable' rather than 'essentially due' to that area. The definition of a PGI merely requires a link between the product and the reputation of the place. The product does not have to originate entirely from the defined area; it need only have one particular quality that is attributable to the geographical area. The choice between a PDO and PGI will depend upon whether all or some of the production is done within a geographical area.

The legal implications of each category of protection are not spelt out in the **3.38** Regulation. Article 13(1) defines what 'registered names' shall be protected against. It does not differentiate between the categories of registered name. As registered PGIs and PDOs are available to all producers who meet the qualifying terms of the registered specification, it will obviously be more demanding for a producer to comply with all the elements of a PDO.

Recital (23) of the Regulation explains that an agricultural product or **3.39** foodstuff bearing such a geographical description should meet certain conditions set out in a specification, such as specific requirements aimed at protecting the natural resources or landscape of the production area or improving the welfare of farm animals. Recital (24) states that the protection afforded by this Regulation upon registration should be equally available to designations of origin and GIs of third countries that meet the corresponding criteria and that are protected in their country of origin.

3. Defining the geographical area of production/protection

3.40 The Regulation contains no specific rules for delimiting the geographic area to be the subject of a PDO or PGI. In *Germany v Commission (Agriculture)*[35] the ECJ pointed out that the terms 'region' and 'place' mentioned in Art 2(3) of Regulation (EEC) No 2081/92 'may be interpreted only from a geomorphological and non-administrative viewpoint, in so far as the natural and human factors inherent in a given product are likely to transcend administrative borders'. In that case, which concerned the name 'FETA', the defined geographical area covered only the territory of mainland Greece and the department of Lesbos. All other Greek islands and archipelagos were excluded because the necessary natural and/or human factors did not apply there, including the feed for goats based on the particular flora present in the pastures of eligible regions and the ancestral tradition of transhumance, which produced small native breeds of sheep and goats 'fitted for survival in an environment that offers little food in quantitative terms but, in terms of quality, is endowed with an extremely diversified flora, thus giving the finished product its own specific aroma and flavour'.[36]

3.41 The question of relevant territory is usually raised where the definition of the geographical area excludes producers from the protection of a PDO or PGI. This was the nub of the litigation in the cases discussed below concerning the PGO 'ALTENBURGER ZIEGENKÄSE' and the PGI 'MELTON MOWBRAY PORK PIE'.

3.42 If products under the name in question have been lawfully produced outside the geographical area, this will be taken into account. This was of relevance in 'MÜNCHNER WEIßWURST',[37] which concerned a boiled sausage popular for breakfast in southern Germany. Although the relevant geographical area was supposed to be the city and administrative district of Munich, the German Federal Patent Court noted that 95 per cent of 'MÜNCHNER WEIßWURST' was being produced outside the geographical area. The Court held that it is of particular relevance if products from outside the geographical area are being imported lawfully and unopposed on a large scale into the geographical area.[38]

---

35 [2005] EUECJ C-465/02 at para 35.
36 Ibid., at para. 36.
37 German Federal Patent Court, Case 30 W (pat) 22/06 Münchner Weißwurst [2009], MarkenR 2009, 166 discussed in O. Günzel, 2012, 247.
38 Ibid., at 174.

(a) 'ALTENBURGER ZIEGENKÄSE'

Case T-109/97[39] under Council Regulation 2081/92 concerned the PDO **3.43** 'ALTENBURGER ZIEGENKÄSE' (goat cheese made in the Altenburg region, which must contain a minimum percentage of goat's milk), which was registered by Germany under Regulation No 2081/92. This registration was preceded by several legislative and administrative measures in Germany. On 20 December 1993 the German authorities adopted regulations on cheese, which identified 'ALTENBURGER ZIEGENKÄSE' as a designation of origin, the geographical area of manufacture corresponding to that designation comprised the districts of Altenburg, Schmölln, Gera, Zeitz, Geithain, Grimma, Wurzen and Borna and the city of Gera. The names of these districts were subsequently changed; for example, Schmölln and Altenburg became Altenburger Land, but the geographical area covered by the 'ALTENBURGER ZIEGENKÄSE' designation remained unchanged.

Before the registration by Regulation No 123/97 of the name 'ALTEN- **3.44** BURGER ZIEGENKÄSE', the applicants complained to the relevant German ministry that the German regulations on cheese had defined the area of manufacture of 'ALTENBURGER ZIEGENKÄSE' too widely, by including in particular the district of Wurzen in Saxony, the place of establishment of the cheesemaker Zimmermann GmbH, which has since 1936 likewise manufactured a cheese sold under the name 'ALTENBURGER ZIEGEN-KÄSE'. The applicants requested that the area of manufacture should be limited to the district of Altenburger Land, as the product 'ALTEN-BURGER ZIEGENKÄSE' could come only from the district which had given it its name. The ministry rejected that request. The applicants complained to the Commission, asking for an action for failure to fulfil obligations to be brought against Germany under Art 169 of the EC Treaty.

The Court of First Instance took the view that the German legislature was **3.45** better placed than the Community legislature to define the geographical area, taking account of the particular features of production and marketing in the region. In the present case, it was for the applicants to produce, at the admissibility stage, specific evidence of disadvantage to themselves and they had not succeeded at national level in having the designation restricted to a smaller geographical area, namely the district of Altenburger Land. They had not produced any evidence to show that the contested provisions weakened their rights. Consequently, the application was dismissed.

---

39 *Molkerei Großbraunshain and Bene Nahrungsmittel v Commission* [1998] ECR II-3533.

3.46 On 7 December 1998 the applicants appealed this decision to the ECJ, which reaffirmed the conclusions of the Court of First Instance.[40] It noted that even if the persons to whom Regulation No 123/97 applied 'were identifiable at the time when it was adopted and it were established that their number could in fact scarcely change, its legislative character would not thereby be called into question, as it envisages only objective legal or factual situations'.[41] Moreover, the ECJ noted that the appellants had not shown that it was not possible for them to bring proceedings in a national court against a competitor marketing a cheese under the name 'ALTENBURGER ZIEGENKÄSE' on the ground that it was not produced in the geographical area.[42] In such proceedings they could argue that Regulation No 123/97 was unlawful, and so enable that court to rule on all complaints brought in that respect, if appropriate after referring a question on the validity of that regulation to the Court of Justice for a preliminary ruling.[43]

(b) 'MELTON MOWBRAY PORK PIE'

3.47 In *Northern Foods plc v The Department for Environment, Food and Rural Affairs & Anor*[44] the claimant sought to challenge the decision of the UK Department of the Environment, Food and Rural Affairs (Defra) to forward to the European Commission an application by the Melton Mowbray Pork Pie Association (MMPPA) for the registration of 'MELTON MOWBRAY PORK PIE' as a PGI under EC Council Regulation 2081/92/EEC. The geographical area defined in the application covered a large area, including Leicestershire, Nottinghamshire and parts of Northamptonshire and Lincolnshire. The claimant asserted that the pork pies should come only from Melton Mowbray in Leicestershire. In rejecting this argument Crane J derived assistance[45] from Art 4.2(f),[46] which required that the specification included details bearing out the link with (for a PGI) the geographical origin within the meaning of Art 2(2)(b). He concluded that the 'defined geographical area' for the purposes of Arts 2.2(b) and 4.2 may be different from the 'specific place'

---

40 Case C-447/98, *Molkerei Großbraunshain and Bene Nahrungsmittel v Commission* [2002] ETMR 55.
41 Ibid., at para 67 citing the order in Case C-87/95 P *CNPAAP v Council* [1996] ECR I-2003 at para 35.
42 Ibid., at para 77.
43 Ibid.
44 [2005] EWHC 2971.
45 Ibid., at para 25.
46 Art 4.2(f) of Regulation 2081/92/EEC provided 'the details bearing out the link with the geographical environment or the geographical origin within the meaning of Article 2(2)(a) or (b), whichever is applicable'. Art 2.2(b), which was applicable in this case, provided that for the purposes of the regulation a PGI:

> means the name of a region, a specific place or, in exceptional cases, a country, used to describe an agricultural product or a foodstuff; originating in that region, specific place or country, and which possesses a specific quality, reputation or other characteristics attributable to that geographical origin and the production and/or processing and/or preparation of which take place in the defined geographical area.

(or 'region') where the foodstuff originated and that Defra was clearly correct in forwarding the application to the Commission.[47]

Incidentally, the judge observed that if the claimant was correct, a number of registrations had been made that did not comply with 'the Regulation instancing the specified area for 'PRUNEAUX D'AGEN' which included not merely Agen but large parts of the departments of Lot-et-Garonne, Gironde, Dordogne, Lot and Tarn-et-Garonne'.[48] The judge noted that the argument put forward by the claimant was novel and not one that has previously met with agreement by the Commission or any of the Member States.[49] This may have had a bearing on the judge's determination. **3.48**

4. Designation of origin

Article 5(1) provides that for the purpose of this Regulation, 'designation of origin' is a name which identifies a product: **3.49**

(a) originating in a specific place, region or, in exceptional cases, a country;
(b) whose quality or characteristics are essentially or exclusively due to a particular geographical environment with its inherent natural and human factors; and
(c) the production steps of which all take place in the defined geographical area.

5. Production steps in the defined geographical area

A number of ECJ cases under Regulation No 2081/92 addressed food processing and packaging as part of a PDO. **3.50**

(a) 'RIOJA'

Case C-47/90[50] concerned the PDO 'RIOJA'. Under Arts 84 et seq. of Law No 25/70, wine produced in the La Rioja region was granted a 'denominación de origen'. At that time, a Governing Council for the designation of origin Rioja was set up. By order of the Spanish Minister for Agriculture, Fisheries and Food of 3 April 1991[51] the rules applicable to that designation and the Rioja were approved. Article 32 of the Rioja Rules provided that wine protected by the denominación de origen calificada Rioja shall be bottled exclusively in the registered cellars authorised by the Governing Council, **3.51**

---

47   [2005] EWHC 2971 at para 30.
48   Ibid., at para 27.
49   Ibid., at para 28.
50   *Établissements Delhaize Frères et Compagnie Le Lion SA v Promalvin SA and AGE Bodegas Unidas SA* ('Rioja 1') [1992] ECR I-3669.
51   BOE No 85 of 9 April 1991, p. 10675.

failing which the wine may not bear that designation and that wines protected by the denominación de origen calificada Rioja may be put into circulation and be despatched solely from registered cellars, in special bottles which do not detract from their quality or prestige and have been approved by the Governing Council. The bottles must be of glass and of a capacity authorised by the European Economic Community with the exception of one-litre bottles.

3.52 The ECJ, in response to a request from the Tribunal de Commerce (Commercial Court), Brussels, for a ruling on the compatibility with Art 34 of the Treaty of national legislation such as Decree No 157/88 and the Rioja Rules adopted under it, held that national provisions applicable to wine of designated origin which limited the quantity of wine that might be exported in bulk but otherwise permitted sales of wine in bulk within the region of production constituted measures having equivalent effect to a quantitative restriction on exports which were prohibited by Art 34 of the EC Treaty. The Spanish government's argument that the supervisory powers vested in the Rioja Governing Council were limited to the region of production, making it necessary for the wine to be bottled in the region of production, was rejected by the Court on the ground that Regulation (EEC) No 986/89 had established a system for verifying that the authenticity of the wine was not affected during transport (para 21). In 1994 the Belgian government drew the Commission's attention to the fact that the Spanish rules at issue in *Delhaize* were still in force, despite the interpretation of Art 34 of the Treaty (now, after amendment, Art 29 EC) given by the Court in that judgment, and called on it to act. On 14 November 1994 the competent member of the Commission replied that the Commission considered it 'inappropriate' to persist with Treaty-infringement cases. The Belgian government and the Danish, Netherlands, Finnish and UK governments, intervening in its support, claimed that, by not amending Decree No 157/88 in order to comply with the *Delhaize* judgment, the Kingdom of Spain had failed to fulfil its obligations under Art 5, as interpreted by the Court of Justice of the European Communities in its judgment of 9 June 1992 and Art 5 of the EC Treaty (now Art 10 EC).

3.53 The Spanish, Italian and Portuguese governments and the Commission adduced new information to demonstrate that the reasons underlying the contested requirement were capable of justifying it. They argued that particularly in the wines sector, Community legislation displays a general tendency to enhance the quality of products within the framework of the CAP, in order to promote the reputation of those products through, inter alia, the use of designations of origin which enjoy special protection. In relation to Rioja wine, the Court accepted that its particular qualities and characteristics result from a combination of natural and human factors that are linked to its geographical area of origin and that vigilance must be exercised and efforts made in order for them to be maintained. It accepted that the rules governing the Rioja denominación de origen calificada were designed to uphold those qualities and characteristics. The control over bottling was accepted as being in pursuit of the aim of better safeguarding the quality of the product and, consequently, the reputation of the designation. The Spanish government, supported by the Italian and Portuguese governments, and by the Commission, submits that, without this requirement, the reputation of the Rioja denominación de origen calificada might in fact be undermined. Transport and bottling outside the region of production would, in its view, put the quality of the wine at risk.

The Court accepted that the bottling of wine is an important operation which, **3.54** if not carried out in accordance with strict requirements, could seriously impair the quality of the product. Bottling does not involve merely filling empty containers but normally entails, before filling, a series of complex oenological operations (filtering, clarifying, cooling, and so on) which, if not carried out in accordance with the prescribed rules of the trade, may adversely affect the quality and alter the characteristics of the wine. It was not contested that bulk transport of wine could seriously impair its quality if not undertaken under optimum conditions. Although the Court accepted that, in the best conditions, a wine's characteristics and quality may indeed be maintained when it has been transported in bulk and bottled outside the region of production, it observed that in the case of bottling, the best conditions are more certain to be assured if bottling is done by undertakings established in the region of those entitled to use the designation and operating under their direct control, since they have specialised experience and, what is more, thorough knowledge of the specific characteristics of the wine in question, which must not be impaired or lost at the time of bottling.

The Court noted that for Rioja wines transported and bottled in the region of **3.55** production, the controls were far-reaching and systematic and were the responsibility of the totality of the producers themselves, who have a fundamental interest in preserving the reputation acquired and that it could be inferred that the risk to which the quality of the product finally offered to consumers is exposed was greater where it has been transported and bottled outside the region of production than when those operations have taken place within the region. Accordingly, it ruled that the requirement at issue, whose aim was to preserve the considerable reputation of Rioja wine by strengthening control over its particular characteristics and its quality, was justified as a measure protecting the denominación de origen calificada, which may be used by all the producers concerned and is of decisive importance to them.

(b) 'GRANA PADANO'

3.56 Case C-469/00[52] concerned the PDO 'GRANA PADANO', which was registered for 'Cheeses'. This registration was subject to the condition that the grating of the cheese be carried out in the region of production and packaging. The defendant imported, grated, pre-packaged and distributed 'GRANA PADANO' cheese in France, marketing it under the designation 'Grana Padano râpé frais'. Two Italian cheese producers brought an action against the defendant in the Tribunal de commerce de Marseille seeking an injunction and damages. The Tribunal granted both applications and on appeal the Cour d'appel d'Aix-en-Provence upheld the judgment, stating that the acts of unfair competition were sufficiently made out by the marketing in France since 1992 of 'GRANA PADANO' cheese in grated form. The Cour de cassation, to which the defendant appealed, sought a ruling from the ECJ as to whether Art 29 [EC] was to be interpreted as precluding national legislation reserving the 'GRANA PADANO' designation of origin for cheese grated in the region of production, in so far as such an obligation is not indispensable for preserving the specific characteristics which the product has acquired.

(c) 'PROSCIUTTO DI PARMA'

3.57 Case C-108/01[53] concerned the Italian Legge No 26, tutela della denominazione di origine 'PROSCIUTTO DI PARMA' (Law No 26 on protection of the designation of origin 'Prosciutto di Parma') of 13 February 1990, which reserved the designation 'PROSCIUTTO DI PARMA' ('Parma Ham') exclusively to ham marked with a distinguishing mark allowing it to be identified at any time, obtained from fresh legs of pigs raised and slaughtered in mainland Italy, produced in accordance with provisions laid down in the law. Article 25 of Decreto No 253, regolamento di esecuzione della legge 13 febbraio 1990, No 26 (Decree No 253 implementing Law No 26 of 13 February 1990) of 15 February 1993 prescribed that the slicing and packaging of Parma Ham must take place at plants in the typical production area which are approved by the Consorzio, responsible for monitoring Parma Ham production. 'PROSCIUTTO DI PARMA' was registered as a PDO under Regulation No 1107/96, under the heading 'Meat-based products'. The Consorzio was registered as an inspection body for the PDO under Art 10(2) of Regulation No 2081/92.

3.58 Asda Stores Ltd, which operated a chain of supermarkets in the UK, purchased pre-sliced ham bearing the description 'Parma ham' from Hygrade

---

52 *Ravil SARL v Bellon Import SARL* [2003] ECR I-5053; [2004] ETMR 22.
53 *Consorzio del Prosciutto di Parma and Salumificio S. Rita SpA v Asda Stores Ltd and Hygrade Foods Ltd* [2003] EUECJ C-108.

Foods Ltd, which itself purchased the ham boned but not sliced from an Italian producer who was a member of the Consorzio. The ham was sliced and hermetically sealed by Hygrade in packets bearing the wording 'ASDA A taste of Italy PARMA HAM Genuine Italian Parma Ham'. The Consorzio brought proceedings by writ in the UK against Asda and Hygrade seeking various injunctions against them, essentially requiring them to cease their activities, on the ground that they were contrary to the rules applicable to Parma Ham.

The House of Lords sought a ruling from the ECJ as to whether the Italian **3.59** legislation read with Commission Regulation (EC) No 1107/96 and the specification for the PDO 'PROSCIUTTO DI PARMA' created a valid Community right, directly enforceable in the court of a Member State, to restrain the retail sale as Parma Ham of sliced and packaged ham derived from hams duly exported from Parma in compliance with the conditions of the PDO but which have not been thereafter sliced, packaged and labelled in accordance with the specification.[54]

The ECJ, applying the 'Rioja' case,[55] ruled that Regulation No 2081/92 must **3.60** be interpreted as not precluding the use of a PDO from being subject to the condition that operations such as the slicing and packaging of the product take place in the region of production, where such a condition was laid down in the specification. Although this was a measure having equivalent effect to a quantitative restriction on exports, the Court accepted that it was justified for the purpose of guaranteeing the authenticity and quality of the product, noting that Community legislation displayed a general tendency to enhance the quality of products within the framework of the common agricultural policy, in order to promote the reputation of those products through, inter alia, the use of designations of origin, which enjoy special protection. Designations of origin, as industrial and commercial property rights, protected those entitled to use them against improper use of those designations by third parties seeking to profit from the reputation which they have acquired. It ruled that the specification of the PDO 'PROSCIUTTO DI PARMA', by requiring the slicing and packaging to be carried out in the region of production, was intended to allow the persons entitled to use the PDO to keep under their control one of the ways in which the product appears on the market. This condition was justified as safeguarding the quality and authenticity of the product, and consequently the reputation of the PDO, for those who are entitled to use it.

---

54   *Consorzio del Prosciutto di Parma v Asda Stores Ltd and Others* [2001] UKHL 7.
55   Case C-388/95 *Belgium v Spain* [2000] ECR I-3123.

3.61 The Court noted that the slicing and packaging of Parma Ham constituted important operations which may harm the quality and hence the reputation of the PDO if they were carried out in conditions that result in a product not possessing the organoleptic qualities expected. Those operations may also compromise the guarantee of the product's authenticity, because they necessarily involve removal of the mark of origin of the whole hams used. Consequently, the Court ruled that the condition of slicing and packaging in the region of production, whose aim was to preserve the reputation of Parma Ham by strengthening control over its particular characteristics and its quality, may be regarded as justified as a measure protecting the PDO which may be used by all the operators concerned and is of decisive importance to them. The resulting restriction was therefore regarded as necessary for attaining the objective pursued, in that there were no alternative less restrictive measures capable of attaining it.

3.62 Finally, it concluded that the PDO 'PROSCIUTTO DI PARMA' would not receive comparable protection from an obligation imposed on operators established outside the region of production to inform consumers, by means of appropriate labelling, that the slicing and packaging has taken place outside that region. Therefore, any deterioration in the quality or authenticity of ham sliced and packaged outside the region of production, resulting from materialisation of the risks associated with slicing and packaging, might harm the reputation of all ham marketed under the PDO, including that sliced and packaged in the region of production under the control of the group of producers entitled to use the PDO.

6. Raw materials

3.63 Article 5(3) provides that (notwithstanding Art 51) certain names shall be treated as designations of origin even though the raw materials for the products concerned come from a geographical area larger than, or different from, the defined geographical area, provided that:

    (a)   the production area of the raw materials is defined;
    (b)   special conditions for the production of the raw materials exist;
    (c)   there are control arrangements to ensure that the conditions referred to in point (b) are adhered to; and
    (d)   the designations of origin in question were recognised as designations of origin in the country of origin before 1 May 2004.

3.64 Article 5(3) provides that only live animals, meat and milk may be considered as raw materials for the purposes of this paragraph.

7. Animal feed

3.65 Article 1(1) of the Delegated Regulation provides that for the purposes of Art 5 of Regulation (EU) No 1151/2012:

> feed shall be sourced entirely from within the defined geographical area in respect of products of animal origin the name of which is registered as a protected designation of origin. Insofar as sourcing entirely from within the defined geographical area is not technically practicable, feed sourced from outside that area can be added, provided that the product quality or characteristic essentially due to the geographical environment are not affected. Feed sourced from outside the defined geographical area shall in no case exceed 50% of dry matter on annual basis.

3.66 One example of a PDO involving materials coming from outside the area is the specification of Parma Ham, which allows for the pigs to come from an area which is larger than the area in which Parma Ham may be produced. Interestingly, with climate change, an argument will be made that raw materials should be sourced from new areas which enjoy the biological features of the original area, eg, grapes for protected 'CHAMPAGNE' wine coming from southern England.

8. Geographical indication

3.67 Article 5(2) provides that for the purpose of this Regulation, 'geographical indication' is a name which identifies a product:

(a) originating in a specific place, region or country;

(b) whose given quality, reputation or other characteristic is essentially attributable to its geographical origin; and

(c) at least one of the production steps of which take place in the defined geographical area.[56]

3.68 A number of cases under Regulation No 2081/92 have addressed the definition of PGIs.

---

56 Contrast with the definition of geographical indication in Art 2(1(b)) of Council Regulation (EC) No 510/2006 of 20 March 2006:

> (b) 'geographical indication' means 'the name of a region, a specific place or, in exceptional cases, a country, used to describe an agricultural product or a foodstuff:
>
> • originating in that region, specific place or country, and
> • which possesses a specific quality, reputation or other characteristics attributable to that geographical origin, and
> • the production and/or processing and/or preparation of which take place in the defined geographical area.

(a) 'SPREEWÄLDER GURKEN'

3.69 Case C-269/99[57] concerned an application under Art 17 of Regulation No 2081/92 from the German government on 26 January 1994 for gherkins originating in the geographical area defined as 'the glacial valley of the Spree between the northern edge of the town of Cottbus and the Neuendorfer See, north of the town of Lübben'. Following various requests made by Spreewald-verein eV, the German authorities on several occasions amended the original application so that, finally, according to the amended specification, it sought the registration of the designation 'SPREEWÄLDER GURKEN' as a PGI. The geographical area was the territory along the Spree between Jänschwalde and Dürrenhofe and within the boundaries of an economic region determined by decisions of the local legislative bodies, called Wirtschaftsraum Spreewald (Spreewald economic zone), with the result that the geographical area defined in the original specification was more than doubled. During the course of the national phase of the simplified procedure under Art 17 of Regulation No 2081/92, a number of interested third parties raised objections to the application for registration of the designation 'SPREEWÄLDER GURKEN'. They claimed that the special geographical and climatic conditions referred to in the application applied at most to the Spreewald, in the strict sense of the inland delta region, and not to the entire Wirtschaftsraum Spreewald, and that the processed product should not contain any raw materials from other production areas.

3.70 The defendant, Jütro, had its registered office and production facility in Jüterbog, a town outside the geographical area of the PGI 'SPREEWÄLDER GURKEN'. It produced, among other things, pickled gherkins called 'Jütro Gurkenfäßchen', which were distributed throughout Germany under the description 'Spreewälder Art' (Spreewald style). A number of other producers of pickled gherkins brought an action in the Landgericht Hamburg seeking an order prohibiting Jütro from using the designation 'Spreewälder Art' for its pickled gherkins on the ground that the use of that designation was invalid.

3.71 The Landgericht Hamburg referred to the ECJ the question whether Regulation (EC) No 590/1999 of 18 March 1999 supplementing, by the designation 'SPREEWÄLDER GURKEN', the Annex to Regulation (EC) No 1107/96 on the registration of geographical indications and designations of origin under the procedure laid down in Art 17 of Regulation (EEC) No 2081/92 was compatible with European Community law. It took the view that the registration procedure provided for by Art 17 of Regulation No 2081/92

---

57   *Carl Kühne and Others v Jütro Konservenfabrik GmbH & Co. KG* [2001] ECR I-9517.

was not applicable to the designation 'SPREEWÄLDER GURKEN' because that designation was neither legally protected nor established by usage as a GI within the meaning of that article. It was not legally protected because there was no system of formal legal protection for GIs in Germany. Further, the national court was of the view that registration of the designation 'SPREE-WÄLDER GURKEN' as a PGI may have infringed Arts 2 and 4 of Regulation No 2081/92 since the nature of the product and the expectations of consumers mean that it should have been registered as a PDO. In its view, the designation 'SPREEWÄLDER GURKEN' told consumers that all the gherkins came from the Spreewald proper and were, consequently, of a particular quality. Finally, the national court considered that, since the specifications relating to the geographical area did not reflect consumer expectations of a product carrying the designation 'SPREEWÄLDER GURKEN', the registration of the latter as a PGI gives approval to the misleading of consumers.

The ECJ ruled that it was for the national courts to rule on the lawfulness of **3.72** an application for registration of a designation. Similarly as the national court had made its own assessment, which was not tainted by a manifest error, the Commission could properly register the designation 'SPREEWÄLDER GURKEN' under the simplified procedure. The registration of the designation 'SPREEWÄLDER GURKEN' as a PGI was because a foodstuff may be treated as originating from the geographical area concerned if it is processed or produced in that area, even if the raw materials are produced in another region.

The same principle applied to the registration of the designation 'SPREE- **3.73** WÄLDER GURKEN' for the geographical area defined in the amended specification.

9. Generic indications

Recital (52) maintained that existing rules concerning the continued use of **3.74** names that are generic should be clarified so that generic terms that are similar to or form part of a name or term that is protected or reserved should retain their generic status. This issue is addressed in Art 6 of the Regulation.

10. Definition of 'generic terms'

Article 3(6) of the Regulation defines 'generic terms' to mean 'the names of **3.75** products which, although relating to the place, region or country where the product was originally produced or marketed, have become the common name of a product in the Union'.

3.76 Article 41(1) provides that without prejudice to Art 13, this Regulation shall not affect the use of terms that are generic in the Union, even if the generic term is part of a name that is protected under a quality scheme.

3.77 Article 41(2) provides that to establish whether or not a term has become generic, account shall be taken of all relevant factors, in particular:

    (a)   the existing situation in areas of consumption;
    (b)   the relevant national or Union legal acts.

3.78 Article 41(3) provides that in order to fully protect the rights of interested parties, the Commission shall be empowered to adopt delegated acts, in accordance with Art 56, laying down additional rules for determining the generic status of terms referred to in Art 41(1).

11. Non-registration of generic terms

3.79 Article 6(1) provides that 'generic terms shall not be registered as protected designations of origin or protected geographical indications'.

12. Protection of registered PDOs and PGIs

3.80 Article 13(2) of the Regulation provides that PDOs and PGIs shall not become generic.

3.81 Under Art 3(3) of EEC Regulation 2081/92, the Council was supposed to draw up a non-exhaustive, indicative list of the names of products which were regarded as generic under Art 3(1) and not able to be registered. This list was to have been published in the *Official Journal* before that regulation entered into force, but the Member States were unable to agree on these designations and the list has never been published. No equivalent provision appears in the Regulation.

3.82 However, generic terms can be protected, if they are part of a composite product name. For example the generic cheese names Emmentaler, Cheddar and Gouda have been protected as: *Allgäuer Emmentaler PGI*,[58] *Emmentaler de*

---

58   EU No: DE/PDO/0017/0459 – 24.01.1997 (Allgäuer Emmentaler).

Savoie PDO,[59] *West Country Farmhouse Cheddar PDO,*[60] *Orkney Scottish Island Cheddar PGI*[61] and *Gouda Holland PDO.*[62]

13. Case law

In Case C-317/95[63] Advocate General Colomer, said that a sign or term that **3.83** represents a product is generic if it forms 'part of the general cultural and gastronomic stock and may, in principle, be used by any producer'.[64] Once an indication becomes generic, it loses its geographic meaning and acquires another meaning based on qualities that do not necessarily relate to specific characteristics from the initial geographical origin.[65]

In Case C-446/07[66] the ECJ ruled that a name could not be presumed to be **3.84** generic until such time as it had become registered as a PDO.

(a) 'FETA'

The question of genericity under Regulation No 2082/92 was considered in **3.85** Cases C-289/96, C-293/96 and C-299/96, which concerned the use of the name 'FETA' for cheese. At the time of Greece's accession to the Community in 1981 the name 'FETA' was not protected by law, but by usage. In July 1992 the Commission had asked the Member States to give it the names of the products which they regarded as capable of being recognised as generic names. In 1994 Greece finalised rules governing the production of 'FETA' cheese[67] and on this basis it sought protection under Regulation No 2081/92. By letter dated 21 January 1994, the Greek government requested registration of the word 'Feta' as a PDO under the simplified procedure laid down by Art 17 of Regulation No 2081/92.

In response to the request, the Commission indicated that it was concerned **3.86** that the name 'FETA' might have become generic. In April 1994 the

---

59   EU No: FR/PGI/0017/0179 – 21.06.1996 (Emmentaler de Savoie).
60   EU No: UK/PDO/0017/0279 – 21.06.1996 (West Country farmhouse Cheddar).
61   EU No: GB/PGI/0005/00908 – 03.11.2011 (Orkney Scottish Island Cheddar).
62   EU No: NL/PGI/0005/0328 – 27.11.2003 (Gouda Holland).
63   Opinion of the Advocate General Ruiz-Jarabo Colomer in *Canadane Cheese Trading AMBA and Adelfi G. Kouri Anonymos Emoriki Kai Viomichaniki Etaireia v Hellenic Republic* [1997] ECR I-4681.
64   Ibid., at 28.
65   See WIPO, *About Geographical Indications: What is a 'Generic' Geographical Indication?* http://www.wipo.int/geo_indications/en/about.html#generic.
66   *Alberto Severi v Regione Emilia Romagna* [2009] EUECJ C-446/07.
67   By an order of the Deputy Minister for Agriculture (313025/94) the denomination of origin 'FETA' was established and protected in Greece. Art 1(2) of that order stated that 'the milk used for the manufacture of "FETA" must come exclusively from the regions of Macedonia, Thrace, Epirus, Thessaly, Central Greece, Peloponnese and Lesbos'.

Commission arranged for a survey of the opinions of some 12,800 nationals of the then 12 EC Member States. The Commission also submitted its file to the Scientific Committee. Having regard to the results of the market survey and the opinion of the Scientific Committee, the Commission concluded that the name 'FETA' had not become generic within the meaning of Art 3 of Regulation No 2081/92 and on 12 June 1996 adopted Regulation No 1107/1996 by which 'FETA' was registered as a PDO.[68]

3.87 The ECJ ruled that it was not permissible for the Commission to minimise the importance to be attached to the situation existing in the Member States other than the state of origin and that account must be taken of the existence of products which are legally on the market and have therefore been legally marketed under that name in Member States other than the state of origin by which registration is applied for. Thus as the Commission did not take due account of all the factors which Art 3(1) of the basic regulation required it to take into consideration, the ECJ ruled that the contested regulation had to be annulled to the extent to which it registered the name 'FETA' as a PDO.

3.88 Joined Cases C-465/02 and C-466/02[69] considered an objection by some Member States to the Commission Regulation adopted following the above judgment, on 25 May 1999, which deleted the name 'FETA' from the Register of protected designations of origin and geographical indications.[70] By letter of 15 October 1999, the Commission sent the Member States a questionnaire on the manufacture and consumption of cheeses known as 'feta' and on how well known that name was amongst consumers in each of the states. The information received in response to that questionnaire was presented to the Scientific Committee, which gave its unanimous opinion on 24 April 2001 that the name 'feta' was not generic in nature. On 14 October 2002 the Commission adopted a regulation under which the name 'Φ|AaETA' ('FETA') was once again registered as a PDO.[71]

3.89 In its consideration of the objections to the regulation by Germany, Denmark, France and the UK, the ECJ noted that it was common ground in the present proceedings that the term 'feta' was derived from the Italian word meaning

---

68 Commission Regulation 1107/96 of 12 June 1996 on the registration of geographical indications and designations of origin under the procedure laid down in Article 17 of Council Regulation 2081/92, OJ L 148, 21/06/1996, p. 1.

69 *Germany v Commission (Agriculture)* [2005] EUECJ C-465/02, [2005] ECR I-9115, [2006] ETMR 16.

70 Commission Regulation (EC) No 1070/1999 of 25 May 1999 amending the Annex to Regulation (EC) No 1107/96 (OJ 1999 L 130, p. 18).

71 Commission Regulation (EC) No 1829/2002 of 14 October 2002 amending the Annex to Regulation (EC) No 1107/96 with regard to the name 'Feta' (OJ 2002 L 277, p. 10).

'slice', which had entered the Greek language in the seventeenth century.[72] It was also common ground that 'feta' was not the name of a region, place or country within the meaning of Art 2(2)(a) of Regulation (EEC) No 2081/92 and so could not be registered as a designation of origin pursuant to that provision, but at most could be registered under Art 2(3) of Regulation No 2081/92, which extended the definition of designation of origin, in particular, to certain traditional non-geographical names.[73]

Combining these two provisions, the ECJ observed that the place or region **3.90** referred to in Art 2(3) must be defined as a geographical environment with specific natural and human factors, which is capable of giving an agricultural product or foodstuff its specific characteristics, and thus the area of origin referred to must present homogeneous natural factors which distinguish it from the areas adjoining it.[74]

Applying these criteria the ECJ noted that the Commission had based its **3.91** decision on the Greek legislation governing the matter,[75] Art 1 of Ministerial Order No 313025/1994 of 11 January 1994 recognising the PDO of feta cheese, which required that the milk used for the manufacture of 'FETA' must come exclusively from the regions of Macedonia, Thrace, Epirus, Thessaly, Central Greece, Peloponnese and the department (*Nomos*) of Lesbos and which excluded the island of Crete and the archipelagos of Sporades, the Cyclades, the Dodecanese Islands and the Ionian Islands. According to the information submitted to the Court, the geographical area was defined by reference, inter alia, to geomorphology (mountainous or semi-mountainous nature of the terrain); climate (mild winters, hot summers and a great deal of sunshine); and to botanical characteristics (the typical vegetation of the Balkan medium mountain range). The Court took this into account in deciding that the area in question in the case was not determined in an artificial manner.[76]

On the question of whether 'FETA' had become generic, the Court noted that **3.92** it was common ground that white cheeses soaked in brine have been produced for a long time, not only in Greece but in various countries in the Balkans and

---

72 [2005] EUECJ C-465/02 at para 46.
73 Art 2(3) of Reg No 2081/92 provided:

> Certain traditional geographical or non-geographical names designating an agricultural product or a foodstuff originating in a region or a specific place, which fulfil the conditions referred to in the second indent of paragraph 2(a) shall also be considered as designations of origin.

74 [2005] EUECJ C-465/02 at para 50.
75 Art 1 of Ministerial Order No 313025/1994 of 11 January 1994 recognising the PDO of feta cheese.
76 Ibid., at para 58.

the south-east of the Mediterranean basin, but that in those countries those cheeses are known under names other than 'FETA'.

3.93 Although the Court observed that the production of cheese under the name 'FETA' was quite large and of substantial duration in other countries such as Denmark and Germany, the Court took note of the Scientific Committee that the production and consumption of this cheese has remained concentrated in Greece.[77] The information provided to the Court indicated that the majority of consumers in Greece considered that the name 'FETA' carries a geographical and not a generic connotation, whereas in Denmark the majority of consumers believed the name to be generic.[78] However, the evidence adduced to the Court of usage in Member States other than Greece was that feta was commonly marketed with labels referring to Greek cultural traditions and civilisation, from which the Court said that it was legitimate to infer that consumers in those Member States perceived feta as a cheese associated with the Hellenic Republic, even if in reality it has been produced in another Member State.[79] The Court ruled that those various factors relating to the consumption of feta in the Member States tended to indicate that the name 'FETA' was not generic in nature.[80]

(b) 'GRANA BIRAGHI'

3.94 Case T-291/03[81] concerned an application filed at the Office for Harmonization in the Internal Market (OHIM) on 2 February 1998, by Biraghi SpA for registration of the word mark 'GRANA BIRAGHI' as a Community trade mark for cheeses. The Consorzio per la tutela del formaggio Grana Padano filed an application with OHIM for a declaration that the Community trade mark 'was invalid as contrary to the protection of the "PDO GRANA PADANO" registered under to Regulation 2081/92 and, relying on the registration of the earlier national and international marks "GRANA" and "GRANA PADANO"'. The Cancellation Division of OHIM allowed an application for a declaration of invalidity under Art 14 of Regulation No 2081/92. Biraghi appealed against that decision on the grounds of the generic and descriptive nature of the term 'GRANA'. The First Board of Appeal allowed the appeal, annulling the Cancellation Division's decision and rejecting the application for a declaration that the Community trade mark 'GRANA BIRAGHI' was invalid. The Board of Appeal found that the word 'grana' was generic and described an essential quality of the goods in question.

---

77   Ibid., at paras 83–85.
78   Ibid., at para 86.
79   Ibid., at para 87.
80   Ibid., at para 88.
81   *Consorzio per la tutela del formaggio Grana Padano v OHIM* [2007] ECR II-3081.

Therefore, according to the Board of Appeal decision, the existence of the PDO 'GRANA PADANO' did not preclude the registration of the sign 'GRANA BIRAGHI' as a Community trade mark.

This decision was reversed by the Court of First Instance of the European **3.95** Communities. The Court looked at the legislative history of the protection of 'grana' and 'grana padano'. The first legislative recognition of the name 'grana' dates back to 1938 (Regio Decreto Legge No 1177). In a decree, which prescribed the minimum fat content in the different Italian cheeses, reference was made to different granas (parmigiano reggiano, lodigiano, emiliano, lombardo and veneto), all produced in the area of the plain of the Po.[82] The Court took this decree and subsequent legislation introducing the name 'grana padano' whilst abandoning the earlier names as an indication that grana was a cheese traditionally produced in numerous areas of the plain of the Po, and the qualifier 'padano' was inserted not to restrict the scope of the PDO to certain granas only, but in order to place them all under the same increased protection, conferred initially by Italian legislation and subsequently by Regulation No 2081/92.[83] The Court therefore ruled that the changes in the Italian legal context indicated that the name 'grana' was not generic.[84]

(c) 'BAYERISCHES BIER'

In Case C-343/07, *Bavaria and Bavaria Italia*[85] it was argued that the name **3.96** 'BAYERISCHES BIER' was a 'generic name' within the meaning of Arts 3(1) and 17(2) of Regulation No 2081/92 because of the national application since 1906 of the Law on beer purity of 1516 ('Reinheitsgebot') and the international spread of the Bavarian bottom-fermentation brewing method in the course of the nineteenth century. It was also argued that the word 'Bayerisches' or translations of it were used as synonyms for 'beer' in at least three Member States (Denmark, Sweden and Finland) and as synonyms for the Bavarian bottom-fermentation brewing method in names, trade marks and labels of commercial companies the world over, including in Germany. The ECJ observed that it must be borne in mind that when assessing the generic character of a name, it is necessary, under Art 3(1) of Regulation No 2081/92, to take into account the places of production of the product concerned both inside and outside the Member State which obtained the registration of the name at issue, the consumption of that product and how it is perceived by consumers inside and outside that Member State, the existence of national

---

82 Ibid., at para 77.
83 Ibid., at para 78.
84 Ibid.
85 [2009] ECR I-5491.

legislation specifically relating to that product, and the way in which the name has been used in Community law.[86]

3.97 The ECJ did not consider that the evidence as it was presented established genericity. It stated that as regards a PGI:

> a name becomes generic only if the direct link between, on the one hand, the geographical origin of the product and, on the other hand, a specific quality of that product, its reputation or another characteristic of the product, attributable to that origin, has disappeared, and that the name does no more than describe a style or type of product.[87]

3.98 In the present case, the Community institutions had found that the PGI 'BAYERISCHES BIER' had not become generic and the ECJ added that the existence between 1960 and 1970 of the collective marks 'BAYRISCH BIER' and 'BAYERISCHES BIER' and of five different bilateral agreements relating to the protection of the name 'BAYERISCHES BIER' as a geographical name showed that that name had no generic character.[88]

(d) 'PARMESAN'

3.99 The issue of the possible genericity of 'Parmesan' was raised for the first time in Case C-66/00,[89] which concerned a criminal prosecution of a person for selling as 'Parmesan' a dried, grated pasteurised cheese in powder form, made from a mixture of several types of cheese of various origins, which did not conform to the specification for the PDO 'PARMIGIANO REGGIANO'. The Tribunale di Parma referred a number of questions to the ECJ for a preliminary ruling. The German government intervened, contending that the reference for a preliminary ruling was inadmissible on the ground that the designation 'Parmesan' used by the accused was a generic name and not a PDO within the meaning of Regulation No 2081/92. The Court did not have to deal with this issue, but it commented that 'in the present case it is far from clear that the designation "parmesan" has become generic'.[90]

3.100 The question of the genericity of 'Parmesan' was finally dealt with by the Court in Case C-132/05.[91] Following a complaint filed by several economic

---

86   Ibid., at para 101, citing Case C-132/05 *Commission v Federal Republic of Germany* [2008] ECR I-957; [2008] ETMR 32, para 53.
87   Ibid., at para 107.
88   Ibid., at para 109.
89   *Criminal proceedings against Dante Bigi* [2002] ECR I-5917.
90   Ibid., at para 20.
91   *Commission of the European Communities v Federal Republic of Germany* [2008] ETMR 32.

operators, the Commission requested the German authorities, by letter of 15 April 2003, to give clear instructions to the government bodies responsible for the combating of fraud to bring to an end the marketing on German territory of products designated as 'Parmesan' which did not comply with the specification for the PDO 'PARMIGIANO REGGIANO'. The German government replied by letter of 13 May 2003 that, although the term 'Parmesan' had historical roots in the region of Parma, it had become a generic name for hard cheeses of diverse origins, grated or intended to be grated, distinct from the PDO 'PARMIGIANO REGGIANO'. On an application by the Commission, the ECJ ruled that the Federal Republic of Germany had failed to show that the name 'Parmesan' had become generic.[92] It had merely restricted itself to providing quotations from dictionaries and specialist literature and did not 'provide any comprehensive view of how the word "Parmesan" is perceived by consumers in Germany and other Member States, and failed even to give any figures as to the production or consumption of the cheese marketed under the name "Parmesan" in Germany or in other Member States'.[93] Finally, the Court noted that at the hearing, the Federal Republic of Germany was also unable to provide information on the quantity of cheese produced in Italy under the PDO 'PARMIGIANO REGGIANO' and imported into Germany, making it impossible for the Court to use the factors relating to the consumption of that cheese as indicators of the generic character of the name 'Parmesan'.[94]

The Court noted in a *dictum* that a geographical designation could, over time and through use, become a generic name in the sense that consumers cease to regard it as an indication of the geographical origin of the product, and come to regard it only as an indication of a certain type of product. 'That shift in meaning occurred for instance in the case of the designations "Camembert" and "Brie".'[95] **3.101**

14. Names of plant or animal breeds

Article 6(2) disqualifies from registration as a designation of origin or geographical indication 'where it conflicts with a name of a plant variety or an animal breed and is likely to mislead the consumer as to the true origin of the product'. **3.102**

---

92 Ibid., at para 57.
93 Ibid., at para 54.
94 Ibid., at para 56.
95 Ibid., at para 36.

3.103 Council Regulation 2100/94[96] on Community variety rights requires that for protection a plant variety must be designated by a denomination in accordance with the provisions of Art 63.[97] The use of a geographical name as a part of the denomination of the plant variety is not prohibited. O'Connor[98] refers to the name 'Genova', which is used for the plant variety *Ocimum basilicum L.* and the fact that Alicante, Ankara, Athene, Barcelona, Bari, Bordeaux, Calcutta, Cannes and Copenhagen are registered for new varieties of Rosemallow (*Hibiscus L.*) and Baltimore, Barcelona, Chianti, Colorado, Flandria, Guadelope and Liguria for Lettuce (*Lactuca sativa L.*).

3.104 There is no requirement for a link between the particular plant variety and its geographical location.

3.105 Article 42(1) of the Regulation provides that it shall not prevent the placing on the market of products the labelling of which includes a name or term protected or reserved under a quality scheme described in Title II, Title III, or Title IV that contains or comprises the name of a plant variety or animal breed, provided that the following conditions are met:

(a) the product in question comprises or is derived from the variety or breed indicated;
(b) consumers are not misled;
(c) the usage of the name of the variety or breed name constitutes fair competition;
(d) the usage does not exploit the reputation of the protected term; and
(e) in the case of the quality scheme described in Title II, production and marketing of the product had spread beyond its area of origin prior to the date of application for registration of the geographical indication.

3.106 Article 42(2) provides that in order to further clarify the extent of rights and freedoms of food business operators to use the name of a plant variety or of an animal breed referred to in Art 42(1), the Commission shall be empowered to adopt delegated acts, in accordance with Art 56, concerning rules for determining the use of such names.

15. Homonyms

3.107 Article 6(3) provides that a name proposed for registration

---

96 Council Regulation 2100/94 of 27 July 1994 on Community plant variety rights, OJ L 227, 1/09/1994, p. 1.
97 See Art 63 of Council Regulation 2100/94 and Commission Regulation 930/2000 of 4 May 2000, establishing implementing rules as to the suitability of the denomination of varieties of agricultural plant species and vegetable species.
98 O'Connor, 2004, n 171.

that is wholly or partially homonymous with a name already entered in the register established under Art 11 may not be registered unless there is sufficient distinction in practice between the conditions of local and traditional usage and presentation of the homonym registered subsequently and the name already entered in the register, taking into account the need to ensure equitable treatment of the producers concerned and that consumers are not misled.

16.   Misleading designations of origin or geographical indications

3.108 Article 6(4) of the Regulation provides that a name proposed for registration as a designation of origin or geographical indication shall not be registered where, in the light of a trade mark's reputation and renown and the length of time it has been used, registration of the name proposed as the designation of origin or geographical indication would be liable to mislead the consumer as to the true identity of the product.

3.109 Article 6(3) provides that a homonymous name which misleads the consumer into believing that products come from another territory shall not be registered even if the name is accurate as far as the actual territory, region or place of origin of the products in question is concerned.

17.   Product specification

(a)   Content of specification

3.110 Article 7(1) provides that a PDO or a PGI shall comply with a specification which shall include at least:

Name

(a)   the name to be protected as a designation of origin or geographical indication, as it is used, whether in trade or in common language, and only in the languages which are or were historically used to describe the specific product in the defined geographical area;

Description

(b)   a description of the product, including the raw materials, if appropriate, as well as the principal physical, chemical, microbiological or organoleptic characteristics of the product;

Geographical area

(c)   the definition of the geographical area delimited with regard to the link referred to in point (f)(i) or (ii) of this paragraph, and, where appropriate, details indicating compliance with the requirements of Article 5(3);

Proof of origin

(d) evidence that the product originates in the defined geographical area referred to in Article 5(1) or (2);

Packaging

(e) a description of the method of obtaining the product and, where appropriate, the authentic and unvarying local methods as well as information concerning packaging, if the applicant group so determines and gives sufficient product-specific justification as to why the packaging must take place in the defined geographical area to safeguard quality, to ensure the origin or to ensure control, taking into account Union law, in particular that on the free movement of goods and the free provision of services;

Link

(f) details establishing the following:
   (i) the link between the quality or characteristics of the product and the geographical environment referred to in Article 5(1); or
   (ii) where appropriate, the link between a given quality, the reputation or other characteristic of the product and the geographical origin referred to in Article 5(2).

(b) Raw materials

3.111 Article 5(3) provides that only live animals, meat and milk may be considered as raw materials for the purposes of this paragraph.

3.112 Article 1(2) of the Delegated Regulation provides that '[a]ny restrictions to the origin of raw materials provided in the product specification of a product the name of which is registered as a protected geographical indication shall be justified in relation to the link referred to in point (f)(ii) of Art 7(1) of Regulation (EU) No 1151/2012'.

G. REGULATION (EU) NO 1169/2011 ON THE PROVISION OF FOOD INFORMATION TO CONSUMERS

3.113 Regulation (EU) No 1169/2011 of the European Parliament and of the Council of 25 October 2011 on the provision of food information to consumers[99] contains a number of provisions dealing with the labelling of country of origin or place of provenance.

---

99   OJ L 304, 22.11.2011, pp. 18–63.

Recital (29) to this Regulation explains that the indication of the country of **3.114** origin or of the place of provenance of a food should be provided whenever its absence is likely to mislead consumers as to the true country of origin or place of provenance of that product and that in all cases, the indication of country of origin or place of provenance should be provided in a manner which does not deceive the consumer and on the basis of clearly defined criteria.

Recital (30) suggests that in some cases, food business operators may want to **3.115** indicate the origin of a food on a voluntary basis to draw consumers' attention to the qualities of their product. In this case such indications should also comply with harmonised criteria.

1. Relationship with the Foodstuffs Regulation

Article 26(1) of Regulation (EU) No 1169/2011 provides that: **3.116**

> This Article shall apply without prejudice to labelling requirements provided for in specific Union provisions, in particular Council Regulation (EC) No 509/2006 of 20 March 2006 on agricultural products and foodstuffs as traditional specialties guaranteed[100] and Council Regulation (EC) No 510/2006 of 20 March 2006 on the protection of geographical indications and designations of origin for agricultural products and foodstuffs.[101]

As both these regulations have been repealed by Regulation (EU) No 1151/2012, it is expected that there will be a consequential amendment to Art 26(1) to replace these references with Regulation (EU) No 1151/2012.

2. Mandatory indication of country of origin or place of provenance

Article 26(2) of Regulation (EU) No 1169/2011 lists the following as **3.117** situations where the indication of the country of origin or place of provenance shall be mandatory:

(a) where failure to indicate this might mislead the consumer as to the true country of origin or place of provenance of the food, in particular if the information accompanying the food or the label as a whole would otherwise imply that the food has a different country of origin or place of provenance;

---

100   OJ L 93, 31.3.2006, p. 1.
101   Ibid., p. 12.

    (b) for meat falling within the Combined Nomenclature ('CN') codes listed in Annex XI.[102]

The application of this point shall be subject to the adoption of implementing acts referred to in para 8.[103]

3.118 Recital (31) to Regulation (EU) No 1169/2011 explains that the indication of origin is currently mandatory for beef and beef products[104] in the EU following the bovine spongiform encephalopathy crisis and it has created consumer expectations. 'The impact assessment of the Commission confirms that the origin of meat appears to be consumers' prime concern.' Recital (31) points out that as there are other meats widely consumed in the EU, such as swine, sheep, goat and poultry meat, it is appropriate to impose a mandatory declaration of origin for those products. The specific origin requirements could differ from one type of meat to another according to the characteristics of the animal species. The Recital indicates that it is appropriate to provide for the establishment through implementing rules of mandatory requirements that could vary from one type of meat to another 'taking into account the principle of proportionality and the administrative burden for food business operators and enforcement authorities'.

3. Ingredients

3.119 Article 26(3) of Regulation (EU) No 1169/2011 provides that where the country of origin or the place of provenance of a food is given and where it is not the same as that of its primary ingredient:

    (a) the country of origin or place of provenance of the primary ingredient in question shall also be given; or

    (b) the country of origin or place of provenance of the primary ingredient shall be indicated as being different to that of the food.

---

102   Annex XI provides as follows:

      Types of Meat for which the Indication of the Country of Origin or Place of Provenance is Mandatory
CN codes (Combined Nomenclature 2010) | Description |
0203 | Meat of swine, fresh, chilled or frozen |
0204 | Meat of sheep or goats, fresh, chilled or frozen |
Ex0207 | Meat of the poultry of heading 0105, fresh, chilled or frozen |.

103   Art 26(8) provides that by 13 December 2013, following impact assessments, the Commission shall adopt implementing acts concerning the application of Art 26(2)(b) and the application of Art 26(3). Those implementing acts shall be adopted in accordance with the examination procedure referred to in Art 48(2).

104   Regulation (EC) No 1760/2000 of the European Parliament and of the Council of 17 July 2000 establishing a system for the identification and registration of bovine animals and regarding the labelling of beef and beef products, OJ L 204, 11.8.2000, p. 1.

The application of this paragraph shall be subject to the adoption of the implementing acts referred to in para 8.[105]

4. Reports on mandatory indications of country of origin or place of provenance

Recital (32) to Regulation (EU) No 1169/2011 reports that mandatory origin **3.120** provisions have been developed on the basis of vertical approaches, for instance for honey,[106] fruit and vegetables,[107] fish,[108] beef and beef products,[109] and olive oil.[110] There is a need to explore the possibility to extend mandatory origin labelling for other foods. It is therefore appropriate to request the Commission to prepare reports covering the following foods: types of meat other than beef, swine, sheep, goat and poultry meat; milk; milk used as an ingredient in dairy products; meat used as an ingredient; unprocessed foods; single-ingredient products; and ingredients that represent more than 50 per cent of a food. Milk being one of the products for which an indication of origin is considered of particular interest, the Commission report on this product should be made available as soon as possible. Based on the conclusions of such reports, the Commission may submit proposals to modify the relevant Union provisions or may take new initiatives, where appropriate, on a sectoral basis.

Article 26(4) of Regulation (EU) No 1169/2011 provides that within five **3.121** years from the date of application of Art 26(2)(b), the Commission shall submit a report to the European Parliament and the Council to evaluate the mandatory indication of the country of origin or place of provenance for products referred to in that provision.

Article 26(5) of Regulation (EU) No 1169/2011 provides that by 13 Decem- **3.122** ber 2014, the Commission shall submit reports to the European Parliament and the Council regarding the mandatory indication of the country of origin or place of provenance for the following foods:

---

105   Ibid.

106   Council Directive 2001/110/EC of 20 December 2001 relating to honey, OJ L 10, 12.1.2002, p. 47.

107   Commission Regulation (EC) No 1580/2007 of 21 December 2007 laying down implementing rules of Council Regulations (EC) No 2200/96, (EC) No 2201/96 and (EC) No 1182/2007 in the fruit and vegetable sector, OJ L 350, 31.12.2007, p. 1.

108   Council Regulation (EC) No 104/2000 of 17 December 1999 on the common organisation of the markets in fishery and aquaculture products, OJ L 17, 21.1.2000, p. 22.

109   Regulation (EC) No 1760/2000.

110   Commission Regulation (EC) No 1019/2002 of 13 June 2002 on marketing standards for olive oil, OJ L 155, 14.6.2002, p. 27.

    (a) types of meat other than beef and those referred to in Art 26(2)(b);
    (b) milk;
    (c) milk used as an ingredient in dairy products;
    (d) unprocessed foods;
    (e) single-ingredient products;
    (f) ingredients that represent more than 50 per cent of a food.

3.123   Article 26(6) of Regulation (EU) No 1169/2011 provides that by 13 December 2013, the Commission shall submit a report to the European Parliament and the Council regarding the mandatory indication of the country of origin or place of provenance for meat used as an ingredient.

3.124   Article 26(7) of Regulation (EU) No 1169/2011 provides that the reports referred to in Art 26(5) and (6) shall take into account the need for the consumer to be informed, the feasibility of providing the mandatory indication of the country of origin or place of provenance and an analysis of the costs and benefits of the introduction of such measures, including the legal impact on the internal market and the impact on international trade.

3.125   The Commission may accompany those reports with proposals to modify the relevant Union provisions.

3.126   Article 26(8) of Regulation (EU) No 1169/2011 provides that by 13 December 2013, following impact assessments, the Commission shall adopt implementing acts concerning the application of Art 26(2)(b) and the application of Art 26(3). Those implementing acts shall be adopted in accordance with the examination procedure referred to in Art 48(2).

3.127   Article 26(9) of Regulation (EU) No 1169/2011 provides that in the case of foods referred to in Art 26(2)(b), in Art 26(5)(a) and in Art 26(6), the reports and the impact assessments under this Article shall consider, inter alia, the options for the modalities of expressing the country of origin or place of provenance of those foods, in particular with respect to each of the following determining points in the life of the animal:

    (a) place of birth;
    (b) place of rearing;
    (c) place of slaughter.

5. National measures on additional mandatory particulars

Article 39(1) of Regulation (EU) No 1169/2011 provides that in addition to **3.128** the mandatory particulars referred to in Art 9(1)[111] and in Art 10, Member States may, in accordance with the procedure laid down in Art 45, adopt measures requiring additional mandatory particulars for specific types or categories of foods, justified on grounds of at least one of the following:

(a) the protection of public health;
(b) the protection of consumers;
(c) the prevention of fraud;
(d) the protection of industrial and commercial property rights, indications of provenance, registered designations of origin and the prevention of unfair competition.

Article 39(2) of Regulation (EU) No 1169/2011 provides that by means of Art **3.129** 39(1):

Member States may introduce measures concerning the mandatory indication of the country of origin or place of provenance of foods only where there is a proven link between certain qualities of the food and its origin or provenance. When notifying such measures to the Commission, Member States shall provide evidence that the majority of consumers attach significant value to the provision of that information.

---

111 Art 9(1) of Regulation (EU) No 1169/2011 provides that:

in accordance with Articles 10 to 35 and subject to the exceptions contained in this Chapter, indication of the following particulars shall be mandatory:

(a) the name of the food;
(b) the list of ingredients;
(c) any ingredient or processing aid listed in Annex II [Annex II lists Substances or products causing allergies or intolerances] or derived from a substance or product listed in Annex II causing allergies or intolerances used in the manufacture or preparation of a food and still present in the finished product, even if in an altered form;
(d) the quantity of certain ingredients or categories of ingredients;
(e) the net quantity of the food;
(f) the date of minimum durability or the 'use by' date;
(g) any special storage conditions and/or conditions of use;
(h) the name or business name and address of the food business operator referred to in Article 8(1) [Art 8(1) provides that the food business operator responsible for the food information shall be the operator under whose name or business name the food is marketed or, if that operator is not established in the Union, the importer into the Union market];
(i) the country of origin or place of provenance where provided for in Article 26;
(j) instructions for use where it would be difficult to make appropriate use of the food in the absence of such instructions;
(k) with respect to beverages containing more than 1,2 % by volume of alcohol, the actual alcoholic strength by volume;
(l) a nutrition declaration.

6. Commission guidelines on labelling

3.130 Recital (32) explains that when PDOs or PGIs are used as ingredients, the Commission Communication entitled 'Guidelines on the labelling of foodstuffs using protected designations of origin (PDOs) or protected geographical indications (PGIs) as ingredients' should be taken into account. These Guidelines were issued by the Commission in December 2010.[112] The Communication made it clear that adoption of the guidelines is voluntary and that they should not be deemed to constitute a legally binding interpretation of EU legislation on PDOs and PGIs or the Labelling Directive. Referring to the ECJ's decision in Case C-446/07 *Alberto Severi v Regione Emilia Romagna*,[113] the Communication cautioned that the issue of whether a specific product's labelling could mislead purchasers or consumers, or any decision regarding the potentially misleading nature of a trade name was the responsibility of domestic courts.

3.131 According to the Commission, a name registered as a PDO or PGI may legitimately be included in the list of ingredients of a foodstuff and a name registered as a PDO or PGI may be mentioned in or close to the trade name of a foodstuff incorporating products benefiting from a registered name, as well as in the labelling, presentation and advertising relating to that foodstuff, provided that the following conditions are met:

- The foodstuff in question should not contain *any other 'comparable ingredient'*, ie any other ingredient which may partially or totally replace the ingredient benefiting from a PDO or PGI. As a non-restrictive example of the concept of 'comparable ingredient', the Commission considers that a blue-veined cheese (commonly known as 'blue cheese') could be considered comparable to 'Roquefort' cheese.
- This ingredient should also be used in *sufficient quantities* to confer an essential characteristic on the foodstuff concerned. However, given the wide range of possible scenarios, the Commission is not able to suggest a minimum percentage to be uniformly applied. As an example, the incorporation of a minimum amount of a spice benefiting from a PDO/PGI in a foodstuff could, if appropriate, be sufficient to confer an essential characteristic on that foodstuff. By contrast, the incorporation of a minimum amount of meat benefiting from a PDO/PGI in a

---

112 'Guidelines on the labelling of foodstuffs using protected designations of origin (PDOs) or protected geographical indications (PGIs) as ingredients' 2010/C 341/03.
113 [2009] ECR I-8041 at para 60.

foodstuff would not a priori be sufficient to confer an essential characteristic on a foodstuff.

- The *percentage of incorporation* of an ingredient with a PDO or PGI
  should ideally be indicated in or in close proximity to the trade name of
  the relevant foodstuff or, failing that, in the list of ingredients, in direct
  relation to the ingredient in question.[114]

The Commission indicated that on the assumption that the conditions above **3.132**
are met, the EU terms, abbreviations or symbols accompanying the registered
name should be used in labelling, within or close to the trade name or in the
list of ingredients of the foodstuff only if it is made clear that the said foodstuff
is not itself a PDO or PGI.[115] Otherwise, the Commission indicated that this
would result in the undue exploitation of the reputation of the PDO or PGI
and result in consumers being misled. It gave the example of the trade names
'Pizza au Roquefort' (Pizza with Roquefort) or 'Pizza élaborée avec du
Roquefort AOP' (Pizza prepared with Roquefort PDO) as hardly giving rise
to a dispute contrasting with the trade name 'Pizza au Roquefort AOP' (Pizza
with Roquefort PDO) which 'would clearly be ill-advised, in as much as it
could give the consumer the impression that the pizza as such was a product
benefiting from a PDO'.[116]

Where an ingredient comparable to an ingredient benefiting from a PDO/ **3.133**
PGI has been incorporated in a foodstuff, the name registered as a PDO/PGI,
the Commission takes the view that it *should appear only in the list of
ingredients*, in accordance with rules similar to those applicable to the other
ingredients mentioned.[117] In particular, it would be appropriate to use characters that are identical in terms of font, size, colour, etc.

According to the Commission, provisions governing the use of a name **3.134**
registered as a PDO or PGI in the labelling of other foodstuffs should not be
included, in principle, in the specification for that name but may be included
by way of exception only in order to resolve a specific, clearly identified
difficulty and provided they are objective, proportionate and non-
discriminatory. In any case, any provisions contained in the specifications
could not be aimed at or result in modifying the legislation in force.[118]

---

114 2010/C 341/03 at 2.1(1)–(2).
115 Ibid., at 2.1(3).
116 Ibid.
117 Ibid., at 2.1(4).
118 Ibid., at 2.2.

7. Verification of compliance with product specification

3.135 Article 37(1) provides that in respect of PDOs, PGIs and TSGs that designate products originating within the Union, verification of compliance with the product specification, before placing the product on the market, shall be carried out by:

(a) one or more of the competent authorities as referred to in Art 36 of this Regulation; and/or

(b) one or more of the control bodies within the meaning of point (5) of Art 2 of Regulation (EC) No 882/2004[119] operating as a product certification body.

The costs of such verification of compliance with the specifications may be borne by the operators that are subject to those controls. The Member States may also contribute to these costs.

3.136 Article 37(2) provides that in respect of designations of origin, GIs and TSGs that designate products originating in a third country, the verification of compliance with the specifications before placing the product on the market shall be carried out by:

(a) one or more of the public authorities designated by the third country; and/or

(b) one or more of the product certification bodies.

H. APPLICATION FOR REGISTRATION

3.137 It has been pointed out that the application process has tended to be quite lengthy, up to five or six years, because of the time taken by the Home Office before an application is forwarded to the Commission, the possibility of objection proceedings both at the national and Community level as well as the problem of lack of resources to deal with applications.[120]

1. Scope of application processes

3.138 Article 48 provides that the provisions of Chapter IV: Application and registration processes for designations of origin, GIs, and TSGs (Arts 49–54) shall apply in respect of the quality schemes set out in Title II (PDOs and

---

119 Regulation (EC) No 882/2004 of the European Parliament and of the Council of 29 April 2004 on official controls performed to ensure the verification of compliance with feed and food law, animal health and animal welfare rules, OJ L 299, 8.11.2008, p. 25.

120 See Profeta et al, 2009, 634–7.

PGIs) and Title III (TSGs – 'traditional speciality guaranteed'). These are discussed in the last section of this chapter.

2. Content of application for registration

Article 8(1) provides that an application for registration of a designation of **3.139** origin or geographical indication pursuant to Art 49(2) or (5) shall include at least:

(a) the name and address of the applicant group and of the authorities or, if available, bodies verifying compliance with the provisions of the product specification;
(b) the product specification provided for in Art 7;
(c) a single document setting out the following:
    (i) the main points of the product specification: the name, a description of the product, including, where appropriate, specific rules concerning packaging and labelling, and a concise definition of the geographical area;
    (ii) a description of the link between the product and the geographical environment or geographical origin referred to in Art 5(1) or (2), as the case may be, including, where appropriate, the specific elements of the product description or production method justifying the link.

An application as referred to in Art 49(5) shall, in addition, include proof that **3.140** the name of the product is protected in its country of origin.

3. Dossier

Article 8(2) provides that an application dossier referred to in Art 49(4) shall **3.141** comprise:

(a) the name and address of the applicant group;
(b) the single document referred to in point (c) of paragraph 1 of this Article;
(c) a declaration by the Member State that it considers that the application lodged by the applicant group and qualifying for the favourable decision meets the conditions of this Regulation and the provisions adopted pursuant thereto;
(d) the publication reference of the product specification.

4. Transitional national protection

Article 9 of the Regulation provides that a Member State may, on a **3.142** transitional basis only, grant protection to a name under this Regulation at national level, with effect from the date on which an application is lodged with the Commission.

3.143 Such national protection shall cease on the date on which either a decision on registration under this Regulation is taken or the application is withdrawn.

3.144 Where a name is not registered under this Regulation, the consequences of such national protection shall be the sole responsibility of the Member State concerned.

3.145 The measures taken by Member States under the first paragraph shall produce effects at national level only, and they shall have no effect on intra-Union or international trade.

5. Grounds for opposition

3.146 Article 10(1) provides that a reasoned statement of opposition as referred to in Art 51(2) shall be admissible only if it is received by the Commission within the time limit set out in that paragraph and if it:

    (a)   shows that the conditions referred to in Art 5 and Art 7(1) are not complied with;

    (b)   shows that the registration of the name proposed would be contrary to Art 6(2), (3) or (4);

    (c)   shows that the registration of the name proposed would jeopardise the existence of an entirely or partly identical name or of a trade mark or the existence of products which have been legally on the market for at least five years preceding the date of the publication provided for in point (a) of Art 50(2); or

    (d)   gives details from which it can be concluded that the name for which registration is requested is a generic term.

3.147 Article 10(2) provides that the grounds for opposition shall be assessed in relation to the territory of the Union.

I. REGISTER OF PROTECTED DESIGNATIONS OF ORIGIN AND PROTECTED GEOGRAPHICAL INDICATIONS

1. The Register

3.148 Article 11(1) of Regulation (EU) No 1151/2012 provides that the Commission shall adopt implementing acts, without applying the procedure referred to in Art 57(2), establishing and maintaining a publicly accessible updated register of PDOs and PGIs recognised under this scheme.

2. Registration of third country geographical indications

Recital (27) explains that the Union negotiates international agreements, **3.149** including those concerning the protection of designations of origin and GIs, with its trade partners. In order to facilitate the provision to the public of information about the names so protected, and in particular to ensure protection and control of the use to which those names are put, the names may be entered in the register of PDOs and PGIs.

Article 11(2) provides that geographical indications pertaining to products of **3.150** third countries that are protected in the Union under an international agreement to which the Union is a contracting party may be entered in the register. Unless specifically identified in the said agreement as PDOs under this Regulation, such names shall be entered in the register as PGIs.

A recent illustration of a third country registration under the Regulation is for **3.151** Thai Hom Mali rice (Khao Hom Mali Thung Kula Rong-Hai).[121] An application had been made to register this designation pursuant to Art 6(2) of Council Regulation (EC) No 510/2006. This had been objected to by Belgium, France, Italy, the Netherlands and the UK, because it contained the requirement that packaging should take place in the area of production,[122] which the objecting nations considered inadequately justified or unnecessarily restrictive. In the absence of agreement between the objectors and Thailand the Commission resolved the question in Thailand's favour.

3. Form and content of the Register

Article 11(3) provides that the Commission may adopt implementing acts **3.152** laying down detailed rules on the form and content of the register. Those implementing acts shall be adopted in accordance with the examination procedure referred to in Art 57(2).

---

121 Commission Implementing Regulation (EU) No 120/2013 of 11 February 2013 entering a name in the register of protected designations of origin and protected geographical indications (Khao Hom Mali Thung Kula Rong-Hai) (PGI), OJ L 41/3 12.2.2013.

122 The packaging requirement was that it:

shall take place in Roi Et, Surin, Sisaket, Mahasarakham, and Yasothon Provinces, which are the five provinces of the Thung Kula Rong-Hai area. This is to give consumers an effective guarantee of the origin, the quality of the rice and in order to ensure the retention of 2-acetyl-1-pyrroline (0,1–0,2 micrograms at the growing field), unique to Khao Hom Mali grown within the identified geographical area. The repackaging is not allowed in order to minimise possible dilution in concentration, which would undermine its distinctive aroma and to prevent any possible contamination or alteration of the product.

Ibid., clause 3.6.

4. List of international agreements

3.153 Recital (27) informs in order to facilitate the provision to the public of information about the names protected under international agreements, including those concerning the protection of designations of origin and GIs, with its trade partners and in particular to ensure protection and control of the use to which those names are put, the names may be entered in the register of PDOs and PGIs. Unless specifically identified as designations of origin in such international agreements, Recital (27) proposes that the names should be entered in the register as PGIs.

3.154 Article 11(4) provides that the Commission shall make public and regularly update the list of the international agreements referred to in Art 11(2) as well as the list of GIs protected under those agreements.

J. NAMES, SYMBOLS AND INDICATIONS

3.155 Recital (28) to the Regulation recommends that in view of their specific nature, special provisions concerning labelling should be adopted in respect of PDOs and PGIs that require producers to use the appropriate Union symbols or indications on packaging. In the case of Union names, the use of such symbols or indications should be made obligatory in order to make this category of products, and the guarantees attached to them, better known to consumers and in order to permit easier identification of these products on the market, thereby facilitating checks. Taking into account the requirements of the WTO, the use of such symbols or indications should be made voluntary for third country GIs and designations of origin.

1. Permitted use of PDOs and PGIs

3.156 Article 12(1) provides that PDOs and PGIs may be used by any operator marketing a product conforming to the corresponding specification.

2. Union symbols

3.157 Article 12(2) provides that Union symbols designed to publicise PDOs and PGIs shall be established. Article 2 of the Delegated Regulation provides that the Union symbols referred to in Art 12(2) 'are established as laid down in the Annex to this Regulation'.

Article 12(3) provides that in the case of products originating in the Union **3.158** that are marketed under a PDO or a PGI registered in accordance with the procedures laid down in this Regulation, the Union symbols associated with them shall appear on the labelling. In addition, the registered name of the product should appear in the same field of vision. The indications 'protected designation of origin' or 'protected geographical indication' or the corresponding abbreviations 'PDO' or 'PGI' may appear on the labelling.

Article 59 provides that Art 12(3) 'shall apply from 4 January 2016, without **3.159** prejudice to products already placed on the market before that date'.

3. Protection of indications and symbols

Article 44(1) provides that indications, abbreviations and symbols referring to **3.160** the quality schemes may only be used in connection with products produced in conformity with the rules of the quality scheme to which they apply. This applies in particular to the following indications, abbreviations and symbols: '(a) "protected designation of origin", "protected geographical indication", "geographical indication", "PDO", "PGI", and the associated symbols, as provided for in Title II'.

4. Other symbols

Article 12(4) provides that in addition, the following may also appear on the **3.161** labelling: depictions of the geographical area of origin, as referred to in Art 5, and text, graphics or symbols referring to the Member State and/or region in which that geographical area of origin is located.

5. Collective marks

Article 12(5) provides that without prejudice to Directive 2000/13/EC,[123] the **3.162** collective geographical marks referred to in Art 15 of Directive 2008/95/ EC[124] may be used on labels, together with the PDO or PGI.

---

123 Directive 2000/13/EC of the European Parliament and of the Council of 20 March 2000 on the approximation of the laws of the Member States relating to the labelling, presentation and advertising of foodstuffs, OJ 2000 L 109, p. 29.
124 Directive 2008/95/EC of the European Parliament and of the Council of 22 October 2008 to approximate the laws of the Member States relating to trade marks, OJ L 299, 8.11.2008.

6. Third-country products

3.163 Article 12(6) provides that in the case of products originating in third countries marketed under a name entered in the register, the indications referred to in Art 12(3) or the Union symbols associated with them may appear on the labelling.

K. PROTECTION

3.164 Article 13(1) provides that registered names shall be protected against:

(a) any direct or indirect commercial use of a registered name in respect of products not covered by the registration where those products are comparable to the products registered under that name or where using the name exploits the reputation of the protected name, including when those products are used as an ingredient;

(b) any misuse, imitation or evocation, even if the true origin of the products or services is indicated or if the protected name is translated or accompanied by an expression such as 'style', 'type', 'method', 'as produced in', 'imitation' or similar, including when those products are used as an ingredient;

(c) any other false or misleading indication as to the provenance, origin, nature or essential qualities of the product that is used on the inner or outer packaging, advertising material or documents relating to the product concerned, and the packing of the product in a container liable to convey a false impression as to its origin;

(d) any other practice liable to mislead the consumer as to the true origin of the product.

Where a PDO or a PGI contains within it the name of a product which is considered to be generic, the use of that generic name shall not be considered to be contrary to point (a) or (b) of the first subparagraph.

3.165 Article 13(3) provides that Member States shall take appropriate administrative and judicial steps to prevent or stop the unlawful use of PDOs and PGIs, as referred to in para 1, that are produced or marketed in that Member State. To that end Member States shall designate the authorities that are responsible for taking these steps in accordance with procedures determined by each individual Member State. 'These authorities shall offer adequate guarantees of objectivity and impartiality, and shall have at their disposal the qualified staff and resources necessary to carry out their functions.'

L. RIGHT TO BRING AN ACTION IN RESPECT OF A GEOGRAPHICAL INDICATION

Under Art 173 of the EC Treaty, a natural or legal person may bring an action **3.166**
against a decision which, although in the form of a regulation, is of direct and
individual concern to him. Registering a PDO or a PGI gives all economic
operators whose products satisfy the prescribed geographical and quality
requirements, as they appear from the specification referred to in Art 7 of the
Regulation and annexed to the application for registration, the right to market
them under the protected name. It thus produces legal effects for economic
operators who satisfy the relevant conditions.

In Case C-447/98[125] two cheese companies objected to the adoption by the **3.167**
German authorities, on 20 December 1993, of regulations on cheese in which
the name 'ALTENBURGER ZIEGENKÄSE' was identified as a designation of origin and which by letter of 26 January 1994 the Federal Republic
of Germany had requested the Commission to register the name as a PDO
pursuant to Art 17 of Regulation No 2081/92. By the adoption of Regulation
No 123/97, the Commission registered, inter alia, the name 'ALTEN-
BURGER ZIEGENKÄSE' as a PDO within the meaning of Regulation No
2081/92. The appellants argued that the geographical area defined in the
German regulations on cheese and the request for registration made to the
Commission as the area of manufacture of 'ALTENBURGER ZIEGEN-
KÄSE' was too extensive. The Appeal Court sustained the decision of the
court of first instance that Regulation No 123/97 concerned the appellants
only in their objective capacity of undertakings producing the cheese in
question in the geographical area defined in the specification and marketing it
on the same basis as any other economic operator currently or potentially in
the same position, and they could not therefore complain about whether other
undertakings might be included in that designation.

In Case T-215/00[126] the applicant producer of duck-based products objected **3.168**
to the application on 5 May 1999 by the French government of the registration as a PGI of the name 'CANARD À FOIE GRAS DU SUD-OUEST',
from the Association pour la défense du palmipède du Sud-Ouest. The
applicant in this case objected that the procedure for registering canard à foie
gras du Sud-Ouest as a PGI had not been adequately publicised at national
level and that the specifications accompanying the application for registration
had nothing to do with the protection of geographical origin, particularly the

---

125 *Molkerei Großbraunshain and Bene Nahrungsmittel v Commission* [1998] ECR II-3533.
126 *La Conqueste SCEA v The Commission of the EC*, Case T-215/00 [2002] ECR I-1179.

requirements relating to the maximum production capacity of the structures for rearing and force-feeding ducks for foie gras and maintained that those requirements had very serious consequences for health, hygiene and safety in the traditional small units of production.

3.169 The applicant's annual production of ducks was in excess of the limits prescribed in the French regulation and it was therefore precluded from marketing the products obtained from its ducks under the name in question. The Court ruled that this economic impact was not relevant to the validity of the PGI.

1. Infringement actions

3.170 As a matter of general practice, infringement actions in relation to GIs concern either: (a) wrongful use of a PGI or a PDO, in breach of Art 13(1)(a) of the Regulation, in which case an action will be brought by the entity responsible for preserving the integrity of the geographical indication; or (b) in relation to a misleading use of a PGI or a PDO, in breach of Art 13(1)(b), (c) or (d) of the Regulation.

3.171 In Cases C-129/97 and C-130/97 the ECJ was requested by the Tribunal de Grande Instance, Dijon, France, to provide a preliminary ruling in the criminal proceedings pending before that court concerning, inter alia, whether an action lay against an undertaking which used part of a compound PDO. French legislation had provided for the registration of 'ÉPOISSES DE BOURGOGNE' as a PDO. Two enterprises were prosecuted under this legislation for using the name 'Époisses' for their cheeses. In response to a question from the Tribunal de Grande Instance, the ECJ ruled that in relation to a compound designation of origin, the absence of a footnote in the relevant regulation specifying that registration was not sought for one of the parts of that designation did not necessarily mean that each of its parts was protected.

3.172 Case C-312/98[127] concerned proceedings between the Schutzverband gegen Unwesen in der Wirtschaft eV, an association founded to combat unfair competition ('the Schutzverband'), and Warsteiner Brauerei Haus Cramer GmbH & Co. KG ('Warsteiner Brauerei') concerning the use by the latter of the name 'WARSTEINER' on labels on bottles for certain types of beer which it brewed at a brewery in Paderborn, 40 km from the town of Warstein. The German law, the Gesetz über den Schutz von Marken und sonstigen

---

127 *Schutzverband gegen Unwesen in der Wirtschaft v Warsteiner Brauerei Haus Cramer GmbH & Co. KG* [2000] ECR I-9187.

Kennzeichen (Law on Protection of Trade Marks and Other Signs, 'the Markengesetz') of 25 October 1994, which entered into force on 1 January 1995, defined PGIs of source to mean names of places, areas, regions or countries and other indications or signs used commercially to designate the geographical provenance of goods or services. Paragraph 127 of the Markengesetz provided that:

> geographical indications of source may not be used commercially for goods or services which do not come from the place, area, region or country which they designate, if with the use of such names, indications or signs for goods or services of other origin there is a risk of misleading as to the geographical provenance.

Warsteiner was the owner of the trade mark 'WARSTEINER' for 'beer of Pilsener style', registered on 24 October 1990 at the Deutsche Patentamt (German Patents Office). It was common ground that beer brewed in Warstein had no special characteristics attributable to that locality and that the beer called 'Warsteiner' owed its reputation to the quality of the beer and promotion of the 'Warsteiner' brand. In autumn 1990, Warsteiner Brauerei acquired a brewery located in Paderborn, 40 km from Warstein, where it brewed 'Light'- and 'Fresh'-type beers until the end of 1991. The labels on the front of the bottles for these beers bore, inter alia the name 'Warsteiner' or 'Marke Warsteiner' (Warsteiner Brand). The back labels indicated, inter alia, that the beers were brewed and bottled 'in unserer neuen Paderborner Brauerei' (in our new Paderborn Brewery). As it considered that those labels were misleading, the Schutzverband brought an action against Warsteiner Brauerei before the Landgericht (Regional Court), Mannheim, seeking an injunction, pursuant to para 3 of the UWG (Gesetz gegen den unlauteren Wettbewerb – Act Against Unfair Competition), restraining it from using 'Warsteiner' as a geographical indication of source for beer brewed in Paderborn. **3.173**

Before the Landgericht, Mannheim, Warsteiner Brauerei argued, inter alia, that the name 'Warsteiner' was not a reference to geographical provenance, in as much as the locality of Warstein was largely unknown to the general public, and, in any event, the reputation of its beer did not depend on particular characteristics attributable to that locality. It also pointed out that there were other beers bearing names referring to a geographical source which did not come exclusively from the place thereby designated. **3.174**

After ordering a consumer survey, the Landgericht, Mannheim, granted the injunction sought by the Schutzverband. On appeal, the Oberlandesgericht (Higher Regional Court), Karlsruhe, by order of 14 February 1996, quashed **3.175** the judgment of the Landgericht and dismissed the action of the Schutzverband. It held that a market survey that had been ordered by the lower court showed that the name at issue did not significantly mislead consumers.

3.176 The Bundesgerichtshof then observed that the prohibition on labelling a product with inaccurate information as to its geographical source was justified in order to protect competitors, so that GIs of source should also be protected where the source of a product has no influence on the consumer's purchasing decision. According to the Bundesgerichtshof, the protection of simple GIs of source provided for in para 127(1) of the Markengesetz was not subject to the condition that such indications should be familiar to the public as such, that is to say, in the case in the main proceedings, as a reference to a place called 'Warstein', but simply required that the locality indicated should not be wholly inconceivable as the place of production because of its specific character or the particular nature of the product. Nor was that protection subject to the condition that the consumer should associate particular qualities with that indication, attributable to regional or local characteristics.

3.177 Since it considered that the case turned on the interpretation of Regulation No 2081/92, the Bundesgerichtshof decided to stay proceedings and referred to the ECJ the question whether Regulation No 2081/92 precluded application of a national provision which prohibits the misleading use of a simple geographical designation of source, that is, an indication in the case of which there is no link between the characteristics of the product and its geographical provenance.

3.178 The Court observed that in the absence of common rules relating to the production and marketing of a product, it was in principle for the Member States to regulate all matters relating to the marketing of that product on their own territory, including its description and labelling, subject to any Community measure adopted with a view to approximating national laws in these fields. Regulation No 2081/92 only concerned GIs in respect of which there was a direct link between both a specific quality, reputation or other characteristic of the product and its specific geographical origin. Thus, simple GIs of source where there was no link between the characteristics of the product and its geographical provenance did not fall within that definition and were not protected under Regulation No 2081/92. The Court ruled that this did not preclude national legislation on the subject.

Case C-216/01[128] and Case C-245/02[129] concern the on-going dispute **3.179**
between the US brewery Anheuser-Busch and various European opponents
concerning the use of the names: 'BUDWEISER', 'BUDWEISER BUD-
VAR' and 'BUD'. In Case C-216/01 the 'Budéjovický Budvar' brewery
(Budvar) brought an action against an Austrian company (Ammersin) which
imported and sold the Anheuser-Busch's beer called 'American Bud'. Budvar
applied to the Handelsgericht (Commercial Court) in Vienna for an order
restraining Ammersin from importing 'American Bud' claiming that the name
'American Bud', which was registered as a US trade mark by Anheuser-Busch,
was similar to its own priority trade marks protected in Austria (namely
'Budweiser', 'Budweiser Budvar' and 'Bud') and was likely to cause confusion
within the terms of the Austrian law on unfair competition. Budvar also
argued that the use of the name 'American Bud' was an abuse of the indication
of origin protected under the Austro-Czechoslovakian Treaty of 1976 under
which Austria granted to the geographical designations of agricultural products from Czechoslovakia a protection similar to that subsequently laid down,
in respect of Community products, by Community laws on PDOs. The ECJ
held on the basis of the findings of the national court that the name 'Bud' did
not directly or indirectly identify any region or place in the territory of the
Czech Republic. The protection of the name in question could not be justified
on the grounds of protection of industrial and commercial property within the
meaning of Art 30 of the EC Treaty.

M. 'IMITATION OR EVOCATION'

It will be recalled that Art 13(1)(b) prohibits any 'misuse, imitation or **3.180**
evocation, even if the true origin of the products or services is indicated'.
Profeta et al[130] question whether producers can evade the requirements of a
specification by using geographical names indicating places within an area of
production, eg brewers from Nuremberg (in the Bavarian region of Franken)
might call their product 'NÜRNBERGER BIER' or 'FRANKEN BIER' to
avoid the specification of 'BAVARIAN BEER'. This question would be
decided on the basis of whether or not such designations constitute an
'imitation or evocation' or a 'misleading indication'. This in turn would depend
upon whether the relevant consumers would regard the relevant designation of
a sub-region as referring to the registered designation.

---

128   *Budéjovický Budvar v Rudolf Ammersin GmbH* [2003] ECR I-13617.
129   *Anheuser-Busch v Budéjovický Budvar* [2004] ECR I-10989; [2005] ETMR 286.
130   Profeta et al, 2009, 629.

3.181 The question raised in Case C-87/97[131] was whether a PDO 'GORGON-ZOLA (ITALY)' was infringed if the packaging of the cheese designated as 'CAMBOZOLA' bore a clearly visible indication of the country of manufacture (Deutscher Weichkäse [German soft cheese]), also where that cheese was as a rule not displayed and sold to consumers in the form of whole cheeses, but in pieces, sometimes without the original packaging.

3.182 The ECJ ruled that since the product at issue is a soft blue cheese which was not dissimilar in appearance to Gorgonzola, it was reasonable to conclude that a protected name was evoked, within the meaning of Art 13(1)(b) of Regulation No 2081/92, 'where the term used to designate that product ends in the same two syllables and contains the same number of syllables, with the result that the phonetic and visual similarity between the two terms is obvious'. In that connection, the ECJ stated that it was appropriate for the national court to take into account advertising material published by the defendant which suggested that the phonetic similarity between the two names was not fortuitous.

3.183 It will be recalled that in Case C-132/05[132] the German government had argued unsuccessfully that it did not need to enforce the PDO 'PARMIGIANO REGGIANO' in its territory on the grounds that the term 'Parmesan' had become a generic name for hard cheeses of diverse origins, grated or intended to be grated. Another unsuccessful argument of the Federal Republic of Germany was that the use of the word 'Parmesan' did not infringe Art 13(1)(b) of Regulation No 2081/92, given that it was distinct from the full PDO 'PARMIGIANO REGGIANO'. This involved a consideration by the Court of whether in the terms of Art 13(1)(b) of that regulation, there was 'any misuse, imitation or evocation' of the PDO.

3.184 With regard to the evocation of a PDO, the Court noted that it had held that that term covered a situation where the term used to designate a product incorporates part of a protected designation, so that when the consumer is confronted with the name of the product, the image brought to his mind is that of the product whose designation is protected.[133] In the present case, the Court noted that there was 'phonetic and visual similarity' between the names 'Parmesan' and 'Parmigiano Reggiano', and in a situation where the products at issue are hard cheeses, grated or intended to be grated, namely, where they

---

131 *Consorzio per la Tutela del Formaggio Gorgonzola v Käserei Champignon Hofmeister GmbH & Co. KG and Eduard Bracharz GmbH* [1999] ECR I-1301.
132 *Commission of the European Communities v Germany* [2008] ECR I-957; [2008] ETMR 32.
133 Case C-87/97 *Consorzio per la tutela del formaggio Gorgonzola* [1999] ECR I-1301, para 25.

have a similar appearance.[134] In addition, regardless whether the name 'Parmesan' was or was not an exact translation of the PDO 'PARMIGIANO REGGIANO' or of the term 'Parmigiano', the Court held that the conceptual proximity between those two terms emanating from different languages must also be taken into account.[135] It accepted that proximity and the phonetic and visual similarities in this case 'brought to the mind of the consumer the cheese protected by the PDO "PARMIGIANO REGGIANO", when he is confronted by a hard cheese, grated or intended to be grated, bearing the name "Parmesan"'.[136] Thus the Court held the use of the name 'Parmesan' must be regarded, in the sense of Art 13(1)(b) of Regulation No 2081/92, as an evocation of the PDO 'PARMIGIANO REGGIANO'.[137]

1. Defence of good faith registration

The defendant in the 'GORGONZOLA' case[138] sought to rely on its good **3.185** faith defence in Art 14(2) of Regulation No 2081/92 in that the registration of the trade mark 'CAMBOZOLA' in Austria, was made in good faith before the date when the application for registration of the designation of origin was lodged. The ECJ ruled that this defence was not open because in 1983, when the trade mark 'CAMBOZOLA' was lodged in Austria, the protection enjoyed there by the designation 'GORGONZOLA' was essentially similar to the protection guaranteed since 1996 by Community law. It observed that 'the concept of good faith referred to ... must be viewed in the light of the entire body of legislation, both national and international, in force at the time when the application for registration of the trade mark was lodged'. However, it was for the national court to decide whether the facts of the case allowed it to find good faith.

N. RELATIONS BETWEEN TRADE MARKS, DESIGNATIONS OF ORIGIN AND GEOGRAPHICAL INDICATIONS

Recital (53) to the Regulation indicates that the date for establishing the **3.186** seniority of a trade mark and of a designation of origin or a GI should be that of the date of application of the trade mark for registration in the Union or in the Member States and the date of application for protection of a designation of origin or a geographical indication to the Commission.

---

134 [2008] ECR I-957 at para 46.
135 Ibid., at para 47.
136 Ibid., at para 48.
137 Ibid., at para 49.
138 Case C-87/97.

3.187 Recital (54) proposes that the provisions dealing with the refusal or coexistence of a designation of origin or a geographical indication on the ground of conflict with a prior trade mark should continue to apply.

3.188 Recital (55) indicates that the criteria by which subsequent trade marks should be refused or, if registered, invalidated on the ground that they conflict with a prior designation of origin or GI should correspond to the scope of protection of designation of origin or a GI laid down.

1. Legislation

3.189 Article 14 deals with the problems arising when a trade mark that includes a geographical name clashes with a PDO or a PGI.

3.190 The simplest case of conflict, which is dealt with in Art 14(1) of the Regulation, provides that where a PDO or a PGI is registered under the Regulation, the application for registration of a trade mark corresponding to one of the situations referred to in Art 13 and relating to the same class of product shall be refused if the application for registration of the trade mark is submitted after the date of submission of the registration application to the Commission. In this case, Art 14(1) gives priority to the geographical name as it provides that trade marks 'registered in breach of Article 14(1) shall be invalidated'.

3.191 Article 14(1) provides that the provisions of this paragraph shall apply notwithstanding the provisions of the Trade Marks Directive.[139]

3.192 The second case, referred to in Art 14(2), provides for coexistence in certain cases. A conflicting trade mark can only continue to be used if, with due regard to Community law:

- the trade mark was applied for, registered or established by use in good faith before the date of protection in the country of origin or the date of submission to the Commission of the application for registration of the PGI or PDO;

---

139 First Council Directive 89/104/EEC of 21 December 1988 to approximate the laws of the Member States relating to trade marks, OJ L 40, 11.2.1989, p. 1.

- there are no grounds for its invalidity or revocation exist under the Community trade mark Regulation[140] or under the Trade Marks Directive.[141]

In such cases, the use of the PDO or PGI shall be permitted as well as use of the relevant trade marks.

Kireeva suggests that the provision for coexistence of trade marks with GIs in the previous foodstuffs Regulation was influenced by the conflict between the 'MIGUEL TORRES' trade mark, which had been registered in Spain and used for wine for many years, and the Portuguese government's designation of 'TORRES VEDRAS' as a geographical indication for wine.[142] **3.193**

Finally where there is a registered trade mark, Art 3(4) provides that a designation of origin or GI shall not be registered where, 'in the light of a trademark's reputation and renown and the length of time it has been used, registration is liable to mislead the consumer as to the true identity of the product'. **3.194**

2. Case law

(a) 'CAMBOZOLA'

Case C-87/97[143] concerned an order sought by the Consorzio per la Tutela del Formaggio Gorgonzola against Käserei Champignon Hofmeister GmbH & Co KG and Eduard Bracharz GmbH (Austria) to prohibit the marketing in Austria of a blue cheese under the designation 'CAMBOZOLA' and requiring cancellation of the 'CAMBOZOLA' trade mark. The applicant referred to Art 3 of the International Stresa Convention for the Use of Designations of Origin and Names of Cheeses, which provided that only 'cheese manufactured or matured in traditional regions, by virtue of local, loyal and uninterrupted usages' could benefit from designations of origin governed by national legislation. **3.195**

The ECJ ruled that the principle of free movement of goods did not preclude Member States from taking the measures incumbent upon them in order to ensure the protection of PDOs registered under Regulation 2081/92. It also **3.196**

---

140   Council Regulation (EC) No 40/94 of 20 December 1993 on the Community trade mark, OJ L 11, 14.1.1994, p. 1.

141   OJ L 40, 11.2.1989, p. 1.

142   Kireeva, 2009, at 203.

143   *Consorzio per la Tutela del Formaggio Gorgonzola v Käserei Champignon Hofmeister GmbH & Co. KG and Eduard Bracharz GmbH* [1999] ECR I-1301.

ruled that it was for the national court to decide whether, on the facts, the conditions laid down in Art 14(2) of Regulation 2081/92 allow use of an earlier trade mark to continue notwithstanding the registration of the PDO 'GORGONZOLA', having regard in particular to the law in force at the time of registration of the trade mark, in order to determine whether such registration could have been made in good faith.

(b) 'GRANA BIRAGHI' and 'GRANA PADANO'

3.197 Case T-291/03[144] concerned an application filed at OHIM on 2 February 1998 by Biraghi SpA for registration of the word mark 'GRANA BIRAGHI' as a Community trade mark for cheeses. The Consorzio per la tutela del formaggio Grana Padano filed an application with OHIM for a declaration that the Community trade mark was invalid as contrary to the protection of the PDO 'GRANA PADANO' registered under Regulation 2081/92 and, relying on the registration of the earlier national and international marks 'GRANA' and 'GRANA PADANO'. The Cancellation Division of OHIM allowed an application for a declaration of invalidity under Art 14 of Regulation No 2081/92. Biraghi appealed against that decision on the grounds of the generic and descriptive nature of the term 'grana'. The First Board of Appeal allowed the appeal, annulling the Cancellation Division's decision and rejecting the application for a declaration that the Community trade mark 'GRANA BIRAGHI' was invalid. The Board of Appeal found that the word 'grana' was generic and described an essential quality of the goods in question. Therefore, according to the Board of Appeal decision, the existence of the PDO 'GRANA PADANO' did not preclude the registration of the sign 'GRANA BIRAGHI' as a Community trade mark.

3.198 One of the issues which was addressed by the Court of First Instance of the European Communities on appeal was whether the term 'grana' designated a geographical area as such. The Court noted that a PDO may also be constituted by a traditional non-geographical name designating a foodstuff originating in a region or specific place which presents homogeneous natural factors which distinguish it from the areas adjoining it and that in that regard, it was not disputed that 'grana' cheese originates in the region of the plain of the Po and thus met the conditions provided for in Art 2(3) of Regulation No 2081/92.[145]

---

144 *Consorzio per la tutela del formaggio Grana Padano v OHIM* [2007] ECR II-3081.
145 Ibid., at para 81.

(c) 'BAYERISCHES BIER'

In Case C-120/08[146] Bayerischer Brauerbund, a German association with the **3.199**
objective of protecting the common interests of Bavarian brewers, was the
proprietor of the registered collective trade marks 'GENUINE BAVARIAN
BEER' (since 1958), 'BAYRISCH BIER' and 'BAYERISCHES BIER'
(since 1968), and 'Reinheitsgebot seit 1516 Bayrisches Bier' (since 1985).
Bavaria was a Netherlands commercial company which began to use the word
'BAVARIA' in 1925, and it became part of its name in 1930. Bavaria was and
is the proprietor of several registered trade marks and figurative elements
containing the word 'Bavaria', including an international trade mark.

On 28 September 1993 Bayerischer Brauerbund, in agreement with two other **3.200**
Bavarian associations, submitted to the German government an application
for registration of a PGI pursuant to Art 17(1) of Regulation No 2081/92. On
20 January 1994 the German government informed the Commission of the
application for registration of 'Bayerisches Bier' as a PGI in accordance with
the simplified procedure under that provision. The Regulatory Committee on
Geographical Indications and Designations of Origin discussed two draft
Commission regulations for registration of 'Bayerisches Bier' as a PGI. The
existence of marks which also include the words 'Bayerisches Bier' or translations of them was one of the issues discussed. Following discussions as to
whether 'Bayerisches' had become generic, the Committee was unable to agree
within the period prescribed within the Regulation, therefore the Commission
converted its last draft into a proposal for a Council regulation, and the
Council then adopted Regulation No 1347/2001 which registered 'Bayerisches Bier' as a PGI by including it among the names listed in the Annex to
Regulation (EC) No 1107/96.

Following similar proceedings in other Member States, Bayerischer Brauer- **3.201**
bund applied to the Landgericht München for an order requiring Bavaria to
agree to renounce the protection of its international trade mark protected in
Germany with priority from 28 April 1995. The Landgericht München
granted Bayerischer Brauerbund's application by a judgment which was
upheld on appeal by the Oberlandesgericht München (Higher Regional
Court, Munich). Bavaria appealed on a point of law to the Bundesgerichtshof
(Federal Court of Justice). The Bundesgerichtshof decided to stay the proceedings and to refer questions to the ECJ under Art 234 EC for a preliminary
ruling on the interpretation of Council Regulation (EC) No 510/2006 of 20
March 2006.

---

146 *Bavaria NVl v Bayerischer Brauerbund eV* [2011] ETMR 225.

3.202 By decision of the President of the ECJ of 8 May 2008, the proceedings were stayed pending delivery of the judgment in Case C-343/07, *Bavaria and Bavaria Italia* [2009] ECR I-5491. which was a reference for a preliminary ruling from the Corte d'appello di Torino (Appeal Court, Turin) (Italy) in a dispute which concerned, inter alia, the validity of Regulation No 1347/2001 and was also between Bavaria and Bayerischer Brauerbund.

3.203 The ECJ observed that both Art 14(1) of Regulation No 2081/92, in its original version and as amended by Regulation No 692/2003, and Art 14(1) of Regulation No 510/2006 were designed to resolve a conflict between a name registered as a PGI and an application for registration of a trade mark corresponding to one of the situations referred to in Art 13 of Regulation No 2081/92 and Regulation No 510/2006 respectively.[147] The solution provided for in the case of such a conflict was refusal of the application for registration of the trade mark at issue, or, in the alternative, invalidation of the trade mark registered, where that application was submitted after the date respectively provided for in those various provisions.[148]

3.204 However, the Court noted that these provisions could not be applied retroactively in order to govern the current conflict between a name validly registered as a PGI in accordance with the simplified procedure under Art 17 of Regulation No 2081/92 and a trade mark the application for registration of which was submitted before the entry into force of Regulation No 692/2003.[149] Thus in the present case it was a matter of establishing whether, when the trade mark 'Bavaria' at issue was registered in 1995, the PGI 'Bayerisches Bier' already enjoyed priority which could justify invalidation of that mark. That question must be answered in the light of the rule which governed the conflict at issue at the time when it arose.

3.205 The Court observed that it was immaterial that, according to Recital (19) in the preamble to Regulation No 510/2006 and under Art 17 of that regulation, names registered as a PGI under Regulation No 2081/92 are entitled to protection under Regulation No 510/2006[150] as the conflict that gave rise to the dispute in these proceedings was governed by Art 14(1) of Regulation No 2081/92. Consequently, the ECJ ruled that this provision was applicable for resolving the conflict between a name validly registered as a PGI in accordance with the simplified procedure under Art 17 of that regulation and a trade mark corresponding to one of the situations referred to in Art 13 of that

---

147   Ibid., at para 36.
148   Ibid., at para 37.
149   Ibid., at para 38.
150   Ibid., at para 45.

regulation relating to the same type of product, the application for registration of which was submitted both before the registration of that name and before the entry into force of Regulation No 692/2003.[151]

O. EUROPEAN GEOGRAPHICAL INDICATIONS IN NON-EUROPEAN TRADE MARK PROCEEDINGS

The globalisation of trade has inevitably resulted in the globalisation of intellectual property disputes. Among these are fights between those asserting European GIs in trade marks proceedings. For example the conflict between Bayerischer Brauerbund and Bavaria NV, described above, was fought out in trade mark opposition proceedings in Australia.[152] Bayerischer Brauerbund opposed the registration of the 'BAVARIA' trade mark for beer by Bavaria NV on a number of grounds, one of which was that 'Bavaria' is a geographical indication within the meaning of s 6 of the Australian Trade Marks Act (the Act) so that the registration of the trade mark should be refused pursuant to s 61 of that Act. The other grounds were that the trade mark 'BAVARIA' was not capable of distinguishing, nor was it inherently adapted to distinguish, Bavaria NV's goods from the goods of other persons.[153] Bayerischer Brauerbund also argued that the word mark 'BAVARIA' suggested an erroneous and therefore misleading origin to Australian consumers in breach of Australia's consumer protection legislation[154] and was therefore contrary to law and should be rejected under s 42 of the Act. On the same reasoning it argued that the use of the trade mark would be likely to deceive or cause confusion, and registration should be refused under s 43 of the Act.

3.206

On the GIs issue, Bayerischer Brauerbund called in aid its PGI registration for 'BAYERISCHES BIER'. However, the Federal Court held that the critical question was whether 'BAVARIA' was a geographical indication and disqualified from registration under s 61 of the Act. It found no evidence that this was a GI or that it was deceptively similar to the PGI 'BAYERISCHES BIER' and rejected the opposition on this ground.[155] The Court also ruled that as Bayerischer Brauerbund had not shown that Australian consumers equated 'Bavaria' as a source of beer there was no evidence of confusion or of consumers being misled, so the opposition failed on these bases also.[156]

3.207

---

151 Ibid., at para 69.
152 *Bavaria NV v Bayerischer Brauerbund eV* [2009] FCA 428.
153 Trade Marks Act 1995 (Cth), s 41.
154 Trade Practices Act 1974 (Cth), s 52 and/or ss 53(a), 53(c), 53(d) or 53(e).
155 [2009] FCA 428, at para 162.
156 Ibid., at paras 91, 94, 106.

P. TRANSITIONAL PERIODS FOR USE OF PROTECTED DESIGNATIONS OF ORIGIN AND PROTECTED GEOGRAPHICAL INDICATIONS

3.208 Article 15(1) provides that without prejudice to Art 14, the Commission may adopt implementing acts granting a transitional period of up to five years to enable products originating in a Member State or a third country the designation of which consists of or contains a name that contravenes Art 13(1) to continue to use the designation under which it was marketed on condition that an admissible statement of opposition under Art 49(3) or Art 51 shows that:

(a) the registration of the name would jeopardise the existence of an entirely or partly identical name; or

(b) such products have been legally marketed with that name in the territory concerned for at least five years preceding the date of the publication provided for in point (a) of Art 50(2).

Those implementing acts shall be adopted in accordance with the examination procedure referred to in Art 57(2).

3.209 Article 15(2) provides that without prejudice to Art 14, the Commission may adopt implementing acts extending the transitional period mentioned in Art 15(1) to 15 years in duly justified cases where it is shown that:

(a) the designation referred to in Art 15(1) has been in legal use consistently and fairly for at least 25 years before the application for registration was submitted to the Commission;

(b) the purpose of using the designation referred to in Art 15(1) has not, at any time, been to profit from the reputation of the registered name and it is shown that the consumer has not been nor could have been misled as to the true origin of the product.

Those implementing acts shall be adopted in accordance with the examination procedure referred to in Art 57(2).

3.210 Article 15(3) provides that when using a designation referred to in Art 15(1) and (2), the indication of country of origin shall clearly and visibly appear on the labelling.

3.211 Article 15(4) provides that to overcome temporary difficulties with the long-term objective of ensuring that all producers in the area concerned comply with the specification, a Member State may grant a transitional period of up to ten years, with effect from the date on which the application is lodged with the Commission, on condition that the operators concerned have legally marketed the products in question, using the names concerned continuously for at least the five years prior to the lodging of the application to the authorities of the Member State and have made that point in the national opposition procedure referred to in Art 49(3).

The first subparagraph shall apply *mutatis mutandis* to a PGI or PDO referring to a geographical area situated in a third country, with the exception of the opposition procedure. **3.212**

Such transitional periods shall be indicated in the application dossier referred to in Art 8(2). **3.213**

Q. PRESERVED REGISTRATIONS

Article 16(1) provides that names entered in the register provided for in Art 7(6) of Regulation (EC) No 510/2006 shall automatically be entered in the register referred to in Art 11 of this Regulation. The corresponding specifications shall be deemed to be the specifications referred to in Art 7 of this Regulation. Any specific transitional provisions associated with such registrations shall continue to apply. **3.214**

Article 16(2) provides that this Regulation shall apply without prejudice to any right of coexistence recognised under Regulation (EC) No 510/2006 in respect of designations of origin and GIs, on the one hand, and trade marks, on the other. **3.215**

R. TRADITIONAL SPECIALITIES GUARANTEED

Recital (34) to the Regulation explains that the specific objective of the scheme for TSGs 'is to help the producers of traditional products to communicate to consumers the value-adding attributes of their product'. It noted that only a few names had been registered under the preceding legislation[157] and that to realise its potential, provisions should be improved, clarified and sharpened in order to make the scheme more understandable, operational and attractive to potential applicants. **3.216**

---

157 Council Regulation (EC) No 509/2006 of 20 March 2006 on agricultural products and foodstuffs as traditional specialities guaranteed.

3.217 The previous scheme had provided the option to register a name for identification purposes without reservation of the name in the Union. This option, according to Recital (35) has not been well understood by stakeholders and should be discontinued with the scheme dealing only with the reservation of names across the Union.

3.218 Recital (36) explained that to ensure that names of genuine traditional products are registered under the scheme, the criteria and conditions for registration of a name should be adapted, in particular those concerning the definition of 'traditional', which should cover products that have been produced for a significant period of time.

3.219 Recital (37) proposed that to ensure that TSGs comply with their specification and are consistent, producers organised into groups should themselves define the product in a specification. Also the option of registering a name as a TSG should be open to third country producers.

3.220 The Protection of Traditional Specialities Guaranteed is contained in Title III of the Regulation.

1. Objective

3.221 The objective of the protection regime is set out in Art 17, which provides that a scheme for TSGs 'is established to safeguard traditional methods of production and recipes by helping producers of traditional product in marketing and communicating the value-adding attributes of their traditional recipes and products to consumers'.

2. Criteria

(a) Traditional use

3.222 Article 3(3) of the Regulation defines 'traditional' to mean 'proven usage on the domestic market for a period that allows transmission between generations; this period is to be at least 30 years'.

3.223 Article 18(1) provides that a name shall be eligible for registration as a TSG where it describes a specific product or foodstuff that:

(a) results from a mode of production, processing or composition corresponding to traditional practice for that product or foodstuff; or

(b) is produced from raw materials or ingredients that are those traditionally used.

For a name to be registered as a TSG, Art 18(2) provides that it shall: **3.224**

  (a) have been traditionally used to refer to the specific product; or
  (b) identify the traditional character or specific character of the product.

3. Relation to intellectual property

Article 43 provides that the quality schemes described in Titles III and IV   **3.225**
shall apply without prejudice to Union rules or to those of Member States
governing intellectual property, and in particular to those concerning designations of origin and GIs and trade marks, and rights granted under those rules.

4. Exclusion of 'generic terms'

Article 3(6) of the Regulation defines 'generic terms' to mean 'the names of   **3.226**
products which, although relating to the place, region or country where the
product was originally produced or marketed, have become the common name
of a product in the Union'.

Article 41(1) provides that without prejudice to Art 13, this Regulation shall   **3.227**
not affect the use of terms that are generic in the Union, even if the generic
term is part of a name that is protected under a quality scheme.

Article 41(2) provides that to establish whether or not a term has become   **3.228**
generic, account shall be taken of all relevant factors, in particular:

  (a) the existing situation in areas of consumption;
  (b) the relevant national or Union legal acts.

Article 41(3) provides that in order to fully protect the rights of interested   **3.229**
parties, the Commission shall be empowered to adopt delegated acts, in
accordance with Art 56, laying down additional rules for determining the
generic status of terms referred to in Art 41(1).

5. Plant varieties and animal breeds

Article 42(1) of the Regulation provides that it shall not prevent the placing on   **3.230**
the market of products the labelling of which includes a name or term
protected or reserved under a quality scheme described in Title II, Title III, or
Title IV that contains or comprises the name of a plant variety or animal
breed, provided that the following conditions are met:

    (a) the product in question comprises or is derived from the variety or breed indicated;

    (b) consumers are not misled;

    (c) the usage of the name of the variety or breed name constitutes fair competition;

    (d) the usage does not exploit the reputation of the protected term; and

    (e) in the case of the quality scheme described in Title II, production and marketing of the product had spread beyond its area of origin prior to the date of application for registration of the geographical indication.

3.231 Article 42(2) provides that in order to further clarify the extent of rights and freedoms of food business operators to use the name of a plant variety or of an animal breed referred to in Art 42(1), the Commission shall be empowered to adopt delegated acts, in accordance with Art 56, concerning rules for determining the use of such names.

6. Use in another Member State or third country

3.232 Recital (39) proposes that in order to avoid creating unfair conditions of competition, any producer, including a third country producer, should be able to use a registered name of a TSG, provided that the product concerned complies with the requirements of the relevant specification and the producer is covered by a system of controls. For TSGs produced within the Union, the Union symbol should be indicated on the labelling and it should be possible to associate it with the indication 'traditional speciality guaranteed'.

3.233 Article 18(3) provides that if it is demonstrated in the opposition procedure under Art 51 that the name is also used in another Member State or in a third country, in order to distinguish comparable products or products that share an identical or similar name, the decision on registration taken in accordance with Art 52(3) may provide that the name of the TSG is to be accompanied by the claim 'made following the tradition of' immediately followed by the name of a country or a region thereof.

7. Exclusion from registration

3.234 Article 18(4) provides that a name may not be registered if it refers only to claims of a general nature used for a set of products, or to claims provided for by particular Union legislation.

8. Delegated acts

3.235 Article 18(5) provides that in order to ensure the smooth functioning of the scheme, the Commission shall be empowered to adopt delegated acts, in accordance with Art 56, concerning further details of the eligibility criteria laid down in this Article.

9. Product specification

(a) Content of specification

Article 19(1) provides that a TSG shall comply with a specification which **3.236** shall comprise:

(a) the name proposed for registration, in the appropriate language versions;
(b) a description of the product including its main physical, chemical, microbiological or organoleptic characteristics, showing the product's specific character;
(c) a description of the production method that the producers must follow, including, where appropriate, the nature and characteristics of the raw materials or ingredients used, and the method by which the product is prepared; and
(d) the key elements establishing the product's traditional character.

Article 19(2) provides that in order to ensure that product specifications **3.237** provide relevant and succinct information, the Commission shall be empowered to adopt delegated acts, in accordance with Art 56, laying down rules which limit the information contained in the specification referred to in paragraph 1 of this Article, where such a limitation is necessary to avoid excessively voluminous applications for registration. Subsequently, Art 3 of the Delegated Regulation provides that the product specification referred to in Art 19 'shall be concise and shall not exceed 5,000 words, except in duly justified cases'.

The Commission may adopt implementing acts laying down rules on the form **3.238** of the specification. Those implementing acts shall be adopted in accordance with the examination procedure referred to in Art 57(2).

10. Verification of compliance with product specification

Article 37(1) provides that in respect of TSGs that designate products **3.239** originating within the Union, verification of compliance with the product specification, before placing the product on the market, shall be carried out by:

(a) one or more of the competent authorities as referred to in Art 36 of this Regulation; and/or
(b) one or more of the control bodies within the meaning of point (5) of Art 2 of Regulation (EC) No 882/2004 operating as a product certification body.

3.240 The costs of such verification of compliance with the specifications may be borne by the operators that are subject to those controls. The Member States may also contribute to these costs.

3.241 Article 37(2) provides that in respect of TSGs that designate products originating in a third country, the verification of compliance with the specifications before placing the product on the market shall be carried out by:

    (a)   one or more of the public authorities designated by the third country; and/or

    (b)   one or more of the product certification bodies.

11. Content of application for registration

3.242 Article 20(1) provides that an application for registration of a name as a TSG referred to in Art 49(2) or (5) shall comprise:

    (a)   the name and address of the applicant group;

    (b)   the product specification as provided for in Art 19.

12. Dossier

3.243 Article 20(2) provides that an application dossier referred to in Art 49(4) shall comprise:

    (a)   the elements referred to in paragraph 1 of this Article; and

    (b)   a declaration by the Member State that it considers that the application lodged by the group and qualifying for the favourable decision meets the conditions of this Regulation and the provisions adopted pursuant thereto.

13. Grounds for opposition

3.244 Article 21(1) provides that a reasoned statement of opposition as referred to in Art 51(2) shall be admissible only if it is received by the Commission before expiry of the time limit and if it:

    (a)   gives duly substantiated reasons why the proposed registration is incompatible with the terms of this Regulation; or

    (b)   shows that use of the name is lawful, renowned and economically significant for similar agricultural products or foodstuffs.

Article 21(2) provides that the criteria referred to in Art 21(1)(b) shall be assessed in relation to the territory of the Union.

14. Register of traditional specialities guaranteed

Article 22(1) provides that the Commission shall adopt implementing acts, **3.245** without applying the procedure referred to in Art 57(2), establishing and maintaining a publicly accessible updated register of TSGs recognised under this scheme.

Article 22(2) provides that the Commission may adopt implementing acts **3.246** laying down detailed rules on the form and content of the register. Those implementing acts shall be adopted in accordance with the examination procedure referred to in Art 57(2).

15. Names, symbol and indication

(a) Use

Article 23(1) provides that a name registered as a TSG may be used by any **3.247** operator marketing a product that conforms to the corresponding specification.

(b) Union symbol

Article 23(2) provides that a Union symbol shall be established in order to **3.248** publicise the TSGs. Article 2 of the Delegated Regulation provides that the Union symbols referred to in Art 23(2) 'are established as laid down in the Annex to this Regulation'.

In the case of products originating in the Union that are marketed under a **3.249** TSG that is registered in accordance with this Regulation, Art 23(3) provides that the symbol referred to in Art 23(2) shall, without prejudice to Art 23(4), appear on the labelling. In addition, the name of the product should appear in the same field of vision. The indication 'traditional speciality guaranteed' or the corresponding abbreviation 'TSG' may also appear on the labelling.

The symbol shall be optional on the labelling of TSGs which are produced **3.250** outside the Union.

Article 59 provides that Art 23(3) shall apply from 4 January 2016, without **3.251** prejudice to products already placed on the market before that date.

(c) Protection of indications and symbols

Article 44(1) provides that indications, abbreviations and symbols referring to **3.252** the quality schemes may only be used in connection with products produced in conformity with the rules of the quality scheme to which they apply. This applies in particular to the following indications, abbreviations and symbols: '(b) "traditional speciality guaranteed", "TSG", and the associated symbol, as provided for in Title III'.

(d) Delegated acts

3.253 Article 23(4) provides that in order to ensure that the appropriate information is communicated to the consumer, the Commission shall be empowered to adopt delegated acts, in accordance with Art 56, establishing the Union symbol.

3.254 The Commission may adopt implementing acts defining the technical characteristics of the Union symbol and indication, as well as the rules of their use on the products bearing the name of a TSG, including as to the appropriate linguistic versions to be used. Those implementing acts shall be adopted in accordance with the examination procedure referred to in Art 57(2).

S. RESTRICTION ON USE OF REGISTERED NAMES

1. Misleading use

3.255 Article 24(1) provides that registered names shall be protected against any misuse, imitation or evocation, or against any other practice liable to mislead the consumer.

2. Confusing sales descriptions

3.256 Article 24(2) provides that Member States shall ensure that sales descriptions used at national level do not give rise to confusion with names that are registered.

3. Implementing acts

3.257 Article 24(3) provides that the Commission may adopt implementing acts laying down rules for the protection of TSGs. Those implementing acts shall be adopted in accordance with the examination procedure referred to in Art 57(2).

4. Preserved registrations

Article 25(1) provides that 'names registered in accordance with Art 13(2) of **3.258**
Regulation (EC) No 509/2006 shall be automatically entered in the register
referred to in Art 22 of this Regulation. The corresponding specifications shall
be deemed to be the specifications referred to in Art 19 of this Regulation'.
Any specific transitional provisions associated with such registrations shall
continue to apply.

Article 25(2) provides that names registered in accordance with the require- **3.259**
ments laid down in Art 13(1) of Regulation (EC) No 509/2006, including
those registered pursuant to applications referred to in the second subparagraph of Art 58(1) of this Regulation, may continue to be used under the
conditions provided for in Regulation (EC) No 509/2006 until 4 January 2023
unless Member States use the procedure set out in Art 26 of this Regulation.

5. Delegated acts

Article 25(1) provides that in order to protect the rights and legitimate **3.260**
interests of producers or stakeholders concerned, the Commission shall be
empowered to adopt delegated acts, in accordance with Art 56, laying down
additional transitional rules.

6. Simplified procedure

(a) Names registered under Regulation (EC) No 509/2006

Article 26(1) provides that at the request of a group, a Member State may **3.261**
submit, no later than 4 January 2016, to the Commission names of TSGs that
are registered in accordance with Art 13(1) of Regulation (EC) No 509/2006
and that comply with this Regulation.

(b) Mandatory opposition procedure

Article 26(1) provides that before submitting a name, the Member State shall **3.262**
initiate an opposition procedure as defined in Art 49(3) and (4).

If it is demonstrated in the course of this procedure that the name is also used **3.263**
in reference to comparable products or products that share an identical or
similar name, the name may be complemented by a term identifying its
traditional or specific character.

Article 26(3) provides that Arts 51 and 52 shall apply. **3.264**

3.265 Article 26(1) provides that once the opposition procedure has finished, the Commission shall, where appropriate, adjust the entries in the register set out in Art 22. The corresponding specifications shall be deemed to be the specifications referred to in Art 19.

(c) Third country applications

3.266 Article 26(1) provides that a group from a third country may submit such names to the Commission, either directly or through the authorities of the third country.

(d) Publication of application

3.267 Article 26(1) provides that the name, together with the specifications for each such name, is published in the *Official Journal of the European Union* within two months from reception.

T. OPTIONAL QUALITY TERMS

3.268 Recital (44) to the Regulation proposes that a second tier of quality systems, based on quality terms which add value, should be introduced. Those optional quality terms should refer to specific horizontal characteristics, with regard to one or more categories of products, farming methods or processing attributes which apply in specific areas.

3.269 The scheme for the protection of Optional Quality Terms is contained in Title IV of the Regulation.

1. Objective

3.270 Article 27 provides that a scheme for optional quality terms is established in order to facilitate the communication within the internal market of the value-adding characteristics or attributes of agricultural products by the producers thereof.

2. National rules

3.271 Article 28 permits Member States to maintain national rules on optional quality terms which are not covered by the Regulation, 'provided that such rules comply with Union law'.

3. Criteria for optional quality terms

Article 29(1) provides that optional quality terms shall satisfy the following **3.272** criteria:

(a) the term relates to a characteristic of one or more categories of products, or to a farming or processing attribute which applies in specific areas;

(b) the use of the term adds value to the product as compared to products of a similar type; and

(c) the term has a European dimension.

4. Relation to intellectual property

Recital (56) explains that the provisions of systems establishing intellectual **3.273** property rights, and particularly of those established by the quality scheme for designations of origin and GIs or those established under trade mark law, should not be affected by the reservation of names and the establishment of indications and symbols pursuant to the quality schemes for TSGs and for optional quality terms. Consequently, Art 43 provides that the quality schemes described in Titles III and IV shall apply without prejudice to Union rules or to those of Member States governing intellectual property, and in particular to those concerning designations of origin and GIs and trade marks, and rights granted under those rules.

5. Excluded optional quality terms in relation to compulsory marketing standards

Article 29(2) provides that optional quality terms that describe technical **3.274** product qualities with the purpose of putting into effect *compulsory marketing standards* and that are not intended to inform consumers about those product qualities shall be excluded from this scheme.

Article 29(3) provides that optional quality terms shall exclude *optional* **3.275** *reserved terms*, which support and complement specific marketing standards determined on a sectoral or product category basis.

6. 'Generic terms'

Article 41(1) provides that without prejudice to Art 13, this Regulation shall **3.276** not affect the use of terms that are generic in the Union, even if the generic term is part of a name that is protected under a quality scheme.

7. Delegated acts

3.277 Article 29(4) provides that in order to take into account the specific character of certain sectors as well as consumer expectations, the Commission shall be empowered to adopt delegated acts, in accordance with Art 56, laying down detailed rules relating to the criteria referred to in para 1 of this Article.

8. Implementing acts

3.278 Article 29(5) provides that the Commission may adopt implementing acts laying down all measures related to forms, procedures or other technical details, necessary for the application of this Title. Those implementing acts shall be adopted in accordance with the examination procedure referred to in Art 57(2).

9. International standards

3.279 Article 29(3) provides that when adopting delegated and implementing acts in accordance with paras 4 and 5 of this Article, the Commission shall take account of any relevant international standards.

10. Reservation and amendment

3.280 Article 30(1) provides that in order to take account of the expectations of consumers, developments in scientific and technical knowledge, the market situation, and developments in marketing standards and in international standards, the Commission shall be empowered to adopt delegated acts, in accordance with Art 56, reserving an additional optional quality term and laying down its conditions of use.

3.281 Article 30(2) provides that in duly justified cases and in order to take into account the appropriate use of the additional optional quality term, the Commission shall be empowered to adopt delegated acts, in accordance with Art 56, laying down amendments to the conditions of use referred to in paragraph 1 of this Article.

11. 'Mountain product'

3.282 In explaining the rationale for the protection of optional quality terms Recital (44) suggests that the term 'mountain product' will add value to the product on the market. In order to facilitate the application of Directive 2000/13/EC[158] where the labelling of foodstuffs may give rise to consumer confusion in relation to optional quality terms, including in particular 'mountain products', Recital (44) suggests that the Commission may adopt guidelines.

(a) Precursor legislation

The first optional quality term specifically identified in the Regulation is **3.283** 'mountain product'. This had been the subject of litigation under Regulation No 2081/92, which considered the relationship between that Regulation and domestic legislation. Cases C-321/94, C-322/94, C-323/94 and C-324/94,[159] which concerned a number of criminal prosecutions under French legislation which sought to protect the designation 'MOUNTAIN' for agricultural products.[160] The ECJ ruled that domestic legislation which prescribed conditions governing the use, for agricultural products and foodstuffs, of the description 'mountain' could not be regarded as covering a designation of origin or a geographical indication within the meaning of Regulation No 2081/92. The description 'mountain' was quite general in character and transcended national frontiers, whereas, according to Art 2 of Regulation No 2081/92, a direct link must exist between the quality or characteristics of the product and its specific geographical origin.

Recital (45) to the Regulation explains that: **3.284**

> in order to provide mountain producers with an effective tool to better market their product and to reduce the actual risks of consumer confusion as to the mountain provenance of products in the market place, provision should be made for the definition at Union level of an optional quality term for mountain products.

It proposes that the definition of mountain areas should build on the general classification criteria employed to identify a mountain area in Council Regulation (EC) No 1257/1999 of 17 May 1999 on support for rural development from the European Agricultural Guidance and Guarantee Fund (EAGGF).[161]

---

158 Directive 2000/13/EC of the European Parliament and of the Council of 20 March 2000 on the approximation of the laws of the Member States relating to the labelling, presentation and advertising of foodstuffs, OJ 2000 L 109, p. 29.

159 Cases C-321/94, C-322/94, C-323/94 and C-324/94, Judgment of 7 May 1997, *Criminal proceedings against Jacques Pistre* (C-321/94), *Michèle Barthes* (C-322/94), *Yves Milhau* (C-323/94) *and Didier Oberti* (C-324/94) [1997] ECR I-2343.

160 Law No 85–30 of 9 January 1985 on the development and protection of mountain regions (*Journal Officiel de la République Française* (JORF) of 10 January 1985, p. 320, hereinafter 'Law No 85–30') and Decree No 88–194 of 26 February 1988 laying down the conditions governing the use of indications of 'mountain' provenance for agricultural products and foodstuffs (JORF) of 27 February 1988, p. 2747.

161 OJ L 160, 26.6.1999, p. 80.

(b) Definition

3.285 Article 31(1) provides that the term 'mountain product' is established as an optional quality term. This term shall only be used to describe products intended for human consumption listed in Annex I to the Treaty in respect of which:

(a) both the raw materials and the feedstuffs for farm animals come essentially from mountain areas;

(b) in the case of processed products, the processing also takes place in mountain areas.

3.286 Article 31(2) provides that for the purposes of this Article, mountain areas within the Union are those delimited pursuant to Art 18(1) of Regulation (EC) No 1257/1999.[162] For third country products, mountain areas include areas officially designated as mountain areas by the third country or that meet criteria equivalent to those set out in Art 18(1) of Regulation (EC) No 1257/1999.

(c) Derogations

3.287 Article 31(2) provides that in duly justified cases and in order to take into account natural constraints affecting agricultural production in mountain areas, the Commission shall be empowered to adopt delegated acts, in accordance with Art 56, laying down derogations from the conditions of use referred to in para 1 of this Article. In particular, the Commission shall be empowered:

to adopt a delegated act laying down the conditions under which raw materials or feedstuffs are permitted to come from outside the mountain areas, the conditions under which the processing of products is permitted to take place outside of the mountain areas in a geographical area to be defined, and the definition of that geographical area.

(d) Protection of indications and symbols

3.288 Article 44(1) provides that indications, abbreviations and symbols referring to the quality schemes may only be used in connection with products produced in conformity with the rules of the quality scheme to which they apply. This applies in particular to the following indications, abbreviations and symbols: '(c) "mountain product", as provided for in Title IV'.

---

162 Council Regulation (EC) No 1257/1999 of 17 May 1999 on support for rural development from the European Agricultural Guidance and Guarantee Fund (EAGGF) and amending and repealing certain Regulations, OJ L 160 of 26.6.1999.

(e)   Delegated acts concerning methods of production

Article 31(2) provides that in order to take into account natural constraints **3.289** affecting agricultural production in mountain areas, the Commission shall be empowered to adopt delegated acts, in accordance with Art 56, concerning the establishment of the methods of production, and other criteria relevant for the application of the optional quality term established in para 1 of this Article.

12.   Product of island farming

Article 32 provides that no later than 4 January 2014 the Commission shall **3.290** present a report to the European Parliament and to the Council on the case for a new term, 'product of island farming'. The term may only be used to describe the products intended for human consumption that are listed in Annex I to the Treaty, the raw materials of which come from islands. In addition, for the term to be applied to processed products, processing must also take place on islands in cases where this substantially affects the particular characteristics of the final product.

That report shall, if necessary, be accompanied by appropriate legislative **3.291** proposals to reserve an optional quality term 'product of island farming'.

13.   Restrictions on use

Article 33(1) provides that an optional quality term may only be used to **3.292** describe products that comply with the corresponding conditions of use.

Article 33(2) provides that the Commission may adopt implementing acts **3.293** laying down rules for the use of optional quality terms. Those implementing acts shall be adopted in accordance with the examination procedure referred to in Art 57(2).

14.   Monitoring

Article 34 requires Member States to undertake checks, based on a risk **3.294** analysis, to ensure compliance with the requirements of this Title and, in the event of breach, shall apply appropriate administrative penalties.

U. COMMON PROVISIONS

3.295 Title V of the Regulation contains a number of common provisions applicable equally to PDOs, PGIs and TSGs. Chapter I deals with official controls, Chapter II with exceptions for certain prior uses, Chapter III with quality scheme indications and symbols and role of producers and Chapter IV with application and registration processes for designations of origin, GIs, and TSGs. Chapter IV and aspects of Chapter II have already been dealt with in connection with the sections of this chapter dealing first with PDOs and PGIs and then with TSGs.

1. Official controls of protected designations of origin, protected geographical indications and traditional specialities guaranteed

3.296 Recital (46) to the Regulation explains that the added value of the GIs and TSGs is based on consumer trust which is only credible if accompanied by effective verification and controls. It proposes a monitoring system of official controls, in line with the principles set out in Regulation (EC) No 882/2004 of the European Parliament and of the Council of 29 April 2004 on official controls performed to ensure the verification of compliance with feed and food law, animal health and animal welfare rules[163] and should include a system of checks at all stages of production, processing and distribution.

3.297 Recital (47) explains that to guarantee to the consumer the specific characteristics of GIs and TSGs, operators should be subject to a system that verifies compliance with the product specification.

3.298 In order to ensure that they are impartial and effective, Recital (48) requires that the competent authorities should meet a number of operational criteria and that provisions on delegating some competences of performing specific control tasks to control bodies should be envisaged.

3.299 Recital (49) proposes that the European standards (EN standards) developed by the European Committee for Standardization (CEN) and The international standards developed by the International Organization for Standardization (ISO) should be used for the accreditation of the control bodies as well as by those bodies for their operations. The accreditation of those bodies should take place in accordance with Regulation (EC) No 765/2008 of the European Parliament and of the Council of 9 July 2008 setting out the

---

163   OJ L 299, 8.11.2008, p. 25.

requirements for accreditation and market surveillance relating to the marketing of products.[164]

2. Scope

Article 35 provides that the provisions of this Chapter shall apply in respect of the quality schemes set out in Title II (PDOs and PGIs) and Title III (TSGs). **3.300**

3. Designation of competent authority

(a) Quality schemes

Article 36(1) provides that in accordance with Regulation (EC) No 882/ 2004,[165] Member States shall designate the competent authority or authorities responsible for official controls carried out to verify compliance with the legal requirements related to the quality schemes established by this Regulation. **3.301**

Article 36(1) provides that procedures and requirements of Regulation (EC) No 882/2004 shall apply *mutatis mutandis* to the official controls carried out to verify compliance with the legal requirement related to the quality schemes for all products covered by Annex I to this Regulation. **3.302**

(b) Objectivity and impartiality

Article 36(2) provides that the competent authorities referred to in Art 36(1) shall offer adequate guarantees of objectivity and impartiality, and shall have at their disposal the qualified staff and resources necessary to carry out their functions. **3.303**

(c) Scope of official controls

Article 36(3) provides that official controls shall cover: **3.304**

(a) verification that a product complies with the corresponding product specification; and
(b) monitoring of the use of registered names to describe product placed on the market, in conformity with Art 13 for names registered under Title II and in conformity with Art 24 for names registered under Title III.

---

164   OJ L 218, 13.8.2008, p. 30.
165   Regulation 882/2004 on official controls performed to ensure the verification of compliance with feed and food law, animal health and animal welfare rules.

4. Verification of compliance with product specification

3.305 Article 37(1) provides that in respect of PDOs, PGIs and TSGs that designate products originating within the Union, verification of compliance with the product specification before placing the product on the market shall be carried out by:

(a) one or more of the competent authorities as referred to in Art 36 of this Regulation; and/or

(b) one or more of the control bodies within the meaning of point (5) of Art 2 of Regulation (EC) No 882/2004 operating as a product certification body.

The costs of such verification of compliance with the specifications may be borne by the operators that are subject to those controls. The Member States may also contribute to these costs.

3.306 Article 37(2) provides that in respect of designations of origin, GIs and TSGs that designate products originating in a third country, the verification of compliance with the specifications before placing the product on the market shall be carried out by:

(a) one or more of the public authorities designated by the third country; and/or

(b) one or more of the product certification bodies.

3.307 Article 37(3) provides that Member States shall make public the name and address of the authorities and bodies referred to Art 37(1) of this Article, and update that information periodically.

3.308 The Commission shall make public the name and address of the authorities and bodies referred to in Art 37(2) of this Article and update that information periodically.

3.309 Article 37(4) provides that the Commission may adopt implementing acts, without applying the procedure referred to in Art 57(2), defining the means by which the name and address of product certification bodies referred to in Art 37(1) and (2) of this Article shall be made public.

5. Surveillance of the use of the name in the market place

3.310 Article 38 requires that Member States shall inform the Commission of the names and addresses of the competent authorities referred to in Art 36. The Commission shall make public the names and addresses of those authorities.

Member States shall carry out checks, based on a risk analysis, to ensure **3.311** compliance with the requirements of this Regulation and, in the event of breaches, Member States shall take all necessary measures.

6. Delegation by competent authorities to control bodies

Article 39(1) provides that competent authorities may delegate, in accordance **3.312** with Art 5 of Regulation (EC) No 882/2004, specific tasks related to official controls of the quality schemes to one or more control bodies.

Article 39(2) requires that such control bodies shall be accredited in accord- **3.313** ance with European Standard EN 45011 or ISO/IEC Guide 65 (General requirements for bodies operating product certification systems).

Article 39(3) provides that the accreditation referred to in Art 39(2) of this **3.314** Article may only be performed by:

(a) a national accreditation body in the Union in accordance with the provisions of Regulation (EC) No 765/2008; or
(b) an accreditation body outside the Union that is a signatory of a multilateral recognition arrangement under the auspices of the International Accreditation Forum.

7. Planning and reporting of control activities

Article 40(1) requires that Member States shall ensure that activities for the **3.315** control of obligations under this Chapter are specifically included in a separate section within the multi-annual national control plans in accordance with Arts 41, 42 and 43 of Regulation (EC) No 882/2004.

Article 40(2) requires that the annual reports concerning the control of the **3.316** obligations established by this Regulation shall include a separate section comprising the information laid down in Art 44 of Regulation (EC) No 882/2004.

8. Role of groups

Recital (29) to the Regulation maintains that protection should be granted to **3.317** names included in the register with the aim of ensuring that they are used fairly and in order to prevent practices liable to mislead consumers. In addition, the means of ensuring that GIs and designations of origin are protected should be clarified, particularly as regards the role of producer groups and competent authorities of Member States.

3.318 Recital (57) refers to the role of groups which play an essential role in the application process for the registration of names of designations of origin and GIs and TSGs, as well as in the amendment of specifications and cancellation requests. Recital (57) also mentions the role of groups in: the surveillance of the enforcement of the protection of the registered names; the compliance of production with the product specification: the promotion and improving the value of the registered names and effectiveness of the quality schemes; and monitoring the position of the products on the market.

3.319 Article 45(1) provides that without prejudice to specific provisions on producer organisations and inter-branch organisations as laid down in Regulation (EC) No 1234/2007, a group is entitled to:

    (a) contribute to ensuring that the quality, reputation and authenticity of their products are guaranteed on the market by monitoring the use of the name in trade and, if necessary, by informing competent authorities as referred to in Art 36, or any other competent authority within the framework of Art 13(3);

    (b) take action to ensure adequate legal protection of the PDO or PGI and of the intellectual property rights that are directly connected with them;

    (c) develop information and promotion activities aiming at communicating the value-adding attributes of the product to consumers;

    (d) develop activities related to ensuring compliance of a product with its specification;

    (e) take action to improve the performance of the scheme, including developing economic expertise, carrying out economic analyses, disseminating economic information on the scheme and providing advice to producers;

    (f) take measures to enhance the value of products and, where necessary, take steps to prevent or counter any measures which are, or risk being, detrimental to the image of those products.

3.320 Article 45(2) provides that Member States may encourage the formation and functioning of groups on their territories by administrative means. Moreover, Member States shall communicate to the Commission the name and address of the groups referred to in point 2 of Art 3. The Commission shall make this information public.

(a) Administrative support for groups

3.321 Article 44(2) provides that in accordance with Art 5 of Regulation (EC) No 1290/2005, the European Agricultural Fund for Rural Development (EAFRD) may, on the initiative of the Commission or on its behalf, finance, on a centralised basis, administrative support concerning the development, preparatory work, monitoring, administrative and legal support, legal defence, registration fees, renewal fees, trade mark watching fees, litigation fees and any other related measure required to protect the use of the indications, abbreviations and symbols referring to the quality schemes from misuse, imitation, evocation or any other practice liable to mislead the consumer, within the Union and in third countries.

3.322 Article 44(3) provides that the Commission shall adopt implementing acts laying down rules for the uniform protection of the indications, abbreviations and symbols referred to in para 1 of this Article. Those implementing acts shall be adopted in accordance with the examination procedure referred to in Art 57(2).

9. Right to use the schemes

3.323 Article 46(1) provides that Member States shall ensure that any operator complying with the rules of a quality scheme set out in Titles II and III is entitled to be covered by the verification of compliance established pursuant to Art 37.

3.324 Article 46(2) provides that operators who prepare and store a product marketed under the TSG, PDO or PGI schemes or who place such products on the market shall also be subject to the controls laid down in Chapter I of this Title.

3.325 Article 46(2) provides that Member States shall ensure that operators willing to adhere to the rules of a quality scheme set out in Titles III and IV are able to do so and do not face obstacles to participation that are discriminatory or otherwise not objectively founded.

10. Fees

3.326 Article 47 provides that without prejudice to Regulation (EC) No 882/2004 and in particular the provisions of Chapter VI of Title II thereof, Member States may charge a fee to cover their costs of managing the quality schemes, including those incurred in processing applications, statements of opposition, applications for amendments and requests for cancellations provided for in this Regulation.

11. Scope of application processes

3.327 Article 48 provides that the provisions of Chapter IV: Application and registration processes for designations of origin, GIs, and TSGs (Arts 49–54) shall apply in respect of the quality schemes set out in Title II (PDOs and PGIs) and Title III (TSGs).

12. Application for registration of names

3.328 Recital (58) to the Regulation proposes that to ensure that registered names of designations of origin and GIs and TSGs meet the conditions laid down by this Regulation, applications should be examined by the national authorities of the Member State concerned, in compliance with minimum common provisions, including a national opposition procedure. The Commission should subsequently scrutinise applications to ensure that there are no manifest errors and that Union law and the interests of stakeholders outside the Member State of application have been taken into account.

3.329 Recital (61) indicates that the registration procedure for PDOs, PGIs and TSGs, including the scrutiny and the opposition periods, should be shortened and improved, in particular as regards decision-making. The Commission, in certain circumstances acting with the assistance of Member States, should be responsible for decision-making on registration. Procedures should be laid down to allow the amendment of product specifications after registration and the cancellation of registered names, in particular if the product no longer complies with the corresponding product specification or if a name is no longer used in the market place.

3.330 Recital (62) indicates that in order to facilitate cross-border applications for joint registration of PDOs, PGIs or TSGs, provision should be made for appropriate procedures.

13. Eligible applicants

3.331 Article 49(1) provides that applications for registration of names under the quality schemes referred to in Art 48 may only be submitted by groups who work with the products with the name to be registered. In the case of a 'protected designations of origin' or 'protected geographical indications' name that designates a trans-border geographical area or in the case of a 'traditional specialities guaranteed' name, several groups from different Member States or third countries may lodge a joint application for registration.

Article 4 of the Delegated Regulation provides that in case of joint appli- **3.332** cations as referred to in Art 49(1) 'the related national opposition procedures shall be carried out in all the Member States concerned'.

Article 49(1) provides that a single natural or legal person may be treated as a **3.333** group where it is shown that both of the following conditions are fulfilled:

(a) the person concerned is the only producer willing to submit an application;
(b) with regard to PDOs and PGIs, the defined geographical area possesses characteristics which differ appreciably from those of neighbouring areas or the characteristics of the product are different from those produced in neighbouring areas.

14. Grounds of opposition

The grounds of opposition are suggested by the reference in Art 49(2) to **3.334** scrutiny by the Member State 'in order to check that it is justified and meets the conditions of the respective scheme' and by the reference in Art 49(3) to the obligation of the Member State to examine the admissibility of oppositions to PDOs and PGIs in the light of the criteria referred to in Art 10(1)[166] or the admissibility of oppositions to TSGs in the light of the criteria referred to in Art 21(1).[167]

Günzel suggests that the description of the properties of the product or the **3.335** methods of production may also be objected to.[168] In particular, the description must not contain any restrictions which would lead to an unlawful

---

166 Art 10(1) provides:

A reasoned statement of opposition as referred to in Article 51(2) shall be admissible only if it is received by the Commission within the time limit set out in that paragraph and if it:
(a) shows that the conditions referred to in Article 5 and Article 7(1) are not complied with;
(b) shows that the registration of the name proposed would be contrary to Article 6(2), (3) or (4);
(c) shows that the registration of the name proposed would jeopardise the existence of an entirely or partly identical name or of a trade mark or the existence of products which have been legally on the market for at least five years preceding the date of the publication provided for in point (a) of Article 50(2); or
(d) gives details from which it can be concluded that the name for which registration is requested is a generic term.

167 Art 21(1) provides:

A reasoned statement of opposition as referred to in Article 51(2) shall be admissible only if it is received by the Commission before expiry of the time limit and if it:
(a) gives duly substantiated reasons why the proposed registration is incompatible with the terms of this Regulation; or
(b) shows that use of the name is lawful, renowned and economically significant for similar agricultural products or foodstuffs.

168 Günzel, 2012, at pp. 246–7.

monopolisation in favour of one or several producers. This was an issue in the decision of the German Federal Patent Court rendered on 22 September 2011[169] concerning 'OBAZDA', comprising Camembert cheese, butter, paprika, and other spices. This beer garden food is popular in Bavaria. The product specification set out that the only permissible means of stabilising the product should be by use of heat, and that the use of chemical preserving agents was forbidden. However, as only one of the producers based in the defined geographical area used heat for stabilising its 'Obazda', as opposed to chemical stabilisers, the German Federal Patent Court held that the German Patent and Trademark Office should examine how the specification could be changed in order to prevent unjustified restrictions.

15. Application to Member States

3.336 Article 49(2) provides that where the application under the scheme set out in Title II relates to a geographical area in a Member State, or where an application under the scheme set out in Title III is prepared by a group established in a Member State, the application shall be addressed to the authorities of that Member State.

16. Member State scrutiny of opposition

3.337 Article 49(2) requires that the Member State shall scrutinise the application by appropriate means in order to check that it is justified and meets the conditions of the respective scheme.

3.338 Article 49(3) provides that as part of the scrutiny referred to in the second subparagraph of Art 49(2), the Member State shall initiate a national opposition procedure that ensures adequate publication of the application and that provides for a reasonable period within which any natural or legal person having a legitimate interest and established or resident on its territory may lodge an opposition to the application.

3.339 As mentioned above, the Member State shall examine the admissibility of oppositions received under the scheme set out in Title II (PDOs and PGIs) in the light of the criteria referred to in Art 10(1), or the admissibility of oppositions received under the scheme set out in Title III (TSGs) in the light of the criteria referred to in Art 21(1).

---

169   Case 30 W (pat) 9/10, BeckRS 2011, 25376, at II.5 discussed in ibid.

17. Member State notification of opposition to the Commission

Article 49(4) provides that if, after assessment of any opposition received, the **3.340** Member State considers that the requirements of this Regulation are met, it may take a favourable decision and lodge an application dossier with the Commission. It shall in such a case inform the Commission of admissible oppositions received from a natural or legal person that has legally marketed the products in question, using the names concerned, continuously for at least five years preceding the date of the publication referred to in Art 49(3).

18. Publication of opposition by Member State

Article 49(4) provides that the Member State shall ensure that its favourable **3.341** decision is made public and that any natural or legal person having a legitimate interest has an opportunity to appeal.

19. Publication of specification by Member State

Article 49(4) provides that the Member State shall ensure that the version of **3.342** the product specification on which its favourable decision is based is published, and shall provide electronic access to the product specification.

With reference to PDOs and PGIs, the Member State shall also ensure **3.343** adequate publication of the version of the product specification on which the Commission takes its decision pursuant to Art 50(2).

20. Third-country applications

Article 49(5) provides that where the application under the scheme set out in **3.344** Title II relates to a geographical area in a third country, or where an application under the scheme set out in Title III is prepared by a group established in a third country, the application shall be lodged with the Commission, either directly or via the authorities of the third country concerned.

21. Language of documents

Article 49(6) provides that the documents referred to in this Article which are **3.345** sent to the Commission shall be in one of the official languages of the Union.

22. Delegated acts

3.346 Article 49(7) provides that in order to facilitate the application process, the Commission shall be empowered to adopt delegated acts, in accordance with Art 56, defining the rules for carrying out the national objection procedure for joint applications concerning more than one national territory and complementing the rules of the application process.

23. Implementing acts

3.347 The Commission may adopt implementing acts laying down detailed rules on procedures, form and presentation of applications, including for applications concerning more than one national territory. Those implementing acts shall be adopted in accordance with the examination procedure referred to in Art 57(2).

24. Scrutiny of application for opposition by the Commission

3.348 Article 50(1) provides that the Commission shall scrutinise by appropriate means any application that it receives pursuant to Art 49, in order to check that it is justified and that it meets the conditions of the respective scheme. This scrutiny should not exceed a period of six months. Where this period is exceeded, the Commission shall indicate in writing to the applicant the reasons for the delay.

25. Publication of opposition by the Commission

3.349 The Commission shall, at least each month, make public the list of names for which registration applications have been submitted to it, as well as their date of submission.

3.350 Article 50(2) provides that where, based on the scrutiny carried out pursuant to the first subparagraph of Art 50(1), the Commission considers that the conditions laid down in this Regulation are fulfilled, it shall publish in the *Official Journal of the European Union*:

> (a) for applications under the scheme set out in Title II, the single document and the reference to the publication of the product specification;
> (b) for applications under the scheme set out in Title III, the specification.

26. Opposition procedure at the Commission

(a) Notice of opposition

Article 51(1) provides that within three months from the date of publication **3.351** in the *Official Journal of the European Union*, the authorities of a Member State or of a third country, or a natural or legal person having a legitimate interest and established in a third country may lodge a notice of opposition with the Commission.

(b) Eligible opponents

Article 51(1) provides that any natural or legal person having a legitimate **3.352** interest, established or resident in a Member State other than that from which the application was submitted, may lodge a notice of opposition with the Member State in which it is established within a time limit permitting an opposition to be lodged pursuant to the first subparagraph.

(c) Required declaration

Article 51(1) provides that a notice of opposition shall contain a declaration **3.353** that the application might infringe the conditions laid down in this Regulation. A notice of opposition that does not contain this declaration is void.

(d) Commission forwards notice of opposition to applicant

Article 51(1) provides that the Commission shall forward the notice of **3.354** opposition to the authority or body that lodged the application without delay.

(e) Reasoned statement of opposition

Article 51(2) provides that if a notice of opposition is lodged with the **3.355** Commission and is followed within two months by a reasoned statement of opposition, the Commission shall check the admissibility of this reasoned statement of opposition.

(f) Consultations with Commission

i. Invitation from the Commission

Article 51(3) provides that within two months after the receipt of an **3.356** admissible reasoned statement of opposition, the Commission shall invite the authority or person that lodged the opposition and the authority or body that lodged the application to engage in appropriate consultations for a reasonable period that shall not exceed three months.

ii. Provision of information

3.357 The authority or person that lodged the opposition and the authority or body that lodged the application shall start such appropriate consultations without undue delay. They shall provide each other with the relevant information to assess whether the application for registration complies with the conditions of this Regulation. If no agreement is reached, this information shall also be provided to the Commission.

iii. Notification of agreement to the Commission

3.358 Article 5 of the Delegated Regulation provides that when the interested parties reach an agreement following the consultations referred to in Art 51(3), the authorities of the Member State or of the third country from which the application was lodged shall notify the Commission of all the factors which enabled that agreement to be reached, including the opinions of the applicant and of the authorities of a Member State or of a third country or other natural and legal persons having lodged an opposition.

iv. Extension of deadline

3.359 Article 51(3) of the Regulation provides that at any time during these three months, the Commission may, at the request of the applicant, extend the deadline for the consultations by a maximum of three months.

v. Scrutiny of amendments

3.360 Article 51(4) provides that where, following the appropriate consultations referred to in Art 51(3), the details published in accordance with Art 50(2) have been substantially amended the Commission shall repeat the scrutiny referred to in Art 50.

vi. Language

3.361 Article 51(5) provides that the notice of opposition, the reasoned statement of opposition and the related documents which are sent to the Commission in accordance with Art 51(1) to (4) shall be in one of the official languages of the Union.

vii. Delegated acts

3.362 Article 51(6) provides that in order to establish clear procedures and deadlines for opposition, the Commission shall be empowered to adopt delegated acts, in accordance with Art 56, complementing the rules of the opposition procedure.

viii. Implementing acts

The Commission may adopt implementing acts laying down detailed rules on **3.363** procedures, form and presentation of the oppositions. Those implementing acts shall be adopted in accordance with the examination procedure referred to in Art 57(2).

27. Decision on registration

(a) Rejection of application

Article 52(1) provides that where, on the basis of the information available to **3.364** the Commission from the scrutiny carried out pursuant to the first subparagraph of Art 50(1), the Commission considers that the conditions for registration are not fulfilled, it shall adopt implementing acts rejecting the application. Those implementing acts shall be adopted in accordance with the examination procedure referred to in Art 57(2).

(b) Adoption of implementing acts

Article 52(2) provides that if the Commission receives no notice of opposition **3.365** or no admissible reasoned statement of opposition under Art 51, it shall adopt implementing acts, without applying the procedure referred to in Art 57(2), registering the name.

(c) Determination of application for opposition

Article 52(3) provides that if the Commission receives an admissible reasoned **3.366** statement of opposition, it shall, following the appropriate consultations referred to in Art 51(3), and taking into account the results thereof, either:

(a) if an agreement has been reached, register the name by means of implementing acts adopted without applying the procedure referred to in Art 57(2), and, if necessary, amend the information published pursuant to Art 50(2) provided such amendments are not substantial; or

(b) if an agreement has not been reached, adopt implementing acts deciding on the registration. Those implementing acts shall be adopted in accordance with the examination procedure referred to in Art 57(2).

(d) Publication

Article 52(4) provides that acts of registration and decisions on rejection shall **3.367** be published in the *Official Journal of the European Union*.

28. Scientific Committee

3.368 Under the legislation which preceded the Regulation the Commission could be assisted by the Standing Committee on Protected Geographical Indications and Protected Designations of Origin. Commission Decision of 20 December 2006[170] provided for the establishment of a scientific group of experts to assist the Commission on its evaluations of applications for designations of origin, GIs and TSGs.

3.369 The precursor Scientific Committee was established by Commission Decision 93/53/EEC of 21 December 1992[171] to assist the Commission in the field of designations of origin, GIs and certificates of specific character. At the request of the Commission, the Scientific Committee examined all technical problems involved in the registration of names of agricultural products and foodstuffs and any disputes between the Member States, in particular:

- the factors to be taken into account when defining GIs and designations of origin and exceptions thereto, particularly exceptional reputation and renown;
- whether a name is generic;
- the assessment of the traditional nature of the product;
- the assessment of criteria regarding fair competition in commercial transactions and the risk of confusing consumers in cases of conflict between the designation of origin or geographical indication and a trade mark, a homonym or existing product which are legally marketed.[172]

The Regulation makes no reference to the Scientific Committee.

(a) Case law

3.370 In Joined Cases C-465/02 and C-466/02[173] concerning whether the PDO 'FETA' was generic, it was argued that the Commission had merely adopted the decision of the Scientific Committee that it was not. The ECJ rejected this argument, as the Scientific Committee was set up by the Commission, who also appointed its members. It met at the request of a representative of the Commission and the proceedings of the committee related to matters on

---

170 OJ L 32, 6.2.2007, pp. 177–9.
171 Commission Decision of 21 December 1992 setting up a scientific committee for designations of origin, geographical indications and certificates of specific character, [1993] OJ L13/16, as amended by Commission Decision of 14 June 1994, [1994] OJ L 180/47 and Commission Decision of 2 October 1997, [1997] OJ L 277/30.
172 Art 2 of the Commission Decision.
173 *Germany v Commission (Agriculture)* [2005] EUECJ C-465/02, [2005] ECR I-9115, [2006] ETMR 16.

which the Commission has requested an opinion.[174] It was free, as it determined, to refer questions relating to designation of origin to the experts appointed to the Committee in order to help elucidate the problem, as it did in the present case. It was for the Commission to decide to what extent it would follow the opinion provided by the Committee.[175]

29. Amendment to a product specification

(a) Application for amendment

Article 53(1) provides that a group having a legitimate interest may apply for approval of an amendment to a product specification and that applications shall describe and give reasons for the amendments requested. **3.371**

Article 6(1) of the Delegated Regulation provides that the application for an amendment to a product specification as referred to in Art 53(1) 'which is not minor shall contain an exhaustive description and the specific reasons for each amendment'. The description 'shall compare in detail, for each amendment, the original product specification and, where relevant, the original single document with the amended versions proposed'. **3.372**

Article 6(1) of the Delegated Regulation provides 'that application shall be self-sufficient' and 'shall contain all amendments to the product specification and, where relevant, to the single document for which approval is sought'. **3.373**

An application for an amendment which is not minor that does not comply with the first and the second subparagraphs shall not be admissible. The Commission shall inform the applicant if the application is deemed inadmissible. **3.374**

(b) Non-minor amendments

Article 53(2) provides that where the amendment involves one or more amendments to the specification that are not minor, the amendment application shall follow the procedure laid down in Arts 49–52. **3.375**

Article 6(1) of the Delegated Regulation provides that the approval by the Commission 'of an application for an amendment to a product specification which is not minor shall only cover the amendments as included in the application itself'. **3.376**

---

174   [2005] EUECJ C-465/02 at para 103.
175   Ibid., at para 104.

(c) Minor amendments

3.377 However, if the proposed amendments are minor, Art 53(2) provides that the Commission shall approve or reject the application. In the event of the approval of amendments implying a modification of the elements referred to in Art 50(2), the Commission shall publish those elements in the *Official Journal of the European Union.*

(d) Definition of minor amendment

3.378 Article 53(2) provides that for an amendment to be regarded as minor in the case of the quality scheme described in Title II (PDOs and PGIs), it shall not:

(a) relate to the essential characteristics of the product;
(b) alter the link referred to in point (f)(i) or (ii) of Art 7(1);
(c) include a change to the name, or to any part of the name of the product;
(d) affect the defined geographical area; or
(e) represent an increase in restrictions on trade in the product or its raw materials.

3.379 For an amendment to be regarded as minor in the case of the quality scheme described in Title III (TSGs), it shall not:

(a) relate to the essential characteristics of the product;
(b) introduce essential changes to the production method; or
(c) include a change to the name, or to any part of the name of the product.

Article 53(2) requires that the scrutiny of the application shall focus on the proposed amendment.

(e) Submission to Member State

3.380 Article 6(2) of the Delegated Regulation provides that applications for a minor amendment to a product specification concerning PDOs or PGIs 'shall be submitted to the authorities of the Member State the geographical area of the designation or indication relates to'.

3.381 Article 6(2) of the Delegated Regulation provides that 'applications for a minor amendment of a product specification concerning TSGs shall be submitted to the authorities of the Member State in which the group is established'. If the application for a minor amendment of a product specification does not come from the group which had submitted the application for registration of the name or names the product specification refers to, 'the Member State shall give that group the opportunity to make comments on the application if that group still exists'.

(f) Application dossier

If the Member State considers that the requirements of Regulation (EU) No **3.382**
1151/2012 and of the provisions adopted pursuant thereto are met, Art 6(2) of
the Delegated Regulation provides that 'it may lodge a minor amendment
application dossier with the Commission'.

(g) Minor amendments concerning third countries

Article 6(2) of the Delegated Regulation provides that applications for a minor **3.383**
amendment to a product specification concerning products originating in
third countries may be submitted 'by a group having a legitimate interest
either directly to the Commission or via the authorities of that third country'.

(h) Contents of application for minor amendment

Article 6(2) of the Delegated Regulation provides that the application for a **3.384**
minor amendment shall only propose minor amendments within the meaning
of Art 53(2) of Regulation (EU) No 1151/2012. It shall describe those minor
amendments, provide summary reasons therefor and show that the proposed
amendments are indeed to be qualified as minor according to Art 53(2) of
Regulation (EU) No 1151/2012. It shall compare, for each amendment, the
original product specification and, where relevant, the original single document with the amended version proposed.

Article 6(2) of the Delegated Regulation provides that the application shall be **3.385**
'self-sufficient and shall contain all amendments to the product specification
and, where relevant, to the single document for which approval is sought'.

(i) Approval of minor amendment

Article 6(2) of the Delegated Regulation provides that minor amendments **3.386**
referred to in the second subparagraph of Art 53(2) of Regulation (EU) No
1151/2012 'shall be deemed approved if the Commission does not inform
the applicant otherwise within three months from the reception of the
application'.

Article 6(2) of the Delegated Regulation provides that an application for a **3.387**
minor amendment that does not comply with the second subparagraph of this
paragraph shall not be admissible. 'Tacit approval referred to in the third
subparagraph of this Article shall not apply to such applications.' The
Commission shall inform the applicant if the application is deemed inadmissible within three months from the receipt of the application.

(j)   Publication of approval

3.388   Article 6(2) of the Delegated Regulation provides that the Commission shall make public the approved minor amendment to a product specification not implying a modification of the elements referred to in Art 50(2) of Regulation (EU) No 1151/2012.

30.   Temporary change in product specification due to natural disasters, etc

3.389   Article 6(3) of the Delegated Regulation provides that the procedure laid down in Arts 49–52 of Regulation (EU) No 1151/2012 'shall not apply to amendments concerning a temporary change in the product specification resulting from the imposition of obligatory sanitary and phytosanitary measures by the public authorities or linked to natural disasters or adverse weather conditions formally recognised by the competent authorities'.

3.390   Article 6(3) of the Delegated Regulation provides that Member States or third countries shall publish such temporary amendments to the product specification. Those amendments, together with the reasons for them, shall be communicated to the Commission not later than two weeks following approval in the Member State. In communications concerning a temporary amendment to a product specification relating to a PDO or a PGI, Member States shall only enclose the reference to the publication.

3.391   In communications concerning a temporary amendment to the product specification relating to a TSG, Art 6(3) of the Delegated Regulation provides that 'they shall enclose the temporary amendment to the product specification as published'.

3.392   Article 6(3) of the Delegated Regulation provides that third countries shall communicate published temporary amendments to the product specification in the three types of communications.

3.393   Article 6(3) of the Delegated Regulation provides that evidence of the sanitary and phytosanitary measures and a copy of the act recognising natural disasters or adverse weather conditions shall be provided for the three types of communications both by Member States and third countries.

3.394   Article 6(3) of the Delegated Regulation provides that the Commission shall make public such amendments.

31. Cancellation

(a) Procedure

Article 7(1) of the Delegated Regulation provides that the procedure laid **3.395** down in Arts 49–52 of Regulation (EU) No 1151/2012 'shall apply *mutatis mutandis* to the cancellation of a registration as referred to in the first and second subparagraphs of Article 54(1) of that Regulation'.

(b) On the Commission's initiative

Article 54(1) provides that the Commission may, on its own initiative or at the **3.396** request of any natural or legal person having a legitimate interest, adopt implementing acts to cancel the registration of a PDO or of a PGI or of a TSG in the following cases:

(a) where compliance with the conditions of the specification is not ensured;
(b) where no product is placed on the market under the TSG, the PDO or the PGI for at least seven years.

(c) On the initiative of Member States

Article 7(2) of the Delegated Regulation provides that 'Member States shall **3.397** be allowed to submit a request for cancellation on their own initiative pursuant to the first subparagraph of Article 54(1) of Regulation (EU) No 1151/2012'.

(d) At the request of producers

Article 54(1) provides that the Commission may, at the request of the **3.398** producers of product marketed under the registered name, cancel the corres-ponding registration.

(e) Examination procedure

Those implementing acts shall be adopted in accordance with the examination **3.399** procedure referred to in Art 57(2). Article 57(2) provides that where reference is made to this paragraph, Art 5 of Regulation (EU) No 182/2011 shall apply.

(f) Opportunity to defend

Article 54(2) provides that in order to ensure legal certainty all parties have the **3.400** opportunity to defend their rights and legitimate interests. The Commission shall be empowered to adopt delegated acts, in accordance with Art 56 complementing the rules regarding the cancellation process.

3.401 Article 7(4) of the Delegated Regulation provides that 'reasoned statements of opposition as regards cancellation shall be admissible only if they show *continued commercial reliance by an interested person on the registered name*'.

(g) Publicity

3.402 Article 7(3) of the Delegated Regulation provides that 'the request for cancellation shall be made public pursuant to the second paragraph of Art 50(1) of Regulation (EU) No 1151/2012.'

32. Transitional rules

3.403 Article 8 of the Delegated Regulation contains the following transitional rules:

1. In respect of protected designations of origin and protected geographical indications registered prior to 31 March 2006, the Commission shall, at the request of a Member State, publish a single document submitted by that Member State in the *Official Journal of the European Union*. That publication shall be accompanied by the reference of publication of the product specification.
2. Until 3 January 2016 the following rules shall apply:
    (a) for products originating in the Union, where the registered name is used on the labelling, it shall be accompanied either by the relevant Union symbol or by the relevant indication referred to in Art 12(3) or Art 23(3) of Regulation (EU) No 1151/2012;
    (b) for products which are produced outside the Union, the indication referred to in Art 23(3) of Regulation (EU) No 1151/2012 shall be optional on the labelling of traditional specialities guaranteed.

3.404 Article 10 of the Delegated Regulation provides that Art 5 shall only apply to opposition procedures for which the three-month period established in the first subparagraph of Art 51(1) of Regulation (EU) No 1151/2012 has not expired on the date of entry into force of this Regulation.

V. REPEAL OF REGULATIONS

3.405 Article 58(1) repeals Regulations (EC) No 509/2006 and (EC) No 510/2006.

3.406 Article 58(1) provides that Art 13 of Regulation (EC) No 509/2006 shall continue to apply in respect of applications concerning products falling outside the scope of Title III (TSGs) received by the Commission prior to the date of entry into force of this Regulation.

Article 9 of the Delegated Regulation provides for the repeal of Regulations **3.407** (EC) No 1898/2006 and (EC) No 1216/2007.

W. ENTRY INTO FORCE

Article 59 of the Regulation provides for its entry into force on the 20th day **3.408** following that of its publication in the *Official Journal of the European Union* (ie 3 January 2013).

However, Art 59 provides that Art 12(3)[176] and Art 23(3)[177] shall apply from **3.409** 4 January 2016, without prejudice to products already placed on the market before that date.

---

176 Art 12(3) provides:

In the case of products originating in the Union that are marketed under a protected designation of origin or a protected geographical indication registered in accordance with the procedures laid down in this Regulation, the Union symbols associated with them shall appear on the labelling. In addition, the registered name of the product should appear in the same field of vision. The indications 'protected designation of origin' or 'protected geographical indication' or the corresponding abbreviations 'PDO' or 'PGI' may appear on the labelling.

177 Art 23(3) provides:

In the case of the products originating in the Union that are marketed under a traditional speciality guaranteed that is registered in accordance with this Regulation, the symbol referred to in paragraph 2 shall, without prejudice to paragraph 4, appear on the labelling. In addition, the name of the product should appear in the same field of vision. The indication 'traditional speciality guaranteed' or the corresponding abbreviation 'TSG' may also appear on the labelling.

The symbol shall be optional on the labelling of traditional specialities guaranteed which are produced outside the Union.

4

PROTECTION OF GEOGRAPHICAL INDICATIONS AND DESIGNATIONS OF ORIGIN AND TRADITIONAL TERMS FOR WINES IN EUROPE

---

1   OJ L 39, 13.2.2008, p. 16.

A. INTRODUCTION

4.01 European legislation regulating the designations for wines and spirits dates back to 1970.[2] That Regulation 817/70 and its successors – Council Regulations 338/79,[3] 823/87,[4] 1493/1999[5] and Commission Regulation 1607/2000[6] – laid down the rules and standards for 'quality wine produced in specified regions'. Commission Regulations 2133/74,[7] 2392/89,[8] 01/1990,[9] 881/98[10] and 753/2002[11] deal with the use of geographical names for wines.

4.02 As part of the implementation of Agenda 2000 a new common market organisation for wine was established by Regulation 1493/1999[12] on the

---

2   Council Regulation 817/70 of 28 April 1970 laying down special provisions relating to quality wines produced in specified regions, OJ L 99, 5/05/1970, p. 20, no longer in force.

3   Council Regulation 338/79 of 5 February 1979 laying down special provisions relating to quality wines produced in specified regions, OJ L 54, 5/03/1979 p. 48, no longer in force.

4   Council Regulation 823/87 of 16 March 1987 laying down special provisions relating to quality wines produced in specified regions, OJ L 84, 27/03/1987 p. 59, no longer in force.

5   Council Regulation 1493/1999 of 17 May 1999 on the common organisation of the market in wine, OJ L 179, 14/07/1999, p. 16.

6   Commission Regulation 1607/2000 of 24 July 2000 laying down detailed rules for implementing Regulation 1493/1999 on the common organisation of the market in wine, in particular the title relating to quality wine produced in specified regions, OJ L 185, 25/07/2000, p. 17.

7   Council Regulation 2133/74 of 8 August 1974 laying down general rules for the description and presentation of wines and grape musts, OJ L 240, 3/09/1974, p. 16, no longer in force.

8   Council Regulation 2392/89 of 24 July 1989 laying down general rules for the description and presentation of wines and grape musts, OJ L 232, 09/08/1989, p. 13, no longer in force.

9   Commission Regulation 3201/90 of 16 October 1990 laying down detailed rules for the description and presentation of wines and grape musts, OJ L 309, 08/11/1990, p. 1 and Commission Regulation 1640/2000 of 25 July 2000 amending Regulation 3201/90 laying down detailed rules for the description and presentation of wines and grape musts, OJ L 187, 26/07/2000, p. 41.

10   Commission Regulation 881/98 of 24 April 1998 laying down detailed rules for the protection of the additional traditional terms used to designate certain types of quality wine produced in specified regions (*quality wine psr*), OJ L 124, 25/04/1998, p. 22 and Commission Regulation 2253/1999 of 25 October 1999 amending Regulation 881/98 laying down detailed rules for the protection of the additional traditional terms used to designate certain types of quality wine produced in specified regions (*quality wine psr*), OJ L 275, 26/10/1999, p. 8, no longer in force.

11   Commission Regulation 753/2002 of 29 April 2002 laying down certain rules for applying Council Regulation 1493/1999 as regards the description, designation, presentation and protection of certain wine sector products, OJ L 118, 4/05/2002, p. 1, as amended by Regulation 2086/2002, OJ L 321, 26/11/2002, p. 8.

12   Council Regulation 1493/1999 of 17 May 1999 on the common organisation of the market in wine, OJ L 179, 14/07/1999, p. 16, as last amended by Council Regulation 806/2003 of 14 April 2003 adapting to Decision 1999/468/EC the provisions relating to committees which assist the Commission in the exercise of

common organisation of the market in wine. This applied to fresh grapes other than table grapes, grape juice and musts, wine of fresh grapes (including sparkling wines, liqueur wines and semi-sparkling wines), wine vinegar, piquette, wine lees and grape marc.

Regulation 1493/1999 distinguished two categories of wines: quality wines **4.03** produced in specific regions, so-called quality wines psr (produced in specific regions), and table wines. The recognition and control of quality wines psr was left with each Member State. Some, eg Germany, Luxembourg and Austria, classified almost all their wines in the quality wine category, whereas Spain, Italy and France have both table wines with indications of origin and quality wines produced in specified regions.

Some wine labelling rules were included in Directive 2000/13/EC of 20 **4.04** March 2000 on the approximation of the laws of the Member States relating to the labelling, presentation and advertising of foodstuffs. Commission Regulation 753/2002 of 29 April 2002 on the description, designation and protection of certain wine sector products added more specific rules for the labelling of wine.[13] The Wine Regulation also introduced a comprehensive regime dealing with traditional names for wines.

Wine labelling, as well as the use of designations of origin and GIs for wines, **4.05** was regularised by Council Regulation 479/2008 of 29 April 2008 on the common organisation of the market in wine (hereinafter 'the Wine Regulation').[14] This Regulation was updated by Commission Regulation (EC) No 607/2009 of 14 July 2009, which detailed procedures for application, opposition, alteration and cancellation.[15] This Regulation was repealed by Commission Delegated Regulation (EU) No 2019/33, following the Repeal and replacement of Council Regulation (EC) No 1234/2007 by Regulation (EU)

---

its implementing powers laid down in Council instruments adopted in accordance with the consultation procedure (qualified majority), OJ L 122, 16/05/2003, p. 1.

13 Commission Regulation (EC) No 753/2002 of 29 April 2002 laying down certain rules for applying Council Regulation 1493/99 as regards the description, designation and protection of certain wine sector products; OJ L 118, 4/05/2002, p. 1, as last amended by Commission Regulation 261/2006 of 15 February 2006, OJ L 46, 16/2/2006, p. 18.

14 Council Regulation (EC) No 479/2008 of 29 April 2008 on the common organisation of the market in wine, amending Regulations (EC) No 1493/1999, (EC) No 1782/2003, (EC) No 1290/2005, (EC) No 3/2008 and repealing Regulations (EEC) No 2392/86 and (EC) No 1493/1999, OJ L 148, 6/6/2008, p. 1.

15 Commission Regulation (EC) No 607/2009 of 14 July 2009 laying down certain detailed rules for the implementation of Council Regulation (EC) No 479/2008 as regards protected designations of origin and geographical indications, traditional terms, labelling and presentation of certain wine sector products, OJ L 193/6, 9 24.7.2009.

No 1308/2013 establishing a common organisation of the markets in agricultural products.[16] The European Parliament had formulated a Common Agricultural Policy embodied in Council Regulation (EC) No 1234/2007 of 22 October 2007 establishing a common organisation of agricultural markets and on specific provisions for certain agricultural products.[17] In 2013 this was repealed and replaced by Regulation (EU) No 1308/2013. Sections 2 and 3 of Chapter I of Title II of Part II of Regulation No 1308/2013 prescribed rules on designations of origin, geographical indications, traditional terms and labelling and presentation in the wine sector. This was supplemented by Commission Delegated Regulation (EU) No 2019/33 of 17 October 2018 as regards applications for protection of designations of origin, geographical indications and traditional terms in the wine sector, the objection procedure, restrictions of use, amendments to product specifications, cancellation of protection, and labelling and presentation. Regulation 1308/2013 was implemented by Commission Implementing Regulation (EU) No 2019/34 of 17 October 2018.[18]

4.06 Article 100(4) of Regulation No 1308/2013 provided that the protection of designations of origin and GIs of products covered by Art 93 of this Regulation were without prejudice to protected geographical indications applying to spirit drinks as defined in Art 2 of the Wine Regulation.

4.07 The European Union developed the E-Bacchus database[19] which consists of the register of designations of origin and GIs protected in the EU in accordance with Council Regulation (EC) No 1234/2007.[20] It lists non-EU countries' GIs and names of origin protected in the EU in accordance with bilateral agreements on trade in wine concluded between the EU and the non-EU countries concerned and lists the traditional terms protected in the EU in accordance with Council Regulation (EC) No 1234/2007. Regulation (EU) No 1308/2013 provided for this information to be transferred to the Register which it established.

---

16 OJ L 347, 20.12.2013, pp. 671–854.
17 OJ L 299, 16.11.2007, p. 1.
18 C/2018/6621, OJ L 9, 11.1.2019, pp. 46–76.
19 http://ec.europa.eu/agriculture/markets/wine/e-bacchus/index.cfm?event=pwelcome &language=EN.
20 Council Regulation (EC) No 1234/2007 of 22 October 2007 establishing a common organisation of agricultural markets and on specific provisions for certain agricultural products (Single CMO Regulation), OJ L 299, 16.11.2007, pp. 1–149.

B. THE WINE REGULATION

1. Introduction

The Wine Regulation was enacted out of the concern for the steady decline in   **4.08**
wine consumption in the Community and the slow increase in wine exports
compared with the growth in imports.[21] It was perceived that the existing
legislation had become ineffective in steering the wine sector towards a
competitive and sustainable development as the market mechanism measures
had encouraged structural surpluses without requiring structural improvements and had unduly constrained the activities of competitive producers.[22] In
the light of previous experience it was considered appropriate to make a
fundamental change to the Community wine regime with a view to achieving
the following objectives:

- increasing the competitiveness of the Community's wine producers;
- strengthening the reputation of Community quality wine as the best in
  the world;
- recovering old markets and winning new ones in the Community and
  worldwide;
- creating a wine regime that operates through clear, simple and effective
  rules that balance supply and demand;
- creating a wine regime that preserves the best traditions of Community
  wine production;
- reinforcing the social fabric of many rural areas, and ensuring that all
  production respects the environment.[23]

The Wine Regulation therefore repealed the previous Regulation[24] and   **4.09**
established a structure of support measures for wine producers[25] and a
regulatory structure which included the regulation of oenological practices[26]
and rules dealing with designations of origin, GIs and traditional terms.[27] The
Regulation also deals with trade with third countries[28] and production
potential.[29] This chapter deals only with the rules concerning designations of
origin, GIs and traditional terms.

---

21   The Wine Regulation, Recital (2).
22   Ibid.
23   Ibid., Recital (5).
24   Regulation (EC) No 1493/1999.
25   The Wine Regulation, Title II.
26   Ibid., Title III, chapter I.
27   Ibid., Title III, chapters III and IV.
28   Ibid., Title IV.
29   Ibid., Title V.

2. Scope of the rules concerning designations

4.10 Chapter IV of the Wine Regulation deals with designations of origin and GIs. Recital (27) explains that the concept of quality wines in the Community is based, inter alia, on the specific characteristics attributable to the wine's geographical origin, which are identified for consumers via protected designations of origin and GIs. It proposes that in order to allow for a transparent and more elaborate framework underpinning the claim to quality by the products concerned, 'a regime should be established under which applications for a designation of origin or a geographical indication are examined in line with the approach followed under the Community's horizontal quality policy applicable to foodstuffs other than wine and spirits'.[30]

4.11 Recital (28) proposes that to preserve the particular quality characteristics of wines with a designation of origin or a GI, 'Member States should be allowed to apply more stringent rules in that respect.' Thus to qualify for protection in the Community Recital (29) explains that designations of origin and GIs should be recognised and registered at Community level with applications being examined by the national authorities of the Member State concerned, subject to compliance with minimum common provisions, including a national objection procedure. The Commission will subsequently scrutinise these decisions to ensure that the conditions laid down by the Wine Regulation are satisfied and that the approach to applications is uniform across the Member States.

4.12 In relation to third countries Recital (30) suggests that protection should be open to designations of origin and GIs of third countries where these are protected in their country of origin and Recital (31) states that the registration procedure should enable any natural or legal person having a legitimate interest in a Member State or a third country to exercise his rights by notifying his objections.

4.13 Recital (32) states that registered designations of origin and GIs should enjoy protection against 'uses which unduly take advantage of the reputation that complying products command' and that to promote fair competition and not to mislead consumers, 'this protection should also affect products and services not covered by this Regulation, including those not found in Annex I to the Treaty'.

---

30 In Council Regulation (EC) No 510/2006 of 20 March 2006 on the protection of geographical indications and designations of origin for agricultural products and foodstuffs OJ L 93, 31.3.2006, p. 12. Regulation as amended by Regulation (EC) No 1791/2006, OJ L 363, 20.12.2006, p. 1.

In relation to amendment of product specifications after protection, and **4.14** cancellation of the designation of origin or GI, Recital (33) proposes that procedures should be provided for these matters to ensure in particular if compliance with the corresponding product specification is no longer ensured.

Recital (34) proposes that the designations of origin and GIs protected on **4.15** Community territory should be subject to controls, where possible in compliance with Regulation (EC) No 882/2004 of 29 April 2004 on official controls performed to ensure the verification of compliance with feed and food law, animal health and animal welfare rules,[31] including a system of checks to ensure compliance with the product specifications of the wines concerned.

Finally Recital (36) states that existing designations of origin and GIs in the **4.16** Community should for reasons of legal certainty be exempt from the application of the new examination procedure. However, the Member States concerned should provide the Commission with the basic information and acts under which they have been recognised at national level, failing which they should lose their protection as designations of origin or GIs. 'The scope for cancellation of existing designations of origin and geographical indications should be limited for reasons of legal certainty.'

The objectives of the Wine Regulation, which are outlined in the previous **4.17** section, are reflected in Art 33 of the Wine Regulation. This provides in Art 33(1) that the rules relating to designations of origin, GIs and traditional terms laid down in Chapters IV and V shall apply to certain wines designated in Annex IV of the Regulation.[32]

According to Art 33(2) the rules referred to in Art 32(1) shall be based on: **4.18**

---

31 OJ L 165, 30.4.2004, p. 1; corrected by OJ L 191, 28.5.2004, p. 1. Regulation as last amended by Council Regulation (EC) No 301/2008, OJ L 97, 9.4.2008, p. 85.
32 Art 33(1) listed the products referred to and defined in paras 1, 3–6, 8, 9, 11, 15 and 16 of Annex IV, namely:

    1. Wine
    3. Liqueur wine
    4. Sparkling wine
    5. Quality sparkling wine
    6. Quality aromatic sparkling wine
    8. Semi-sparkling wine
    9. Aerated semi-sparkling wine
   11. Partially fermented grape must
   15. Wine from raisined grapes
   16. Wine of overripe grapes.

    (a)   the protection of legitimate interests of:
        (i)   consumers; and
        (ii) producers;
    (b)   ensuring the smooth operation of the common market in the products concerned;
    (c)   promoting the production of quality products, whilst allowing national quality policy measures.

C. DEFINITIONS

1. Designation of origin

4.19 Article 34(1) provides that for the purposes of the Wine Regulation, the following definitions shall apply:

    (a)   'designation of origin' means the name of a region, a specific place or, in exceptional cases, a country used to describe a product referred to in Art 33(1) that complies with the following requirements:
        (i)   its quality and characteristics are essentially or exclusively due to a particular geographical environment with its inherent natural and human factors;
        (ii) the grapes from which it is produced come exclusively from this geographical area;
        (iii) its production takes place in this geographical area;
        (iv) it is obtained from vine varieties belonging to *Vitis vinifera.*

4.20 Article 34(2) provides that certain traditionally used names shall constitute a designation of origin where they:

    (a)   designate a wine;
    (b)   refer to a geographical name;
    (c)   meet the requirements referred to in Art 34(1) (a)(i) to (iv);
    (d)   undergo the procedure conferring protection on designations of origin and GIs laid down in this Chapter.

4.21 In Case 12–74,[33] which concerned German legislation stating that the appellations 'SEKT' and 'WEINBRAND' shall describe vine products originating in the Federal Republic of Germany or coming from other countries throughout the whole of which German was an official language, the Court ruled that an:

> area of origin which is defined on the basis either of the extent of national territory or a linguistic criterion cannot constitute a geographical area within the meaning referred

---

33 *Commission of the European Communities v The Federal Republic of Germany* [1975] ECR 181.

to above, capable of justifying an indication of origin, particularly as the products in question may be produced from grapes of indeterminate origin.[34]

2. Geographical indication

Article 34(1) provides that for the purposes of the Wine Regulation, the **4.22** following definitions shall apply:

(b) 'geographical indication' means an indication referring to a region, a specific place or, in exceptional cases, a country, used to describe a product referred to in Article 33(1) which complies with the following requirements:
   (i) it possesses a specific quality, reputation or other characteristics attributable to that geographical origin;
   (ii) at least 85 per cent of the grapes used for its production come exclusively from this geographical area;
   (iii) its production takes place in this geographical area;
   (iv) it is obtained from vine varieties belonging to *Vitis vinifera or* a cross between the *Vitis vinifera* species and other species of the genus *Vitis*.

3. Production in the demarcated geographical area

(a) 'Production'

Article 5(1) of Commission Regulation (EC) No 607/2009[35] provides that for **4.23** the purpose of application of Art 34(1)(a)(iii) and (b)(iii) of the Wine Regulation and of this Article *'production'* covers all the operations involved, from the harvesting of the grapes to the completion of the wine-making process, with the exception of any post-production processes.

(b) PGIs

Article 5(2) of Commission Regulation (EC) No 607/2009 provides that for **4.24** products with a PGI, the portion of grapes, of up to 15 per cent, which may originate outside the demarcated geographical area as provided for in Art 34(1)(b)(ii) of the Wine Regulation, shall come from the Member State or third country concerned in which the demarcated area lies.

---

34 Ibid., at para 8.
35 Commission Regulation (EC) No 607/2009 of 14 July 2009 laying down certain detailed rules for the implementation of Council Regulation (EC) No 479/2008 as regards protected designations of origin and geographical indications, traditional terms, labelling and presentation of certain wine sector products, OJ L 193/6, 9 24.7.2009.

4. Amendment of lists of wines

4.25 Article 5(3) of Commission Regulation (EC) No 607/2009 by way of derogation from Art 34(1)(a)(ii) of Regulation (EC) No 479/2008, Annex III, Part B, paragraph 3 of Commission Regulation (EC) No 606/2009 on wine-making practices and restrictions applies.[36] This provision is as follows:

> The lists of wines bearing a protected designation of origin or a protected geographical indication given in subparagraphs (c), (d) and (e) of paragraph 2 may be amended where the production conditions of the wines concerned are amended or the designation of origin or geographical indication is changed. The Member States shall provide the Commission, in advance, with all the necessary technical information for the wines concerned, including their product specifications and the annual quantities produced.

5. Wines made in areas adjacent to protected areas or in trans-border areas

4.26 Article 5(4) of Commission Regulation (EC) No 607/2009 provides by way of derogation from Art 34(1)(a)(iii) and (1)(b)(iii) of the Wine Regulation, and on condition that the product specification so provides, that:

(a) in an area in the immediate proximity of the demarcated area concerned; or
(b) in an area located within the same administrative unit or within a neighbouring administrative unit, in conformity with national rules; or
(c) in the case of a trans-border designation of origin or GI, or where an agreement on control measures exists between two or more Member States or between one or more Member State(s) and one or more third country(-ies),a product with a PDO or GI may be made into wine in an area situated in the immediate proximity of the demarcated area in question.

4.27 Article 5(4) of Commission Regulation (EC) No 607/2009 provides by way of derogation from Art 34(1)(b)(iii) of Regulation (EC) No 479/2008, and on condition that the product specification so provides, that wines with a PGI may continue to be made into wine beyond the immediate proximity of the demarcated area in question until 31 December 2012.

4.28 Article 5(4) of Commission Regulation (EC) No 607/2009 provides by way of derogation from Art 34(1)(a)(iii) of the Wine Regulation, and on condition that the product specification so provides, that a product may be made into sparkling wine or semi-sparkling wine with a PDO beyond the immediate

---

36   Ibid.

proximity of the demarcated area in question if this practice was in use prior to 1 March 1986.

6. Traditional term

Recital (38) of the Wine Regulation explains that certain terms are tradition- **4.29** ally used in the Community and convey information to consumers about particularities and quality of wines complementing the information conveyed by designations of origin and GIs. Recital (12) to Commission Regulation (EC) No 607/2009, which lays down certain detailed rules for the implementation of Wine Regulation, as regards, inter alia, traditional terms, states that such terms 'evoke in the minds of consumers a production or ageing method or a quality, colour or type of place or a particular event linked to the history of the wine'.

Consequently, 'so as to ensure the working of the internal market and fair **4.30** competition and to avoid consumers being misled, those traditional terms should be eligible for protection in the Community'.

Article 54(1) provides that 'traditional term' shall mean a term traditionally **4.31** used in Member States for products referred to in Art 33(1) to designate:

(a) that the product has a PDO or GI under Community or Member State law;
(b) the production or ageing method or the quality, colour, type of place, or a particular event linked to the history, of the product with a PDO or GI.

7. Third countries

Article 23(3) provides that designations of origin and GIs, 'including those **4.32** relating to geographical areas in third countries', shall be eligible for protection in the Community in accordance with the rules laid down in Chapter IV of the Wine Regulation.

D. APPLICATION FOR PROTECTION

1. Content of applications – technical file

Article 35(1) provides that applications for protection of names as desig- **4.33** nations of origin or GIs shall include a technical file containing:

(a) the name to be protected;

    (b)   the name and address of the applicant;
    (c)   a product specification as referred to in paragraph 2;
    (d)   a single document summarising the product specification referred to in paragraph 2.

4.34 Article 3 of Commission Regulation (EC) No 607/2009 provides that an application for protection shall consist of the documents required under Arts 35 or 36 and an electronic copy of the product specification and the single document. Annexes I and II to this Regulation set out models for an application for protection, as well as the single document and Art 3 requires that the application for protection shall comply with these.

2. Specification

4.35 Article 35(2) provides that the product specification 'shall enable interested parties to verify the relevant conditions of production of the designation of origin or geographical indication' and shall consist at least of the following items in the language which appears in italics:

name

    (a)   the name to be protected;

4.36 Article 4(1) of Commission Regulation (EC) No 607/2009 provides that the name to be protected shall be registered only in the language(s) used to describe the product in question in the demarcated geographical area and Art 4(2) requires that the name shall be registered with its original spelling(s).

description of the wine(s)

    (b)   a description of the wine(s):
        (i)   for wines with a designation of origin, its principal analytical and organoleptic characteristics;
        (ii) for wines with a geographical indication, its principal analytical characteristics as well as an evaluation or indication of its organoleptic characteristics;

specific oenological practices

    (c)   where applicable, the specific oenological practices used to make the wine(s) as well as the relevant restrictions on making the wine(s);

demarcation of the geographical area

    (d)   the demarcation of the geographical area concerned;

4.37 Article 5 of Commission Regulation (EC) No 607/2009 provides the area shall be 'demarcated in a detailed, precise and unambiguous manner'.

maximum yields per hectare

(e)   the maximum yields per hectare;

indication of the wine grape variety

(f)   an indication of the wine grape variety or varieties the wine(s) is obtained from;

details of the link

(g)   the details bearing out the link referred to in Article 34(1)(a)(i) or, as the case may be, in Article 34(1)(b)(i);

Article 7(1) of Commission Regulation (EC) No 607/2009 provides that the **4.38** details bearing out the geographical link referred to in Art 35(2)(g) shall explain to what extent the features of the demarcated geographical area influence the final product.

In case of applications covering different categories of grapevine products, the **4.39** details bearing out the link shall be demonstrated for each of the grapevine products concerned.

Article 7(2) of Commission Regulation (EC) No 607/2009 provides that in **4.40** the case of a *designation of origin*, the product specification shall set out:

(a)   details of the geographical area, and in particular natural and human factors, relevant to the link;
(b)   details of the quality or characteristics of the product essentially or exclusively attributable to the geographical environment;
(c)   a description of the causal interaction between the details referred to in point (a) and those referred to in point (b).

Article 7(3) of Commission Regulation (EC) No 607/2009 provides that in **4.41** the case of a *geographical indication*, the product specification shall set out:

(a)   details of the geographical area relevant to the link;
(b)   details of the quality, reputation or other specific characteristics of the product attributable to its geographical origin;
(c)   a description of the causal interaction between the details referred to in point (a) and those referred to in point (b).

Article 7(4) of Commission Regulation (EC) No 607/2009 provides that the **4.42** product specification for a GI shall state whether it is based on a specific quality or reputation or other characteristics linked to its geographical origin.

4.43   Case C-47/90[37] considered whether Spanish Law 25/70 laying down the basic rules on vines, wines and spirits requires that wine could require that wine which fulfilled the conditions laid down for eligibility for the 'Rioja denominación de origen calificada' could be bottled outside the region without being deprived of that designation. Wine transported in bulk within the region retained its entitlement to the 'denominación de origen calificad' when bottled in authorised cellars. Belgium commenced proceedings under Art 170 of the EC Treaty against Spain for infringement of Art 34 (now Art 29) of the EC Treaty. Spain argued that by ensuring that operators in the wine-growing sector of the Rioja region could obtain a designation of origin and also control bottling, the quality of the product was better safeguarded, and consequently, so was the reputation of the designation, for which operators assumed full and collective responsibility. In this case, it was undisputed that the bottling of wine is an important operation and one which, if not carried out in accordance with strict requirements, may seriously impair the quality of the product. The best conditions for bottling are met if it is undertaken by operators established in the same region as those entitled to use the designation and operating under their direct control. Such operators have specialised experience and thorough knowledge of the specific characteristics of the wine in question, which must not be impaired or lost at the time of bottling. Taking into account these circumstances, the ECJ concluded that the challenged requirement was not contrary to Art 34 of the EC Treaty and dismissed the action of Belgium.

objective and non-discriminatory requirements compatible with community law

(h)   applicable requirements laid down in Community or national provisions or, where foreseen by Member States, by an organisation which manages the protected designation of origin or geographical indication, having regard to the fact that such requirements shall be objective and non-discriminatory and compatible with Community law;

4.44   Article 8 of Commission Regulation (EC) No 607/2009 provides that if a product specification indicates that packaging of the product must take place within the demarcated geographical area or in an area in the immediate proximity of the demarcated area in question, in accordance with a requirement referred to in Art 35(2)(h) 'justification for this requirement shall be given in respect of the product concerned'.

---

37   Case C-47/90, Judgment of 9 June 1992, *Établissements Delhaize frères et Compagnie Le Lion SA v Promalvin SA and AGE Bodegas Unidas SA* [1992] ECR I-3669 and ECJ Case C-388/95, Judgment of 16 May 2000, *Kingdom of Belgium v Kingdom of Spain* [2000] ECR I-3123.

name and address of verifying authorities and bodies

(i)   the name and address of the authorities or bodies verifying compliance with the provisions of the product specification and their specific tasks.

3.   Application for protection relating to a geographical area in a third country

Article 36(1) provides that where the application for protection concerns a geographical area in a third country, it shall contain in addition to the elements provided for in Art 35 proof that the name in question is protected in its country of origin.   **4.45**

Article 36(2) requires the application to be sent to the Commission, either directly from the applicant or via the authorities of the third country concerned. Article 36(3) requires the application for protection to be filed in one of the official languages of the Community or accompanied by a certified translation into one of those languages.   **4.46**

(a)   Applicants

Article 37(1) provides that 'any interested group of producers, or in exceptional cases a single producer, may apply for the protection of a designation of origin or geographical indication' and that other interested parties may participate in the application.   **4.47**

Commission Regulation (EC) No 607/2009 of 14 July 2009 provides in Art 2(1) that a single producer may be an applicant within the meaning of Art 37(1) if it is shown that: **4.48**

(a)   the person in question is the only producer in the demarcated geographical area; and

(b)   where the relevant demarcated geographical area is surrounded by areas with designations of origin or GIs, this relevant area possesses features which are substantially different from those of the surrounding demarcated areas or characteristics of the product differ from those of the products obtained in the surrounding demarcated areas.

In Art 2(2) Commission Regulation (EC) No 607/2009 provides that a Member State or third country, or the respective authorities thereof, shall not be an applicant within the meaning of Art 37.   **4.49**

Article 37(2) restricts producers to lodging an application for protection 'only for wines which they produce'.   **4.50**

4.51   Article 37(3) permits a joint application 'in the case of a name designating a trans-border geographical area or a traditional name connected to a trans-border geographical area'.

4.   Preliminary national procedure

4.52   Article 38(1) provides that applications for protection of a designation of origin or a GI of wines in accordance with Art 34 originating in the Community shall be subject to a preliminary national procedure in accordance with Art 38.

4.53   Article 38(2) requires the application for protection to be filed with the Member State in which territory the designation of origin or GI originates.

4.54   Article 38(3) requires the Member State to examine the application for protection as to whether it meets the conditions set out in Chapter IV of the Wine Regulation. This requires the Member State to carry out a national procedure ensuring adequate publication of the application and providing for a period of at least two months from the date of publication within which any natural or legal person having a legitimate interest and established or resident on its territory may object to the proposed protection by lodging a duly substantiated statement with the Member State.

4.55   If the Member State considers that the designation of origin or GI does not meet the relevant requirements, including the eventuality that it is incompatible with Community law in general, Art 38(4) requires it to reject the application.

4.56   On the other hand, if the Member State considers that the relevant requirements are met, Art 38(5) requires the Member State to:

    (a)   publish the single document and the product specification at least on the Internet; and

    (b)   forward to the Commission an application for protection containing the following information:

        (i)   the name and address of the applicant;

        (ii)   the single document referred to in Art 35(1)(d);

        (iii)   a declaration by the Member State that it considers that the application lodged by the applicant meets the conditions of this Regulation;

        (iv)   the reference to publication, as referred to in (a).

This information shall be forwarded in one of the official languages of the Community or accompanied by a certified translation into one of those languages.

Article 38(6) required Member States to introduce the laws, regulations or **4.57** administrative provisions necessary to comply with this Article by 1 August 2009.

Article 38(7) provides that where a Member State has no national legislation **4.58** concerning the protection of designations of origin and GIs, it may, on a transitional basis only, grant protection to the name in accordance with the terms of Chapter IV of the Wine Regulation at national level with effect from the day the application is lodged with the Commission. Such transitional national protection shall cease on the date on which a decision on registration or refusal under this Chapter is taken.

5. Commission examination procedure

Article 39(1) of Commission Regulation (EC) No 607/2009 requires the **4.59** Commission to make public the date of submission of the application for protection of the designation of origin or GI.

Article 39(2) requires the Commission to examine whether the applications **4.60** for protection referred to in Art 38(5) meet the conditions laid down in Chapter IV of the Wine Regulation.

Where the Commission considers that the conditions laid down in Chapter **4.61** IV of the Wine Regulation are met, Art 39(3) requires it to publish in the *Official Journal of the European Union* the single document referred to in Art 35(1)(d) and the reference to the publication of the product specification referred to in Art 38(5).

Where this is not the case, it shall be decided, in accordance with the **4.62** procedure referred to in Art 113(2), to reject the application.

The details of the Commission examination procedure were considerably **4.63** supplemented by Section 2 of Commission Regulation (EC) No 607/2009.

6. Receipt of the application

Article 9(1) of Commission Regulation (EC) No 607/2009 provides that the **4.64** application shall be submitted to the Commission in paper or electronic form.

The date of submission of an application to the Commission shall be the date on which the application is entered in the Commission's mail registry. This date is made available to the public by appropriate means.

4.65 Article 9(2) requires the Commission to mark the documents making up the application with the date of receipt and the file number allocated to the application.

4.66 The Member State or the third-country authorities or the applicant established in the third country in question shall receive an acknowledgement of receipt indicating at least the following:

> (a) the file number;
> (b) the name to be registered;
> (c) the number of pages received; and
> (d) the date of receipt of the application.

7. Submission of a trans-border application

4.67 Article 10(1) of Commission Regulation (EC) No 607/2009 provides that in the case of a trans-border request, a joint application may be submitted for a name designating a trans-border geographical area by more than one group of producers representing that area.

4.68 Article 10(2) of Commission Regulation (EC) No 607/2009 provides that where only Member States are concerned, the preliminary national procedure referred to in Art 38 of Regulation (EC) No 479/2008 applies in all the Member States concerned.

4.69 For the purposes of application of Art 38(5) of Regulation (EC) No 479/2008, a trans-border application shall be forwarded to the Commission by one Member State on behalf of the others, and shall include an authorisation from each of the other Member States concerned authorising the Member State forwarding the application to act on its behalf.

4.70 Article 10(3) of Commission Regulation (EC) No 607/2009 provides that where a trans-border application involves only third countries, the application shall be forwarded to the Commission either by one of the applicant groups on behalf of the others or by one of the third countries on behalf of the others and shall include:

(a) the elements proving that the conditions laid down in Arts 34 and 35 of the Wine Regulation are fulfilled;

(b) the proof of protection in the third countries concerned; and

(c) an authorisation as referred to in paragraph 2 from each of the other third countries concerned.

Article 10(4) of Commission Regulation (EC) No 607/2009 provides that **4.71** where a trans-border application involves at least one Member State and at least one third country, the preliminary national procedure referred to in Art 38 of Regulation (EC) No 479/2008 applies in all the Member States concerned. The application shall be forwarded to the Commission by one of the Member States or third countries or by one of the third-country applicant groups and shall include:

(a) the elements proving that the conditions laid down in Arts 34 and 35 of Regulation (EC) No 479/2008 are fulfilled;

(b) the proof of protection in the third countries concerned; and

(c) an authorisation as referred to in paragraph 2 from each of the other Member States or third countries concerned.

Article 10(5) of Commission Regulation (EC) No 607/2009 provides that the **4.72** Member State, third countries or groups of producers established in third countries which forward to the Commission a trans-border application as referred to in paras 2, 3 and 4 of this Article, become the consignee of any notification or decision issued by the Commission.

8. Admissibility of application for protection

Article 11(1) of Commission Regulation (EC) No 607/2009 provides that for **4.73** the purposes of determining whether an application for protection is admissible, the Commission shall verify that the application for registration set out in Annex I has been completed and that the supporting documents have been attached to the application.

Article 11(2) of Commission Regulation (EC) No 607/2009 provides that any **4.74** application for registration that is deemed admissible shall be notified to the Member State or the third-country authorities or the applicant established in the third country in question.

If the application has not been completed or has only been partially completed, **4.75** or if the supporting documents referred to in para 1 have not been produced at the same time as the application for registration or some are missing, the Commission shall inform the applicant accordingly and shall invite it to remedy the deficiencies noted within a period of two months. If the deficiencies are not remedied before the time limit expires, the Commission shall reject the application as inadmissible. The decision on inadmissibility shall be notified to the Member State or the third-country authorities or the applicant established in the third country in question.

9. Scrutiny of the conditions of validity

4.76 Article 12(1) of Commission Regulation (EC) No 607/2009 provides that if an admissible application for the protection of a designation of origin or GI does not meet the requirements laid down in Arts 34 and 35 of the Wine Regulation, the Commission shall inform the Member State or the third-country authorities or the applicant established in the third country in question of the grounds for refusal, setting a deadline for the withdrawal or amendment of the application or for the submission of comments.

4.77 If the obstacles to registration are not remedied by the Member State or third-country authorities or the applicant established in the third country in question within the deadline, Art 12(2) requires the Commission to reject the application in accordance with Art 39(3) of the Wine Regulation.

4.78 Article 12(3) requires such decision on rejection to be notified to the Member State or the third-country authorities or the applicant established in the third country in question.

10. Verification of compliance with specifications

4.79 Article 48(1) of Commission Regulation (EC) No 607/2009 requires annual verification of compliance with the product specification, during the production and during or after conditioning of the wine in respect of protected designations of origin and GIs relating to a geographical area within the Community.

4.80 Article 48(1) requires the annual verification to be ensured by:

(a) the competent authority or authorities referred to in Art 47(1); or

(b) one or more control bodies within the meaning of point 5 of the second subparagraph of Art 2 of Regulation (EC) No 882/2004[38] operating as a product certification body in accordance with the criteria laid down in Art 5 of that Regulation.

---

38 Regulation (EC) No 882/2004 of 29 April 2004 on official controls performed to ensure the verification of compliance with feed and food law, animal health and animal welfare rules, OJ L 191, 28.5.2004, p. 1.

Article 48(1) requires the costs of such verification to be borne by the operators subject to it.

11. Verification of compliance with specifications in third countries

Article 48(2) of Commission Regulation (EC) No 607/2009 requires that in **4.81** third countries annual verification of compliance with the product specification, during the production and during or after conditioning of the wine in respect of protected designations of origin and GIs relating to a geographical area in a third country, shall be ensured by:

(a) one or more public authorities designated by the third country; or
(b) one or more certification bodies.

12. Amendments to product specifications

(a) Applicants for amendment

Article 49(1) of the Wine Regulation provides that an applicant satisfying the **4.82** conditions of Art 37 (dealing with the eligibility of applicants) may apply for approval of an amendment to the product specification of a PDO or GI, in particular to take account of developments in scientific and technical knowledge or to redefine the geographical area referred to in (d) of the second subparagraph of Art 35(2) of the Wine Regulation.

Article 20(5) of Commission Regulation (EC) No 607/2009 provides that **4.83** where the application for approval of amendments to the product specification is submitted by an applicant other than the initial applicant, the commission shall communicate the application to the initial applicant.

(b) Form of application for amendment

Article 20(1) of Commission Regulation (EC) No 607/2009 provides that an **4.84** application for approval of amendments to the product specification submitted by an applicant as referred to in Art 37 of the Wine Regulation of a PDO or GI shall be drawn up in accordance with Annex IV to Commission Regulation (EC) No 607/2009.

(c) Verification of admissibility of applications

Article 20(2) of Commission Regulation (EC) No 607/2009 provides that for **4.85** the purposes of determining whether an application for the approval of amendments to the product specification pursuant to Art 49(1) of the Wine Regulation is admissible, the Commission shall verify that it has been sent the information required under Art 35(2) of that Regulation and a completed application as referred to in Art 20(1) of Commission Regulation (EC) No 607/2009.

4.86 Article 20(3) of Commission Regulation (EC) No 607/2009 provides that for the purposes of the application of the first sentence of Art 49(2) of the Wine Regulation, Arts 9, 10, 11, 12, 13, 14, 15, 16, 17 and 18 of Commission Regulation (EC) No 607/2009 shall apply *mutatis mutandis*.

(d) Reasons for amendment

4.87 Article 49(1) of the Wine Regulation requires applications to describe and give reasons for the amendments requested.

(e) Amendments to the single document

4.88 Article 49(2) of the Wine Regulation provides that where the proposed amendment involves one or more amendments to the single document referred to in Art 35(1)(d) (technical file containing the specification), Art 49(2) provides also that Arts 38–41 (covering the national procedure and scrutiny by the Commission) shall apply *mutatis mutandis* to the amendment application.

(f) Minor amendments

4.89 However, if the proposed amendment is only minor, Art 49(2) of the Wine Regulation provides that it shall be decided, in accordance with the procedure referred to in Art 113(2),[39] whether to approve the application without following the procedure laid down in Art 39(2) and Art 40 and in the case of approval, the Commission shall proceed to publication of the elements referred to in Art 39(3) of the Wine Regulation.

4.90 Article 20(4) of Commission Regulation (EC) No 607/2009 provides that an amendment is considered to be minor if:

(a) it does not relate the essential characteristics of the product;
(b) it does not alter the link;
(c) it does not include a change in the name or any part of the name of the product;
(d) it does not affect the demarcated geographical area;
(e) it does not entail any further restrictions on the marketing of the product.

---

39 Art 113(2) provides that:

where reference is made to this paragraph:

(a) the Commission shall be assisted by a Regulatory Committee;
(b) Articles 5 and 7 of Decision 1999/468/EC shall apply;
(c) the period referred to in Article 5(6) of Decision 1999/468/EC shall be three months.

(g) No changes to the single document

Article 49(3) of the Wine Regulation provides that: **4.91**

> where the proposed amendment does not involve any change to the single document, the following rules shall apply:
> (a) where the geographical area is in a given Member State, that Member State shall express its position on the amendment and, if it is in favour, shall publish the amended product specification and inform the Commission of the amendments approved and the reasons for them;
> (b) where the geographical area is in a third country, the Commission shall determine whether to approve the proposed amendment.

(h) Acceptance of amendment

Article 20(4) of Commission Regulation (EC) No 607/2009 provides that **4.92** where the Commission decides to accept an amendment to the product specification that affects or comprises an amendment to the information recorded in the Register, it shall delete the original data from the Register and enter the new data with effect from the date on which the relevant decision takes effect.

13. Objection procedure

(a) Eligible objector

Article 40 provides that within two months from the date of publication **4.93** provided for in the first subparagraph of Art 39(3), any Member State or third country, or any natural or legal person having a legitimate interest, established or resident in a Member State other than that applying for the protection or in a third country, may object to the proposed protection by lodging with the Commission a duly substantiated statement relating to the conditions of eligibility as laid down in Chapter IV of the Wine Regulation.

In the case of natural or legal persons established or resident in a third country, **4.94** such a statement shall be lodged, either directly or via the authorities of the third country concerned, within the time limit of two months referred to in the first paragraph.

(b) Form of objection

Article 14(1) of Commission Regulation (EC) No 607/2009 requires the **4.95** objections referred to in Art 40 to be drawn up on the basis of the form set out in Annex III to Regulation No 607/2009. The objection shall be submitted to the Commission in paper or electronic form. The date of submission of the objection to the Commission shall be the date on which the objection is entered in the Commission's mail registry. This date is made available to the public by appropriate means.

(c) Acknowledgement of receipt of objection

4.96 Article 14(2) of Commission Regulation (EC) No 607/2009 requires the Commission to mark the documents making up the objection with the date of receipt and the file number allocated to the objection. The objector shall receive an acknowledgement of receipt indicating at least the following:

    (a) the file number;
    (b) the number of pages received; and
    (c) the date of receipt of the request.

(d) Admissibility under Community procedure

i. Prior rights

4.97 Article 15(1) of Commission Regulation (EC) No 607/2009 provides that for the purposes of determining whether an objection is admissible, in accordance with Art 40 of the Wine Regulation, the Commission shall verify that the objection mentions the prior right(s) claimed and the ground(s) for the objection and was received by the Commission within the deadline.

ii. Earlier trade mark

4.98 Article 15(2) of Commission Regulation (EC) No 607/2009 provides that if the objection is based on the existence of an earlier trade mark of reputation and renown, in accordance with Art 43(2) of the Wine Regulation, the objection shall be accompanied by proof of the filing, registration or use of that earlier trade mark, such as the certificate of registration or proof of its use, and proof of its reputation and renown.

4.99 Article 15(2) of Commission Regulation (EC) No 607/2009 requires that the information and evidence to be produced in support of the use of an earlier trade mark shall comprise particulars of the location, duration, extent and nature of the use made of the earlier trade mark, and of its reputation and renown.

iii. Details of objection

4.100 Article 15(3) of Commission Regulation (EC) No 607/2009 requires that any duly substantiated objection shall contain details of the facts, evidence and comments submitted in support of the objection, accompanied by the relevant supporting documents.

iv. Remedying deficiencies

Article 15(4) of Commission Regulation (EC) No 607/2009 provides that if **4.101** the details of the prior right(s) claimed, ground(s), facts, evidence or comments, or the supporting documents, as referred to in Art 15(1)–(3), have not been produced at the same time as the objection or if some are missing, the Commission shall inform the opponent accordingly and shall invite him to remedy the deficiencies noted within a period of two months. If the deficiencies are not remedied before the time limit expires, the Commission shall reject the objection as inadmissible. The decision on inadmissibility shall be notified to the objector and to the Member State or the third-country authorities or the applicant established in the third country in question.

v. Notification of admissibility

Article 15(5) of Commission Regulation (EC) No 607/2009 provides that an **4.102** objection that is deemed admissible shall be notified to the Member State or the third-country authorities or the applicant established in the third country in question.

(e) Scrutiny of an objection under Community procedure

i. Communication of invitation to file observations

Article 16(1) of Commission Regulation (EC) No 607/2009 provides that if **4.103** the Commission has not rejected the objection in accordance with Art 15(4), it shall communicate the objection to the Member State or the third-country authorities or the applicant established in the third country in question and shall invite him to file observations within two months from the issuance date of such communication. Any observations received within this two-month period shall be communicated to the objector.

ii. Request for comments on observations

Article 16(1) of Commission Regulation (EC) No 607/2009 provides that in **4.104** the course of the scrutiny of an objection, the Commission shall request the parties to submit comments, if appropriate, within a period of two months from the issuance date of such request, on the communications received from the other parties.

iii. Ruling by Commission

Article 16(2) of Commission Regulation (EC) No 607/2009 provides that if **4.105** the Member State or the third-country authorities or the applicant established in the third country in question or the objector files no observations in response, or does not respect the time periods, the Commission gives a ruling on the opposition.

4.106 Article 16(3) of Commission Regulation (EC) No 607/2009 provides that any decision to reject or register the designation of origin or GI concerned shall be taken by the Commission on the basis of the evidence available to it. The decision on rejection shall be notified to the objector and to the Member State or the third-country authorities or the applicant established in the third country in question.

iv. Multiple objectors

4.107 Article 16(4) of Commission Regulation (EC) No 607/2009 provides that in the event of multiple objectors, following a preliminary examination of one or more such objections, it may not be possible to accept the application for registration; in such cases, the Commission may suspend the other objection procedures. The Commission shall inform the other objectors of any decision affecting them which was taken in the course of the procedure.

4.108 Where an application is rejected, objection procedures which have been suspended shall be deemed to be closed and the objectors concerned shall be duly informed.

14. Protection

(a) Decision on protection

4.109 Article 41 of the Wine Regulation provides that on the basis of the information available to the Commission, it shall be decided, in accordance with the procedure referred to in Art 113(2), either to confer protection on the designation of origin or GI which meets the conditions laid down in Chapter IV of the Wine Regulation and is compatible with Community law, or to reject the application where those conditions are not satisfied.

4.110 Article 72(2) of Commission Regulation (EC) No 607/2009 provides that where the Commission decides not to confer protection to a designation of origin or GI pursuant to Art 41 of the Wine Regulation, wines labelled in accordance with Art 72(1) of this Article shall be withdrawn from the market or re-labelled in accordance with Chapter IV of this Regulation.

4.111 Article 17(1) of Commission Regulation (EC) No 607/2009 provides that unless applications for protection of designations of origin or GIs are rejected pursuant to Arts 11, 12, 16 and 28 of that Regulation, the Commission shall decide to protect the designations of origin or GIs.

(b) Publication of decision

Article 17(2) of Commission Regulation (EC) No 607/2009 provides that **4.112** decisions on protection taken pursuant to Art 41 of the Wine Regulation shall be published in the *Official Journal of the European Union.*

(c) Commencement of protection

Article 19(1) of Commission Regulation (EC) No 607/2009 provides that the **4.113** protection of a designation of origin or GI shall run from the date on which it is entered in the Register.

Article 19(3) of Commission Regulation (EC) No 607/2009 provides that the **4.114** protection of a designation of origin or GI shall apply to the whole denomination including its constitutive elements provided they are distinctive in themselves. A non-distinctive or generic element of a PDO or GI shall not be protected.

15. Grounds for refusal of protection

(a) Generic names

Article 43(1) provides that names that have become generic shall not be **4.115** protected as a designation of origin or GI.

For the purposes of Chapter IV of the Wine Regulation, Art 43(1) provides **4.116** that a 'name that has become generic' means the name of a wine which, although it relates to the place or the region where this product was originally produced or marketed, has become the common name of a wine in the Community. It provides that to establish whether or not a name has become generic, account shall be taken of all relevant factors, in particular:

(a) the existing situation in the Community, notably in areas of consumption;
(b) the relevant national or Community legal provisions.

Article 45(3) provides that protected designations of origin or PGIs shall not **4.117** become generic in the Community within the meaning of Art 43(1).

Article 55(2) provides that traditional terms shall not become generic in the **4.118** Community.

(b) Misleading names

4.119 Article 43(2) provides that a name shall not be protected as a designation of origin or GI 'where, in the light of a trademark's reputation and renown, protection is liable to mislead the consumer as to the true identity of the wine'.

(c) Homonyms

4.120 Article 42(1) provides that a name, for which an application is lodged, which is wholly or partially homonymous with that of a name already registered under this Regulation shall be registered with due regard for local and traditional usage and the risk of confusion. On the other hand, a homonymous name which misleads the consumer into believing that products come from another territory shall not be registered even if the name is accurate as far as the actual territory, region or place of origin of the products in question is concerned.

4.121 The use of a registered homonymous name shall be subject to there being a sufficient distinction in practice between the homonym registered subsequently and the name already on the register, having regard to the need to treat the producers concerned in an equitable manner and not to mislead the consumer.

4.122 Article 42(2) applies para 1 *mutatis mutandis* if a name, for which an application is lodged, is wholly or partially homonymous with a GI protected as such under the legislation of Member States.

4.123 However, Art 42(2) provides that Member States shall not register non-identical GIs for protection under their respective legislation on GIs if a designation of origin or GI is protected in the Community by virtue of the Community law relevant to designations of origin and GIs.

(d) Homonymous grape variety

4.124 Article 42(3) provides that save as otherwise provided for in Commission implementing measures, where the name of a wine grape variety contains or consists of a PDO or GI that name shall not be used for purposes of labelling the products covered by this Regulation.

4.125 Article 62(3) of Regulation 607/2009 provides that by way of derogation from Art 42(3) of the Wine Regulation, the wine grape variety names and their synonyms listed in Part A of Annex XV to this Regulation, that consist of or contain a PDO or GI may only appear on the label of a product with PDO or GI or GI of a third country if they were authorised under Community rules in force on 11 May 2002 or on the date of accession of Member States, whichever is later.

E. REGISTER

Article 46 requires the Commission to establish and maintain an electronic **4.126** register of protected designations of origin and GIs for wine which shall be publicly accessible.

Article 18(2) of Commission Regulation (EC) No 607/2009 provides a **4.127** designation of origin or GI which has been accepted shall be entered in the Register.

In the case of names registered under Art 51(1) of the Wine Regulation, the **4.128** Commission shall enter in the Register the data provided for in Art 18(3), with the exception of that of point (f).

Article 18(3) provides that the Commission shall enter the following data in **4.129** the Register:

(a) registered name of the product(s);
(b) record of the fact that the name is protected as a GI or designation of origin;
(c) name of the country or countries of origin;
(d) date of registration;
(e) reference to the legal instrument registering the name;
(f) reference to the single document.

F. SPIRITS

Article 42(4) of Commission Regulation (EC) No 607/2009 provides that the **4.130** protection of designations of origin and GIs for products covered in Art 34 shall be without prejudice to PGIs applying in relation to spirit drinks within the meaning of Regulation (EC) No 110/2008 of the European Parliament and of the Council of 15 January 2008 on the definition, description, presentation, labelling and the protection of GIs of spirit drinks[40] and vice versa.

---

40   OJ L 39, 13.2.2008, pp. 16–54.

G. RELATIONSHIP WITH TRADE MARKS

1. Registration of trade mark after date of application for a geographical indication

4.131   Article 44(1) of Commission Regulation (EC) No 607/2009 provides that where a designation of origin or a GI is protected under this Regulation, the registration of a trade mark corresponding to one of the situations referred to in Art 45(2) and relating to a product falling under one of the categories listed in Annex IV shall be refused if the application for registration of the trade mark is submitted after the date of submission of the application for protection of the designation of origin or GI to the Commission and the designation of origin or GI is subsequently protected.

4.132   Trade marks registered in breach of the first subparagraph shall be invalidated.

2. Registration of trade mark prior to date of application for a geographical indication

4.133   Article 44(2) of Commission Regulation (EC) No 607/2009 provides that without prejudice to Art 43(2), a trade mark the use of which corresponds to one of the situations referred to in Art 45(2), which has been applied for, registered or established by use, if that possibility is provided for by the legislation concerned, in the territory of the Community before the date on which the application for protection of the designation of origin or GI is submitted to the Commission, may continue to be used and renewed notwithstanding the protection of a designation of origin or GI, provided that no grounds for the trade mark's invalidity or revocation exist as specified by the First Council Directive 89/104/EEC of 21 December 1988 to approximate the laws of the Member States relating to trade marks[41] or Council Regulation (EC) No 40/94 of 20 December 1993 on the Community trade mark.[42]

4.134   In such cases the use of the designation of origin or GI shall be permitted alongside the relevant trade marks.

---

41   OJ L 040, 11/02/1989 P. 0001–0007.
42   Ibid.

H. RIGHT TO USE DESIGNATION OF ORIGIN AND GEOGRAPHICAL INDICATION

Article 45(1) of Commission Regulation (EC) No 607/2009 provides that **4.135** protected designations of origins and GIs may be used by any operator marketing a wine which has been produced in conformity with the corresponding product specification.

1. Exclusive rights

Article 45(2) of Commission Regulation (EC) No 607/2009 provides that **4.136** protected designations of origins and GIs and the wines using those protected names in conformity with the product specification shall be protected against:

(a) any direct or indirect commercial use of a protected name:
  (i) by comparable products not complying with the product specification of the protected name; or
  (ii) in so far as such use exploits the reputation of a designation of origin or a GI;
(b) any misuse, imitation or evocation, even if the true origin of the product or service is indicated or if the protected name is translated or accompanied by an expression such as 'style', 'type', 'method', 'as produced in', 'imitation', 'flavour', 'like' or similar;
(c) any other false or misleading indication as to the provenance, origin, nature or essential qualities of the product, on the inner or outer packaging, advertising material or documents relating to the wine product concerned, and the packing of the product in a container liable to convey a false impression as to its origin;
(d) any other practice liable to mislead the consumer as to the true origin of the product.

Article 45(4) requires Member States to take the steps necessary to stop **4.137** unlawful use of protected designations of origin and GIs as referred to in Art 45(2).

2. *Ex officio* action by Member States

Article 19(2) of Commission Regulation (EC) No 607/2009 provides that in **4.138** the event of unlawful use of a PDO or GI, the competent authorities of the Member States shall on their own initiative, pursuant to Art 45(4) of the Wine Regulation, or at the request of a party, take the steps necessary to stop such unlawful use and to prevent any marketing or export of the products at issue.

3. Designation of competent control authority

4.139 Article 47(1) of the Wine Regulation requires Member States to designate the competent authority or authorities responsible for controls in respect of the obligations established by this Chapter in accordance with the criteria laid down in Art 4 of Regulation (EC) No 882/2004.[43]

4.140 Article 47(3) of the Wine Regulation requires Member States to inform the Commission of the competent authority or authorities referred to in Art 47(1). The Commission shall make their names and addresses public and update them periodically.

4.141 Article 47(2) of the Wine Regulation requires that Member States shall ensure that any operator complying with Chapter IV of the Wine Regulation is entitled to be covered by a system of controls.

4. Declaration by operators

4.142 Article 24 of Commission Regulation (EC) No 607/2009 requires each operator wishing to participate in all or part of the production or packaging of a product with a PDO or GI to be declared to the competent control authority referred to in Art 47 of the Wine Regulation.

5. Certification bodies

4.143 Article 48(3) of the Wine Regulation requires the certification bodies referred to in Art 48(1)(b) and Art 48(2)(b) to comply with, and from 1 May 2010 be accredited in accordance with, the European standard EN 45011 or ISO/IEC Guide 65 (General requirements for bodies operating product certification systems).

4.144 Article 48(4) of the Wine Regulation requires such authority or authorities to offer adequate guarantees of objectivity and impartiality and have at their disposal the qualified staff and resources needed to carry out their tasks.

---

43 Regulation (EC) No 882/2004 of the European Parliament and of the Council of 29 April 2004 on official controls performed to ensure the verification of compliance with feed and food law, animal health and animal welfare rules, OJ L 191, 28.5.2004, p. 1.

6. Annual verification

(a) Testing

Article 25(1) of Commission Regulation (EC) No 607/2009 requires that the **4.145** annual verification carried out by the competent control authority as referred to in Art 48(1) of the Wine Regulation shall consist of:

    (a) an organoleptic and analytical testing for products covered by a designation of origin;

    (b) either analytical testing only or both organoleptic and analytical testing for products covered by a GI; and

    (c) a check on the conditions set out in the product specification.

i. Analytical and organoleptic testing

Article 26 of Commission Regulation (EC) No 607/2009 provides that the **4.146** analytical and organoleptic testing referred to in Art 25(1)(a) and (b) consists of:

    (a) an analysis of the wine in question measuring the following characteristic properties:

        (i) determined on the basis of a physical and chemical analysis:

- total and actual alcoholic strength,
- total sugars expressed in terms of fructose and glucose (including any sucrose, in the case of semi-sparkling and sparkling wines),
- total acidity,
- volatile acidity,
- total sulphur dioxide.

        (ii) determined on the basis of an additional analysis:

- carbon dioxide (semi-sparkling and sparkling wines, excess pressure in bar at 20 °C),
- any other characteristic properties provided for in Member States legislation or product specifications of protected designations of origin and GIs concerned;

    (b) an organoleptic test covering visual appearance, odour and taste.

(b) Procedure

Article 25(1) of Commission Regulation (EC) No 607/2009 requires this **4.147** annual verification to be conducted in the Member State in which production took place in accordance with the product specification and shall be carried out either through:

    (a) random checks based on a risk analysis; or

    (b) sampling; or

    (c) systematically.

i.   Random checks

4.148 In the case of random checks, Art 25(1) of Commission Regulation (EC) No 607/2009 requires Member States to select the minimum number of operators to be subjected to those checks.

ii.   Sampling

4.149 In the case of sampling, Art 25(1) of Commission Regulation (EC) No 607/2009 requires Member States to ensure that by their number, nature and frequency of controls, they are representative of the whole of the demarcated geographical area concerned and correspond to the volume of wine-sector products marketed or held with a view to their marketing.

4.150 Random checks may be combined with sampling.

(c) Objective of testing

4.151 Article 25(2) of Commission Regulation (EC) No 607/2009 requires the testing referred to in Art 25(1)(a) and (b) to be performed on anonymous samples, demonstrate that the product tested complies with the characteristics and qualities described in the product specification for the relevant designation of origin or GI, and be carried out at any stage in the production process, including even the packaging stage, or later. Each sample taken shall be representative of the relevant wines held by the operator.

4.152 Article 25(4) of Commission Regulation (EC) No 607/2009 requires that the annual verification shall ensure that a product cannot use the PDO or GI relating to it unless:

(a)   the results of the testing referred to in Art 25(1) (a) and (b) and in Art 25(2) prove that the product in question complies with the limit values and possesses all the appropriate characteristics of the designation of origin or GI concerned;

(b)   the other conditions listed in the product specification are met in accordance with the procedures laid down in Art 25(3).

(d) Testing procedure

4.153 Article 25(3) of Commission Regulation (EC) No 607/2009 requires that for the purposes of checking compliance with the product specification referred to in Art 25(1)(c) the control authority shall check:

(a)   the premises of operators, consisting in checking that the operators are actually able to meet the conditions laid down in the product specification; and

(b)   the products at any stage of the production process, including the packaging stage, on the basis of an inspection plan which is drawn up in advance by the control authority and of which operators are aware, covering every stage of production of the product.

(e) Marketing without designation of origin or geographical indication

Article 25(5) of Commission Regulation (EC) No 607/2009 requires that any **4.154** product failing to meet the conditions set out in this Article may be placed on the market, but without the relevant designation of origin or GI, provided that the other legal requirements are satisfied.

(f) Verification of trans-border designations

Article 25(6) of Commission Regulation (EC) No 607/2009 provides that in **4.155** the case of a protected trans-border designation of origin or GI, the verification may be performed by a control authority of either of the Member States affected by this designation of origin or GI.

(g) Verification at the packaging stage

Article 25(7) of Commission Regulation (EC) No 607/2009 provides that in **4.156** the case where annual verification is carried out at the packaging stage of the product in the territory of a Member State which is not the Member State where the production took place, Art 84 of Commission Regulation (EC) No 555/2008[44] applies.

(h) Application of Article 25 of Commission Regulation (EC) No 607/2009

Article 25(7) of Commission Regulation (EC) No 607/2009 provides that Art **4.157** 25(1)–(7) applies to wines bearing a designation of origin or a GI, whose designation of origin or GI concerned meet the requirements as referred to in Art 38(5) of the Wine Regulation.

(i) Checks on products originating in third countries

Article 27 of Commission Regulation (EC) No 607/2009 provides that if a **4.158** third country's wines benefit from the protection of a PDO or GI, the third country concerned shall send the Commission, at its request, information on the competent authorities referred to in Art 48(2) of the Wine Regulation and on the aspects covered by the check, as well as proof that the wine in question fulfils the conditions of the relevant designation of origin or GI.

---

44 Commission Regulation (EC) No 555/2008 of 27 June 2008 laying down detailed rules for implementing Council Regulation (EC) No 479/2008 on the common organisation of the market in wine as regards support programmes, trade with third countries, production potential and on controls in the wine sector, OJ L 170, 30.6.2008, p. 1.

I. CANCELLATION

1. Procedure – general rules

4.159 Article 50 of the Wine Regulation provides that it may be decided, in accordance with the procedure referred to in Art 113(2), at the initiative of the Commission or at a duly substantiated request of a Member State, of a third country or of a natural or legal person having a legitimate interest, to cancel the protection of a designation of origin or a GI if compliance with the corresponding product specification is no longer ensured. Article 50 provides that Arts 38–41 (covering the national procedure and scrutiny by the Commission) shall apply *mutatis mutandis*.

(a) Submission of a request for cancellation

4.160 Article 21(1) of Commission Regulation (EC) No 607/2009 provides that a request for cancellation pursuant to Art 50 of the Wine Regulation shall be drawn up in accordance with the form set out in Annex V to Commission Regulation (EC) No 607/2009. The request for cancellation shall be submitted to the Commission in paper or electronic form. The date of submission of the request for cancellation to the Commission shall be the date on which the request is entered in the Commission's mail registry. That date is made available to the public by appropriate means.

2. Procedure – specific rules

4.161 Article 21(2) of Commission Regulation (EC) No 607/2009 provides that the Commission shall mark the documents making up the request for cancellation with the date of receipt and the file number allocated to the request for cancellation.

4.162 The author of the request for cancellation shall receive an acknowledgement of receipt indicating at least:

    (a) the file number;
    (b) the number of pages received; and
    (c) the date of receipt of the request.

3. Cancellation initiated by the Commission

4.163 Article 21(3) of Commission Regulation (EC) No 607/2009 provides that Art 21(1) and (2) does not apply when the cancellation is initiated by the Commission.

4. Admissibility of request for cancellation

Article 22(1) of Commission Regulation (EC) No 607/2009 provides that for **4.164** the purposes of determining whether a request for cancellation is admissible, in accordance with Art 50 of the Wine Regulation, the Commission shall verify that the request:

(a) mentions the legitimate interest, the reasons and justification of the author of the request for cancellation;
(b) explains the ground for cancellation; and
(c) refers to a statement from the Member State or third country where the residence or registered office of the author of the request is located supporting the request for cancellation.

Case T-194/10, *Hungary v Commission*,[45] concerned an annulment action **4.165** brought by Hungary, seeking to overturn a protected Slovakian designation of origin for wine produced in the Tokaj region, which both countries share. The Commission had registered the PDO 'Vinohradnicka oblast' Tokaj' on Slovakia's behalf in the 2006 and 2007 lists of quality wines produced in specified regions (QWPSR). On 31 July 2009, the day before the EU established the E-Bacchus database to publish the QWPSR lists, Slovakia requested a modified designation: 'Tokajská/Tokajské/Tokajsky vinohradnicka oblast' which became the new protected designation on the electronic database. Several months later, Slovakia requested that the Commission revert to the original designation of origin, and the Commission amended the designation as requested.

Hungary then contested the amendment, claiming violations of applicable **4.166** regulations and contending that the name 'Tokajská/Tokajské/Tokajsky vinohradnicka oblast' enjoyed Community protection, on 1 August 2009, 'the date of the entry into force of the new legislation of the Union on the market in the wine sector'. The Court found that wine names protected in the EU before the E-Bacchus database was introduced 'are automatically protected under the legislation in force since that database was introduced'. Thus, the protection 'did not depend on the registration of those names in the database'. According to the Court, the registration was simply the result of an automatic transition 'from one regulatory regime to another, of protection that has already been granted and is not a condition for the grant of that protection'.

---

45 Gen. Ct., Judgment, 8 November 2012.

5. Documents accompanying request for cancellation

4.167 Article 22(2) of Commission Regulation (EC) No 607/2009 provides that any request for cancellation shall contain details of the facts, evidence and comments submitted in support of the cancellation, accompanied by the relevant supporting documents.

4.168 Article 22(3) of Commission Regulation (EC) No 607/2009 provides that if detailed information concerning the grounds, facts, evidence and comments, as well as the supporting documents referred to in paras 1 and 2, have not been produced at the same time as the request for cancellation, the Commission shall inform the author of the request for cancellation accordingly and shall invite him to remedy the deficiencies noted within a period of two months. If the deficiencies are not remedied before the time limit expires, the Commission shall reject the request as inadmissible. The decision on inadmissibility shall be notified to the author of the request for cancellation and to the Member State or the third-country authorities or the author of the request for cancellation established in the third country in question.

6. Notification of admissible application for cancellation

4.169 Article 22(4) of Commission Regulation (EC) No 607/2009 provides that any request for cancellation that is deemed admissible, as well as a Commission own-initiative cancellation procedure, shall be notified to the Member State or the third-country authorities or the applicants established in the third country whose designation of origin or GI is affected by the cancellation.

7. Invitation to file observations and comments

4.170 Article 23(1) of Commission Regulation (EC) No 607/2009 provides that if the Commission has not rejected the request for cancellation in accordance with Art 22(3), it shall communicate the cancellation to the Member State or the third-country authorities or the producers concerned established in the third country in question and shall invite them to file observations within two months from the issuance date of such communication. Any observations received within this two-month period shall be communicated, where applicable, to the author of the request for cancellation.

4.171 In the course of the scrutiny of a cancellation, the Commission shall request the parties to submit comments, if appropriate, within a period of two months from the issuance date of such request, on the communications received from the other parties.

8. Decision by Commission in absence of observations

Article 23(2) of Commission Regulation (EC) No 607/2009 provides that if **4.172** the Member State or the third-country authorities or the applicant established in the third country in question or the author of a request for cancellation files no observations in response, or does not respect the time periods, the Commission decides upon the cancellation.

9. Basis of the Commission's decision on cancellation

Article 23(3) of Commission Regulation (EC) No 607/2009 provides that any **4.173** decision to cancel the designation of origin or GI concerned shall be taken by the Commission on the basis of the evidence available to it. It shall consider whether compliance with the product specification for a wine sector product covered by a PDO or GI is no longer possible or can no longer be guaranteed, particularly if the conditions laid down in Art 35 of the Wine Regulation are no longer fulfilled or may no longer be fulfilled in the near future.

Such decision on cancellation shall be notified to the author of the request for **4.174** cancellation and to the Member State or the third-country authorities or the applicant established in the third country in question.

10. Multiple requests for cancellation

Article 23(4) of Commission Regulation (EC) No 607/2009 provides that in **4.175** the event of multiple requests for cancellation, following a preliminary examination of one or more such requests for cancellation, it may not be possible to accept the continuation of protection of a designation or origin or GI, in which case the Commission may suspend the other cancellation procedures. In this case the Commission shall inform the other authors of the requests for cancellation of any decision affecting them which was taken in the course of the procedure.

Where a PDO or GI is cancelled, cancellation procedures which have been **4.176** suspended shall be deemed to be closed and the authors of the request for cancellation concerned shall be duly informed.

11. Deletion from the Register

Article 23(5) of Commission Regulation (EC) No 607/2009 provides that **4.177** when a cancellation takes effect, the Commission shall delete the name from the Register.

J. CONVERSION OF A PDO INTO A PGI

4.178 Article 28(1) of Commission Regulation (EC) No 607/2009 provides that a Member State or third-country authority or the applicant established in the third country in question may request the conversion of a PDO into a PGI if compliance with the product specification of a PDO is no longer possible or can no longer be guaranteed.

1. Request

4.179 Article 28(1) of Commission Regulation (EC) No 607/2009 provides that the request for conversion submitted to the Commission shall be drawn up in accordance with the model set out in Annex VI to that Regulation. The request for conversion shall be submitted to the Commission in paper or electronic form. The date of submission of the request for conversion to the Commission is the date on which the request is entered in the Commission's mail registry.

2. Verification by the Commission

4.180 Article 28(2) of Commission Regulation (EC) No 607/2009 provides that if the request for conversion into a GI does not meet the requirements laid down in Arts 34 and 35 of the Wine Regulation, the Commission shall inform the Member State or the third-country authorities or the applicant established in the third country in question of the grounds for refusal, and shall invite them to withdraw or amend the request or submit comments within a period of two months.

3. Rejection by the Commission

4.181 Article 28(3) of Commission Regulation (EC) No 607/2009 provides that if the obstacles to the conversion into a GI are not remedied by the Member State or third-country authorities or the applicant established in the third country in question before the time limit expires, the Commission shall reject the request.

4.182 Article 28(4) of Commission Regulation (EC) No 607/2009 requires that any decision to reject the conversion request shall be taken by the Commission on the basis of the documents and information available to it. Such decision on rejection shall be notified to the Member State or the third-country authorities or the applicant established in the third country in question.

Article 28(5) of Commission Regulation (EC) No 607/2009 provides that **4.183** Arts 40 (objection procedure) and 49(1) (amendment procedure) of the Wine Regulation shall not apply.

4. Existing protected wine names

Article 51(1) of the Wine Regulation provides that wine names which are **4.184** protected in accordance with Arts 51 and 54 of Regulation (EC) No 1493/1999[46] and Art 28 of Regulation (EC) No 753/2002[47] shall automatically be protected under this Regulation. The Commission shall list them in the register provided for in Art 46 of this Regulation.

Article 28 of Regulation 753/2002 provides that each wine-producing Mem- **4.185** ber State has to notify to the EC Commission the list of names of geographical units smaller than the Member State, as referred to in Art 51(1) of Regulation (EC) No 1493/1999,[48] that may be used as GIs and the provisions regulating the use of the terms and unit names. The Commission publishes the names of the geographical units notified in the *Official Journal of the European Communities*. Member States may adopt stricter rules on the use of these terms for wine produced in their territory.

Annex VII(A)(2)(b) to Regulation (EC) No 1493/1999 provides that the sales **4.186** description of table wines with GIs must consist of the words 'table wine' and the name of the geographical unit. Where special terms are used such as 'Landwein', 'vin de pays', 'indicazione geografica tipica', 'vino de la tierra', 'vinho regional', 'regional wine' and the others specified by Art 28 of Regulation (EC) No 753/2002, the words 'table wine' are not required.

Article 28 Commission Regulation (EC) No 753/2002 provides that with **4.187** regard to the table wines described as:

- 'Landwein' in the case of table wines originating in Germany, Austria and in the Province of Bolzano in Italy,
- 'vin de pays' in the case of table wines originating in France, Luxembourg and the Region of Valle d'Aosta in Italy,

---

46 Council Regulation (EC) No 1493/1999 of 17 May 1999 on the common organisation of the market in wine, OJ L 179, 14.7.1999, pp. 1–84.

47 Commission Regulation (EC) No 753/2002 laying down certain rules for applying Council Regulation (EC) No 1493/1999 as regards the description, designation, presentation and protection of certain wine sector products, OJ L 118, 4 May 2002, pp. 1–54.

48 Council Regulation (EC) No 1493/1999 of 17 May 1999 on the common organisation of the market in wine, OJ L 179, 14.7.1999, pp. 1–84.

- 'indicazione geografica tipica' or 'IGT' in the case of table wines originating in Italy,
- 'vino de la tierra' in the case of table wines originating in Spain,
- 'ονομασία κατά παράδοση' (appellation traditionnelle) or 'τοπικός οίνος' (vin de pays) in the case of table wines originating in Greece,
- 'vinho regional' in the case of table wines originating in Portugal,
- 'regional wine' in the case of table wines originating in the UK,
- 'landwijn' in the case of table wines originating in the Netherlands,
- 'zemské víno' in the case of table wines originating in the Czech Republic,
- 'Τοπικός Οίνος' or '(Regional Wine)' in the case of table wines originating in Cyprus,
- 'tájbor' in the case of table wines originating in Hungary,
- 'Inbid ta' lokalita tradizzjonali ('I.L.T.')' in the case of table wines originating in Malta,
- 'deželno vino s priznano geografsko oznako' or 'deželno vino PGO' in the case of table wines originating in Slovenia,
- 'регионално вино' in the case of table wines originating in Bulgaria,
- 'Vin cu indicație geografică' in the case of table wines originating in Romania,
- 'regional vin' in the case of table wines originating in Denmark.

Each producer Member State is required to notify to the Commission,

> in accordance with the third indent of Annex II(A)(2)(b) to Regulation (EC) No 1493/1999:
> (a) the list of names of geographical units smaller than the Member State as referred to in Art 51(1) of Regulation (EC) No 1493/1999 that may be used and the provisions regulating the use of the terms and unit names;
> (b) any subsequent change to the list and to the provisions referred to in (a).

4.188 The national rules on the use of the terms given in the first subparagraph must require the terms concerned to be linked to use of a specified GI smaller than the Member State and reserved for table wines meeting certain production requirements, notably regarding the vine variety, minimum natural alcoholic strength by volume and an evaluation or indication of the organoleptic characteristics.

4.189 The rules referred to in the second paragraph may, however, allow the term 'ονομασία κατά παράδοση' (traditional designation) to be used in conjunction with 'Ρετσίνα' (retsina) without necessarily being linked to a specified GI.

Article 28 provides that the producer Member States may adopt stricter rules **4.190** on the use of these terms for wine produced in their territory. The Commission shall publish the names of the geographical units notified to it under the first subparagraph in the 'C' series of the *Official Journal of the European Communities.*

Annex VII(A)(2)(c) to Regulation (EC) No 1493/1999 provides that the sales **4.191** description of quality wines psr must consist of:

- the name of the production area,
- the specific words indicating the particular quality such as 'quality wine produced in a specified region' or 'quality wine psr', 'quality liqueur wine produced in a specified region' or 'quality liqueur wine psr', 'quality semi-sparkling wine produced in a specified region' or 'quality semi-sparkling wine psr';
- traditional specific particulars regulated by Art 29 of Regulation 753/2002.

By way of derogation from the compulsory list of sales description indicated in **4.192** Annex VII(A)(2)(c) to Regulation (EC) No 1493/1999 and according to Art 30 of Regulation (EC) No 753/2002, wines carrying one of the following specified regional names under the applicable EC and national provisions may be marketed using certain names only:

    (a)   Greece: 'Σάμος' ('Samos');
    (b)   Spain: 'Cava', 'Jerez', 'Xérès' or 'Sherry', 'Manzanilla';
    (c)   France: 'Champagne';
    (d)   Italy: 'Asti', 'Marsala', 'Franciacorta';
    (e)   Portugal: 'Madeira' or 'Madère', 'Porto' or 'Port';
    (f)   Cyprus: 'Κουμανδαρία' (Commandaria).

Provisions applying to third-country wines marketed in the EC are also **4.193** included in the Regulation. In the context of third-country wines, Regulation 752/2002 provides for national treatment. This means that third-country wines with GIs are treated the same as EC wines with GIs. In terms of the use of GIs, there must be full compliance with the TRIPS obligations. For WTO Members, GIs may be used if they meet the definition provided in the TRIPS Agreement. Also, the use of homonymous GIs is permitted in accordance with the TRIPS Agreement commitments.

Article 51(2) of the Wine Regulation requires Members to transmit to the **4.194** Commission in respect of existing protected wine names referred to in Art 51(1):

    (a) the technical files as provided for in Art 35(1);
    (b) the national decisions of approval.

4.195 Article 51(3) of the Wine Regulation provides that wine names referred to in Art 51(1), for which the information referred to in Art 51(2) is not submitted by 31 December 2011, shall lose protection under this Regulation.

4.196 Article 51(4) of the Wine Regulation requires the Commission to take the corresponding formal step of removing such names from the register provided for in Art 46.

4.197 Article 51(4) provides that Art 50 of the Wine Regulation shall not apply in respect of existing protected wine names referred to in Art 51(1).

4.198 Article 51(4) also provides that it may be decided, until 31 December 2014, at the initiative of the Commission and in accordance with the procedure referred to in Art 113(2) of the Wine Regulation, to cancel protection of existing protected wine names referred to in para 1 if they do not meet the conditions laid down in Art 34 of the Wine Regulation.

K. IMPLEMENTING MEASURES

4.199 Article 52 of the Wine Regulation provides that the measures necessary for the implementation of Chapter IV of the Wine Regulation shall be adopted in accordance with the procedure referred to in Art 113(1). Those measures may in particular include derogations from the applicability of the rules and requirements laid down in Chapter IV:

    (a) in so far as pending applications for protection of designations of origin or GIs are concerned;
    (b) in so far as the production of certain wines with a PDO or GI in a geographical area in proximity of the geographical area where the grapes originate is concerned;
    (c) in so far as traditional production practices of certain wines with a PDO are concerned.

L. TRADITIONAL TERMS

1. Definition

Article 54 (2) of the Wine Regulation provides that 'traditional terms'[49] shall **4.200** be recognised, defined and protected in accordance with the procedure referred to in Art 113(1) (under Art 195(2) of Regulation (EC) No 1234/ 2007).[50]

The traditional specific terms listed in Art 29 of Regulation (EC) No **4.201** 753/2002 such as (Belgium), 'gecontroleerde oorsprongsbenaming', 'appellation d'origine contrôlée'; (Germany) 'Qualitätswein garantierten Ursprungs'; (Spain) 'Denominación de origen', 'Denominación de origen calificada'; (France) 'appellation d'origine contrôlée', 'appellation contrôlée'; (Italy) 'Denominazione di origine controllata', 'Denominazione di origine controllata e garantita', 'vino dolce natural'; (Portugal) 'Denominação de origem', 'Denominação de origem controlada', 'Indicação de proveniência regulamentada', 'vinho generoso', 'vinho dolce natural'; (UK) 'English vineyard quality wine psr' and 'Welsh vineyard quality wine psr' are reserved by particular Member States. These traditional terms could only be used as specified by the Member States reserving these terms.

2. Production

Article 55(1) of the Wine Regulation provides that a protected traditional **4.202** term may only be used for a product which has been produced in conformity with the definition referred to in Art 54(2).

Article 55(1) of the Wine Regulation provides that traditional terms shall be **4.203** protected against unlawful use and that Member States shall take the steps necessary to stop the unlawful use of protected traditional terms.

---

49 Art 54(1) defines 'traditional term' as:

   a term traditionally used in Member States for products referred to in Article 33(1) to designate:

   (a) that the product has a protected designation of origin or geographical indication under Community or Member State law;

   (b) the production or ageing method or the quality, colour, type of place, or a particular event linked to the history, of the product with a protected designation of origin or geographical indication.

50 Council Regulation (EC) No 1234/2007 of 22 October 2007 establishing a common organisation of agricultural markets and on specific provisions for certain agricultural products (Single CMO Regulation), OJ L 299, 16.11.2007, pp. 1–149.

4.204 A comprehensive regime for the protection of traditional terms is detailed in Chapter III of Commission Regulation (EC) No 607/2009. Recital (12) to that regulation explains that the use, regulation and protection of certain terms (other than designations of origin and GIs) to describe wine sector products is a long-established practice in the Community. The Recital continues that such traditional terms evoke in the minds of consumers a production or ageing method or a quality, colour or type of place or a particular event linked to the history of the wine and that so as to ensure fair competition and avoid misleading consumers, a common framework should be laid down regarding the definition, recognition, protection and use of such traditional terms.

3. Applicants for traditional terms

4.205 Article 29(1) of Regulation (EC) No 607/2009 provides that the competent authorities of Member States or third countries or representative professional organisations established in third countries may submit to the Commission an application for protection of traditional terms within the meaning of Art 54(1) of the Wine Regulation.

4.206 Article 29(2) of Regulation (EC) No 607/2009 defines 'representative professional organisation' to mean:

> any producer organisation or association of producer organisations having adopted the same rules, operating in a given or more wine designation of origin or geographical indication area(s) where it includes in its membership at least two thirds of the producers in the designation of origin or geographical indication area(s) in which it operates and accounts for at least two thirds of that areas' production.

Article 29(2) of Regulation (EC) No 607/2009 provides that a representative professional organisation may lodge an application for protection only for wines which it produces.

4. Application for protection of traditional terms

4.207 Article 30(1) of Regulation (EC) No 607/2009 provides that the application for protection of a traditional term shall conform to the model set out in Annex VII and shall be accompanied by a copy of the rules regulating the use of the term concerned.

Commission Regulation (EU) No 538/2011 of 1 June 2011[51] amends Art **4.208** 30(2) of Regulation No 607/2009 to provide that in the case of an application filed by a representative professional organisation established in a third country, the details of the representative professional organisation shall also be communicated. The Commission shall publish on the Internet the list of third countries concerned, the names of the representative professional organisations and the members of these representative professional organisations.

5. Language

Article 31(1) of Regulation (EC) No 607/2009 provides that the term to be **4.209** protected shall be either:

(a) in the official language(s), regional language(s) of the Member State or third country where the term originates; or

(b) in the language used in commerce for this term.

Article 31(1) of Regulation (EC) No 607/2009 requires that the term used in a certain language shall refer to specific products referred to in Art 33(1) of the Wine Regulation.

Article 31(2) of Regulation (EC) No 607/2009 requires that the term shall be **4.210** registered with its original spelling(s).

6. Rules on traditional terms of third countries

Recital (13) to Commission Regulation (EC) No 607/2009 explains that the **4.211** use of traditional terms on third countries' products is allowed provided they fulfil the same or equivalent conditions to those required from Member States in order to ensure that consumers are not misled. Furthermore, given that several third countries do not have the same level of centralised rules as the community legal system, some requirements for 'representative professional organisations' of third countries should be laid down to ensure the same guarantees as those provided for in the Community rules.

Commission Regulation (EU) No 538/2011 of 1 June 2011[52] replaces Art **4.212** 30(2) of Regulation (EC) No 607/2009 with the following provisions:

---

51 Commission Regulation (EU) No 538/2011 of 1 June 2011, amending Regulation (EC) No 607/2009 laying down certain detailed rules for the implementation of Council Regulation (EC) No 479/2008 as regards protected designations of origin and geographical indications, traditional terms, labelling and presentation of certain wine sector products, OJ L 147, 2.6.2011, p. 6.

52 Ibid.

1. The definition of traditional terms provided for in Article 118u(1) of Regulation (EC) No 1234/2007 shall apply *mutatis mutandis* to terms traditionally used in third countries for wine products covered by geographical indications or names of origin under the legislation of those third countries.

2. Wines originating in third countries whose labels bear traditional indications other than the traditional terms listed in the electronic database 'E-Bacchus' may use these traditional indications on wine labels in accordance with the rules applicable in the third countries concerned, including those emanating from representative professional organisations.

7. Examination procedure

(a) Filing of the application

4.213 Article 33 of Regulation (EC) No 607/2009 requires that the Commission shall mark the documents making up the application with the date of its receipt and the file number of the application. The application shall be submitted to the Commission in paper or electronic form. The date of submission of the application to the Commission shall be the date on which the application is entered in the Commission's mail registry. This date and the traditional term are made available to the public by appropriate means.

4.214 The applicant shall receive an acknowledgement of receipt indicating at least:

(a) the file number;
(b) the traditional term;
(c) the number of the documents received; and
(d) the date of their receipt.

(b) Admissibility

4.215 Article 34 of Regulation (EC) No 607/2009 requires the Commission to verify that the application form is fully completed and is accompanied by the requested documentation as provided for in Art 30 of Regulation (EC) No 607/2009.

4.216 If the application form is incomplete or the documentation is missing or incomplete, the Commission shall inform the applicant accordingly and shall invite it to remedy the deficiencies noted within a period of two months. If the deficiencies are not remedied before the time limit expires, the Commission shall reject the application as inadmissible. The decision on inadmissibility shall be notified to the applicant.

(c)   Conditions of validity

Article 35(1) of Regulation (EC) No 607/2009 provides that the recognition **4.217** of a traditional term shall be accepted if: '(a) it fulfils the definition as laid down in Art 54(1)(a) or (b) of the Wine Regulation and the conditions laid down in Art 31 of Regulation No 607/2009'.

i.   Traditional use

Article 35(1) of Regulation (EC) No 607/2009 provides that the recognition **4.218** of a traditional term shall be accepted if:

(b)   the term exclusively consists of either:
  (i)   a name traditionally used in commerce in a large part of the territory of the Community or of the third country concerned, to distinguish specific categories of grapevine products referred to in Article 33(1) of the Wine Regulation; or
  (ii)   a reputed name traditionally used in commerce in at least the territory of the Member State or third country concerned, to distinguish specific categories of grapevine products referred to in Article 33(1) of the Wine Regulation;

Article 35(2) of Regulation (EC) No 607/2009 requires that for the purpose of **4.219** Art 35(1)(b), traditional use means:

(a)   at least five years in case of terms filed in language(s) referred to in Art 31(a) of Regulation No 607/2009;
(b)   at least 15 years in case of terms filed in a language referred to in Art 31(b) of Regulation No 607/2009.

Article 35(4) of Regulation (EC) No 607/2009 provides that the condition **4.220** listed in Art 35(1)(b) do not apply to traditional terms referred to in Art 54(1)(a) of the Wine Regulation.

An illustration of the way in which these provisions might operate is Case **4.221** C-309/89, *Codorníu SA v Council of the European Union*,[53] concerned the use of the term 'crémant', Regulation (EEC) No 3309/85 laying down general rules for the description and presentation of sparkling wines and aerated sparkling wines[54] had reserved this term for vineyards in France and Luxembourg. This reservation was reiterated in an amending Council Regulation (EEC) No 2045/89.[55] Codorníu, a Spanish company manufacturing and

---

53   [1994] ECR I-1853.
54   OJ 1989 L 202, p. 12.
55   Council Regulation (EEC) No 2045/89 of 19 June 1989, amending Regulation (EEC) No 3309/85 laying down general rules for the description and presentation of sparkling wines and aerated sparkling wines, OJ 1989 L 202, p. 12.

marketing quality sparkling wines psr, was the holder of the Spanish trade mark 'Gran Cremant de Codorníu', which it has been using since 1924 to designate one of its quality sparkling wines psr. Codorníu was the main Community producer of quality sparkling wines psr. It objected to the designation the term 'crémant' as traditional for France and Luxembourg.

4.222 As it was common ground that the first national measures providing in France and Luxembourg for the use of the term 'crémant' as a 'traditional description' were adopted only in 1975, the Court observed that the reservation of the term 'crémant' for quality sparkling wines psr manufactured in France and Luxembourg could not validly be justified on the basis of traditional use, since it disregarded the traditional use of that mark by Codorníu since 1924.[56]

ii.   Non-genericity

4.223 Article 35(1) of Regulation (EC) No 607/2009 provides that the recognition of a traditional term shall be accepted if:

> (c)   the term shall:
>> (i)   not be generic;
>> (ii) be defined and regulated in the Member State's legislation; or
>> (iii) be subject to conditions of use as provided for by rules applicable to wine producers in the third country concerned, including those emanating from representative professional organisations.

4.224 Article 35(3) of Regulation (EC) No 607/2009 provides that for the purpose of 35(1)(c)(i), 'generic' means the name of a traditional term, although it relates to a specific production method or ageing method, or the quality, colour, type of place, or a particular method linked to the history of a grapevine product, has become the common name of the grapevine product in question in the Community.

4.225 The issue of genericity in relation to wine production methods was considered in Case C-306/93, *SMW Winzersekt GmbH v Land Rheinland-Pfalz*,[57] which involved a dispute concerning the use of the term 'Flaschengaerung im Champagnerverfahren' ('bottle-fermented by the champagne method') to describe certain quality sparkling wines produced in a specified region ('quality sparkling wines psr'). Regulation No 2333/92 provided, inter alia, that the method of production known as 'méthode champenoise'[58] may, if such a usage were traditional, be used together with an equivalent expression relating to

---

56   [1994] ECR I-1853, at paras 31–32.
57   [1994] ECR I-5555.
58   Fermentation takes place in the bottle and the *cuvée* is separated from the lees by disgorging.

that method of production for five wine-growing years terminating on 31 August 1994 for wines not entitled to the registered designation 'Champagne'.

Winzersekt, an association of wine-growers which produced sparkling wine **4.226** from wines of the Mosel-Saar-Ruwer region using the 'méthode champenoise' process and which marketed it under the description 'Flaschengaerung im Champagnerverfahren' ('bottle-fermented by the champagne method') or 'klassische Flaschengaerung, méthode champenoise' ('classical bottle fermentation, champagne method') applied to the Ministry of Agriculture, Viticulture and Forests of the Land Rheinland-Pfalz for a 'binding statement' as to whether it would be lawfully entitled to continue to use these terms after 31 August 1994.

It argued that the designation 'méthode champenoise' was of fundamental **4.227** importance for its commercial activity in so far as that designation enabled it to make the public aware of its method of production and that if it was unable to continue to use the designation 'méthode champenoise', it would be placed at a competitive disadvantage and its very existence jeopardised.[59]

The ECJ pointed out that among the objectives pursued by Regulation No **4.228** 2333/92 was that of the protection of registered designations or indications of the geographical origin of wines. The Court said that this implied that 'a wine producer cannot be authorized to use, in descriptions relating to the method of production of his products, geographical indications which do not correspond to the actual provenance of the wine'.[60] The Regulation in Art 6(5) had specifically provided for the discontinuation of the designation 'méthode champenoise' by those not in the Champagne region and Winzersekt could have had recourse to the alternative expressions contained in Art 6(4) of Regulation No 2333/92, such as 'bottle-fermented by the traditional method', 'traditional method', 'classical method' or 'classical traditional method' and any expressions resulting from a translation of those terms.[61]

(d) Grounds for refusal

Article 36(1) of Regulation (EC) No 607/2009 provides that if an application **4.229** for a traditional term does not meet the definition laid down in Art 54(1) of the Wine Regulation and the requirements laid down in Arts 31 and 35, the Commission shall inform the applicant of the grounds for refusal, setting a

---

59 [1994] ECR I-5555, at para 20.
60 Ibid., at para 25.
61 Ibid., at para 28.

deadline of two months from the issuance date of such communication, for the withdrawal or amendment of the application, or for the submission of comments.

4.230 Article 36(1) of Regulation (EC) No 607/2009 requires the Commission to decide on the protection based on the information available to it.

4.231 Article 36(2) of Regulation (EC) No 607/2009 provides that if the obstacles are not remedied by the applicant within the deadline referred to in para 1, the Commission shall reject the application. Any decision to reject the traditional term concerned shall be taken by the Commission on the basis of the documents and information available to it. Such decision on rejection shall be notified to the applicant.

8. Objection procedures

(a) Submission of a request of objection

4.232 Article 37(1) of Regulation (EC) No 607/2009 provides that within two months from the date of publication provided for in Art 33(1), any Member State or third country, or any natural or legal person having a legitimate interest, may object to the proposed recognition by lodging a request of objection.

4.233 Article 37(2) of Regulation (EC) No 607/2009 requires that the request of objection shall be drawn up on the basis of the form set out in Annex VIII and shall be submitted to the Commission in paper or electronic form. The date of submission of the request of objection to the Commission is the date on which the request is entered in the Commission's mail registry.

4.234 Article 37(2) of Regulation (EC) No 607/2009 requires the Commission to mark the documents making up the request of objection with the date of receipt and the file number allocated to the request of objection.

4.235 The objector shall receive an acknowledgement of receipt indicating at least the following:

(a) the file number;
(b) the number of pages received; and
(c) the date of receipt of the request.

(b) Admissibility

i. Verification of receipt of application within the deadline

4.236 Article 38(1) of Regulation (EC) No 607/2009 provides that for the purposes of determining whether an objection is admissible, the Commission shall verify that the request of objection mentions the prior right(s) claimed and the ground(s) for the objection and was received by the Commission within the deadline provided for in Art 37(1) of Regulation (EC) No 607/2009.

ii. Objection based upon earlier trade mark

4.237 Article 38(2) of Regulation (EC) No 607/2009 provides that if the objection is based on the existence of an earlier trade mark of reputation and renown, in accordance with Art 41(2) of the Wine Regulation, the request of objection shall be accompanied by proof of the filing, registration or use of that earlier trade mark, such as the certificate of registration and proof of its reputation and renown.

4.238 Article 38(3) of Regulation (EC) No 607/2009 requires that the information and evidence to be produced in support of the use of an earlier trade mark shall comprise particulars of the location, duration, extent and nature of the use made of the earlier trade mark, and of its reputation and renown.

iii. Details of facts and evidence

4.239 Article 38(3) of Regulation (EC) No 607/2009 requires that any duly substantiated request of objection shall contain details of the facts, evidence and comments submitted in support of the objection, accompanied by the relevant supporting documents.

iv. Failure to provide details

4.240 Article 38(4) of Regulation (EC) No 607/2009 provides that if the details of the prior right(s) claimed, ground(s), facts, evidence or comments, or the supporting documents, as referred to in Art 38(1)–(3), have not been produced at the same time as the request of objection or if some are missing, the Commission shall inform the opponent accordingly and shall invite him to remedy the deficiencies noted within a period of two months. If the deficiencies are not remedied before the time limit expires, the Commission shall reject the request as inadmissible. The decision on inadmissibility shall be notified to the objector and to the Member State or the third-country authorities or the representative professional organisation established in the third country in question.

v. Notification of objection

4.241 Article 38(5) of Regulation (EC) No 607/2009 requires any request of objection that is deemed admissible shall be notified to the Member State or the third-country authorities or the representative professional organisation in the third country in question.

(c) Scrutiny of an objection

i. Communication of objection

4.242 Article 39(1) of Regulation (EC) No 607/2009 provides that if the Commission has not rejected the request of opposition in accordance with Art 38(4) of Regulation (EC) No 607/2009, it shall communicate the objection to the Member State or the third-country authorities or the representative professional organisation established in the third country in question and shall invite it to file observations within two months from the issuance date of such communication. Any observations received within this two-month period shall be communicated to the objector.

ii. Request for comments

4.243 Article 39(1) of Regulation (EC) No 607/2009 provides that in the course of its scrutiny of an objection, the Commission shall request the parties to submit comments on the communications received from the other parties, if appropriate, within a period of two months from the issuance date of such request.

iii. Commission ruling in absence of response

4.244 Article 39(2) of Regulation (EC) No 607/2009 provides that if the Member State or the third-country authorities or the representative professional organisation established in the third country in question or the objector file no observations in response, or do not respect the time periods, the Commission gives a ruling on the opposition.

iv. Decision by Commission

4.245 Article 39(3) of Regulation (EC) No 607/2009 provides that any decision to reject or recognise the traditional term concerned shall be taken by the Commission on the basis of the evidence available to it. It shall consider whether the conditions referred to in Art 40(1), or laid down in Art 41(3) or 42 are not fulfilled. The decision on rejection shall be notified to the objector and to the Member State or the third-country authorities or the representative professional organisation established in the third country in question.

v. Multiple requests of objection

Article 39(4) of Regulation (EC) No 607/2009 provides that in the event of **4.246** multiple requests of objection, following a preliminary examination of one or more such requests of objection, it may not be possible to accept the application for recognition; in such cases, the Commission may suspend the other objection procedures. The Commission shall inform the other objectors of any decision affecting them which was taken in the course of the procedure.

Where an application is rejected, objection procedures which have been **4.247** suspended shall be deemed to be closed and the objectors concerned shall be duly informed.

9. Protection

(a) General protection

Commission Regulation (EU) No 538/2011 of 1 June 2011[62] replaces Art 40 **4.248** of Regulation (EC) No 607/2009 with the following provisions:

> 1. If an application for the protection of a traditional term satisfies the conditions laid down in Article 118u(1) of Regulation (EC) No 1234/2007 and in Articles 31 and 35 of this Regulation and is not rejected under Articles 36, 38 and 39 of this Regulation, the traditional term shall be included in the electronic database 'E-Bacchus' with an indication of:
>   (a) the language as referred to in Article 31;
>   (b) an indication of the grapevine product category or categories concerned by the protection;
>   (c) a reference to the national legislation of the Member State in which the traditional term is defined and regulated, or rules applicable to wine producers in third countries, including those emanating from representative professional organisations; and
>   (d) a summary of the definition or conditions of use.

Protection against misuse

> 2. The traditional terms listed in the electronic database 'E-Bacchus', are protected only in the language and for the categories of grapevine products claimed in the application, against:
>   (a) any misuse even if the protected term is accompanied by an expression such as 'style', 'type', 'method', 'as produced in', 'imitation', 'flavour', 'like' or similar;

---

62 Commission Regulation (EU) No 538/2011 of 1 June 2011, amending Regulation (EC) No 607/2009 laying down certain detailed rules for the implementation of Council Regulation (EC) No 479/2008 as regards protected designations of origin and geographical indications, traditional terms, labelling and presentation of certain wine sector products, OJ L 147, 2.6.2011, p. 6.

(b) any other false or misleading indication as to the nature, characteristics or essential qualities of the product, on the inner or outer packaging, advertising material or documents relating to it;

(c) any other practice liable to mislead the consumer, in particular to give the impression that the wine qualifies for the protected traditional term.

(b) Relationship with trade marks

i. Refusal of application for trade mark submitted after application for protection of traditional term

4.249 Commission Regulation (EU) No 538/2011 of 1 June 2011 replaces Art 41(1) of Regulation No 607/2009 with the following provisions:

> 1. Where a traditional term is protected under this Regulation, the registration of a trade mark, the use of which would contravene Article 40(2), shall be assessed in accordance with Directive 2008/95/EC of the European Parliament and of the Council[63] or Council Regulation (EC) No 207/2009.[64]
>
> Trade marks registered in breach of the first subparagraph shall be declared invalid upon request in accordance with the applicable procedures as specified by Directive 2008/95/EC or Regulation (EC) No 207/2009.

ii. Coexistence of trade mark applied for or registered prior to application for traditional term

4.250 Article 41(2) of Regulation (EC) No 607/2009 provides that a trade mark which corresponds to one of the situations referred to in Art 40 of Regulation No 607/2009, and which has been applied for, registered or established by use, if that possibility is provided for by the legislation concerned, in the territory of the Community before 4 May 2002 or before the date of submission of the application for protection of the traditional term to the Commission, may continue to be used and renewed notwithstanding the protection of the traditional term. In such cases the use of the traditional term shall be permitted alongside the relevant trade mark.

iii. Non-registration of misleading traditional terms

4.251 Article 41(3) of Regulation (EC) No 607/2009 provides that a name shall not be protected as a traditional term, where in the light of a trade mark's reputation and renown, such protection is liable to mislead the consumer as to the true identity, nature, characteristic or quality of the wine.

---

63 OJ L 299, 8.11.2008, p. 25.
64 OJ L 78, 24.3.2009, p. 1.

(c) Homonyms

Commission Regulation (EU) No 538/2011 of 1 June 2011 replaces Art 42(1) **4.252**
of Regulation (EC) No 607/2009 with the following provisions:

General protection of homonyms

A term, for which an application is lodged and which is wholly or partially homonymous with that of a traditional term already protected under this Chapter shall be
protected with due regard to local and traditional usage and the risk of confusion.

Misleading homonyms not to be registered

A homonymous term which misleads consumers as to the nature, quality or the true
origin of the products shall not be registered even if the term is accurate.

Distinction between subsequent homonym and traditional term

The use of a protected homonymous term shall be subject to there being a sufficient
distinction in practice between the homonym protected subsequently and the traditional term already listed in the electronic database 'E-Bacchus', having regard to the
need to treat the producers concerned in an equitable manner and not to mislead the
consumer.

Partial homonyms

Article 42(2) of Regulation No 607/2009 provides that Article 42(1) shall apply
mutatis mutandis for traditional terms protected before 1 August 2009, which are
partially homonymous with a protected designation of origin or geographical indication or a wine grape variety name or its synonym listed in Annex XV.

10. Modification of traditional term

Commission Regulation (EU) No 538/2011 of 1 June 2011 inserts Art 42a, **4.253**
which provides that an applicant as referred to in Art 29 may apply for an
approval of a modification of a traditional term, the language indicated, the
wine or wines concerned or of the summary of the definition or conditions of
use of the traditional term concerned.

Article 42a provides that Arts 33 to 39 of Regulation (EC) No 607/2009 apply **4.254**
mutatis mutandis to applications for modification.

11. Enforcement of the protection

Article 43 of Regulation (EC) No 607/2009 provides that for the purposes of **4.255**
the application of Art 55 of the Wine Regulation, in case of illegal use of
protected traditional terms, competent national authorities, on their own

initiative or at the request of a party, shall take all measures to stop the marketing, including any export, of the products concerned.

12. Cancellation procedure

(a) Grounds for cancellation

4.256 Article 44 of Regulation (EC) No 607/2009 provides that the grounds for cancelling a traditional term shall be that it no longer meets the definition laid down in Art 54(1) of the Wine Regulation or the requirements laid down in Arts 31, 35, 40(2), 41(3) or 42 of Regulation No 607/2009.

(b) Submission of a request for cancellation

4.257 Article 45(1) of Regulation (EC) No 607/2009 provides that a duly substantiated request for cancellation may be filed with the Commission by a Member State, a third country or a natural or legal person having a legitimate interest in accordance with the form set out in Annex IX. The request for cancellation shall be submitted to the Commission in paper or electronic form. The date of submission of the request for cancellation to the Commission is the date on which the request is entered in the Commission's mail registry. This date shall be made available to the public by appropriate means.

4.258 Article 45(2) of Regulation (EC) No 607/2009 requires the Commission to mark the documents making up the request for cancellation with the date of receipt and the file number allocated to the request for cancellation.

4.259 The author of the request for cancellation shall receive an acknowledgement of receipt indicating at least:

    (a)   the file number;
    (b)   the number of pages received; and
    (c)   the date of receipt of the request.

4.260 Article 45(3) of Regulation (EC) No 607/2009 provides that Art 45(1) and (2) does not apply when the cancellation is initiated by the Commission.

(c) Admissibility

i. Contents of application

4.261 Article 46(1) of Regulation (EC) No 607/2009 provides that for the purposes of determining whether a request for cancellation is admissible, the Commission shall verify that the request:

(a) mentions the legitimate interest of the author of the request for cancellation;

(b) identifies the ground(s) for cancellation; and

(c) refers to a statement from the Member State or third country where the residence or registered office of the author of the request is located explaining the legitimate interest, reasons and justification of the author of the cancellation.

Article 46(2) of Regulation (EC) No 607/2009 provides that any request for cancellation shall contain details of the facts, evidence and comments submitted in support of the cancellation, accompanied by the relevant supporting documents. **4.262**

ii. Failure to provide information

Article 46(3) of Regulation (EC) No 607/2009 provides that if detailed information concerning the grounds, facts, evidence and comments, as well as the supporting documents referred to in Art 46(1) and (2), have not been produced at the same time as the request for cancellation, the Commission shall inform the author of the request for cancellation accordingly and shall invite him to remedy the deficiencies noted within a period of two months. If the deficiencies are not remedied before the time limit expires, the Commission shall reject the request as inadmissible. The decision on inadmissibility shall be notified to the author of the request for cancellation and to the Member State or the third-country authorities or the author of the request for cancellation established in the third country in question. **4.263**

iii. Notification

Article 46(4) of Regulation (EC) No 607/2009 provides that any request for cancellation that is deemed admissible, including the Commission's own-initiative cancellation procedure, shall be notified to the Member State or the third-country authorities or the author of the request for cancellation established in the third country whose traditional term is affected by the cancellation. **4.264**

(d) Scrutiny of a cancellation

i. Request for observations

Article 47(1) of Regulation (EC) No 607/2009 provides that if the Commission has not rejected the request for cancellation in accordance with Art 46(3), it shall communicate the request for cancellation to the Member State or the third-country authorities or the applicant established in the third country in question and shall invite it to file observations within two months from the issuance date of such communication. Any observations received within this **4.265** two-month period shall be communicated to the author of the request for cancellation.

4.266 In the course of the scrutiny of a cancellation, the Commission shall request the parties to submit comments on the communications received from the other parties, if appropriate, within a period of two months from the issuance date of such request.

ii. Ruling by Commission in absence of observations

4.267 Article 47(2) of Regulation (EC) No 607/2009 provides that if the Member State or the third-country authorities or the applicant established in the third country in question or the author of a request for cancellation files no observations in response, or does not respect the time periods, the Commission gives a ruling on the cancellation.

iii. Ruling by Commission on basis of evidence

4.268 Article 47(3) of Regulation (EC) No 607/2009 provides that any decision to cancel the traditional term concerned shall be taken by the Commission on the basis of the evidence available to it. It shall consider whether the conditions referred to in Art 44 are no longer fulfilled.

4.269 Such decision on cancellation shall be notified to the author of the request for cancellation and to the Member State or the third-country authorities in question.

iv. Multiple requests for cancellation

4.270 Article 47(4) of Regulation (EC) No 607/2009 provides that in the event of multiple requests for cancellation, following a preliminary examination of one or more such requests for cancellation, it may not be possible to accept the continuation of protection of a traditional term, in which case the Commission may suspend the other cancellation procedures. In this case the Commission shall inform the other authors of the request for cancellation of any decision affecting them which was taken in the course of the procedure.

v. Closure of cancellation procedures

4.271 Article 47(4) of Regulation (EC) No 607/2009 provides that where a traditional term is cancelled, cancellation procedures which have been suspended shall be deemed to be closed and the authors of the request for cancellation concerned shall be duly informed.

vi. *Removal of name after cancellation*

Article 47(4) of Regulation (EC) No 607/2009 provides that when a cancel- **4.272** lation takes effect, the Commission shall remove the name concerned from the list set out in Annex XII.

13. Existing protected traditional terms

Commission Regulation (EU) No 538/2011 of 1 June 2011 replaces Art 47(5) **4.273** of Regulation No (EC) 607/2009 with the following: 'When a cancellation takes effect, the Commission shall remove the name concerned from the list set out in the electronic database "E-Bacchus".'

M. LABELLING OF WINE AND INDICATIONS OF ORIGIN

Prior to 2008 the regulation of wine labelling was largely left to EU Member **4.274** States. This regime was replaced by Council Regulation (EC) No 479/2008[65] ('the Wine Regulation') which repealed and replaced the earlier legislation.[66] Recital (39) of the Wine Regulation explains that 'the description, designation and presentation of products covered by this Regulation can have significant effects on their marketability' and that, consequently, differences between the laws of the Member States on the labelling of wine products may impede the smooth functioning of the internal market. Recital (40) takes this as the justification for laying down Community rules 'which take into account the legitimate interests of consumers and producers'.

Recital (41) proposes that these rules should provide for the obligatory use of **4.275** certain terms 'so as to identify the product in accordance with the sales categories and provide consumers with certain important items of information'.

Recital (42) proposes that the labelling rules in the wine sector should, in the **4.276** main, be complementary to those laid down in Directive 2000/13/EC of 20 March 2000 on the approximation of the laws of the Member States relating to the labelling, presentation and advertising of foodstuffs.[67]

---

65 Council Regulation (EC) No 479/2008 of 29 April 2008 on the common organisation of the market in wine, amending Regulations (EC) No 1493/1999, (EC) No 1782/2003, (EC) No 1290/2005, (EC) No 3/2008 and repealing Regulations (EEC) No 2392/86 and (EC) No 1493/1999.

66 Ie Regulations (EEC) No 2392/86 and (EC) No 1493/1999.

67 OJ L 109, 6.5.2000, p. 29. Directive as last amended by Commission Directive 2007/68/EC, OJ L 310, 28.11.2007, p. 11.

4.277 Because experience had shown that a differentiation in terms of labelling rules according to the category of wine product was often not expedient, Recital (42) recommends that the rules should in principle apply to all the different categories of wine, including imported products. 'In particular, they should allow the indication of a wine grape variety and a vintage on wines without a designation of origin or a geographical indication, subject to requirements and exceptions concerning the veracity of the labelling and the respective monitoring as well as the risk of confusion of consumers.'

1. Legislation

4.278 Explaining the repeal of existing labelling legislation by the Wine Regulation, it was explained in Recital (42) to the Wine Regulation that experience had shown that different terms of labelling rules across Member States, according to the category of wine product, were often not expedient and that common rules should in principle apply to all the different categories of wine, including imported products. In particular, they should 'allow the indication of a wine grape variety and a vintage on wines without a designation of origin or a geographical indication, subject to requirements and exceptions concerning the veracity of the labelling and the respective monitoring as well as the risk of confusion of consumers'.

4.279 Recital (51) indicated that products imported from third countries should be subject to the Community rules on labelling and designations of origin and GIs.

4.280 Labelling and presentation is dealt with in Chapter VI of the Wine Regulation. This is supplemented by Commission Regulation (EC) No 607/2009 of 14 July 2009 which provides in Art 49 that:

> Save as otherwise provided for in this Regulation, the labelling of the products referred to in paragraphs 1 to 11, 13, 15 and 16 of Annex IV to Regulation (EC) No 479/2008 (hereinafter 'products') may not be supplemented by any particulars other than those provided for in Article 58 and those regulated in Article 59(1) and 60(1) of that Regulation, unless they satisfy the requirements of Article 2(1)(a) of Directive 2000/13/EC.[68]

2. Definitions

4.281 Article 57 provides that for the purposes of the Wine Regulation:

---

68   Ibid.

(a) 'labelling' shall mean any words, particulars, trademarks, brand name, pictorial matter or symbol placed on any packaging, document, notice, label, ring or collar accompanying or referring to a given product.

Case C-46/94[69] considered whether moulded inlays and prints carried on a **4.282** bottle which described the town where the bottles were being offered for sale constituted the misleading labelling of Bordeaux and Champagne wine. This case considered the definition of labelling under repealed Regulation 2392/89 laying down general rules for the description and presentation of wines and grape musts. This defined labelling in the same terms as contained in the Wine Regulation. The Court held that decorative material on bottles which was liable to mislead purchasers as to the provenance of the wine or the vine variety fell within the definition of labelling.

(b) 'presentation' shall mean any information conveyed to consumers by virtue of the **4.283** packaging of the product concerned including the form and type of bottles.

3. Compulsory particulars

Article 59(1) of the Wine Regulation provides that the labelling and presen- **4.284** tation of the products referred to in paras 1 to 11, 13, 15 and 16 of Annex IV[70] marketed in the Community or for export shall contain the following compulsory particulars:

(a) the designation for the category of the grapevine product in accordance with Annex IV;
(b) for wines with a protected designation of origin or geographical indication:
    (i) the term 'protected designation of origin' or 'protected geographical indication'; and
    (ii) the name of the protected designation of origin or geographical indication;
    ...
(d) an indication of provenance;
(e) an indication of the bottler or, in the case of sparkling wine, aerated sparkling wine, quality sparkling wine or quality aromatic sparkling wine, the name of the producer or vendor;
(f) an indication of the importer in the case of imported wines;

---

69 *Criminal proceedings against Michèle Voisine* [1995] ECR I-1859.

70 These categories are: 1. Wine, 2. New wine still in fermentation, 3. Liqueur wine, 4. Sparkling wine, 5. Quality sparkling wine, 6. Quality aromatic sparkling wine, 7. Aerated sparkling wine, 8. Semi-sparkling wine, 9. Aerated semi-sparkling wine, 10. Grape must, 11. Partially fermented grape must, 13. Concentrated grape must, 15. Wine from raisined grapes, 16. Wine of overripe grapes.

4. Indication of the provenance

4.285 Article 55(1) of Regulation (EC) No 607/2009 provides that the indication of provenance as referred to in Art 59(1)(d) of the Wine Regulation shall be indicated as follows:

(a) for wines referred to in paragraphs 1, 2, 3, 7 to 9, 15 and 16 of Annex IV to Regulation (EC) No 479/2008, without protected designation of origin or geographical indication, one of the following:

   (i) the words '*wine of* (…)', '*produced in* (…)', or '*product of* (…)', or expressed in equivalent terms, supplemented by the name of the Member State or third country where the grapes are harvested and turned into wine in that territory; In the case of a trans-border wine produced from certain wine grapes varieties as referred to in Article 60(2)(c) of Regulation (EC) No 479/2008, only the name of one or more Member State(s) or third countrie(s) may be mentioned.

   (ii) either the words '*European Community wine*', or expressed in equivalent terms, or '*blend of wines from different countries of the European Community*' in the case of wine resulting from a blending of wines originating in a number of Member States, or the words '*blend of wines from different countries outside the European Community*' or '*blend from* (…)' citing the names of the third countries in question, in the case if wine resulting from a blending of wines originating in a number of third countries;

   (iii) either the words '*European Community wine*', or expressed in equivalent terms, or '*wine obtained in from grapes harvested in* (…)', supplemented by the names of the Member States concerned in the case of wines produced in a Member State from grapes harvested in another Member State, or the words '*wine obtained in (…) from grapes harvested in* (…)' citing the names of the third countries in question, for wines made in a third country from grapes harvested in another third country;

(b) for wines referred to in paragraphs 4, 5 and 6 to Annex IV of Regulation (EC) No 479/2008, without protected designation of origin or geographical indication, one of the following:

   (i) the words '*wine of* (…)', '*produced in* (…)', '*product of* (…)' or '*sekt of* (…)', or expressed in equivalent terms, supplemented by the name of the Member State or third country where the grapes are harvested and turned into wine in that territory;

   (ii) the words '*produced in* (…)', or expressed in equivalent terms, supplemented by the name of the Member State where the second fermentation takes place;

(c) for wines with protected designation of origin or geographical indication, the words '*wine of* (…)', '*produced in* (…)' or '*product of* (…)', or expressed in equivalent terms, supplemented by the name of the Member State or third country where the grapes are harvested and turned into wine in that territory.

In the case of a trans-border protected designation of origin or geographical indication, only the name of one or more Member State(s) or third countrie(s) shall be mentioned.

This paragraph is without prejudice to Articles 56 and 67.

Article 55(2) of Regulation (EC) No 607/2009 provides that the indication of **4.286** provenance as referred to in Art 59(1)(d) of the Wine Regulation, on labels of grape must, grape must in fermentation, concentrated grape must or new wine still in fermentation shall be indicated as follows:

(a) *'must be of (…)'* or *'must produced in (…)'* or expressed in equivalent terms, supplemented by the name of the Member State, an individual country forming part of the Member State where the product is produced;

(b) *'blend made from the produce of two or more European Community* countries' in case of coupage of products produced in two or more Member States;

(c) *'must be obtained in (…) from grapes harvested in (…)'* in case of grape must which has not been made in the Member State where the grapes used were harvested.

Article 55(3) provides that in the case of the UK, the name of the Member **4.287** State may be replaced by the name of an individual country forming part of the UK.

5. Indication of the bottler

Article 59(1)(e) of the Wine Regulation provides as compulsory particulars: **4.288**

(e) an indication of the bottler or, in the case of sparkling wine, aerated sparkling wine, quality sparkling wine or quality aromatic sparkling wine, the name of the producer or vendor;

6. Indication of the bottler, producer, importer and vendor

(a) Definitions

Article 56(1) of Regulation (EC) No 607/2009 provides that for the purposes **4.289** of the application of Art 59(1)(e) and (f) of the Wine Regulation and of this Article:

(a) 'bottler' means a natural or legal person or a group of such persons carrying out bottling or having bottling carried out on their behalf;

(b) 'bottling' means putting the product concerned in containers of a capacity not exceeding 60 litres for subsequent sale;

(c) 'producer' means a natural or legal person or a group of such persons by whom or on whose behalf the processing of the grapes, grape musts and wine into sparkling wines, aerated sparkling wine, quality sparkling wine or quality aromatic sparkling wines is carried out;

(d) 'importer' means a natural or legal person or group of such persons established within the Community assuming responsibility for bringing into circulation non-Community goods within the meaning of Art 4(8) of Council Regulation (EEC) No 2913/92(1);

(e) 'vendor' means a natural or legal person or a group of such persons, not covered by the definition of producer, purchasing and then putting sparkling wines, aerated sparkling wine, quality sparkling wine or quality aromatic sparkling wines into circulation;

(f) 'address' means the indications of the local administrative area and the Member State in which the head office of the bottler, producer, vendor or importer is situated.

(b) Reference to bottler

4.290 Article 56(2) of Regulation (EC) No 607/2009 requires that the name and address of the bottler shall be supplemented either,

(a) by the words 'bottler' or 'bottled by (...)'; or
(b) by terms, whose conditions of use are defined by Member States, where bottling of wines with protected designation of origin or GI takes place:
  (i) on the producer's holding; or
  (ii) on the premises of a producer group; or
  (iii) in an enterprise located in the demarcated geographical area or in the immediate proximity of the demarcated geographical area concerned.

(c) Contract bottling

4.291 Article 56(2) of Regulation (EC) No 607/2009 requires that in case of contract bottling, the indication of the bottler shall be supplemented by the words 'bottled for (...)' or, where the name, address of the person who has carried out the bottling on behalf of a third party are indicated, by the words 'bottled for (...) by (...)'.

(d) Bottling in another place

4.292 Article 56(2) of Regulation (EC) No 607/2009 requires that where bottling takes place in another place than that of the bottler, the particulars referred to in this paragraph shall be accompanied by a reference to the exact place where the operation took place and, if it is carried out in another Member State, the name of that state.

4.293 In case of containers other than bottles, the words 'packager' and 'packaged by (...)' shall replace the words 'bottler' and 'bottled by (...)' respectively, except when the language used does not indicate by itself such a difference.

(e) Indication of producer

4.294 Article 56(3) of Regulation (EC) No 607/2009 requires that the name and address of the producer or vendor shall be supplemented by the words 'producer' or 'produced by' and 'vendor' or 'sold by', or equivalent. Member States may make compulsory the indication of the producer.

(f) Indication of importer

Article 56(4) of Regulation (EC) No 607/2009 requires that the name and **4.295** address of the importer shall be preceded by the words 'importer' or 'imported by (...)'.

(g) Grouping of compulsory particulars

Article 56(5) of Regulation (EC) No 607/2009 provides that the indications **4.296** referred to in Art 56(2), (3) and (4) can be grouped together, if they concern the same natural or legal person. One of these indications may be replaced by a code determined by the Member State in which the bottler, producer, importer or vendor has its head office. The code shall be supplemented by a reference to the Member State in question. The name and address of another natural or legal person involved in the commercial distribution other than the bottler, producer, importer or vendor indicated by a code shall also appear on the wine label of the product concerned.

(h) Name or address containing protected designation of origin or geographical indication

Article 56(5) provides that where the name or the address of the bottler, **4.297** producer, importer or vendor consists of or contains a PDO or GI, it shall appear on the label:

(a) in characters which are no more than half the size of those used either for the PDO or GIs or for the designation of the category of the grapevine product concerned; or
(b) by using a code as provided for in Art 56(5) second sub-paragraph.

Member States may decide which option applies to products produced in their territories.

7. Marketing and export

Article 55(1) of Regulation (EC) No 607/2009 provides that products whose **4.298** label or presentation does not conform to the corresponding conditions as laid down in this Regulation cannot be marketed in the Community or exported.

Article 55(2) of Regulation (EC) No 607/2009 provides that by way of **4.299** derogation from Chapters V and VI of the Wine Regulation, where the products concerned are to be exported, Member States may allow that particulars which conflict with labelling rules as provided for by Community legislation appear on the label of wines for export, when they are required by the legislation of the third country concerned. These particulars may appear in languages other than the official Community languages.

8. Indication of the holding

4.300 Article 57(1) of Regulation (EC) No 607/2009 provides that the terms referring to a holding listed in Annex XIII, other than the indication of the name of the bottler, producer or vendor, shall be reserved for wines with PDO or GI provided that:

(a) the wine is made exclusively from grapes harvested in vineyards exploited by that holding;
(b) the winemaking is entirely carried out on that holding;
(c) Member States regulate the use of their respective terms listed in Annex XIII. Third countries establish the rules on use applicable to their respective terms listed in Annex XIII, including those emanating from representative professional organisations.

4.301 Article 57(2) of Regulation (EC) No 607/2009 provides that the name of a holding may be used by other operators involved in the marketing of the product only where the holding in question agrees to that use.

4.302 An issue similar to that concerning an indication of a holding that came up under a number of the earlier regulations concerned with wine labelling[71] was whether the term 'château' could be used by a cooperative which included amongst its members both wine-growers whose land derives from the partition of the original estate of a château, and wine-growers who harvested grapes outside that estate. In Case C-403/92 *Claire Lafforgue and François Baux v Château de Calce SCI and Coopérative de Calce*[72] the owner of the original château producing 'Côtes du Roussillon' wine under the registered name 'Château Lafforgue' objected to the members of a cooperative, the Société Coopérative de Calce, using the name the name 'Château de Calce' to market its 'Côtes du Roussillon' wine produced on part of the original château estate. By judgment of 22 September 1988 the Tribunal de Grande Instance

---

71 Council Regulation (EEC) No 338/79 of 5 February 1979 laying down special provisions relating to quality wines produced in specified regions (OJ 1979 L 54, p. 48); Council Regulation (EEC) No 823/87 of 16 March 1987 laying down special provisions relating to quality wines produced in specified regions, OJ 1987 L 84, p. 59.
72 [1994] ECRI-2961.

de Perpignan granted a declaration that Mrs Lafforgue, as owner of the Château de Calce, had the sole right to use the name 'Château de Calce' as it attached to Mrs Lafforgue's property and that its use by the two defendants was capable of misleading consumers, particularly since the Baux-Lafforgues were themselves wine-producers. However, that judgment was reversed on 12 July 1989 by the Court d'Appel de Montpellier. An appeal from this decision to the Cour de Cassation resulted in questions being put to the ECJ concerning the interpretation of the word 'château'.

This word appeared in a number of regulations, now repealed, but was **4.303** retained in identical terms in Commission Regulation (EEC) No 3201/90 of 16 October 1990 laying down detailed rules for the description and presentation of wines and grape musts,[73] which remains in force. The ECJ pointed out that its interpretation of the earlier instruments 'also applies in connection with the regulations at present in force'.[74] The Court ruled that Art 5(1) of Regulation No 997/81, like Art 6 of Regulation No 3201/90, does not preclude the use of the term 'château' by wine-growers producing grapes on lands forming part of the original estate of a château, who have formed a cooperative on whose premises they make wine.[75]

The Court also noted that the fact that some members of the cooperative **4.304** cultivated land which did not belong to the original estate of the château and which, therefore, did not necessarily produce grapes whose quality was comparable to that of the grapes harvested from lands forming part of the original estate, was immaterial, 'provided that reliable procedures are introduced to ensure that the grapes harvested outside the original estate of the château are not mixed with those harvested from the estate'.[76]

9. Derogations

Article 59(2) of the Wine Regulation provides that by way of derogation from **4.305** Art 59(1)(a) the reference to the category of the grapevine product may be omitted for wines whose labels include the protected name of a designation of origin or GI.

---

73   OJ 1990 L 309, p. 1.
74   [1994] ECRI-2961 at para 21.
75   Ibid., at para 22.
76   Ibid., at para. 24.

4.306 Article 59(3) of the Wine Regulation provides that by way of derogation from Art 59(1)(b) the reference to the terms 'protected designation of origin' or 'protected geographical indication' may be omitted in the following cases:

(a) where a traditional term as referred to in Art 54(1)(a) is displayed on the label;

(b) where, in exceptional circumstances to be determined in accordance with the procedure referred to in Art 113(1), the name of the PDO or PGI is displayed on the label.

4.307 Article 59 of Regulation (EC) No 607/2009 provides that in accordance with Art 59(3)(b) to the Wine Regulation the terms 'protected designation of origin' may be omitted for wines bearing the protected designations of origin shown in Table 4.1 below, provided this possibility is regulated in the Member State legislation or in the rules applicable in the third country concerned, including those emanating from representative professional organisations.

Table 4.1   Protected designations of origin

(a)	Cyprus	Κουμανδαρία (Commandaria)
(b)	Greece	Σάμος (Samos)
(c)	Spain	Cava,
		Jerez, Xérès or Sherry,
		Manzanilla
(d)	France	Champagne
(e)	Italy	Asti,
		Marsala,
		Franciacorta
(f)	Portugal	Madeira or Madère,
		Port or Porto

10.   Presentation of the compulsory particulars

4.308 Article 50(1) of Commission Regulation (EC) No 607/2009 of 14 July 2009 provides that the compulsory particulars referred to in Art 58 of the Wine Regulation as well as those listed in Art 59 thereof shall appear in the same field of vision on the container, in such a way as to be simultaneously readable without having to turn the container. However, the compulsory particulars of the lot number and those referred to in Arts 51 and 56(4) of this Regulation may appear outside the visual field in which the other compulsory particulars appear.

4.309 Article 50(2) of Regulation (EC) No 607/2009 provides that the compulsory particulars referred to in Art 50(1) and those applicable by virtue of the legal instruments mentioned in Art 58 of the Wine Regulation shall be presented in indelible characters and shall be clearly distinguishable from surrounding text or graphics.

11. Optional particulars

(a) References to geographical indications and traditional terms

Article 60(1) of the Wine Regulation provides that labelling and presentation **4.310** of products referred to in Art 59(1) may in particular contain the following optional particulars:

> (b) the name of one or more wine grape varieties;
> ...
> (d) for wines with a protected designation of origin or geographical indication, traditional terms as referred to in Article 54(1)(b);
> (e) the Community symbol indicating the protected designation of origin or geographical indication;
> (f) terms referring to certain production methods;
> (g) for wines bearing a protected designation of origin or geographical indication the name of another geographical unit that is smaller or larger than the area underlying the designation of origin or geographical indication.

(b) Name of wine grape variety

Article 62(1) of Regulation (EC) No 607/2009 provides that the names of the **4.311** wine grape varieties or their synonyms referred to in Art 60(1)(b) of the Wine Regulation used for the production of products as referred to in Art 49 of Regulation (EC) No 607/2009 may appear on the labels of the products concerned under the conditions laid down in points (a) and (b) of this Article.

> (a) For wines produced in the European Community, the names of the wine grape varieties or their synonyms shall be those mentioned in the wine grape varieties classification as referred to in Article 24(1) of the Wine Regulation.
>   For Member States exempted from the classification obligation as provided for in Article 24(2) of the Wine Regulation, the names of the wine grape varieties or synonyms shall be mentioned in the 'International list of vine varieties and their synonyms' managed by the International Organisation of Vine and Wine (OIV).
> (b) For wines originating in third countries, the conditions of use of the names of the wine grape varieties or their synonyms shall conform with the rules applicable to wine producers in the third country concerned, including those emanating from representative professional organisations and the names of the wine grape varieties or their synonyms are mentioned in at least one of the following lists:
>   (i)   the International Organisation of Vine and Wine (OIV);
>   (ii) the Union for the Protection of Plant Varieties (UPOV);
>   (iii) the International Board for Plant Genetic Resources (IBPGR).

(c) For products with protected designation of origin or geographical indication or with a geographical indication of a third country, the names of the wine grape varieties or their synonyms may be mentioned:

   (i) if only one wine grape variety or its synonym is named, at least 85 % of the products have been made from that variety, not including:

   - any quantity of products used in sweetening, '*expedition liqueur*' or '*tirage liqueur*'; or
   - any quantity of product as referred to in Annex IV(3)(e) and (f) to the Wine Regulation.

   if two or more wine grape varieties or their synonyms are named, 100% of the products concerned have been made from these varieties, not including:

   - any quantity of products used in sweetening, '*expedition liqueur*' or '*tirage liqueur*'; or
   - any quantity of product as referred to in Annex IV(3)(e) and (f) of the Wine Regulation

   . . .

(d) For products without protected designation of origin or geographical indication, the names of the wine grape varieties or their synonyms may be mentioned provided the requirements laid down in points (a) or (b), and (c) of paragraph 1 and in Article 63 are fulfilled.

12. Derogations

4.312 Article 62(3) of Regulation (EC) No 607/2009 provides that by way of derogation from Art 42(3) of the Wine Regulation, the wine grape variety names and their synonyms listed in Part A of Annex XV to this Regulation that consist of or contain a PDO or GI may only appear on the label of a product with PDO or GI or GI of a third country if they were authorised under Community rules in force on 11 May 2002 or on the date of accession of Member States, whichever is later.

4.313 Article 62(4) of Regulation (EC) No 607/2009 provides that the wine grape variety names and their synonyms listed in Part B of Annex XV to this Regulation that partially contain a PDO or GI and directly refer to the geographical element of the PDO or GI in question, may only appear on the label of a product with PDO or GI or GI of a third country.

13. Name of a smaller or larger geographical unit than the area underlying the designation of origin or geographical indication and geographical area references

4.314 Article 67(1) of Regulation (EC) No 607/2009 provides that as regards Art 60(1)(g) of the Wine Regulation and without prejudice to Arts 55 and 56 of this Regulation, the name of a geographical unit and geographical area references may only appear on labels of wines with PDO or GI or with a GI of a third country.

Article 67(2) of Regulation (EC) No 607/2009 provides that for the use of the **4.315** name of a smaller geographical unit than the area underlying the designation of origin or GI the area of the geographical unit in question shall be well defined. Member States may establish rules concerning the use of these geographical units. At least 85 per cent of the grapes from which the wine has been produced shall originate in that smaller geographical unit. The remaining 15 per cent of the grapes shall originate in the geographical demarcated area of the designation of origin or GI concerned.

Article 67(2) of Regulation (EC) No 607/2009 provides that Member States **4.316** may decide, in the case of registered trade marks or trade marks established by use before 11 May 2002 which contain or consist of a name of a smaller geographical unit than the area underlying the designation of origin or GI and geographical area references of the Member States concerned, not to apply the requirements laid down in the third and fourth sentences of the first subparagraph.

Article 67(3) of Regulation (EC) No 607/2009 provides that the name of a **4.317** smaller or larger geographical unit than the area underlying the designation of origin or GI or a geographical area references shall consist of:

(a) a locality or group of localities;
(b) a local administrative area or part thereof;
(c) a wine-growing sub-region or part thereof;
(d) an administrative area.

14. Specific rules on wine grape varieties and vintage years for wines without protected designation of origin or geographical indication

Article 63(1) of Regulation (EC) No 607/2009 provides that Member States **4.318** shall designate the competent authority or authorities responsible for ensuring certification as provided for in Art 60(2)(a) of the Wine Regulation, in accordance with the criteria laid down in Art 4 of Regulation (EC) No 882/2004.

Certification of wine, at any stage of the production, including during the **4.319** conditioning of the wine, shall be ensured either by:

    (a)   the competent authority or authorities referred to in para 1; or,

    (b)   one or more control bodies within the meaning of point 5 of the second subparagraph of Art 2 of Regulation (EC) No 882/2004[77] operating as a product certification body in accordance with the criteria laid down in Art 5 of that Regulation.

4.320 The authority or authorities referred to in para 1 shall offer adequate guarantees of objectivity and impartiality, and have at their disposal the qualified staff and resources needed to carry out their tasks.

4.321 The certification bodies referred to in point (b) of the first subparagraph shall comply with, and from 1 May 2010 be accredited in accordance with, the European standard EN 45011 or ISO/IEC Guide 65 (General requirements for bodies operating product certification systems).

4.322 The costs of the certification shall be borne by the operators subject to it.

4.323 The Certification procedure as provided for in Art 60(2)(a) of Regulation (EC) No 479/2008 shall ensure administrative evidence to support the veracity of the wine grape variety(-ies) or the vintage year shown on the label of the wine(s) concerned.

4.324 In addition, producing Member States may decide on:

    (a)   an organoleptic test of the wine relating to the odour and the taste with a view to verifying that the essential characteristic of the wine is due to the wine grape variety(-ies), which shall concern anonymous samples;

    (b)   an analytical test in case of a wine made from a single wine grape variety.

4.325 The certification procedure shall be carried out by competent authority(-ies) or control body(-ies) as referred to in paras 1 and 2 in the Member State in which production took place.

4.326 The certification shall be carried out either through:

    (a)   random checks based on a risk analysis;

    (b)   sampling; or

    (c)   systematically.

---

77 Regulation (EC) No 882/2004 on official controls performed to ensure the verification of compliance with feed and food law, animal health and animal welfare rules, OJ L 191, 28.5.2004, p. 1.

In the case of random checks, they shall be based on a control of production of **4.327** the product. The control plan shall be known by the operators. Member States shall select randomly the minimum number of operators to be subjected to this check.

15. Indication of the Community symbols

Article 65(1) of Commission Regulation (EC) No 607/2009 provides that the **4.328** Community symbols referred to in Art 60(1)(e) of the Wine Regulation may appear on labels of wines as laid down in Annex V to Commission Regulation (EC) No 1898/2006).[78] Notwithstanding Art 59, the indications 'PRO-TECTED DESIGNATION OF ORIGIN' and 'PROTECTED GEO-GRAPHICAL INDICATION' within the symbols may be replaced by the equivalent terms in another official language of the Community as laid down in the aforesaid Annex.

Article 65(2) of Commission Regulation (EC) No 607/2009 provides that **4.329** where the Community symbols or the indications referred to in Art 60(1)(e) of the Wine Regulation appear on the label of a product, they shall be accompanied by the corresponding PDO or GI.

16. Temporary labelling

Article 72(1) of Commission Regulation (EC) No 607/2009 provides that by **4.330** way of derogation from Art 65 of this Regulation, wines bearing a designation of origin or a GI, whose designation of origin or GI concerned meet the requirements as referred to in Art 38(5) of the Wine Regulation, shall be labelled in accordance with the provisions laid down in Chapter IV of this Regulation.

Article 72(2) of Commission Regulation (EC) No 607/2009 provides that **4.331** where the Commission decides not to confer protection to a designation of origin or GI pursuant to Art 41 of the Wine Regulation, wines labelled in accordance with Art 72(1) of this Article shall be withdrawn from the market or relabelled in accordance with Chapter IV of this Regulation.

---

78   OJ L 369, 23.12.2006, p. 1.

N. CERTIFICATION PROCEDURES

4.332 Article 60(2) of the Wine Regulation provides that without prejudice to Art 42(3), as regards the use of particulars referred to in Art 60(1)(a) and (b) for wines without a PDO or GI:

> (a) Member States shall introduce laws, regulations or administrative provisions to ensure certification, approval and control procedures so as to guarantee the veracity of the information concerned.

1. Designation of competent authority

4.333 Article 63(1) of Regulation (EC) No 607/2009 provides that Member States shall designate the competent authority or authorities responsible for ensuring certification as provided for in Art 60(2)(a) of the Wine Regulation, in accordance with the criteria laid down in Art 4 of Regulation (EC) No 882/2004.

4.334 Article 63(2) of Regulation (EC) No 607/2009 provides that the certification of wine, at any stage of the production, including during the conditioning of the wine, shall be ensured either by:

> (a) the competent authority or authorities referred to in para 1; or
> (b) one or more control bodies within the meaning of point 5 of the second subparagraph of Art 2 of Regulation (EC) No 882/2004[79] operating as a product certification body in accordance with the criteria laid down in Art 5 of that Regulation.

2. Guarantees of objectivity and impartiality

4.335 Article 63(2) of Regulation (EC) No 607/2009 requires that the authority or authorities referred to in Art 63(1) shall offer adequate guarantees of objectivity and impartiality, and have at their disposal the qualified staff and resources needed to carry out their tasks.

3. Accreditation of certification body

4.336 The certification bodies referred to in point (b) of Art 63(1) of Regulation (EC) No 607/2009 shall comply with, and from 1 May 2010 be accredited in

---

79 Regulation (EC) No 882/2004 on official controls performed to ensure the verification of compliance with feed and food law, animal health and animal welfare rules, OJ L 191, 28.5.2004, p. 1.

accordance with, the European standard EN 45011 or ISO/IEC Guide 65 (General requirements for bodies operating product certification systems) and the costs of the certification shall be borne by the operators subject to it.

4. Evidence to support veracity of grape variety

Article 63(3) of Regulation (EC) No 607/2009 requires that the Certification **4.337** procedure as provided for in Art 60(2)(a) of Regulation (EC) No 479/2008 shall ensure administrative evidence to support the veracity of the wine grape variety(-ies) or the vintage year shown on the label of the wine(s) concerned.

5. Certification tests

Article 63(3) of Regulation (EC) No 607/2009 provides that the certification **4.338** procedure shall be carried out by competent authority(-ies) or control body(-ies) as referred to in paras 1 and 2 in the Member State in which production took place.

The certification shall be carried out through: **4.339**

    (a)   random checks based on a risk analysis;
    (b)   sampling; or
    (c)   systematically.

In the case of random checks, Art 63(3) provides that they shall be based on a **4.340** control plan pre-established by the authority(-ies) covering different stages of production of the product. The control plan shall be known by the operators. Member States shall select randomly the minimum number of operators to be subjected to this check.

In the case of sampling, Art 63(3) of Regulation (EC) No 607/2009 provides **4.341** that Member States shall ensure that by their number, nature and frequency controls, they are representative of the whole of their territory and correspond to the volume of wine-sector products marketed or held with a view to their marketing.

Random checks may be combined with sampling. **4.342**

6. Excluded wine grape varieties

4.343 Article 60(2) of the Wine Regulation provides that without prejudice to Art 42(3), as regards the use of particulars referred to in Art 60(1)(a) and (b) for wines without a PDO or GI:

> (b) Member States may, on the basis of non-discriminatory and objective criteria and with due regard to loyal competition, for wine produced from wine grape varieties on their territory, draw-up lists of excluded wine grape varieties, in particular if:
>
> (i) there is a risk of confusion of consumers as to the true origin of the wine due to the fact that the given wine grape variety forms an integral part of an existing protected designation of origin or geographical indication;
>
> (ii) the relevant controls would not be cost-effective due to the fact that the given wine grape variety represents a very small part of the Member State vineyard.

7. Mixtures of wines

4.344 Article 60(2)(c) of the Wine Regulation provides that, without prejudice to Art 42(3) as regards the use of particulars referred to in Art 60(1)(a) and (b) of the Wine Regulation for wines without a PDO or GI, 'mixtures of wines from different Member States shall not give rise to labelling of the wine grape variety or varieties unless the Member States concerned agree otherwise and ensure the feasibility of the relevant certification, approval and control procedures'.

8. Varietal wines

4.345 Article 63(7) of Regulation (EC) No 607/2009 provides that for wines produced in accordance with Art 60(2) of the Wine Regulation, Member States may decide to use the terms 'varietal wine' supplemented by the name(s) of:

(a) the Member State(s) concerned;
(b) the wine grape variety(-ies).

4.346 Article 63(7) of Regulation (EC) No 607/2009 provides that for wines without PDO, PGI or GI produced in third countries which bear on labels the name of one or more wine grape varieties or the vintage year, third countries may decide to use the terms 'varietal wine' supplemented by the name(s) of the third country(ies) concerned.

O. LANGUAGES

Article 61(1) of the Wine Regulation provides that the compulsory and **4.347** optional particulars referred to in Arts 59 and 60 shall, where expressed in words, appear in one or more of the official languages of the Community.

Article 61(1) provides that notwithstanding Art 61(1) the name of a PDO or **4.348** GI or a traditional term as referred to in Art 54(1)(a) shall appear on the label in the language or languages for which the protection applies.

In the case of protected designations of origin or GIs or national specific **4.349** designations using a non-Latin alphabet, the name may also appear in one or more official languages of the Community.

P. MARKETING AND EXPORT

Article 55(1) of Commission Regulation (EC) No 607/2009 of 14 July 2009 **4.350** provides that products whose label or presentation does not conform to the corresponding conditions as laid down in this Regulation cannot be marketed in the Community or exported.

Article 55(2) provides that by way of derogation from Chapters V and VI of **4.351** the Wine Regulation, where the products concerned are to be exported, Member States may allow that particulars that conflict with labelling rules as provided for by Community legislation appear on the label of wines for export, when they are required by the legislation of the third country concerned. These particulars may appear in languages other than the official Community languages.

Q. ENFORCEMENT

Article 62 provides that the competent authorities of the Member States shall **4.352** take measures to ensure that a product referred to in Art 59(1) not labelled in conformity with this Chapter is not placed on, or is withdrawn from, the market.

R. ADDITIONAL PROVISIONS LAID DOWN BY THE PRODUCER MEMBER STATES RELATING TO LABELLING AND PRESENTATION

4.353 Article 70(1) of Commission Regulation (EC) No 607/2009 provides that for wines with PDO or GI produced on their territory, the particulars referred to in Arts 61, 62 and 64–67 may be rendered compulsory, prohibited or limited as regards their use by introducing conditions stricter than those laid down in this Chapter through the corresponding product specifications of those wines.

4.354 Article 70(2) of Commission Regulation (EC) No 607/2009 provides that as regards wines without PDO or GI produced on their territory, Member States may render compulsory the particulars referred to in Arts 64 and 66.

4.355 Article 70(3) of Commission Regulation (EC) No 607/2009 provides that for control purposes, Member States may decide to define and regulate other particulars than those listed in Arts 59(1) and 60(1) of the Wine Regulation for wines produced in their territories.

4.356 Article 70(4) of Commission Regulation (EC) No 607/2009 provides that for control purposes, Member States may decide to render applicable Arts 58, 59 and 60 of Regulation (EC) No 479/2008 for wines bottled in their territories but not marketed or exported yet.

S. PRODUCER AND INTER-BRANCH ORGANISATIONS

4.357 Recital (43) of the Wine Regulation asserts that the existence and formation of producers' organisations continue to have the potential to contribute to the attainment of the needs of the wine sector at the Community level. 'Their usefulness should lie in the scope and efficiency of the services they offer to their members' and the same holds true for inter-branch organisations.

4.358 Chapter VII of the Wine Regulation deals with the establishment of producer and associated organisations. Article 64(1) provides that Member States may recognise producer organisations which:

(a)   are constituted by producers of products covered by this Regulation;
(b)   are formed on the initiative of producers.

258

Article 64(2) provides that producer organisations recognised in accordance **4.359** with Regulation (EC) No 1493/1999[80] shall be considered as recognised producer organisations under Art 64.

Article 65(1) of the Wine Regulation permits Member States to recognise **4.360** inter-branch organisations which:

(a) are made up of representatives of economic activities in the production of, trade in, or processing of products covered by this Regulation;

(b) are formed on the initiative of all or some of the representatives referred to in (a);

(c) carry out one or more of the following measures in one or more regions of the Community, taking account of public health and the interests of consumers:

   (i) improving knowledge and transparency of production and the market;

   ...

   (vi) providing information on particular characteristics of wine with a protected designation of origin or geographical indication;

   ...

   (xiii) exploiting, protecting and promoting quality labels and protected designations of origin and geographical indications;

(d) have lodged an application for recognition with the Member State concerned and the application contains the following items:

   (i) evidence that the entity meets the requirements laid down in (a) to (c);

   (ii) evidence that the entity carries out its activities in one or more regions in the territory concerned;

   (iii) evidence that the entity represents a significant share of the production of or trade in products covered by this Regulation;

   (iv) evidence that the entity does not engage in the production or processing or marketing of products covered by this Regulation.

Article 65(2) provides that organisations meeting the criteria set out in Art **4.361** 65(1), which have been recognised by Member States, shall be considered as recognised inter-branch organisations under this Article.

T. PROTECTION OF WINE GIS UNDER THE REGULATION ON THE COMMON ORGANISATION OF THE MARKETS IN AGRICULTURAL PRODUCTS

Regulation (EU) No 1308/2013 of the European Parliament and of the **4.362** Council of 17 December 2013 establishing a common organisation of the markets in agricultural products replaced Council Regulation (EC)

---

80 Council Regulation (EC) No 1493/1999 of 17 May 1999 on the common organisation of the market in wine.

No 1234/2007, which had established the Common Agricultural Policy.[81] Regulation (EU) No 1308/2013 sought to 'preserve the particular quality characteristics of wines with a protected designation of origin or a protected geographical indications' in the wine sector and those of third countries.[82] These rules are laid down in subs 2 of this Regulation. These are supplemented by Delegated Regulation (EU) 2019/33 of 17 October 2018[83] (the Delegated Regulation) and Commission Implementing Regulation (EU) No 2019/33 of 17 October 2018[84] (the Implementing Regulation).

1. Definitions

4.363 Article 93(a) defines 'a designation of origin' as 'the name of a region, a specific place or, in exceptional and duly justifiable cases, a country used to describe a product referred to in Article 92(1)[85] fulfilling the following requirements':

    (i)   the quality and characteristics of the product are essentially or exclusively due to a particular geographical environment with its inherent natural and human factors;

    (ii) the grapes from which the product is produced come exclusively from that geographical area;

    (iii) the production[86] takes place in that geographical area; and

    (iv) the product is obtained from vine varieties belonging to *Vitis vinifera*.

4.364 Article 5(1) of the Delegated Regulation provides that by way of derogation from Art 93(a)(iii) and (b)(iii) and on condition that the product specification so provides, a product which has a protected designation of origin or geographical indication may be made into wine in any of the following locations:

    (a) in an area in the immediate proximity of the demarcated area in question;

    (b) in an area located within the same administrative unit or within a neighbouring administrative unit, in conformity with national rules;

    (c) in the case of a trans-border designation of origin or geographical indication, or where an agreement on control measures exists between two or more Member

---

81   Council Regulation (EC) No 1234/2007 of 22 October 2007 establishing a common organisation of agricultural markets and on specific provisions for certain agricultural products (Single CMO Regulation), OJ L 299, 16.11.2007, p. 1.

82   Ibid., Recital 95.

83   C/2018/6622, OJ L 9, 11.1.2019, pp. 2–45.

84   C/2018/6621OJ L 9, 11.1.2019, pp. 46–76.

85   These are 'products referred to in points 1, 3–6, 8, 9, 11, 15 and 16 of Part II of Annex VIII.

86   Production is defined in Art 93(4) as covering 'all the operations involved, from the harvesting of the grapes to the completion of the wine-making processes, with the exception of any post-production processes'.

States or between one or more Member States and one or more third countries, in an area situated in the immediate proximity of the demarcated area in question.

Additionally, by way of derogation from Art 93(a)(iii) and on condition that the product specification so provides, Art 5(2) of the Delegated Regulation provides that a product may be made into sparkling wine or semi-sparkling wine bearing a protected designation of origin beyond the immediate proximity of the demarcated area in question if this practice was in use prior to 1 March 1986 and Art 5(3) of the Delegated Regulation provides with regard to liqueur wines with the protected designation of origin 'Málaga' and 'Jerez-Xérès-Sherry', the must of raisined grapes to which neutral alcohol of vine origin has been added to prevent fermentation, obtained from Pedro Ximénez vine variety, may come from the 'Montilla-Moriles' region.

Article 93(b) defines 'a geographical indication' as 'an indication referring to a **4.365** region, a specific place or, in exceptional and duly justifiable cases, a country, used to describe a product referred to in Article 92(1) fulfilling the following requirements':

(i)   it possesses a specific quality, reputation or other characteristics attributable to that geographical origin;
(ii) at least 85 per cent of the grapes used for its production come exclusively from that geographical area;[87]
(iii) its production takes place in that geographical area; and
(iv) it is obtained from vine varieties belonging to *Vitis vinifera* or a cross between the *Vitis vinifera* species and other species of the genus *Vitis*.

Article 93(2) provides that certain traditionally used names shall constitute a **4.366** designation of origin where they:

(a)   designate a wine;
(b)   refer to a geographical name;
(c)   fulfil the requirements referred to in points (a)(i) to (iv) of paragraph 1; and
(d)   have undergone the procedure conferring protection on designations of origin and geographical indications laid down in this subsection.

Article 93(3) provides that designations of origin and GIs, including those **4.367** relating to geographical areas in third countries, shall be eligible for protection in the EU in accordance with the rules laid down in subs 2 of this Regulation.

---

87 Art 93(5) provides that the maximum 15 per cent share of grapes which may originate outside the demarcated area shall originate from the Member State or third country in which the demarcated area is situated.

Article 5(3) of the Implementing Regulation requires third countries to use the model for single documents set out in Annex I.

2. Applications for protection

4.368 Article 94(1) provides that applications for protection of names as designations of origin or GIs shall include a technical file containing:

(a) the name to be protected;[88]
(b) the name and address of the applicant;
(c) a product specification;[89] and
(d) a single document summarising the product specification.

4.369 The Implementing Regulation in Art 5(1) provides that the single document referred to in para (d) shall include the following main elements of the product specification:

(a) the name to be protected as a designation of origin or a geographical indication;
(b) the Member State or third country to which the demarcated area belongs;
(c) the type of geographical indication;
(d) a description of the wine or wines;
(e) the categories of grapevine products;
(f) the maximum yields per hectare;
(g) the indication of the wine grape variety or varieties from which the wine or wines are obtained;
(h) a concise definition of the demarcated geographical area;[90]
(i) a description of the link referred to in point (a)(i) or in point (b)(i) of Article 93(1).
(j) where applicable, the specific oenological practices used to make the wine or wines, as well as the relevant restrictions on making them;
(k) where applicable, the specific rules concerning packaging and labelling and all other essential relevant requirements.

4.370 The Implementing Regulation in Art 5(2) requires that the description of the link referred to in point (i) of para 1 shall include:

(a) in the case of a designation of origin, a description of the causal link between the quality and characteristics of the product and the geographical environment with

---

88 Art 2(1) of the Delegated Regulation provides that the name to be protected as a designation of origin or GI shall be registered only in the languages which are or were historically used to describe the specific product in the demarcated geographical area.
89 As referred to in Art 94(2).
90 Art 6 of the Implementing Regulation requires the demarcated geographical area to be defined 'in a precise way that presents no ambiguities, referring as far as possible to physical or administrative boundaries'.

its inherent natural and human factors to which they are essentially or exclusively linked, including, where applicable, elements of the product description or production method justifying the link;

(b) in the case of a geographical indication, a description of the causal link between the GI and the relevant specific quality, reputation or other characteristics attributable to the geographical origin of the product, accompanied by a statement indicating on which of the given factors: specific quality, reputation or other characteristics attributable to the geographical origin of the product the causal link is based.

The description may also concern the elements of the product description or production method justifying the causal link. Where an application covers different categories of grapevine products, the details bearing out the link shall be demonstrated for each of the grapevine products concerned.

3. The product specification

Article 94(2) provides that the product specification 'shall enable interested parties to verify the relevant conditions of production relating to the designation of origin or geographical indication' and shall 'at least consist of': **4.371**

(a) the name to be protected;
(b) a description of the wine or wines:
    (i) in respect of a designation of origin, the principal analytical and organoleptic characteristics;
    (ii) in respect of a geographical indication, the principal analytical characteristics as well as an evaluation or indication of its organoleptic characteristics;
(c) where applicable, the specific oenological practices used to make the wine or wines, as well as the relevant restrictions on making them;
(d) the demarcation of the geographical area concerned;
(e) the maximum yields per hectare;
(f) an indication of the wine grape variety or varieties that the wine or wines are obtained from;
(g) the details bearing out the link referred to in point (a)(i) or, as the case may be, in point (b)(i) of Article 93(1);
(h) applicable requirements laid down in EU or national legislation or, where provided for by Member States, by an organisation which manages the protected designation of origin or the protected geographical indication, having regard to the fact that such requirements must be objective, non-discriminatory and compatible with EU law;
(i) the name and address of the authorities or bodies verifying compliance with the provisions of the product specification, and their specific tasks.

4.372 In the case of third countries Art 94(3) requires in addition to the elements provided for in paras 1 and 2, 'proof that the name concerned is protected in its country of origin'.

4.373 Additional requirements for product specifications are contained in Art 4 of the Delegated Regulation. Article 4(2) provides that where the product specification indicates that packaging, including bottling, shall take place within the demarcated geographical area or within an area in the immediate proximity of the demarcated area in question, it shall also include a justification showing why, in the specific case, the packaging must take place in the particular geographical area to safeguard quality, to ensure the origin or to ensure control, taking into account EU law, in particular that on the free movement of goods and the free provision of services.

4. Applicants

4.374 Article 95(1) provides that 'any interested group of producers, or in exceptional and duly justifiable cases a single producer', may apply for the protection of a designation of origin or GI and that other interested parties may participate in the application.

4.375 Article 3 of the Delegated Regulation provides that a single producer may be deemed an applicant within the meaning of Art 95(1) if it is shown that:

(a) the person concerned is the only person willing to submit an application; and

(b) the demarcated geographical area possesses characteristics which differ appreciably from those of neighbouring areas or the characteristics of the product are different from those produced in neighbouring areas It also provides that the circumstance by which a protected designation of origin or GI consists of or contains the name of the holding of the single applicant producer shall not prevent other producers from using that name provided that they comply with the product specification.

4.376 Article 95(2) provides that producers may apply for protection only for wines which they produce. In the case of a name designating a trans-border geographical area or a traditional name connected to a trans-border geographical area, Art 95(3) permits a joint application to be submitted. Article 7 of the Delegated Legislation provides that where joint applications are submitted, the related preliminary national procedures, including the objection stage, shall be carried out in all the Member States concerned.

5. Amendments to product specifications

Article 105 of Regulation (EU) No 1308/2013 provides that an applicant **4.377** satisfying the conditions laid down in Art 95 may apply for approval of an amendment to the product specification of a protected designation of origin or of a protected GI, in particular to take account of developments in scientific and technical knowledge or to re-demarcate the geographical area referred to Art 94(2)(d) and that applications shall describe and state reasons for the amendments requested. Article 17(1) of Delegated Regulation provides that standard amendments shall be approved and made public by Member States to which the geographical area of the designation of origin or GI relates.

(a) Types of amendments

Article 14(1) of the Delegated Regulation provides that for the purposes of **4.378** Art 105 of Regulation (EU) No 1308/2013 amendments to a product specification are classified into two categories as regards their importance:

(i) amendments requiring an objection procedure at EU level ('Union amendments'), and

(ii) amendments to be dealt with at Member State or third-country level ('standard amendments').

An amendment is considered to be a Union amendment where:

(a) it includes a change in the name of the protected designation of origin or protected GI;

(b) it consists of a change, a deletion or an addition of a category of grapevine product, as referred to in Part II of Annex VII to Regulation (EU) No 1308/2013;

(c) it could potentially void the link referred to in point (a)(i) or in point (b)(i) of Article 93(1) of Regulation (EU) No 1308/2013;

(d) it entails further restrictions on the marketing of the product.

Applications for Union amendments submitted by third countries or by third-country producers shall contain proof that the requested amendment complies with the laws on the protection of designations of origin or GIs in force in that third country.

(b) Contents of application

Article 17(1) of Delegated Regulation (EU) 2019/33 requires the application **4.379** for a standard amendment to provide a description of the standard amendments, provide a summary of the reasons for which the amendments are required and demonstrate that the proposed amendments qualify as standard in accordance with Art 14 of the Delegated Regulation. Article 9.1 of the Implementing Regulation provides that an application for a Union amendment to a product specification shall contain:

(a) the reference to the protected name to which the amendment relates;
(b) the name of the applicant and a description of the legitimate interest of the applicant;
(c) the heading in the product specification affected by the amendment;
(d) an exhaustive description of and the specific reasons for each of the amendments proposed;
(e) the consolidated and duly completed single document, as modified;
(f) the electronic reference to the publication of the consolidated and duly completed product specification, as modified.

4.380 Article 9(2) provides that this application for amendment shall be drawn up in accordance with the form made available in the information systems referred to in Art 30(1)(a) of the Implementing Regulation. Third countries shall use the form set out in Annex IV to the Implementing Regulation.

4.381 The amended single document shall be drawn up in accordance with Art 5 of the Implementing Regulation. The electronic reference to the publication of the product specification shall lead to the consolidated version of the proposed product specification. An application from a third country may include a copy of the consolidated version of the product specification instead of the electronic reference to the published copy of the product specification.

(c) Procedure for Union amendments to product specifications

4.382 Article 15(1) of the Delegated Regulation provides that an application for approval of a Union amendment to a product specification, shall follow the procedure laid down in Art 94 and Arts 96–99 of Regulation (EU) No 1308/2013. Where, based on the examination carried out pursuant to Art 97(2) of Regulation (EU) No 1308/2013, Art 15(2) provides that where the Commission considers that the conditions required under Art 97(3) of that Regulation are met, it shall publish the application for a Union amendment in the *Official Journal of the European Union*, C series. The final decision on the approval of the amendment shall be adopted without applying the examination procedure referred to in Art 229(2) of Regulation (EU) No 1308/2013 unless an admissible objection has been lodged or the application for amendment is rejected, in which case the second paragraph of Art 99 of that Regulation shall apply.

Article 15(3) of the Delegated Regulation requires an application for approval **4.383** of Union amendments to contain Union amendments exclusively. If an application for Union amendments also contains standard or temporary amendments the procedure for Union amendments shall apply only to the Union amendments. The standard or temporary amendments shall be deemed as not submitted.

In examining the applications for amendment, Art 15(4) of the Delegated **4.384** Regulation requires the Commission to focus on the proposed amendments.

(d) Admissibility of application for Union amendments

Article 16(1) of the Delegated Regulation provides that applications for **4.385** approval of a Union amendment to a product specification are considered admissible if they are submitted in accordance with Art 105 of Regulation (EU) No 1308/2013 and with Art 3 and Art 9(2) of the Implementing Regulation *mutatis mutandis*, and if they are duly completed. An application for approval of a Union amendment shall be considered to be duly completed where it is comprehensive and exhaustive and where it complies with the requirements set out in Arts 2 and 9(1) of the Implementing Regulation. The approval by the Commission of an application for approval of a Union amendment to a product specification shall only cover the amendments submitted in the application itself.

Article 16(2) of the Delegated Regulation provides that if the application is **4.386** considered inadmissible, the competent authorities of the Member State or those of the third country or the applicant established in a third country shall be informed of the reasons for the inadmissibility.

(e) Standard amendments

Article 17(1) of the Delegated Regulation provides that standard amendments **4.387** shall be approved and made public by Member States to which the geographical area of the designation of origin or GI relates. It provides that applications for approval of a standard amendment to a product specification shall be submitted to the authorities of the Member State to whom the geographical area of the designation or indication relates. Applicants must satisfy the conditions laid down in Art 95 of Regulation (EU) No 1308/2013. If the application for approval of a standard amendment to a product specification does not come from the applicant which had submitted the application for protection of the name or names to which the product specification refers,

Art 17(1) of the Delegated Regulation requires the Member State to give that applicant the opportunity to comment on the application, if that applicant still exists.

4.388 The application for a standard amendment are required by Art 17(1) to provide a description of the standard amendments, provide a summary of the reasons for which the amendments are required and demonstrate that the proposed amendments qualify as standard in accordance with Art 14 of the Delegated Regulation.

4.389 Article 17(2) provides that where the Member State considers that the requirements of Regulation (EU) No 1308/2013 and the provisions adopted pursuant thereto are met, it may approve and make public the standard amendment. The approval decision shall include the modified consolidated single document, where relevant, and the modified consolidated product specification. The standard amendment shall be applicable in the Member State once it has been made public. The Member State shall communicate standard amendments to the Commission not later than one month following the date on which the national decision of approval was made public.

4.390 Decisions approving standard amendments concerning grapevine products originating in third countries, according to Art 17(3) shall be taken in accordance with the system in force in the third country concerned and shall be communicated to the Commission by a single producer within the meaning of Art 3 or a group of producers having a legitimate interest, either directly to the Commission or via the authorities of that third country, not later than one month following the date they are made public.

4.391 Article 17(4) considers the communication of standard amendments to be duly completed when it complies with Art 10 of Implementing Regulation (EU) No 2019/34. In the event that the standard amendment implies a modification of the single document, Art 17(5) requires the Commission to publish the description of the standard amendment referred to in Art 10 of Implementing Regulation (EU) No 2019/34 and the modified single document in the *Official Journal of the European Union*, C series, within three months from the date on which the communication is received from the Member State, third country or third-country single producer or group of producers.

4.392 In the event that the standard amendment does not imply a modification of the single document, Art 17(6) requires the Commission to make public, via the information systems referred to in Art 32 of Implementing Regulation (EU) No 2019/34, the description of the standard amendment within three months from the date on which the communication is received from the Member State, third country or applicant established in the third country. If the geographical area covers more than one Member State, Art 17(8) requires the Member States concerned to apply the procedure for standard amendments separately for the part of the area which falls within their territory. The standard amendment shall be applicable only after the last national decision of approval becomes applicable. The Member State last approving the standard amendment is required by Art 17(8) to send the Commission the communication referred to in Art 17(4) not later than one month following the date on which its decision approving the standard amendment is made public.

If one or more of the Member States concerned do not adopt the national **4.393** decision of approval referred to in the first subparagraph, any of Member States concerned may submit an application under the Union amendment procedure. Such a rule shall also apply *mutatis mutandis* when one or more of the concerned countries is a third country.

(f) Publication of application for amendment

Article 9(3) of the Implementing Regulation requires the information to be **4.394** published in accordance with Art 97(3) of Regulation (EU) No 1308/2013 shall contain the duly completed application as referred to in paras 1 and 2 of Art 9.

Article 17(7) of the Delegated Regulation provides that standard amendments **4.395** shall be applicable in the territory of the Union once they have been published in the *Official Journal of the European Union*, C series or made public by the Commission in the information systems referred to in Art 32 of Implementing Regulation (EU) No 2019/34.

(g) Approval of application for amendment

Where the Member State considers that the requirements of Regulation (EU) **4.396** No 1308/2013 and the provisions adopted pursuant thereto are met, Art 17(2) of Delegated Regulation (EU) No 2019/33 permits it to approve and make public the standard amendment. The approval decision shall include the modified consolidated single document, where relevant, and the modified consolidated product specification. The standard amendment shall be applicable in the Member State once it has been made public. The Member State shall communicate standard amendments to the Commission not later than one month following the date on which the national decision of approval was made public.

4.397 Article 17(4) of Delegated Regulation (EU) No 2019/33 provides that the communication of standard amendments shall be considered to be duly completed when it complies with Art 10 of Implementing Regulation (EU) No 2019/34.

4.398 In the event that the standard amendment implies a modification of the single document, Art 17(5) of Delegated Regulation (EU) No 2019/33 the Commission shall publish the description of the standard amendment referred to in Art 10 of Implementing Regulation (EU) No 2019/34 and the modified single document in the *Official Journal of the European Union*, C series, within three months from the date on which the communication is received from the Member State, third country or third-country single producer or group of producers. In the event that the standard amendment does not imply a modification of the single document, Art 17(6) of the Delegated Regulation permits the Commission to make public, via the information systems referred to in Art 32 of the Implementing Regulation the description of the standard amendment within three months from the date on which the communication is received from the Member State, third country or applicant established in the third country.

4.399 Article 17(7) of the Delegated Regulation provides that standard amendments shall be applicable in the territory of the EU once they have been published in the *Official Journal of the European Union*, C series or made public by the Commission in the information systems referred to in Art 32 of Implementing Regulation (EU) No 2019/34.

(h)   Geographical areas covering more than one Member State

4.400 Article 17(8) of the Delegated Regulation provides that if the geographical area covers more than one Member State, the Member States concerned shall apply the procedure for standard amendments separately for the part of the area which falls within their territory. The standard amendment shall be applicable only after the last national decision of approval becomes applicable.

4.401 The Member State last approving the standard amendment shall send the Commission the communication referred to in para 4 not later than one month following the date on which its decision approving the standard amendment is made public. If one or more of the Member States concerned do not adopt the national decision of approval referred to in the first subparagraph, any of Member States concerned may submit an application under the Union amendment procedure. Such a rule shall also apply *mutatis mutandis* when one or more of the concerned countries is a third country.

(i) Temporary amendments

Article 14(2) of the Delegated Regulation provides that for the purposes of **4.402** Art 105 of Regulation (EU) No 1308/2013, a temporary amendment is a standard amendment concerning a temporary change in the product specification resulting from the imposition of obligatory sanitary and phytosanitary measures by the public authorities or linked to natural disasters or adverse weather conditions formally recognised by the competent authorities. Article 18(1) of the Delegated Regulation provides for temporary amendments to be approved and made public by Member States to which the geographical area of the designation of origin or GI relates. They shall be communicated to the Commission together with the reasons supporting the temporary amendments not later than one month following the date on which the national decision of approval was made public. A temporary amendment is applicable in the Member State once it has been made public. Where the geographical area covers more than one Member State, Art 18(2) provides that the procedure for temporary amendment applies separately in the Member States concerned for the part of the area which falls within their territory.

Temporary amendments shall be applicable only when the last national **4.403** decision of approval becomes applicable. The Member State last approving the temporary amendment shall communicate it to the Commission not later than one month following the date upon which its decision of approval is made public. This rule applies, *mutatis mutandis*, also when one or more of the countries concerned is a third country.

Article 18(3) provides that temporary amendments concerning grapevine **4.404** products originating in third countries shall be communicated to the Commission, together with the reasons supporting the temporary amendments, by a single producer within the meaning of Art 3 or a group of producers having a legitimate interest, either directly or via the authorities of that third country, not later than one month following their approval. Article 18(4) provides that the communication of temporary amendments shall be considered to be duly completed when it contains all the elements referred to in Art 11 of Implementing Regulation (EU) No 2019/34.

Article 18(5) provides that the Commission shall make public such amend- **4.405** ments within three months from the date on which the communication is received from the Member State, third country or third-country single producer or group of producers. A temporary amendment is applicable in the territory of the Union once it has been made public by the Commission.

6. Preliminary national procedure

4.406 Article 96(1) provides that applications for protection of a designation of origin or a GI for wines originating in the EU shall be subject to a preliminary national procedure. This according to Art 96(2) involves an application for protection to be filed with the Member State in the territory of which the designation of origin or GI originates.

4.407 The Member State with which the application for protection is filed is required under Art 96(3) to examine it in order to verify whether it meets the conditions set out in subs 2. This national procedure entails adequate publication of the application and providing for a period of at least two months from the date of publication within which any natural or legal person having a legitimate interest and resident or established on its territory may object to the proposed protection by lodging a duly substantiated statement with that Member State.

4.408 Article 96(4) permits the Member State assessing the application to reject it if its considers that the designation of origin or the GI does not comply with the conditions laid down in this subsection or is incompatible with EU law.

4.409 If the Member State assessing the application considers that the requirements are fulfilled, Art 96(5) requires it to carry out a national procedure which ensures adequate publication of the product specification at least on the Internet and forward the application to the Commission. The Delegated Regulation in Art 6 provides that when forwarding an application for protection to the Commission in accordance with Art 96(5) a Member State shall include a declaration that it considers that the application lodged by the applicant meets the conditions for protection under section 2(2) of Chapter I of Title II of Part II of Regulation (EU) No 1308/2013 and the provisions adopted pursuant thereto and that it certifies that the single document referred to in Art 94(1)(d) of Regulation (EU) No 1308/2013 is a faithful summary of the product specification.

4.410 Member States shall inform the Commission of admissible objections received in the national procedure. Member States shall keep the Commission informed of any national judicial proceedings possibly affecting the application for protection. The Implementing Regulation in Art 2 requires when forwarding an application in accordance with Art 96(5) the Member States shall include the electronic reference to the publication of the product specification referred to in Art 97(3) and the declaration referred to in Art 6 of the Implementing Regulation.

7. Admissibility of the Application

Article 9(1) of the Delegated Regulation provides that applications for **4.411** protection are considered admissible if they are submitted in accordance with Arts 94, 95 and 96 of Regulation (EU) No 1308/2013 and Arts 3 and 5(3) of the Implementing Regulation and if they are duly completed. An application for protection shall be considered to be duly completed when it complies with Art 94(1) and (3) of Regulation (EU) No 1308/2013 and Art 2 of the Implementing Regulation and if the single document is duly completed.

Article 9(1) of the Delegated Regulation provides that the single document **4.412** summarising the product specification, referred to in Art 94(1)(d) of Regulation (EU) No 1308/2013 shall be considered to be duly completed when it complies with the requirements listed in Art 5(1) and (2) of Implementing Regulation (EU) No 2019/34. The product specification shall be considered duly completed when it complies with the requirements set out in Art 94(2) of Regulation (EU) No 1308/2013.

If the Commission considers that an application is inadmissible, Art 9(2) **4.413** requires it to inform the competent authorities of the Member State or those of the third country or the applicant established in a third country of the reasons grounding the finding of inadmissibility.

Article 9(3) obliges the Commission shall make public at least once a month **4.414** the list of names for which it has received applications for protection as designations of origin or GIs, the name of the applicant Member State or third country and the date of submission of the application.

8. Scrutiny by the Commission

On receipt of the application for protection, Art 97(1) requires the Commis- **4.415** sion to make public the date of submission. Then Art 97(2) requires the Commission to examine whether the applications for protection as referred to in Art 94 meet the conditions laid down in subs 2.

4.416 Article 10 of the Delegated Regulation requires that the examination of the application by the Commission, referred to in Art 97(2) to consist of a check that there are no manifest errors in the application and that when examining the application, the Commission shall examine the single document in particular. Article 10 of the Delegated Regulation requires the examination should be completed within a period of six months, but that where this period is exceeded, the Commission shall inform the applicant in writing of the reasons for the delay.

4.417 Where the Commission considers that the conditions are met Art 97(3) requires it to adopt implementing acts concerning the publication, in the *Official Journal of the European Union*, of the single document referred to in Art 94(1)(d) and of the reference to the publication of the product specification made in the course of the preliminary national procedure. However, where the Commission considers that the conditions are not met, Art 94(4) requires it to adopt implementing acts rejecting the application.

4.418 In the case of third countries, Art 7(1) of the Implementing Regulation provides that if an admissible application does not meet the conditions laid down in subs 2 of s 2 of Chapter I of Title II of Part II of Regulation (EU) No 1308/2013, the Commission shall inform the Member State or authorities of the third country or the applicant established in the third country in question of the grounds for refusal, setting a deadline for the withdrawal or modification of the application or for the submission of comments.

4.419 If, following that information, substantial modifications are made to the product specification, before the new version of the single document is sent to the Commission, those modifications shall be made the subject of adequate publication to enable any natural or legal person having a legitimate interest and established or resident in the territory of the Member State in question to lodge an objection. If the obstacles to the conferral of protection are not remedied by the Member State or third-country authorities or the applicant, established in the third country in question, within the given deadline, Art 7(2) requires the Commission to reject the application in accordance with Art 97(4). Article 7(3) of the Implementing Regulation requires that any decision to reject the application shall be taken by the Commission on the basis of the documents and information available to it and the Commission shall notify the Member State or the third-country authorities or the applicant established in the third country in question of the decision to reject the application.

9. Objection procedure

(a) Eligible objectors

4.420 Article 98 provides that within two months[91] from the date of the publication of the single document as referred to in Art 94(1)(d), any Member State or third country, or any natural or legal person having a legitimate interest and resident or established in a Member State other than that applying for the protection or in a third country, may object to the proposed protection by submitting to the Commission a duly substantiated statement concerning the conditions of eligibility as laid down in this subsection. In the case of natural or legal persons resident or established in third countries, such a statement is to be submitted, either directly or via the authorities of the third country concerned, within the two-month period referred to in the first paragraph.

(b) Admissibility and grounds of objection

4.421 Article 11(1) of the Delegated Regulation provides that for the purposes of Art 98 of Regulation (EU) No 1308/2013, a substantiated statement of objection shall be admissible where:

    (a) it is received by the Commission within the deadline set out in Article 98;

    (b) it complies with the requirements set out in Article 8(1) of the Implementing Regulation;

    (c) it shows that the application for protection or amendment to the product specification or for cancellation of the protection is incompatible with the rules on designations of origin and geographical indications because:

        (i) it would conflict with Articles 92 to 95, 105 or 106 of Regulation (EU) No 1308/2013 and with the provisions adopted pursuant thereto;

        (ii) the registration of the proposed name would conflict with Articles 100 or 101 of Regulation (EU) No 1308/2013.

4.422 Article 11(1) of the Delegated Regulation provides that the grounds of objection shall be assessed in relation to the territory of the EU and where an objection is filed by a natural or legal person, the duly substantiated statement of objection shall be admissible only if it shows the legitimate interest of the objector.

4.423 Article 11(1) of the Delegated Regulation provides that where the Commission considers that the objection is inadmissible, it shall inform the authority

---

91 Art 8(2) of the Implementing Regulation provides that the period of three months referred to in Art 12(1) shall commence on the date on which the invitation to engage in consultations is delivered to the interested parties by electronic means.

or natural or legal person that objected of the reasons grounding the finding of inadmissibility.

(c) Procedural rules for objections

4.424 The procedural rules for objections are prescribed in Art 8 of the Implementing Regulation and Art 12 of the Delegated Regulation.

4.425 Article 8 of the Implementing Regulation requires a substantiated statement of objection to contain:

(a) the reference to the name published in the *Official Journal of the European Union*, L series to which the objection relates;

(b) the name and contact details of the authority or person that lodged the objection;

(c) a description of the legitimate interest of the natural or legal person that lodged the objection, with the exclusion of national authorities having legal personality in the national legal order;

(d) an indication of the grounds for objection, the details of the facts, evidence and comments in support of the objection.

The objection may be accompanied by supporting documents, where relevant.

4.426 If the objection is based on the existence of an earlier trade mark of reputation and renown, Art 8 requires objection to be accompanied by:

(a) proof of the filing or the registration of the earlier trade mark or proof of its use; and

(b) proof of its reputation and renown. The information and evidence to be produced in support of the use of an earlier trade mark shall comprise particulars of the location, duration, extent and nature of the use made of the earlier trade mark, and of its reputation and renown.

The substantiated statement of objection must be drawn up in accordance with the form set out in Annex II to the Implementing Regulation.

(d) Consultations

4.427 Article 12(1) of Delegated Regulation (EU) No 2019/33 provides that if the Commission considers that the objection is admissible it shall invite the authority or natural or legal person that lodged the objection and the authority or natural or legal person that lodged the application for protection to engage in appropriate consultations for a period of three months. The invitation shall be issued within a period of four months from the date on which the application for protection, to which the substantiated statement of objection relates, is published in the *Official Journal of the European Union* and it shall be accompanied by a copy of the substantiated statement of objection. At any time during these three months, the Commission may, at the request of the authority or natural or legal person that lodged the application, extend the deadline for the consultations by a maximum of three months.

Article 12(2) of Delegated Regulation (EU) No 2019/33 requires the author- **4.428** ity or person that lodged the objection and the authority or person that lodged the application for protection to 'start such consultations without undue delay'. They are required to provide each other with the relevant information to assess whether the application for protection complies with the conditions of this Regulation and of Regulation (EU) No 1308/2013.

Article 12(3) provides that if the parties reach an agreement, either the **4.429** applicant established in the third country or the authorities of the Member State or of the third country from which the application for protection was lodged shall notify the Commission of the results of the consultations carried out and of all the factors which enabled that agreement to be reached, including the opinions of the parties.

Article 12(3) also provides that if the details published in accordance with Art **4.430** 97(3) of Regulation (EU) No 1308/2013 have been substantially amended, the Commission shall repeat the scrutiny referred to in Art 97(2) of that Regu- lation after a national procedure ensuring adequate publication of those amended details has been carried out. Where, following the agreement, there are no amendments to the product specification or where the amendments are not substantial, the Commission shall adopt a decision in accordance with Art 99 of Regulation (EU) No 1308/2013 conferring protection on the desig- nation of origin or GI.

Where no agreement is reached Art 12(4) of Delegated Regulation (EU) No **4.431** 2019/33 provides that either the applicant established in the third country or the authorities of the Member State or of the third country, from which the application for protection was lodged shall notify the Commission of the results of the consultations carried out and of all the related information and documents. Article 8(3) of the Implementing Regulation requires the Com- mission to be notified of the results of the consultations within one month from the end of the consultations in accordance with the form set out in Annex III to the Implementing Regulation.

Article 12(4) of Delegated Regulation (EU) No 2019/33 requires the Com- **4.432** mission to adopt a decision in accordance with Art 99 of Regulation (EU) No 1308/2013 either conferring protection or rejecting the application.

10. Decision on protection

4.433 On the basis of the information available to the Commission upon the completion of the objection procedure referred to in Art 98, the Commission is required by Art 99 to adopt implementing acts either conferring protection on the designation of origin or GI which meets the conditions laid down in this subsection and is compatible with EU law, or rejecting the application where those conditions are not met.

11. Homonyms

4.434 Homonymous names are defined in Art 100(1) as a name which misleads the consumer into believing that products come from another territory. Article 100(1) provides that these shall not be registered even if the name is accurate as far as the actual territory, region or place of origin of those products is concerned. However, Art 100(1) provides that a name for which an application is submitted, and which is wholly or partially homonymous with a name already registered under this Regulation, shall be registered with due regard to local and traditional usage and any risk of confusion.

4.435 Article 100(1) also provides that a registered homonymous name may be used only if there is a sufficient distinction in practice between the homonym registered subsequently and the name already in the register, having regard to the need to treat the producers concerned in an equitable manner and the need to avoid misleading the consumer. Article 100(2) provides that para (1) shall apply *mutatis mutandis* if a name for which an application is submitted is wholly or partially homonymous with a GI protected under the national law of Member States.

12. Wine designations, agricultural products and spirit drinks

4.436 Where the name of a wine grape variety contains or consists of a protected designation of origin or a protected GI, Art 100(3) of Regulation (EU) No 1308/2013 provides that that name shall not be used for the purposes of labelling agricultural products. Article 100(4) provides that the protection of designations of origin and GIs of products covered by Art 93 of this Regulation shall be without prejudice to protected geographical indications applying to spirit drinks as defined in Art 2 of Regulation (EC) No 110/2008.[92]

---

92   OJ L 39, 13.2.2008, p. 16.

13. Additional grounds for refusal of protection

Article 101(1) of Regulation (EU) No 1308/2013 provides that a name that **4.437** has become generic shall not be protected as a designation of origin or a GI. For the purposes of this section, a 'name that has become generic' means the name of a wine which, although it relates to the place or the region where this product was originally produced or marketed, has become the common name of a wine in the Union. To establish whether or not a name has become generic, Art 101 requires the 'relevant factors' to be taken into account, in particular:

(a) the existing situation in the EU, notably in areas of consumption;
(b) the relevant EU or national law.

Article 101(2) provides that a name shall not be protected as a designation of **4.438** origin or GI where, in the light of a trade mark's reputation and renown, protection could mislead the consumer as to the true identity of the wine.

14. Relationship with trade marks

Article 102(1) of Regulation (EU) No 1308/2013 provides that the registra- **4.439** tion of a trade mark that contains or consists of a protected designation of origin or a GI which does not comply with the product specification con- cerned or the use of which falls under Art 103(2), and that relates to a product falling under one of the categories listed in Part II of Annex VII shall be:

(a) refused if the application for registration of the trade mark is submitted after the date of submission of the application for protection of the designation of origin or GI to the Commission and the designation of origin or GI is subsequently protected; or
(b) invalidated.

Article 102(2) provides that without prejudice to Art 101(2), a trade mark **4.440** referred to in para 1 of this Article which has been applied for, registered or established by use in good faith, if that possibility is provided for by the law concerned, in the territory of the EU either before the date of protection of the designation of origin or GI in the country of origin, or before 1 January 1996, may continue to be used and renewed notwithstanding the protection of a designation of origin or GI, provided that no grounds for the trade mark's invalidity or revocation exist under the EU Trade Marks Directive[93] or under the Community Marks Regulation.[94] In such cases, the use of the designation of origin or GI shall be permitted alongside the relevant trade marks.

15. Protection

4.441 Article 103(1) permits a protected designation of origin and a protected GI to be used by any operator marketing a wine which has been produced in conformity with the corresponding product specification.

4.442 Article 103(2) provides that a protected designation of origin and a protected GI, as well as the wine using that protected name in conformity with the product specifications, shall be protected against:

(a) any direct or indirect commercial use of that protected name:
  (i) by comparable products not complying with the product specification of the protected name; or
  (ii) in so far as such use exploits the reputation of a designation of origin or a GI;

(b) any misuse, imitation or evocation, even if the true origin of the product or service is indicated or if the protected name is translated, transcripted or transliterated or accompanied by an expression such as 'style', 'type', 'method', 'as produced in', 'imitation', 'flavour', 'like' or similar;

(c) any other false or misleading indication as to the provenance, origin, nature or essential qualities of the product, on the inner or outer packaging, advertising material or documents relating to the wine product concerned, as well as the packing of the product in a container liable to convey a false impression as to its origin;

(d) any other practice liable to mislead the consumer as to the true origin of the product.

4.443 Article 16 of the Implementing Regulation requires Member States to carry out checks based on a risk analysis to prevent or stop the unlawful use of protected designations of origin and protected GIs on products produced or marketed in their territories. Member States are required to take all necessary measures to address non-compliance, including administrative and judicial measures.

---

93   Directive 2008/95/EC of the European Parliament and of the Council of 22 October 2008 to approximate the laws of the Member States relating to trade marks, OJ L 299, 8.11.2008, p. 25.
94   Council Regulation (EC) No 207/2009 of 26 February 2009 on the Community trade mark, OJ L 78, 24.3.2009, p. 1.

Member States are required to designate the authorities responsible for taking **4.444** these measures in accordance with procedures determined by each individual Member State. The designated authorities shall offer adequate guarantees of objectivity and impartiality, and shall have at their disposal the qualified staff and resources needed to carry out their tasks.

16. Register

Article 104 requires the Commission to establish and maintain an electronic **4.445** register of protected designations of origin and protected GIs for wine which shall be publicly accessible. Designations of origin and geographical GIs pertaining to products of third countries[95] that are protected in the EU pursuant to an international agreement to which the Union is a contracting party may be entered in the register and unless specifically identified in that agreement as protected designations of origin within the meaning of this Regulation, such names shall be entered in the register as protected GIs.

Article 12(1) of the Implementing Regulation provides that upon the entry **4.446** into force of a decision conferring protection on the name of a designation of origin or GI, the Commission shall record the following data in the electronic register of protected designations of origin and protected GIs established in accordance with Art 104 of Regulation (EU) No 1308/2013:

(a) the name to be protected as a designation of origin or geographical indication;
(b) the file number;
(c) whether the name is protected as either a designation of origin or a GI;
(d) the name of the country or countries of origin;
(e) the date of registration;
(f) the electronic reference to the legal instrument protecting the name;
(g) the electronic reference to the single document;
(h) where the geographical area falls within the territory of Member States, the electronic reference to the publication of the product specification.

Where the Commission approves an amendment to a product specification or **4.447** receives a communication of an approved amendment to a product specification that entails a change to the information recorded in the register, Art 12(2) of the Implementing Regulation requires it to record the new data with effect from the entry into force of the decision approving the amendment.

---

95 Art 2(2) of the Delegated Regulation provides that the name of a designation of origin or a GI shall be registered in its original script. Where the original script is not in Latin characters, a transcription in Latin characters shall be registered together with the name in its original script.

4.448 When a cancellation takes effect, Art 12(3) requires the Commission to delete the name from the register and shall maintain a record of the cancellation.

4.449 Article 12(4) requires that all data present in the electronic database 'E-Bacchus' on the date of entry into force of this Regulation, shall be entered in the electronic register.

4.450 Article 12(5) requires that the register shall be accessible to the public.

17. Cancellation

4.451 Article 106 of Regulation (EU) No 1308/2013 permits the Commission on its own initiative or on a duly substantiated request by a Member State, a third country or a natural or legal person having a legitimate interest, adopt implementing acts cancelling the protection of a designation of origin or a GI if compliance with the corresponding product specification is no longer ensured.

4.452 Article 13 of the Implementing Regulation requires that a request to cancel the protection of a designation of origin or GI as referred to in Art 106 of Regulation (EU) No 1308/2013 shall contain:

    (a) the reference to the protected name to which it relates;
    (b) the name and contact details of the authority or natural or legal person seeking to cancel the protection;
    (c) a description of the legitimate interest of the natural or legal person seeking to cancel the protection, with the exclusion of national authorities having legal personality in the national legal order;
    (d) an indication of the grounds for cancellation;
    (e) the details of the facts, evidence and comments in support of the cancellation request.

It may be accompanied by supporting documents, where relevant.

4.453 A cancellation request shall be drawn up in accordance with the form set out in Annex VII.

4.454 Article 19 of the Delegated Regulation provides that requests to cancel a protected designation of origin or GI, as referred to in Art 106 shall follow the procedure laid down in Art 94 and Arts 96–99 of that Regulation together with provisions of ss 1, 2 and 4 of Chapter II of the Delegated Regulation and of ss 1, 2, 4 and 5 of Chapter II of Implementing Regulation (EU) No 2019/34 *mutatis mutandis*.

Article 19 of the Delegated Regulation requires the Commission to publish **4.455** the cancellation request referred to in Art 13 of the Implementing Regulation in the *Official Journal of the European Union,* C series.

Article 20 of the Delegated Regulation provides that for the purposes of Art **4.456** 106 of Regulation (EU) No 1308/2013 compliance with the product specification shall also be deemed not to be ensured where no product bearing the protected name has been placed on the market for at least seven consecutive years.

Article 21(1) of the Delegated Regulation provides that for the purpose of Art **4.457** 106 of Regulation (EU) No 1308/2013, a substantiated cancellation request shall be admissible where:

(a) the cancellation request complies with the requirements set out in Article 13(1) of Implementing Regulation (EU) 2019/34; and
(b) the cancellation request is based on the grounds referred to in Article 106 of Regulation (EU) No 1308/2013.

Where the Commission considers that the cancellation request is not admissible, Art 21(2) of the Delegated Regulation requires it to inform the Member **4.458** State or third-country authority or the natural or legal person that submitted the request of the reasons supporting the finding of inadmissibility.

Article 20(3) of the Delegated Regulation provides that substantiated state- **4.459** ments of objection to cancellation shall be admissible only where they show commercial reliance by an interested person on the registered name.

18. Existing protected wine names

Article 107(1) continues the protection of wine names referred to in Arts 51 **4.460** and 54 of Council Regulation (EC) No 1493/1999[96] and Art 28 of Commission Regulation (EC) No 753/2002.[97] Article 106(1) requires the Commission to list them in the register provided for in Art 104 of Regulation (EU) No 1308/2013.

---

96 Council Regulation (EC) No 1493/1999 of 17 May 1999 on the common organisation of the market in wine, OJ L 179, 14.7.1999, p. 1.

97 Commission Regulation (EC) No 753/2002 of 29 April 2002 laying down certain rules for applying Council Regulation (EC) No 1493/1999 as regards the description, designation, presentation and protection of certain wine sector products, OJ L 118, 4.5.2002, p. 1.

4.461 Article 107(3) provides that cancellation under Art 106 shall not apply to existing protected wine names referred to in Art 107(1), but that until 31 December 2014, the Commission could on its own initiative, adopt implementing acts cancelling the protection of existing protected wine names if they did not meet the conditions laid down in Art 93. Those implementing acts had to be adopted in accordance with the examination procedure referred to in Art 229(2) of Regulation (EU) No 1308/2013.

4.462 In relation to Croatia, Art 107(4) provided that the wine names published in the *Official Journal of the European Union* shall be protected under this Regulation, subject to a favourable outcome of the objection procedure. The Commission shall list them in the register provided for in Art 104.

19. Transitional national protection

4.463 Article 8(1) of the Delegated Regulation provides that a Member State may, on a transitional basis only, grant protection to a name at national level, with effect from the date upon which an application for protection has been forwarded to the Commission. Such transitional national protection shall cease on the date upon which either a decision on protection under Regulation (EU) No 1308/2013 is taken or the application is withdrawn. Where a name is not protected under this Regulation (EU) No 1308/2013 Art 8(2) of the Delegated Regulation provides that the consequences of such national protection shall be the sole responsibility of the Member State concerned and that the measures taken by Member States under Art 8(1) shall have no effect on intra-EU or international trade.

20. Temporary labelling and presentation

4.464 Article 22 of the Delegated Regulation provides that after an application for protection of a designation of origin or a geographical indication has been forwarded to the Commission, producers may indicate it in labelling and presentation, and use national logos and indications, in compliance with EU law and in particular Regulation (EU) No 1169/2011.[98]

4.465 Union symbols indicating the protected designation of origin or the protected GI, the EU indications 'protected designation of origin' or 'protected GI' and the Union abbreviations 'PDO' or 'PGI' may appear on the labelling only after the publication of the decision conferring protection on that designation of

---

[98] Regulation (EU) No 1169/2011 of the European Parliament and of the Council of 25 October 2011 on the provision of food information to consumers, OJ L 304, 22.11.2011, pp. 18–63.

origin or GI. Where the application is rejected, any grapevine products may be marketed until the stocks are exhausted.

Article 23 of the Delegated Regulation provides that in accordance with Art **4.466** 119(3) of Regulation (EU) No 1308/2013, references to the terms 'protected designation of origin' may be omitted for wines bearing the following protected designations of origin:

(a) Greece: Σάμος (Samos);
(b) Spain: Cava, Jerez, Xérès or Sherry, Manzanilla;
(c) France: Champagne;
(d) Italy: Asti, Marsala, Franciacorta;
(e) Cyprus: Κουμανδαρία (Commandaria);
(f) Portugal: Madeira or Madère, Port or Porto.

21. Restrictions on use of protected designations of origin and protected GIs

Article 13(1) of the Delegated Regulation provides that without prejudice to **4.467** Art 102 of Regulation (EU) No 1308/2013, the Commission may adopt implementing acts granting a transitional period of up to five years to enable products originating in a Member State or a third country, the designation of which consists of or contains a name that contravenes Art 103(2) of Regulation (EU) No 1308/2013, to continue to use the designation under which they were marketed. The granting of such transitional period is conditional upon the submission of an admissible statement of objection under Art 96(3) or Art 98 of Regulation (EU) No 1308/2013 showing that the decision conferring protection over the name would jeopardise the existence:

(a) of an entirely identical name or of a compound name, one term of which is identical to the name to be registered; or
(b) of partially homonymous names or of other names similar to the name to be registered which refer to grapevine products which have been legally on the market for at least five years preceding the date of the publication provided for in Article 97(3) of Regulation (EU) No 1308/2013.

Article 13(2) of the Delegated Regulation provides that the Commission may **4.468** adopt implementing acts extending the transitional period up to 15 years in duly justified cases where it is shown that:

(a) the designation has been in legal use consistently and fairly for at least 25 years before the application for protection was submitted to the Commission;
(b) the purpose of using the designation referred to in paragraph 1 has not, at any time, been to profit from the reputation of the registered name and it is shown

that the consumer has not been nor could have been misled as to the true origin of the product.

4.469 When using a designation referred to in Art 13(1) or (2), Art 13(3) provides that the indication of the country of origin shall clearly and visibly appear on the labelling. Article 13(4) provides that to overcome temporary difficulties, with the long-term objective of ensuring that all producers in the area concerned comply with the product specification, a Member State may grant protection for a transitional period, starting from the date on which the application is forwarded to the Commission, on condition that the operators concerned have legally marketed the grapevine products in question using the names concerned continuously for at least the five years prior to the lodging of the application to the authorities of the Member State and that these temporary difficulties had been raised in the national objection procedure referred to in Art 96(3) of Regulation (EU) No 1308/2013. The transitional period shall be as short as possible and shall not exceed ten years.

4.470 Article 13(1) shall apply *mutatis mutandis* to a protected GI or protected designation of origin referring to a geographical area situated in a third country, with the exception of the objection procedure.

22. Use of the Union symbol

4.471 Article 14 of the Implementing Regulation provides that the Union symbol indicating the protected designation of origin or the protected GI, referred to in Art 120(1)(e) of Regulation (EU) No 308/2013, shall be reproduced as laid down in Annex X to Implementing Regulation (EU) No 668/2014.

23. Traditional terms

(a) Scope of protection

4.472 Article 113(1) provides that a protected traditional term may only be used for a product which has been produced in conformity with the definition provided for in Art 112 and that traditional terms shall be protected against unlawful use.

4.473 Article 113(2) of Regulation (EU) No 1308/2013 provides that traditional terms shall be protected, only in the language and for the categories of grapevine products claimed in the application, against:

(a) any misuse of the protected term, including where it is accompanied by an expression such as 'style', 'type', 'method', 'as produced in', 'imitation', 'flavour', 'like' or similar;

(b) any other false or misleading indication as to the nature, characteristics or essential qualities of the product, placed on the inner or outer packaging, advertising material or documents relating to it;

(c) any other practice likely to mislead the consumer, in particular to give the impression that the wine qualifies for the protected traditional term.

Article 113(3) provides that traditional terms shall not become generic in the EU. **4.474**

(b) Definitions

Article 112(1) defines a 'traditional term' as a term traditionally used in Member States for the products referred to in Art 92(1) to designate: **4.475**

(a) that the product has a protected designation of origin or a protected GI under EU or national law; or

(b) the production or ageing method or the quality, colour, type of place, or a particular event linked to the history of the product with a protected designation of origin or a protected GI.

(c) Language and spelling of the traditional term

Article 24(1) of the Delegated Regulation provides that a traditional term shall be registered: **4.476**

(a) in the official language or regional language of the Member State or third country from which the term originates; or

(b) in the language used in trade for this term.

Article 24(2) provides that a traditional term shall be registered with its original spelling and in its original script. Where the original script is not in Latin characters, a transcription in Latin characters shall be registered together with the name in its original script. **4.477**

(d) Applicants

Article 25(1) of the Delegated Regulation permits competent authorities of the Member States or third countries or representative professional organisations established in third countries to apply for the protection of a traditional term. **4.478**

'Representative professional organisation' is defined in Art 25(2) as any producer organisation or association of producer organisations having adopted **4.479** the same rules, operating in the area of one or more wine designations of origin or GIs where it includes in its membership at least two-thirds of the producers established in the area in which it operates and accounts for at least two-thirds of the production of that area.

4.480 A representative professional organisation may, pursuant to Art 25(2), lodge an application for protection only for grapevine products which it produces.

(e) Applications

4.481 Article 21(1) of the Implementing Regulation provides that the application for protection of a traditional term shall be communicated to the Commission by the competent authorities of the Member States or those of the third countries or by the representative professional organisations established in third countries in accordance with Art 30(3).

4.482 In the case of a request submitted by a representative professional organisation established in a third country, Art 21(2) requires the applicant to communicate the information regarding the representative professional organisation and its members to the Commission in accordance with Art 30(3). The Commission shall make this information public.

(f) Admissibility of the application

4.483 Article 26(1) of the Delegated Regulation provides that applications for protection are considered admissible where they are submitted in compliance with Art 25 of this Regulation and Art 30(1) and 30(3) of the Implementing Regulation and are duly completed. An application is considered to be duly completed, under this provision, where it contains the following information:

(a) the name to be protected as a traditional term;
(b) the type of traditional term, whether it falls under Article 12(a) or (b) of Regulation (EU) No 1308/2013;
(c) the language in which the name to be protected as a traditional term is expressed;
(d) the grapevine product category or categories concerned;
(e) a summary of the definition and conditions of use;
(f) the protected designations of origin or protected geographical indications concerned.

4.484 Article 26(2) requires the application to be accompanied by a copy of the legislation of the Member State concerned or rules applicable to wine producers in the third country or countries concerned, governing the use of the term in question, and a reference to the publication of that legislation or those rules. If these documents are not provided Art 26(3) provides that the application shall be inadmissible.

Article 26(4) provides that in a case of inadmissibility the authorities of the **4.485** Member State or those of the third country or the applicant established in the third country in question shall be informed of the reasons for its inadmissibility and that they are entitled to submit another application duly completed.

(g) Conditions of validity

Article 27(1) of the Delegated Regulation deems an application for the **4.486** protection of a traditional term valid if the name for which the protection is sought:

(a) fulfils the requirements of a traditional term as defined in Article 112 of Regulation (EU) No 1308/2013 as well as the requirements laid down in Article 24 of this Regulation;

(b) consists exclusively of either:

    (i) a name traditionally used in trade in a large part of the territory of the Union or of the third country in question, to distinguish specific categories of grapevine products referred to in Article 92(1) of Regulation (EU) No 1308/2013; or

    (ii) a reputed name traditionally used in trade in at least the territory of the Member State or third country in question, to distinguish specific categories of grapevine products referred to in Article 92(1) of Regulation (EU) No 1308/2013. This shall not apply to traditional terms referred to in Article 112(a) of Regulation (EU) No 1308/2013;

(c) has not become generic;[99] and

(d) is defined and regulated in the Member State's legislation or subject to conditions of use as provided for by rules applicable to wine producers in the third country in question, including those emanating from representative professional organisations.

Article 27(2) of the Delegated Regulation provides that for the purposes of **4.487** Art 27(2)(1)(b), traditional use means:

(a) use amounting to a period of at least five years in case of terms filed in the official language or regional language of the Member State or third country where the term originates;

(b) use amounting to a period of at least 15 years in case of terms filed in the language used for trade.

---

99 Art 27(3) provides that a name that has become 'generic' means the name which, although it relates to a specific production method or ageing method, or the quality, colour, type of place, or a particular event linked to the history of a grapevine product, has become the common name of that product in the EU.

(h) Scrutiny by the Commission

4.488 Article 28(1) of the Delegated Regulation provides that the date of submission of an application for protection of a traditional term shall be the date on which the application is received by the Commission.

4.489 Article 28(2) requires the Commission to examine whether the application for protection meets the conditions laid down in this Chapter and where the Commission considers that the conditions laid down in Arts 26 and 27 are met, Art 28(3) requires it to adopt an implementing act concerning the publication, in the *Official Journal of the European Union*, of the application for protection.

4.490 If an application for the protection of a traditional term does not meet the conditions laid down in this Chapter, Art 28(4) requires the Commission to inform the applicant of the grounds for refusal, setting a deadline for the withdrawal or modification of the application or for the submission of comments. If the obstacles are not remedied by the applicant within the deadline, the Commission shall adopt an implementing act rejecting the application in accordance with Art 115(2) of Regulation (EU) No 1308/2013.

(i) Objection procedure

4.491 Article 29 of the Delegated Regulation provides that the date of submission of an objection shall be the date on which the objection is received by the Commission.

i. Submission of objection

4.492 Article 22(1) of the Implementing Regulation provides that a Member State, third country, or any natural or legal person having a legitimate interest may submit an objection to the application for protection of a traditional term within two months of the date of publication, in the *Official Journal of the European Union*, of the implementing act referred to in Art 28(3) of the Delegated Regulation.

ii. Documents supporting an objection

4.493 Article 23(1) of the Implementing Regulation provides that a duly substantiated objection shall contain details of the facts, evidence and comments submitted in support of the objection, accompanied by the relevant supporting documents. If the objection is based on the existence of an earlier trade mark of reputation and renown, Art 23(2) provides that the objection shall be accompanied by:

(a) proof of the filing or the registration of the earlier trade mark or proof of its use; and

(b) proof of its reputation and renown.

The information and evidence to be produced in support of the use of an **4.494** earlier trade mark shall comprise particulars of the location, duration, extent and nature of the use made of the earlier trade mark, and of its reputation and renown.

If the details of the prior right(s) claimed, ground(s), facts, evidence or **4.495** comments, or the supporting documents, referred to in paras 1 and 2, have not been produced at the date of submission of the objection or if details or documents are missing, Art 23(3) requires the Commission to inform the authority or person that lodged the objection accordingly and shall invite them to remedy the deficiencies noted within a period of two months. If the deficiencies are not remedied before the time limit expires, the Commission shall reject the objection as inadmissible. The decision to reject the objection as inadmissible shall be notified to the authority or person that lodged the objection and to the Member State or the third-country authorities or the representative professional organisation established in the third country in question.

iii. Admissibility and grounds of objection

Article 30(1) provides that a substantiated objection shall be admissible where: **4.496**

(a) it is submitted by any Member State or third country, or any natural or legal person having a legitimate interest;

(b) it is received by the Commission within the deadline provided for in Article 22(1) of Implementing Regulation (EU) 2019/34;

(c) it demonstrates that the application for protection is incompatible with the rules on traditional terms because it does not comply with Article 27 of this Regulation or because the registration of the name proposed would conflict with Article 32 or 33 of this Regulation.

Article 30(2) requires an objection that is deemed admissible to be notified to **4.497** the Member State or the third-country authorities or the representative professional organisation in the third country in question.

iv. Scrutiny of an objection

Where the Commission does not reject the objection in accordance with Art **4.498** 23(3) of the Implementing Regulation, Art 31(1) of the Delegated Regulation requires it to communicate the objection to the applicant that submitted the application and shall invite the applicant to file observations within the time period referred to in Art 24(1) of the Implementing Regulation. Any observations received within this period shall be communicated to the objector.

4.499   In the course of its scrutiny of an objection, Art 31(1) requires the Commission to request the parties to provide comments, if appropriate, within the time period referred to in Art 24(2) of the Implementing Regulation, on the communications received from the other parties. Where the applicant or the objector do not file any observations in response, or where the time periods for filing observations and for submitting comments referred to in Art 24 of the Implementing Regulation are not respected, Art 31(2) of the Delegated Regulation permits the Commission to proceed to rule on the objection.

4.500   Article 31(3) provides that a decision to reject or recognise the traditional term in question shall be taken by the Commission on the basis of the evidence available to it and the Commission shall consider whether the conditions referred to or laid down in Art 27, 32 or 33 of this Regulation are fulfilled. A decision to reject the traditional term shall be notified to the objector and to the applicant.

4.501   Where multiple objections are lodged, Art 31(4) provides that a preliminary examination of one or more such objections may prevent an application for protection from proceeding. In these circumstances, the Commission may suspend the other objection procedures. The Commission shall inform the other objectors of any decision affecting them which was taken in the course of the procedure. Where an application is rejected, objection procedures which have been suspended shall be deemed to be closed and the objectors concerned shall be duly informed.

v.   Submission of observations by the parties

4.502   Where the Commission communicates an objection which is not rejected in accordance with Art 23(3) to the applicant that submitted the application for protection, Art 24 requires the applicant to file observations within a period of two months from the issuance date of such communication.

4.503   Where so requested by the Commission in the course of its scrutiny of an objection, the parties shall provide comments on the communications received from the other parties, if appropriate, within a period of two months from the issuance date of such request.

(j)   Relationship with trade marks

4.504   Article 32(1) of the Delegated Regulation provides that the registration of a trade mark that contains or consists of a traditional term which does not respect the definition and conditions of use of that traditional term as referred to in Art 112 of Regulation (EU) No 1308/2013, and that relates to a product falling under one of the categories listed in Part II of Annex VII thereto shall be:

(a) refused if the application for registration of the trade mark is submitted after the date of submission of the application for protection of the traditional term to the Commission and the traditional term is subsequently protected; or

(b) invalidated.

Article 32(2) provides that a name shall not be protected as a traditional term **4.505** where, in the light of a trade mark's reputation and renown, such protection is liable to mislead the consumer as to the true identity, nature, characteristic or quality of the grapevine product.

Article 32(3) provides that without prejudice to Art 32(2), a trade mark **4.506** referred to in para 1 which has been applied for, registered or established by use in good faith, where national legislation so provides, in the territory of the Union, prior to the date of protection of the traditional term in the country of origin, may continue to be used and renewed notwithstanding the protection of a traditional term, provided that no grounds for the trade mark's invalidity or revocation exist under Directive 2008/95/EC of the European Parliament and of the Council,[100] Directive (EU) 2015/2436 of the European Parliament and of the Council[101] or under Regulation (EU) No 2017/1001 of the European Parliament and of the Council.[102] In such cases, the use of the traditional term shall be permitted alongside the relevant trade marks.

i. Homonyms

Article 33(1) of the Delegated Regulation provides that a term for which an **4.507** application for protection is submitted and which is wholly or partially homonymous with a traditional term already protected under Art 113 of Regulation (EU) No 1308/2013 shall be registered with due regard to local and traditional usage and the risk of confusion. However, a homonymous term which misleads consumers as to the nature, quality or the true origin of the grapevine products shall not be registered even if the term is accurate.

---

100 Directive 2008/95/EC of the European Parliament and of the Council of 22 October 2008 to approximate the laws of the Member States relating to trade marks, OJ L 99, 8.11.2008, p. 25.

101 Directive (EU) 2015/2436 of the European Parliament and of the Council of 16 December 2015 to approximate the laws of the Member States relating to trade marks (Recast), OJ L 336, 23.12.2015, p. 1.

102 Regulation (EU) 2017/1001 of the European Parliament and of the Council of 14 June 2017 on the European Union trade mark, OJ L 54, 16.6.2017, p. 1.

4.508   Article 33(1) provides that a registered homonymous term may be used only if there is a sufficient distinction in practice between the homonym registered subsequently and the term already in the register, having regard to the need to treat the producers concerned in an equitable manner and the need to avoid misleading the consumer. Article 33(2) provides that paragraph 1 shall apply *mutatis mutandis* for traditional terms protected before 1 August 2009 which are wholly or partially homonymous with a protected designation of origin or geographical indication or a wine grape variety name or its synonym listed in Annex IV.

(k)   Modification of a traditional term

4.509   Article 34 of the Delegated Regulation provides that an applicant satisfying the conditions of Art 25 may apply for approval of a modification of a registered traditional term concerning the elements referred to in Art 26(1)(b), (c) and (d). Articles 26–31 shall apply *mutatis mutandis* to applications for modification.

(l)   Cancellation

4.510   Under Art 115(2) of Regulation (EU) No 1308/2013, the Commission may, on a duly substantiated request by a Member State, a third country or a natural or legal person having a legitimate interest, adopt implementing acts cancelling the protection of a traditional term.

i.   Grounds for cancellation

4.511   The grounds for cancellation are set out in Art 36 of the Delegated Regulation. It provides that protection of a traditional term shall be cancelled where: that term no longer meets the requirements of Art 27, 32 or 33, or where compliance with the corresponding definition and conditions of use is no longer ensured.

ii.   Cancellation request

4.512   Article 28(1) of the Implementing Regulation provides that a request to cancel the protection of a traditional term shall contain:

(a)   the reference to the traditional term it refers to;
(b)   the name and contact details of the natural or legal person seeking cancellation;
(c)   a description of the legitimate interest of the natural or legal person that lodged the cancelation request;
(d)   an indication of the grounds for cancellation, referred to in Article 36 of Delegated Regulation (EU) 2019/33;

(e) the details of the facts, evidence and comments in support of the cancellation request.

It may be accompanied by supporting documents, where relevant. However, if **4.513** detailed information concerning the grounds, facts, evidence and comments, as well as the supporting documents have not been furnished at the same time as the cancellation request, Art 28(2) requires the Commission to inform the author of the cancellation request accordingly and shall invite him to remedy the deficiencies noted within a period of two months. If the deficiencies are not remedied before the time limit expires, the Commission shall deem the cancellation request inadmissible and shall reject it. The decision deeming the request inadmissible shall be notified to the author of the cancellation request.

iii. Admissibility of a cancellation request

Article 37(1)of the Delegated Regulation provides that a substantiated cancel- **4.514** lation request shall be admissible where:

(a) it was submitted to the Commission by a Member State, a third country or a natural or legal person having a legitimate interest; and
(b) it is based on one of the grounds referred to in Article 36.

The duly substantiated cancellation request shall be admissible only if it demonstrates the legitimate interest of the applicant.

Where the Commission considers that the cancellation request is not admis- **4.515** sible, Art 37(2) requires it to inform the authority or person that sent the request of the reasons for inadmissibility.

Article 37(3) requires the Commission to make the cancellation request **4.516** available to the authorities and persons affected in accordance with Art 30(4) of the Implementing Regulation.

Article 37(4) provides that substantiated statements of objection to cancel- **4.517** lation requests shall be admissible only if they show continued commercial reliance on the registered name by an interested person.

iv. Scrutiny of a cancellation request

Article 29(1) of the Implementing Regulation provides that if the Commis- **4.518** sion does not deem the cancellation request to be inadmissible in accordance with Art 28(2), it shall communicate the cancellation request to the Member State or the third-country authorities or the applicant established in the third country in question and shall invite him to file observations within two months from the issuance date of such invitation. Any observations received within this two-month period shall be communicated to the author of the request.

4.519 In the course of the examination of a cancellation request, the Commission shall invite the parties to submit comments on the communications received from the other parties within a period of two months from the issuance date of such request.

4.520 If the Member State or the third-country authorities or the applicant established in the third country in question or the author of a cancellation request does not file any comments in response, or does not respect the time periods, Art 29(2) requires the Commission to rule on the request.

4.521 Article 29(3) provides that a decision to cancel the protection of the traditional term concerned shall be taken by the Commission on the basis of the evidence available to it. It shall consider whether the grounds referred to in Art 36 of the Delegated Regulation are fulfilled. The decision to cancel the protection of the traditional term shall be notified to the author of the cancellation request and to the Member State or the third-country authorities in question.

4.522 Article 29(4) provides that where multiple cancellation requests are lodged in respect of a traditional term and where it can be concluded from a preliminary examination of one or more such requests that it is no longer possible to continue to protect a traditional term, the Commission may suspend the other cancellation procedures. The Commission shall notify the parties that submitted the other cancellation requests of any decision affecting them which was taken in the course of the procedure.

4.523 Where a decision cancelling a traditional term is adopted, cancellation procedures which have been suspended shall be deemed to be closed and the authors of the cancellation requests in question shall be duly informed.

4.524 Article 29(5) provides that when a decision cancelling a traditional term takes effect, the Commission shall remove the name from the register, while maintaining a record of the cancellation.

(m) Traditional terms in third countries

4.525 Article 38(1) of the Delegated Regulation provides that the definition of traditional terms provided for in Art 112 of Regulation (EU) No 1308/2013 shall apply *mutatis mutandis* to terms traditionally used in third countries for grapevine products covered by GIs or designations of origin under the legislation of those third countries.

Article 38(2) of Regulation provides that grapevine products originating in **4.526** third countries whose labels bear traditional indications other than the traditional terms listed in the electronic database 'E-Bacchus', may use these traditional indications on wine labels in accordance with the rules applicable in the third countries concerned, including those emanating from representative professional organisations.

(n) Existing protected traditional terms

Article 39 of the Delegated Regulation provides that a traditional term which **4.527** is protected under Regulation (EC) No 607/2009 shall automatically be protected under this Regulation.

(o) Registration

Article 25(1) of the Implementing Regulation provides that up to the entry **4.528** into force of a decision conferring protection over a traditional term, the Commission shall record the following data in the electronic register of protected traditional terms:

(a) the name to be protected as a traditional term;
(b) the type of traditional term according to Article 112 of Regulation (EU) No 1308/2013;
(c) the language referred to in Article 24 of the Delegated Regulation;
(d) the grapevine product category or categories concerned by the protection;
(e) a reference to the national legislation of the Member State or third country in which the traditional term is defined and regulated, or to the rules applicable to wine producers in the third country, including those originating from representative trade organisations, in the absence of national legislation in those third countries;
(f) a summary of the definition or conditions of use;
(g) the name of the country or countries of origin;
(h) the date of inclusion in the register.

Article 25(2) provides that the electronic register of protected traditional terms **4.529** shall be made available to the public.

i. Enforcement of the protection

Article 26 of the Implementing Regulation provides that for the purposes of the **4.530** application of Art 113 of Regulation (EU) No 1308/2013, where there is unlawful use of protected traditional terms, competent national authorities, on their own initiative or at the request of a party, shall take all measures to prevent or stop the marketing, including any export, of the products in question.

U. CASE LAW

4.531 *Comité Interprofessionnel du Vin de Champagne v Aldi Süd Dienstleistungs-GmbH & Co and Galana NV*[103] concerned the use of the protected designation of origin (PDO) 'Champagne' in the name of a frozen product manufactured by Galena and distributed by Aldi under the name 'Champagner Sorbet' and contained, among its ingredients, 12 per cent champagne. The CIVC, an association of champagne producers, brought proceedings before the Landgericht München I (Regional Court, Munich I, Germany) in order to obtain an injunction, on the basis of Art 118m of Regulation 1234/2007 and Art 103 of Regulation 1308/2013, prohibiting Aldi from using that name on the frozen goods market. The decision of that court, which granted the application, was reversed on appeal by decision of the Oberlandesgericht München (Higher Regional Court, Munich, Germany), which dismissed the application.

4.532 The CIVC then lodged an appeal to the Bundesgerichtshof (Federal Court of Justice, which referred the following questions to the CJEU for a preliminary ruling:

> (1) Are Article 118m(2)(a)(ii) of Regulation No 234/2007 and Article 103(2)(a)(ii) of Regulation No 1308/2013 to be interpreted as meaning that the scope of those provision also covers a case in which a [PDO] is used as part of the name of a foodstuff which does not correspond to the product specifications but to which an ingredient has been added which does correspond to the product specifications?

> (2) If the first question is answered in the affirmative: Are Article 118m(2)(a)(ii) of Regulation No 1234/2007 and Article 103(2)(a)(ii) of Regulation No 1308/2013 to be interpreted as meaning that the use of a [PDO] as part of the name of a foodstuff which does not correspond to the product specifications but to which an ingredient has been added which does correspond to the product specifications constitutes exploitation of the reputation of the designation of origin where the name of the foodstuff corresponds to the name usually used by the relevant public to refer to that foodstuff and the ingredient has been added in a quantity which is sufficient to give the product one of its essential characteristics?

> (3) Are Article 118m(2)(b) of Regulation No 1234/2007 and Article 103(2)(b) of Regulation No 1308/2013 to be interpreted as meaning that the use of a [PDO] in the circumstances set out in Question 2 constitutes unlawful misuse, imitation or evocation?

---

103   Case C-393/16, Judgment, 20 December 2017.

(4) Are Article 118m(2)(c) of Regulation No 1234/2007 and Article 103(2)(c) of Regulation No 1308/2013 to be interpreted as meaning that they are applicable only to false or misleading indications which, for the relevant public, are liable to convey a false impression as to a product's geographical origin?

In answer to the first question the CJEU concluded that Art 118m(2)(a)(ii) of **4.533** Regulation No 1234/2007 and Art 103(2)(a)(ii) of Regulation No 1308/2013 were applicable to the commercial use of a PDO, such as 'Champagne', as part of the name of a foodstuff, such as 'Champagner Sorbet', containing an ingredient which corresponds to the product specifications of the PDO.[104]

In relation to the second question, the CJEU note the observation by the **4.534** referring court, that the use of the name 'Champagner Sorbet' to refer to a sorbet containing champagne is likely to extend to that product the reputation of the PDO 'Champagne', which conveys an image of luxury and prestige, and therefore to take advantage of that reputation. However, in order to determine whether it undermines the protection afforded by Art 118m(2)(a)(ii) of Regulation No 1234/2007 and Art 103(2)(a)(ii) of Regulation No 1308/2013, it was necessary to examine whether such use constituted a means of taking unfair advantage of the reputation of that PDO.

The CJEU observed that the use of a PDO as part of the name under which is **4.535** sold a foodstuff that does not correspond to the product specifications for that PDO but contains an ingredient which does correspond to those specifications cannot be regarded, in itself, as an unfair use, but it was for the national courts to determine, in the light of the particular circumstances of each individual case, whether such use was intended to take unfair advantage of the reputation of a PDO.[105]

In response to the argument that 'Champagner Sorbet' was the name com- **4.536** monly used by the relevant public to refer to that foodstuff the CJEU said that this would be tantamount to accepting that that PDO may be used generically and would therefore be at odds with the GIs legislation.[106]

The Court took the view that the use of a PDO as part of the name under **4.537** which is sold a foodstuff that does not correspond to the product specifications for that PDO but contains an ingredient which does correspond to those specifications is intended to take unfair advantage of the reputation of the

---

104   Ibid., at para 35.
105   Ibid., at para 46.
106   Ibid., at para 48.

PDO if that ingredient does not confer on that foodstuff one of its essential characteristics.[107]

4.538 The answer to the second question was that the statutory provisions mentioned in that question were to be interpreted as meaning that the use of a PDO as part of the name under which is sold a foodstuff that does not correspond to the product specifications for that PDO but contains an ingredient that does correspond to those specifications, such as 'Champagner Sorbet', constitutes exploitation of the reputation of a PDO, within the meaning of those provisions, if that foodstuff does not have, as one of its essential characteristics, a taste attributable primarily to the presence of that ingredient in the composition of the foodstuff.[108]

4.539 In considering the third question, the CJEU observed that the use of a PDO in the name of a foodstuff does not appear such as to constitute misuse, imitation or evocation within the meaning of Art 118m(2)(b) of Regulation No 1234/2007 and Art 103(2)(b) of Regulation No 1308/2013. 'By incorporating in the name of the foodstuff in question the name of the ingredient protected by a PDO, direct use is made of the PDO to claim openly a gustatory quality connected with it, which does not amount to misuse, imitation or evocation.'[109] Applying *Viiniverla*[110] the CJEU ruled that the incorporation of the name of the PDO in its entirety in that of the foodstuff concerned to indicate the taste of the foodstuff did not amount to an 'evocation' and did not constitute misuse, imitation or evocation within the meaning of those provisions.[111]

4.540 The answer to the fourth question was that Art 118m(2)(c) of Regulation No 234/2007 and Art 103(2)(c) of Regulation No 1308/2013 are to be interpreted as being applicable both to false or misleading indications which are liable to create a false impression as to the geographical origin of the product concerned and to false or misleading indications relating to the nature or essential qualities of the product.[112]

107 Ibid., at para 50.
108 Ibid., at para 53.
109 Ibid., at para 57.
110 C-75/15, EU:C:2016:35, para 21.
111 Case C-393/16, Judgment, 20 December 2017, para 59.
112 Ibid., at para 64.

PROTECTION OF GEOGRAPHICAL INDICATIONS AND DESIGNATIONS OF ORIGIN FOR SPIRITS IN EUROPE

A. INTRODUCTION

5.01 Council Regulation (EEC) No 1576/89 of 29 May 1989 laying down general rules on the definition, description and presentation of spirit drinks[1] and Commission Regulation (EEC) No 1014/90 of 24 April 1990 laying down detailed implementing rules on the definition, description and presentation of spirit drinks[2] have proved successful in regulating the spirit drinks sector. However, in order to clarify the rules applicable to the definition, description, presentation and labelling of spirit drinks as well as on the protection of geographical indications of certain spirit drinks, while taking into account traditional production methods, Regulation (EEC) No 1576/89 was repealed and replaced by Regulation (EC) No 110/2008 of 15 January 2008 of the European Parliament and of the Council of 15 January 2008 on the definition, description, presentation, labelling and the protection of geographical indications of spirit drinks (hereinafter 'the Spirits Regulation').[3] This came into effect from 20 May 2008.[4] Recital (4) to Regulation (EC) No 110/2008 explained that to ensure a more systematic approach in the legislation governing spirit drinks, 'this Regulation should set out clearly defined criteria for the production, description, presentation and labelling of spirit drinks as well as on the protection of geographical indications'.

5.02 In order to clarify certain provisions of Regulation (EC) No 110/2008 and to ensure their uniform implementation in the Member States, detailed rules were promulgated in Commission Implementing Regulation (EU) No 716/2013 of 25 July 2013[5] dealing in particular with the use of compound terms, allusions, sales denominations and GIs for the presentation of spirit drinks and the application, objection and cancellation procedure. Article 23 of Commission Implementing Regulation (EU) No 716/2013 provides that it shall apply from 1 September 2013, but that Arts 3 and 4 shall apply from 1 March 2015.

5.03 On 13 March 2019, the European Parliament adopted at first reading the terms of a new regulation repealing Regulation (EC) No 110/2008 covering 'the definition, description, presentation and labelling of spirit drinks, the use

---

1 OJ C 324, 30.12.2006, p. 12.
2 OJ L 105, 25.4.1990, p. 9. Regulation as last amended by Regulation (EC) No 2140/98, OJ L 270, 7.10.1998, p. 9.
3 Recital (1) of Regulation (EC) No 110/2008 and repealing Council Regulation (EEC) No 1576/89, OJ L 39/16, 13.2.2008.
4 Ibid., Art 30.
5 Commission Implementing Regulation (EU) No 716/2013 of 25 July 2013 laying down rules for the application of Regulation (EC) No 110/2008 of the European Parliament and of the Council on the definition, description, presentation, labelling and the protection of geographical indications of spirit drinks, OJ L 201/21, 26.7.2013, pp. 21–30.

of the names of spirit drinks in the presentation and labelling of other foodstuffs, the protection of geographical indications for spirit drinks, the use of ethyl alcohol and distillates of agricultural origin in alcoholic beverages'. This is discussed in section E below.

B. SUBJECT MATTER AND SCOPE OF REGULATION (EC) NO 110/2008

1. Includes geographical indications

Article 1(1) provides that the Spirits Regulation lays down rules on the **5.04** definition, description, presentation and labelling of spirit drinks as well as on the protection of GIs of spirit drinks.

2. EU connection

Article 1(2) provides that the Spirits Regulation shall apply to all spirit drinks **5.05** placed on the market in the Community whether produced in the Community or in third countries, as well as to those produced in the Community for export. It also applies to the use of ethyl alcohol and/or distillates of agricultural origin in the production of alcoholic beverages and to the use of the names of spirit drinks in the presentation and labelling of foodstuffs.

3. Derogation for third countries

Article 1(3) provides that in exceptional cases where the law of the importing **5.06** third country so requires, a derogation may be granted from the provisions of Annexes I and II in accordance with the regulatory procedure with scrutiny referred to in Art 25(3).

4. Definition of spirit drink

Article 2(1) provides that for the purpose of the Spirits Regulation 'spirit **5.07** drink' means an alcoholic beverage:

    (a)   intended for human consumption;
    (b)   possessing particular organoleptic qualities;
    (c)   having a minimum alcoholic strength of 15 per cent vol;
    (d)   having been produced:
        (i)   either directly:
            •   by the distillation, with or without added flavourings, of naturally fermented products, and/or

- by the maceration or similar processing of plant materials in ethyl alcohol of agricultural origin and/or distillates of agricultural origin, and/or spirit drinks within the meaning of this Regulation, and/or
- by the addition of flavourings, sugars or other sweetening products listed in Annex I(3) and/or other agricultural products and/or food-stuffs to ethyl alcohol of agricultural origin and/or to distillates of agricultural origin and/or to spirit drinks, within the meaning of this Regulation,

(ii) or by the mixture of a spirit drink with one or more:
- other spirit drinks, and/or
- ethyl alcohol of agricultural origin or distillates of agricultural origin, and/or
- other alcoholic beverages, and/or
- drinks.

Excluded from the Spirits Regulation by Art 2(2) are drinks falling within CN codes 2203, 2204, 2205, 2206 and 2207.

5.08 Article 2(3) provides that the minimum alcoholic strength provided for in paragraph 1(c) shall be without prejudice to the definition for the product in category 41 in Annex II.

5.09 Article 2(4) states that for the purpose of the Spirits Regulation the technical definitions and requirements are laid down in Annex I.

5.10 The ECJ in Joined Cases C-4/10 and C-27/10 *Bureau national interprofession-nel du Cognac, v Gust. Ranin Oy*[6] held that 'spirit drinks' covers drinks 'which have common objective characteristics and which are consumed, from the point of view of the relevant public, on occasions which are largely identical' and 'they are frequently distributed through the same channels and subject to similar marketing rules'.[7]

5. Origin of ethyl alcohol

5.11 Article 3(1) provides that the ethyl alcohol used in the production of spirit drinks and all of their components shall not be of any origin other than agricultural, within the meaning of Annex I to the Treaty.

---

6   [2011] ETMR 53.
7   Ibid.

Recital (8) to the Spirits Regulation explains that this requirement is to meet **5.12** consumer expectations and conform to traditional practices and ensure an outlet for basic agricultural products.

Article 3(2) provides that the ethyl alcohol used in the production of spirit **5.13** drinks shall comply with the definition provided for in Annex I(1) to the Spirits Regulation.[8]

Article 3(3) provides that the ethyl alcohol used to dilute or dissolve colorants, **5.14** flavourings or any other authorised additives used in the preparation of spirit drinks shall be ethyl alcohol of agricultural origin.

Article 3(4) provides that alcoholic beverages shall not contain alcohol of **5.15** synthetic origin, nor other alcohol of non-agricultural origin within the meaning of Annex I to the Treaty.

6. Categories of spirit drinks

Article 4 provides that spirit drinks shall be classified into categories according **5.16** to the definitions laid down in Annex II to the Spirits Regulation.

7. General rules concerning the categories of spirit drinks

Article 5(1) of the Spirits Regulation provides that without prejudice to the **5.17** specific rules laid down for each of the categories numbered 1 to 14 in Annex II,[9] the spirit drinks defined therein shall:

---

8 Annex I(1) provides:

Ethyl alcohol of agricultural origin possesses the following properties:

(a) organoleptic characteristics: no detectable taste other than that of the raw material;
(b) minimum alcoholic strength by volume: 96.0%;
(c) maximum level of residues:
  (i) total acidity, expressed in grams of acetic acid per hectolitre of 100% vol. alcohol: 1,5,
  (ii) esters expressed in grams of ethyl acetate per hectolitre of 100% vol. alcohol: 1,3,
  (iii) aldehydes expressed in grams of acetaldehyde per hectolitre of 100% vol. alcohol: 0,5,
  (iv) higher alcohols expressed in grams of methyl2 propanol1 per hectolitre of 100% vol. alcohol: 0,5,
  (v) methanol expressed in grams per hectolitre of 100% vol. alcohol: 30,
  (vi) dry extract expressed in grams per hectolitre of 100% vol. alcohol: 1,5,
  (vii) volatile bases containing nitrogen expressed in grams of nitrogen per hectolitre of 100% vol. alcohol: 0,1,
  (viii) furfural: not detectable.

9 These categories of spirits are: 1. Rum, 2. Whisky or Whiskey, 3. Grain spirit, 4. Wine Spirit, 5. Brandy or Weinbrand, 6. Grape marc spirit or grape marc, 7. Fruit marc spirit, 8. Raisin spirit or raisin brandy, 9. Fruit spirit, 10. Cider spirit and perry spirit, 11. Honey spirit, 12. Hefebrand or lees spirit, 13. Bierbrand or eau de vie de bière, 14. Topinambur or Jerusalem artichoke spirit.

(a) be produced by the alcoholic fermentation and distillation exclusively obtained from the raw material provided for in the relevant definition for the spirit drink concerned;

(b) have no addition of alcohol as defined in Annex I(5), diluted or not;

(c) not contain added flavouring substances;

(d) only contain added caramel as a means to adapt colour;

(e) solely be sweetened to round off the final taste of the product, according to Annex I(3).

5.18 The maximum level for the products used for rounding off listed under Annex I(3)(a) to (f) shall be decided upon in accordance with the regulatory procedure with scrutiny referred to in Art 25(3). The particular legislation of the Member States shall be taken into account.

5.19 Article 5(1) provides that without prejudice to the specific rules laid down for each of the categories numbered 15 to 46 in Annex II,[10] the spirit drinks defined therein may:

(a) be obtained from any agricultural raw material listed in Annex I to the Treaty;

(b) have addition of alcohol as defined in Annex I(5) to this Regulation;

(c) contain natural or nature-identical flavouring substances and preparations as defined in Article 1(2)(b)(i) and (ii) and in Article 1(2)(c) of Directive 88/388/EEC;

(d) contain colouring as defined in Annex I(10) to this Regulation;

(e) be sweetened to correspond to particular product characteristics and according to Annex I(3) to this Regulation and taking into account the particular legislation of the Member States.

5.20 Article 25(3) provides that without prejudice to the specific rules laid down in Annex II, other spirit drinks which do not meet the requirements of categories 1 to 46 may:

(a) be obtained from any agricultural raw material listed in Annex I to the Treaty and/or foodstuff suitable for human consumption;

(b) have addition of alcohol as defined in Annex I(5) to this Regulation;

---

10 These categories of spirit are: 15. Vodka, 16. Spirit (preceded by the name of the fruit) obtained by maceration and distillation, 17. Geist (with the name of the fruit or the raw material used), 18. Gentian, 19. Juniper-flavoured spirit drinks, 20. Gin, 21. Distilled gin, 22. London gin, 23. Caraway-flavoured spirit drinks, 24. Akvavit or aquavit, 25. Aniseed-flavoured spirit drinks, 26. Pastis, 27. Pastis de Marseille, 28. Anis, 29. Distilled anis, 30. Bitter-tasting spirit drinks or bitter, 31. Flavoured vodka, 32. Liqueur, 33. Crème de (followed by the name of a fruit or the raw material used), 34. Crème de cassis, 35. Guignolet, 36. Punch au rhum, 37. Sloe gin, 38. Sambuca, 39. Maraschino, Marrasquino or Maraskino, 40. Nocino, 41. Egg liqueur or advocaat or avocat or advokat, 42. Liqueur with egg, 43. Mistrà, 44. Väkevä glögi or spritglögg, 45. Berenburg or Beerenburg, 46. Honey or mead nectar, 47. Other spirit drinks, eg Rum-Verschnitt and Slivovice.

(c) contain one or more of the flavourings as defined in Article 1(2)(a) of Directive 88/388/EEC;

(d) contain colouring as defined in Annex I(10) to this Regulation;

(e) be sweetened to correspond to particular product characteristics and according to Annex I(3) to this Regulation.

8. Member States' legislation

Article 6(1) of the Spirits Regulation provides that in applying a quality policy **5.21** for spirit drinks which are produced on their own territory and in particular for GIs registered in Annex III or for the establishment of new GIs, Member States may lay down rules stricter than those in Annex II on production, description, presentation and labelling in so far as they are compatible with Community law.

Article 6(2) provides that Member States shall not prohibit or restrict the **5.22** import, sale or consumption of spirit drinks which comply with the Spirits Regulation.

C. DESCRIPTION, PRESENTATION AND LABELLING OF SPIRIT DRINKS

Rules dealing with GIs are included in Chapter II of the Spirits Regulation, **5.23** which regulates the description, presentation and labelling of spirit drinks. This Regulation repeals and replaces Council Regulation (EEC) No 1576/89.[11]

In Joined Cases C-4/10 and C-27/10 *Bureau national interprofessionnel du* **5.24** *Cognac v Gust. Ranin Oy*[12] the ECJ ruled that Regulation No 110/2008 applied to the assessment of the conditions for registration of a trade mark, containing a GI protected by that regulation, which was applied for on 19 December 2001 and registered on 31 January 2003. The Court observed that under Art 23(1) of Regulation No 110/2008 there was 'no reference to a time-frame imposing some sort of temporal restriction as regards the date of registration it is intended to apply to marks registered before that regulation entered into force'.[13]

---

11   See n 1 above.
12   [2011] ETMR 53.
13   Ibid., at para 31.

5.25 Article 8 provides that 'in accordance with Art 5 of Directive 2000/13/EC, the name under which a spirit drink is sold (sales denomination) shall be subject to the provisions laid down in this Chapter'.

1. Definitions

5.26 Article 7 provides that for the purpose of the Spirits Regulation the terms 'description', 'presentation' and 'labelling' are defined in Annex I(14), (15) and (16).

5.27 Annex I(14) defines 'description' to mean 'the terms used on the labelling, presentation and packaging; on the documents accompanying the transport of a drink; on the commercial documents, particularly the invoices and delivery notes; and in its advertising'.

5.28 Annex I(15) defines 'presentation' as 'the terms used on the labelling and on the packaging, including in advertising and sales promotion, in images or such like, as well as on the container, including the bottle and the closure'.

5.29 Annex I(16) defines 'labelling' as 'all descriptions and other references, signs, designs or trade marks which distinguish a drink and which appear on the same container, including its sealing device or the tag attached to the container and the sheathing covering the neck of the bottle'.

5.30 It will be recalled, from the previous chapter, that Case C-46/94[14] held that moulded inlays and prints carried on a wine bottle that described the town where the bottles were being offered for sale constituted misleading labelling of Bordeaux and Champagne wine as the decorative material on the bottles was liable to mislead purchasers as to the provenance of the wine or the vine variety and fell within the definition of labelling laid down in Art 38(1) of Regulation No 2392/89. This reasoning would probably apply to the definition of labelling in Annex I(16) as it uses the word 'including' in referring to 'design' appearing on the container.

2. Specific rules concerning sales denominations

(a) Products in categories 1 to 46 of Annex II

5.31 Article 9(1) of the Spirits Regulation provides that spirit drinks which meet the specifications for the products defined in categories 1 to 46 of Annex II

---

14 *Criminal proceedings against Michèle Voisine* [1995] ECR I-1859.

shall bear in their description, presentation and labelling the sales denomination assigned therein.

(b) Products not in categories 1 to 46 of Annex II

5.32 Article 9(2) of the Spirits Regulation provides that spirit drinks which meet the definition laid down in Art 2 but which do not meet the requirements for inclusion in categories 1 to 46 of Annex II shall bear in their description, presentation and labelling the sales denomination 'spirit drink' and that without prejudice to Art 9(5), that sales denomination shall not be replaced or altered.

(c) Products in more than one category of spirit drink in Annex II

5.33 Article 9(3) of the Spirits Regulation provides that where a spirit drink meets the definition of more than one category of spirit drink in Annex II, it may be sold under one or more of the names listed for those categories in Annex II.

(d) Restriction of names to spirit drinks

5.34 Article 9(4) of the Spirits Regulation provides that without prejudice to Art 9(9) and to Art 10(1), the names referred to in Art 9(1) shall not be used to describe or present in any way whatsoever any drink other than the spirit drinks for which those names are listed in Annex II and registered in Annex III.

(e) Sales denominations and geographical indications

5.35 Article 9(5) of the Spirits Regulation provides that sales denominations may be supplemented or replaced by a GI registered in Annex III and in accordance with Chapter III, or supplemented in accordance with national provisions by another GI, provided that this does not mislead the consumer.

5.36 Article 9(6) of the Spirits Regulation provides that the GIs registered in Annex III may only be supplemented either:

(a) by terms already in use on 20 February 2008 for established GIs within the meaning of Article 20, or
(b) according to the relevant technical file provided for under Article 17(1).

(f) Prohibition of the use of 'like', 'type', 'style', 'made', 'flavour' or any other similar terms

5.37 Article 9(7) of the Spirits Regulation provides that an alcoholic beverage not meeting one of the definitions listed under categories 1 to 46 of Annex II 'shall not be described, presented or labelled by associating words or phrases such as "like", "type", "style", "made", "flavour" or any other similar terms with any of the sales denominations provided for in the Spirits Regulation and/or geographical indications registered in Annex III'.

(g) Prohibition of trade mark, etc for sales denomination

5.38 Article 9(8) of the Spirits Regulation provides that 'no trade mark, brand name or fancy name may be substituted for the sales denomination of a spirit drink'.

(h) Ingredients for foodstuffs

5.39 Article 9(9) of the Spirits Regulation provides that the names referred to in categories 1 to 46 of Annex II may be included in a list of ingredients for foodstuffs provided that the list is in accordance with Directive 2000/13/EC.

3. Specific rules concerning the use of sales denominations and geographical indications

(a) Compound terms

5.40 Article 10(1) of the Spirits Regulation provides that without prejudice to Directive 2000/13/EC, the use of a term listed in categories 1 to 46 of Annex II, or of a GI registered in Annex III in a compound term or the allusion in the presentation of a foodstuff to any of them shall be prohibited unless the alcohol originates exclusively from the spirit drink(s) referred to.

5.41 This provision was amplified by Art 3 of Commission Implementing Regulation (EU) No 716/2013 of 25 July 2013.[15] Article 3(1) provides that the term 'spirit drink' shall not be part of a compound term describing an alcoholic beverage. Article 2(c) of that regulation defines 'compound term' as:

> the combination of a term listed in categories 1 to 46 of Annex II to the Spirits Regulation or a GI of a spirit drink, from which all the alcohol of the final product originates, with:
> (i) the name of one or more foodstuffs other than those used for the production of that spirit drink in accordance with Annex II to Regulation (EC) No 110/2008, or adjectives deriving from those names; and/or
> (ii) the term 'liqueur'.

---

15 OJ L 201/21, 26.7.2013, pp. 21–30.

The term 'geographical indication' is defined in the Spirits Regulation to mean 'one of the geographical indications registered in Annex III to Regulation (EC) No 110/2008'.

Article 3(2) of Commission Implementing Regulation (EU) No 716/2013 **5.42** provides that a compound term describing an alcoholic beverage shall not consist of a combination of the term 'liqueur' with the name of one of the categories 33 to 40 of Annex II to Regulation (EC) No 110/2008.

Article 3(3) of Commission Implementing Regulation (EU) No 716/2013 **5.43** provides that a compound term shall not replace the sales denomination of a spirit drink.

Article 3(4) of Commission Implementing Regulation (EU) No 716/2013 **5.44** provides that the compound term describing an alcoholic beverage shall appear in uniform characters of the same font, size and colour. It shall not be interrupted by any textual or pictorial element which does not form part of it and shall not appear in a larger font size than that of the sales denomination.

(b) Dilution of a spirit drink

Article 10(2) of the Spirits Regulation provides that the use of a compound **5.45** term as referred to in Art 10(1) shall also be prohibited where a spirit drink has been diluted so that the alcoholic strength is reduced to below the minimum strength specified in the definition for that spirit drink.

Article 5 of Commission Implementing Regulation (EU) No 716/2013 **5.46** provides that for the purpose of Art 10(2) of the Spirits Regulation, the reduction of the alcoholic strength of a spirit drink below the minimum alcoholic strength established for that spirit drink in the corresponding category in Annex II to that Regulation, exclusively by the addition of water, shall be considered as dilution.

(c) Allusions

Article 4 of Commission Implementing Regulation (EU) No 716/2013 **5.47** provides that the allusion to any spirit drink category or GI, for the presentation of a foodstuff, shall not be in the same line as the sales denomination. For alcoholic beverages, the allusion shall appear in a font size smaller than those used for the sales denomination and compound term.

Article 2(d) of Commission Implementing Regulation (EU) No 716/2013 **5.48** defines 'allusion' to mean 'the direct or indirect reference to one or more spirit drink categories or geographical indications, other than the reference in a compound term or list of ingredients referred to in Article 9(9) of Regulation (EC) No 110/2008'.

(d) Derogations

5.49 Article 10(3) of the Spirits Regulation provides that by way of derogation from Art 10(1), the provisions of this Regulation shall not affect the possible use of the terms 'amer' or 'bitter' for products not covered by this Regulation.

5.50 Article 10(4) of the Spirits Regulation provides that by way of derogation from Art 10(1) and in order to take account of established production methods, the compound terms listed in category 32(d)[16] of Annex II may be used in the presentation of liqueurs produced in the Community under the conditions set out therein.

4. Description, presentation and labelling of mixtures

(a) Addition of alcohol

5.51 Article 11(1) of the Spirits Regulation provides that where there has been addition of alcohol, as defined in Annex I(5), diluted or not, to a spirit drink listed in categories 1 to 14 of Annex II, that spirit drink shall bear the sales denomination 'spirit drink'. It may not bear in any form a name reserved in categories 1 to 14.

(b) Mixture of spirit drinks

5.52 Article 11(2) provides that:

---

16 Category 32(d) of Annex II is as follows:

> (d) The following compound terms may be used in the presentation of liqueurs produced in the Community where ethyl alcohol of agricultural origin is used to mirror established production methods:
> - *prune brandy,*
> - *orange brandy,*
> - *apricot brandy,*
> - *cherry brandy,*
> - *solbaerrom,* also called blackcurrant rum.
>
> As regards the labelling and presentation of those liqueurs, the compound term must appear on the labelling in one line in uniform characters of the same font and colour and the word 'liqueur' must appear in immediate proximity in characters no smaller than that font. If the alcohol does not come from the spirit drink indicated, its origin must be shown on the labelling in the same visual field as the compound term and the word 'liqueur' either by stating the type of agricultural alcohol or by the words 'agricultural alcohol' preceded on each occasion by 'made from' or 'made using'.

where a spirit drink listed in categories 1 to 46 of Annex II is mixed with:
(a)   one or more spirit drinks, and/or
(b)   one or more distillates of agricultural origin,
it shall bear the sales denomination 'spirit drink'. This sales denomination shall be shown clearly and visibly in a prominent position on the label and shall not be replaced or altered.

Article 11(3) provides that Art 11(2) shall not apply to the description, **5.53** presentation or labelling of a mixture referred to in that paragraph if it meets one of the definitions laid down in categories 1 to 46 of Annex II.

(c)   'Mixed spirit drink'

Article 11(4) of the Spirits Regulation provides that without prejudice to **5.54** Directive 2000/13/EC, the description, presentation or labelling of the spirit drinks resulting from the mixtures referred to in para 2 of this Article may show one or more of the terms listed in Annex II only if that term does not form part of the sales denomination but is solely listed in the same visual field in the listing of all the alcoholic ingredients contained in the mixture, preceded by the term 'mixed spirit drink'.

'The term "mixed spirit drink" shall be labelled in uniform characters of the **5.55** same font and colour as those used for the sales denomination. The characters shall be no larger than half the size of the characters used for the sales denomination.'

(d)   Listed proportions

Article 11(5) of the Spirits Regulation provides that for the labelling and **5.56** presentation of the mixtures referred to in Art 11(2) and to which the requirement to list alcoholic ingredients under Art 11(4) applies, the proportion of each alcoholic ingredient shall be expressed as a percentage in descending order of quantities used. That proportion shall be equal to the percentage by volume of pure alcohol it represents in the total pure alcohol content by volume of the mixture.

5.   Specific rules concerning the description, presentation and labelling of spirit drinks

(a)   Indication of raw material

Article 12(1) of the Spirits Regulation provides that where the description, **5.57** presentation or labelling of a spirit drink indicates the raw material used to produce the ethyl alcohol of agricultural origin, each agricultural alcohol used shall be mentioned in descending order of quantity used.

(b)   Blends

5.58   Article 12(2) of the Spirits Regulation provides that the description, presentation or labelling of a spirit drink may be supplemented by the term 'blend',
'blending' or 'blended' only where the spirit drink has undergone blending, as
defined in Annex I(7).[17]

5.59   Article 12(3) of the Spirits Regulation provides that without prejudice to any
derogation adopted in accordance with the regulatory procedure with scrutiny
referred to in Art 25(3), a maturation period or age may only be specified in
the description, presentation or labelling of a spirit drink where it refers to the
youngest alcoholic component and provided that the spirit drink was aged
under revenue supervision or supervision affording equivalent guarantees.

6.   Prohibition of lead-based capsules or foil

5.60   Article 13 of the Spirits Regulation provides that spirit drinks shall not be held
with a view to sale or placed on the market 'in containers fitted with closing
devices covered by lead-based capsules or foil'.

7.   Use of language in the description, presentation and labelling of spirit drinks

(a)   Use of official languages

5.61   Article 14(1) of the Spirits Regulation provides that the particulars provided
for in this Regulation shall be given in one or more official languages of the
European Union in such a way that the final consumer can easily understand
each of those items of information, unless the consumer is provided with the
information by other means.

---

17   Annex I(7) provides as follows:

> Blending means combining two or more spirit drinks of the same category, distinguished only by minor
> differences in composition due to one or more of the following factors:
>
>   (a)   the method of preparation;
>   (b)   the stills employed;
>   (c)   the period of maturation or ageing;
>   (d)   the geographical area of production.
>
> The spirit drink so produced shall be of the same category of spirit drink as the original spirit drinks before
> blending.

(b) Prohibition of translations

Article 14(2) of the Spirits Regulation provides that the terms in italics in **5.62** Annex II and the GIs registered in Annex III shall not be translated on the label nor in the presentation of the spirit drink.

(c) Languages of third countries

Article 14(3) of the Spirits Regulation provides that in the case of spirit drinks **5.63** originating in third countries, use of an official language of the third country in which the spirit drink was produced shall be authorised if the particulars provided for in this Regulation are also given in an official language of the European Union in such a way that the final consumer can easily understand each item.

(d) Exports

Article 14(4) of the Spirits Regulation provides that without prejudice to Art **5.64** 14(2), in the case of spirit drinks produced in the Community and intended for export, the particulars provided for in this Regulation may be repeated in a language other than an official language of the European Union.

D. GEOGRAPHICAL INDICATIONS

Chapter III of the Spirits Regulation deals specifically with GIs. **5.65**

Article 42(4) of Commission Regulation (EC) No 607/2009 provides that the **5.66** protection of designations of origin and GIs for products covered in Art 34 of Commission Regulation (EC) No 607/2009 shall be without prejudice to PGIs applying in relation to spirit drinks within the meaning of the Spirits Regulation[18] and vice versa.

1. Definitions

(a) 'Geographical indication'

Article 15(1) of the Spirits Regulation provides that for the purpose of the **5.67** Spirits Regulation a geographical indication shall be 'an indication which identifies a spirit drink as originating in the territory of a country, or a region

---

18 OJ L 39, 13.2.2008, pp. 16–54.

or locality in that territory, where a given quality, reputation or other characteristic of that spirit drink is essentially attributable to its geographical origin'.

(b) Geographical indications in Annex III

5.68 Article 15(2) of the Spirits Regulation provides that the GIs referred to in Art 15(1) are registered in Annex III. Annex III lists 20 product categories: Rum, Whisky/Whiskey, Grain spirit, Wine spirit, Brandy/Weinbrand, Grape marc spirit, Fruit spirit, Cider spirit and perry spirit, Vodka, Geist, Gentian, Juniper-flavoured spirit drinks, Akvavit/aquavit, Aniseed-flavoured spirit drinks, Distilled Anis, Bitter-tasting spirit drinks/bitter, Liqueur, Crème de cassis, Nocino, Other spirit drinks such as the Pommeaux de Bretagne, du Maine and de Normandie, Svensk Punsch/Swedish Punch, Pacharán Navarro, Pacharán, Inländerrum and Bärwurz.

5.69 Article 15(4) provides that spirit drinks bearing a GI registered in Annex III shall comply with all the specifications of the technical file provided for under Art 17(1).

2. Registration of geographical indications

(a) Form of application

5.70 Article 17(1) of the Spirits Regulation provides that an application for a GI to be registered in Annex III shall be submitted to the Commission in one of the official languages of the European Union or accompanied by a translation into one of those languages. That application shall be duly substantiated and shall include a technical file setting out the specifications with which the spirit drink concerned must comply.

(b) Application for the registration of a geographical indication

5.71 Article 6 of Commission Implementing Regulation (EU) No 716/2013 provides that the application for registration of a GI in Annex III to the Spirits Regulation shall be submitted to the Commission and consist of:

(a) the application form, according to the model set out in Annex I to this Regulation;

(b) the technical file, according to the model set out in Annex II to this Regulation;

(c) the main specifications of the technical file referred to in point (b).

(c) Technical file

Article 17(4) provides that the technical file referred to in Art 17(1) shall **5.72** include at least the following main specifications:

(a) the name and category of the spirit drink including the GI;

(b) a description of the spirit drink including the principal physical, chemical and/or organoleptic characteristics of the product as well as the specific characteristics of the spirit drink as compared to the relevant category;

(c) the definition of the geographical area concerned;

(d) a description of the method for obtaining the spirit drink and, if appropriate, the authentic and unvarying local methods;

(e) the details bearing out the link with the geographical environment or the geographical origin;

(f) any requirements laid down by Community and/or national and/or regional provisions;

(g) the name and contact address of the applicant;

(h) any supplement to the GI and/or any specific labelling rule, according to the relevant technical file.

(d) Packaging in the geographical area concerned

Article 10 of Commission Implementing Regulation (EU) No 716/2013 **5.73** provides that if the technical file sets out that packaging of the spirit drink must take place within the demarcated geographical area or in an area in its immediate proximity, justification for this requirement shall be given in respect of the product concerned.

(e) Eligible applicants

Article 17(2) provides that with regard to GIs within the Community, the **5.74** application referred to in Art 17(1) shall be made by the Member State of origin of the spirit drink.

(f) Third country applications

Article 17(3) provides that with regard to GIs within a third country, the **5.75** application referred to in Art 17(1) shall be sent to the Commission, either directly or via the authorities of the third country concerned, and shall include proof that the name in question is protected in its country of origin.

(g) Trans-border applications

Article 7(1) of Commission Implementing Regulation (EU) No 716/2013 **5.76** provides that where a trans-border GI involves only Member States, the relevant application shall be submitted jointly or by one of the Member States in the name of the others. In the latter case, the application shall include a document from each of the other Member States concerned authorising the Member State forwarding the application to act on its behalf.

5.77 Article 7(1) of Commission Implementing Regulation (EU) No 716/2013 provides that where a trans-border GI involves only third countries, the relevant application shall be submitted to the Commission either by one of the applicants on behalf of the others or by one of the third countries on behalf of the others and shall include:

(a) the proof of protection in the third countries concerned; and
(b) a document from each of the other third countries concerned authorising the third country submitting the application to act on its behalf.

5.78 Article 7(1) of Commission Implementing Regulation (EU) No 716/2013 provides that where a trans-border GI involves at least one Member State and at least one third country, the application shall be submitted to the Commission by one of the Member States, third-country authorities or private entities from the third country in question and shall include:

(a) the proof of protection in the third countries concerned; and
(b) a document from each of the Member States or third countries concerned authorising the party forwarding the application to act on its behalf.

5.79 Article 7(2) of Commission Implementing Regulation (EU) No 716/2013 provides that the Member State or the third-country authority or the private entity from the third country in question which submits to the Commission a trans-border application shall become the consignee of any notification or decision issued by the Commission.

(h) Receipt of the application

5.80 Article 8(1) of Commission Implementing Regulation (EU) No 716/2013 provides that the date of submission of an application shall be the date of its receipt by the Commission.

5.81 Article 8(2) provides that the Member State or the third-country authority or the private entity from the third country in question shall receive an acknowledgement of receipt indicating at least the following:

(a) the file number;
(b) the name to be registered;
(c) the number of pages received;
(d) the date of receipt of the application.

(i) Admissibility of the application

Article 11(1) of Commission Implementing Regulation (EU) No 716/2013 **5.82** provides that the application is admissible if it consists of all the elements referred to in Art 6 of Commission Implementing Regulation (EU) No 716/2013.[19]

Article 11(2) of Commission Implementing Regulation (EU) No 716/2013 **5.83** provides that if the application is not complete the Commission shall invite the applicant to remedy the deficiency within a period of two months. If the deficiency is not remedied within that time limit, the Commission shall reject the application as inadmissible.

(j) Scrutiny by the Commission

Article 17(5) of the Spirits Regulation provides that the Commission shall **5.84** verify, within 12 months of the date of submission of the application referred to in Art 17(1), whether that application complies with this Regulation.

Article 17(6) of the Spirits Regulation provides that if the Commission **5.85** concludes that the application referred to in para 1 complies with this Regulation, the main specifications of the technical file referred to in Art 17(4) shall be published in the *Official Journal of the European Union*, C Series.

(k) Scrutiny of the conditions of validity

Article 12(1) of Commission Implementing Regulation (EU) No 716/2013 **5.86** provides that if a GI does not comply with Art 15 of the Spirits Regulation or if the application for registration does not meet the requirements laid down in Art 17 of the Spirits Regulation, the Commission shall set a time period for its amendment or withdrawal or for the submission of comments by the Member State, the third-country authority or the private entity from the third country in question.

Article 12(2) provides that if the deficiencies are not remedied by the Member **5.87** State, the third-country authority or the private entity from the third country in question within the time period referred to in Art 12(1) of Commission Implementing Regulation (EU) No 716/2013, the Commission shall reject the application.

---

19 Art 6 provides that the application for registration of a GI in Annex III to Regulation (EC) No 110/2008 shall be submitted to the Commission and consist of:

    (a)   the application form, according to the model set out in Annex I to this Regulation;

    (b)   the technical file, according to the model set out in Annex II to this Regulation;

    (c)   the main specifications of the technical file referred to in point (b).

(l)   Correcting deficiencies in the technical file

5.88   Article 9(1) of Commission Implementing Regulation (EU) No 716/2013 provides that if the technical file for an established GI, submitted pursuant to Art 20(1) of the Wine Regulation, does not demonstrate that the requirements laid down in Art 15(1) of that Regulation are fulfilled, the Commission shall set a time period for its amendment or withdrawal or for the submission of comments by the Member State.

5.89   Article 9(2) of Commission Implementing Regulation (EU) No 716/2013 provides that if such deficiencies are not remedied by the Member State within the time period referred to in the first paragraph, the technical file shall be deemed not to have been submitted and Art 20(3) of the Wine Regulation shall apply.

(m)   Objections

5.90   Article 17(7) of the Spirits Regulation provides that within six months of the date of publication of the technical file, any natural or legal person that has a legitimate interest may object to the registration of the GI in Annex III on the grounds that the conditions provided for in this Regulation are not fulfilled. The objection, which must be duly substantiated, shall be submitted to the Commission in one of the official languages of the European Union or accompanied by a translation into one of those languages.

(n)   Objection to the registration

5.91   Article 13(1) of Commission Implementing Regulation (EU) No 716/2013 provides that Objections referred to in Art 17(7) of the Spirits Regulation shall be drawn up in accordance with the form set out in Annex III to this Regulation and submitted to the Commission. The date of submission of the objection shall be the date of its receipt by the Commission.

5.92   Article 13(2) of Commission Implementing Regulation (EU) No 716/2013 provides that the objector shall receive an acknowledgement of receipt indicating at least the following:

(a)   the file number;
(b)   the number of pages received;
(c)   the date of receipt of the objection.

(o)   Admissibility of an objection

5.93   Article 14(1) of Commission Implementing Regulation (EU) No 716/2013 provides that the objection is admissible if it mentions the prior right(s) claimed, where relevant, and the ground(s) for the objection and it was received within the time period referred to in Art 17(7) of the Spirits Regulation.

Article 14(2) of Commission Implementing Regulation (EU) No 716/2013 **5.94** provides that if the objection is based on the existence of an earlier trade mark of reputation and renown already used in the Union, in accordance with Art 23(3) of the Spirits Regulation, it shall be accompanied by proof of the filing of an application for registration, registration or use of that trade mark, such as the certificate of registration or proof of its use, and proof of its reputation and renown.

Article 14(3) of Commission Implementing Regulation (EU) No 716/2013 **5.95** provides that any objection shall contain details of the facts, evidence and comments submitted in support of the objection and be accompanied by the relevant supporting documents.

The information and evidence produced in support of the use of an earlier **5.96** trade mark shall refer to location, duration, extent and nature of use and of its reputation and renown.

Article 14(4) of Commission Implementing Regulation (EU) No 716/2013 **5.97** provides that if the information and the documents referred to in Art 14(1), (2) and (3) have not been produced, the Commission shall invite the objector to remedy the deficiencies within a period of two months. If the deficiencies are not remedied within the time limit, the Commission shall reject the objection as inadmissible.

(p) Scrutiny of an objection

Article 15(1) of Commission Implementing Regulation (EU) No 716/2013 **5.98** provides that if the objection is admissible, the Commission shall communicate it to the Member State, the third-country authority or the private entity from the third country in question and invite them to file observations within a period of two months. Any observations received within this time period shall be communicated to the objector.

Article 15(2) of Commission Implementing Regulation (EU) No 716/2013 **5.99** provides that the Commission shall request the parties to submit comments on the observations received from the other parties within a period of two months.

5.100 Article 15(3) of Commission Implementing Regulation (EU) No 716/2013 provides that if the Commission considers that the objection is founded, it shall reject the application for registration.

5.101 Article 15(5) of Commission Implementing Regulation (EU) No 716/2013 provides that where an application for registration is rejected, objection procedures which have been suspended shall be deemed to be closed and the objectors concerned shall be duly informed.

5.102 Article 15(4) of Commission Implementing Regulation (EU) No 716/2013 provides that if, in the event of multiple objections, following a preliminary examination of one or more such objections, it may not be possible to accept the application for registration, the Commission may suspend the other objection procedures. The Commission shall inform the other objectors of any decision affecting them.

(q) Decisions of the Commission

5.103 Article 16(1) of Commission Implementing Regulation (EU) No 716/2013 provides that decisions taken by the Commission pursuant to Arts 9(2), 11(2), 12(2) and 15(3) shall be based on the documents and information available to it. The decisions, including grounds for them, shall be notified to the Member State, the third-country authority or the private entity from the third country in question, and, if appropriate, to the objector.

5.104 Article 16(2) of Commission Implementing Regulation (EU) No 716/2013 provides that unless the application for the registration of a GI is rejected pursuant to Arts 11(2), 12(2) and 15(3) of this Regulation, the Commission shall decide pursuant to Art 17(8) of the Spirits Regulation to register the GI in Annex III to that Regulation.

5.105 Article 17(8) of the Spirits Regulation provides that the Commission shall take the decision on registration of the GI in Annex III in accordance with the regulatory procedure with scrutiny referred to in Art 25(3), taking into account any objection raised in accordance with Art 17(7). That decision shall be published in the *Official Journal of the European Union*, C Series.

3. Cancellation of a geographical indication

5.106 Article 18 of the Spirits Regulation provides that if compliance with the specifications in the technical file is no longer ensured, the Commission shall take a decision cancelling the registration in accordance with the regulatory procedure with scrutiny referred to in Art 25(3). That decision shall be published in the *Official Journal of the European Union*, C Series.

(a) Submission of a request for cancellation

Article 18(1) of Commission Implementing Regulation (EU) No 716/2013 **5.107** provides that a request for cancellation of a GI shall be drawn up in accordance with the form set out in Annex IV and shall be submitted to the Commission. The date of submission of the request for cancellation shall be the date of its receipt by the Commission.

Article 18(2) of Commission Implementing Regulation (EU) No 716/2013 **5.108** provides that the author of the request for cancellation shall receive an acknowledgement of receipt indicating at least:

(a) the file number;
(b) the number of pages received; and
(c) the date of receipt of the request.

(b) Admissibility of a request for cancellation

Article 19(1) of Commission Implementing Regulation (EU) No 716/2013 **5.109** provides that a request for cancellation is admissible if it clearly states the legitimate interest of the author of the request for cancellation and explains the ground(s) for such cancellation.

Article 19(2) of Commission Implementing Regulation (EU) No 716/2013 **5.110** provides that any request for cancellation shall contain details of the facts, evidence and comments submitted in support of cancellation. It shall be accompanied by the relevant supporting documents and, in particular, by a statement from the Member State or the third-country authority where the residence or registered office of the author of the request is located.

Article 19(3) of Commission Implementing Regulation (EU) No 716/2013 **5.111** provides that if the information and documents referred to in Art 19(1) and (2) have not been provided at the same time as the request for cancellation, the Commission shall invite the author of the request to remedy the deficiencies within a period of two months. If the deficiencies are not remedied within the time limit, the Commission shall reject the request as inadmissible.

4. Generic names

5.112 Article 15(3) of the Spirits Regulation provides that the GIs registered in Annex III may not become generic and that names that have become generic may not be registered in Annex III.

5.113 Article 15(3) provides that a name that has become generic means that the name of a spirit drink which, although it relates to the place or region where this product was originally produced or placed on the market, has become the common name of a spirit drink in the Community.

5. Homonymous geographical indications

5.114 Article 19 of the Spirits Regulation provides that a homonymous GI meeting the requirements of this Regulation shall be registered with due regard for local and traditional usage and the actual risk of confusion, in particular:

- a homonymous name which misleads the consumer into believing that products come from another territory shall not be registered even if the name is accurate as far as its wording is concerned for the actual territory, region or place of origin of the spirit drink in question;
- the use of a registered homonymous GI shall be subject to there being a clear distinction in practice between the homonym registered subsequently and the name already on the register, having regard to the need to treat the producers concerned in an equitable manner and not to mislead consumers.

6. Established geographical indications

5.115 Article 20(1) of the Spirits Regulation provides that for each GI registered in Annex III on 20 February 2008, Member States shall submit a technical file as provided for under Art 17(1) to the Commission not later than 20 February 2015.

5.116 Article 20(2) requires that Member States shall ensure that this technical file is accessible to the public.

5.117 Article 20(3) provides that where no technical file has been submitted to the Commission by 20 February 2015, the Commission shall remove the GI from Annex III in accordance with the regulatory procedure with scrutiny referred to in Art 25(3).

7. Alteration of the technical file

Article 21 of the Spirits Regulation provides that the procedure provided for in **5.118**
Art 17 shall apply *mutatis mutandis* where the technical file referred to in Arts
17(1) and 20(1) is to be altered.

8. Verification of compliance with the specifications in the technical file

(a) Authorised verifying bodies

Article 22(1) of the Spirits Regulation provides that in respect of the GIs **5.119**
within the Community, verification of compliance with the specifications in
the technical file, before placing the product on the market, shall be ensured
by:

- one or more competent authorities referred to in Art 24(1), and/or
- one or more control bodies within the meaning of Art 2 of Regulation
  (EC) No 882/2004[20] of the European Parliament and of the Council of
  29 April 2004 on official controls performed to ensure the verification of
  compliance with feed and food law, animal health and animal welfare
  rules,[21] operating as a product certification body.

Notwithstanding national legislation, the costs of such verification of compliance with the specifications in the technical file shall be borne by the operators
subject to those controls.

(b) Verifying bodies in third countries

Article 22(2) of the Spirits Regulation provides that in respect of the GIs **5.120**
within a third country, verification of compliance with the specifications in the
technical file, before placing the product on the market, shall be ensured by:

- one or more public authorities designated by the third country, and/or
- one or more product certification bodies.

(c) Standards for verification

Article 22(3) of the Spirits Regulation requires that the product certification **5.121**
bodies referred to in Art 22(1) and (2) shall comply with, and from 1 May

---

20 Regulation (EC) No 882/2004 of the European Parliament and of the Council on official controls performed
   to ensure the verification of compliance with feed and food law, animal health and welfare rules, OJ L 191,
   28.5.2004, pp. 1–52.
21 OJ L 165, 30.4.2004, p. 1, corrected by OJ L 191, 28.5.2004, p. 1. Regulation as last amended by Council
   Regulation (EC) No 1791/2006.

2010 be accredited in accordance with, European standard EN 45011 or ISO/IEC Guide 65 (General requirements for bodies operating product certification systems).

(d) Competence of verifying bodies

5.122 Article 22(4) requires that where the authorities or bodies referred to in Art 22(1) and (2) have chosen to verify compliance with the specifications in the technical file, they shall offer adequate guarantees of objectivity and impartiality and have at their disposal the qualified staff and resources necessary to carry out their functions.

9. Use of languages

5.123 Article 17 of Commission Implementing Regulation (EU) No 716/2013 provides that the GI shall be registered in the language(s) used to describe the product in question in the geographical area concerned and with its original spelling.

10. Protection of geographical indications

5.124 Article 16 of the Spirits Regulation provides that without prejudice to Art 10, the GIs registered in Annex III shall be protected against:

(a) any direct or indirect commercial use in respect of products not covered by the registration in so far as those products are comparable to the spirit drink registered under that GI or insofar as such use exploits the reputation of the registered GI;

(b) any misuse, imitation or evocation, even if the true origin of the product is indicated or the GI is used in translation or accompanied by an expression such as 'like', 'type', 'style', 'made', 'flavour' or any other similar term;

(c) any other false or misleading indication as to the provenance, origin, nature or essential qualities on the description, presentation or labelling of the product, liable to convey a false impression as to its origin;

(d) any other practice liable to mislead the consumer as to the true origin of the product.

E. PROPOSED NEW REGULATION 2019

5.125 The modernisation of Regulation (EC) No 110/2008 has been considered by the European Parliament on a number of occasions. On 13 March 2019, it adopted at first reading a legislative resolution on the proposal for a regulation of the European Parliament and of the Council on the definition, presentation and labelling of spirit drinks, the use of the names of spirit drinks in the presentation and labelling of other foodstuffs and the protection of geographical indications for spirit drinks.[22] The resolution envisaged that the rules applicable to spirit drinks 'should contribute to attaining a high level of consumer protection, removing information asymmetry, preventing deceptive practices and attaining market transparency and fair competition'.[23] It explained that technological innovation should also be taken into account in respect of spirit drinks, 'where it serves to improve quality, without affecting the traditional character of the spirit drinks concerned'.[24] It noted that the rules applicable to spirit drinks constituted a special case compared with the general rules laid down for the agri-food sector and should also take into account the traditional production methods in use in the different Member States[25] and further that in order to meet consumer expectations and to conform to traditional practices, 'ethyl alcohol and distillates used for the production of spirit drinks should be exclusively of agricultural origin'.[26]

1. Subject matter and scope

Article 1(1) of the draft Regulation defines its scope as laying down rules on: **5.126**

- the definition, description, presentation and labelling of spirit drinks, as well as on the protection of geographical indications of spirit drinks;
- ethyl alcohol and distillates used in the production of alcoholic beverages; and
- the use of legal names of spirit drinks in the presentation and labelling of foodstuffs other than spirit drinks.

Article 1(2) applies the draft Regulation to the products mentioned above that **5.127** are placed on the market in the EU, whether produced in the EU or in third countries, as well as to those produced in the EU for export.

As regards the protection of geographical indications, Art 1(3) provides that **5.128** Chapter III of the draft Regulation also applies to goods entering the customs territory of the EU without being released for free circulation there.

---

22 European Parliament, P8_TA-PROV(2019)0178 (COM(2016)0750 – C8-0496/2017 – 2016/0392(COD)) available at http://www.europarl.europa.eu/sides/getDoc.do?pubRef=-//EP//NONSGML+TA+P8-TA-2019-0178+0+DOC+PDF+V0//EN, accessed 21 March 2019.
23 Ibid., Recital (2).
24 Ibid.
25 Ibid., Recital (4).
26 Ibid., Recital (6).

2.   Definitions

5.129   Article 2 of the draft Regulation defines a 'spirit drink' as an alcoholic beverage which:

(a)   is intended for human consumption;

(b)   possesses particular organoleptic qualities;

(c)   has a minimum alcoholic strength by volume of 15 per cent, except in the case of spirit drinks that comply with the requirements of category 39 of Annex I;

(d)   has been produced either:

(i)   directly by using, individually or in combination, any of the following methods:

- distillation, with or without added flavourings or flavouring foodstuffs, of fermented products,
- the maceration or similar processing of plant materials in ethyl alcohol of agricultural origin, distillates of agricultural origin or spirit drinks or a combination thereof,
- the addition, individually or in combination, to ethyl alcohol of agricultural origin, distillates of agricultural origin or spirit drinks of any of the following:
- flavourings used in accordance with Regulation (EC) No 1334/2008,
- colours used in accordance with Regulation (EC) No 1333/2008,
- other authorised ingredients used in accordance with Regulations (EC) No 1333/2008 and (EC) No 1334/2008,
- sweetening products,
- other agricultural products,
- foodstuffs; or

(ii)   by adding, individually or in combination, to it any of the following:

- other spirit drinks,
- ethyl alcohol of agricultural origin,
- distillates of agricultural origin,
- other foodstuffs;

(e)   it does not fall within CN codes 2203, 2204, 2205, 2206 and 2207;

(f)   if water, which may be distilled, demineralised, permuted or softened, has been added in its production:

(i)   the quality of that water complies with Council Directive 98/83/EC[27] and Directive 2009/54/EC of the European Parliament and of the Council;[28] and

(ii)   the alcoholic strength of the spirit drink, after the addition of the water, still complies with the minimum alcoholic strength by volume provided for in point (c) of this Article or under the relevant category of spirit drinks as set out in Annex I.

---

27   Council Directive 98/83/EC of 3 November 1998 on the quality of water intended for human consumption, OJ L 330, 5.12.1998, p. 32.

28   Directive 2009/54/EC of the European Parliament and of the Council of 18 June 2009 on the exploitation and marketing of natural mineral waters, OJ L 164, 26.6.2009, p. 45.

'Distillation' is defined in Art 4(6) as: **5.130**

a thermal separation process involving one or more separation steps intended to achieve certain organoleptic properties or a higher alcoholic concentration or both, regardless of whether such steps take place under normal pressure or under vacuum, due to the distilling device used; and can be single or multiple distillation or re-distillation.

'Distillates of agricultural origin' are defined in Art 4(7) as an alcoholic liquid 'which is the result of the distillation, after alcoholic fermentation, of agricultural products listed in Annex I to the Treaty, and which does not have the properties of ethyl alcohol and which retains the aroma and taste of the raw materials used'.

'Addition of alcohol' is defined in Art 4(10) to mean the addition of ethyl **5.131** alcohol of agricultural origin or distillates of agricultural origin or both to a spirit drink, but such addition does not include the use of alcohol for dilution or dissolution of colours, flavourings or any other authorised ingredients used in the production of spirit drinks.

'Sweetening products' are defined in Art 4(9) to mean: **5.132**

    (a) semi-white sugar, white sugar, extra-white sugar, dextrose, fructose, glucose syrup, sugar solution, invert sugar solution and invert sugar syrup, as defined in Part A of the Annex to Council Directive 2001/111/EC;[29]

    (b) rectified concentrated grape must, concentrated grape must and fresh grape must;

    (c) burned sugar which is the product obtained exclusively from the controlled heating of sucrose without bases, mineral acids or other chemical additives;

    (d) honey as defined in point 1 of Annex I to Council Directive 2001/110/EC;[30]

    (e) carob syrup;

    (f) any other natural carbohydrate substances having a similar effect as the products referred to in points (a) to (e).

Article 5 defines 'ethyl alcohol of agricultural origin' as a liquid which **5.133** complies with the following requirements:

    (a) it has been obtained exclusively from products listed in Annex I to the Treaty;

    (b) it has no detectable taste other than that of the raw materials used in its production;

    (c) its minimum alcoholic strength by volume is 96.0 per cent;

---

29 Council Directive 2001/111/EC of 20 December 2001 relating to certain sugars intended for human consumption, OJ L 10, 12.1.2002, p. 53.

30 Council Directive 2001/110/EC of 20 December 2001 relating to honey, OJ L 10, 12.1.2002, p. 47.

    (d) its maximum levels of residues do not exceed the following:

        (i)   total acidity (expressed in acetic acid): 1.5 grams per hectolitre of 100 per cent vol. alcohol;

       (ii) esters (expressed in ethyl acetate): 1.3 grams per hectolitre of 100 per cent vol. alcohol;

     (iii) aldehydes (expressed in acetaldehyde): 0.5 grams per hectolitre of 100 per cent vol. alcohol;

     (iv) higher alcohols (expresssed in 2-methyl-1-propanol): 0.5 grams per hecto-litre of 100 per cent vol. alcohol;

      (v) methanol: 30 grams per hectolitre of 100 per cent vol. alcohol;

     (vi) dry extract: 1.5 grams per hectolitre of 100 per cent vol. alcohol;

    (vii) volatile bases containing nitrogen (expressed in nitrogen): 0.1 grams per hectolitre of 100 per cent vol. alcohol;

   (viii) furfural: not detectable.

5.134   Detailed definitions of each category of spirit are set out in Annex I to the draft Regulation. Annex II contains detailed rules for *Rum-Verschnitt* from Germany, *Slivovice* from Czechia and *Guignolet Kirsch from France*.

3. Description and labelling of spirit drinks

5.135   The description, presentation and labelling of spirit drinks and use of the names of spirit drinks in the presentation and labelling of other foodstuffs is set out in Chapter II of the draft Regulation. This includes provisions dealing with geographical indications. Article 9 provides that spirit drinks placed on the EU market shall comply with the presentation and labelling requirements set out in Regulation (EU) No 1169/2011, unless otherwise provided for in this Regulation. This chapter is only concerned with those requirements of the draft Regulation which relate to geographical indications.

(a) *Legal names of spirit drinks*

5.136   Article 10 of the draft Regulation deals with the requirements in relation to the depiction of the legal names of spirit drinks. In para 6(a) it permits the supplementation of the legal name by a name or 'geographical reference' provided for in the laws, regulations and administrative provisions applicable in a Member State in which the spirit drink is placed on the market, 'provided that this does not mislead the consumer'.

(b) *Allusions*

5.137   Article 12 of the draft Regulation provides, inter alia, that in the presentation and labelling of a foodstuff other than an alcoholic beverage, an allusion to 'one or more geographical indications for spirit drinks' shall be authorised on condition that the alcohol used in the production of the foodstuff originates exclusively from the spirit drink or the spirit drinks referred to in the allusion, except as regards the alcohol that may be present in flavourings, colours or other authorised ingredients used for the production of that foodstuff.

(c) Indication of place of provenance

Article 14 provides that where the place of provenance of a spirit drink, other **5.138** than a GI or trade mark, is indicated in its description, presentation or labelling, it shall correspond to the place or region where the stage in the production process which conferred on the finished spirit drink its character and essential definitive qualities took place, but this does not extend to primary ingredient as referred to in Regulation (EU) No 1169/2011.

(d) Use of Union symbol for GIs

The Union symbol for protected GIs established pursuant to Art 12(7) of **5.139** Regulation (EU) No 1151/2012 is permitted by Art 16 to be used in the description, presentation and labelling of spirit drinks the names of which are geographical indications.

4. Geographical indications

Chapter III of the draft Regulation deals with the use of GIs in relation to **5.140** spirit drinks. Article 3(4) defines 'geographical indication' as 'an indication which identifies a spirit drink as originating in the territory of a country, or a region or locality in that territory, where a given quality, reputation or other characteristic of that spirit drink is essentially attributable to its geographical origin'.

(a) Scope of protection

Article 21(1) provides that GIs protected under this Regulation may be used **5.141** by any operator marketing a spirit drink produced in conformity with the corresponding product specification.

Article 21(2) provides that the GIs protected under this Regulation shall be **5.142** protected against:

  (a) any direct or indirect commercial use of a registered name in respect of products not covered by the registration where those products are comparable to the products registered under that name or where using the name exploits the reputation of the protected name, including where those products are used as an ingredient;
  (b) any misuse, imitation or evocation, even if the true origin of the products or services is indicated or if the protected name is translated or accompanied by an

expression such as 'style', 'type', 'method', 'as produced in', 'imitation', 'flavour', 'like' or similar, including when those products are used as an ingredient;

(c) any other false or misleading indication as to the provenance, origin, nature or essential qualities of the product in the description, presentation or labelling of the product liable to convey a false impression as to the origin of the product;

(d) any other practice liable to mislead the consumer as to the true origin of the product.

5.143 Article 21(4) provides that this protection 'shall also apply with regard to goods entering the customs territory of the Union without being released for free circulation there'.

(b) Genericity

5.144 Article 21(3) provides that geographical indications protected under this Regulation shall not become generic in the EU.

(c) Product specification

5.145 A GI protected under the draft Regulation is required by Art 22 to comply with a product specification which shall include at least:

(a) the name to be protected as a geographical indication, as it is used, whether in trade or in common language, only in the languages which are or were historically used to describe the specific product in the defined geographical area, in the original script and in Latin transcription if different;

(b) the category of the spirit drink or the term 'spirit drink' if the spirit drink does not comply with the requirements laid down for the categories of spirit drinks set out in Annex I;

(c) a description of the characteristics of the spirit drink, including the raw materials from which it is produced, if appropriate, as well as the principal physical, chemical or organoleptic characteristics of the product and the specific characteristics of the product compared to spirit drinks of the same category;

(d) the definition of the geographical area delimited with regard to the link referred to in point (f);

(e) a description of the method of producing the spirit drink and, where appropriate, the authentic and unvarying local production methods;

(f) details establishing the link between a given quality, reputation or other characteristic of the spirit drink and its geographical origin;

(g) the names and addresses of the competent authorities or, if available, the names and addresses of the bodies that verify compliance with the provisions of the product specification pursuant to Article 38 and their specific tasks;

(h) any specific labelling rule for the geographical indication in question.

Article 22 also provides that where applicable, requirements regarding pack- **5.146** aging shall be included in the product specification, accompanied by a justification showing why the packaging must take place in the defined geographical area to safeguard quality, to ensure the origin or to ensure control, taking into account EU law, in particular EU law on the free movement of goods and the free provision of services.

Article 38 deals with the verification of compliance with the product specifi- **5.147** cation and in Art 38(1) requires Member States to draw up and keep up to date a list of operators that produce spirit drinks with a geographical indica- tion registered under this Regulation.

Article 38(2) requires that the verification of compliance with the product **5.148** specification referred to in Art 22, before placing the product on the market, shall be carried out by:

   (a) one or more competent authorities referred to in Article 43(1); or
   (b) control bodies within the meaning of point 5 of the second subparagraph of Article 2 of Regulation (EC) No 882/2004 (on official controls performed to ensure the verification of compliance with feed and food law, animal health and animal welfare rules), operating as a product certification body.

Notwithstanding the national law of Member States, the costs of such **5.149** verification of compliance with the product specification may be borne by the operators which are subject to those controls.

In respect of the GIs that designate spirit drinks originating within a third **5.150** country registered under this Regulation, Art 38(3) provides that verification of compliance with the product specification, before placing the product on the market, shall be carried out by:

   (a) a public competent authority designated by the third country; or
   (b) a product certification body.

Article 38(4) requires Member States to make public the names and addresses **5.151** of the competent authorities and bodies referred to in Art 38(2) and update that information periodically. The Commission is required to make public the name and address of the competent authorities and bodies referred to in Art 38(3) and update that information periodically.

(d) Content of an application for registration

5.152 Article 23(1) requires an application for registration of a GI shall include at least:

    (a)   the name and address of the applicant group and of the competent authorities or, if available, the bodies that verify compliance with the provisions of the product specification;

    (b)   the product specification provided for in Article 22;

    (c)   a single document setting out the following:

        (i)   the main points of the product specification, including the name to be protected, the category to which the spirit drink belongs or the term 'spirit drink', the production method, a description of the characteristics of the spirit drink, a concise definition of the geographical area, and, where appropriate, specific rules concerning packaging and labelling;

        (ii)   a description of the link between the spirit drink and its geographical origin as referred to in point (4) of Article 3, including, where appropriate, the specific elements of the product description or production method justifying the link.

5.153 Where the application relates to a geographical area in a Member State, Art 24(5) requires that the application be submitted to the authorities of that Member State and the Member State shall scrutinise the application by appropriate means in order to check that it is reasoned and meets the requirements of Chapter III.

(e) Amendments to applications

5.154 Article 31(1) permits any group having a legitimate interest to apply for approval of an amendment to a product specification. Such applications are required to describe and give reasons for the amendments requested.

5.155 Article 31(2) classifies amendments to product specifications into two categories as regards their importance:

    (a)   Union amendments requiring an opposition procedure at Union level;

    (b)   standard amendments to be dealt with at Member State or third-country level.

5.156 Article 31(3) provides that an amendment shall be considered a Union amendment if it:

    (a)   includes a change in the name or any part of the name of the geographical indication registered under this Regulation;

    (b)   consists of a change of the legal name or the category of the spirit drink;

(c)   risks voiding the given quality, reputation or other characteristic of the spirit drink that is essentially attributable to its geographical origin; or

(d)   entails further restrictions on the marketing of the product.

Any other amendments are considered to be standard amendments.

Article 31(4) provides that Union amendments shall be approved by the Commission. The approval procedure shall follow, *mutatis mutandis*, the procedure laid down in Art 24 and Arts 26–30. Applications for Union amendments submitted by a third country or by third-country producers have to contain proof that the requested amendment complies with the laws applicable in that third country to the protection of GIs.   **5.157**

Article 31(5) provides that standard amendments shall be approved by the Member State in whose territory the geographical area of the product concerned is located. As regards third countries, amendments have to be approved in accordance with the law applicable in the third country concerned.   **5.158**

(f) Eligible applicants

Article 24(1) provides that applications for the registration of a GI under this Chapter may only be submitted by 'groups who work with the spirit drink, the name of which is proposed for registration'. Article 24(2) envisages that a Member State may designate an authority designated 'if it is not feasible for the producers concerned to form a group by reason of their number, geographical locations or organisational characteristics'.   **5.159**

Article 24(3) provides that a single natural or legal person may be deemed to be a group for the purpose of this Chapter if both of the following conditions are fulfilled: **5.160**

(a)   the person concerned is the only producer willing to submit an application; and

(b)   the defined geographical area possesses characteristics which differ appreciably from those of neighbouring areas, the characteristics of the spirit drink are different from those produced in neighbouring areas or the spirit drink has a special quality, reputation or other characteristic which is clearly attributable to its geographical origin.

In such case, the application dossier referred to in Art 23(2) is required to state those reasons.   **5.161**

An application dossier as referred to in Art 24(7) shall include: **5.162**

(a) the name and address of the applicant group;

(b) the single document referred to in point (c) of paragraph 1 of this Article;

(c) a declaration by the Member State that it considers that the application meets the requirements of this Regulation and the provisions adopted pursuant thereto;

(d) the publication reference of the product specification.

5.163 Article 24(9) requires the documents referred to in this Article which are sent to the Commission to be in one of the official languages of the EU.

(g)   Cross-border applications

5.164 In the case of a GI that designates a cross-border geographical area, Art 24(4) provides that several groups from different Member States or third countries may submit a joint application for registration. Where a joint application is submitted, it shall be submitted to the Commission by a Member State concerned, or by an applicant group in a third country concerned, directly or through the authorities of that third country after consultation of all the authorities and applicant groups concerned.

5.165 The joint application shall include the declaration referred to in Art 23(2)(c) from all the Member States concerned. The requirements laid down in Art 23 shall be fulfilled in all Member States and third countries concerned.

5.166 In the case of joint applications, the related national opposition procedures shall be carried out in all the Member States concerned.

(h)   Applications from third countries

5.167 Article 24(8) provides that where the application relates to a geographical area in a third country, the application shall be submitted to the Commission, either directly or via the authorities of the third country concerned. Such an application is required by Art 23(1) to also include the publication reference of the product specification and proof that the name of the product is protected in its country of origin.

(i)   Scrutiny by the Commission

5.168 The Commission is required by Art 26 to 'scrutinise by appropriate means any application that it receives pursuant to Article 24', in order to check that it is reasoned, that it meets the requirements of this Chapter, and that the interests of stakeholders outside the Member State of application have been taken into account.

Such scrutiny shall be based on the single document referred to in Art 23(1)(c) **5.169** and shall consist of a check that there are no manifest errors in the application. The Commission is required by Art 26, at least each month, to make public the list of names for which registration applications have been submitted to it, as well as their date of submission. The list shall also contain the name of the Member State or third country from which the application came.

Where, based on the scrutiny carried out under the Article, the Commission **5.170** considers that the requirements of this Chapter are met, it is required to publish in the *Official Journal of the European Union* the single document referred to in Art 23(1)(c) and the publication reference of the product specification.

(j) Opposition proceedings

As part of the scrutiny of an application under Art 24(5), a Member State is **5.171** required by Art 24(6) to initiate a national opposition procedure that ensures adequate publication of the application and that provides for a reasonable period within which any natural or legal person having a legitimate interest and resident or established on its territory may submit an opposition to the application. The Member State is required to examine the admissibility of any opposition received in accordance with the criteria referred to in Art 28.

Article 24(7) requires a Member State to ensure that where it takes a **5.172** favourable decision, that decision is to be made, providing any natural or legal person having a legitimate interest with an opportunity to appeal. The Member State is also required to ensure that the version of the product specification on which its favourable decision is based is published made available electronically. The Member State is also required to ensure adequate publication of the version of the product specification on which the Commission took its decision pursuant to Art 26(2).

Within three months from the date of publication in the *Official Journal of the* **5.173** *European Union*, the authorities of a Member State or of a third country, or a natural or legal person having a legitimate interest and resident or established in a third country may submit a notice of opposition to the Commission.

The procedure for oppositions is set out in Art 27. Article 27(1) provides that **5.174** any natural or legal person having a legitimate interest and resident or established in a Member State other than that from which the application was submitted, may submit a notice of opposition to the Member State in which that person is resident or established within a time limit permitting an opposition to be submitted.

5.175 The notice of opposition shall contain a declaration that the application might infringe the requirements of Chapter III, without this the notice of opposition shall be void. The Commission is required by Art 27(1) to forward the notice of opposition without delay to the authority or body that submitted the application.

5.176 Article 27(2) provides that if a notice of opposition is submitted to the Commission and is followed within two months by a reasoned statement of opposition, the Commission is required to check the admissibility of this reasoned statement of opposition. Article 27(3) prescribes that within two months from the receipt of an admissible reasoned statement of opposition, the Commission shall invite the authority or person that submitted the opposition and the authority or body that submitted the application to engage in appropriate consultations for a period that shall not exceed three months. That deadline shall start on the date when the invitation to the interested parties is delivered by electronic means.

5.177 The authority or person that submitted the opposition and the authority or body that submitted the application is required to start such appropriate consultations without undue delay and shall 'provide each other with the relevant information to assess whether the application for registration complies with the requirements of this Chapter'. If no agreement is reached, this information shall also be provided to the Commission.

5.178 When the interested parties reach an agreement, Art 27(3) requires the authorities of the Member State or of the third country from which the application was submitted to notify the Commission of all the factors which enabled that agreement to be reached, including the opinions of the applicant and of the authorities of a Member State or of a third country, or of other natural and legal persons having submitted an opposition.

5.179 Irrespective of whether an agreement has been reached or not, the notification to the Commission shall be made within one month from the end of the consultations.

5.180 At any time during those three months, the Commission may, at the request of the applicant, extend the deadline for the consultations by a maximum of three months.

In the case of substantial amendment of the details published in accordance **5.181** with Art 26(2) the Commission is required by Art 27(4) to repeat the scrutiny referred to in Art 26.

Article 27(5) requires the notice of opposition, the reasoned statement of **5.182** opposition and the related documents which are sent to the Commission to be in one of the official languages of the Union.

Article 28(1) provides that the reasoned statement of opposition referred to in **5.183** Art 27(2) shall be admissible only if it is received by the Commission within the time limit set out in that Article and that grounds for opposition are set out in that notice.

The grounds for opposition listed in Art 28(1) are: **5.184**

    (a)   the proposed geographical indication does not comply with the definition in Article 3(4) or with the requirements referred to in Article 22;

    (b)   the registration of the proposed geographical indication would be contrary to Article 34 (homonymous names) or 35 (generic names);

    (c)   the registration of the proposed geographical indication would jeopardise the existence of an entirely or partly identical name or of a trade mark or the existence of products which have been legally on the market for at least five years preceding the date of the publication provided for in Article 26(2); or

    (d)   the requirements referred to in Articles 31 (amendment) and 32 (cancelled mark) are not complied with.

Article 28(2) requires the grounds for opposition to be assessed in relation to **5.185** the territory of the EU.

(k) Decision on registration

Article 30(1) provides that where, on the basis of the information available to **5.186** the Commission from the scrutiny carried out pursuant to Art 26(1), the Commission considers that the conditions for the registration of a proposed GI are not fulfilled, it shall inform the Member State or third-country applicant concerned of the reasons for rejection and shall give it two months to submit observations.

If the Commission receives no observations or, if, despite the observations **5.187** received, it still considers that the conditions for registration are not fulfilled it shall, by means of implementing acts, reject the application unless the application is withdrawn. Those implementing acts shall be adopted in accordance with the examination procedure referred to in Art 47(2).

5.188 Where, however, the Commission receives no notice of opposition or no admissible reasoned statement of opposition under Art 27, Art 30(2) permits it to adopt implementing acts, without applying the procedure referred to in Art 47(2), to register the name.

5.189 Article 30(3) provides that if the Commission receives an admissible reasoned statement of opposition, it shall, following the appropriate consultations referred to in Art 27(3), and taking into account the results thereof, either:

    (a)   if an agreement has been reached, register the name by means of implementing acts adopted without applying the procedure referred to in Article 47(2), and, if necessary, amend the information published pursuant to Article 26(2) provided such amendments are not substantial; or

    (b)   if an agreement has not been reached, adopt implementing acts deciding on the registration.

5.190 Article 30(4) provides that acts of registration and decisions on rejection shall be published in the *Official Journal of the European Union* and that the act of registration shall grant the protection referred to in Art 21 to the GI.

(l) Transitional periods for use of geographical indications

5.191 Article 29 permits the Commission to adopt implementing acts granting a transitional period of up to five years to enable spirit drinks originating in a Member State or a third country, and the name of which contravenes Art 21(2), to continue to use the designation under which they were marketed on condition that an admissible statement of opposition under Art 24(6) or Art 27 shows that the registration of the name would jeopardise the existence of:

    (a)   an entirely identical name or of a compound name, one term of which is identical to the name to be registered; or

    (b)   other names similar to the name to be registered which refer to spirit drinks which have been legally on the market for at least five years preceding the date of the publication provided for in Article 26(2).

5.192 Article 29(2) permits the Commission, without prejudice to Art 36, to adopt implementing acts extending the transitional period granted under Art 26(1) up to 15 years, or allowing continued use for up to 15 years in duly justified cases, provided it is shown that:

    (a)   the designation referred to in Article 26(1) has been in legal use consistently and fairly for at least 25 years before the application for protection was submitted to the Commission;

(b) the purpose of using the designation referred to in Article 26(1) has not, at any time, been to profit from the reputation of the registered geographical indication; and

(c) the consumer has not been nor could have been misled as to the true origin of the product.

(m) Cancellation

Article 32(1) provides that the Commission may, on its own initiative or at the **5.193** request of any natural or legal person having a legitimate interest, adopt implementing acts to cancel the registration of a GI:

(a) where compliance with the requirements for the product specification can no longer be ensured;

(b) where no product has been placed on the market under the geographical indication for at least seven consecutive years.

Article 32(2) permits the Commission, at the request of the producers of the **5.194** spirit drink marketed under the registered GI, to adopt implementing acts cancelling a registration.

In the above situations, Art 32(3) requires the Commission, before adopting **5.195** the implementing act, to consult the authorities of the Member State, the authorities of the third country or, where possible, the third-country producer which had originally applied for the registration of the GI concerned, unless the cancellation is directly requested by those original applicants.

The implementing acts referred to in this Article shall be adopted in accord- **5.196** ance with the examination procedure referred to in Art 47(2).

(n) Register of geographical indications of spirit drinks

Article 33 requires the Commission to establish a register of GIs of spirit **5.197** drinks. In relation to GIs registered under the new Regulation, Art 33(2) requires direct access to be provided to the single documents and shall also contain the publication reference of the product specification. For GIs registered before the Regulation, direct access is to be provided to the main specifications of the technical file as set out in Art 17(4) of Regulation (EC) No 110/2008.

Article 33(3) permits the registration of GIs of spirit drinks produced in third **5.198** countries that are protected in the EU pursuant to an international agreement to which the EU is a contracting party.

(o)   Homonymous geographical indications

5.199   Where a name for which an application is submitted is a whole or partial homonym of a name already registered under the draft Regulation, Art 34(1) permits the name to be registered 'with due regard to local and traditional usage and any risk of confusion'. A homonymous name is defined in Art 34(2) as a name which misleads the consumer into believing that products come from another territory and provides that it shall not be registered 'even if the name is accurate as far as the actual territory, region or place of origin of those products is concerned'.

5.200   Article 34(3) provides that the use of a registered homonymous GI shall be subject to there being a sufficient distinction in practice between the homonym registered subsequently and the name already in the register, having regard to the need to treat the producers concerned in an equitable manner and not to mislead the consumer.

5.201   Article 34(4) provides that the protection of GIs of spirit drinks referred to in Art 21 of the draft Regulation shall be without prejudice to the protected GIs and designations of origin of products under Regulations (EU) No 1308/2013 (establishing a common organisation of the markets in agricultural products) and (EU) No 251/2014 (on the definition, description, presentation, labelling and the protection of GIs of aromatised wine products).

(p)   Specific grounds for refusal of protection

5.202   Article 35(1) provides that a generic name shall not be protected as a GI and that to establish whether or not a name has become a generic name, account shall be taken of all relevant factors, in particular: (a) the existing situation in the EU, in particular in areas of consumption; and (b) the relevant EU or national legislation.

5.203   Well-known marks are dealt with in Art 35(2) which provides that a name shall not be protected as a GI where, in the light of a trade mark's reputation and renown, protection could mislead the consumer as to the true identity of the spirit drink.

5.204   Article 35(3) provides that a name shall only be protected as a GI if the production steps which give the spirit drink the quality, reputation or other characteristic that is essentially attributable to its geographical origin, take place in the relevant geographical area.

(q) Relationship between trade marks and geographical indications

Article 36(1) provides that the registration of a trade mark the use of which **5.205** corresponds or would correspond to one or more of the situations referred to in Art 21(2) shall be refused or invalidated.

In the case of a trade mark which has been applied for, registered, or **5.206** established by use, before the date on which the application for protection of the GI was submitted to the Commission, Art 36(2) allows the trade mark to continue to be used and renewed, if that possibility is provided for by the legislation concerned, in good faith within the territory of the Union, notwithstanding the registration of a GI, provided that no grounds for its invalidity or revocation exist under Directive (EU) 2015/2436 (to approximate the laws of the Member States relating to trade marks) and Regulation (EU) No 2017/1001 (on the European trade mark).

(r) Existing registered geographical indications

Article 37 provides that GIs of spirit drinks registered in Annex III to **5.207** Regulation (EC) No 110/2008 and thus protected under that Regulation shall automatically be protected as GIs under the draft Regulation and the Commission shall list them in the register referred to in Art 33 of the draft Regulation.

(s) Surveillance of names in the market place

Article 39 requires Member States to carry out checks, based on a risk analysis, **5.208** as regards the use, in the market place, of the GIs registered under the draft Regulation and shall take all necessary measures in the event of breaches of the requirements of Chapter III.

Member States have to take appropriate administrative and judicial steps to **5.209** prevent or stop the unlawful use of the names of products or services that are produced or marketed in their territory and that are covered by geographical indications registered under the draft Regulation.

Member States are required to designate the authorities responsible carrying **5.210** out checks and are required to inform the Commission of the names and addresses of the competent authorities responsible for checking, which the Commission shall make public.

F. PROTECTED DESIGNATIONS – CASE LAW

1. 'Whisky'

5.211 In Case C-136/96, *The Scotch Whisky Association v COFEPP*,[31] the ECJ considered that the use of the words 'Blended Whisky Spirit' and 'spiritueux au whisky' ('whisky-based spirit') in relation to a drink diluted below the 40 per cent alcohol level required for the designation of 'whisky' under Council Regulation (EEC) No 1576/89 of 29 May 1989 laying down general rules on the definition, description and presentation of spirit drinks,[32] breached that Regulation.

5.212 The Scotch Whisky Association brought proceedings before the Tribunal de Grande Instance, Paris, against COFEPP, Prisunic SA and Centrale d'Achats et de Services Alimentaires SARL (Casal), seeking, inter alia, a finding that they had engaged in unfair competition against it by marketing their diluted whisky-based drinks on the same shelves as complying whiskies. In relation to questions put to the ECJ it held that Art 1(4) of Regulation No 1576/89, specifically provided that the term 'whisky' may not appear in the sales description of such a product.[33]

5.213 COFEPP also argued that 'whisky' was a generic term inside a compound term and exonerated by Art 7(b) of Commission Regulation (EEC) No 1014/90 of 24 April 1990 laying down detailed implementing rules on the definition, description and presentation of spirit drinks.[34]

5.214 The Court followed the approach of the Advocate General who observed that the words 'spiritueux au whisky' did not constitute a compound term within the meaning of Art 7b of Regulation No 1014/90, as by 'compound term', 'the Community legislature intended to refer to a combination of the names of two different drinks, not the combination of the words "spirit" and "whisky", whisky being itself a spirit'.[35]

5.215 *Scotch Whisky Association v JD Vintners Ltd*[36] concerned an action by the trade association of the proprietors of the vast majority of the leading brands of Scotch Whisky. The defendant sold a spirit with an alcoholic strength of 30

---

31 [1996] ECR I-04571.
32 OJ 1989 L 160, p. 1.
33 [1996] ECR I-04571, at para 33.
34 OJ 1990 L 105, p. 9.
35 [1996] ECR I-04571, at para 43.
36 [1997] EuLR 446.

per cent called 'Canadian Whisky'. After the coming into force of Council Regulation (EEC) No 1576/89 of 29 May 1989 laying down general rules on the definition, description and presentation of spirit drinks,[37] which provided that a spirit which was to have the name of 'whisky' or 'whiskey' was to have a minimum alcoholic strength of 40 per cent, the defendant changed the name of the spirit to 'Light Canadian Rye'. The plaintiffs issued proceedings claiming that the sale of the spirit as 'Light Canadian Rye' represented a breach of the provision in the Regulation that required spirit with an alcoholic strength of under 40 per cent to be described and sold as 'spirit' or a 'spirit drink'.

The defendant applied for the part of the cause of action based in breaches of the Regulation to be struck out. It was contended that any breach of the Regulation did not give rise to a private action in damages because the allegation of the breach of the Regulation was an allegation of breach of statutory duty, and since the duty imposed by the Regulation was for the benefit of consumers, not rival traders, a breach of the Regulation could not support a private action by rival traders. It was contended that, in any event, the Regulation could not support a private action by a trade association such as the first plaintiff. **5.216**

Sir Richard Scott V-C ruled that as a matter of construction of the Regulation as a whole it could be concluded that its purposes included not only the protection of the consumer but also the maintenance of the quality of the products and the protection of traders in those products from unfair competition from rival traders who described and sold as 'whisky' spirit with an alcoholic content that was less than 40 per cent. Therefore, it was at least arguable that the Regulation gave right to a private right of action for breach and, accordingly, the application to strike out the allegations based on breaches of the Regulation was dismissed.[38] As the Regulation had direct effect in the UK, the Court ruled that private actions could be brought by persons falling in the requisite class or classes of those adversely affected by a breach of the Regulation. **5.217**

In *Scotch Whisky Association v Glen Kella Distillers Ltd*[39] a trade association, whose members included the majority of the makers of the leading brands of Scotch Whisky, objected to the sale by the defendant of a drink known as Glen Kella, which was called 'white whisky' and which was made by the **5.218**

---

37   OJ 1989 L 160, p. 1 (*no longer in force*).
38   [1997] EuLR 446, at pp. 450–51.
39   [1997] ETMR 470.

re-distilling of matured and blended Scotch Whisky in the Isle of Man. The plaintiffs issued proceedings and sought an injunction in the UK High Court to prevent the defendant selling the drink as whisky. They contended that Glen Kella was not whisky by reason of the fact that it was not matured after distillation and accordingly, its sale as whisky was in breach of Art 1(4)(b) of Regulation No 1576/89, which required that the 'spirit drink' concerned should have undergone a process of maturation for at least three years in wooden casks after its production as a liquid by distillation. The defendant contended that Glen Kella was whisky within the definition contained in the Regulation since it had undergone a process of maturation for at least three years prior to the defendant's re-distillation of the spirit. It was submitted that in any event the plaintiffs had no *locus standi* to enforce the provisions of the Regulation, which could only be enforced by government agencies.

5.219   Rattee J held that there was no justification for ignoring the clearly expressed requirement in Art 1(4)(b) of the Regulation that the 'spirit drink' concerned should have undergone a process of maturation for at least three years after its production as a liquid by distillation. The liquid produced by the defendant's re-distillation process was not the same as the liquid which had undergone the prior maturation process and it had not been subsequently matured. There-fore, Glen Kella was not 'whisky' within the definition in Art 1(4)(b) of the Regulation, and to sell it as whisky was in breach of the Regulation.

5.220   Following *Scotch Whisky Association v JD Vintners Ltd*,[40] the Court also observed that as the purposes of the Regulation included not only the protection of the consumer but also the maintenance of the quality of the products and the protection of traders in those products from unfair com-petition from rival traders, a producer was entitled to enforce the Regulation.

5.221   *Scotch Whisky Association v Michael Klotz*[41] concerned an objection by the Scotch Whisky Association (SWA) to the use of the name of a whisky 'Glen Buchenbach', that was produced by the Waldhorn distillery in Berglen, situated in the Buchenbach valley in Swabia (Baden-Württemberg, Germany).

5.222   The label on the whisky bottles in question included, in addition to a stylised depiction of a hunting horn (*Waldhorn* in German), the following infor-mation: "'*Waldhornbrennerei*" (Waldhorn distillery), "Glen Buchenbach",

---

40   [1997] EuLR 446.
41   Case C-44/17, Judgment 7 June 2018.

"Swabian Single Malt Whisky", "500 ml", "40% vol", *"Deutsches Erzeugnis"* (German product), *"Hergestellt in den Berglen"* (produced in the Berglen)'.

The SWA brought an action before the Landgericht Hamburg (Regional **5.223** Court, Hamburg, Germany) seeking an order that Mr Klotz, inter alia, cease to market his whisky, under the designation 'Glen Buchenbach', on the ground that use of that designation infringed, in particular, Art 16(a)–(c) of Reg No 10/2008, which protected the GIs registered in Annex III to that regulation, which included 'Scotch Whisky'.

The Landgericht Hamburg referred three questions to the CJEU for a **5.224** preliminary ruling:

(1) Does 'indirect commercial use' of a registered geographical indication of a spirit drink in accordance with Article 16(a) of Regulation No 110/2008 require that the registered geographical indication be used in identical or phonetically and/or visually similar form, or is it sufficient that the disputed element evokes in the relevant public some kind of association with the registered geographical indication or the geographical area?

If the latter is sufficient, when determining whether there is any 'indirect commercial use', does the context in which the disputed element is embedded then also play a role, or can that context not counteract indirect commercial use of the registered geographical indication, even if the disputed element is accompanied by an indication of the true origin of the product?

(2) Does an 'evocation' of a registered geographical indication in accordance with Article 16(b) of Regulation No 110/2008 require that there be a phonetic and/or visual similarity between the registered geographical indication and the disputed element, or is it sufficient that the disputed element evokes in the relevant public some kind of association with the registered geographical indication or the geographical area?

If the latter is sufficient: When determining whether there is any 'evocation', does the context in which the disputed element is embedded also play a role, or can that context not counteract any unlawful evocation of the registered geographical indication, even if the disputed element is accompanied by an indication of the true origin of the product?

(3) When determining whether there is any 'other false or misleading indication' in accordance with Article 16(c) of Regulation No110/2008, does the context in which the disputed element is embedded play a role, or can that context not counteract any misleading indication, even if the disputed element is accompanied by an indication of the true origin of the product?

5.225 Applying its previous decisions in *Viiniverla*,[42] *EUIPO v Instituto dos Vinhos do Douro e do Porto*[43] and *Comité Interprofessionnel du Vin de Champagnev Aldi Süd Dienstleistungs-GmbH & Co OHG*,[44] the CJEU answered the first question by advising that Art 16(a) must be interpreted as meaning that, for the purpose of establishing that there is 'indirect commercial use' of a registered GI, the disputed element must be used in a form that is either identical to that indication or phonetically and/or visually similar to it. 'Accordingly, it is not sufficient that that element is liable to evoke in the relevant public some kind of association with the indication concerned or the geographical area relating thereto.'[45] Having regard to this answer to the first part of the first question, the CJEU considered that there was no need to answer the second part.[46]

5.226 In relation to the second question concerning evocation, the Court noted that its case law has established that the notion of 'evocation' covers a situation in which the term used to designate a product incorporates part of a protected GI, so that when the consumer is confronted with the name of the product in question, the image triggered in his mind is that of the product whose indication is protected.[47]

5.227 Thus, the CJEU followed its earlier rulings that for the purpose of finding there to be an 'evocation' within the meaning of Art 6(b) of Regulation 110/2008 it was up to the national court to determine not only whether the term used to designate the product at issue incorporated a part of a protected GI but also whether, when the consumer is confronted with the name of the product, the image triggered in his mind is that of the product whose indication is protected.[48] It advised that the national court must, in making that assessment, refer to 'the perception of an average European consumer who is reasonably well-informed and reasonably observant and circumspect'.[49] In addition, the Court noted its rulings that it is legitimate to consider there to be an evocation of a protected GI where, concerning products which are similar in appearance, the sales names are phonetically and visually similar.[50]

5.228 In addition to the criteria relating to the incorporation of a part of a protected GI in the disputed designation and to the phonetic and visual similarity

---

42 C-75/15, EU:C:2016.
43 C-56/16 P, EU:C:2017:693.
44 C-393/16, EU:C:2017:99.
45 Case C-44/17, Judgment at para 39.
46 Ibid., at para 40.
47 Referring to *Viiniverla*, C-75/15, EU:C:2016:35, para 21 and the case law cited.
48 Case C-44/17, Judgment at para 45.
49 Ibid., at para 47.
50 Ibid., at para 48.

between the designation and the indication, it was noted that the Court has ruled that it is necessary, where appropriate, to take account of the criterion of 'conceptual proximity' between terms emanating from different languages, since such proximity, like the other criteria mentioned above, may also trigger an image in the consumer's mind which is that of the product whose GI is protected, when he is confronted with a similar product bearing the disputed name.[51]

Thus in the main proceedings, the CJEU ruled that the referring court would **5.229** have to determine whether an average European consumer who is reasonably well-informed and reasonably observant and circumspect thinks directly of the protected GI, namely 'Scotch Whisky', when he is confronted with a comparable product bearing the disputed designation, in this case 'Glen', that court taking account, in the absence of (i) any phonetic and/or visual similarity between the disputed designation and the protected GI and (ii) any partial incorporation of that indication in that designation, of conceptual proximity between the protected GI and the disputed designation.[52]

As regards the second part of the second question, concerning the role that the **5.230** context in which the disputed designation is embedded plays in the national court's assessment of whether there is an 'evocation' within the meaning of Art 16(b), the CJEU noted that it was 'apparent from the wording of that provision that there may be an "evocation" even if the true origin of the product is indicated'.[53]

Finally, the Court ruled in answer to the third question that Art 16(c) must be **5.231** interpreted as meaning that, for the purpose of establishing that there is a 'false or misleading indication', as prohibited by that provision, account is not be taken of the context in which the disputed element is used.[54]

The Hamburg court in applying the CJEU decision[55] found that no infringe- **5.232** ment of Art 16(a) had occurred, since 'Glen Buchenbach' does not make actual use of the registered indication 'Scotch Whisky'. The court also found that no 'evocation' in the sense of Art 16(b) had occurred, since there was no conceptual proximity between 'Glen' and 'Scotch Whisky'. The fact that it

---

51 Ibid., at para 50.
52 Ibid., at para 52.
53 Ibid., at para 57.
54 Ibid., at para 71.
55 Referred to in http://ipkitten.blogspot.com/2019/02/glen-buchenbach-is-misleading.html, accessed 4 April 2019.

might cause a chain of associations ending with 'Scotch Whisky' was held not to be a sufficient evocation in an Art 16(b) sense.

5.233 However, the Court found that the use of the indication 'Glen' on a whisky that was not 'Scotch Whisky' constituted a 'misleading indication', liable to convey a false impression as to the product's origin under Art 16(c) because the designation 'Glen' gives the average European consumer who is reasonably well-informed and reasonably observant and circumspect the impression that this is a 'Scotch Whisky'. It noted that almost all whiskies with the designation 'Glen' in their name were Scotch whiskies, even though not all Scotch whiskies bore the designation 'Glen', because the question was whether there was a risk that consumers would think of Scotch whisky when they heard of a whisky bearing the name 'Glen' and not whether they thought of 'Glen' when they heard 'Scotch whisky'.

5.234 The Court ruled that the additional information on the disputed product, such as 'Swabian Single Malt Whisky' and 'Deutsches Erzeugnis' (produce of Germany) could not be used to restrict the protection of GIs and must not be taken into account when assessing the misleading indication.

2. 'Cognac'

5.235 In Joined Cases C-4/10 and C-27/10 *Bureau national interprofessionnel du Cognac v Gust Ranin Oy*.[56] Gust. Ranin Oy applied to register in Finland two figurative trade marks: HIENOA KONJAKKIA mark for 'cognac', and CAFÉ COGNAC trade mark for 'liqueur including cognac'. The Bureau National Interprofessionnel du Cognac ('BNIC') opposed the registration of both marks, objecting to the use of the word 'Cognac' in the labels. The Finnish Patent and Registration Office (Patentti- ja rekisterihallitus) rejected the opposition against the 'HIENOA KONJAKKIA' label, but accepted the opposition against the 'CAFÉ COGNAC' label. The reason for the different result was due to the legend 'Product of France' in the 'HIENOA KONJAKKIA' label, which was considered to remove any misconception about the origin of the product. The BNIC sought to annul the adverse decision. By a decision of 22 October 2007, the Board of Appeal of the Finnish Patent and Registration Office (Patentti- ja rekis-terihallituksen valituslautakunta) dismissed the BNIC's appeal and upheld the decision of 10 September 2004 confirming the registration of the 'HIENOA KONJAKKIA' mark. It also upheld the appeal brought by

---

56   [2011] ETMR 53.

Gust. Ranin Oy and set aside the decision cancelling the 'CAFÉ COGNAC' registration.

In proceedings before the Supreme Administrative Court (Korkein hallinto-oikeus) the BNIC sought the annulment of the decision of 22 October 2007 or the referral of the case back to the Finnish Patent and Registration Office in order for it to undertake a fresh examination of the case. These proceedings were stayed for a referral of questions to the ECJ. **5.236**

One question was whether Arts 16 and 23 of Regulation No 110/2008 preclude the registration of a mark which contains a PGI of origin, or such an indication in the form of a generic term and a translation of the latter, and which is registered for spirit drinks which do not satisfy the conditions for the use of that GI. **5.237**

The Court observed that the clear and unconditional wording of Art 23(1) of Regulation No 110/2008, under which the registration of a mark which contains a GI registered in Annex III is to be refused or invalidated if its use would lead to any of the situations referred to in Art 16 of that Regulation, requires the national authorities to refuse or to invalidate the registration of a mark if it is used in such circumstances. The term 'Cognac' appears both in Annex III to Regulation No 110/2008 and in Annex II to Regulation No 1576/89 as a GI identifying a spirit drink originating from France. The Court ruled that independently of the protection it enjoys under French law, the term 'Cognac' has therefore been protected as a GI under EU law since 15 June 1989, the date on which Regulation No 1576/89 entered into force.[57] **5.238**

The Court observed that the protection thus conferred on GIs by Art 16 of Regulation No 110/2008 must be interpreted in the light of the objective pursued through the registration of those indications, 'namely, as is clear from recital 14 to that regulation, to enable the identification of spirit drinks as originating in a particular area, where a given quality, reputation or other characteristic of those drinks is essentially attributable to its geographical origin'.[58] Specifically, the extent of that protection must be assessed in the light of the fundamental rule laid down in Art 15(4) of Regulation No 110/2008, in accordance with which a GI registered in Annex III to that regulation may be borne only by spirit drinks which meet all the specifications in the technical file provided to the Commission by the Member State of origin, pursuant to Art 17 of Regulation No 110/2008, when the application **5.239**

---

57   [2011] ETMR 53, at para 43.
58   Ibid., at para 44.

for registration of the indication concerned is made.[59] The question whether a particular spirit drink meets all the specifications applicable to a PGI is a question of fact which is a matter to be determined by the competent national authorities and which must be decided before the examination as to whether Art 16 of Regulation No 110/2008 may be applicable.[60]

5.240 In so far as that question refers to a mark containing the generic term corresponding to a PGI and its translation, the Court noted that, pursuant to the first subparagraph of Art 15(3) of Regulation No 110/2008, the GIs registered in Annex III thereto cannot become generic. Conversely, the second subparagraph of Art 15(3) states that names which have become generic may not be registered in Annex III. It follows that, for the purposes of determining the validity of the registration of the marks at issue in the main proceedings, it cannot be argued that the indication 'Cognac', registered in Annex III, has become generic.[61]

5.241 It should be added that, in accordance with Art 14(2) of Regulation No 110/2008, the GIs registered in Annex III thereto, such as 'Cognac', cannot be translated either on the label or in the presentation of a spirit drink.[62]

5.242 In Joined Cases C-4/10 and C-27/10 *Bureau national interprofessionnel du Cognac v Gust. Ranin Oy*[63] the ECJ considered the concept of 'evocation', as referred to in Art 16(b) of Regulation No 110/2008. It pointed out that that concept covered 'a situation in which the term used to designate a product incorporates part of a protected designation, so that when the consumer is confronted with the name of the product, the image triggered in his mind is that of the product whose designation is protected'.[64] It also instanced the situation where the Court has held that that could be the position in the case of products with visual similarities and sales names which are phonetically and visually alike.[65]

5.243 The Court ruled that the use of a mark containing the element 'Cognac' for spirit drinks which did not meet the relevant specifications could be categorised as an 'evocation' for the purposes of Art 16(b) of Regulation No 110/

---

59   Ibid., at para 48.
60   Ibid., at para 49.
61   Ibid., at para 53.
62   Ibid., at para 52.
63   [2011] ETMR 53.
64   Ibid., at para 56, citing Case C-87/97 *Consorzio per la tutela del formaggio Gorgonzola* [1999] ECR I-1301, para 25 and Case C-132/05 *Commission v Germany* [2008] ECR I-957, para 44.
65   Ibid., at para 57 citing *Consorzio per la tutela del formaggio Gorgonzola*, para 27 and *Commission v Germany*, para 46.

2008.[66] It added that, in accordance with that provision, the mention of the actual origin of the product or the use of the GI in translation or accompanied by an expression such as 'like', 'type', 'style', 'made', 'flavour', or any other similar term, would not alter that categorisation.[67]

3. 'Calvados'

Viiniverla Oy v Sosiaali- ja terveysalan lupa- ja valvontavirasto[68] concerned a   **5.244**
request made in proceedings between Viiniverla Oy ('Viiniverla'), a company established under Finnish law, and the Sosiaali- ja terveysalan lupa- ja valvontavirasto (Social and Health Sector Licensing and Supervisory Author-ity, 'the Authority') concerning the latter's decision of 18 November 2013 to prohibit Viiniverla from marketing a drink named 'Verlados'. Viiniverla, had manufactured and marketed cider spirits named 'Verlados' since 2001. On 23 November 2012, following a complaint relating to the alleged misuse of the French geographic indication 'Calvados', the European Commission sent the Finnish authorities a request for clarification relating to the use of the name 'Verlados'. In their reply of 31 January 2013, the Finnish authorities stated that the drink named 'Verlados' was a local product whose name refers directly to the place of its manufacture, that is to say the village of Verla and the Verla winery. On 6 March 2013 the Commission indicated that the name 'Verlados' was not authorised under Art 16(b) of Regulation No 110/2008, and that it intended to open infringement proceedings against the Republic of Finland. Consequently, the Authority adopted, on the basis of Art 49(2) of the Law on alcohol, a decision prohibiting Viiniverla from marketing the drink named 'Verlados' as from 1 February 2014. Viiniverla brought before the mark-kinaoikeus (Market Court) an action for annulment of that decision. Before that court, it claimed that the use of the name 'Verlados' did not constitute any misuse, imitation or evocation of the product 'Calvados' and did not therefore infringe EU law on the protection of geographical indications.

The Market Court stayed the proceedings and referred a number of questions   **5.245**
to the CJEU, including:

> (1) whether when assessing whether to prohibit the use of the name Verlados in order to protect the geographical indication 'Calvados', what importance should be given to the following facts in the interpretation of the concept of 'evocation' in Article 16(b) of Regulation No 110/2008 and the application of that regulation:

---

66   Ibid., at para 58.
67   Ibid., at para 59.
68   Case C-75/15 (26 Jan. 2016).

(a) the first part of the name Verlados, Verla, is a village in Finland whose name may be recognised by Finnish consumers;

(b) the first part of the name Verlados, Verla, refers to the producer of Verlados, Viiniverla Oy;

(c) Verlados is a local product produced in Verla village of which a few hundred litres on average are sold each year in the winery's own restaurant and a limited amount by order from the state-owned alcohol business referred to in the Law on alcohol;

(d) the words Verlados and Calvados have only one syllable in common ('dos') out of three, although the last four letters ('ados') of the words, that is, half of the total number of letter in each word, are identical?

(2) If there is considered to be an 'evocation' within the meaning of Article 16(b) of Regulation No.110/2008, may the use of the name Verlados nevertheless be authorised on one of the grounds mentioned above or on other grounds, such as that Finnish consumers at least are unlikely to imagine that Verlados is produced in France?

5.246 In assessing whether the name 'Verlados' constituted an 'evocation' within the meaning of Art 16(b), the Court said that the national court had to take into consideration, in addition to the phonetic and visual relationship between the names, the existence of circumstances which tended to indicate that the use of the name 'Verlados' was not likely to deceive Finnish consumers.[69] This involved a consideration whether, when confronted with the name 'Verlados', the image triggered in the mind of consumers was that of the product benefiting from the protected GI, namely, 'Calvados'.[70]

5.247 It was noted that before the referring court, it had not been disputed that the name 'Verlados' had been used in Finland for products similar to those with the protected GI 'Calvados', that those products had objective characteristics in common, and were consumed, by the relevant public, on occasions which were largely identical.[71] On the question of the visual and phonetic relationship between the two names, the Court ruled that the referring court must take into account the fact that they both contain eight letters, the last four of which were identical, with the same number of syllables, and that they shared the suffix 'dos', which conferred on them 'a certain visual and phonetic similarity'.[72] The Court noted that it was also for the referring court to take into account possible information capable of indicating that the visual and phonetic relationship between the two names was not fortuitous.[73] Given that the suffix 'dos' was added only following a significant growth in exports of

---

69 Ibid., at para 29.
70 Ibid., at para 32.
71 Ibid., at para 37.
72 Ibid., at para 38.
73 Ibid, para 39 referring to *Consorzio per la tutela del formaggio Gorgonzola*, C-87/97, EU:C:1999:115, para 28.

'Calvados' to Finland between 1990 and 2001 and that the suffix had no particular meaning in the Finnish language, the Court ruled that if those facts were established by the referring court, they were capable of constituting evidence from which it may be concluded that the relationship was not fortuitous.[74]

The referring court had pointed out that the name 'Verlados' referred both to **5.248** the name of the undertaking Viiniverla, which manufactured that drink, and to the village of Verla, which was known to Finnish consumers, so that that name was not capable of misleading those consumers. However, the CJEU noted that, under Art 16(b) there may be an 'evocation' even if the true origin of the product was indicated.[75] It noted that the concept of 'consumer' covered European consumers and not only consumers of the Member State in which the product giving rise to the evocation of the protected GI was manufactured and it referred to its earlier decisions which held that there can be 'evocation' even in the absence of any likelihood of confusion between the products concerned.[76] Thus in answer to the second question the Court held that Art 16(b) must be interpreted as meaning that, in order to assess whether the name 'Verlados' constitutes an 'evocation' within the meaning of that provision of the protected GI 'Calvados' with respect to similar products, the referring court must take into consideration the phonetic and visual relationship between those names and any evidence that may show that such a relationship is not fortuitous, so as to ascertain whether, when the average European consumer, reasonably well-informed and reasonably observant and circumspect, is confronted with the name of a product, the image triggered in his mind is that of the product whose GI is protected.[77]

In relation to the third question, the CJEU ruled that Art 16(b) must be **5.249** interpreted as meaning that the use of a name classified as an 'evocation' within the meaning of that provision of a GI referred to in Annex III to Regulation No 110/2008 may not be authorised, even in the absence of any likelihood of confusion.[78]

---

74 Ibid., at para 41.
75 Ibid., at para 43.
76 Ibid para 45 referring to judgments in *Consorzio per la tutela del formaggio Gorgonzola*, C-87/97, EU:C:1999:115, para 26, and *Commission v Germany*, C-132/05, EU:C:2008:117, para 45.
77 Case C-75/15 at para 48.
78 Ibid., at para 52.

G. RELATION BETWEEN TRADE MARKS AND GEOGRAPHICAL INDICATIONS

1. Where registered geographical indication exists

5.250 Article 23(1) of the Spirits Regulation provides that the registration of a trade mark which contains or consists of a GI registered in Annex III shall be refused or invalidated if its use would lead to any of the situations referred to in Art 16.

2. Registration of trade mark prior to geographical indication

5.251 Article 23(2) provides that with due regard to Community law, a trade mark the use of which corresponds to one of the situations referred to in Art 16, which has been applied for, registered, or established by use, if that possibility is provided for by the legislation concerned, in good faith within the territory of the Community, before either the date of protection of the GI in the country of origin or before 1 January 1996, may continue to be used notwithstanding the registration of a GI, provided that no grounds for its invalidity or revocation exist as specified by First Council Directive 89/104/ EEC of 21 December 1988 to approximate the laws of the Member States relating to trade marks[79] Council Regulation (EC) No 40/94 of 20 December 1993 on the Community trade mark.[80]

3. Registration of geographical indication after trade mark

5.252 Article 23(3) of the Spirits Regulation provides that a GI shall not be registered where, in the light of a trade mark's reputation and renown and the length of time it has been used in the Community, registration is liable to mislead the consumer as to the true identity of the product.

4. Control and protection of spirit drinks by Member States

5.253 Article 24(1) of the Spirits Regulation provides that Member States shall be responsible for the control of spirit drinks. They shall take the measures necessary to ensure compliance with the provisions of this Regulation and in

---

79   OJ L 40, 11.2.1989, p. 1. Directive as amended by Council Decision 92/10/EEC OJ L 6, 11.1.1992, p. 35.
80   OJ L 11, 14.1.1994, p. 1. Regulation as last amended by Regulation (EC) No 1891/2006, OJ L 386, 29.12.2006, p. 14.

particular they shall designate the competent authority or authorities responsible for controls in respect of the obligations established by this Regulation in accordance with Regulation (EC) No 882/2004.[81]

Article 24(2) provides that Member States and the Commission shall communicate to each other the information necessary for the application of this Regulation. **5.254**

Article 24(3) provides that the Commission, in consultation with the Member States, shall ensure the uniform application of this Regulation and if necessary shall adopt measures in accordance with the regulatory procedure referred to in Art 25(2). **5.255**

---

81 Regulation (EC) No 882/2004 of the European Parliament and of the Council of 29 April 2004 on official controls performed to ensure the verification of compliance with feed and food law, animal health and animal welfare rules, OJ L 165, 30.4.2004, p. 1, corrected by OJ L 191, 28.5.2004, p. 1. Regulation as last amended by Council Regulation (EC) No 1791/2006.

6

TRADE MARKS, COLLECTIVE MARKS, CERTIFICATION MARKS, PASSING OFF AND DOMAIN NAMES

6.01 Trade mark laws invariably refuse to allow geographical marks to be registered on the ground that they are insufficiently distinctive, as well as the public interest of leaving to traders the names of the geographical areas in which they are located, particularly where a positive commercial reputation is associated with products coming from those areas. Similarly, trade mark laws provide as a defence to infringement the use of a person's address or an indication of the geographical origin of goods or services. Excepted from the trade mark rules that disqualify the registration or enforcement of geographical marks are collective marks and certification marks, as well as registered GIs.

The European rules that relate to these categories of trade marks are discussed **6.02** in this chapter.

A. EUROPEAN TRADE MARKS LEGISLATION

Both Council Regulation (EC) No 207/2009 of 26 February 2009 on the **6.03** Community trade mark[1] (Community Trade Mark Regulation) and Directive 2008/95/EC of the European Parliament and of the Council of 22 October 2008 to approximate the laws of the Member States relating to trade marks[2] (Trade Marks Directive) define as 'signs of which a trade mark may consist' those signs which 'are capable of distinguishing the goods or services of one undertaking from those of other undertakings'.[3]

In 2007 the European Council, recalling that the Community trade mark **6.04** system had been designed to co-exist with the national trade mark systems and that more than a decade had passed since the creation of the Community trade mark, identified the need for an overall assessment of the functioning of the Community trade mark system.[4] It invited the Commission to start work on identifying whether the existing instruments of cooperation between OHIM and national trade mark offices could be intensified and broadened. In its 2008 Small Business Act the Commission pledged to make the Community trade mark system more accessible to small- and medium-sized businesses (SMEs).[5] The Commission's 2008 Communication on an Industrial Property Rights Strategy for Europe reiterated its commitment to an effective and efficient trade mark system and concluded that an overall evaluation of the trade marks system was appropriate.[6] Finally, in its 2011 IPR strategy for Europe,[7] the Commission announced a review of the trade mark system in Europe with a view to modernising the system, both at EU and at national level, by making it more effective, efficient and consistent overall. The main component of the evaluation was a study that the Max Planck Institute for Intellectual Property and Competition Law undertook on behalf of the Commission. The study

---

1 (OJ 2009 L 78, p. 1) codified and repealed Council Regulation (EC) No 40/94 of 20 December 1993 on the Community trade mark, OJ 1994 L 11, p. 1.
2 OJ L 299, 8.11.2008, p. 1.
3 Art 4, Community Trade Mark Regulation, Art 2, Trade Marks Directive.
4 Competitiveness Council Conclusions of 21 and 22 May 2007, Council document 9427/07.
5 Communication from the Commission '"Think Small First", A "Small Business Act" for Europe', COM(2008) 394 final of 25 June 2008.
6 COM(2008) 465 final of 16 July 2008.
7 A Single Market for Intellectual Property Rights: Boosting creativity and innovation to provide economic growth, high quality jobs and first class products and services in Europe', COM(2011) 287.

was carried out between November 2009 and February 2011[8] and involved consultations with stakeholders. The Final Report found that further convergence of trade mark laws and practices in the EU was required. The Council accepted the findings of this report in its Conclusions of 25 May 2010.[9] On 2 April 2013 the EU Council released a proposed amending regulation.[10] Article 1 of this instrument proposes that as a consequence of the entry into force of the Lisbon Treaty, the terminology of the Community Trade Mark Regulation should be updated by changing 'Community trade mark' to 'European trade mark'. It also proposed that Art 2(1) be amended to replace 'the Office for Harmonisation in the Internal Market' with the 'European Union Trade Marks and Designs Agency'.

6.05 In this chapter the previous terminology is used. A subsequent edition of this book will update the terminology when the proposed regulation is adopted.

6.06 This chapter addresses those aspects of European trade marks law which bear on geographical marks.

1. Distinctiveness

6.07 Article 3(1)(b) of the Trade Marks Directive[11] and Art 7(1)(c) of the Community Trade Marks Regulation provide that 'trade marks which are devoid of any distinctive character' shall not be registered or if registered shall be liable to be declared invalid.

6.08 As the OHIM Trade Marks Examination Manual[12] emphasises, Art 7(1)(c) of the Community Trade Marks Regulation does not exclude GIs as such from registration, but 'trade marks which consist exclusively of signs or indications which may serve, in trade, to designate the kind, quality, geographical origin or other characteristics of the goods or services'.[13] As with all other descriptive terms, the test is whether the geographic term describes objective characteristics of the goods and services, assessed with reference to

---

8   See Max Planck Institute for Intellectual Property and Competition Law, *Study on the Overall Functioning of the European Trade Mark System*, Munich, 15.02.2011 http://ec.europa.eu/internal_market/indprop/tm/index_en.htm.

9   Competitiveness Council Conclusions of 25 May 2010 on the future revision of the Trade Mark system in the EU, OJ C 140, 29.5.2010, p. 22.

10 Proposal for a Regulation of the European Parliament and of the Council amending Council Regulation (EC) No 207/2009 on the Community trade mark, COM(2013) 161 final, 2 April 2013.

11 Article 7(1)(b) of the Community Trade Mark Regulation.

12 OHIM, Manual Concerning Proceedings before the Office for Harmonization in the Internal Market (Trade Marks and Designs), Part B, Examination (hereinafter 'the OHIM Trade Marks Manual').

13 Ibid., at 37.

the goods and services claimed and with reference to the perception by the relevant public.[14] The OHIM Trade Marks Manual points out that the descriptive character of the geographical term may pertain to:

- the place of production of the goods,
- the subject matter of a good (for example, what city or region a travel guide is about, or the area covered by a newspaper),
- the place at which the services are rendered,
- the place where the company rendering the services has its seat and from where the rendering of the services is managed and controlled,
- the nature of the goods to which the service relates (eg 'Chinese restaurant').[15]

The OHIM Trade Marks Manual requires that the trade mark is not **6.09** descriptive in any of these respects.[16]

The OHIM Trade Marks Manual states that an individual trade mark which **6.10** consists exclusively of a PGI/PDO for wines or spirits (eg word mark 'Tequila') must be refused under Art 7(1)(c) and can only be registered as a collective mark.[17] Moreover, this objection will naturally be appropriate where a trade mark consists exclusively of a geographical name which is famous for the goods even where this geographical name has no protection as an official PGI/PDO.[18]

The UK Trade Marks Manual identifies the following factors which will be **6.11** considered by examiners in order to assess the potential for other traders to use a sign as a geographical designation:

(a) whether the geographical location has a reputation for the goods/services listed in the application;
(b) if not, whether the characteristics of the geographical location concerned indicate that the place is, or in the future is liable to become, a geographical source for the goods/services listed in the application;
(c) the extent to which the location is known to the relevant class of persons in the UK – and what it is known for.

The UK Trade Marks Manual advises that examiners will pay particularly **6.12** close attention to the following types of applications:

---

14 Ibid.
15 Ibid.
16 Ibid.
17 Ibid., at 46.
18 Ibid.

(i) **Geographical indications with a reputation (or in an area with a reputation) for the goods/services listed in the application or for *closely* related goods/services**

Such applications are likely to be refused unless the applicant can show why the name applied for is nevertheless unlikely to be used by other undertakings in relation to the goods or services concerned. For example, the name of a particular spring may be registrable for water even though it is in an area with a reputation for that product, if

(1) the applicant can show that he is the sole owner of the rights to exploit the spring water and no other water in that area is entitled to be sold under the name of the spring, and

(2) the name is not so well known as being *merely* the name of a spring as to be incapable of also designating the trade source of the product.

(ii) **The goods are natural produce**

The names of places which are likely to be the source of natural produce are unlikely to be registrable as trade marks for such goods even if the place identified by the mark has no specific reputation. However, the names of very small locations (small in this sense means area as well as population) are unlikely to be used in trade as designations of geographical origin because – without reputation – the place is unlikely to mean anything to the relevant public. A place will have to be obscure before its name could be registered as a trade mark for *unprocessed* products of the kind frequently sold from roadsides and farm shops, such as fruit and vegetables, flowers, potatoes, water, eggs and milk. A slightly more relaxed view may be taken where the product is *processed* natural produce. Again, without a specific reputation, the goods are more likely to be identified with the (generally larger) place of processing, or the name of the wider area, rather than the small villages where the raw materials were grown.

(iii) **Local Services**

A cautious approach will be taken to the registration of geographical names for local services such as hairdressing, window cleaning and retail-type services such as the organisation of car boot sales. However, each case will be judged on its merits and the names of very small places (population of less than 5,000) may still be registrable.

6.13 In relation to applications for signs which are the names of other places with no reputation for the goods/services in the application and where the application does not include natural produce or local services the UK Trade Marks Manual lists the following criteria against which registrability will be assessed:

(a) How well-known the name is as a geographical location. Names that are well-known as being a geographical location are less likely to be registrable compared to the names of obscure or remote places. However, a name which is well-known but which is fanciful or exotic in relation to the type of goods or services listed in the application will not be refused simply because it is well-known. For example, 'Marrakech' may be seen as simply a fancy and exotic name for motor cars (but may be a plausible indication of the geographical source of other goods, such as carpets, and therefore not registrable for those goods).

(b)   The goods and services with which the place is associated (if any). For example, if the mark consists of the name of a town with significant manufacturing industry it will be reasonable to assume that the town is, or will become, a source of other manufactured products. On the other hand a rural location is less likely to be the source of a product which requires heavy industry, such as vehicles or their parts and fittings.

(c)   Other characteristics of the place, including its size.

The UK Trade Marks Manual points out that for most goods, the larger the location the more likely it will appear as a source of goods. Consequently, there are likely to be difficulties in registering the names of well-known towns and cities in the UK as trade marks for many types of products. In the case of London it is pointed out that the well-known central districts, such as Mayfair and Westminster, have little or no manufacturing industry and their names would probably not be taken as the geographical origin of goods unless the area has a specific reputation. The same applies to services, although a more cautious approach would be justified with local services. It suggests that suburbs or outlying districts of London, such as Wimbledon, should be treated the same as a town of a comparable size. However, it may be possible to register names where, because of the type of place it is, the name appears to be an unlikely description of the geographical origin of the goods or services, eg HENLEY for steel.   **6.14**

An early illustration of this principle was *Magnolia Metal Company's Trade-Marks*[19] where the Court of Appeal, noting the existence of obscure towns in the USA named 'Magnolia', held that its primary significance for UK consumers was not geographical.   **6.15**

A recent UK illustration of the successful registration of a geographical trade mark was the decision of the Examiner in *OZARK (Trade Mark: Invalidity)*,[20] which concerned the word mark 'OZARK' which was opposed by Wal-Mart Stores, Inc, a US-based department store group. The objection was based on the fact that the word 'OZARK' was an indication of geographical origin, an area of high lands in central southern USA. The Hearing Officer considered that it would not be seen by consumers in the UK as anything other than an invented word. He said that in the unlikely event that UK consumers understood the geographical significance of OZARK he did not accept that they would be deceived into believing that it had some direct reference to the goods. Interestingly, it was pointed out that Wal-Mart Stores, Inc had   **6.16**

---

19   [1897] 2 Ch 371.
20   [2002] UKIntelP o14902.

no connection with the goods such as *Byblos* (Class 25), which is the ancient name for the Lebanese town of Jubayl, have a level of inherent adaptation to distinguish that will allow prima facie acceptance. Other names which have been officially superseded recently but are still in popular usage may require some evidence or could be accepted if there are any other circumstances which support doing so. These could include names such as 'Peking', 'Ceylon' and 'Leningrad' where the original geographical meaning is still very much the primary signification of the name and is still being used interchangeably with the new name. Some ancient place names which are no longer population centres presently have tourist significance and therefore could attract a ground for rejection, depending on the services claimed.[25]

3. Acquired distinctiveness of geographical signs

In Case C-353/03, *Société des produits Nestlé SA v Mars UK Ltd* the ECJ **6.22** determined that a mark may acquire a distinctive character as a result of being used as part of, or in conjunction with, another mark. Thus a mark that, for example, comprises in part a geographical reference, which could be regarded as descriptive, could be registered if part of a trade mark which includes a distinctive sign. The UK Trade Marks Manual gives the example of 'HARD-CASTLE'S YORKSHIRE BITTER' as a sign which is registrable.

As the case law set out below indicates, it must first be ascertained whether the **6.23** term is known to the relevant public as a geographical term. Secondly, the relevant public must understand it as a reference to the geographic place used in connection with the claimed goods or services. In other words, the geographic term must not be understood as having a mere suggestive or fanciful association with the relevant products, eg Mont Blanc would not be understood as a place of production for writing instruments. Thirdly, the geographical place must be currently associated, in the mind of the relevant public, with the category of goods in question, or the geographical name must be liable to be used in future by the undertakings concerned as an indication of the geographical origin of that category of goods. In this assessment, regard must be had to the degree of familiarity amongst the public with the geographical name, with the characteristics of the place designated by the name, and with the category of the goods concerned.[26]

---

25 Australian Trade Marks Manual, at 15.4.
26 Ibid., para 32.

6.24 Registration is excluded also for those geographical names that are liable to be used by undertakings,[27] however the registration of geographical names is not excluded when the public is unlikely to believe that the category of goods concerned originates there.[28]

6.25 The OHIM Trade Marks Manual points out that whether an existing geographical term will, for the relevant goods, be understood as having an informational value about the place of production, or rather as a fanciful term, also largely depends on the nature of the goods.[29] For example, it points out that for wine, a geographical name is always perceived as an indicator of origin because wine must carry a correct indication of its origin and for agricultural products or drinks (mineral water, beer), geographic names usually are meant to refer to the place of production.[30] On the other hand for textile and body care products, there may be a tradition of production in some places whereas for other places the term might be fanciful.

6.26 The OHIM Trade Marks Manual refers to the widespread practice of using fashionable city names for goods unrelated to the ground for which the city is known (Hollywood for chewing gum) or names of certain fashionable suburbs or shopping streets (Champs Élysées, Manhattan) and considers that as these will be perceived as suggestive terms, registration should not be refused.[31]

6.27 The OHIM Trade Marks Manual acknowledges that it is current branding practice for city names to be used as a basis for series of model designations for mechanical goods such as cars (eg SEAT Cordoba, Toledo, Malaga) which are unrelated to the place of production and the case is also true for high-technology goods such as computers, telecommunication products and consumer electronics (eg Germansat).[32]

6.28 For services, a geographic term will, in many instances, be perceived as the place of the location of the enterprise and registration will be refused to keep that location free (eg Munich financial services, Zürich insurance).[33] However, the mere fact that the service can be rendered at the place concerned does not justify a refusal (eg 'Cloppenburg' for retail services[34]).

---

27 *Nordmilch eG v Office for Harmonisation in the Internal Market (Trade Marks and Designs) (OHIM)* (Community trade mark) [2003] EUECJ T-295/01 at para 31.
28 Ibid., para 33.
29 OHIM Trade Marks Manual at 39.
30 Ibid.
31 Ibid.
32 Ibid.
33 Ibid.
34 See Case T-379/03, *Peek & Cloppenburg v OHMI* [2005] EUECJ T-379/03.

Community trade mark law allows that through use in the course of trade, **6.29** geographical marks may acquire the distinctiveness necessary for registration.[35] This will mean that registrable geographical marks will have attracted the secondary meaning of having the origin of the applicant undertaking.

4. Case law

(a) 'CHIEMSEE'

Joined Cases C-108/97 and C-109/97[36] concerned an enterprise 'Windsurfing **6.30** Chiemsee' which was located near the shores of the Chiemsee, the largest lake in Bavaria, which was a tourist destination with surfing as one of the activities carried on there. It sold sports fashion clothing, shoes and other sports goods bearing the designation 'Chiemsee'. Between 1992 and 1994, Windsurfing Chiemsee registered that designation in Germany as a picture trade mark in the form of various graphic designs, in some cases with additional features or words such as 'Chiemsee Jeans' and 'Windsurfing – Chiemsee – Active Wear'. It had not obtained a German word mark as the German registration authorities regarded the word 'Chiemsee' as an indication which may serve to designate geographical origin and which is consequently incapable of registration as a trade mark.

Messrs Huber and Attenberger had sold sports clothing since 1995 in a town **6.31** situated near the shores of the Chiemsee. The clothing carried the designation 'Chiemsee', but this was depicted in a different graphic form from that of the trade marks which identified Windsurfing Chiemsee's products. Windsurfing Chiemsee challenged the use by Huber and Mr Attenberger of the name 'Chiemsee', claiming that there was a likelihood of confusion with its designation 'Chiemsee' with which, it claims, the public is familiar and which had in any case been in use since 1990. The defendants contended, inter alia, that since the word 'Chiemsee' was an indication which designated geographical origin it must consequently remain available and thus was not capable of protection. The applicant claimed that the word 'Chiemsee' had acquired the secondary meaning under Art 3 of the Trade Marks Directive of referring to products emanating from it. The ECJ listed the following factors to be considered in establishing acquired distinctiveness: the market share held by the mark; how intensive, geographically widespread and long-standing use of

---

35 For example, Art 7 of the Community Trade Mark Regulation states: '3. Paragraph 1(b), (c) and (d) shall not apply if the trade mark has become distinctive in relation to the goods or services for which registration is requested in consequence of the use which has been made of it.'

36 *Windsurfing Chiemsee* [1999] [2000] 2 WLR 205, [1999] EUECJ C-108/97, [2000] Ch 523, [1999] ECR I-2779.

the mark has been; the amount invested by the undertaking in promoting the mark; the proportion of the relevant class of persons who, because of the mark, identify goods as originating from a particular undertaking; and statements from chambers of commerce and industry or other trade and professional associations.[37]

6.32 The Court concluded that:

> if, on the basis of those factors, the competent authority finds that the relevant class of persons, or at least a significant proportion thereof, identify goods as originating from a particular undertaking because of the trade mark, it must hold that the requirement for registering the mark laid down in Art 3(3) of the Directive is satisfied.[38]

As regards the method to be used to assess the distinctive character of a mark in respect of which registration is applied for, the ECJ noted that Community law did not preclude the competent authority, where it has particular difficulty in that connection, from having recourse, under the conditions laid down by its own national law, to an opinion poll as guidance for its judgment.[39]

i. Designation of geographical area

6.33 Joined Cases C-108/97 and C-109/97[40] also concerned an evaluation by the ECJ of what constituted a geographical area for the purposes of the Directive. The relevant national law which implemented the Directive was the German Markengesetz (Law on Trade Marks), which has been applicable since 1 January 1995. Under s 8(2)(2) of the Markengesetz, trade marks 'which consist exclusively of indications which may serve in trade to designate the geographical origin or other characteristics of the goods are to be refused registration'. Pursuant to s 8(3) of the Markengesetz, s 8(2)(2) does not apply 'if the mark, before the time of the decision on registration, as a result of its use for the goods in respect of which registration has been applied for, has gained acceptance among the relevant class of persons'. These provisions applied Arts 3(1)(c) and 3(3) of the Trade Marks Directive concerning the registrability of geographical words.

6.34 In language which has been repeated in its subsequent decisions on geographic marks, the ECJ explained that Art 3(1)(c) of the Directive 'pursues an aim

---

37 Ibid., at para 51.
38 Ibid., at para 52.
39 Ibid., at para 53, referring to Case C-210/96 *Gut Springenheide and Tusky* v *Oberkreisdirektor des Kreises Steinfurt-Amt für Lebensmittelüberwachung* [1998] ECR I-4657, at para 37.
40 *Windsurfing Chiemsee (Law relating to undertakings)* [1999] [2000] 2 WLR 205, [1999] EUECJ C-108/97, [2000] Ch 523, [1999] ECR I-2779.

which is in the public interest, namely that descriptive signs or indications relating to the categories of goods or services in respect of which registration is applied for may be freely used by all, including as collective marks or as part of complex or graphic marks'.[41] Thus Art 3(1)(c) prevents 'such signs and indications from being reserved to one undertaking alone because they have been registered as trade marks'.[42] As regards, more particularly, signs or indications which may serve to designate the geographical origin of the categories of goods in relation to which registration of the mark is applied for, especially geographical names, the Court observed that:

> [I]t is in the public interest that they remain available, not least because they may be an indication of the quality and other characteristics of the categories of goods concerned, and may also, in various ways, influence consumer tastes by, for instance, associating the goods with a place that may give rise to a favourable response.[43]

The Court noted that the public interest underlying the provision:

> is also evident in the fact that it is open to the Member States, under Article 15(2) of the Directive, to provide, by way of derogation from Article 3(1)(c), that signs or indications which may serve to designate the geographical origin of the goods may constitute collective marks.[44]

Also in language repeated in its subsequent decisions the ECJ ruled that Art **6.35** 3(1)(c) is to be interpreted as meaning that:

- it does not prohibit the registration of geographical names as trade marks solely where the names designate places which are, in the mind of the relevant class of persons, currently associated with the category of goods in question; it also applies to geographical names which are liable to be used in future by the undertakings concerned as an indication of the geographical origin of that category of goods;
- where there is currently no association in the mind of the relevant class of persons between the geographical name and the category of goods in question, the competent authority must assess whether it is reasonable to assume that such a name is, in the mind of the relevant class of persons, capable of designating the geographical origin of that category of goods;
- in making that assessment, particular consideration should be given to the degree of familiarity amongst the relevant class of persons with the

---

41 [1999] EUECJ C-108/97, at para 25.
42 Ibid.
43 Ibid., at para 26.
44 Ibid., at para 27.

geographical name in question, with the characteristics of the place designated by that name, and with the category of goods concerned;

- it is not necessary for the goods to be manufactured in the geographical location in order for them to be associated with it.[45]

(b) 'CLOPPENBURG'

6.36 Case T-379/03, *Peek & Cloppenburg v OHMI*,[46] concerned an application with OHIM for a Community trade mark for the word sign 'CLOPPEN-BURG'[47] in relation to retail trade services that fall within Class 35 of the Nice Agreement. The application was rejected under Art 7(1)(c) of the Community Trade Mark Regulation on the ground, inter alia, that the word Cloppenburg designated a German town in Lower Saxony and that the Landkreis Cloppenburg, a territorial district to which that town had given its name, numbered more than 152,000 inhabitants in 2002. This decision was affirmed by the Fourth Board of Appeal of OHIM and the applicant appealed to the Court of First Instance.

6.37 The Court followed the public interest approach to Art 7(1)(c), which it formulated in *Windsurfing Chiemsee*,[48] concerning leaving free signs or indications which may serve to designate the geographical origin of the categories of goods in relation to which registration of the mark is applied for, especially geographical names.

> [I]t is in the public interest that they remain available, not least because they may be an indication of the quality and other characteristics of the categories of goods concerned, and may also, in various ways, influence consumer tastes by, for instance, associating the goods with a place that may give rise to a favourable response.[49]

It observed further that the registration of geographical names as trade marks solely where they designate specified geographical locations which are already famous, or are known for the category of goods concerned, and which are therefore associated with those goods in the mind of the relevant class of persons, is excluded, as is the registration of geographical names which are

---

45 Ibid., at para 37.
46 [2005] EUECJ T-379/03.
47 Pursuant to Council Regulation (EC) No 40/94 of 20 December 1993 on the Community trade mark, OJ 1994 L 11, p. 1.
48 [1999] ECR I-2779 at para 26.
49 [2005] EUECJ T-379/03 at paras 32–33.

liable to be used by undertakings and must remain available to such undertakings as indications of the geographical origin of the category of goods concerned.[50]

The Court noted that Art 7(1)(c) of the Regulation did not in principle **6.38** preclude the registration of geographical names which are unknown to the relevant class of persons – or at least unknown as the designation of a geographical location – or of names in respect of which, because of the type of place they designate, such persons are unlikely to believe that the category of goods concerned originates there or was conceived of there.[51] It ruled, therefore, that 'a sign's descriptiveness cannot be assessed other than by reference to the goods or services concerned, on the one hand, and by reference to the understanding which the relevant persons have of it, on the other'.[52]

The Court said that in making that assessment the Office was bound to **6.39** establish that the geographical name was known to the relevant class of persons as the designation of a place.[53]

> What is more, the name in question must suggest a current association, in the mind of the relevant class of persons, with the category of goods or services in question, or else it must be reasonable to assume that such a name may, in the view of those persons, designate the geographical origin of that category of goods or services. In making that assessment, particular consideration should be given to the relevant class of persons degree of familiarity with the geographical name in question, with the characteristics of the place designated by that name, and with the category of goods or services concerned.[54]

In this case, the Court's examination must be confined to the question **6.40** whether, for the relevant public in Germany, the sign for which registration is sought consists exclusively of an indication that may serve, in trade, to designate the geographical origin of the services designated, the Court defining the relevant public as average German consumers of retail trade services, who would not necessarily consider that 'CLOPPENBURG' was a specific geographical location.[55] It doubted evidence that a town the size of Cloppenburg was mentioned in weather reports, or that it appeared on other than local road signs and that there was any economic activity for which the

---

50   Ibid., at para 34.
51   Ibid., at para 36.
52   Applying Case T-295/01, *Nordmilch v OHIM (OLDENBURGER)* [2003] ECR II-4365, at paras 27–34.
53   Ibid., at para 38.
54   Ibid.
55   Ibid., at para 42.

town would be familiar to consumers throughout Germany.[56] On this issue the Court did not consider that the required legal standard had been met that there existed, in the eyes of the public concerned, any link between the town or region of Cloppenburg and the category of services concerned, or that the word 'CLOPPENBURG' might reasonably be supposed, in the eyes of that public, to designate the geographical origin of the category of services at issue.[57]

6.41 Finally, the Court observed that even if the relevant public did know of the town of Cloppenburg, it did not automatically follow that the sign may serve, in trade, to designate geographical origin as account had to be taken of all the relevant circumstances, such as the nature of the goods or services designated, the greater or lesser reputation, especially within the economic sector involved, of the geographical location in question and the relevant public's greater or lesser familiarity with it, the customs obtaining in the area of activity concerned and the question to what extent the geographical origin of the goods or services at issue may be relevant, in the view of the persons concerned, to the assessment of the quality or other characteristics of the goods or services concerned.[58]

6.42 Applying these principles, the Court observed that the relevant public was, at the very most, only moderately familiar with the town of Cloppenburg and that the Board of Appeal had not mentioned any class of goods or services for which that town enjoyed a reputation as the place where the goods are produced or the services rendered.[59] The Board of Appeal has not established that it is current practice in trade to indicate the geographical origin of retail trade services and that it was not reasonable to imagine that the indication at issue might in the future designate the geographical origin of those services.[60]

(c) 'OLDENBURGER'

6.43 Case T-295/01[61] concerned an application for a community trade mark for the word 'OLDENBURGER' in relation to milk and dairy products within Classes 29, 30 and 32 of the Nice Agreement. The examiner at OHIM rejected the application on the ground that the word claimed was capable of constituting an indication of geographical origin that referred to a German

---

56 Ibid., at paras 44–45.
57 Ibid., at para 47.
58 Ibid., at paras 48–49.
59 Ibid., at para 50.
60 Ibid., para 51.
61 *Nordmilch eG v Office for Harmonisation in the Internal Market (Trade Marks and Designs) (OHIM)* (Community trade mark) [2003] EUECJ T-295/01 (15 October 2003).

region known for producing the goods identified in the application, and that there was a public interest in its remaining freely available. This rejection was supported by the Board of Appeal of OHIM.

On appeal to the Court of First Instance, the applicant did not dispute that **6.44** the term 'OLDENBURG' designates the principal town of the region of Weser-Ems in the Land of Niedersachsen (Lower Saxony) and a town of the same name in the Land of Schleswig-Holstein in Germany, nor did it deny that goods of the kind covered by the application for registration were manufactured in the district of Weser-Ems. However, the applicant denied that the mark sought, 'OLDENBURGER', was composed exclusively of an indication which, taken alone, designates or could designate the geographical origin of the goods to which it is affixed and that the Board of Appeal extended the absolute ground for refusal relating to terms that are exclusively descriptive of origin to cover an indication which merely refers to a GI or is derived from one.

Applying *Windsurfing Chiemsee*,[62] the Court explained that as regards signs or **6.45** indications which may serve to designate the geographical origin of the categories of goods in relation to which registration of the mark is applied for, especially geographical names, it was in the public interest that they remain available, not least because they may be an indication of the quality and other characteristics of the categories of goods concerned, and may also, in various ways, influence consumer tastes by, for instance, associating the goods with a place that may give rise to a favourable response.[63] Furthermore, the registration of geographical names as trade marks solely where they designate specified geographical locations which are already famous, or are known for the category of goods concerned, and which are therefore associated with those goods in the mind of the relevant class of persons, was excluded, as well as the registration of geographical names which are liable to be used by undertakings and must remain available to such undertakings as indications of the geographical origin of the category of goods concerned.[64]

The Court observed, however, that Art 7(1)(c) of the Regulation did not, in **6.46** principle, preclude the registration of geographical names which were unknown to the relevant class of persons – or at least unknown as the designation of a geographical location – or of names in respect of which, because of the type of place they designate, such persons are unlikely to believe

---

62 [1999] ECR I-2779 at para 26.
63 [2003] EUECJ T-295/01 at para 31.
64 Ibid.

that the category of goods concerned originates there.[65] Thus, the Court ruled, a sign's descriptiveness could not be assessed other than by reference to the goods or services concerned, on the one hand, and by reference to the understanding which the relevant persons have of it, on the other.[66]

6.47 In the present case the Court noted the agricultural reputation of Oldenburg included dairy, livestock and meat-processing industries, thus the relevant public may have perceived the geographical name as an indication of the geographical origin of those goods.[67] The Court approved the approach of the Board of Appeal, which was careful to avoid confirming that the contested mark designated the geographical origin of the goods claimed, but that the relevant public perceived the sign in question as an indication of the origin of those goods.[68] It therefore found that the sign in question consisted exclusively of a word 'which indicates or is capable of indicating to the relevant persons the geographical origin of the designated goods'.[69]

(d) 'SALAME FELINO'

6.48 Case C-46/07[70] concerned the interpretation of Art 2 of Directive 2000/13/EC of the European Parliament and of the Council of 20 March 2000 on the approximation of the laws of the Member States relating to the labelling, presentation and advertising of foodstuffs,[71] of Arts 3(1) and 13(3) of Council Regulation (EEC) No 2081/92 of 14 July 1992 on the protection of geographical indications and designations of origin for agricultural products and foodstuffs and of Art 15(2) of the Trade Marks Directive.[72] On 12 December 2002 the Milan municipal police informed Mr Severi, in his own name and as the legal representative of Grandi Salumifici Italiani SpA (GSI) that GSI was charged with infringing Art 2 of Legislative Decree No 109/92 relating to labelling, presentation and advertising of foodstuffs,[73] by having marketed a sausage, produced in Modena, the labelling of which bore the expression

---

65 Ibid., at para 34.
66 Ibid.
67 Ibid., at para 38.
68 Ibid., at para 43.
69 Ibid., at para 45.
70 *Alberto Severi v Regione Emilia Romagna* [2009] EUECJ C-446/07.
71 OJ 2000 L 109, p. 29.
72 First Council Directive 89/104/EEC of 21 December 1988 to approximate the laws of the Member States relating to trade marks, OJ 1989 L 40, p. 1.
73 Legislative Decree No 109/92 transposed the provisions of Art 2(1)(a)(i) of Council Directive 79/112/EEC of 18 December 1978 on the approximation of the laws of the Member States relating to the labelling, presentation and advertising of foodstuffs for sale to the ultimate consumer and provided:

   1. The labelling and the methods used are intended to provide the consumer with clear and accurate information. They must be such as:

'Salame tipo Felino'. That name was said to refer to a traditional method of production and to a place of production – the territory of the commune of Felino, in Emilia Romagna, in the province of Parma – which did not correspond to the defendant's foodstuffs which were produced in the province of Modena.

An administrative penalty of €3,108.33 was imposed upon the defendant for infringement of Art 2 of Legislative Decree No 109/92. Mr Severi challenged the penalty of 16 May 2006 before the Tribunale civile di Modena (Civil Court, Modena) on the basis that until 'Salame Felino' was registered as a PDO, it remained generic and available for use in the European market by producers who have used it in good faith and uninterruptedly for a considerable period before the entry into force of Regulation No 2081/92 (now Regulation No 510/2006) and in the period following the entry into force of that regulation. This was put as a question by the Modena Court to the ECJ. The ECJ rejected a presumption of genericity arising from the fact that a PDO had not yet been registered.[74] **6.49**

The defendant also argued that the qualification 'tipo' (type) prevented the deception of consumers. The ECJ ruled that the question of whether consumers were misled was a matter for national courts, but that it was clear from the Court's case law that, in order to assess the capacity to mislead of a description to be found on a label, the national court must in essence take account of the presumed expectations, in light of that description, of an average consumer who is reasonably well-informed, and reasonably observant and circumspect, as to the origin, provenance, and quality associated with the foodstuff, the critical point being that the consumer must not be misled and must not be induced to believe, incorrectly, that the product has an origin, provenance or quality which are other than genuine.[75] For the purpose of assessing whether labelling might be misleading, the ECJ ruled that national courts may have regard to the length of time during which the name has been used and that any good faith on the part of the manufacturer or retailer is irrelevant in that regard.[76] **6.50**

(a)   not to mislead the purchaser as to the characteristics of the foodstuff and, in particular, as to its nature, identity, properties, composition, quantity, durability, origin or provenance, method of manufacture or production of the foodstuff in question.

74   [2009] EUECJ C-446/07 at para 49.

75   Ibid., at para 61 applying: Case C-470/93, *Verein gegen Unwesen in Handel und Gewerbe Köln e.V. v Mars GmbH* [1995] ECR I-1923, at para 24; *Gut Springenheide and Tusky v Oberkreisdirektor des Kreises Steinfurt-Amt für Lebensmittelüberwachung* [1998] ECR I-4657, at para 31; and Case C-220/98 Estée *Lauder Cosmetics GmbH & Co OHG v Lancaster Group GmbH* [2000] ECR I-117 at para 30.

76   Ibid., at para 63.

5. Absolute bars to registration of geographical marks

6.51 Both the Community Trade Marks Regulation and the Trade Marks Directive list the grounds for refusal of registration or invalidity of signs which cannot constitute a trade mark. For example, the Community Trade Marks Regulation in Art 7(1) lists as absolutely barred from registration:

...

(b) trade marks which are devoid of any distinctive character;
(c) trade marks which consist exclusively of signs or indications which may serve, in trade, to designate the kind, quality, quantity, intended purpose, value, geographical origin, or the time of production of the goods or of rendering of the service, or other characteristics of the goods or service;
(d) trade marks which consist exclusively of signs or indications which have become customary in the current language or in the *bona fide* and established practices of the trade;

...

(g) trade marks which are of such a nature as to deceive the public, for instance as to the nature, quality or geographical origin of the goods or service;[77]

...

6. Absolute bars aligned with geographical indications protection

6.52 The Community Trade Marks Regulation in Art 7(1) refuses registration to:

(j) trade marks for wines which contain or consist of a geographical indication identifying wines or for spirits which contain or consist of a geographical indication identifying spirits with respect to such wines or spirits not having that origin;
(k) trade marks which contain or consist of a designation of origin or a geographical indication registered in accordance with Council Regulation (EC) No 510/2006 of 20 March 2006 on the protection of geographical indications and designations of origin for agricultural products and foodstuffs;
(l) when they correspond to one of the situations covered by Article 13 of the said Regulation and regarding the same type of product, on condition that the application for registration of the trade mark has been submitted after the date of filing with the Commission of the application for registration of the designation of origin or geographical indication.

---

77   Art 7(1), Community Trade Mark Regulation, Art 3, Trade Marks Directive.

Concerned that these provisions do not offer the same degree of protection to **6.53** GIs as provided in the European GIs legislation,[78] the proposed amending regulation[79] replaces these provisions with the following:

(j)   trade marks which are excluded from registration and shall not continue to be used pursuant to Union legislation or international agreements to which the Union is party, providing for protection of designations of origin and geographical indications;

(k)   trade marks which are excluded from registration pursuant to Union legislation or international agreements to which the Union is party, providing for protection of traditional terms for wine and traditional specialities guaranteed;

(l)   trade marks which contain or consist of an earlier variety denomination registered in accordance with Council Regulation (EC) No 2100/94 of 27 July 1994 on Community plant variety rights with respect to the same type of product.

7.   Absolute bar to partially non-registrable signs

Article 7(2) provides that the absolute bars in Art 7(1) shall apply notwith- **6.54** standing that the grounds of non-registrability obtain in only part of the Community. The proposed amending regulation[80] proposes the replacement of Art 7(2) with the following:

2.   Paragraph 1 shall apply notwithstanding that the grounds of non-registrability obtain:
(a) in only part of the Union;
(b) only where a trade mark in a foreign language or script is translated or transcribed in any script or official language of a Member State.

Sub-paragraph (b) is explained by Recital (13) to the proposed amending regulation that trade marks 'applied for in a script or language not intelligible in the Union should not deserve protection if their registration would have to be refused on absolute grounds when translated or transcribed in any official language of the Member States'.

---

78 Specifically: Arts 13 and 14 of Regulation (EU) No 1151/2012 of 21 November 2012 on quality schemes for agricultural products and foodstuffs, OJ L 343, 14.12.2012, p. 1; Arts 118l and 118m of Regulation (EC) No 1234/2007 of 22 October 2007 establishing a common organisation of agricultural markets and on specific provisions for certain agricultural products, as amended by Regulation (EC) No 491/2009 of 25 May 2009, OJ L 154, 17.6.2009, p. 1; and Art 16 of Regulation (EC) No 110/2008 of 15 January 2008 on the protection of GIs of spirit drinks, OJ L 39, 13.2.2008, p. 16.

79 Proposal for a Regulation of the European Parliament and of the Council amending Council Regulation (EC) No 207/2009 on the Community trade mark, COM(2013) 161 final, 2 April 2013.

80 Proposal for a Regulation of the European Parliament and of the Council amending Council Regulation (EC) No 207/2009 on the Community trade mark, COM(2013) 161 final, 2 April 2013.

8. Limitation of the effects of a registered geographical trade mark

(a) Defence to infringement

6.55 Most trade mark laws allow a defendant in an infringement action to rely on the geographical implications of an allegedly infringing mark to be called in aid in an infringement action brought in relation to a registered trade mark. Thus Art 12(b) of the Community Trade Marks Regulation and Art 6(1)(b) of the Trade Marks Directive prevent a proprietor, inter alia, from prohibiting a third party from using in the course of trade indications concerning the geographical origin of the goods or service, in respect of which the mark has been registered provided that they are used in accordance with 'honest practices in industrial or commercial matters'. In the UK that defence is contained in s 11(2)(b) of the UK Trade Marks Act 1994.

(b) Use of an indication concerning geographical origin

6.56 A recent illustration of the operation of this defence in a UK case is *Samuel Smith Old Brewery (Tadcaster) v Lee (t/a Cropton Brewery)*,[81] which concerned a complaint by a Yorkshire brewery about the use by another Yorkshire brewery of its stylised white rose device, which was part of its registered trade marks. The white rose is the traditional symbol of the county of Yorkshire, having been the emblem of the House of York during the Wars of the Roses, fought between 1455 and 1485. Arnold J ruled that the emblem was intended to be, and would be, perceived by the average consumer as an indication that the two beers are brewed in (or otherwise associated with) Yorkshire.[82] As is usual in cases involving geographical marks, passing off was also pleaded in this action.

(c) Use in accordance with honest practices in industrial or commercial matters

6.57 The principles applying to this defence from the ECJ case law were usefully summarised by Arnold J in *Samuel Smith Old Brewery (Tadcaster) v Lee (t/a Cropton Brewery)*[83] as follows:

> [114] First, the requirement to act in accordance with honest practices in industrial or commercial matters 'constitutes in substance the expression of a duty to act fairly in relation to the legitimate interests of the trade mark proprietor': see *Bayerische Motorenwerke AG v Deenik* (C-63/97) [1999] E.C.R. I-905; [1998] E.T.M.R. 348 at [61], *Gerolsteiner Brunnen GmbH & Co v Putsch* GmbH (C-100/02) [2004] E.C.R. I-691; [2004] E.T.M.R. 40; [2004] R.P.C. 39 at [24], *Anheuser-Busch Inc v Budjovický*

---

81 [2011] EWHC 1879 (Ch).
82 Ibid., at para 111.
83 [2011] EWHC 1879 (Ch).

Budvar, Národní Podnik (C-245/02) [2004] E.C.R. I-10989; [2005] E.T.M.R. 27 at [82], *Gillette Co v LA-Laboratories Ltd Oy* (C-228/03) [2005] E.C.R. I-2337; [2005] E.T.M.R. 67; [2005] F.S.R. 37 at [41] and *Céline Sarl v Céline SA* (C-17/06) [2007] E.C.R. I-7041; [2007] E.T.M.R. 80 at [33].

[115] Secondly, the court should 'carry out an overall assessment of all the relevant circumstances', and in particular should assess whether the defendant 'can be regarded as unfairly competing with the proprietor of the trade mark': see *Gerolsteiner* [2004] E.T.M.R. 40 at [26], *Anheuser-Busch* [2005] E.T.M.R. 27 at [84] and *Céline* [2007] E.T.M.R. 80 at [35].

[116] Thirdly, an important factor is whether the use of the sign complained of either gives rise to consumer deception or takes unfair advantage of, or is detrimental to, the distinctive character or repute of the trade mark. If it does, it is unlikely to qualify as being in accordance with honest practices: see *Gillette* [2005] F.S.R. 37 at [49], *Anheuser-Busch* [2005] E.T.M.R. 27 at [83] and *Céline* [2007] E.T.M.R. 80 at [34].

[117] Fourthly, a mere likelihood of confusion will not disqualify the use from being in accordance with honest practices if there is a good reason why such a likelihood of confusion should be tolerated. Thus in *Gerolsteiner* [2004] E.T.M.R. 40, which was an art. 6(1)(b) case, the Court of Justice held at [25]:

'The mere fact that there exists a likelihood of aural confusion between a word mark registered in one Member State and an indication of geographical origin from another Member State is therefore insufficient to conclude that the use of that indication in the course of trade is not in accordance with honest practices. In a Community of 15 Member States, with great linguistic diversity, the chance that there exists some phonetic similarity between a trade mark registered in one Member State and an indication of geographical origin from another Member State is already substantial and will be even greater after the impending enlargement.'

In *Samuel Smith Old Brewery (Tadcaster) v Lee (t/a Cropton Brewery)*[84] Arnold **6.58** J ruled that the defendant's use of the white rose emblem met the defence until he was informed by the plaintiff of the conflict between their two marks.

The principles enumerated by Arnold J were approved by Asplin J in *Evegate* **6.59** *Publishing Ltd v Newsquest Media (Southern) Ltd.*[85] That case concerned a dispute arising out of the launch by the defendant of a farming newspaper called *The Southern Farmer*, which the plaintiff claimed infringed its registered trade mark 'SOUTH EAST FARMER', which was registered in Class 16 in respect of 'periodicals, magazines and newspapers'. The judge did not in fact have to apply the defence as the case turned on whether the registered mark was sufficiently distinctive to be valid.

---

84 Ibid.
85 [2013] EWHC 1975 (Ch).

6.60   A useful analysis of the defence under the Trade Marks Directive was the ECJ's decision in Case C-100/02 *Gerolsteiner Brunnen GmbH & Co v Putsch GmbH*.[86] This case concerned the marketing of bottled mineral water and soft drinks with a mineral water base, which were marketed by Gerolsteiner Brunnen in Germany. It was also the proprietor of trade marks in Germany including the word mark 'GERRI' covering those products. Since the mid-1990s Putsch had marketed soft drinks in Germany bearing labels including the words 'KERRY SPRING'. Those drinks were manufactured and bottled in Ballyferriter in County Kerry, Ireland, by the Irish company Kerry Spring Water using water from a spring called Kerry Spring. Gerolsteiner Brunnen commenced proceedings against Putsch in the German courts for infringement of its trade mark rights. At first instance, the Landgericht München (Munich Regional Court) found for Gerolsteiner Brunnen and restrained Putsch from using the distinctive sign 'KERRY SPRING' for mineral water or soft drinks. On appeal by Putsch the Oberlandesgericht München (Munich Higher Regional Court) dismissed Gerolsteiner Brunnen's claims and in relation to questions put to the ECJ, the issues of geographical marks and whether use had been in accordance with honest practices in industrial or commercial matters was addressed.

6.61   The referring court had found that there existed a likelihood of aural confusion for the purposes of Art 5(1)(b) of the Trade Marks Directive between GERRI and KERRY. The Commission emphasised the geographical nature of the expression 'KERRY SPRING' by noting that Kerry Spring was included in the list of mineral waters recognised by Ireland for the purposes of Council Directive 80/777/EEC of 15 July 1980 on the approximation of the laws of the Member States relating to the exploitation and marketing of natural mineral waters.[87] The question which the ECJ addressed was whether such a likelihood of confusion between a word mark and an indication of geographical origin entitled the proprietor of the trade mark to rely upon Art 5(1)(b) of the Trade Marks Directive to prevent a third party from using the indication of geographical origin. In answering that question, the Court noted that the only test mentioned in Art 6(1) of the Trade Marks Directive was whether the indication of geographical origin is used in accordance with honest practices in industrial or commercial matters. The Court held that the 'condition of honest practice constitutes in substance the expression of a duty to act fairly in relation to the legitimate interests of the trade mark owner'.[88] The mere fact that there existed a likelihood of aural

---

86   [2004] ECR I-691; [2004] ETMR 40; [2004] RPC 39.
87   OJ 1980 L 229, p. 1.
88   [2004] ECR I-691 at para 24.

confusion between a word mark registered in one Member State and an indication of geographical origin from another Member State was held to be 'insufficient to conclude that the use of that indication in the course of trade is not in accordance with honest practices'.[89]

The *Gerolsteiner* case was applied and amplified by the ECJ in Case C-245/02 **6.62** *Anheuser-Busch Inc v Budějovický Budvar*.[90] It held that:

> In assessing whether the condition of honest practice is satisfied, account must be taken first of the extent to which the use of the third party's trade name is understood by the relevant public, or at least a significant section of that public, as indicating a link between the third party's goods and the trade-mark proprietor or a person authorised to use the trade mark, and secondly of the extent to which the third party ought to have been aware of that. Another factor to be taken into account when making the assessment is whether the trade mark concerned enjoys a certain reputation in the Member State in which it is registered and its protection is sought, from which the third party might profit in selling his goods.[91]

In the case, which involved a complaint about the use of the plaintiff's trade **6.63** mark on the defendant's beer bottles, the ECJ observed that it is for the national court to carry out an overall assessment of all the relevant circumstances, 'which include the labelling of the bottle in order to assess, more specifically, whether the producer of the drink bearing the trade name can be regarded as unfairly competing with the proprietor of the trade mark'.[92]

The proposed regulation to amend the Community Trade Marks Regulation **6.64** proposes the addition to Art 12 a definition of 'in accordance with honest practices' in the following terms:

> 2. The usle by a third party shall be considered not to be in accordance with honest practices, in particular in any of the following cases:
>   (a) it gives the impression that there is a commercial connection between the third party and the proprietor of the trade mark;
>   (b) it takes unfair advantage of, or is detrimental to, the distinctive character or the repute of the trade mark without due cause.

(d) Generic marks

The Community Trade Mark Regulation and the Trade Marks Directive **6.65** exclude the registration of trade marks which consist exclusively of signs or

---

89   Ibid., at para 25.
90   [2005] ETMR 286.
91   Ibid., at para 83.
92   Ibid., at para 85.

indications which have become customary in the current language or in the *bona fide* and established practices of the trade. Where a sign designating a geographical place is a GI or a generic term (eg Frankfurt sausages) registration will be refused in both instances. Whether or not a given term is considered generic is a matter of consumer perception and the applicable legal framework.

6.66 In the European context it will be recalled that Council Regulation (EC) No 510/2006 of 20 March 2006 on the protection of geographical indications and designations of origin for agricultural products and foodstuffs in Art 3(1) provides that names that have become generic may not be registered and that for the purposes of the Regulation, 'a name that has become generic' means the name of an agricultural product or a foodstuff which, although it relates to the place or the region where this product or foodstuff was originally produced or marketed, has become the common name of an agricultural product or a foodstuff in the Community. Article 3(1) requires that in establishing whether or not a name has become generic, 'account shall be taken of all factors, in particular: (a) the existing situation in the Member States and in areas of consumption; (b) the relevant national or Community laws'.

6.67 A national example of legislation on genericity is s 126(2) of the German Trademark Law, which provides that 'names, indications or signs of a generic nature shall not be eligible for protection as indications of geographical origin'. This provision defines as designations of a generic nature those 'which – although containing an indication of geographical origin within the meaning of subsection (1) or being derived therefrom – have lost their original meaning and serve as names of goods or services or as designations for or indications of the kind, nature, type or other properties or characteristics of goods or services'.

6.68 In the USA and Canada determinations of genericity in relation to wines are delegated to government agencies.[93]

6.69 As regards multilateral agreements, the Lisbon Agreement and the TRIPS Agreement contain references to generic terms. Article 6 of the Lisbon

---

93 See WIPO Secretariat, Addendum to Document SCT/6/3 Rev. (Geographical Indications: Historical Background, Nature of Rights, Existing Systems for Protection and obtaining protection in other Countries), Standing Committee on The Law of Trademarks, Industrial Designs and Geographical Indications, Eighth Session, Geneva, 27–31 May 2002, WIPO Doc, SCT/8/5 April 2, 2002, paras 37–8.

Agreement provides that an appellation cannot be deemed to have become generic, as long as it is protected as an appellation of origin in the country of origin.

(e) Deceptive marks

The Community Trade Mark Regulation and the Trade Marks Directive both **6.70** provide an absolute bar to trade marks which are of such a nature as to deceive the public as to the geographical origin of goods or service. The OHIM Trade Marks Manual points out that this ground for refusal also applies where the mark contains elements other than the geographical term.[94]

The UK Trade Marks Examination Manual, referring to s 3(3)(b) of the **6.71** Trade Marks Act 1994, which enacts this aspect of the Trade Marks Directive, explains that objections should only be taken at the first examination stage to place names or figurative marks indicating geographical origin where the place has a reputation for the goods or services and gives the examples of:

- PIAZZA D'ITALIA for 'clothing', because the public would be deceived if the goods or the cloth were not made in Italy, which has a strong reputation for quality cloth and clothing;
- SOMERSET GOLD for 'cider', because Somerset is well known for its cider;
- SWISSTEX for 'watches', because Switzerland is famous for high-quality watches.

The UK Trade Marks Examination Manual provides that s 3(3)(b) may be **6.72** overcome by restricting the specification to goods *manufactured in* the appropriate place for manufactured goods or *produced in* for other goods, for example:

SWISSTEX: 'Watches and horological instruments; all manufactured in Switzerland';
LOCH DOUGLAS: 'Salmon and salmon products; all the produce of Scotland'.

---

94   OHIM Trade Marks Manual at 41.

9. Trade Marks and Protected Geographic Indications (PGIs) or Protected Denominations of Origin (PDOs)

(a) Signs which consist of or contain a PGI/PDO for wines

6.73 It will be recalled that Art 7(1)(j) of the Community Trade Mark Regulation No 40/94 provides that trade marks for wines which contain or consist of a GI identifying wines with respect to such wines not having that origin are not to be registered.

6.74 The OHIM Trade Marks Manual states that an application may only be registered for the goods protected by a PGI/PDO if it is limited to such goods originating from the relevant PGI/PDO and says that the following wording should be used for the limitation: '[name of product] in conformity with the specifications of the [name PDO/PGI]'.[95]

6.75 For 'comparable goods' the OHIM Trade Marks Manual observes that 'such a limitation is inoperable given that the PGI/PDO specifications only relate to the goods for which the PGI/PDO protection exists'.[96]

6.76 EU case law requires that the provisions of the Community Trade Mark Regulation which deal with the protection of PGIs and PDOs must be interpreted as far as possible in conformity with the specific EU legislation on those subjects and international agreements concluded by the EU, such as the TRIPS Agreement, as well as with the national laws of Member States.

(b) Case law

i. 'CUVÉE PALOMAR'

6.77 Case T-237/08 *Abadía Retuerta, SA v OHIM*[97] concerned an application for a Community trade mark for the sign 'CUVÉE PALOMAR' in Class 33 under the Nice Agreement for wines. The examiner, taking the view that the mark applied for was inadmissible on the basis of the absolute ground for refusal referred to in Art 7(1)(j) of Regulation No 40/94, refused the application for registration by decision of 5 June 2007. The applicant appealed against the examiner's decision and this appeal was dismissed by the First Board of Appeal largely on the ground that 'el Palomar' is the name of a local administrative area in the sub-region Clariano and constitutes, pursuant to the

---

95 OHIM Trade Marks Manual at 44.
96 Ibid.
97 Judgment 11 May 2010.

applicable Community and national law, an area of production protected by the registered designation of origin 'VALENCIA'.

The applicant appealed to the General Court (Third Chamber), which stated **6.78** that in order to apply Art 7(1)(j) of Regulation No 40/94 it is necessary to determine the scope of the concept of 'geographical indication identifying wines'.[98] In the absence of a definition of the concept of GI identifying wines, the Court referred to the fourth Recital in the preamble to Regulation No 3288/94, which inserted Art 7(1)(j) into Regulation No 40/94. This states that 'Article 23(2) of the TRIPS Agreement provides for the refusal or invalidation of trade marks which contain or consist of false geographical indications for wines and spirits without the condition that they are of such a nature as to deceive the public' and that 'a new subparagraph (j) has to be added to Article 7(1) of Regulation (EC) No 40/94'.[99] The Court recalled that since the Community is a party to the TRIPS Agreement, it is required to interpret its trade mark legislation, as far as possible, in the light of the wording and purpose of that Agreement.[100] Furthermore, the Court noted that the concept of a GI identifying wines, within the meaning of Art 7(1)(j) of Regulation No 40/94, must be read in the light of the relevant provisions of Community law on determining and protecting GIs relating to wines, refer-ring to Regulation No 1493/1999, which is also intended to ensure that Community law is consistent with the provisions of the TRIPS Agreement.[101] Article 47(1) of Regulation No 1493/1999 provides that the rules relating to the description, designation and presentation of certain products covered by the Regulation are set out in this Chapter and in Annexes VII and VIII. Point A of Annex VI deals with the definition of 'Specified region', which includes 'the name of a local administrative area, a part thereof or a small locality to designate a quality wine'.[102] Article 4(1) of the Regulation dealing with the PDO 'VALENCIA' provided that the area of production protected by the PDO consisted of, inter alia, the sub-region Clariano, which includes, inter alia, a local administrative area with the name el Palomar. Thus the Court ruled that the name el Palomar is a GI for a quality wine and therefore constitutes a GI identifying wines within the meaning of Art 7(1)(j) of Regulation No 40/94.[103] The Court also referred to references to the name 'Palomar' in the annex to the Agreement between the European Community

---

98 Ibid., para 60.
99 Ibid., para. 61.
100 Citing Case C-245/02 *Anheuser-Busch Inc. v Budějovický Budvar* [2004] ECR I-10989 at para 42.
101 Judgment 11 May 2010 at paras 73–74.
102 Ibid., at para 75.
103 Ibid., at para 88.

and the Republic of South Africa on trade in wine[104] the Agreement between the European Community and the Swiss Confederation on trade in agricultural products.[105]

6.79 As it was not in dispute that the applicant's wine did not come from the local administrative area el Palomar, the Court ruled that the mark applied for consisted of a GI which identifies a quality wine psr even though the wine in respect of which the mark is sought does not have that origin and therefore the Board of Appeal was correct in finding that the mark applied for 'was inadmissible on the basis of the absolute ground for refusal laid down in Article 7(1)(j) of Regulation No 40/94'.[106]

(c)   Signs which are evocative of a PGI/PDO

6.80 The OHIM Trade Marks Manual provides than a Community trade mark application which contains or consists of a term or a sign which is 'evocative' of the PGI/PDO should also be refused, which covers the situation where the term used to designate the product incorporates part of a protected designation, so that when the consumer is confronted with the name of the product, the image triggered in his mind is that of the product whose designation is protected.[107] It provides the example of 'PRO SECKO' for *wine* as evocative of the Italian PDO 'PROSECCO'[108] stating that

> the question is whether the elements (visual, phonetic and conceptual) that the trade mark and the PGI/PDO have in common, and the proximity between the products, are such as to trigger associations ('the image') of the product bearing the protected name in the mind of the relevant public when encountering the trade mark applied for.[109]

6.81 The OHIM Trade Marks Manual points out that an objection based on Art 7(1)(j) of the Community Trade Mark Regulation also arises in the case of applications which contain or evoke a constituent part of a PGI/PDO. It provides the example of the PGI 'COTEAUX DU PONT DU GARD' which would be evoked by a Community trade mark application which contains or evokes 'PONT DU GARD'.[110]

---

104   Ibid., at para 104.
105   Ibid., at para 106.
106   Ibid., at paras 111–112.
107   Ibid., citing judgment of 04/03/1999, C-87/97, 'CAMBOZOLA', [1999] ECR I-1301 at para 25; and judgment of 26/02/2008, C-132/05, 'PARMESAN'.
108   OHIM Trade Marks Manual at 44.
109   Ibid.
110   Ibid.

However, the OHIM Trade Marks Manual warns that it is important to **6.82** distinguish between parts of a PGI/PDO with geographical significance and other parts with only a generic or non-geographical significance (such as 'vin' or 'vallé'). Whether a term is generic or non-geographical needs to be determined on the basis of the understanding in the Member State in which the GI has its origin. Thus in the case of Italian PGIs/PDOs the Italian-speaker's view is the relevant one, suggesting that in the case of 'ASTI SPUMANTE', only 'Asti' is geographically significant since 'spumante' is a generic term meaning 'sparkling'.

(d) Identical and comparable products

This absolute ground for refusal applies not only where the Community trade **6.83** mark application and the PGI/PDO cover identical goods, but also where the application covers 'comparable products' to those protected under the PGI/PDO. The ECJ provided some guidance on comparable products in Joined Cases C-4/10 and C-27/10 *Bureau national interprofessionnel du Cognac v Gust. Ranin Oy*[111] when it observed that

> it seems reasonable to hold that that situation may concern products comparable to the spirit drink registered under that geographical indication: regardless of their various categories, 'spirit drinks' covers drinks which have common objective characteristics and which are consumed, from the point of view of the relevant public, on occasions which are largely identical. Furthermore, they are frequently distributed through the same channels and subject to similar marketing rules.

On this basis OHIM suggests that '*spirits* and *spirit-based mixtures (alcoholic drinks)*, are "comparable" pursuant to the "COGNAC criteria". On the other hand, *spirits* and *fruit juices* (eg CALVADOS, an apple-based brandy, and apple juice) cannot be considered comparable.'[112] In the case of wines, OHIM observes that protection for comparable goods is limited to those set out in Annex XIb of Regulation EC 1234/2007.[113] This annex lists the categories of 'grapevine products', including various types of wines, liqueur wines, sparkling wines and wine-based products, such as must and vinegar. Thus a Community trade mark application that conflicts with a PGI/PDO for wines must also be refused for *must* (Class 32) or *vinegar* (Class 30).

---

111   [2011] ETMR 53.
112   OHIM Trade Marks Manual at 44.
113   Ibid.

(e) Translations

6.84 In Joined Cases C-4/10 and C-27/10 *Bureau national interprofessionnel du Cognac v Gust. Ranin Oy*[114] it will be recalled that an application was made to register in Finland a Community trade mark containing the Finnish translation 'KONJAKKIA' for 'cognac'. The ECJ held that the use of a mark containing a GI, or a term corresponding to that indication and its translation, with respect to spirit drinks which do not meet the relevant specifications constitutes, for the purposes of Art 16(a) of Regulation No 110/2008, a direct commercial use of a GI in respect of products which are comparable to the spirit drink registered under that indication, but which are not covered by the registration.[115]

B. COLLECTIVE AND CERTIFICATION MARKS

6.85 Signs or indications which may serve, in trade, to designate the geographical origin of the goods or services under the trade mark laws of a number of European Member States may be registered as collective or certification marks. The Community Trade Mark Regulation provides for the registration of Community collective marks in Title VIII (Arts 66–74), but currently contains no provisions for the registration of certification marks.

6.86 Regulation (EU) No 2017/1001 of the European Parliament and of the Council of 14 June 2017 on the European Union trade mark (codification) contained specific provisions on EU collective marks and certification marks.[116] This Regulation was implemented by Commission Implementing Regulation (EU) No 2018/626 of 5 March 2018.[117] These are discussed below.

6.87 The Trade Marks Directive in Art 15(2) permits Member States by way of derogation from Art 3(1)(c) to provide that signs or indications which may serve, in trade, to designate the geographical origin of the goods or services may constitute collective, guarantee or certification marks. However, it also provides that such a mark does not entitle the proprietor to prohibit a third party from using in the course of trade such signs or indications, provided he uses them in accordance with honest practices in industrial or commercial matters; in particular, such a mark may not be invoked against a third party who is entitled to use a geographical name.

---

114 [2011] ETMR 53.
115 Ibid., at para 55.
116 OJ L 154, 16.6.2017, pp. 1–99.
117 OJ L 104, 24.4.2018, pp. 37–56.

1. Community collective marks

Title VIII of the Community Trade Mark Regulation provides for the **6.88** registration of collective marks. However, very few of these marks have been registered. Only 89 were registered in 2012 and from 1996 to 2013 1,268 collective marks were registered at OHIM compared with more than 1.1 million individual Community trade marks over that period.[118] This is attributed to their 'lack of promotion', an unclear legal framework and 'confusion arising due to an overlap with other rights, such as geographical indications and certification trademarks' and 'wrong filing strategies'.[119]

The Community trade mark provisions apply to Community collective marks, **6.89** unless Arts 67–74 Community Trade Mark Regulations provide otherwise. A Community collective trade mark is subject to broadly the same examination procedure and conditions as individual marks. In general terms, the classification of goods and services, examination of formalities and of absolute grounds for refusal is done according to the same procedure as that applied to individual trade marks. The OHIM Trade Marks Manual explains that examiners will check the list of goods and services or the language requirements in the same way as they do with individual trade marks.[120] Likewise, whether the Community Collective Trade Mark falls under one of the grounds for refusal of Art 7 Community Trade Mark Regulation will also be examined.

The examination of a Community Collective Trade Mark will also consider **6.90** the exceptions and particularities of this kind of mark. These exceptions and particularities refer both to the formal and substantive provisions. As regards formalities, the requirement of the regulations governing use of the mark is, for example, a specific characteristic of a Community collective trade mark.

(a) Definition

Article 66(1) provides that: **6.91**

> A Community collective mark shall be a Community trade mark which is described as such when the mark is applied for and is capable of distinguishing the goods or services of the members of the association which is the proprietor of the mark from those of other undertakings. Associations of manufacturers, producers, suppliers of

---

118   Dimitris Botis, Deputy Director for Legal Affairs at OHIM, *'Collective and certification marks in the EU'* www.worldipreview.com/news/ecta-2013-explaining-the-mysterious-collective-ctm.

119   Ibid.

120   OHIM Trade Marks Manual, Part B: Examination, Section 2: Examination of Formalities, 7.2 Collective Marks.

services, or traders which, under the terms of the law governing them, have the capacity in their own name to have rights and obligations of all kinds, to make contracts or accomplish other legal acts and to sue and be sued, as well as legal persons governed by public law, may apply for Community collective marks.

6.92 A Community collective mark is thus aimed at distinguishing the goods and services of the members of an association which owns the mark from those of other companies which do not belong to that association. Therefore, the Community collective mark qualifies the commercial origin of certain goods and services by informing the consumer that the producer of the goods or the service provider belongs to a certain association and that it has the right to use the mark.

6.93 Case R0675/2010–2,[121] which concerned an application by a group of farmers for the collective mark 'BIODYNAMIC', was held by the Second Board of Appeal of OHIM to be a descriptive word and not registrable under Art 7(1)(c) as it described the characteristics of the goods which other enterprises might legitimately wish to use in the course of trade.

6.94 Unlike certification marks which are available in some countries, collective marks do not necessarily certify the quality of the goods, although this is sometimes the case. For example, the OHIM Trade Marks Manual has pointed out that regulations governing use frequently contain provisions to certify the quality of the goods and services of the members of the association and this is acceptable.[122] It is for the applicant to decide whether the trade mark is applied for as a collective mark or as an individual mark.

(b) Eligible applicants

6.95 The OHIM Trade Marks Manual points out that ownership of collective community trade marks is limited to (i) associations of manufacturers, producers, suppliers of services, or traders which, under the terms of the law governing them, have the capacity in their own name to have rights and obligations of all kinds, to make contracts or accomplish other legal acts and to sue and be sued; and (ii) legal persons governed by public law.[123] The first category of owners typically comprises private associations with a common purpose or interest with their own legal personality and capacity to act. Therefore, multiple applicants with separate legal personality or temporary unions of companies cannot be owners of a Community collective mark. As

---

121 Decision of 15 February 2011.
122 OHIM Trade Mark Manual, 83, citing OHIM decision of 10/05/2012, R 1007/2011–2, para 13.
123 Ibid., at 84.

regards the second type of owners, the concept 'legal persons governed by public law' is broadly interpreted by OHIM to include for example, 'Consejos Reguladores' or 'Colegios Profesionales' under Spanish Law and other legal persons governed by public law such as, for example, the European Union, states or municipalities, which do not necessarily have a corporate structure.[124] When the applicant for a Community collective mark is such a legal person governed by public law OHIM does not require details concerning membership in the regulations to be filed.[125]

(c) Permitted use of a geographical name in accordance with honest practices in industrial or commercial matters

Article 66(2) provides that a collective mark shall not entitle the proprietor to **6.96** prohibit a third party from using in the course of trade such signs or indications, provided he uses them in accordance with honest practices in industrial or commercial matters; in particular, such a mark may not be invoked against a third party who is entitled to use a geographical name.

For example, an application for the word mark 'ALICANTE' applied for **6.97** tourist services, should be refused under Art 7(1)(c) of the Community Trade Mark Regulation if it is applied for as an individual Community trade mark, however if it is validly applied for as a Community collective mark (ie it is applied for by an association or a legal person governed by public law and it complies with the other requirements of Community collective marks) and the regulations governing use of the mark contain the authorisation foreseen in Art 67(2), it will be accepted under Art 7(1)(c) of the Community Trade Mark Regulation.[126]

The EU Intellectual Property Office Trade Marks Manual points out that the **6.98** exception in Art 66(2) exclusively applies to those signs which are descriptive of the geographical origin of the goods and services and that if the Community collective mark is descriptive of other characteristics of the goods or services, this exception does not apply and the application will be refused under Art 7(1)(c).[127]

(d) Prohibited applications

Article 68(1) provides that in addition to the grounds for refusal of a **6.99** Community trade mark, application for non-compliance with formalities

---

124 Ibid.
125 Ibid., at 85.
126 Ibid.
127 Ibid.

(Art 36) and rejection upon examination (Art 38) and where Art 66 and regulations promulgated under Art 67 are not satisfied, and application can be refused if 'contrary to public policy or to accepted principles of morality'.

6.100 The EU Intellectual Property Office Trade Marks Manual points out that this ground for refusal must be differentiated from that contained in Art 7(1)(f) of the Community Trade Marks Regulation, which prohibits registration of those trade marks which are by themselves contrary to public policy or to accepted principles of morality.[128] The refusal foreseen in Art 68(1) is said to refer to situations where, regardless of the trade mark, the regulations governing use of the mark contain a provision which is contrary to public policy or to accepted principles of morality, for instance rules which discriminate on the grounds of sex, creed or race. For example, if the regulations contain a clause which prohibits women from using the mark, the Community collective mark will be refused, even if the trade mark does not fall under Art 7(1)(f) of the Community Trade Mark Regulation.[129]

6.101 The EU Intellectual Property Office Trade Marks Manual states that the examiner's objection can be waived if the regulations are amended in order to remove the conflicting provision.[130]

(e) Community trade marks and opposition proceedings

6.102 In Case C-393/12P, *Foundation for the Protection of the Traditional Cheese of Cyprus named Halloumi v OHIM* ,[131] on 24 October 2005 German manufacturer Garmo AG filed an application to register the word mark 'Hellim' (the Turkish word for halloumi) as a Community trade mark for 'milk and milk products'. A Cypriot firm filed a notice of opposition against the registration of the above mark based on its own earlier registered Community collective trade mark 'HALLOUMI'. The opposition was based on the likelihood of confusion under Art 8(1)(b) of the Community Trade Mark Regulation. The opposition was dismissed on 10 March 2010, despite the fact that the goods concerned were identical and/or similar on the basis that there was no visual or phonetic similarity between the two marks. This decision of the opposition division was unsuccessfully appealed pursuant to the Board of Appeal of OHIM. The Board held that the 'HALLOUMI' mark was of weak character and coupled with the low visual similarities, there was no likelihood of confusion. The applicant applied to the General Court to annul the Board of

---

128 Ibid., at para 86.
129 Ibid.
130 Ibid.
131 Judgment 13 June 2013.

Appeal's decision, but it upheld the decision of the Board of Appeal. The applicant had argued that its mark was at least of average distinctiveness due to its collective status. This argument was rejected by the court which held that the mere fact that 'HALLOUMI' is a collective mark does not automatically make it a mark of great or even average distinctiveness.

A successful opposition to the registration of a trade mark was an application **6.103** to the Spanish Patent and Trade Mark Office (SPTO), filed on 30 August 2012, to register the figurative trade mark 'CAFÉ NARIÑO' for coffee and artificial coffee in Class 30. It was rejected on the ground (among others) that it conflicted with a Colombian GI, 'CAFÉ DE COLOMBIA', which enjoyed protection in the EU.[132]

(f) Misleading applications

Article 68(2) provides that an application for a Community collective mark **6.104** shall also be refused 'if the public is liable to be misled as regards the character or the significance of the mark, in particular if it is likely to be taken to be something other than a collective mark'. Case R0675/2010–2[133] concerned an application by a group of farmers for the collective mark 'BIODYNAMIC'. The term refers to an organic type of agriculture. The application was rejected and an appeal refused by the Second Board of Appeal of OHIM on the ground that the application in truth concerned a guarantee or certification in breach of Art 68(2) of the Community Trade Mark Regulation as 'the public is liable to be misled as regards the character or the significance of the mark, in particular if it is likely to be taken to be something other than a collective mark'.

The EU Intellectual Property Office Trade Marks Manual gives as examples **6.105** of misleading applications those which mislead as regards the character or the meaning of the mark, in particular if it is likely to be perceived as something other than a collective mark and a collective mark which is available for use only by members of an association which owns the mark which gives the impression that it is available for use by anyone who is able to meet certain objective standards.[134]

The issue of a misleading application for a Community collective was raised **6.106** recently in an application for the mark 'BARCELONA' for all 45 Nice classes, which authorised persons linked with the city of Barcelona or with its

---

132   See www.marques.org/class46/Default.asp?XID=BHA3257.
133   Decision of 15 February 2011.
134   Ibid.

metropolitan area to use this mark. This was said to be misleading as it excluded persons with a link to the province of Barcelona.

(g) Observations by third parties

6.107 Article 69 provides that in addition to the opposition procedure provided for in Art 41, any person, group or body referred to in that Article may submit to the Office written observations based on the particular grounds on which the application for a Community collective mark should be refused under the terms of Art 66.

6.108 The proposed regulation to amend the Community Trade Marks Regulation proposes the replacement of Art 69 by the following:

> Where written observations on a European collective mark are submitted to the Agency pursuant to Article 40, those observations may also be based on the particular grounds on which the application for a European collective mark shall be refused pursuant to Article 68.

(h) Use of marks

6.109 Article 70 provides that use of a Community collective mark by any person who has authority to use it shall satisfy the requirements of this Regulation, provided that the other conditions which this Regulation imposes with regard to the use of Community trade marks are fulfilled.

6.110 Where regulations concerning use are amended, Art 71(1) requires the proprietor of a Community collective mark to submit to OHIM any amended regulations governing use.

6.111 Article 12(5) of Regulation (EU) No 1151/2012 of the European Parliament and of the Council of 21 November 2012 on quality schemes for agricultural products and foodstuffs[135] provides that without prejudice to Directive 2000/13/EC,[136] the collective geographical marks referred to in Art 15 of Directive 2008/95/EC[137] may be used on labels, together with the PDO or PGI.

---

135 OJ L 343, 14.12.2012, p. 1.
136 Directive 2000/13/EC of the European Parliament and of the Council of 20 March 2000 on the approximation of the laws of the Member States relating to the labelling, presentation and advertising of foodstuffs, OJ 2000 L 109, p. 29.
137 Directive 2008/95/EC of the European Parliament and of the Council of 22 October 2008 to approximate the laws of the Member States relating to trade marks, OJ L 299, 8.11.2008, pp 29–33.

(i) Grounds for revocation

Article 73 provides that apart from the grounds for revocation provided for in **6.112**
Art 51[138] the rights of the proprietor of a Community collective mark shall be
revoked on application to the Office or on the basis of a counterclaim in
infringement proceedings, if:

(a) the proprietor does not take reasonable steps to prevent the mark being used in a
manner incompatible with the conditions of use, where these exist, laid down in
the regulations governing use, amendments to which have, where appropriate,
been mentioned in the Register;

(b) the manner in which the mark has been used by the proprietor has caused it to
become liable to mislead the public in the manner referred to in Art 68(2);

(c) an amendment to the regulations governing use of the mark has been mentioned
in the Register in breach of the provisions of Art 71(2), unless the proprietor of
the mark, by further amending the regulations governing use, complies with the
requirements of those provisions.

(j) Grounds for invalidity

Article 74 provides that apart from the grounds for invalidity provided for in **6.113**
Arts 52 and 53, a Community collective mark which is registered in breach of
the provisions of Art 68 shall be declared invalid on application to the Office
or on the basis of a counterclaim in infringement proceedings, unless the
proprietor of the mark, by amending the regulations governing use, complies
with the requirements of those provisions.

(k) Delegation of powers

To deal with the period referred to in Art 67(1) within which an applicant for **6.114**
a Community collective mark must submit regulations governing its use, the
proposed regulation to amend the Community Trade Mark Regulation
proposes the insertion of Art 74a which provides:

The Commission shall be empowered to adopt delegated acts in accordance with
Article 163 specifying the period referred to in Article 67(1) for submitting the

---

138 Ie:

(a) within a continuous period of five years, the trade mark has not been put to genuine use in the
Community in connection with the goods or services in respect of which it is registered, and there
are no proper reasons for non-use;

(b) if, in consequence of acts or inactivity of the proprietor, the trade mark has become the common
name in the trade for a product or service in respect of which it is registered;

(c) if, in consequence of the use made of it by the proprietor of the trade mark or with his consent in
respect of the goods or services for which it is registered, the trade mark is liable to mislead the
public, particularly as to the nature, quality or geographical origin of those goods or services.

regulations governing use of the European collective mark to the Agency and the content of those regulations as set out in Article 67(2).

(m) Community trade marks and the Trade Marks Directive

6.115 Article 15(1) of the Trade Marks Directive provides that without prejudice to Art 4 (which deals with grounds for refusal or invalidity concerning conflicts with earlier rights) Member States whose laws authorise the registration of collective marks may provide that such marks shall not be registered, or shall be revoked or declared invalid, on grounds additional to those specified in Arts 3 (grounds for refusal of validity) and 12 (grounds for revocation) where the function of those marks so requires.

6.116 Article 15(2) provides that by way of derogation from Art 3(1)(c) (absolute bar to the registration of trade marks which consist exclusively of signs or indications which may serve, in trade, to designate the geographical origin of the goods or services),

> Member States may provide that signs or indications which may serve, in trade, to designate the geographical origin of the goods or services may constitute collective, guarantee or certification marks. Such a mark does not entitle the proprietor to prohibit a third party from using in the course of trade such signs or indications, provided he uses them in accordance with honest practices in industrial or commercial matters; in particular, such a mark may not be invoked against a third party who is entitled to use a geographical name.

2. Collective marks

(a) Introduction

6.117 The EU Trademarks Regulation[139] provides for the registration of collective marks. Article 74(1) defines an EU collective mark as 'an EU trade mark which is described as such when the mark is applied for and is capable of distinguishing the goods or services of the members of the association which is the proprietor of the mark from those of other undertakings'. It provides that associations of manufacturers, producers, suppliers of services, or traders which, under the terms of the law governing them, have the capacity in their own name to have rights and obligations of all kinds, to make contracts or accomplish other legal acts, and to sue and be sued, as well as legal persons governed by public law, may apply for EU collective marks.

---

139   Regulation (EU) No 2017/1001 of the European Parliament and of the Council of 14 June 2017 on the European Union trade mark (codification), OJ L 154, 16.6.2017, pp. 1–99.

Article 74(3) applies the general provisions of the Regulation in Chapters **6.118** I–VII and IX to XIV to EU collective marks to the extent that this section does not provide otherwise.

(b) Definition

Article 74(2) provides that by way of derogation from Art 7(1)(c), signs or **6.119** indications which may serve, in trade, to designate the geographical origin of the goods or services may constitute EU collective marks within the meaning of para 1.

(c) Entitlement to use

Article 74(2) provides that an EU collective mark shall not entitle the **6.120** proprietor to prohibit a third party from using in the course of trade such signs or indications, provided that he uses them in accordance with honest practices in industrial or commercial matters; in particular, such a mark shall not be invoked against a third party who is entitled to use a geographical name.

(d) Regulations

Article 75(1) requires an applicant for an EU collective mark to submit regu- **6.121** lations governing use within two months of the date of filing. These regulations governing use are required by Art 75(2) to specify the persons authorised to use the mark, the conditions of membership of the association and, where they exist, the conditions of use of the mark, including sanctions.

The Implementing Regulation in Art 16 requires that the regulations govern- **6.122** ing EU collective marks shall specify:

(a) the name of the applicant;
(b) the object of the association or the object for which the legal person governed by public law is constituted;
(c) the bodies authorised to represent the association or the legal person governed by public law;
(d) in the case of an association, the conditions for membership;
(e) the representation of the EU collective mark;
(f) the persons authorised to use the EU collective mark;
(g) where appropriate, the conditions governing use of the EU collective mark, including sanctions;
(h) the goods or services covered by the EU collective mark including, where appropriate, any limitation introduced as a consequence of the application of Article 7(1)(j), (k) or (l) of Regulation (EU) 2017/1001;
(i) where appropriate, the authorisation referred to in the second sentence of Article 5(2) of Regulation (EU) 2017/1001.

(e) Refusal of application

6.123 Article 76 1 provides that in addition to the grounds for refusal of an EU trade mark application provided for in Arts 41 and 42 of the Regulation, an application for an EU collective mark shall be refused where the provisions of Art 74 or 75 are not satisfied, or where the regulations governing use are contrary to public policy or to accepted principles of morality. Also Art 76(2) provides that an application for an EU collective mark shall also be refused if the public is liable to be misled as regards the character or the significance of the mark, in particular if it is likely to be taken to be something other than a collective mark. Article 76(3) provides for amendment of regulations to meet the requirements of paras 1 and 2.

6.124 Article 77 allows for observations of third parties 'on the particular grounds on which the application for an EU collective mark should be refused pursuant to Article 76'.

(f) Use of a mark

6.125 Article 78 provides that use of an EU collective mark by any person who has authority to use it shall satisfy the requirements of this Regulation, provided that the other conditions which this Regulation imposes with regard to the use of EU trade marks are fulfilled.

(g) Amendment of regulations governing use

6.126 Amendment of the regulations governing use of the EU collective mark may be submitted by the proprietor of an EU collective mark to the EU Intellectual Property Office pursuant to Art 79(1). Article 79(3) also permits written observations made in accordance with Art 77 to be submitted with regard to amended regulations governing use.

6.127 Article 79(2) provides that the amendments shall not be mentioned in the Register if they do not satisfy the requirements of Art 75 or involve one of the grounds for refusal referred to in Art 76.

6.128 Article 75(4) provides that for the purposes of applying this Regulation, amendments to the regulations governing use shall take effect only from the date of entry of the mention of the amendment in the Register.

(h) Infringement actions

6.129 The persons who are entitled to bring an action for infringement are identified in Art 80(1) as every person who has authority to use an EU collective mark. Article 80(2) permits the proprietor of an EU collective mark to be entitled to claim compensation on behalf of persons who have authority to use the mark where they have sustained damage in consequence of unauthorised use of the mark.

(i) Revocation

Apart from the grounds for revocation provided for in Art 58, Art 81 provides that the rights of the proprietor of an EU collective mark shall be revoked on application to the Office or on the basis of a counterclaim in infringement proceedings, if: **6.130**

(i)   the proprietor does not take reasonable steps to prevent the mark being used in a manner incompatible with the conditions of use, where these exist, laid down in the regulations governing use, amendments to which have, where appropriate, been mentioned in the Register;

(ii) the manner in which the mark has been used by the proprietor has caused it to become liable to mislead the public in the manner referred to in Article 76(2);

(iii) an amendment to the regulations governing use of the mark has been mentioned in the Register in breach of the provisions of Article 79(2), unless the proprietor of the mark, by further amending the regulations governing use, complies with the requirements of those provisions.

(j) Grounds for invalidity

Article 82 provides that apart from the grounds for invalidity provided for in Arts 59[140] and 60,[141] an EU collective mark which is registered in breach of the provisions of Art 76 shall be declared invalid on application to the Office or on the basis of a counterclaim in infringement proceedings, unless the proprietor of the mark, by amending the regulations governing use, complies with the requirements of those provisions. **6.131**

3. Certification marks

It will be recalled that collective marks require a holder whose members use the mark. This is to be contrasted with certification marks, which allow a certifying organisation or person to permit traders who comply with the certification requirements to use the mark as a sign for goods or services. In **6.132**

---

140   Ie, where the EU trade mark has been registered contrary to the provisions of Art 7; (b) where the applicant was acting in bad faith when he filed the application for the trade mark.

141   Ie, where there is an earlier trade mark as referred to in Art 8(2) and the conditions set out in paras 1 or 5 of that Article are fulfilled; where there is a trade mark as referred to in Art 8(3) and the conditions set out in that paragraph are fulfilled; (c) where there is an earlier right as referred to in Art 8(4) and the conditions set out in that paragraph are fulfilled; where there is an earlier designation of origin or GI as referred to in Art 8(6) and the conditions set out in that paragraph are fulfilled; or on the basis of a counterclaim in infringement proceedings.

this way certification marks are said to be signs of supervised quality contrasting with collective marks, which do not necessarily imply a claim of quality. The EU Trademarks Regulation[142] (the Regulation) provides for the registration of certification marks. Article 83(3) provides that chapters I to VII and IX to XIV apply to certification marks, as well as the specific provisions in Arts 83–93.

(a) Definition

6.133 Article 83(1) provides that an EU certification mark shall be an EU trade mark which is described as such when the mark is applied for and is capable of distinguishing goods or services which are certified by the proprietor of the mark in respect of material, mode of manufacture of goods or performance of services, quality, accuracy or other characteristics, with the exception of geographical origin, from goods and services which are not so certified.

(b) Eligible applicants

6.134 Article 83(2) provides that any natural or legal person, including institutions, authorities and bodies governed by public law, may apply for EU certification marks provided that such person does not carry on a business involving the supply of goods or services of the kind certified.

(c) Regulations governing use of a certification mark

6.135 Article 84(1) provides that an applicant for an EU certification mark shall submit regulations governing the use of the EU certification mark within two months of the date of filing. Article 84(2) requires that the regulations governing use shall specify the persons authorised to use the mark, the characteristics to be certified by the mark, how the certifying body is to test those characteristics and to supervise the use of the mark. Those regulations shall also specify the conditions of use of the mark, including sanctions.

6.136 The Implementing Regulation in Art 17 requires the regulations governing use of EU certification marks to specify:

(a) the name of the applicant;
(b) a declaration that the applicant complies with the requirements laid down in Article 83(2) of Regulation (EU) No 2017/1001;
(c) the representation of the EU certification mark;
(d) the goods or services covered by the EU certification mark;
(e) the characteristics of the goods or services to be certified by the EU certification

---

142 Regulation (EU) No 2017/1001 of the European Parliament and of the Council of 14 June 2017 on the European Union trade mark (codification), OJ L 154, 16.6.2017, pp. 1–99.

mark, such as the material, mode of manufacture of goods or performance of services, quality or accuracy;

(f) the conditions governing the use of the EU certification mark, including sanctions;

(g) the persons authorised to use the EU certification mark.

6.137 Article 84(3) requires the Commission to adopt implementing acts specifying the details to be contained in the regulations referred to in para 2 of this Article. Those implementing acts shall be adopted in accordance with the examination procedure referred to in Art 207(2).

(d) Refusal of the application

6.138 Article 85(1) provides that in addition to the grounds for refusal of an EU trade mark application provided for in Arts 41 and 42, an application for an EU certification mark shall be refused where the conditions set out in Arts 83 and 84 are not satisfied, or where the regulations governing use are contrary to public policy or to accepted principles of morality. Article 85(2) provides that an application for an EU certification mark shall also be refused if the public is liable to be misled as regards the character or the significance of the mark, in particular if it is likely to be taken to be something other than a certification mark.

6.139 Article 85(3) provides that an application shall not be refused if the applicant, as a result of an amendment of the regulations governing use, meets the requirements of paras 1 and 2.

6.140 Article 86 permits written observations on an EU certification mark to be submitted to the EU Intellectual Property Office pursuant to Art 45, which may be based on the particular grounds on which the application for an EU certification mark should be refused pursuant to Art 85.

(e) Use of a certification mark

6.141 Article 87 provides that use of an EU certification mark by any person who has authority to use it pursuant to the regulations governing use referred to in Art 84 shall satisfy the requirements of the EU Trademarks Regulation provided that the other conditions laid down in this Regulation with regard to the use of EU trade marks are fulfilled.

(f) Amendment of the regulations governing use of the EU certification mark

6.142 Article 88(1) requires the proprietor of an EU certification mark to submit to the EU Intellectual Property Office any amended regulations governing use.

obtained the registration of the trade mark 'OZARK TRAIL' in the USA, where its geographical significance was likely to be known.

6.17 In relation to overseas place names, the UK Trade Marks Manual points out that in practice, it may be easier to register the name of a small- or medium-size overseas location than it would be to register the name of a comparable size location in the UK for the same product.

6.18 In Case C-265/00, *Campina Melkunie BV v Benelux-Merkenbureau*,[21] the ECJ determined that a trade mark which is composed of a number of elements, each of which is descriptive of the goods/services in the application, is excluded from registration under unless the trade mark is perceptibly more than the sum of the meanings of its descriptive parts. That case concerned the sign 'BIOMILD' for food products in Classes 29, 30 and 32. This was considered to be merely descriptive of the qualities of those goods, namely: 'biological' and 'mild'.

6.19 In a geographical marks context, the mark EUROLAMB was found to be unregistrable on the grounds that the element EURO is commonly used to indicate 'European' and conjoining EURO and LAMB therefore results in nothing more than a composite description of the kind and geographical origin of the goods, which is no more registrable than the term 'European Lamb'.[22]

6.20 Similarly, in Australia a word of prima facie geographical signification will be rejected for registration, particularly if goods of the kind for which it is sought to be registered are produced at the place or in the area,[23] or if it is reasonable to suppose that such goods would be produced there in the future.[24]

2. Superseded geographical names

6.21 The Australian Trade Marks Examination Manual contains a chapter on superseded geographical names which might provide some guidance for European practice. It provides that superseded geographical names that have

---

21 [2004] ECR I-01699.

22 EUROLAMB trade mark case [1997] RPC 279.

23 MICHIGAN for earth moving equipment, *Clark Equipment Company v Registrar of Trade Marks* (1964) 111 CLR 511 at pp. 515–16 (High Court).

24 OXFORD for printed publications, *Chancellor, Masters and Scholars of the University of Oxford (Trading as Oxford University Press) v Registrar of Trade Marks* (1990) 24 FCR 1 at 23 (Full Federal Court); COLORADO refused for outdoor bags, *Colorado Group Ltd v Strandbags Group Pty Ltd* (2007) 164 FCR 506 (Federal Court).

6.143   Article 88(2) provides that amendments shall not be mentioned in the Register where the regulations as amended do not satisfy the requirements of Art 84 or involve one of the grounds for refusal referred to in Art 85.

6.144   Written observations in accordance with Art 86 may also be submitted with regard to amended regulations governing use, pursuant to Art 88(3).

6.145   For the purposes of this Regulation, Art 88(4) provides that amendments to the regulations governing use shall take effect only as from the date of entry of the mention of the amendment in the Register.

(g)   Transfer

6.146   Article 89 provides that by way of derogation from Art 20(1), an EU certification mark may only be transferred to a person who meets the requirements of Art 83(2).

(h)   Persons who are entitled to bring an action for infringement

6.147   Article 90(1) provides that only the proprietor of an EU certification mark, or any person specifically authorised by him to that effect, shall be entitled to bring an action for infringement.

(i)   Remedies

6.148   Article 90(2) provides that the proprietor of an EU certification mark shall be entitled to claim compensation on behalf of persons who have authority to use the mark where they have sustained damage as a consequence of unauthorised use of the mark.

(j)   Grounds for revocation

6.149   Article 91 provides that in addition to the grounds for revocation provided for in Art 58, the rights of the proprietor of an EU certification mark shall be revoked on application to the Office or on the basis of a counterclaim in infringement proceedings, where any of the following conditions is fulfilled:

    (i)   the proprietor no longer complies with the requirements set out in Article 83(2);

    (ii) the proprietor does not take reasonable steps to prevent the EU certification mark being used in a manner that is incompatible with the conditions of use laid down in the regulations governing use, amendments to which have, where appropriate, been mentioned in the Register;

    (iii) the manner in which the EU certification mark has been used by the proprietor has caused it to become liable to mislead the public in the manner referred to in Article 85(2);

(iv) an amendment to the regulations governing use of the EU certification mark has been mentioned in the Register in breach of Article 88(2), unless the proprietor of the mark, by further amending the regulations governing use, complies with the requirements of that Article.

(k) Grounds for invalidity

In addition to the grounds for invalidity provided for in Arts 59 and 60, Art 92 **6.150** provides that an EU certification mark which is registered in breach of Art 85 shall be declared invalid on application to the Office or on the basis of a counterclaim in infringement proceedings, unless the proprietor of the EU certification mark, by amending the regulations governing use, complies with the requirements of Art 85.

(l) Conversion

Article 93 provides that without prejudice to Art 139(2), conversion of an **6.151** application for an EU certification mark or of a registered EU certification mark shall not take place where the national law of the Member State concerned does not provide for the registration of guarantee or certification marks pursuant to Art 28 of Directive (EU) 2015/2436.[143]

4. Choice between collective and certification marks

A certification mark is only available where the applicant is connected with **6.152** those who wish to use the mark only through the certification process, whereas members of the association may use, or not, a collective mark to indicate membership and compliance with the conditions for membership. A certification mark in distinguishing the goods or services which are certified is considered to be more protective of consumers.[144]

A certification mark is not used by its owner. The certification mark owner **6.153** controls the use of the mark by others on the certified goods or services by taking steps to ensure that the mark is applied only to products that contain or display the requisite characteristics or meet the specified requirements that the certifier has established or adopted for the certification.

Collective marks indicate commercial origin of goods or services in members **6.154** of a group rather than origin in any one member or party. All members of the group use the mark; therefore, no one member can own the mark, and the

---

143 Directive (EU) 2015/2436 of the European Parliament and of the Council of 16 December 2015 to approximate the laws of the Member States relating to trade marks, OJ L 336, 23.12.2015, pp. 1–26.
144 Belson, 2002 at 3–01.

collective organisation holds the title to the collectively used mark for the benefit of all members of the group. The collective organisation might conduct advertising or other promotional activities to publicise the mark and promote the business of the members.

5. Choice between trade mark protection and geographical indications protection

6.155 The Community trade mark is a unitary right providing registered trade mark protection throughout the European Union renewable at ten intervals, indefinitely, while the mark continues in use. The rights accorded PGIs and PDOs are of indefinite duration, so long as the conditions of the product specification continue to be met.

6.156 The Community trade mark system has the procedural advantage of convenience and cost effectiveness of registration. Any natural or legal person can apply for a Community trade mark or a Community collective trade mark registration either through the trade mark office of an EU Member State or directly at the OHIM. With the accession of the EU to the Madrid Protocol for the International Registration of Marks, applicants can simply designate the Community trade mark system when applying for an international registration. With the extension of the Community Trade Marks Act to certification marks these advantages will extend to that category of marks.

6.157 The EU system for the registration of GIs, on the other hand, requires applications to the national authorities, which forward them to the European Commission for further scrutiny. Third countries, however, benefit from a one-step process, either filing applications online or sending them to the Commission via their national authorities.[145]

6.158 It is pointed out that despite the similarity between trade mark protection and the protection of GIs, there are substantive differences that impact upon their respective registrability and scope of protection. For example, applicants for geographical Community trade marks are likely to spend proportionately more on prosecuting or defending opposition actions, due to trade mark law's presumption that geographical names are prima facie descriptive, and therefore available for the use of other traders throughout the European market.[146]

---

145 See, http://ec.europa.eu/agriculture/quality/schemes/index_en.htm.
146 See Evans, 2010 at 651.

Within the GIs regime account should be taken of the different requirements **6.159** for PDO and PGI protection. To be designated as a PDO a product must not only originate in a particular place but its quality must be exclusively due to its geographical environment with its inherent natural and human factors. In comparison, to be designated as a PGI the product must be produced, processed, or prepared in the geographical area, and the quality, reputation, or other characteristics must be generally 'attributable' rather than 'essentially due' to that area. A PDO will confer stronger protection as usually all elements of production and processing will be included in the specification.

The choice between PDO and PGI will invariably turn on the proximity of **6.160** the product with the place of production.[147] For example, where production requires the sourcing of some raw materials from outside the defined geographical area, then the PGI will be the only available option.

In the absence of the necessary linkage of a product's reputation with the place **6.161** of production, protection under the trade mark system will be the only practical option. For example, the government of Ethiopia was unable to establish the geographical link for its speciality coffees 'HARRAR', 'YIRGACHEFFE' and 'SIDAMO' and thus decided upon Community trade marks protection.[148]

Trade marks registration enjoys the flexibility of the availability of licensing **6.162** the mark and it also avoids the obligation of ensuring the monitoring of production standards, which GIs protection obliges.

Of course the advantages of both systems can be enjoyed through dual **6.163** protection. Invariably, a PGO or PGI will be accompanied by a registered house brand. This is certainly a characteristic of the wine trade.

C. RELEVANCE OF TRIPS AND INTERNATIONAL INSTRUMENTS IN THE INTERPRETATION OF EUROPEAN TRADE MARKS LAW

Probably because of the recent history of the EU before a WTO Dispute **6.164** Panel interpreting the GIs and trade marks provisions of the TRIPS Agreement, the ECJ has taken account of the WTO TRIPS Agreement in its interpretation of the language of its legislation. In Case C-245/02 *Anheuser-Busch Inc v Budějovický Budvar* the ECJ said that since the Community is a

---

147   Ibid, at 652.
148   See Mengistie, 2010.

party to the TRIPS Agreement, 'it is indeed under an obligation to interpret its trade-mark legislation, as far as possible, in the light of the wording and purpose of that agreement'.[149] It observed that:

> when called upon to apply national rules with a view to ordering measures for the protection of rights in a field to which the TRIPS Agreement applies and in which the Community has already legislated, as is the case with the field of trade marks, the national courts are required under Community law to do so, as far as possible, in the light of the wording and purpose of the relevant provisions of the TRIPs Agreement.[150]

1. Temporal application of the TRIPS Agreement

6.165 In Case C-245/02 *Anheuser-Busch Inc v Budějovický Budvar*[151] the Court held that applying Art 70(2) of the TRIPS Agreement, obligations arising from that Agreement apply in respect of 'all subject-matter existing ... and which is protected' on the date of application of that Agreement to a Member of the WTO so that, 'from that date, such a member is required to fulfil all the obligations arising from that agreement in respect of that existing subject-matter'.[152]

6.166 Furthermore, the Court pointed out that Art 70(4) of the TRIPS Agreement applied to acts in respect of specific objects embodying protected subject matter which become infringing under the terms of legislation in conformity with that Agreement, and which were commenced, or in respect of which a significant investment was made, before the date of acceptance of the WTO Agreement. In such a situation, Art 70(4) allows the members to provide for limitations of the remedies available to the holder of the right against continued performance of such acts after the date of application of the TRIPS Agreement to the WTO member concerned.[153] Thus in the case before the acts which the defendant was alleged to have committed had occurred before the date of application of the TRIPS Agreement but continued after that date, so the Court ruled that the TRIPS Agreement applied to that situation.[154]

---

149   [2005] ETMR 286, at para 42.
150   Ibid., at para 42.
151   [2005] ETMR 286.
152   Ibid., at para 49.
153   Ibid., at para 50.
154   Ibid., at para 52.

2. Relevant signs

The Court in Case C-245/02 *Anheuser-Busch Inc v Budějovický Budvar*[155] **6.167** ruled that the relevant provisions of national trade mark law must be applied and interpreted to the effect that the exercise of the exclusive right conferred on the proprietor of the trade mark to prevent the use of the sign of which that mark consists or of a sign similar to that mark must be reserved to cases in which a third party's use of the sign prejudices or is liable to prejudice the functions of the trade mark. It privileged the essential function of a trade mark in guaranteeing consumers the correct origin of the goods to which they are applied.[156] It noted that 'this interpretation was moreover, supported by the general purpose of the TRIPS Agreement' which is to ensure that a balance is maintained between the aim of reducing distortions and impediments to international trade and that of promoting effective and adequate protection of intellectual property rights so as to ensure that the measures and procedures to enforce intellectual property rights do not themselves become barriers to legitimate trade.[157] The Court considered that distinction also 'to be appropriate in the light of the specific object of Article 16 of the TRIPS Agreement, which is to guarantee a minimum standard of exclusive rights agreed at international level'.[158]

The ECJ also considered applicable the exceptions provided for in Art 17 of **6.168** the TRIPS Agreement, which 'are intended, inter alia, to enable a third party to use a sign which is identical or similar to a trade mark to indicate his trade name, provided that such use is in accordance with honest practices in industrial or commercial matters'.[159]

3. 'Existing prior right'

The final question raised in Case C-245/02 *Anheuser-Busch Inc v Budějovický* **6.169** *Budvar*[160] was whether and, if so, under what conditions, a trade name which is not registered or established by use in the state in which the trade mark is registered and in which protection against the trade name in question is sought may be regarded as an existing prior right within the meaning of the third sentence of Art 16(1) of the TRIPS Agreement, having regard in

---

155 [2005] ETMR 286.
156 Ibid., at para 71.
157 Ibid., at para 72.
158 Ibid., at para 73.
159 Ibid., at para 85.
160 [2005] ETMR 286.

particular to that Member State's obligations to protect the trade name under Art 8 of the Paris Convention and Art 2(1) of the TRIPS Agreement.[161]

6.170 The Court observed that it is apparent from the examinations to be carried out by the national court that the use made of the trade name falls within the scope of the first sentence of Art 16(1) of the TRIPS Agreement; the proprietor of the trade mark has an exclusive right to prevent such use, subject to the provisions of Art 17 of that Agreement.[162] However, the third sentence of Art 16(1) of the TRIPS Agreement provides that that exclusive right must not prejudice any 'existing prior right' which the Court took to mean that, where the proprietor of a trade name has a right falling within the scope of the TRIPS Agreement which arose prior to that conferred by the trade mark with which it is alleged to conflict and which entitles him to use a sign identical or similar to that trade mark, such use cannot be prohibited by virtue of the exclusive right conferred by the trade mark on its proprietor under the first sentence of Art 16(1) of the TRIPS Agreement.[163]

4. Protection of trade names

6.171 The Court in Case C-245/02 *Anheuser-Busch Inc v Budějovický Budvar*[164] observed that a trade name is a right falling within the scope of the term 'intellectual property' within the meaning of Art 1(2) of the TRIPS Agreement. Article 2(1) of the TRIPS Agreement expressly incorporates the protection of trade names, for which specific provision is made in Art 8 of the Paris Convention, and thus the ECJ ruled that the members of the WTO are under an obligation to protect trade names.[165]

6.172 Applying Art 8 of the Paris Convention the ECJ noted that the protection of trade names may not be made subject to any registration requirement.[166]

6.173 In referring to the specific issues raised by the case it concluded that a trade name which is not registered or established by use in the Member State in which the trade mark is registered and in which protection against the trade name in question is sought may be regarded as an existing prior right within the meaning of the third sentence of Art 16(1) of the TRIPS Agreement if the proprietor of the trade name has a right falling within the substantive and

---

161 Ibid., at para 86.
162 Ibid., at para 87.
163 Ibid., at para 89.
164 [2005] ETMR 286.
165 Ibid., at para 92.
166 Ibid., at para 96.

temporal scope of that Agreement which arose prior to the trade mark with which it is alleged to conflict and which entitles him to use a sign identical or similar to that trade mark.[167]

D. UNREGISTERED TRADE MARKS – PASSING OFF

In situations where a trade mark is absolutely barred from registrability **6.174** because of a reference to a geographical place or region, an alternative mode of protection is reliance upon the tort of passing off. This has long been used to protect geographical designations in common law jurisdictions. In civil law jurisdictions, unfair competition law performs an equivalent role.

1. Elements of the action in passing off

The law of passing off is concerned with the protection of reputation and **6.175** goodwill from misrepresentations made in the course of trade which cause damage. In the UK the elements of the action were set out by Lord Diplock in *Erven Warnink bv v J Townend & Sons Ltd*[168] (the *Advocaat* case) and abbreviated to three requirements by Lord Oliver in *Reckitt & Colman Products Ltd v Borden Inc*[169] (the *Jif lemon* case):

> First, he must establish a goodwill or reputation attached to the goods or services which he supplies in the mind of the purchasing public by association with the identifying 'get-up' (whether it consists simply of a brand name or a trade description, or the individual features of labelling or packaging) under which his particular goods or services are offered to the public, such that the get-up is recognised by the public as distinctive specifically of the plaintiff's goods or services. Secondly, he must demonstrate a misrepresentation by the defendant to the public (whether or not intentional) leading or likely to lead the public to believe that goods or services offered by him are the goods or services of the plaintiff. Whether the public is aware of the plaintiff's identity as the manufacturer or supplier of the goods or services is immaterial, as long as they are identified with a particular source which is in fact the plaintiff. For example, if the public is accustomed to rely upon a particular brand name in purchasing goods of a particular description, it matters not at all that there is little or no public awareness of the identity of the proprietor of the brand name. Thirdly, he must demonstrate that he suffers or, in a *quia timet* action that he is likely to suffer, damage by reason of the erroneous belief engendered by the defendant's misrepresentation that the source of the defendant's goods or services is the same as the source of those offered by the plaintiff.

---

167   Ibid., at para 100.
168   [1979] AC 731, at p. 742 D–E.
169   [1990] RPC 341 at p. 406.

6.176 The *Advocaat* case had concerned the claim by the Dutch producers of an egg-flavoured alcoholic drink that the use of the word 'Advocaat' used by the UK-based defendants suggested a Dutch origin for their product. Lord Fraser in outlining the elements of a passing off action said that:

> It is essential for the plaintiff in a passing-off action to show at least the following facts: – (1) that his business consists of, or includes, selling in England a class of goods to which the particular trade name applies; (2) that the class of goods is clearly defined, and that in the minds of the public, or a section of the public, in England, the trade name distinguishes that class from other similar goods; (3) that because of the reputation of the goods, there is goodwill attached to the name; (4) that he, the plaintiff, as a member of the class of those who sell the goods, is the owner of goodwill in England which is of substantial value; (5) that he has suffered, or is really likely to suffer, substantial damage to his property in the goodwill by reason of the defendants selling goods which are falsely described by the trade name to which the goodwill is attached.[170]

2. Geographical marks and passing off

6.177 From its earliest development the British law of passing off prevented the misuse of geographical terms. In *Dunnachie v Young & Sons*[171] the defendants were enjoined from marking their fire bricks 'Young Glenboig' and advertising them as 'made from Glenboig clay', because they were made from a seam of clay about two miles from Glenboig.

6.178 The principal development of passing off law in relation to GIs occurred with the *Spanish Champagne* case,[172] which formed the basis of protection for champagne not only in England but also other common law jurisdictions. The question which the court had to consider in that case was whether use of the term 'Spanish Champagne' could be used in relation to a sparkling wine not produced in the French Champagne district. The suit was instituted by one of the French champagne houses on behalf of themselves and all other persons who produce wine in the Champagne district and supply such wine to England and Wales. The plaintiffs alleged that wine produced by the champagne houses and each of them and supplied by them to England and Wales, was a naturally sparkling wine produced in the Champagne district by a process of double fermentation from the grapes grown in the Champagne district and that it was long known to the trade and public throughout the UK as champagne and had as such acquired a high reputation. They alleged that

---

170   [1979] AC 731, pp. 755G–756A.
171   (1883), 10 R. (Ct. of Sess.) 874.
172   *HP Bollinger v Costa Brava Wine Co Ltd* [1959] 3 All ER 800.

any member of the trade or public in the UK ordering champagne or seeing wine advertised or offered for sale as champagne, would expect the wine so ordered, advertised or offered for sale, to be a naturally sparkling wine produced in the Champagne district from grapes grown in the Champagne district and no other.

The trial judge observed that: **6.179**

> The region in which the Champagne vineyards are found is about 100 miles east of Paris around Rheims and Epernay, where there is a chalky, flinty soil and the climate is subject to extreme variations of heat and cold. It appears that these factors give to the wine its particular qualities. since 1927 the Champagne Viticole District has been strictly limited by law, and only certain vineyards are allowed in France to use the name 'Champagne'. Wines produced from these vineyards are sold as 'Champagne', but goodwill has also become attached to the names of the shippers, or 'brand names' as they are called. The wine is a naturally sparkling wine made from the grapes produced in the Champagne district by a process of double fermentation which requires a considerable amount of care.

He ruled that it was established that 'Champagne' in England meant the product produced in the Champagne district of France by the plaintiffs and the other growers and shippers of that district.

This decision was followed in the '*Sherry case*'[173] in which Spanish sherry **6.180** producers claimed exclusive rights in the mark 'Sherry' which they derived from the Jerez district of Spain. They sought to enjoin the use of the mark, 'British Sherry'. The Court found that the term 'Sherry' was indeed a GI, but that the plaintiffs were disqualified from a remedy because they had acquiesced for a long time in the use in the English market of marks such as 'Australian Sherry' and 'South African Sherry'.

The *Scotch Whisky* case[174] was the third in the line of English cases on **6.181** protecting GIs. The questionable practice was the export of Scotch whisky to Ecuador where it was to be resold under the labels 'White Abbey' and 'Scottish Archer' Scotch whisky after being admixed with local cane spirit. The evidence in the case disclosed that there were two basic types of Scotch whisky: that made from malted barley only, and grain whisky, which is made from malted barley together with unmalted barley in varying proportions. These whiskies were produced by two different processes: the pot-still process for malt whisky and the patent or Coffey Still process for grain whisky.

---

173 *Vine Products Ltd & Others v Mackenzie & Co Ltd & Others* [1969] RPC 1.
174 *John Walker & Sons Ltd v Henry Ost & Co Ltd* [1970] 2 All ER 106.

Almost all of the whisky sold to the public is blended whisky, where a number of malt whiskies are blended with a number of grain whiskies to produce the whisky sold to the public under brand names. The formula for each brand is secret. There was evidence that there were no blenders of Scotch outside Scotland and England. The Court held that producers of Scotch fell within the principle enunciated in the *Spanish Champagne* case and were entitled to have upheld the description of their product as 'Scotch whisky'.

6.182 Similar results were obtained by the Scotch whisky manufacturers in passing off cases in South Africa. In *William Grant v Cape Wine & Distillers*[175] the Court held that a blend of Scotch whisky with local spirit, together with advertising material showing a Scotsman in full Highland dress and carrying the slogan 'ten years in Scotland makes all the difference', was actionable. In *Long John International v Stellenbosch Wine Trust*[176] the Court enjoined the sale of a product called 'Ben Nevis Scotch Whisky Liquor' with a Scottish theme to the label. The drink actually consisted of whisky distilled with water and sweetened with sugar.

3. Geographical marks and protectable reputation

6.183 The problem for claimants in relying on passing off to protect their geographical marks is that where the relevant mark is descriptive of a geographical region or location as the place of manufacture, a claimant will fail if he can establish no more than that. In *Chocosuisse Union des Fabricants Suisses de Chocolat v Cadbury*[177] the Court of Appeal pointed out that something more is necessary. This requirement was explained by Chadwick LJ:[178]

> The words 'Swiss chocolate' are, [as Laddie J pointed out at first instance[179]] ... descriptive in nature. They are clearly apt to describe chocolate made in Switzerland. But they are also apt to describe chocolate made to a Swiss recipe with Swiss expertise by a Swiss manufacturer. If the words are no more than descriptive – whether of the place of manufacture or of the identity of the manufacturer – they cannot found an action in passing-off. The judge identified the point, correctly in my view, in the following passage of his judgment[180] 'It is only if they [the words "Swiss chocolate"] are taken by a significant part of the public to be used in relation to and indicating a particular group of products having a discrete reputation as a group that a case of passing off can get off the ground. I have had to bear this in mind when assessing the

---

175 (1990) 3 SA 897.
176 [1990] 4 SA 136.
177 [1999] RPC 826.
178 Ibid., at p. 832.
179 [1998] RPC 117, at p. 129.
180 Ibid., lines 31–6.

evidence of what the words mean to members of the public. If they convey nothing more than their descriptive meaning the action must fail.'

There were, therefore, two questions to be addressed on this part of the case: **6.184** (i) would the words 'Swiss chocolate' have been taken by a significant section of the public in England at the relevant time to mean, and to mean only, chocolate made in Switzerland; and if so, (ii) did chocolate made in Switzerland have a discrete reputation, distinct from other chocolate, which the Swiss Chocolate Manufacturers were entitled to protect?

It is not necessary that the 'something more' must consist of a reputation for **6.185** higher quality or cachet. As Patten LJ explained in *Diageo North America Inc v Intercontinental Brands (ICB) Ltd*[181] (the *Vodkat* case):

> But there is no legal requirement that the distinctiveness of the claimant's mark should also be a badge of quality. Whether it generates goodwill in relation to the goods or services sold will inevitably be determined by the impact which they have on consumers. Doubtless the better the quality or the more fashionable they are, the more likely it is that the necessary reputation and goodwill will be acquired. But this factor is evidential in character and largely co-incidental. The law of passing-off is there to protect the unlawful appropriation of goodwill through misrepresentation. It is not there to guarantee to the general consumer the quality of what he buys. For that he must look elsewhere.[182]

In *Fage UK Ltd v Chobani UK Ltd*[183] Briggs J analysed the earlier cases by **6.186** identifying that the fundamental question 'is whether the geographical trade name has a pulling power that brings in custom, so that reputation and goodwill can properly be said to be enjoyed by all producers within the class which use that name for their product'.[184] This case concerned the term 'Greek yoghurt', which Briggs J held had attracted substantial goodwill beyond a mere description of its place of origin to which consumers were indifferent.[185]

In *Taittinger v Allbev* the High Court was concerned with the use of the name **6.187** 'Elderflower Champagne' for the use of a soft drink.[186] Despite the unlikelihood of English consumers thinking that the champagne houses of France were now involved in the production of soft drinks, the Court took the view

---

181 [2010] EWCA Civ 920; [2011] RPC 110.
182 Ibid., at para 29.
183 [2013] EWHC 630 (Ch).
184 Ibid., at para 125.
185 Ibid., at para 133.
186 [1994] 4 All ER 75 CA.

that the international significance of appellations of origin prevented their misuse, even in an apparently innocuous context.

4. Geographical marks and product processing

6.188   The Scottish passing off case *Argyllshire Weavers v Macauley*[187] discussed an issue which has been raised in a number of European GIs cases, namely whether the place of processing is part of the protectable reputation of a product. The defendants in the case were a London-based company which had used the words 'Harris Tweed' in its advertising for cloth made from pure virgin Scottish wool in the Islands of Harris and Lewis and the adjacent islands of the Outer Hebrides for a period exceeding 25 years. The plaintiffs claimed that all the cloth-making processes, including dyeing, spinning, hand weaving and finishing, had to be carried out in the Outer Hebrides.[188]

6.189   In *Scotch Whisky Association v Glen Kella Distillers Ltd*[189] the plaintiff trade association, whose members included the majority of the makers of the leading brands of Scotch whisky, brought an action in the High Court objecting to the sale by the defendant of a drink known as 'Glen Kella', which was called 'white whisky' and which was made by the re-distilling of matured and blended Scotch whisky in the Isle of Man. The plaintiffs contended that Glen Kella was not whisky by reason of the fact that it was not matured after distillation and accordingly, its sale as whisky was in breach of Art 1(4)(b) of Council Regulation (EEC) No 1576/89 of 29 May 1989 laying down general rules on the definition, description and presentation of spirit drinks,[190] which required that the 'spirit drink' concerned should have undergone a process of maturation for at least three years in wooden casks after its production as a liquid by distillation and that the sale of Glen Kella under the name 'whisky' amounted to passing off.

6.190   Rattee J upheld the passing off claim as there was a real risk of damage if the defendant were allowed to continue to call its product 'whisky' when it was not, the damage being an insidious erosion of the reputation or 'aura' of true whisky in the minds of potential consumers.

---

187   [1962] ScotCS CSIH_2 1962 SLT 310, 1962 SC 388, [1962].
188   *Macaulay (A.) (Tweeds) Ltd v Independent Harris Tweed Producers Ltd* [1961] PCR, Part 8, p. 184.
189   [1997] ETMR 470.
190   OJ 1989 L 160, p. 1 *(no longer in force).*

5. Genericity

As with trade marks and GIs, genericity can be an obstacle to a successful **6.191** action in passing off. This was raised incidentally in the 1913 case *Anderson v Britcher*.[191] The respondent had been charged with unlawfully selling as 'Demerara sugar' a sugar that was 'cane sugar crystals coloured with an organic dye foreign to genuine Demerara sugar, so that the sugar was not of the quality, substance, or nature of the article demanded by the purchaser'. It was found by a police magistrate that the sugar was a crystallised cane sugar grown in Mauritius and coloured with dye. The magistrate dismissed the charge, finding that the term 'Demerara sugar' was a:

> generic term applicable to any sugar of the substance, kind, and colour of the sugar in question wherever produced, and that therefore the said sugar was of the nature, substance, and quality of the article demanded by the appellant, the purchaser, and that accordingly the sale was not to his prejudice, and that no offence had been committed by the respondent.

The case was appealed to the King's Bench Court. In dismissing the appeal, **6.192** the Court agreed with the magistrate's view on the genericity of 'Demerara' and observed that:

> It would appear that 'Demerara sugar' does not mean sugar having certain qualities peculiar to Demerara sugar, but it means a sugar which is cane sugar and which has a particular colour owing to certain treatment, and it is stated that Demerara sugar as originally produced was white, and probably if a person asked for Demerara sugar and was offered real Demerara sugar in its natural state he would refuse it. This sugar which the appellant got when he asked for Demerara sugar was Demerara sugar in every single particular as understood by everybody who deals with such things, except that it was grown, not in Demerara, but in Mauritius.

> It was stated and admitted that with regard to Demerara sugar the word 'Demerara,' as applied to sugar, does not mean sugar grown only in Demerara; it means sugar grown in Demerara, or in Grenada, Martinique, or St. Kitts or Tobago, or Barbados, or Dominics [sic] or in many other islands of the West India group, and therefore the case really is hardly distinguishable from that of a Brussels carpet, which nobody supposes to be necessarily a carpet made in Brussels, or the case of a Cambridge sausage, which I suppose nobody believes to come necessarily from Cambridge.[192]

---

191 (1913) 24 Cox's Criminal Law Cases, 60.
192 Ibid., at 65.

E. DOMAIN NAMES AND GEOGRAPHICAL INDICATIONS

1. Internet Corporation for Assigned Names and Numbers (ICANN)

6.193 ICANN is responsible for the allocation of generic Top Level Domains (gTLDs), such as .com, .net, and .org. Since 2006 it has been considering the extension of the categories of gTLDs. At its meeting in Singapore in June 2011, ICANN formally approved an expansion of these domains by introducing up to 1,400 new gTLDs. ICANN is currently considering in excess of 2,000 applications.[193] These include in addition to the names of cities:

.bzh   (Breton community)
.eus   (Basque Language)
.gal   (Galician language)
.lat   (Latin America)
.africa (African and Pan African communities)
.scot   (Scots community).

6.194 The Government Advisory Committee (GAC) to the ICANN Board has expressed concerns about the use and protection of new geographic domains in the new gTLDs. In 2007 it issued 'GAC Principles regarding New gTLDs',[194] which advised that ICANN should avoid delegation of new gTLDs concerning country, territory or place names, and regional language or people descriptions, unless in agreement with the relevant governments or public authorities. Those GAC Principles also stated that new registries should adopt procedures for blocking/challenge of names with national or geographical significance at the second level upon demand of governments. The GAC has expressed reservations regarding a number of new gTLD applications on grounds of correspondence to geographical or other terms, advising the ICANN Board not to proceed beyond initial evaluation for these, and seeking further clarification from the Board on the scope for applicants to modify their new gTLD applications to address specific GAC concerns.

6.195 In 1999 ICANN adopted the Uniform Domain Name Dispute Resolution Policy (UDRP), which went into effect on 1 December 1999, for all ICANN-accredited registrars of Internet domain names. As is discussed below, the WIPO Arbitration and Mediation Centre is the principal ICANN-accredited domain name dispute resolution provider.

---

193   See https://gtldresult.icann.org/application-result/applicationstatus.
194   See http://gac.icann.org/web/home/gTLD_principles.pdf.

In anticipation of the July 2013 meeting of ICANN in Durban, the Organ- **6.196**
ization for an International Geographical Indications Network (oriGIn) called
on ICANN to set up a dispute resolution system so that prior rights for
geographic indications could be taken into account in the process for the
attribution of new gTLDs.[195] However, the participating countries were
unable to agree. Ermert[196] reported that US and Australian representatives
criticised as discriminatory the European Federation of Origin Wines
(EFOW) action to use an ICANN GAC recommendation to the ICANN
Board to block the application process for .vin and .wine. Ermert noted that
'Governments at ICANN in the past were able to agree on stern protection of
trademark rights in the new TLD procedure, but the protection of geographical indications is an unresolved issue in ongoing international negotiations'.[197]

Although the UDRP will remain as the principal avenue for the resolution of **6.197**
new gTLD disputes, ICANN has proposed a Uniform Rapid Suspension
(URS) System for appropriate cases.[198] This provides for (i) a URS Lock,
which prevents a domain name from being updated, transferred or deleted;
(ii) URS Suspension; or (iii) URS Rollback, the reversion of a domain name to
a Non-URS state.

2. Domain names at WIPO

Under the UDRP, WIPO is the leading ICANN-accredited domain name **6.198**
dispute resolution provider.[199] While the mandatory application of the UDRP
is limited to domain names registered in gTLDs, such as .com, .net, and .org,
WIPO's arbitration centre also assists country code top level domain (ccTLD)
registries in their establishment of registration conditions and dispute resolution procedures, which are mostly modelled after the UDRP, but may take
account of the particular circumstances and needs of individual ccTLDs. The
WIPO Arbitration and Mediation Centre in September 2013 provided
domain name dispute resolution services to 69 ccTLD registries.[200]

The possible need for the protection of GIs in the Domain Name System **6.199**
(DNS) was discussed in the final report of the first WIPO Internet Domain

---

195   Saez, 2013.
196   Ermert, 2013.
197   Ibid.
198   See http://newgtlds.icann.org/en/applicants/urs.
199   See Forrest, 2013.
200   Standing Committee on the Law of Trademarks, Industrial Designs and Geographical Indications,
      Thirtieth Session, 4–8 November 2013, WIPO Doc, SCT/30/5, 'Update on Trademark-Related Aspects of
      the Domain Name System', 20 September 2013, para 7.

Name Process dated 30 April 1999. The possibility of extending the UDRP to GIs was considered premature because of the lack of global harmonisation of international GIs norms.[201]

6.200 On 28 June 2000 WIPO received a letter of request from the government of Australia, as well as 19 governments of its other Member States, to initiate a second WIPO process to address 'the issues raised, in the domain name space, inter alia, by bad faith, abusive, misleading or unfair use of [among other identifiers] geographical indications ...'[202] In response to this request, on 10 July 2000, WIPO commenced the Second WIPO Internet Domain Name Process.

6.201 The final report of the Second WIPO Internet Domain Name Process of 3 September 2001 referred to problems experienced in the DNS by a number of organisations concerned with protecting the interests of the users of GIs. These included the Office international de la vigne et du vin (OIV) and the Institut national des appellations d'origine (INAO). The OIV reported that 'a very large number of Internet domain names consist of geographical indications of recognised traditional denominations that are regulated by the Member States of the OIV and have been communicated to the OIV by them' and that among these domain names, 'there are a number which are particularly confusing for Internet users and constitute commercial piracy or a misappropriation of notoriety ... certain registrations are offered for sale to the highest bidder or are linked to inactive sites, evidencing bad faith'.[203]

6.202 The OIV submitted a study conducted by the Fédération des syndicats de producteurs de Châteauneuf du Pape (the Federation of Producers' Associations of Châteauneuf du Pape), which argued that 'a large number of domain names have been registered which correspond to appellations of origin and geographical indications of wine-derived growing products, as well as wine varieties, without there being any relationship between the domain name registrants and the persons who hold rights in these distinctive signs'.[204]

6.203 Although it accepted the evidence of abuse the final Report of the Second WIPO Internet Domain Name Process concluded that because views were divided it was 'recommended that no modification be made to the UDRP, at

---

201 See WIPO Standing Committee on the Law of Trademarks, Industrial Designs and Geographical Indications, Tenth Session, 28 April–2 May 2003, 'Internet Domain Names and Geographical Indications' WIPO Doc, SCT/10/6, 3 April 2003, at 2.

202 Ibid., at 3.

203 Ibid., at 4.

204 Ibid. A representative selection of domain names covered by this study were submitted by OIV and INAO.

this stage, to permit complaints to be made concerning the registration and use of domain names in violation of the prohibition against false indications of source or the rules relating to the protection of geographical indications'.[205]

The final Report was also submitted to Special Sessions of the WIPO **6.204** Standing Committee on the Law of Trademarks, Industrial Designs and Geographical Indications (SCT) which were held from 29 November– 4 December 2001, and from 21–24 May 2002. The SCT was also unable to reach consensus on this subject for much the same reasons that the WTO discussions on the extension of Art 23 of the TRIPS Agreement and the establishment of the multilateral system for the protection of GIs for wines and spirits has faltered.

3. WIPO DNS panel decisions on geographical domain names

(a) Uniform Domain Name Dispute Resolution Policy

Under para 4(a) of the Policy, a complainant has the burden of proving the **6.205** following:

(i) that the disputed domain name is identical or confusingly similar to a trade mark or service mark in which the complainant has rights; and
(ii) that the respondent has no rights or legitimate interests in respect of the disputed domain name; and
(iii) that the disputed domain name has been registered and is being used in bad faith.

A respondent to demonstrate 'rights or legitimate interest' had to demonstrate **6.206** in accordance with para 4(c) of the Policy:

(a) that he used or has made preparations to use the domain name or a name corresponding to the domain name in connection with a *bona fide* offering of goods or services prior to the dispute;
(b) that he is commonly known by the domain name, even if he has not acquired any trade mark rights; or
(c) that he intends to make a legitimate, non-commercial or fair use of the domain name without intent for commercial gain to misleadingly divert consumers or to tarnish the trade mark.

For the purpose of para 4(a)(iii) of the Policy, the following circumstances, in **6.207** particular but without limitation, if found by the Panel to be present, shall be evidence of the registration and use of the domain name in bad faith:

---

205   Ibid., at 9.

(i)   circumstances indicating that the holder has registered or has acquired the domain name primarily for the purpose of selling, renting, or otherwise transferring the domain name registration to the complainant who is the owner of the trade mark or service mark or to a competitor of that complainant, for valuable consideration in excess of the holder's documented out-of-pocket costs directly related to the domain name; or

(ii) the holder has registered the domain name in order to prevent the owner of the trade mark or service mark from reflecting the mark in a corresponding domain name, provided that the holder has engaged in a pattern of such conduct; or

(iii) the holder has registered the domain name primarily for the purpose of disrupting the business of a competitor; or

(iv) by using the domain name, the holder has intentionally attempted to attract, for commercial gain, Internet users to the holder's website or other online location, by creating a likelihood of confusion with the complainant's mark as to the source, sponsorship, affiliation, or endorsement of the holder's website or location or of a product or service on the holder's website or location.

6.208 Paragraph 15(a) of the Rules requires the panel to 'decide a complaint on the basis of the statements and documents submitted in accordance with the Policy, these Rules and any Rules and principles of law that it deems applicable'.

6.209 Decisions of WIPO Panellists applying its UDRP have held that some geographical terms can be protected under the UDRP if the complainant has shown that it has rights in the term and that the term is being used as a trade mark for goods or services other than those that are described by or related to the geographical meaning of the term. The fact that a domain is a GI protected under European law is considered, applying the final report of the Second WIPO Internet Domain Name Process, to be a matter outside the policy.

6.210 A number of the important Panel decisions dealing with geographical marks and GIs are digested below.

(b) Comité Interprofessionnel du vin de Champagne v Steven Vickers[206]

6.211 The Complainant was Comité Interprofessionnel du vin de Champagne of Épernay, France, established by statute under the laws of France to defend, preserve and promote the interests of all those involved in the production and marketing of the wines sold under the appellation of origin 'Champagne'. All producers of champagne in the Champagne district of France are required by law to subscribe to the complainant. According to the complainant, the

---

206   [2011] ETMR 56.

expression 'champagne' is distinctive only of wine produced in the Champagne region of France and is registered as a PDO under Regulation (EC) No 491/2009. The complainant held 27 gTLDs and ccTLDs consisting of the word 'champagne', and a further 101 domain names which include 'champagne' as part of the name. These domain names include <champagne.eu>, <champagne.biz>, <champagne.com>, <champagne.fr> and <champagne-.co.uk>. The domain names <champagne.co.uk> and <champagne.com> both revert to the complainant's websites. The respondent, Steven Vickers of London, registered the disputed domain name <champagne.co>. He operated an IT consultancy and computer sales business in London and did not trade in champagne or beverages of any kind. The respondent stated that he decided to register a batch of generic '.co' domain names with a view to future sale. He applied for over 100 such domain names, and all were registered in July/August 2010. A sub-group of these domain names consisted of 13 names which related generally to food or drink. One of them was the domain name <champagne.com>; two others were <brandy.co> and <gin.co>.

6.212 The complainant contended that the domain name was identical or confusingly similar to a trade mark or service mark in which the complainant had rights, namely that it had become an unregistered trade mark and was protected in the UK under the common law of passing off, and had been so protected in a number of decided cases, including *Taittinger and Others v Allbev Ltd*,[207] discussed above.

6.213 The claimant pointed out that 'CHAMPAGNE' was protected as a PDO under Regulation (EC) No 491/2009 and the reputation and rights associated with the name Champagne had been recognised in numerous cases throughout the world.

6.214 As the respondent did not trade in champagne or beverages of any kind and the domain name bore no resemblance to the respondent's personal name or to the corporate names with which the respondent was connected, it was argued by the claimant that the domain name was registered and was being used in bad faith. The respondent submitted that the complainant offered no clear explanation as to why and how the term 'champagne', which is both a dictionary and a highly descriptive word, should be considered as capable of generating unregistered rights for the purposes of the UDRP.

---

207   [1993] FSR 641.

i. That the disputed domain name is identical or confusingly similar to a trade mark or service mark in which the complainant has rights

6.215 Appling para 4(a) of the UDRP, the Panellist addressed first 'what rights does the Ccomplainant hold in the expression "Champagne"?' The Panel accepted on the evidence as a whole, including an Irish[208] and French[209] domain name decision and the decision of the Nominet UK appeal panel in *CIVC v Jackson*, that the complainant held rights in the expression 'Champagne' as an appellation of origin, or as a PDO, or geographical identifier, under relevant European Regulations. However, acknowledging the refusal of the Second WIPO Internet Domain Name Process to recommend specifically extending protection to geographical terms under the UDRP, the Panellist ruled that rights in a PDO or a geographical identifier were not sufficient for the Complainant to make out a case of 'rights' under para 4(a)(i) of the UDRP.[210]

6.216 As the complainant did not hold any registered trade mark or service mark (including any certification mark or collective mark) that would have placed it within the policy, it relied on its unregistered trade mark rights, which it said existed under the English law of passing off. The Panellist observed, in this regard, that while a trader may in appropriate circumstances have recourse to the English law of passing off to protect unregistered rights which it has in a trade mark or service mark, the converse did not necessarily apply, that the fact that a trader might have a right to sue in passing off did not necessarily imply that the trader holds an unregistered trade mark or service mark.[211] The Panellist observed that permitting a claimant to assert an unregistered trade mark right under the law of passing off would defeat the intention of the framers of the UDRP that GIs or 'protected designations of origin' should not provide a basis as such for a 'right' under para 4(a)(i) of the Policy.[212] On this basis the complaint was denied.[213]

ii. Registered and used in bad faith

6.217 In view of the Panel's findings on the lack of the complainant's justiciable right it was not necessary for the Panel to make any finding on the issue of bad faith, but the Panel noted that it would also have found for the respondent on this issue.[214]

---

208 *CIVC v Richard Doyle*, Case No DIE 2007–0005.
209 *VC v Internet SARL*, Case No DFR2005–0006.
210 Ibid., at paras 71–74.
211 Ibid., at para 76.
212 Ibid., at para 79 applying the decision of the Nominet UK appeal panel in *CIVC v Jackson* (Nominet UK DRS Case No 4479).
213 Ibid., at para 80.
214 Ibid., at para 86.

It was pointed out that the complainant had not alleged that the respondent's **6.218** intention was to sell, rent or otherwise transfer the domain name *to the Complainant or to a competitor of the Complainant* – just that the respondent's primary intention was to rent, sell or otherwise transfer the domain name *to a third party*.[215] Even if the complainant had said that the respondent's intention was to sell, rent or otherwise transfer the domain name to the complainant at a profit, the Panel found that the complainant was not in fact 'the owner of the trademark or service mark', as those words are used in para 4(b)(i).

It was also noted that trading in domain names is not per se contrary to the **6.219** Policy.[216]

iii. Reverse domain name hijacking

Under para 15(e) of the UDRP a Panel is obliged to state in its decision any **6.220** conclusion it might reach that a complainant has brought the complaint in bad faith, for example in an attempt at reverse domain name hijacking. 'Reverse domain name hijacking' is defined in the Rules as 'using the Policy in bad faith to attempt to deprive a registered domain name holder of a domain name'.

Jazeera Space Channel TV Station v AJ Publishing aka Aljazeera Publishing[217] **6.221** ruled by majority that the onus of proving that a complainant has acted in bad faith is on the respondent, and that mere lack of success of the complaint is not of itself sufficient to constitute reverse domain name hijacking. The Panellist in the current case referred to the three-member panel decision in *Yell Ltd v Ultimate Search*,[218] which had observed that whether a complainant should have appreciated at the outset that its complaint could not succeed will often be an important consideration.[219] The respondent submitted that the complainant could not seriously have thought that it had a real prospect of winning the case because of its failure to secure modification of the UDRP to bring GIs within its ambit and because of the general lack of detail of its claim.[220] However, given the complexity of the law in relation to unregistered trade marks, despite a finding that the complainant's arguments were inadequately documented, the Panel was unable to conclude with sufficient confidence that the complainant acted in bad faith in bringing the complaint.[221]

---

215   Ibid.
216   Ibid., applying *Media General Communications Inc v Rarenames WebReg WIPO*, Case No D2006–0964.
217   WIPO Case No D2005–0309.
218   WIPO Case No D2005–0091.
219   [2011] ETMR 56 at para 90.
220   Ibid., at para 92.
221   Ibid., at para 97.

(c)   *Consejo Regulador del Cava v Adrian Lucas*[222]

6.222   The complainant's name translates into English as The Regulating Council of Cava. It is a trade body attached to the Spanish Ministry of the Environment and Rural and Marine Affairs. It was established in 1993. Its functions include control of production processes for a particular variety of sparkling wine called 'Cava' originating primarily from certain specified municipalities mainly in and around the Catalonian region of Spain. The complainant was the registered proprietor of a collective device mark filed with OHIM on 12 December 2003 'CONSEJO REGULADOR CAVA' for 'sparkling wine (cava)' and services relating to the sale and distribution of sparkling wine (cava). The complainant was also the proprietor of a Community trade mark application filed on 28 May 2008 'CAVA DE LA TIERRA AL CORAZON (device)' for the same goods and services as the previous registration. The complainant was also the proprietor of the domain name <crcava.es>, which it registered in 1999.

6.223   The disputed domain name, <cava.com>, was registered on 26 November 1996. This domain name was connected to a directory page featuring sponsored links to a variety of sites ranging from hotel sites to sites offering sparkling wine for sale. Other links led to sites concerned with other wines and a range of soft drinks. The respondent's site indicated that the domain <cava.com> may be for sale by its owner.

i.   Identical or confusingly similar

6.224   The Panel accepted as fact that 'Cava' was protected in Spain and the European Community as a reserved denomination and a GI. However, the Panel noted that under the UDRP the complainant was not able to rely on these. In relation to the fact that the applicant's registered trade mark had as its most prominent feature the word 'CAVA' in upper case, the Panel found it not difficult to conclude that the disputed domain name was confusingly similar to it.

6.225   As for the complainant's domain name, <crcava.es>, the Panel had insufficient information to enable it to decide whether the complainant's domain name was an unregistered trade mark in which the complainant had rights. For example, the Panel did not know when the complainant first started making active use of that domain name, nor did the Panel know the extent to which (if at all) the complainant had promoted that domain name such as to give it the status of a trade mark or service mark.

---

222   WIPO Case No D2008–1939.

ii. Rights or legitimate interests

In light of the evidence put forward by the complainant, the Panel considered **6.226** it probable that the respondent had no connection with 'Cava' such as to give him any right or legitimate interest in respect of 'Cava'.

iii. Registered and used in bad faith

The Panel was unable to agree with the complainant that the disputed domain **6.227** name was registered in bad faith. First, the complaint was launched more than a decade after the domain name was registered. While a delay of this length need not have been fatal to a complaint under the Policy, it was nonetheless likely to give rise to evidentiary difficulties.

Secondly, the domain name was not a trade mark or service mark, but a **6.228** generic term for a genus of wine. Thirdly, there was no direct evidence of intent on the part of the respondent to target the complainant at the time of registration. Fourthly, at the date of registration of the disputed domain name, the complainant did not own any trade mark rights in respect of the word 'cava' per se. While the complainant was in existence when the domain name was registered, the Panel did not believe that the respondent could be expected to have anticipated at that time that the complainant would be able to obtain trade mark rights in respect of the word 'cava'. The Panel also regarded it as unlikely that when the respondent registered the domain name he had in mind the complainant and/or any future trade mark rights of the complainant. The Panel was therefore not persuaded that the respondent registered the domain name in bad faith within the meaning of para 4(a)(iii) of the Policy.

(d) Consorzio del Prosciutto di Parma v Domain Name Clearing Company, LLC[223]

The complainant was a consortium of certified manufacturers of Parma Ham **6.229** and the owner of the certification mark 'PARMA HAM', registered in the USA on 12 November 1996 in relation to 'ham products'. The certificate of registration bears the following mention: 'The certification mark is used by persons authorised by the certifier to certify the regional origin of the product to which the mark is applied'. The respondent registered the domain name <parmaham.com> on 26 April 1997. On 30 January 1997 it had registered the domain names <prosciutto.com> and <parmaprosciutto.com>, 'Prosciutto' being the Italian word for ham.

---

223   WIPO Case No. D2000–0629.

6.230 The complainant contended that the domain name was identical or confusingly similar to a trade mark in which it had rights, that the respondent had no rights or legitimate interests in respect of the domain name, and that the respondent had registered and used the domain name in bad faith.

i. Identity or confusing similarity

6.231 The Panel held that this was satisfied by the complainant's ownership of a US registration for the certification word mark 'PARMA HAM', which was identical to the respondent's domain name.

ii. Rights or legitimate interests

6.232 In the absence of the assertion of such rights or interests by the respondent, the Panellist inferred from this default that such rights or legitimate interests in fact did not exist.

iii. Registration and use in bad faith

6.233 As regards sub-para 4(b)(i) of the UDRP, the Panellist observed that the file did not contain any indication that the respondent had at any time tried to sell the domain name to the complainant or a competitor. As regards sub-para 4(b)(iii), it was not alleged that the respondent and complainant were competitors, therefore the registration could not have had the purpose of disrupting a competitor's business. As regards sub-para 4(b)(iv), as the respondent did not use the domain name to designate a website, it did not appear that it tried to attract consumers by causing a confusion with the complainant's company, services or products. Thus, the requirements of sub-paras (i), (iii) and (iv) were not satisfied in the present case and the Panellist ruled that the complainant had not demonstrated that the respondent had engaged in a pattern of registering domain names in order to prevent the owner of trade marks to register them in corresponding domain names.

6.234 In relation to other circumstances that may constitute evidence that a domain name was registered or is being used in bad faith, the complainant referred to its registered certification mark. The Panellist pointed out that as this mark was registered only in November 1996, it was quite possible that the respondent did not know of this in 1997. Consequently, the complainant had not satisfied its burden of proof as far as registration in bad faith was concerned.

(e) Consorzio del Prosciutto di Parma v Matthias Gasser, Hanslmeier Fleischwarenfabrik[224]

The complainant was a consortium of certified producers of Parma Ham **6.235** and the owner of registrations of the certification marks 'PARMA', 'PROSCIUTTO DI PARMA' and 'PARMA HAM' in several countries. In 1996 Parma Ham was registered as a PDO. The respondent registered the domain name <parma-schinken.com> on 7 February 2001. 'Schinken' is the German word for ham. The domain name was used on a website on which the respondent offered various meat products including products advertised as Parma Ham.

Among the arguments of the complainant were that the domain name was **6.236** confusingly similar to its registered certification marks because 'Schinken' translates into 'prosciutto' in Italian and 'ham' in English; that the respondent was aware of the complainant's rights, and therefore acted in bad faith, because it placed on its website a reference to the PDO status of Parma Ham; and that the respondent advertised as 'Parmaschinken' certain ham products, which did not appear to originate from producers allowed to sell original Parma Ham.

i. Domain name identical or confusingly similar

The Panel noted that the European PDO status of Parma Ham was irrelevant **6.237** because it was outside the UDRP, however the complainant's certification marks brought it within the policy and because 'Schinken' was the literal German translation of the generic words 'prosciutto' and 'ham', the Panel found that the domain name was confusingly similar to the complainant's certification marks.

ii. Rights and legitimate interest

The Panel pointed out that in determining whether a reseller or service agent **6.238** of trade-marked goods can use the trade mark at issue in its domain names, previous decisions have held that a respondent must at the minimum: (i) actually be offering the goods or services at issue; (ii) use the site to sell only the trade-marked goods; (iii) accurately disclose the registrant's relationship with the trade mark owner; and (iv) not try to corner the market in all domain names.[225] In this case the Panel considered that the respondent's use of the reference to 'Parma Ham' was not in good faith. It distinguished the decision

---

224 Case No D2003–0474.
225 *Oki Data Americas, Inc. v ASD, Inc*, WIPO Case No D2001–0903.

Consorzio del Prosciutto di Parma v Domain Name Clearing Company, LLC[226] because of the significantly different factual basis, and because in that case the Panel considered that the respondent had not yet actually used that domain name and concluded that it was possible to conceive of a legitimate use of the term 'Parma Ham'. In the present case, however, the respondent actually used the domain name in a way which did not qualify as 'bona fide'. The Panel therefore found that the complainant had shown that the respondent had no rights or legitimate interests in respect of the domain name, according to para 4(a)(ii) of the Policy.

iii. Registration and use in bad faith

6.239 The Panel held that by using the domain name to sell a multitude of different competing meat products (and not only Parma ham), the respondent attempted to attract, for commercial gain, Internet users looking for Parma Ham to its website. The respondent's use of the complainant's certification marks created a likelihood of confusion in that Internet users might assume that the respondent's website was affiliated to or otherwise sponsored by the certified producers of Parma Ham. Therefore, the Panel found that the complainant had shown that the respondent registered and used the domain name in bad faith in the sense of para 4(b)(iv) of the Policy.

6.240 The Administrative Panel ordered that the registration of the domain name <parma-schinken.com> be transferred to the complainant.

(f) Province of Brabant Wallon v Domain Purchase, NOLDC, Inc[227]

i. The parties

6.241 Brabant Wallon is the geographic denomination of the Belgian province of Brabant Wallon. The complainant was the public body which governs that geographic area. Since 15 June 1999, it had been the owner of OHIM-registered trade mark No 000613638, comprising the words 'Brabant wallon' (written vertically) and 'la jeune Province' (written horizontally) together with relatively large figurative elements (Vienna classifications 26.3.4, 26.4.1 and 26.13.25). In 1996 the complainant engaged a company called Aleph One to register domain names related to the province, with registrations for one year. However, Aleph One kept and renewed, on its own behalf, the domain name <brabant-wallon.org>. This domain name was subsequently transferred to different entities before being registered by the respondent, Domain Purchase, NOLDC, Inc, of New Orleans, Louisiana, USA on 21 November 2003.

---

226 WIPO Case No D2000–0629.
227 WIPO Case No D2006–0778.

The complainant submitted that the contested domain name was identical or **6.242** confusingly similar to a trade mark or service mark in which the complainant had rights, namely the trade mark 'BRABANT WALLON' and that the respondent had no rights or legitimate interests in respect of the domain name and could not prove any link with the Province of Brabant Wallon that would justify the use of the trade mark as a domain name. These facts were also asserted in support of the complainant's argument that the domain name was registered and used in bad faith. The respondent did not reply to the complainant's contentions.

ii.   The complainant's rights in a geographical trade mark

Although it was acknowledged by the Panellist that geographical terms are not **6.243** protected as such under the UNDP, it was generally accepted amongst Panellists that geographical terms can be so protected if shown by evidence of their use or by registration to have become or to be distinctive of the goods or services of a particular trader. It was a matter of evidence in each case as to whether a complainant had proved that the geographical name functioned as a trade mark.[228] In this case the complainant had established that it has rights in a registered trade mark.

iii.   Identical or confusingly similar

The Panel observed that the dominant and immediately striking feature of the **6.244** registered trade mark on which the complainant relied was its figurative element comprising a combination of triangles, squares and other shapes forming a design somewhat reminiscent, for example, of a silhouette of sails. This overshadowed the words 'Brabant wallon – la jeune Province'. As the figurative element was an essential element of the complainant's mark in comparing the disputed domain name with the complainant's mark, it was apparent that the two were neither identical nor virtually identical, so the Panel ruled that the complainant had failed to establish this element of its case and that it was therefore unnecessary to consider the issues of legitimacy and bad faith.

(g)   Warendorfer Küchen GmbH v MDNH Inc [229]

The complainant, Warendorfer Küchen GmbH of Warendorf, Nordrhein- **6.245** Westfalen, Germany, is a German corporation in the business of the development, production and distribution of kitchen furniture. The respondent, MDNH Inc of Las Vegas, Nevada, USA, registered the domain name

---

228   Applying *Consejo de Promoción Turística de México, SA de CV v Latin America Telecom Inc*, WIPO Case No D2004–0242.
229   WIPO Case No D2009–1067.

<warendorf.com>. On 15 June 2009 the complainant applied to register in Germany a trade mark consisting of the word 'Warendorf' together with a motif consisting of various triangles. The trade mark was entered on the register on 11 August 2009 and the opposition period began. There are currently three other trade marks registered in Germany that include the word 'Warendorf'.

6.246 The complainant argued that the disputed domain name was confusingly similar to the company name Warendorfer Küchen GmbH, and also to the complainant's service mark 'Warendorfer'. The complainant stated that the respondent had no rights or legitimate interests in the disputed domain name, as it did not own any trade mark rights in 'Warendorf' or 'Warendorfer' or offer goods or services under the disputed domain name. The complainant also stated that the respondent had acted in bad faith within the meaning of the Policy.

6.247 The respondent argued that this dispute concerned a geographical term, and in particular the name of a municipality in Germany, which it had been using as a domain name to provide travel-related advertising.

i. Identical or confusingly similar

6.248 The Panel ruled that the disputed domain name was not identical or confusingly similar to the complainant's corporate name 'Warendorfer Küchen' for the following reasons: (i) Warendorf is a geographical name, used by numerous businesses; (ii) 'Warendorfer Küchen' is a descriptive term, meaning 'kitchens of Warendorf', and so has little inherent distinctiveness; (iii) the complainant's trade name consists of two descriptive words in German and does not confer any rights to the two individual words or any derivative of the individual words; (iv) the complainant uses 'Warendorfer Küchen' as a business name rather than in the active marketing of its products; (v) there was no evidence of actual confusion by Internet users between the respondent's website and the complainant's business (such evidence is not routinely required in a UDRP proceeding); and (vi) there was no evidence that the sponsored links on the respondent's website had ever generated any links to the complainant or its products. For these reasons, the Panel found that the complainant had failed to prove the first element of the Policy, and the complaint was dismissed.

7

ENFORCEMENT OF GEOGRAPHICAL INDICATIONS IN EUROPE

A. INTRODUCTION

Until recently, most of the attention paid to the exponential growth in the **7.01** international trade in infringing products has been focused upon counterfeit pharmaceuticals, branded fashion products and various pirated copyright works. However, most products are capable of being imitated in industrial quantities and products protected by GIs, particularly wines and spirits, are no exception.[1] The TRIPS Agreement had directed criminal enforcement primarily against 'cases of wilful trademark counterfeiting or copyright piracy on a commercial scale'[2] and this focus was replicated in the EU in Council Regulation (EC) No 1383/2003 of 22 July 2003 concerning customs action against goods suspected of infringing certain IPRs and the measures to be taken against goods found to have infringed such rights.[3] This Regulation has now been replaced by Regulation (EU) No 608/2013 of the European Parliament and of the Council of 12 June 2013 concerning customs enforcement of intellectual property.[4]

7.02   The new Regulation includes in the definition of 'counterfeit goods': 'goods which are subject of an action infringing a geographical indication and bear or are described by a name or term protected in respect of that geographical indication'.

7.03   For various constitutional reasons, the EU has not yet been able to enact an instrument providing for criminal sanctions against IPR infringements,[5] although the EU has participated in the negotiation of the Anti-counterfeiting Trade Agreement (ACTA), which contains a suite of such sanctions.[6] However, on 4 July 2012 (ACTA) was rejected by the European Parliament.[7]

7.04   In the absence of criminal sanctions, EU enforcement of GIs is left to civil enforcement under the terms of the 'Enforcement Directive' (Directive 2004/48/EC of the European Parliament and of the Council of 29 April 2004 on the enforcement of intellectual property rights)[8] and 'the Customs Regulation' (Council Regulation (EC) No 1383/2003 of 22 July 2003 concerning customs action against goods suspected of infringing certain intellectual property rights and the measures to be taken against goods found to have infringed such rights).[9]

---

1   See Zanzig, 2013.
2   TRIPS Agreement, Art 61.
3   OJ L 196, 2.8.2003, pp. 7–14 (hereinafter 'the Customs Regulation').
4   OJ L 181/15, 29.6.13, pp. 15–34.
5   In an environmental law case decided in 2005 (Case C-176/03, *Commission of the European Communities v Council of the European Union* [2005] ECR I-07879), the ECJ indicated that the EU had a limited competence in the field of criminal law if the application of effective, proportionate, and dissuasive criminal penalties is necessary to ensure the efficiency of important Community policies.
6   See Blakeney, 2012a.
7   http://www.europarl.europa.eu/news/en/press-room/20120703IPR48247/european-parliament-rejects-acta.
8   OJ L 195, 02/06/2004, pp. 16–25.
9   OJ L 196, 2.8.2003, pp. 7–14.

On 29 November 2017 the Commission issued a communication concerning **7.05**
initiatives concerning IP enforcement.[10] These include stepping up the fight
against counterfeiting and piracy by providing new guidance on how to apply
the 2004 Enforcement Directive; supporting industry-led initiatives to combat
IP infringements, including voluntary agreements on advertising on websites,
on payment services and on transport and shipping and assessing the
implementation of the EU Customs Action Plan on IP infringements and
proposing more targeted assistance to national customs authorities.

B. AVAILABILITY OF CRIMINAL OFFENCES UNDER EUROPEAN LAW

The criminalisation of IPR wrongs was attempted in the controversial EU **7.06**
Draft Directive on criminal measures aimed at ensuring the enforcement of
intellectual property rights.[11] The controversy resulted from the constitutional
objections which EU Member States had to the European Parliament legis-
lating on criminal law matters. This was an area of competency which they
regarded as within the exclusive competence of national parliaments. However, the European Court of Justice of the European Communities (ECJ) in
Commission and European Parliament v Council, Case C-176/03 of 13 September 2005, had indicated that the Community could adopt criminal measures in
relation to environmental policy where these were 'essential' for combating
serious environmental offences and where the Community legislature considered such measures to be necessary to ensure that the Community rules on
environmental protection were fully effective. Article 1 of the Draft Directive
on criminal law enforcement had described the Directive as laying down the
criminal measures which were 'necessary' to ensure the enforcement of IPRs
and provided that the measures were to apply to IPRs under both Community
and national law. However, various Member States argued that the judgment
of the ECJ in Case C-176/03 should be interpreted restrictively and that any
obligations created must be limited to Community law and not general
criminal law.

1. Knowledge

Article 61 permits the institution of criminal penalties in the case of wilful **7.07**
infringement. As a matter of practice it is not uncommon in intellectual
property disputes for a complainant to send a cease and desist notice to an
alleged infringer to put them on notice that they may be infringing the

---

10 http://europa.eu/rapid/press-release_IP-17-4942_en.htm.
11 8866/06 COM(06) 168.

complainant's IPRs. This may, however, be unrealistic in cases of large-scale copyright piracy and trade mark counterfeiting, particularly where the perpetrators may be involved in organised crime. Although it is usual for intellectual property statutes to insist upon wilfulness before criminal sanctions can be invoked, in analogous areas of the law, 'involving economic or social regulation', legislatures have imposed strict liability and have not required proof of *mens rea*.

2. Quantification of penalties

7.08 The degree of wilfulness or deliberation in the infringing conduct will have a bearing on the size of any pecuniary penalties which are imposed. Also relevant as a quantification factor will be the multiplicity of offences by a defendant and the recurrence of similar offences. Article 61 also refers to the deterrent effect of penalties. This will involve a consideration of the capacity of the defendant to pay, the incentives for wrongdoing and the likelihood of recurrence.

7.09 Article 61 was analysed in the WTO's Dispute Panel determination in relation to the US complaint about copyright enforcement in China.[12] The US argued that China's copyright laws did not apply to copyright piracy on a commercial scale and therefore were also inconsistent with China's obligations under the second sentence of that Article to make the necessary remedies 'available' or sufficient to deter piracy and counterfeiting. The Panel considered it unnecessary to rule on the question of deterrence as the US had made this claim contingent upon the outcome of its claims under the first sentence of Art 61 of the TRIPS Agreement and the Panel ruled that the US had been unable to establish that China did not impose criminal liability in relation to infringements on a commercial scale.[13]

7.10 The issue of deterrence is also mentioned in Art 41.1 of TRIPS, which requires that enforcement procedures specified in the Agreement are 'available' so as to permit 'effective action' against any act of infringement of the IPRs covered by the Agreement, including 'remedies which constitute a deterrent to further infringements'. The WTO's Dispute Panel determination in relation to the US complaint about copyright enforcement in China suggested that enforcement procedures under Art 41 permitted effective action if they were

---

12   *China – Measures Affecting the Protection and Enforcement of Intellectual Property Rights*, WT/DS362, 26 January 2009, paras 7.670ff.
13   Interestingly, ACTA was characterised as the 'Anti-China Trade Alliance' (Yu, 2011 at 128) (citing Remarks of Howard P. Knopf, at the 18th Fordham Annual International Intellectual Property and Policy Conference, Fordham University School of Law, in New York (9 April 2010)).

'available'.[14] Article 46 of TRIPS, which refers to 'other remedies', provides that in order to 'create an effective deterrent to infringement', the judicial authorities 'shall have the authority to order that goods that they have found to be infringing be, without compensation of any sort, disposed of outside the channels of commerce in such a manner as to avoid any harm caused to the right holder'. Thus confiscation of infringing goods seems to be a category of deterrent remedy, although it is a remedy other than a criminal remedy.

Footnote 12 to Art 24 provides that 'it is understood that there is no **7.11** obligation for a Party to provide for the possibility of imprisonment and monetary fines to be imposed in parallel'.

C. DIRECTIVE 2004/48/EC OF THE EUROPEAN PARLIAMENT AND OF THE COUNCIL OF 29 APRIL 2004 ON THE ENFORCEMENT OF INTELLECTUAL PROPERTY RIGHTS

1. Objective and scope

The Enforcement Directive was promulgated at the same time as the TRIPS **7.12** Agreement and represents the EU's attempt to implement at least the civil enforcement provisions of the TRIPS Agreement. This is acknowledged in Recital (4) to the Enforcement Directive, which points out that at the international level, 'all Member States, as well as the Community itself as regards matters within its competence, are bound by the [TRIPS] Agreement ... approved, as part of the multilateral negotiations of the Uruguay Round, by Council Decision 94/800/EC (3) and concluded in the framework of the World Trade Organization'.

Another objective of the Enforcement Regulation identified in Recital (3) is **7.13** the general role of IPR enforcement in encouraging innovation and creativity and associated investment as well as the specific role to ensure that the substantive law on intellectual property is applied effectively in the Community in supporting the internal market.

Recital (8) notes the disparities between the systems of the Member States as **7.14** regards the means of enforcing IPRs which are prejudicial to the proper functioning of the internal market causing, according to Recital (9), a loss of confidence in the internal market in business circles, with a consequent

---

14 *China – Measures Affecting the Protection and Enforcement of Intellectual Property Rights*, WT/DS362, 26 January 2009, paras 7.177–7.181.

reduction in investment in innovation and creation. Thus as Recital (10) explains, the objective of the Directive 'is to approximate legislative systems so as to ensure a high, equivalent and homogeneous level of protection in the internal market'.

(a) Subject matter

7.15 Article 1 provides that 'this Directive concerns the measures, procedures and remedies necessary to ensure the enforcement of intellectual property rights'. Interestingly, the Directive, does not define the term 'intellectual property rights' beyond saying that it 'includes industrial property rights'. Neither is 'industrial property' defined. The definition of this term in Art 2(2) of the Paris Convention for the Protection of Industrial Property provides that the protection of industrial property has as its object '... trademarks, service marks, trade names, indications of source or appellations of origin, and the repression of unfair competition'.

7.16 As was mentioned above, Recital (4) to the Enforcement Directive mentions that all Member States, as well as the Community itself, are bound by the TRIPS Agreement. This Agreement in Art 1(2) provides that for the purposes of the Agreement, the term 'intellectual property' refers to all categories of intellectual property 'that are the subject of Sections 1 through 7 of Part II'. Section 2 deals with trade marks and section 3 with geographical indications. Also Art 2(1) of the TRIPS Agreement obliges signatories to comply with Arts 1 to 12, and Art 19, of the Paris Convention, which includes the definition of industrial property.

(b) Scope

7.17 Article 2(1) provides that without prejudice to the means which are or may be provided for in Community or national legislation, in so far as those means may be more favourable for right holders, the measures, procedures and remedies provided for by the Directive shall apply, in accordance with Art 3, to any infringement of IPRs as provided for by Community law and/or by the national law of the Member State concerned.

7.18 These infringements would obviously include those under the European legislation dealing with GIs and trade marks.

7.19 Article 2(3) provides that this Directive shall not affect:

(a) the Community provisions governing the substantive law on intellectual property, Directive 95/46/EC,[15] Directive 1999/93/EC[16] or Directive 2000/31/EC, in general, and Arts 12 to 15 of Directive 2000/31/EC[17] in particular;

(b) Member States' international obligations and notably the TRIPS Agreement, including those relating to criminal procedures and penalties;

(c) any national provisions in Member States relating to criminal procedures or penalties in respect of infringement of IPRs.

2. Measures, procedures and remedies

(a) General obligation

Article 3(1) provides that Member States shall provide for the measures, procedures and remedies necessary to ensure the enforcement of the IPRs covered by this Directive. Those measures, procedures and remedies shall be fair and equitable and shall not be unnecessarily complicated or costly, or entail unreasonable time limits or unwarranted delays. **7.20**

This provision replicates the terms of TRIPS Art 41.2, which provides that '[p]rocedures concerning the enforcement of intellectual property rights shall be fair and equitable. They shall not be unnecessarily complicated or costly, or entail unreasonable time-limits or unwarranted delays.' **7.21**

The high cost of IPR enforcement was considered by the fifth session of the WIPO's Advisory Committee on Enforcement (ACE), held in Geneva from 2 to 4 November 2009, taking into consideration Recommendation 45 of the WIPO Development Agenda. Recommendation 45 is that IPR enforcement should be approached with the objectives of the TRIPS Agreement in mind, ie that **7.22**

> the protection and enforcement of intellectual property rights should contribute to the promotion of technological innovation and to the transfer and dissemination of technology, to the mutual advantage of producers and users of technological knowledge and in a manner conducive to social and economic welfare, and to a balance of rights and obligations,

---

15 Directive 95/46/EC of the European Parliament and of the Council of 24 October 1995 on the protection of individuals with regard to the processing of personal data and on the free movement of such data, OJ L 281, 23/11/1995, pp. 31–50.

16 Directive 1999/93/EC of the European Parliament and of the Council of 13 December 1999 on a Community framework for electronic signatures, OJ L 13, 19.1.2000.

17 Directive 2000/31/EC of the European Parliament and of the Council of 8 June 2000 on certain legal aspects of information society services, in particular electronic commerce, in the Internal Market ('Directive on electronic commerce'), OJ L 178, 17.07.2000, pp. 1–16.

in the context of broader societal interests and especially development-oriented concerns. Concern was expressed by participants about the often costly evidential burden in IPR cases, high attorneys' fees and the possibility of meeting some of these expenses through the greater use of presumptions or litigation on a contingency basis.[18]

7.23 Article 3(2) requires that those measures, procedures and remedies shall also be effective, proportionate and dissuasive and shall be applied in such a manner as to avoid the creation of barriers to legitimate trade and to provide for safeguards against their abuse.

(b) Persons entitled to apply for the application of the measures, procedures and remedies

7.24 Article 4 provides that Member States shall recognise as persons entitled to seek application of the measures, procedures and remedies referred to in this chapter:

(a) the holders of IPRs, in accordance with the provisions of the applicable law;

(b) all other persons authorised to use those rights, in particular licensees, in so far as permitted by and in accordance with the provisions of the applicable law;

(c) intellectual property collective rights-management bodies which are regularly recognised as having a right to represent holders of IPRs, in so far as permitted by and in accordance with the provisions of the applicable law;

(d) professional defence bodies which are regularly recognised as having a right to represent holders of IPRs, in so far as permitted by and in accordance with the provisions of the applicable law.

The language of Art 4 would appear to cover those producer associations and certification bodies which monitor specific GIs.

(c) Evidence

7.25 Article 6(1) provides that Member States shall ensure that, on application by a party which has presented reasonably available evidence sufficient to support its claims, and has, in substantiating those claims, specified evidence which lies in the control of the opposing party, the competent judicial authorities may order that such evidence be presented by the opposing party, subject to the protection of confidential information. For the purposes of this paragraph, Member States may provide that a reasonable sample of a substantial number

---

18 See 'IP Litigation Costs Special Edition' *WIPO Magazine*, February 2010, http://www.wipo.int/wipo_magazine/en/pdf/2010/wipo_pub_121_2010_01.pdf.

of copies of a work or any other protected object be considered by the competent judicial authorities to constitute reasonable evidence.

i. Disclosure of documents

Article 6(2) provides that under the same conditions, in the case of an **7.26** infringement 'committed on a commercial scale' Member States shall take such measures as are necessary to enable the competent judicial authorities to order, where appropriate, on application by a party, the communication of banking, financial or commercial documents under the control of the opposing party, subject to the protection of confidential information.

'Commercial scale' is not defined in the body of the Enforcement Directive **7.27** but Recital (14) states that 'acts carried out on a commercial scale are those carried out for direct or indirect economic or commercial advantage; this would normally exclude acts carried out by end consumers acting in good faith'. In an analysis of the implementation of the Civil Enforcement Directive an EC Staff Working Document points out that only in a few Member States does the law provides for a definition of this term.[19] In those states it observed that the definition is often given by using the notion of 'commercial purpose' and defining it as 'purposes aimed at direct or indirect economic or commercial gain' or similar.[20]

The interpretation of the expression 'commercial scale' within Art 61 of the **7.28** TRIPS Agreement was raised in *China – Measures Affecting the Protection and Enforcement of Intellectual Property Rights*,[21] which arose on a complaint by the US about the threshold number of infringements which were required before the criminal sanctions concerning IP crimes under China's criminal law were activated. The US submitted that the concept of 'commercial scale' extended both to those who engage in commercial activities in order to make a 'financial return' in the market place, and who are, by definition, therefore operating on a commercial scale, as well as to those whose actions, regardless of motive or purpose, are of a sufficient extent or magnitude to qualify as 'commercial scale' in the relevant market.[22] It observed that whether a particular counterfeiting or piracy activity is 'on a commercial scale' would depend on the facts and circumstances surrounding that activity, such as the market for the infringed goods, the object of the infringement, the value of the infringed goods, the

---

19 Eg Germany, Czech Republic, Romania, Slovenia.
20 EC, Commission Staff Working Document, Analysis of the application of Directive 2004/48/EC of the European Parliament and the Council of 29 April 2004 on the enforcement of intellectual property rights in the Member States, SEC(2010) 1589 final, Brussels, 22.12.2010, at 9.
21 *Report of the Panel* WT/DS362/R, 26 January 2009.
22 Ibid., at para 7.480.

means of producing the infringed goods, and the impact of the infringement on the right holder.[23] It conceded that some activity would be so trivial or of a *de minimis* character so as *not* to be 'on a commercial scale' in some circumstances, 'such as occasional infringing acts of a purely personal nature carried out by consumers, or the sale of trivial volumes for trivial amounts unless there are circumstances indicating to the contrary'.[24]

7.29 The Dispute Panel pointed out that the ordinary meaning of the word 'scale' includes both the concept of quantity, in terms of magnitude or extent, as well as the concept of relative size. For the purposes of Art 61 the relevant size was indicated by the word 'commercial'. The Panel adopted the following dictionary definition of 'commercial': 'Engaged in commerce; of, pertaining to, or bearing on commerce' in the sense of buying and selling, especially on a large scale.[25] The Panel pointed out that the use of the word 'scale' was a deliberate choice and reflects the intention of the negotiators that the limitation on the obligation depended on the *size* of acts of counterfeiting and piracy.[26] Thus the combination of the primary definition of 'commercial' and the definition of 'scale' can be reconciled with the context of Art 61 if it is assessed not solely according to the nature of an activity but also in terms of relative size, as a market benchmark.

7.30 The Panel observed that the phrase 'on a commercial scale' has been used in the IPR legislation of various countries, particularly in patent laws which refer to the working of inventions, or failure to work inventions, 'on a commercial scale'.[27] The term was also used in the specific context of trade mark counterfeiting and copyright piracy in the WIPO Committee of Experts on Measures Against Counterfeiting and Piracy in 1988. Article A(1), (2) and (3) of the Draft Model Provisions for National Laws included the proviso to manufacturing as an act of counterfeiting or piracy that it be 'on a commercial scale'. The explanatory memorandum advised that in deciding upon commercial scale the courts will have to take into consideration the circumstances accompanying the manufacture, 'the quantity of the goods manufactured, the way in which they were, are or are intended to be used and the will to make profit'.[28]

---

23 Ibid.
24 Ibid.
25 Ibid., at para 7.535.
26 Ibid., at para 7.543.
27 See, eg, the Australian Patent Act 1990, s 135(1); Indian Patents Act 1970, ss 83–84; South African Patent Act 1978, s 56; UK Patent Act 1977–1988, s 50; Zimbabwean Patents Act 1971, s 31. The UK Patents and Design Act 1919, s 27, had referred to working a patent 'on a commercial scale'.
28 WIPO document C&P/CE/2 of 18, 19 February 1988, para 17.

The Panel concluded that counterfeiting or piracy 'on a commercial scale' **7.31** refers to counterfeiting or piracy carried on at the magnitude or extent of typical or usual commercial activity with respect to a given product in a given market.[29]

> It followed that what constitutes a commercial scale for counterfeiting or piracy of a particular product in a particular market will depend on the magnitude or extent that is typical or usual with respect to such a product in such a market, which may be small or large. The magnitude or extent of typical or usual commercial activity relates, in the longer term, to profitability.[30]

The free trade agreements (FTA) which the US has negotiated with Australia, **7.32** Peru and Singapore require each party to 'provide criminal procedures and penalties to be applied at least in cases of wilful trademark counterfeiting or copyright or related rights piracy on a commercial scale.' 'Wilful copyright or related rights piracy on a commercial scale' is defined to include: '(i) significant wilful infringements of copyright or related rights that have no direct or indirect motivation of financial gain, as well as (ii) wilful infringements for purposes of commercial advantage or financial gain'.[31]

The confidentiality concern mirrors Art 42 of TRIPS, which requires that **7.33** making available to right holders of civil judicial enforcement procedures, 'a means' shall be provided 'to identify and protect confidential information, unless this would be contrary to existing constitutional requirements'.

ii. Measures for preserving evidence

Seizure order
Article 7(1) of the Enforcement Directive provides that Member States shall **7.34** ensure that, even before the commencement of proceedings on the merits of the case, the competent judicial authorities may, on application by a party who has presented reasonably available evidence to support his/her claims that his/her IPR has been infringed or is about to be infringed, order prompt and effective provisional measures to preserve relevant evidence in respect of the alleged infringement, subject to the protection of confidential information. Such measures may include the detailed description, with or without the taking of samples, or the physical seizure of the infringing goods,' and, in appropriate cases, 'the materials and implements used in the production and/or distribution of these goods and the documents relating thereto'. Those

---

29   Ibid., at para 7.577.
30   Ibid.
31   US–Australia FTA, Art 26; US–Peru FTA, Art 26; US–Singapore FTA, Art 21.

measures shall be taken, if necessary without the other party having been heard, in particular where any delay is likely to cause irreparable harm to the right holder or where there is a demonstrable risk of evidence being destroyed.

7.35 A question raised by Cottier and Véron[32] is whether 'documents relating thereto' means 'documents relating to the evidence of the reality of the infringement or the disclosure of all the commercial information by which it would be possible to determine the distribution network and the extent of the prejudice suffered by the victim of the infringement'. They mention that the French case law is divided on this point However, the Paris Court of Appeal in a decision of 16 June 2010 considered that the wording was not intended solely to remove the obstacle of confidentiality but, on the contrary, to allow the seizure of any document with evidential value, without making any distinction between measures to establish the actual physical reality of the infringement and to establish the total infringing sales ('*masse contrefaisante*'). 'The Court considered that the primary purpose of the right of information was to make it possible to retrace the concealed links in the infringement chain, rather than to determine the extent of the prejudice suffered by the victim of the infringement.'[33]

7.36 The second paragraph of Art 7(1) of the Enforcement Directive provides that where measures to preserve evidence are adopted without the other party having been heard, the parties affected shall be given notice, without delay after the execution of the measures at the latest. A review, including a right to be heard, shall take place upon request of the parties affected with a view to deciding, within a reasonable period after the notification of the measures, whether the measures shall be modified, revoked or confirmed.

7.37 Article 7(1) of the Enforcement Directive replicates Art 50.2 of TRIPS, which provides for applications for provisional measures to be made on the application of a single party. This procedure is available, in particular where any delay is likely to cause irreparable harm to the right holder, or where there is a demonstrable risk of evidence being destroyed. In cases of copyright piracy or trade mark counterfeiting, the defendant, who will often be involved in serious criminality, will not usually remain available to answer interrogatories or to discover documents. Indeed, on detection, relevant evidence will immediately be removed or destroyed. To deal with this situation the Court of Appeal of England and Wales in *Anton Piller v Manufacturing Processes*[34]

---

32   Cottier and Véron, 2011 at 531–2.
33   Ibid., at 533.
34   [1976] RPC 719.

approved a procedure whereby on an *ex parte* application in camera, an order would be granted to an applicant that the defendant, advised by his legal representative, grant access to the applicant to inspect the defendant's premises to seize, copy or photograph material which may be used as evidence of the alleged infringement. The defendant may be obliged to deliver up infringing goods and tooling and may also be obliged to provide information about sources of supply and about the destination of infringing products.

A similar procedure, the *saisie-contrefaçon*, has been developed by the French **7.38** courts. Because of the exceptional nature of these orders, in their impact upon an individual's civil rights, after the demonstration that there is a very strong prima facie case of infringement, the courts have insisted upon proof that there is a strong possibility that evidence in the possession of a defendant is likely to be destroyed before an application *inter partes* can be made. Additionally, the British courts have insisted upon the safeguards of the attendance upon a search, conducted in business hours, by both parties' legal representatives, sometimes with a neutral supervising solicitor who has experience in the execution of these orders. Refusal to comply with a seizure order will result in a contempt of court. On the other hand, the use of the order for abusive purposes may result in the grant of substantial compensation to a defendant.

Security
Article 7(2) of the Enforcement Directive provides that Member States shall **7.39** ensure that the measures to preserve evidence may be subject to the lodging by the applicant of adequate security or an equivalent assurance intended to ensure compensation for any prejudice suffered by the defendant as provided for in Art 7(4).

Article 10.4 of the ACTA contains the additional qualification that any **7.40** security or equivalent assurance imposed by the courts shall not 'unreasonably deter' applicants for provisional measures.

Revocation of seizure orders
Article 7(3) of the Enforcement Directive provides that Member States shall **7.41** ensure that the measures to preserve evidence are revoked or otherwise cease to have effect, upon request of the defendant, without prejudice to the damages which may be claimed, if the applicant does not institute, within a reasonable period, proceedings leading to a decision on the merits of the case before the competent judicial authority, the period to be determined by the judicial authority ordering the measures where the law of a Member State so permits or, in the absence of such determination, within a period not exceeding 20 working days or 31 calendar days, whichever is the longer.

Compensation

7.42 Article 7(5) of the Enforcement Directive provides that where the measures to preserve evidence are revoked, or where they lapse due to any act or omission by the applicant, or where it is subsequently found that there has been no infringement or threat of infringement of an IPR, the judicial authorities shall have the authority to order the applicant, upon request of the defendant, to provide the defendant with appropriate compensation for any injury caused by those measures.

7.43 This provision emulates Art 50.7 of the TRIPS Agreement, which provides that where a provisional measure is revoked or where it is subsequently found that there is no IPR infringement, the judicial authorities shall have the authority *upon the request* of the defendant to provide the defendant with appropriate compensation for any injury caused by these measures.

Protection of witnesses' identity

7.44 Article 7(5) of the Enforcement Directive provides that Member States may take measures to protect witnesses' identity.

(d) Right of information

7.45 Article 8(1) provides that Member States shall ensure that, in the context of proceedings concerning an infringement of an IPR and in response to a justified and proportionate request of the claimant, the competent judicial authorities may order that information on the origin and distribution networks of the goods or services which infringe an IPR be provided by the infringer and/or any other person who:

(a) was found in possession of the infringing goods on a commercial scale;
(b) was found to be using the infringing services on a commercial scale;
(c) was found to be providing on a commercial scale services used in infringing activities; or
(d) was indicated by the person referred to in point (a), (b) or (c) as being involved in the production, manufacture or distribution of the goods or the provision of the services.

7.46 Article 8(2) provides that the information referred to in Art 8(1) shall, as appropriate, comprise:

(a) the names and addresses of the producers, manufacturers, distributors, suppliers and other previous holders of the goods or services, as well as the intended wholesalers and retailers;
(b) information on the quantities produced, manufactured, delivered, received or ordered, as well as the price obtained for the goods or services in question.

Article 8(3) provides that Art 8(1) and (2) shall apply without prejudice to **7.47** other statutory provisions which:

(a) grant the right holder rights to receive fuller information;
(b) govern the use in civil or criminal proceedings of the information communicated pursuant to this Article.

A study by the European Observatory on Counterfeiting and Piracy indicated **7.48** that the law and practice in relation to the application of this provision varied widely between Member States.[35] In some cases the measures are available only in the case of infringements committed on a commercial scale which, combined with variances in the interpretation and application of the commercial scale requirement, leads to inconsistencies.

In the UK, responding to complaints from right holders that for the purposes **7.49** of civil litigation they were unable to obtain information from the Trading Standards Office, which, among other things, conducts investigations into counterfeiting, changes were made to Part 9 of the Enterprise Act 2002. Section 241A of that Act enables public authorities subject to competition law concerns to disclose information where the information is to be used for civil proceedings 'relating to or arising out of the infringement of an intellectual property right or relating to or arising out of passing off or the misuse of a trade secret'.[36]

(e) Provisional and precautionary measures

i. Interlocutory injunction

Article 9(1) of the Enforcement Directive provides that Member States shall **7.50** ensure that the judicial authorities may, at the request of the applicant:

(a) issue against the alleged infringer an interlocutory injunction intended to prevent any imminent infringement of an intellectual property right, or to forbid, on a provisional basis and subject, where appropriate, to a recurring penalty payment where provided for by national law, the continuation of the alleged infringements of that right, or to make such continuation subject to the lodging of guarantees intended to ensure the compensation of the rightholder ...

---

35 European Observatory on Counterfeiting and Piracy, *Evidence and Right of Information in Intellectual Property Rights*, (2010) available at http://ec.europa.eu/internal.market/iprenforcement/docs/evidence. en.pdf.

36 Department for Business, Enterprise and Regulatory Reform, 'A Guidance Note on Information Disclosure to Consumers and Intellectual Property Rights Holders for Civil Proceedings', March 2008, accessed at http://www.bis.gov.uk/files/file41381.pdf.

7.51   Article 44.1 of the TRIPS Agreement, in relation to imports, exempts from injunctions 'in respect of protected subject matter acquired or ordered by a person prior to knowing or having reasonable grounds to know that dealing in such subject matter would entail the infringement of an intellectual property right'.

7.52   The remedy of injunction is usually granted by common law courts on a discretionary basis. Among the factors considered by the court are whether:

    (a)   damages provides an adequate remedy;

    (b)   the order will require constant supervision by the court;

    (c)   the applicant has engaged in some disentitling conduct, such as its own infringing activity; and

    (d)   the applicant has delayed in seeking its remedy or has acquiesced in the respondent's conduct.

ii.   Injunction to prevent goods entering channels of commerce

7.53   Article 9(1)(b) of the Enforcement Directive provides that Member States shall ensure that the judicial authorities may, at the request of the applicant 'order the seizure or delivery up of the goods suspected of infringing an intellectual property right so as to prevent their entry into or movement within the channels of commerce'.

iii.   Precautionary seizure of immovable property

7.54   Article 9(2) of the Enforcement Directive provides that in the case of an infringement committed on a commercial scale, the Member States shall ensure that, if the injured party demonstrates circumstances likely to endanger the recovery of damages, the judicial authorities may order the precautionary seizure of the movable and immovable property of the alleged infringer, including the blocking of his/her bank accounts and other assets. To that end, the competent authorities may order the communication of bank, financial or commercial documents, or appropriate access to the relevant information.

iv.   Required evidence

7.55   Article 9(3) of the Enforcement Directive provides that the judicial authorities shall, in respect of the measures referred to in Art 9(1) and (2), have the authority to require the applicant to provide any reasonably available evidence in order to satisfy themselves with a sufficient degree of certainty that the applicant is the right holder and that the applicant's right is being infringed, or that such infringement is imminent.

v. Ex parte *applications*

Article 9(4) of the Enforcement Directive provides that the Member States **7.56** shall ensure that the provisional measures referred to in Art 9(1) and (2) may, in appropriate cases, be taken without the defendant having been heard, in particular where any delay would cause irreparable harm to the right holder. In that event, the parties shall be so informed without delay after the execution of the measures at the latest.

A review, including a right to be heard, shall take place upon request of the **7.57** defendant with a view to deciding, within a reasonable time after notification of the measures, whether those measures shall be modified, revoked or confirmed.

vi.   Revocation of provisional measures

Article 9(5) of the Enforcement Directive provides that the Member States **7.58** shall ensure that the provisional measures referred to in Art 9(1) and (2) are revoked or otherwise cease to have effect, upon request of the defendant, if the applicant does not institute, within a reasonable period, proceedings leading to a decision on the merits of the case before the competent judicial authority, the period to be determined by the judicial authority ordering the measures where the law of a Member State so permits or, in the absence of such determination, within a period not exceeding 20 working days or 31 calendar days, whichever is the longer.

vii.   Security

Article 9(6) of the Enforcement Directive provides that the competent judicial **7.59** authorities may make the provisional measures referred to in Art 9(1) and (2) subject to the lodging by the applicant of adequate security or an equivalent assurance intended to ensure compensation for any prejudice suffered by the defendant as provided for in para 7.

viii.   Compensation

Article 9(7) of the Enforcement Directive provides that where the provisional **7.60** measures are revoked or where they lapse due to any act or omission by the applicant, or where it is subsequently found that there has been no infringement or threat of infringement of an IPR, the judicial authorities shall have the authority to order the applicant, upon request of the defendant, to provide the defendant appropriate compensation for any injury caused by those measures.

(f) Measures resulting from a decision on the merits of the case

i. Corrective measures

7.61 Recital (24) to the Enforcement Directive explains that there should be corrective measures, where appropriate, at the expense of the infringer, such as the recall and definitive removal from the channels of commerce, or destruction, of the infringing goods and, in appropriate cases, of the materials and implements principally used in the creation or manufacture of these goods. These corrective measures should take account of the interests of third parties including, in particular, consumers and private parties acting in good faith.

7.62 Article 10(1) provides that without prejudice to any damages due to the right holder by reason of the infringement, and without compensation of any sort, Member States shall ensure that the competent judicial authorities may order, at the request of the applicant, that appropriate measures be taken with regard to goods that they have found to be infringing an IPR and, in appropriate cases, with regard to materials and implements principally used in the creation or manufacture of those goods. Such measures shall include:

(a) recall from the channels of commerce;
(b) definitive removal from the channels of commerce; or
(c) destruction.

Article 10(1) provides that the judicial authorities shall order that those measures be carried out at the expense of the infringer, unless particular reasons are invoked for not doing so.

7.63 Article 10(3) provides that in considering a request for corrective measures, the need for proportionality between the seriousness of the infringement and the remedies ordered as well as the interests of third parties shall be taken into account.

ii. Injunctions

7.64 Article 11 provides that Member States shall ensure that, where a judicial decision is taken finding an infringement of an IPR, the judicial authorities may issue against the infringer an injunction aimed at prohibiting the continuation of the infringement. Where provided for by national law, non-compliance with an injunction shall, where appropriate, be subject to a recurring penalty payment, with a view to ensuring compliance. Member States shall also ensure that right holders are in a position to apply for an injunction against intermediaries whose services are used by a third party to infringe an IPR, without prejudice to Art 8(3) of Directive 2001/29/EC.[37]

The question of whether injunctions could be obtained against third-party **7.65** distributors of infringing products was considered by UK High Court in *L'Oréal SA & Ors v EBay International AG & Ors*.[38] In that case L'Oréal called in aid Art 11 of the EU Civil Enforcement Directive as entitling it to an injunction against eBay Europe even if the latter was not liable for trade mark infringement. The final sentence of Art 11 required that EU Member States should ensure that 'rightholders are in a position to apply for an injunction against intermediaries whose services are used by a third party to infringe an intellectual property right ...'. Although it was accepted that the UK had not specifically implemented this provision, Arnold J observed that the court's power to grant injunctions against third parties was part of the law of equity which applied to the grant of injunctions.[39] He stated that he was 'not treating Article 11 as having direct effect; but as providing a principled basis for the exercise of an existing jurisdiction in a new way'.[40] The question then is whether, and if so to what extent, that is what Art 11 requires. As to what Art 11 required, Arnold J applied three decisions of the Bundesgerichtshof, concerned with Internet auctions in which the defendant provided an online auction-style service, offering for sale imitation 'ROLEX' watches explicitly described as such.[41] In these cases the Bundesgerichtshof held that the Rolex applicant companies would be entitled to an order requiring the defendant to take reasonable measures, such as filtering, to prevent further infringements, but could not be required to take steps which would jeopardise its entire business model. Arnold J referred to an extrajudicial explanation of this case by Prof Dr Joachim Bornkamm, the President of the First Civil Chamber and a party to the decision.[42] In his paper Judge Bornkamm explained that German courts may grant orders against a third person whom it is reasonable to burden with a duty to examine goods he has to carry in regard to possible trade mark infringements. Although there can be no *ex ante* examination of any infringing content of the vendors may want to put up for sale, a duty to react in the case of infringement would, however, be reasonable once a clear infringement has

---

37 Directive 2001/29/EC of the European Parliament and of the Council of 22 May 2001 on the harmonisation of certain aspects of copyright and related rights in the information society, OJ L 167 of 22.6.2001, p. 10.

38 [2009] EWHC 1094 (Ch).

39 Ibid., at paras 447ff.

40 Ibid., at para 454.

41 Case I ZR 304/01 *Internet Auction I* (reported in English at [2006] ECC 9, [2005] ETMR 25 and [2005] IIC 573), Case I ZR 35/04 *Internet Auction II* (reported in English at [2007] ETMR 70) and Case I ZR 73/05 *Internet Auction III*.

42 Bornkamm, 2007.

been shown by the right holder. In this case the host provider should indeed be obliged to remove the infringing object from the platform and to install measures in order to prevent a repetition of such an infringement.

iii.   Alternative measures

7.66 Article 12 of the Enforcement Directive provides that Member States may provide that, in appropriate cases and at the request of the person liable to be subject to the measures provided for in this section, the competent judicial authorities may order pecuniary compensation to be paid to the injured party instead of applying the measures provided for in this section if that person acted unintentionally and without negligence, if execution of the measures in question would cause him/her disproportionate harm and if pecuniary compensation to the injured party appears reasonably satisfactory.

iv.   Damages

Compensatory damages

7.67 Article 13(1) of the Enforcement Directive provides that Member States shall ensure that the competent judicial authorities, on application of the injured party, order the infringer who knowingly, or with reasonable grounds to know, engaged in an infringing activity, to pay the right holder damages appropriate to the actual prejudice suffered by him/her as a result of the infringement.

7.68 The general principles of damages computation in an IPR infringement action are usefully summarised by Kitchin J in a patent infringement case: *Ultraframe (UK) Ltd v Eurocell Building Plastics Ltd & Anor*,[43] where he stated that 'the general principles to be applied in assessing damages for infringement of patent are now well established':[44]

(a)   Damages are compensatory. The general rule is that the measure of damages is to be, as far as possible, that sum of money that will put the claimant in the same position as he would have been in if he had not sustained the wrong.

(b)   The claimant can recover loss which was:
(i)   foreseeable;
(ii)   caused by the wrong; and
(iii)   not excluded from recovery by public or social policy. It is not enough that the loss would not have occurred but for the tort. The tort must be, as a matter of common sense, a cause of the loss.

(c)   The burden of proof rests on the claimant. Damages are to be assessed liberally. But the object is to compensate the claimant and not to punish the defendant.

(d)   It is irrelevant that the defendant could have competed lawfully.

---

43   [2006] EWHC 1344 (Pat).
44   Citing *Gerber Garment Technology v Lectra Systems* [1995] RPC 383 (HC) and [1997] RPC 443 (CA).

(e) Where a claimant has exploited his patent by manufacture and sale he can claim:
(i) lost profit on sales by the defendant that he would have made otherwise;
(ii) lost profit on his own sales to the extent that he was forced by the infringement to reduce his own price; and
(iii) a reasonable royalty on sales by the defendant which he would not have made.

(f) As to lost sales, the court should form a general view as to what proportion of the defendant's sales the claimant would have made.

(g) The assessment of damages for lost profits should take into account the fact that the lost sales are of 'extra production' and that only certain specific extra costs (marginal costs) have been incurred in making the additional sales. Nevertheless, in practice costs go up and so it may be appropriate to temper the approach somewhat in making the assessment.

(h) The reasonable royalty is to be assessed as the royalty that a willing licensor and a willing licensee would have agreed. Where there are truly comparable licences in the relevant field these are the most useful guidance for the court as to the reasonable royalty. Another approach is the profits available approach. This involves an assessment of the profits that would be available to the licensee, absent a licence, and apportioning them between the licensor and the licensee.

(i) Where damages are difficult to assess with precision, the court should make the best estimate it can, having regard to all the circumstances of the case and dealing with the matter broadly, with common sense and fairness.

7.69 However, it should be noted that although this may summarise the situation in the UK, the practice of awarding damages in IPR cases varies between countries. For example, the European Observatory on Counterfeiting and Piracy, found varying standards in EU Member States for the award of damages in IPR cases.[45] It noted that in some countries right holders often cannot recover in full the compensation appropriate to an infringement, or the full costs that the right holder has borne to redress the infringement. Different methods were also found to be used to calculate lost profits. To deal with variations in damages calculation, it recommended that Member States 'should provide that lump-sum damages, reflecting all negative economic consequences that the rightholder has been reasonably found to have suffered, are available at the rightholder's discretion at least as an alternative to any lost profits that can be proved'.[46]

Calculation of damages

7.70 The second paragraph of Art 13(1) of the Enforcement Directive provides that when the judicial authorities set the damages:

---

45 European Observatory on Counterfeiting and Piracy, *Damages in Intellectual Property Rights* (2010), accessed at http://ec.europa.eu/internal_market/iprenforcement/docs/damages_en.pdf.
46 Ibid., at 5.

(a) they shall take into account all appropriate aspects, such as the negative economic consequences, including lost profits, which the injured party has suffered, any unfair profits made by the infringer and, in appropriate cases, elements other than economic factors, such as the moral prejudice caused to the right holder by the infringement; or

(b) as an alternative to (a), they may, in appropriate cases, set the damages as a lump sum on the basis of elements such as at least the amount of royalties or fees which would have been due if the infringer had requested authorisation to use the IPR in question.

Recovery of profits

7.71 Article 13(2) provides that where the infringer did not knowingly, or with reasonable grounds, engage in infringing activity, Member States may lay down that the judicial authorities may order the recovery of profits or the payment of damages, which may be pre-established.

7.72 Account of profits is a useful remedy in trade mark and GI counterfeiting cases, where the purchaser of a counterfeited product would be under no illusion as to its legitimacy, given its price, quality or the place where it was being offered for sale. As a consequence, it would be difficult to say that the purchaser had been diverted away from a much higher-priced genuine product and thus that compensatory damages were appropriate.

7.73 Similarly, it would be difficult to quantify the reputational harm suffered by a brand-owner from the sale of cheap imitations. Taking the profits made by the wrongdoer may also be an effective deterrent. Because even lump-sum damages calculations can be difficult to quantify precisely or consistently the European Observatory on Counterfeiting and Piracy recommended that Member States should provide that a 'predetermined' calculation method for determining lump-sum damages, reflecting a reasonable approximation of all negative economic consequences that the right holder is likely to have suffered, is available as an alternative to any other means of determining damages – at a minimum in copyright and trade mark cases.[47] It noted that several Member States allow double awards[48] or triple awards[49] of proven damages in certain cases as a measurement of the full range of damage incurred by the right holder.

v. Legal costs

7.74 Article 14 of the Enforcement Directive provides that Member States shall ensure that reasonable and proportionate legal costs and other expenses

---

47   Ibid.
48   Eg Austria, Czech Republic, Germany, Greece and Poland.
49   Belgium, Poland, Romania.

incurred by the successful party shall, as a general rule, be borne by the unsuccessful party, unless equity does not allow this.

vi. Publication of judicial decisions

Recital (27) of the Enforcement Directive explains that to act as a supplementary deterrent to future infringers and to contribute to the awareness of the public at large, it is useful to publicise decisions in intellectual property infringement cases. **7.75**

Article 15 of the Enforcement Directive provides that Member States shall **7.76** ensure that, in legal proceedings instituted for infringement of an IPR, the judicial authorities may order, at the request of the applicant and at the expense of the infringer, appropriate measures for the dissemination of the information concerning the decision, including displaying the decision and publishing it in full or in part. Member States may provide for other additional publicity measures which are appropriate to the particular circumstances, including prominent advertising.

D. SANCTIONS BY MEMBER STATES

Chapter III of the Enforcement Directive envisages that Member States may **7.77** provide for enforcement which is beyond the power of the European Parliament. Thus Art 16 provides that 'without prejudice to the civil and administrative measures, procedures and remedies laid down by this Directive, Member States may apply other appropriate sanctions in cases where intellectual property rights have been infringed'.

Recital (28) to the Enforcement Directive explains that in addition to the civil **7.78** and administrative measures, procedures and remedies provided for under this Directive, 'criminal sanctions also constitute, in appropriate cases, a means of ensuring enforcement of intellectual property rights'.

1. Codes of conduct and administrative cooperation

Article 17 of the Enforcement Directive requires Member States to encourage: **7.79**

    (a) the development by trade or professional associations or organisations of codes of conduct at Community level aimed at contributing towards the enforcement of the intellectual property rights ... ;

(b) the submission to the Commission of draft codes of conduct at national and Community level and of any evaluations of the application of these codes of conduct.

2. Assessment

7.80 Article 18(1) requires that three years after the date for implementation of the Directive each Member State shall submit to the Commission a report on its implementation and on the basis of those reports, the Commission shall draw up a report assessing the effectiveness of the measures taken, as well as an evaluation of its impact on innovation.

7.81 This report was submitted by the Commission in December 2012.[50] Although it acknowledged an overall improvement of enforcement procedures in Europe, it noted the alarming increase in IPR infringements, largely because of the opportunities to infringe IPRs offered by the Internet. It observed that the Directive was not designed with this challenge in mind and made a number of proposals in this regard, which dealt with online copyright piracy.

3. Border control (customs) enforcement of intellectual property rights

7.82 Regulation (EU) No 608/2013 of the European Parliament and of the Council of 12 June 2013 concerning customs enforcement of intellectual property rights[51] repealed Council Regulation (EC) No 1383/2003 of 22 July 2003 on the same subject[52] and is the current European instrument concerned with customs control of the entry into the EU and the export and re-export from the EU of goods infringing certain IPRs. This Regulation in the main takes effect from 1 January 2014.[53]

7.83 The Customs Regulation was enacted partly to clarify the earlier customs regulations which gave effect to the border control provisions of the TRIPS Agreement. In particular the Customs Regulation expanded the categories of IPRs within its purview, for example 'trade names' were added as a category of IPR. More fundamentally, the European Parliament and Council acknowledged the practical importance of customs controls in interdicting the

---

50 Report from the Commission to the European Parliament, the Council, the European Economic and Social Committee and the Committee of the Regions, Application of Directive 2004/48/EC of the European Parliament and the Council of 29 April 2004 on the enforcement of intellectual property rights, COM(2010) 779 final, 22.12.2010.
51 OJ L 181/15, 29.6.13, pp. 15–34.
52 OJ L 196, 2.8.2003, pp. 7–14.
53 Art 40(2).

burgeoning trade in infringing goods. Thus Recital (3) to the Customs Regulation points out that enforcing IPRs at the border, wherever the goods are, or should have been, under customs supervision or customs control is an efficient way to quickly and effectively provide legal protection to the right holder as well as the users and groups of producers.

Where the release of goods is suspended or goods are detained by customs authorities at the border, only one legal proceeding should be required, whereas several separate proceedings should be required for the same level of enforcement for goods found on the market, which have been disaggregated and delivered to retailers.

(a) Scope

Article 1(1) provides that the Customs Regulation sets out the conditions and **7.84** procedures for action by the customs authorities where goods suspected of infringing an IPR are, or should have been, subject to customs supervision or customs control within the customs territory of the Union in accordance with Council Regulation (EEC) No 2913/92 of 12 October 1992 establishing the Community Customs Code,[54] particularly goods in the following situations:

(a) when declared for release for free circulation, export or re-export;
(b) when entering or leaving the customs territory of the Union;
(c) when placed under a suspensive procedure or in a free zone or free warehouse.

A number of these terms are described in the Community Customs Code. **7.85** Thus Art 4(14) of the Code defines as 'customs controls':

The specific acts performed by the customs authorities in order to ensure the correct application of customs rules and other legislation governing the entry, exit, transit, transfer and end-use of goods moved between the customs territory of the Community and third countries and the presence of goods that do not have Community status; such acts may include examining goods, verifying declaration data and the existence and authenticity of electronic or written documents, examining the accounts of undertakings and other records, inspecting means of transport, inspecting luggage and other goods carried by or on persons and carrying out official inquiries and other similar acts.

(b) Ex officio border controls

As will be seen below, the border control regime established by the Customs **7.86** Regulation to interdict goods which may infringe IPRs for the most part is initiated on the application of rights holders. However, Art 1(2) provides that

---

54 OJ L 302, 19.10.1992, p. 1, as last amended by Regulation (EC) No 2700/2000, of the European Parliament and of the Council, OJ L 311, 12.12.2000, p. 17.

in respect of the goods subject to customs supervision or customs control, and without prejudice to Arts 17 and 18, the customs authorities shall carry out adequate customs controls and shall take proportionate identification measures as provided for in Art 13(1)[55] and Art 72[56] Regulation (EEC) No 2913/92 in accordance with risk analysis criteria with a view to preventing acts in breach of intellectual property laws applicable in the territory of the Union and in order to cooperate with third countries on the enforcement of IPRs.

(c) Goods in transit

7.87 Although the 2003 Regulation was designed primarily to prevent infringing goods from entering or leaving the customs territory of the Community, it also applied to goods in external transit (ie goods passing through Community customs territory on their way from one non-Member State to another non-Member State). The Customs Regulation similarly applies to goods in transit. This issue has been addressed in a number of ECJ decisions.

7.88 In *The Polo/Lauren Company LP v Pt Dwidua Langgeng Pratam International Freight Forwarders*, the European Court of Justice held that this extended coverage was justified by the risk that goods entering the Community under the external transit procedure may be fraudulently diverted onto the single market.[57]

7.89 The question of goods in internal transit through the EU to be placed on a market in a non-Member country was considered by the ECJ in Case C-115/02, *Rioglass and Transremar*,[58] which concerned goods lawfully manufactured in Spain and detained in France on suspicion of infringement of trade marks in the course of their transport to Poland. The Cour de Cassation

---

55 Art 13(1) of the Customs Code provides that:

> Customs authorities may, in accordance with the conditions laid down by the provisions in force, carry out all the controls they deem necessary to ensure that customs rules and other legislation governing the entry, exit, transit, transfer and end-use of goods moved between the customs territory of the Community and third countries and the presence of goods that do not have Community status are correctly applied. Customs controls for the purpose of the correct application of Community legislation may be carried out in a third country where an international agreement provides for this.

56 Art 72 of the Customs Code provides that:

> 1. The customs authorities shall take the measures necessary to identify the goods where identification is required in order to ensure compliance with the conditions governing the customs procedure for which the said goods have been declared.
> 2. Means of identification affixed to the goods or means of transport shall be removed or destroyed only by the customs authorities or with their permission unless, as a result of unforeseeable circumstances or *force majeure*, their removal or destruction is essential to ensure the protection of the goods or means of transport.

57 Case C-383/98 [2000] ECR I-2519 (ECJ), para 34.
58 [2003] ECR I-12705.

applied for a preliminary ruling as to whether Art 28 EC precluded the implementation of procedures for detention by customs authorities in a Member State of goods lawfully manufactured in Spain which were intended, following their transport through another Member State, to be placed on the market in a non-member country. The ECJ answered the question in the affirmative and, in doing so, observed:

25. With respect to trade marks, it is settled case-law that the specific subject-matter of a trade mark is, in particular, to guarantee to the owner that he has the exclusive right to use that mark for the purpose of putting a product on the market for the first time and thus to protect him against competitors wishing to take unfair advantage of the status and reputation of the trade mark by selling products illegally bearing it (see, in particular, Case 16/74 Centra-farm [1974] ECR 1183, paragraph 8, Case 102/77 Hoffmann-La Roche [1978] ECR 1139, paragraph 7, and Case C-349/95 Loendersloot [1997] ECR I-6227, paragraph 22).

26. The implementation of such protection is therefore linked to the marketing of the goods.

27. Transit, such as that in issue in the main proceedings, which consists in transporting goods lawfully manufactured in a Member State to a non-member country by passing through one or more Member States, does not involve any marketing of the goods in question and is therefore not liable to infringe the specific subject-matter of the trade mark.

28. Furthermore, as Advocate General Mischo noted at point 45 of his Opinion, that conclusion holds good regardless of the final destination of the goods in transit. The fact that the goods are subsequently placed on the market in a non-member country and not in another Member State does not alter the nature of the transit operation which, by definition, does not constitute a placing on the market.

A different rule applies to non-EU goods which are in transit. This was **7.90** considered in Case C-405/03 *Class International BV v Colgate Palmolive Co and Ors*,[59] in which Class International shipped into Rotterdam a container load of toothpaste bearing the 'Aquafresh' trade mark from a source in South Africa. The ECJ was asked, in substance, whether Art 5(1) of the Trade Marks Directive and Art 9(1) and (2)(c) of the Community Trade Mark Regulation must be interpreted as meaning that the trade mark proprietor is entitled to oppose the introduction into the Community, under the external transit procedure or the customs warehousing procedure, of original goods bearing that mark which had not previously been put on the market in the Community by that proprietor or with his consent.

---

59 [2005] ECR I-8735.

7.91   The Court answered that non-Community goods placed under the external transit procedure or the customs warehouse procedure were not to be regarded as 'imported' for the purposes of the Trade Marks Directive or the Community Trade Mark Regulation.[60] The Court noted that the entry of non-Community goods for customs procedures such as external transit or customs warehousing 'is distinguishable from placing them under the customs procedure of release for free circulation, which, pursuant to the first paragraph of Article 79 of the Customs Code, confers on non-Community goods the customs status of Community goods'.[61]

7.92   The Court noted that non-Community goods placed under the external transit procedure or the customs warehousing procedure may at any time be assigned another customs-approved treatment or use such as release for free circulation, or re-export outside the territory of the Community. In the case of customs-approved treatment or use, other than release for free circulation, the Court ruled that 'the mere physical introduction of those goods into the territory of the Community is not "importing" within the meaning of Article 5(3)(c) of the Directive and Article 9(2)(c) of the Regulation'.[62] It concluded that 'placing non-Community goods under a suspensive customs procedure does not make it possible for them to be put on the market in the Community in the absence of release for free circulation'.

7.93   In the field of trade marks and GIs, the external transit of goods would seem to be outside the scope of the Customs Regulation.

7.94   In Case C-281/05 *Montex Holdings v Diesel*,[63] the ECJ had to consider the issue in the context of goods which were not the original goods of the proprietor. Montex manufactured garments by exporting their various different pieces to Poland, having them sewn together on Polish territory and bringing the completed garments bearing the trade mark 'DIESEL' back to Ireland. In the course of transit across Germany, they were detained by the German customs authorities. Diesel argued that the garments infringed its trade marks because of the danger that they could find their way onto the German market. The Court rejected the argument, observing that the external transit of non-Community goods is based on a legal fiction that goods placed under this procedure are treated as if they have not entered the Community

---

60   Ibid., at para 33, applying Joined Cases C-414/99 *Zino Davidoff and Levi Strauss* [2001] ECR I-8691, para 33.
61   Ibid., at para 40.
62   Ibid., at para 44.
63   [2006] ECR I-10881.

and so are subject neither to import duties nor other measures of commercial policy in accordance with its decision in *Polo/Lauren*.[64]

In *Eli Lilly & Company & Anor v 8pm Chemist Ltd*[65] the Court of Appeal of **7.95** England and Wales ruled in 2008 that goods under the control of customs were not imported within the country and thus could not infringe a registered trade mark. This decision was applied by the High Court in 2009 when Kitchin J held in *Nokia Corporation v Revenue & Customs*[66] that goods in transit through the UK could not be seized under the EU Counterfeit Goods Regulation 1383/03. This was because the Regulation focused on infringing goods and that without an importation into the country, there could be no infringement of the plaintiff's trade marks. This case was appealed to the Court of Appeal, which on 9 November 2009 referred the following question to the ECJ:

Are non-Community goods bearing a Community trade mark which are **7.96** subject to customs supervision in a Member State and in transit from a non-Member State to another non-Member State capable of constituting 'counterfeit goods' within the meaning of Article 2(1)(a) of Regulation 1383/2003/EC if there is no evidence to suggest that those goods will be put on the market in the EC, either in conformity with a customs procedure or by means of an illicit diversion?[67]

The question was considered by the ECJ in Joined Cases C-446/09 and **7.97** C-495/09, *Koninklijke Philips Electronics NV v Lucheng Meijing Industrial Co Ltd and others*[68] and it determined as follows:

The temporary detention of goods placed under a suspensive customs procedure

… The transit and customs warehousing procedures are respectively characterised by the movement of goods between customs offices and the storage of goods in a warehouse under customs supervision and those operations cannot, as such, be regarded as the putting of goods on sale in the European Union.[69]

---

64 [2000] ECR I-2519.
65 [2008] EWCA Civ 24.
66 [2009] EWHC 1903 (Ch).
67 While the Court of Appeal found the judgment of Kitchin J persuasive, it decided that a reference to the ECJ was necessary because of another reference by a Belgian court on 4 November 2009 on a similar point in a copyright and designs case and that a highly respected Dutch judge had come to an opposite view to that of Kitchin J.
68 [2012] EUECJ C-446/09.
69 Ibid., at para 55 referring to: Case C-115/02 *Rioglass and Transremar* [2003] ECR I-12705, at para 27, and *Montex Holdings v Diesel* [2006] ECR I-10881, at para 19.

Goods placed under a suspensive customs procedure cannot, merely by the fact of being so placed, infringe intellectual property rights applicable in the European Union.[70]

Those rights may be infringed where, during their placement under a suspensive procedure in the customs territory of the European Union, or even before their arrival in that territory, goods coming from non-member States are the subject of a commercial act directed at European Union consumers, such as a sale, offer for sale or advertising.[71]

Having regard to the secretive nature of the activities of traffickers of goods which are imitations or copies, the detention by customs authorities of goods which they have identified as being imitations or copies cannot, without reducing the effectiveness of Regulations No 3295/94 and No 1383/2003, be made subject to a requirement for proof that those goods have already been sold, offered for sale or advertised to European Union consumers.[72]

A customs authority which has established the presence in warehousing or in transit of goods which are an imitation or a copy of a product protected in the European Union by an intellectual property right can legitimately act when there are indications before it that one or more of the operators involved in the manufacture, consignment or distribution of the goods, while not having yet begun to direct the goods towards European Union consumers, are about to do so or are disguising their commercial intentions.[73]

With regard to the indications required to be before that authority in order for it to suspend release of or detain goods within the meaning of Article 6(1) of Regulation No 3295/94 and Article 9(1) of Regulation No 1383/2003, it is sufficient that there be material such as to give rise to suspicion. That material may include the fact that the destination of the goods is not declared whereas the suspensive procedure requested requires such a declaration, the lack of precise or reliable information as to the identity or address of the manufacturer or consignor of the goods, a lack of cooperation with the customs authorities or the discovery of documents or correspondence concerning the goods in question suggesting that there is liable to be a diversion of those goods to European Union consumers.[74]

Such a suspicion must, in all cases, be based on the facts of the case. If that suspicion and the resulting action were capable of being based merely on the abstract consideration that fraudulent diversion to European Union consumers cannot necessarily be ruled out, all goods in external transit or customs warehousing could be detained without the slightest concrete indication of an irregularity. Such a situation would give

---

70 Ibid., at para 56. In relation to trade marks as regards rights conferred by trade marks the court referred to *Rioglass and Transremar*, at para 27, Case C-405/03 *Class International BV v Colgate-Palmolive Company et al* [2005] ECR I-8735, at para 47, and *Montex Holdings*, at para 21.
71 Ibid., at para 57 referring to *Class International*, at para 61, and Case C-324/09 *L'Oréal SA and Others v eBay International AG and Others*, Case C-324/09 [2011] ECR I-06011, at para 67.
72 Ibid., at para 59.
73 Ibid., at para 60.
74 Ibid., at para 61.

rise to a risk that actions of the Member States' customs authorities would be random and excessive.[75]

It should be borne in mind, in that regard, that imitations and copies coming from a non-member State and transported to another non-member State may comply with the intellectual property provisions in force in each of those States. In the light of the common commercial policy's main objective, set out in Article 131 EC and Article 206 TFEU and consisting in the development of world trade through the progressive abolition of restrictions on trade between States, it is essential that those goods be able to pass in transit, via the European Union, from one non-member State to another without that operation being hindered, even by a temporary detention, by Member States' customs authorities. Precisely such hindrance would be created if Regulations No 3295/94 and No 1383/2003 were interpreted as permitting the detention of goods in transit without the slightest indication suggesting that they could be fraudulently diverted to European Union consumers.[76]

Finally, with regard to goods in respect of which there are suspicions of infringement of an intellectual property right in the presumed non-member State of destination, it must be noted that the customs authorities of the Member States where those goods are in external transit are permitted to cooperate, pursuant to Article 69 of the TRIPS Agreement, with the customs authorities of that non-member State with a view to removing those goods from international trade where appropriate.[77]

The substantive decision following the temporary detention of goods placed under a suspensive customs procedure

Unlike the decision taken by the customs authority to detain the goods temporarily, by means of the detention provided for in Article 6(1) of Regulation No 3295/94 and Article 9(1) of Regulation No 1383/2003, the substantive decision as referred to in Article 6(2)(b) of Regulation No 3295/94 and the first paragraph of Article 10 of Regulation No 1383/2003 cannot be adopted on the basis of a suspicion but must be based on an examination of whether there is proof of an infringement of the right relied upon.[78]

In the event that the judicial or other authority competent to take a substantive decision finds an infringement of the intellectual property right relied upon, the destruction or abandonment of the goods in question is the only customs-approved treatment which they can receive.[79] Consequently, the authority competent to take a substantive decision cannot classify as 'counterfeit goods' and 'pirated goods' or, more generally, 'goods infringing an intellectual property right' goods which a customs authority suspects of infringing an intellectual property right applicable in the European Union but in respect of which, after substantive examination, it is not proven that they are intended to be put on sale in the European Union.[80]

---

75   Ibid., at para 62.
76   Ibid., at para 63.
77   Ibid., at para 65.
78   Ibid., at para 68.
79   Ibid., at para 69.
80   Ibid., at para 70.

With regard to the evidence which the authority competent to take a substantive decision must have in order to find that goods which are imitations or copies and have been brought into the customs territory of the EU without being released for free circulation liable to infringe an intellectual property right applicable in the EU, it must be stated that such evidence may include the existence of a sale of goods to a customer in the EU, of an offer for sale or advertising addressed to consumers in the EU, or of documents or correspondence concerning the goods in question showing that diversion of those goods to EU consumers is envisaged.[81]

Regulations No 3295/94 and No 1383/2003 deal only with combating the entry into the European Union of goods which infringe intellectual property rights. In the interest of correct management of the risks for the health and safety of consumers, it must be stated that the powers and obligations of the Member States' customs authorities as regards goods posing such risks must be assessed on the basis of other provisions of European Union law, such as Articles 56, 58 and 75 of the Customs Code.[82]

7.98 Article 16.2 of the ACTA, which was negotiated by the EU with a number of other countries[83] provides that parties 'may' apply border measures to goods in transit. 'In-transit goods' is defined in Art 5 to mean goods under 'Customs transit' and under 'transhipment'. 'Customs transit' is defined as 'the Customs procedure under which goods are transported under Customs control from one Customs office to another' and 'transhipment' is defined as 'the Customs procedure under which goods are transferred under Customs control from the importing means of transport to the exporting means of transport within the area of one Customs office which is the office of both importation and exportation'.

7.99 The seizure of infringing goods in transit became a controversial issue following the 2008 and 2009 seizures by Dutch customs authorities of at least 19 shipments of generic medicines in transit between India and Brazil, which had not been patented in either country, but which were protected by patents in the Netherlands.[84] On 12 May 2010 India and Brazil initiated separate WTO dispute settlement proceedings against the EU and the Netherlands by requesting consultations over these seizures of generic medicines in transit.[85] Brazil alleged that the EU's Regulation No 1383/2003 under which these

---

81 Ibid., at para 71.
82 Ibid., at para 77.
83 See Blakeney, 2012.
84 See Ruse-Khan, 2011.
85 Request for Consultations by Brazil, *European Union and a Member State Seizure of Generic Drugs in Transit*, WT/DS409/1 (19 May 2010); Request for Consultations by India, *European Union and a Member State Seizure of Generic Drugs in Transit*, WT/DS408/1 (19 May 2010).

medicines were seized was inconsistent with various provisions of the GATT and of the TRIPS Agreement.

4. Exclusions from the Customs Regulation

(a) End-use regime

Article 1(3) provides that the Customs Regulation 'shall not apply to goods **7.100** that have been released for free circulation under the end-use regime'. End-use is a customs procedure whereby goods entered for free circulation in the EU may be given favourable tariff treatment or relief at a reduced or zero rate of duty on condition they are put to a prescribed use.[86] Thus far end-use rules have been promulgated for products which are well outside the current EU GIs regime such as those intended for aircraft, ships, boats and drilling platforms, but in times, for example, of food scarcity it could be envisaged that foodstuffs could be designated in an end-use regime.

(b) Goods of a personal nature

Article 1(4) excludes from the Customs Regulation 'goods of a non- commer- **7.101** cial nature contained in travellers' personal luggage'. This is in line with the permission granted in Art 60 of the TRIPS Agreement for WTO Members to exclude from the application its border control provisions 'small quantities of goods of a non-commercial nature contained in travellers' personal luggage or sent in small consignments'. As is indicated below, small consignments are not exempted under the Customs Regulation.

(c) Parallel imports

Recital (6) of the Customs Regulation explains that goods subject to illegal **7.102** parallel trade, namely goods that have been manufactured with the consent of the right holder but placed on the market for the first time in the European Economic Area without his consent, and overruns, namely goods that are manufactured by a person duly authorised by a right holder to manufacture a certain quantity of goods, in excess of the quantities agreed between that person and the right holder, 'are manufactured as genuine goods and it is therefore not appropriate that customs authorities focus their efforts on such goods'.

---

86 The legal basis for the end-use regime is set out in the Community Customs Code (Arts 21, 82, 86, 87, 88 and 90) and in the Implementing Provisions (Commission Regulation (EEC) No 2454/93 as amended, in particular by Commission Regulation (EC) No 1602/2000 (Arts 291–300)).

7.103 Thus Art 2(5) provides that 'this Regulation shall not apply to goods that have been manufactured with the consent of the right-holder or to goods manufactured, by a person duly authorised by a right-holder to manufacture a certain quantity of goods, in excess of the quantities agreed between that person and the right-holder'.

7.104 Article 3(1) of the Customs Regulation provides that it shall not apply to

> goods bearing a trademark with the consent of the holder of that trademark or to goods bearing a protected designation of origin or a protected geographical indication … and which have been manufactured with the consent of the right-holder but are placed in one of the situations referred to in Article 1(1) without the latter's consent.

Article 3(1) also provides that the Customs Regulation shall similarly not apply to goods referred to in the first subparagraph and which have been manufactured or are protected by another IPR referred to in Art 2(1) under conditions other than those agreed with the right holder.

7.105 The principle of exhaustion states that once right holders, or any authorised party, have sold a genuine product they cannot prohibit the subsequent resale of that product in another country since their rights in respect of that market have been exhausted by the act of selling the product. In most countries the legal rule is that the rights of a trade mark proprietor are exhausted by the first sale of a legitimately trade-marked product. An exception to this principle of universal exhaustion exists in Art 7 of the EU Trade Marks Directive,[87] which provides that a trade mark 'shall not entitle the proprietor to prohibit its use in relation to goods which have been put on the market in the Community under that trademark by the proprietor or with his consent'. This has been interpreted by the ECJ to permit a trade mark owner to object to the importation of trade-marked goods from outside the EU.[88]

7.106 The issue of consent was addressed by the ECJ in *Zino Davidoff SA v A & G Imports Ltd*,[89] which concerned the importation to the UK of Davidoff products which had originally been placed on the market in Singapore. Davidoff denied that it had consented, or could be deemed to have consented, to the products concerned being imported into the European Economic Area (EEA). The question that the case addressed was whether consent could be

---

87 Directive 2008/95/EC of the European Parliament and of the Council of 22 October 2008 to approximate the laws of the Member States relating to trade marks, OJ L 299, 8.11.2008.
88 *Silhouette International v Hartlauer* (Case C-355/96), *Zino Davidoff v A&G Imports* (Case C-414/99) and *van Doren v Lifestyle Sports* (Case C-244/00).
89 [2002] ETMR 109.

inferred from: (i) the fact that the proprietor of the trade mark had not communicated to all subsequent purchasers of the goods placed on the market outside the EEA his opposition to their being marketed within the EEA; (ii) the fact that the goods carried no warning of a prohibition on their being placed on the market within the EEA; and (iii) the fact that the trade mark proprietor had transferred the ownership of the products bearing the trade mark without imposing any contractual reservations. The ECJ ruled that consent must be expressed positively and that the factors taken into consideration in finding implied consent must unequivocally demonstrate that the trade mark proprietor has renounced any intention to enforce his exclusive rights. It was for the trader alleging consent to prove it and not for the trade mark proprietor to demonstrate its absence. Thus, implied consent to the marketing within the EEA of goods put on the market outside that area could not be inferred from the mere silence of the trade mark proprietor or from the fact that a trade mark proprietor had not communicated his opposition to marketing within the EEA or from the fact that the goods do not carry any warning that it was prohibited to place them on the market within the EEA. Finally, consent could not be inferred from the fact that the trade mark proprietor transferred ownership of the goods bearing the mark without imposing contractual reservations.

Under the EU Trade Marks Directive a trade mark owner can object to the **7.107** parallel importation of trade-marked goods 'where there exist legitimate reasons for the proprietor to oppose further commercialization of the goods, especially where the condition of the goods is changed or impaired after they have been put on the market'. This issue has arisen in a number of cases concerning the repackaging of goods.[90] The essence of the current ECJ case law is that an importer who repackages and reapplies a trade mark will infringe, unless it satisfies all five of the following conditions:

- It is 'necessary' to repackage to effectively market the product in the importing country.
- The repackaging has no detrimental effect on the original condition of the product and proper instructions are included.
- There is clear identification of the manufacturer and the importer.

---

90   *Hoffmann-La Roche v Centrafarm* (Case 102/77 [1978] ECR 1139); *Bristol-Myers Squibb and Others v Paranova* (Joined Cases C-427/93, C-429/93 and C-436/93 [1996] ECR I-3457); *Loendersloot v Ballantine* (Case C-349/95); and *Upjohn v Paranova* (Case C-379/97 [1999] ECR I-6927); *Merck, Sharp & Dohme GmbH v Paranova Pharmazeutika Handels GmbH* (Case C-443/99); *Glaxo Group Ltd & Ors v Dowelhurst Ltd & Anr* [2000] EWHC Ch 134; *Boehringer Ingelheim KG v Springward Ltd* [2004] EWCA Civ 129.

465

- The presentation of the repackaged goods causes no harm to the trade mark.
- Proper notice is provided.

7.108 For example, *Merck, Sharp & Dohme GmbH v Paranova Pharmazeutika Handels GmbH*[91] was concerned with the importation to Austria from Spain of pharmaceutical products. The importer had the products repackaged in Denmark, with new outer packaging, and attached instructions translated into German. Merck argued that the marketability of the product would be jeopardised because a significant proportion of the consumers in Austria were suspicious of repackaged pharmaceutical products clearly intended for the market of another state. The ECJ observed that a trade mark proprietor's opposition to the repackaging was not justified if it hinders effective access of the imported product to the market of a state.

(d) Goods involved in criminal procedures

7.109 Article 1(6) provides that the Customs Regulation 'shall not affect national or Union law on intellectual property or the laws of the Member States in relation to criminal procedures'.

5. Application of border controls to geographical indications

(a) Definitions

i. Intellectual property right

7.110 'Intellectual property right' is defined in Art 2(1) to mean, inter alia:

> (a) a trade mark;
>
> ...
>
> (d) a geographical indication;
>
> ...
>
> (l) a trade name in so far as it is protected as an exclusive intellectual property right by national or Union law.

ii. Geographical indication

7.111 'Geographical indication' is defined in Art 2(4) of the Customs Regulation in the following terms:

> (a) a geographical indication or designation of origin protected for agricultural products and foodstuff as provided for in Regulation (EU) No 1151/2012 of the

---

91   [2002] ECR I-03703.

European Parliament and of the Council of 21 November 2012 on quality schemes for agricultural products and foodstuffs;

(b) a designation of origin or geographical indication for wine as provided for in Council Regulation (EC) No 1234/2007 of 22 October 2007 establishing a common organisation of agricultural markets and on specific provisions for certain agricultural products (Single CMO Regulation);

(c) a geographical designation for aromatised drinks based on wine products as provided for in Council Regulation (EEC) No 1601/91 of 10 June 1991 laying down general rules on the definition, description and presentation of aromatised wines, aromatised wine- based drinks and aromatised wine-product cocktails;

(d) a geographical indication of spirit drinks as provided for in Regulation (EC) No 110/2008 of the European Parliament and of the Council of 15 January 2008 on the definition, description, presentation, labelling and the protection of geographical indications of spirit drinks;

(e) a geographical indication for products not falling under points (a) to (d) in so far as it is established as an exclusive intellectual property right by national or Union law;

(f) a geographical indication as provided for in Agreements between the Union and third countries and as such listed in those Agreements.

iii. Trade mark

'Trade mark' is defined in Art 2(2) to mean: **7.112**

(a) a Community trade mark as provided for in Council Regulation (EC) No 207/2009 of 26 February 2009 on the Community trade mark;

(b) a trade mark registered in a Member State, or, in the case of Belgium, Luxembourg or the Netherlands, at the Benelux Office for Intellectual Property;

(c) a trade mark registered under international arrangements which has effect in a Member State or in the Union.

iv. Counterfeit goods

'Counterfeit goods' are defined in Art 2(5) of the Customs Regulation to **7.113** mean:

(a) goods which are the subject of an act infringing a trade mark in the Member State where they are found and bear without authorisation a sign which is identical to the trade mark validly registered in respect of the same type of goods, or which cannot be distinguished in its essential aspects from such a trade mark;

(b) goods which are the subject of an act infringing a geographical indication in the Member State where they are found and, bear or are described by, a name or term protected in respect of that geographical indication;

(c) any packaging, label, sticker, brochure, operating instructions, warranty document or other similar item, even if presented separately, which is the subject of an act infringing a trade mark or a geographical indication, which includes a sign, name or term which is identical to a validly registered trade mark or protected geographical indication, or which cannot be distinguished in its essential aspects from such a trade mark or geographical indication, and which can be used for the same type of goods as that for which the trade mark or geographical indication has been registered.

v. Goods suspected of infringing an intellectual property right

7.114 Finally, Art 2(7) defines 'goods suspected of infringing an intellectual property right' as goods with regard to which there are reasonable indications that, in the Member State where those goods are found, they are prima facie:

(a) goods which are the subject of an act infringing an IPR in that Member State;

(b) devices, products or components which are primarily designed, produced or adapted for the purpose of enabling or facilitating the circumvention of any technology, device or component that, in the normal course of its operation, prevents or restricts acts in respect of works which are not authorised by the holder of any copyright or any right related to copyright and which relate to an act infringing those rights in that Member State;

(c) any mould or matrix which is specifically designed or adapted for the manufacture of goods infringing an intellectual property right, if such moulds or matrices relate to an act infringing an intellectual property right in that Member State.

vi. Right holder

7.115 Article 2(8) provides that for the purposes of the Customs Regulation, 'right-holder' means: 'the holder of an intellectual property right'.

(b) Entitlement to submit an application

7.116 Article 3 of the Customs Regulation deals with 'Union' and 'National' applications to the customs authorities to suspend the clearance of goods until such time as the IPRs in relation to those good have been adjudicated. Thus Art 3 commences with a *chapeau* which provides that:

> the following persons and entities shall, to the extent they are entitled to initiate proceedings, in order to determine whether an intellectual property right has been infringed, in the Member State or Member States where the customs authorities are requested to take action, be entitled to submit:
> (1) a national or a Union application:
>   (a) right-holders;
>   ...
>   (d) groups within the meaning of point (2) of Article 3, and Article 49(1) of Regulation (EU) No 1151/2012,[92] groups of producers within the meaning

---

92 Regulation (EU) No 1151/2012 of the European Parliament and of the Council of 21 November 2012 on quality schemes for agricultural products and foodstuffs, OJ L 343, 14.12.2012, p. 1.

of Article 118e of Regulation (EC) No 1234/2007[93] or similar groups of producers provided for in Union law governing geographical indications representing producers of products with a geographical indication or representatives of such groups, in particular Regulations (EEC) No 1601/91[94] and (EC) No 110/2008[95] and operators entitled to use a geographical indication as well as inspection bodies or authorities competent for such a geographical indication.

A 'Union application' is defined in Art 2(11) as 'an application submitted in one Member State and requesting the customs authorities of that Member State and of one or more other Member States to take action in their respective Member States'.

(2) a national application:
  (a) persons or entities authorised to use intellectual property rights, which have been authorised formally by the right-holder to initiate proceedings in order to determine whether the intellectual property right has been infringed;
  (b) groups of producers provided for in the legislation of the Member States governing geographical indications representing producers of products with geographical indications or representatives of such groups and operators entitled to use a geographical indication, as well as inspection bodies or authorities competent for such a geographical indication.

'National application' is defined in Art 2(10) to mean 'an application requesting the customs authorities of a Member State to take action in that Member State'.

(3) a Union application: holders of exclusive licenses covering the entire territory of two or more Member States, where those licence holders have been authorised formally in those Member States by the right-holder to initiate proceedings in order to determine whether the intellectual property right has been infringed.

---

93 Council Regulation (EC) No 1234/2007 establishing a common organisation of agricultural markets and on specific provisions for certain agricultural products (Single CMO Regulation) relating to wine, OJ L 299, 16.11.2007, p. 1.

94 Council Regulation (EEC) No 1601/91 laying down general rules on the definition, description and presentation of aromatized wines, aromatized wine-based drinks and aromatized wine-product cocktails, OJ No L 149, 14.6.1991, p. 1.

95 Regulation (EC) No 110/2008 of the European Parliament and of the Council of 15 January 2008 on the definition, description, presentation, labelling and the protection of geographical indications of spirit drinks and repealing Council Regulation (EEC) No 1576/89, OJ 2008 L 39, p. 16.

(c)   Intellectual property rights covered by Union applications

7.117   Article 4 provides that a Union application may be submitted only with respect to IPRs based on Union law producing effects throughout the Union. This would include the Community Trade Marks Regulation and the GIs regulations.

(d)   Submission of applications

i.   Designated customs department

7.118   Article 5(1) provides that each Member State shall designate the customs department competent to receive and process applications ('competent customs department'). This is to be notified to the Commission and the Commission shall make public a list of competent customs departments designated by the Member States.

ii.   Application form

7.119   Article 5(2) requires that applications shall be submitted to the competent customs department. The applications shall be completed using the form referred to in Art 6 and shall contain the information required therein.

iii.   Application following customs identification of alleged infringement

7.120   Article 18(3) refers to a procedure under which the customs authorities shall notify persons or entities entitled to submit an application concerning the alleged infringement of the IPRs, of the suspension of the release of the goods or their detention. Article 5(3) provides that in this situation the application for detention shall comply with the following:

(a)   it is submitted to the competent customs department within four working days of the notification of the suspension of the release or detention of the goods;

(b)   it is a national application;

(c)   it contains the information referred to in Art 6(3). The applicant may, however, omit the information referred to in point (g), (h) or (i) of that paragraph.

iv.   Single application

7.121   Article 18(4) provides that except in the case of Union applications mentioned in Art 3(3) involving holders of exclusive licences covering the entire territory of two or more Member States, only one national application and one Union application may be submitted per Member State for the same IPR protected in that Member State.

v. Subsequent applications

Article 5(5) provides that where a Union application is granted for a Member **7.122** State already covered by another Union application granted to the same applicant and for the same IPR, the customs authorities of that Member State shall take action on the basis of the Union application first granted. They shall inform the competent customs department of the Member State where any subsequent Union application was granted, which shall amend or revoke the decision granting that subsequent Union application.

vi. Computerised applications

Article 5(6) provides that where computerised systems are available for the **7.123** purpose of receiving and processing applications, applications as well as attachments shall be submitted using electronic data-processing techniques. Member States and the Commission shall develop, maintain and employ such systems in accordance with the multi-annual strategic plan referred to in Art 8(2) of Decision No 70/2008/EC of the European Parliament and of the Council of 15 January 2008 on a paperless customs environment for customs and trade.[96]

vii. Application form

Article 6(1) provides for the Commission to establish an application form by **7.124** means of implementing acts in accordance with the advisory procedure referred to in Art 34(2). Article 34(2) states that where reference is made to this paragraph, Art 4 of Regulation (EU) No 182/2011[97] shall apply.

Article 6(2) requires that the application form shall specify the information **7.125** that has to be provided to the data subject pursuant to Regulation (EC) No 45/2001[98] and national laws implementing Directive 95/46/EC.[99]

Article 6(3) directs the Commission to ensure that the following information **7.126** is required of the applicant in the application form:

---

96 OJ L 23, 26.1.2008, p. 21.
97 Regulation (EU) No 182/2011 of the European Parliament and of the Council of 16 February 2011 laying down the rules and general principles concerning mechanisms for control by Member States of the Commission's exercise of implementing powers, OJ L 55/13, 28.2.2011, pp. 13–18.
98 Regulation (EC) No 45/2001 of the European Parliament and of the Council of 18 December 2000 on the protection of individuals with regard to the processing of personal data by the Community institutions and bodies and on the free movement of such data, OJ L 8, 12.1.2001, pp. 1–22.
99 Directive 95/46/EC of the European Parliament and of the Council of 24 October 1995 on the protection of individuals with regard to the processing of personal data and on the free movement of such data, OJ L 281, 23.11.1995, pp. 31–50.

(a)   details concerning the applicant;

(b)   the status, within the meaning of Art 3, of the applicant;

(c)   documents providing evidence to satisfy the competent customs department that the applicant is entitled to submit the application;

(d)   where the applicant submits the application by means of a representative, details of the person representing him and evidence of that person's powers to act as representative, in accordance with the legislation of the Member State in which the application is submitted;

(e)   the IPR or rights to be enforced;

(f)   in the case of a Union application, the Member States in which customs action is requested;

(g)   specific and technical data on the authentic goods, including markings such as bar-coding and images where appropriate;

(h)   the information needed to enable the customs authorities to readily identify the goods in question;

(i)   information relevant to the customs authorities' analysis and assessment of the risk of infringement of the IPR or the IPRs concerned, such as the authorised distributors;

(j)   whether information provided in accordance with point (g), (h) or (i) of this paragraph is to be marked for restricted handling in accordance with Art 31(5);

(k)   the details of any representative designated by the applicant to take charge of legal and technical matters;

(l)   an undertaking by the applicant to notify the competent customs department of any of the situations laid down in Art 15;

(m)   an undertaking by the applicant to forward and update any information relevant to the customs authorities' analysis and assessment of the risk of infringement of the IPR(s) concerned;

(n)   an undertaking by the applicant to assume liability under the conditions laid down in Art 28;

(o)   an undertaking by the applicant to bear the costs referred to in Art 29 under the conditions laid down in that Article;

(p)   an agreement by the applicant that the data provided by him may be processed by the Commission and by the Member States;

(q)   whether the applicant requests the use of the procedure referred to in Art 26 and, where requested by the customs authorities, agrees to cover the costs related to destruction of goods under that procedure.

(e)   Decisions on applications

i.   Processing of incomplete applications

7.127   Article 7(1) provides that where, on receipt of an application, the competent customs department considers that the application does not contain all the information required by Art 6(3), the competent customs department shall request the applicant to supply the missing information within ten working days of notification of the request. In such cases, the time limit referred to in Art 9(1) shall be suspended until the relevant information is received.

Article 7(2) provides that where the applicant does not provide the missing **7.128** information within the period referred to in the first subparagraph of para 1, the competent customs department shall reject the application.

ii. Fees

Article 8 provides that the applicant shall not be charged a fee to cover the **7.129** administrative costs resulting from the processing of the application.

iii. Notification of decisions granting or rejecting applications

Article 9(1) requires the competent customs department to notify the appli- **7.130** cant of its decision granting or rejecting the application within 30 working days of the receipt of the application. In the event of rejection, the competent customs department shall provide reasons for its decision and include information on the appeal procedure.

Article 9(2) provides that if the applicant has been notified of the suspension **7.131** of the release or the detention of the goods by the customs authorities before the submission of an application, the competent customs department shall notify the applicant of its decision granting or rejecting the application within two working days of the receipt of the application.

iv. Decisions concerning applications

Article 10(1) provides that a decision granting a national application and any **7.132** decision revoking or amending it shall take effect in the Member State in which the national application was submitted from the day following the date of adoption. A decision extending the period during which customs authorities are to take action shall take effect in the Member State in which the national application was submitted on the day following the date of expiry of the period to be extended.

Article 10(2) provides that a decision granting a Union application and any **7.133** decision revoking or amending it shall take effect as follows:

    (a) in the Member State in which the application was submitted, on the day following the date of adoption;
    (b) in all other Member States where action by the customs authorities is requested, on the day following the date on which the customs authorities are notified in accordance with Article 14(2), provided that the holder of the decision has fulfilled his obligations under Article 29(3) with regard to translation costs.

A decision extending the period during which customs authorities are to take action shall take effect in the Member State in which the Union application was submitted and in all other Member States where action by the customs authorities is requested the day following the date of expiry of the period to be extended.

v. Period during which the customs authorities are to take action

General application

7.134 Article 11(1) provides that when granting an application, the competent customs department shall specify the period during which the customs authorities are to take action. That period shall begin on the day the decision granting the application takes effect, pursuant to Art 10, and shall not exceed one year from the day following the date of adoption.

Application after notification of suspension

7.135 Article 11(2) provides that where an application submitted after notification by the customs authorities of the suspension of the release or detention of the goods in accordance with Art 18(3) does not contain the information referred to in point (g), (h) or (i) of Art 6(3), it shall be granted only for the suspension of the release or detention of those goods, unless that information is provided within ten working days after the notification of the suspension of the release or detention of the goods.

Termination of IPRs

7.136 Article 11(3) provides that where an IPR ceases to have effect or where the applicant ceases for other reasons to be entitled to submit an application, no action shall be taken by the customs authorities. The decision granting the application shall be revoked or amended accordingly by the competent customs department that granted the decision.

vi. Extension of the period during which the customs authorities are to take action

On expiry of initial period

7.137 Article 12(1) provides that on expiry of the period during which the customs authorities are to take action, and subject to the prior discharge by the holder of the decision of any debt owed to the customs authorities under this Regulation, the competent customs department which adopted the initial decision may, at the request of the holder of the decision, extend that period.

Refusal of request for extension of period

7.138 Article 12(2) provides that where the request for extension of the period during which the customs authorities are to take action is received by the competent customs department less than 30 working days before the expiry of the period to be extended, it may refuse that request.

Notification of decision on extension
Article 12(3) provides that the competent customs department shall notify its **7.139** decision on the extension to the holder of the decision within 30 working days of the receipt of the request referred to in Art 12(1). The competent customs department shall specify the period during which the customs authorities are to take action.

Commencement of extension
Article 12(4) provides that the extended period during which the customs **7.140** authorities are to take action shall run from the day following the date of expiry of the previous period and shall not exceed one year.

Revocation of extension on expiry of IPR
Article 12(5) provides that where an IPR ceases to have effect or where the **7.141** applicant ceases for other reasons to be entitled to submit an application, no action shall be taken by the customs authorities. The decision granting the extension shall be revoked or amended accordingly by the competent customs department that granted the decision.

No fee for extension
Article 12(6) provides that the holder of the decision shall not be charged a fee **7.142** to cover the administrative costs resulting from the processing of the request for extension.

Extension request form
Article 12(7) provides that the Commission shall establish an extension **7.143** request form by means of implementing acts. Those implementing acts shall be adopted in accordance with the advisory procedure referred to in Art 34(2).

vii. Amending the decision with regard to IPRs

Article 13 provides that the competent customs department that adopted the **7.144** decision granting the application may, at the request of the holder of that decision, modify the list of IPRs in that decision.

Where a new IPR is added, the request shall contain the information referred **7.145** to in points (c), (e), (g), (h) and (i) of Art 6(3).

In the case of a decision granting a Union application, any modification **7.146** consisting of the addition of IPRs shall be limited to IPRs covered by Art 4.

(f) Notification obligations of the competent customs department

i. National application

7.147 Article 14(1) provides that the competent customs department to which a national application has been submitted shall forward the following decisions to the customs offices of its Member State, immediately after their adoption:

(a) decisions granting the application;
(b) decisions revoking decisions granting the application;
(c) decisions amending decisions granting the application;
(d) decisions extending the period during which the customs authorities are to take action.

ii. Union application

Decisions to be forwarded to relevant Member States

7.148 Article 14(2) provides that the competent customs department to which a Union application has been submitted shall forward the following decisions to the competent customs department of the Member State or Member States indicated in the Union application, immediately after their adoption:

(a) decisions granting the application;
(b) decisions revoking decisions granting the application;
(c) decisions amending decisions granting the application;
(d) decisions extending the period during which the customs authorities are to take action.

Decisions to be forwarded to relevant customs departments

7.149 Article 14(2) provides that the competent customs department of the Member State or Member States indicated in the Union application shall immediately after receiving those decisions forward them to their customs offices.

Request for additional information

7.150 Article 14(3) provides that the competent customs department of the Member State or Member States indicated in the Union application may request the competent customs department that adopted the decision granting the application to provide them with additional information deemed necessary for the implementation of that decision.

Notification of suspension of actions of customs department

7.151 Article 14(4) provides that the competent customs department shall forward its decision suspending the actions of the customs authorities under point (b) of Art 16(1) and Art 16(2) to the customs offices of its Member State, immediately after its adoption.

(g) Notification obligations of the holder of the decision

Article 15 provides that the holder of the decision shall immediately notify the **7.152** competent customs department that granted the application of any of the following:

- (a) an IPR covered by the application ceases to have effect;
- (b) the holder of the decision ceases for other reasons to be entitled to submit the application;
- (c) modifications to the information referred to in Art 6(3).

(h) Failure of the holder of the decision to fulfil his obligations

Article 16(1) provides that where the holder of the decision uses the infor- **7.153** mation provided by the customs authorities for purposes other than those provided for in Art 21, the competent customs department of the Member State where the information was provided or misused may:

- (a) revoke any decision adopted by it granting a national application to that holder of the decision, and refuse to extend the period during which the customs authorities are to take action;
- (b) suspend in their territory, during the period during which the customs authorities are to take action, any decision granting a Union application to that holder of the decision.

Article 16(2) provides that the competent customs department may decide to **7.154** suspend the actions of the customs authorities until the expiry of the period during which those authorities are to take action, where the holder of the decision:

- (a) does not fulfil the notification obligations set out in Article 15;
- (b) does not fulfil the obligation on returning samples set out in Article 19(3);
- (c) does not fulfil the obligations on costs and translation set out in Article 29(1) and (3);
- (d) without valid reason does not initiate proceedings as provided for in Article 23(3) or Article 26(9).

In the case of a Union application, the decision to suspend the actions of the **7.155** customs authorities shall have effect only in the Member State where such decision is taken.

E. ACTION BY THE CUSTOMS AUTHORITIES

7.156 Chapter III of the Customs Regulation deals with actions to be taken by the customs authorities.

7.157 Recital (19) to the Customs Regulation explains that taking into account the provisional and preventive character of the measures adopted by the customs authorities when applying this Regulation and the conflicting interests of the parties affected by the measures, some aspects of the procedures should be adapted to ensure the smooth application of this Regulation, whilst respecting the rights of the concerned parties. Thus, with respect to the various notifications envisaged by this Regulation, the customs authorities should notify the relevant person, on the basis of the documents concerning the customs treatment or of the situation in which the goods are placed. Furthermore, since the procedure for destruction of goods implies that both the declarant or the holder of the goods and the holder of the decision should communicate their possible objections to destruction in parallel, it should be ensured that the holder of the decision is given the possibility to react to a potential objection to destruction by the declarant or the holder of the goods. It should therefore be ensured that the declarant or the holder of the goods is notified of the suspension of the release of the goods or their detention before, or on the same day as, the holder of the decision.

1. Suspension of the release or detention of the goods following the grant of an application

(a) Suspension of goods suspected of infringing an IPR

7.158 Article 17(1) provides that where the customs authorities identify goods suspected of infringing an IPR covered by a decision granting an application, they shall suspend the release of the goods or detain them.

(b) Request for information

7.159 Article 17(2) provides that before suspending the release of or detaining the goods, the customs authorities may ask the holder of the decision to provide them with any relevant information with respect to the goods. The customs authorities may also provide the holder of the decision with information about the actual or estimated quantity of goods, their actual or presumed nature and images thereof, as appropriate.

7.160 'Holder of the decision' is defined in Art 2(13) to mean 'the holder of a decision granting an application'.

(c) Notification of declarant

Article 17(3) provides that the customs authorities shall notify the declarant or the holder of the goods of the suspension of the release of the goods or the detention of the goods within one working day of that suspension or detention. **7.161**

'Declarant' is defined in Art 2(15) to mean 'the declarant as defined in point (18) of Article 4 of Regulation (EEC) No 2913/92'.[100] 'Declarant' means the person making the customs declaration in his own name or the person in whose name a customs declaration is made. **7.162**

(d) Notification of holder of goods

Article 17(3) provides that where the customs authorities opt to notify the holder of the goods and two or more persons are considered to be the holder of the goods, the customs authorities shall not be obliged to notify more than one of those persons. **7.163**

'Holder of the goods' is defined in Art 2(14) to mean 'the person who is the owner of the goods suspected of infringing an intellectual property right or who has a similar right of disposal, or physical control, over such goods'. **7.164**

(e) Notification of the holder of the decision

The customs authorities shall notify the holder of the decision of the suspension of the release of the goods or the detention on the same day as, or promptly after, the declarant or the holder of the goods is notified. **7.165**

(f) Notifications to include procedure on destruction

Article 17(3) provides that the notifications shall include information on the procedure set out in Art 23. **7.166**

(g) Informing of decisions by customs authorities

Article 17(4) provides that the customs authorities shall inform the holder of the decision and the declarant or the holder of the goods of the actual or estimated quantity and the actual or presumed nature of the goods, including available images thereof, as appropriate, whose release has been suspended or which have been detained. The customs authorities shall also, upon request and where available to them, inform the holder of the decision of the names **7.167**

---

100 Council Regulation (EEC) No 2913/92 of 12 October 1992 establishing the Community Customs Code, OJ L 302, 19.10.1992, pp. 1–50.

and addresses of the consignee, the consignor and the declarant or the holder of the goods, of the customs procedure and of the origin, provenance and destination of the goods whose release has been suspended or which have been detained.

2. Suspension of the release or detention of the goods before the grant of an application

(a) Ex officio *action*

7.168 Recital (15) to the Customs Regulation explains that in order to ensure the swift enforcement of IPRs, it should be provided that, where the customs authorities suspect, on the basis of reasonable indications, that goods under their supervision infringe IPRs, they may suspend the release of or detain the goods, whether at their own initiative or upon application, in order to enable a person or entity entitled to submit an application to initiate proceedings for determining whether an IPR has been infringed.

7.169 Article 18(1) provides that where the customs authorities identify goods suspected of infringing an IPR, which are not covered by a decision granting an application, they may, except in the case of perishable goods, suspend the release of those goods or detain them.

7.170 Article 2(20) defines 'perishable goods' as 'goods considered by customs authorities to deteriorate by being kept for up to 20 days from the date of their suspension of release or detention'.

(b) Request for information by customs authorities

7.171 Article 18(2) provides that before suspending the release of or detaining the goods suspected of infringing an IPR, the customs authorities may, without disclosing any information other than the actual or estimated quantity of goods, their actual or presumed nature and images thereof, as appropriate, request any person or entity potentially entitled to submit an application concerning the alleged infringement of the IPRs to provide them with any relevant information.

(c) Notification of declarant of suspension

7.172 Article 18(3) provides that the customs authorities shall notify the declarant or the holder of the goods of the suspension of the release of the goods or their detention within one working day of that suspension or detention.

(d) Notification of holder/s of the goods

Article 18(3) provides that where the customs authorities opt to notify the **7.173** holder of the goods and two or more persons are considered to be the holder of the goods, the customs authorities shall not be obliged to notify more than one of those persons.

(e) Notification of entities entitled to submit an application

Article 18(3) provides that the customs authorities shall notify persons or **7.174** entities entitled to submit an application concerning the alleged infringement of the IPRs of the suspension of the release of the goods or their detention on the same day as, or promptly after, the declarant or the holder of the goods is notified. The customs authorities may consult the competent public authorities in order to identify the persons or entities entitled to submit an application.

(f) Notification of information on destruction

Article 18(3) provides that the notifications shall include information on the **7.175** procedure set out in Art 23.

(g) Release of goods

Article 18(4) provides that the customs authorities shall grant the release of **7.176** the goods or put an end to their detention immediately after completion of all customs formalities in the following cases:

(a) where they have not identified any person or entity entitled to submit an application concerning the alleged infringement of IPRs within one working day from the suspension of the release or the detention of the goods;

(b) where they have not received an application in accordance with Article 5(3), or where they have rejected such an application.

(h) Notification of import information to holder

Article 18(5) provides that where an application has been granted, the customs **7.177** authorities shall, upon request and where available to them, inform the holder of the decision of the names and addresses of the consignee, the consignor and the declarant or the holder of the goods, of the customs procedure and of the origin, provenance and destination of the goods whose release has been suspended or which have been detained.

3. Inspection and sampling of goods whose release has been suspended or which have been detained

(a) Inspection of goods by holder

7.178 Article 19(1) provides that the customs authorities shall give the holder of the decision and the declarant or the holder of the goods the opportunity to inspect the goods whose release has been suspended or which have been detained.

(b) Taking of samples

7.179 Article 19(2) provides that the customs authorities may take samples that are representative of the goods. They may provide or send such samples to the holder of the decision, at the holder's request and strictly for the purposes of analysis and to facilitate the subsequent procedure in relation to counterfeit and pirated goods. Any analysis of those samples shall be carried out under the sole responsibility of the holder of the decision.

7.180 Article 19(3) provides that the holder of the decision shall, unless circumstances do not allow, return the samples referred to in para 2 to the customs authorities on completion of the analysis, at the latest before the goods are released or their detention is ended.

4. Conditions for storage

7.181 Article 20 provides that the conditions of storage of goods during a period of suspension of release or detention shall be determined by the customs authorities.

5. Permitted use of certain information by the holder of the decision

7.182 Article 21 provides that where the holder of the decision has received the information referred to in Art 17(4), Art 18(5), Art 19 or Art 26(8), he may disclose or use that information only for the following purposes:

(a) to initiate proceedings to determine whether an IPR has been infringed and in the course of such proceedings;
(b) in connection with criminal investigations related to the infringement of an IPR and undertaken by public authorities in the Member State where the goods are found;
(c) to initiate criminal proceedings and in the course of such proceedings;
(d) to seek compensation from the infringer or other persons;

(e) to agree with the declarant or the holder of the goods that the goods be destroyed in accordance with Article 23(1);

(f) to agree with the declarant or the holder of the goods of the amount of the guarantee referred to in point (a) of Article 24(2).

6. Sharing of information and data between customs authorities

Recital (21) to the Customs Regulation points out that with a view to **7.183** eliminating international trade in goods infringing IPRs, the TRIPS Agreement provides that WTO Members are to promote the exchange of information between customs authorities on such trade. Accordingly, it should be possible for the Commission and the customs authorities of the Member States to share information on suspected breaches of IPRs with the relevant authorities of third countries, including on goods which are in transit through the territory of the Union and originate in or are destined for those third countries.

Article 22(1) provides that without prejudice to applicable provisions on data **7.184** protection in the Union and for the purpose of contributing to eliminating international trade in goods infringing IPRs, the Commission and the customs authorities of the Member States may share certain data and information available to them with the relevant authorities in third countries according to the practical arrangements referred to in Art 22(3).

Article 22(2) provides that the data and information referred to in Art 22(1) **7.185** shall be exchanged to swiftly enable effective enforcement against shipments of goods infringing an IPR. Such data and information may relate to seizures, trends and general risk information, including on goods which are in transit through the territory of the Union and which have originated in or are destined for the territory of third countries concerned. Such data and information may include, where appropriate, the following:

(a) nature and quantity of goods;
(b) suspected IPR infringed;
(c) origin, provenance and destination of the goods;
(d) information on movements of means of transport, in particular:
    (i) name of vessel or registration of means of transport;
    (ii) reference numbers of freight bill or other transport document;
    (iii) number of containers;
    (iv) weight of load;
    (v) description and/or coding of goods;
    (vi) reservation number;
    (vii) seal number;
    (viii) place of first loading;

      (ix)   place of final unloading;

      (x)   places of transhipment;

      (xi)   expected date of arrival at place of final unloading;

  (e)   information on movements of containers, in particular:

      (i)   container number;

      (ii)   container loading status;

      (iii)   date of movement;

      (iv)   type of movement (loaded, unloaded, transhipped, entered, left, etc);

      (v)   name of vessel or registration of means of transport;

      (vi)   number of voyage/journey;

      (vii) place;

      (viii) freight bill or other transport document.

7.186 Article 22(3) provides that the Commission shall adopt implementing acts defining the elements of the necessary practical arrangements concerning the exchange of data and information referred to in paras 1 and 2 of this Article. Those implementing acts shall be adopted in accordance with the examination procedure referred to in Art 34(3).

F. DESTRUCTION OF GOODS, INITIATION OF PROCEEDINGS AND EARLY RELEASE OF GOODS

7.187 Recital (16) to the Customs Regulation pointed out that its predecessor (Regulation (EC) No 1383/2003) allowed Member States to provide for a procedure allowing the destruction of certain goods without there being any obligation to initiate proceedings to establish whether an IPR has been infringed. The European Parliament Resolution of 18 December 2008 on the impact of counterfeiting on international trade[101] recognised that such a procedure has proved very successful in the Member States where it has been available. Therefore, Recital (16) indicated that the procedure should be made compulsory with regard to all infringements of IPRs and should be applied, where the declarant or the holder of the goods agrees to destruction. Furthermore, the procedure should provide that customs authorities may deem that the declarant or the holder of the goods has agreed to the destruction of the goods where he has not explicitly opposed destruction within the prescribed period.

7.188 Recital (17) to the Customs Regulation explains that in order to reduce the administrative burden and costs to a minimum, a specific procedure should be introduced for small consignments of counterfeit and pirated goods, which

---

101   OJ C 45 E, 23.2.2010, p. 47.

should allow for such goods to be destroyed without the explicit agreement of the applicant in each case. However, a general request made by the applicant in the application should be required in order for that procedure to be applied. Furthermore, customs authorities should have the possibility to require that the applicant covers the costs incurred by the application of that procedure.

The issue of destruction under Art 59,[102] the equivalent provision in the **7.189** TRIPS Agreement, was addressed by the WTO Dispute Panel in *China – Measures Affecting the Protection and Enforcement of Intellectual Property Rights*,[103] this determination addressed, inter alia, whether China's Regulations on Customs Protection of Intellectual Property Rights, 2003 complied with Art 59. The Regulations permitted confiscated goods which infringed IPRs to be used by public welfare bodies for use in social public welfare undertakings. Where the goods concerned could not be disposed of in this way, but the infringing features could be eradicated, they could, according to the Regulation, be auctioned off after eradicating the infringing features. Where the distinguishing features could not be eradicated the goods had to be destroyed. The US claimed that as the Chinese customs authorities were required first to donate seized goods to social welfare bodies, they lacked the discretion to order the destruction or disposal of infringing goods required by Art 59 of the TRIPS Agreement. The response of China was that this donation constituted disposal outside the channels of commerce in such a way as to avoid harm to the right holder.[104]

In interpreting the meaning of 'infringing goods' in Art 59 the Panel read **7.190** down the meaning of these words, by reference to their context, which included the first sentence of Art 51 which provided for the relevant procedures to apply, as a minimum, to 'the importation' of 'counterfeit trademark or pirated copyright goods'.[105] The Panel noted that the IPR infringements covered by the Chinese Customs Regulations included not only counterfeit trade mark goods and pirated copyright goods, but certain other infringements

---

102 TRIPS Agreement in Art 59, provides in the first sentence that:

> Without prejudice to other rights of action open to the right holder and subject to the right of the defendant to seek review by a judicial authority, competent authorities shall have the authority to order the destruction or disposal of infringing goods in accordance with the principles set out in Article 46.

Art 46 of the TRIPS Agreement provides that:

> In order to create an effective deterrent to infringement, the judicial authorities shall have the authority to order that goods that they have found to be infringing be, without compensation of any sort, disposed of outside the channels of commerce in such a manner as to avoid any harm caused to the right holder, or, unless this would be contrary to existing constitutional requirements, destroyed.

103 Report of the Panel, WT/DS362/R, 26 January 2009.
104 Ibid., at paras 7.197–7.198.
105 Ibid., at para 7.221.

such as other trade mark-infringing goods, other copyright-infringing goods, and patent-infringing goods. Thus China's border measures provided a level of protection higher than the minimum standard required by the TRIPS Agreement.

7.191 The obligation in the first sentence of Art 59 of TRIPS was that competent authorities 'shall have the authority' to order certain types of remedies with respect to infringing goods. The Panel noted that the word 'authority' can be defined as 'power or right to enforce obedience; moral or legal supremacy; right to command or give a final decision'. The obligation is to 'have' authority not an obligation to 'exercise' authority.[106] The Panel concluded that the obligation that competent authorities 'shall have the authority' to make certain orders 'is not an obligation that competent authorities shall exercise that authority in a particular way, unless otherwise specified'.[107] The Panel recognised that the obligation that competent authorities 'shall have the authority' to order certain types of remedies left Members free to provide that competent authorities may have authority to order other remedies not required by Art 59 to be within their authority under the Article. The terms of Art 59 did not indicate that the authority to order the specified types of remedies must be exclusive.

7.192 Article 59 requires authority to order 'destruction or disposal'. The Panel observed that it was not disputed that where competent authorities have authority in any given situation within the scope of Art 59 to order either destruction or disposal (in accordance with applicable principles), this was sufficient to implement the obligation in the first sentence of Art 59. Therefore, a condition that precluded the authority from ordering one remedy (eg destruction) could be consistent with Art 59 as long as competent authorities still had the authority to order the other remedy (in this example, disposal).[108]

7.193 The 'authority' required by Art 59 concerns two types of remedies, namely 'destruction or disposal'. The meaning of 'destruction' did not require definition by the Panel as its meaning was considered uncontroversial.

---

106   Ibid., at para 7.236.
107   Ibid., at para 7.238.
108   Ibid., at para 7.246.

1. Destruction of goods and initiation of proceedings

(a) Destruction of goods suspected of infringing an IPR

Article 23(1) provides that goods suspected of infringing an IPR may be **7.194**
destroyed under customs control, without there being any need to determine
whether an IPR has been infringed under the law of the Member State where
the goods are found, where all of the following conditions are fulfilled:

(a) the holder of the decision has confirmed in writing to the customs authorities,
within ten working days, or three working days in the case of perishable goods, of
notification of the suspension of the release or the detention of the goods, that, in
his conviction, an IPR has been infringed;

(b) the holder of the decision has confirmed in writing to the customs authorities,
within ten working days, or three working days in the case of perishable goods, of
notification of the suspension of the release or the detention of the goods, his
agreement to the destruction of the goods;

(c) the declarant or the holder of the goods has confirmed in writing to the customs
authorities, within ten working days, or three working days in the case of
perishable goods, of notification of the suspension of the release or the detention
of the goods, his agreement to the destruction of the goods. Where the declarant
or the holder of the goods has not confirmed his agreement to the destruction of
the goods nor notified his opposition thereto to the customs authorities, within
those deadlines, the customs authorities may deem the declarant or the holder of
the goods to have confirmed his agreement to the destruction of those goods.

(b) Release of goods when IPR infringement not confirmed

Article 23(1) provides that the customs authorities shall grant the release of **7.195**
the goods or put an end to their detention, immediately after completion of all
customs formalities, where within the periods referred to in points (a) and (b)
of the first subparagraph, they have not received both the written confirmation
from the holder of the decision that, in his conviction, an IPR has been
infringed and his agreement to destruction, unless those authorities have been
duly informed about the initiation of proceedings to determine whether an
IPR has been infringed.

(c) Destruction under customs control

Article 23(2) provides that the destruction of the goods shall be carried out **7.196**
under customs control and under the responsibility of the holder of the
decision, unless otherwise specified in the national law of the Member State
where the goods are destroyed. Samples may be taken by competent authorities prior to the destruction of the goods. Samples taken prior to destruction
may be used for educational purposes.

(d) Destruction where holder has not confirmed agreement

7.197 Article 23(3) provides that where the declarant or the holder of the goods has not confirmed his agreement to the destruction in writing and where the declarant or the holder of the goods has not been deemed to have confirmed his agreement to the destruction, in accordance with point (c) of the first subparagraph of Art 23(1) within the periods referred to therein, the customs authorities shall immediately notify the holder of the decision thereof. The holder of the decision shall, within ten working days, or three working days in the case of perishable goods, of notification of the suspension of the release or the detention of the goods, initiate proceedings to determine whether an IPR has been infringed.

(e) Time period for destruction

7.198 Article 23(4) provides that except in the case of perishable goods[109] the customs authorities may extend the period referred to in Art 23(3) by a maximum of ten working days upon a duly justified request by the holder of the decision in appropriate cases.

(f) Release of goods

7.199 Article 23(5) provides that the customs authorities shall grant the release of the goods or put an end to their detention, immediately after completion of all customs formalities, where, within the periods referred to in Art 23(3) and (4), they have not been duly informed, in accordance with Art 23(3), on the initiation of proceedings to determine whether an IPR has been infringed.

(g) Early release of goods

7.200 Article 24(1) provides that where the customs authorities have been notified of the initiation of proceedings to determine whether a design, patent, utility model, topography of semiconductor product or plant variety has been infringed, the declarant or the holder of the goods may request the customs authorities to release the goods or put an end to their detention before the completion of those proceedings.

7.201 Article 24(2) provides that the customs authorities shall release the goods or put an end to their detention only where all the following conditions are fulfilled:

---

109 Art 2(20) defines 'perishable goods' as 'goods considered by customs authorities to deteriorate by being kept for up to 20 days from the date of their suspension of release or detention'.

(a) the declarant or the holder of the goods has provided a guarantee that is of an amount sufficient to protect the interests of the holder of the decision;

(b) the authority competent to determine whether an IPR has been infringed has not authorised precautionary measures;

(c) all customs formalities have been completed.

Article 24(3) provides that the provision of the guarantee referred to in point **7.202** (a) of Art 24(2) shall not affect the other legal remedies available to the holder of the decision.

(h) Goods for destruction

Article 25(1) provides that goods to be destroyed under Art 23 or 26 shall not **7.203** be:

(a) released for free circulation, unless customs authorities, with the agreement of the holder of the decision, decide that it is necessary in the event that the goods are to be recycled or disposed of outside commercial channels, including for awareness-raising, training and educational purposes. The conditions under which the goods can be released for free circulation shall be determined by the customs authorities;

(b) brought out of the customs territory of the Union;

(c) exported;

(d) re-exported;

(e) placed under a suspensive procedure;

(f) placed in a free zone or free warehouse.

Article 25(2) provides that the customs authorities may allow the goods **7.204** referred to in Art 25(1) to be moved under customs supervision between different places within the customs territory of the Union with a view to their destruction under customs control.

(i) Removal of trade marks or geographical indications

An issue which arose under the TRIPS Agreement was whether goods could **7.205** be considered to have been destroyed by the removal of infringing trade marks. In *China – Measures Affecting the Protection and Enforcement of Intellectual Property Rights*,[110] the Panel was concerned with Art 27 of the Chinese Customs IPR Regulations, which allowed confiscated goods that could not be used for social public welfare undertakings and where the right holder had no intention to buy them to be auctioned off with infringing features eradicated. With regard to trade mark-infringing goods, China confirmed that the elimination of infringing features referred to the removal of infringing trade

---

110   Report of the Panel, WT/DS362/R, 26 January 2009.

marks. The question arose whether the Chinese Regulations provided for no more than the 'simple' removal of a trade mark within the meaning of the fourth sentence of Art 46 of the TRIPS Agreement. China argued that its measures did not provide for 'simple' removal of the trade mark because they also provide an opportunity for the trade mark right holder to comment prior to auction. The Panel noted that the word 'simple' could be defined as 'with nothing added; unqualified; neither more nor less than; mere, pure' and thus a situation in which a trade mark is removed from a good and no other action is taken constituted 'simple' removal of the trade mark.[111] This was because where counterfeit trade mark goods are released into the channels of commerce after the simple removal of the trade mark unlawfully affixed, an identical trade mark could be produced or imported separately and unlawfully reaffixed, often with relative ease, so that the goods would infringe once again.[112]

7.206 The Panel noted that this problem applied to counterfeit trade mark goods in particular because, as provided in the definition of 'counterfeit trademark goods' in footnote 14(a) to the TRIPS Agreement, a counterfeit trade mark is *identical* to a valid trade mark or cannot be distinguished in its essential aspects from the valid trade mark.[113] It was observed that counterfeit trade mark goods are more likely to imitate the appearance of genuine goods in their overall appearance and not simply in the affixing of a counterfeit trade mark, as the likelihood that a counterfeit trade mark good will confuse a consumer is related to the degree to which all its features, infringing and non-infringing, resemble the genuine good. Thus, even where the counterfeit trade mark was removed, the resulting state of the goods could still so closely resemble the genuine good that there was a heightened risk of further infringement by means of re-affixing a counterfeit trade mark. The Panel commented that 'the negotiators evidently considered that the heightened risk of further infringement warranted additional measures to create an effective deterrent to further infringement'.[114] It concluded that in light of the objective of the provision, the 'simple' removal of the trade mark was principally a reference to the fact that the state of the goods is not altered in any other way so that the absence of the trade mark is not an effective deterrent to further infringement and that the removal of the trade mark was not 'simple' if the state of the goods is altered sufficiently to deter further infringement.[115]

---

111   Ibid., at para 7.369.
112   Ibid., at para 7.373.
113   Ibid., at para 7.374.
114   Ibid.
115   Ibid., at para 7.375.

The Panel noted that the fourth sentence of Art 46 was not limited to an **7.207** action to render goods non-infringing, which the simple removal of the trade mark would achieve, but imposed an additional requirement beyond rendering the goods non-infringing in order to deter further acts of infringement with those goods. Therefore, it was insufficient, other than in exceptional cases, to show that goods that had already been found to be counterfeit were later unmarked.[116] The Panel observed that the procedure for seeking comment by right holders did not affect the state of the goods, nor was there any obligation to take right holders' comments into account, thus it was irrelevant to the question whether the measures at issue provide for 'simple removal of the trademark unlawfully affixed'.[117]

China argued that auctions of goods confiscated by customs were subject to a **7.208** reserve price that ensures that infringers do not have the opportunity to purchase the seized goods at an unreasonably low cost and reaffix counterfeit marks. This argument was rejected by the Panel as it remained economically viable for the importer or a third party to purchase the goods at auction and reaffix the trade marks in order to infringe again.

Considering all of the foregoing issues the Panel concluded that, in regard to **7.209** counterfeit trade mark goods, China's customs measures provided that the simple removal of the trade mark unlawfully affixed was sufficient to permit release of the goods into the channels of commerce.[118]

The final issue to be considered was what was meant by the words 'other than **7.210** in exceptional cases'. This has the reverse emphasis of Art 17(1)(b) of the Customs Regulation, where trade mark removal is the exceptional case. The Panel considered that the phrase must be interpreted in light of the objective of Art 46 of TRIPS, namely, 'to create an effective deterrent to infringement'.[119] Among the cases suggested by the Panel in which the simple removal of the trade mark prior to release of the goods into the channels of commerce would not lead to further infringement was where an innocent importer who has been deceived into buying a shipment of counterfeit goods has no means of recourse against the exporter and has no means of reaffixing counterfeit trade marks to the goods.[120] However, it acknowledged that such cases must be narrowly circumscribed in order to satisfy the description of 'exceptional' and that even when narrowly circumscribed, application of the

---

116 Ibid., at para 7.379.
117 Ibid., at para 7.380.
118 Ibid., at para 7.385.
119 Ibid., at para 7.391.
120 Ibid.

relevant provision must be rare, 'lest the so-called exception become the rule, or at least ordinary'.[121]

7.211 The Panel did not consider that 'exceptional cases' for the purposes of the fourth sentence of Art 46 could simply be demonstrated by a low rate of cases in which simple removal of the trade mark is treated as sufficient to permit release of goods into the channels of commerce, or in terms of a proportion of all cases of infringing goods seized at the border.[122] Such an approach to goods that have already been found to be counterfeit trade mark goods would amount to a margin of tolerance of further infringement that was not consistent with the objective of Art 46 of creating an effective deterrent. Consequently, the Panel concluded that the customs measures were inconsistent with Art 59 of the TRIPS Agreement, as it incorporates the principle set out in the fourth sentence of Art 46.[123]

(j) Procedure for the destruction of goods in small consignments

7.212 Article 26(1) provides that this Article shall apply to goods where all of the following conditions are fulfilled:

(a) the goods are suspected of being counterfeit or pirated goods;
(b) the goods are not perishable goods;
(c) the goods are covered by a decision granting an application;
(d) the holder of the decision has requested the use of the procedure set out in this Article in the application;
(e) the goods are transported in small consignments.

7.213 'Small consignment' is defined in Art 2(19) as 'a postal or express courier consignment, which:

(a) contains three units or less; or
(b) has a gross weight of less than two kilograms.

7.214 For the purpose of point (a), 'units' means goods as classified under the Combined Nomenclature in accordance with Annex I to Council Regulation (EEC) No 2658/87 of 23 July 1987 on the tariff and statistical nomenclature and on the Common Customs Tariff[124] if unpackaged, or the package of such goods intended for retail sale to the ultimate consumer.

---

121 Ibid.
122 Ibid., at para 7.392.
123 Ibid., at para 7.394.
124 OJ L 256, 7.9.1987, p. 1.

For the purpose of this definition, separate goods falling in the same Combined Nomenclature code shall be considered as different units and goods presented as sets classified in one Combined Nomenclature code shall be considered as one unit. **7.215**

Article 26(2) provides that when the procedure set out in this Article is applied, Art 17(3) and (4) and Art 19(2) and (3) shall not apply. **7.216**

G. LIABILITY, COSTS AND PENALTIES

Liability, costs and penalties are dealt with in Chapter IV of the Customs Regulation **7.217**

1. Liability of the customs authorities

Recital (23) of the Customs Regulation indicates that the liability of the customs authorities should be governed by the legislation of the Member States, though the granting by the customs authorities of an application should not entitle the holder of the decision to compensation in the event that goods suspected of infringing an IPR are not detected by the customs authorities and are released or no action is taken to detain them. **7.218**

Article 27 provides that without prejudice to national law, the decision granting an application shall not entitle the holder of that decision to compensation in the event that goods suspected of infringing an IPR are not detected by a customs office and are released, or no action is taken to detain them. **7.219**

2. Liability of the holder of the decision

Article 28 provides that where a procedure duly initiated pursuant to this Regulation is discontinued owing to an act or omission on the part of the holder of the decision, where samples taken pursuant to Art 19(2) are either not returned or are damaged and beyond use owing to an act or omission on the part of the holder of the decision, or where the goods in question are subsequently found not to infringe an IPR, the holder of the decision shall be liable towards any holder of the goods or declarant who has suffered damage in that regard, in accordance with specific applicable legislation. **7.220**

3. Costs

(a) Customs costs to be reimbursed by the holder of the decision

7.221 Recital (24) to the Customs Regulation explains that given that customs authorities take action upon application, it is appropriate to provide that the holder of the decision should reimburse all the costs incurred by the customs authorities in taking action to enforce his IPRs.

7.222 Article 29(1) provides that where requested by the customs authorities, the holder of the decision shall reimburse the costs incurred by the customs authorities, or other parties acting on behalf of customs authorities, from the moment of detention or suspension of the release of the goods, including storage and handling of the goods, in accordance with Art 17(1), Art 18(1) and Art 19(2) and (3), and when using corrective measures such as destruction of goods in accordance with Arts 23 and 26.

(b) Customs to provide costs information to the holder of the decision

7.223 Article 29(1) provides that the holder of a decision to whom the suspension of release or detention of goods has been notified shall, upon request, be given information by the customs authorities on where and how those goods are being stored and on the estimated costs of storage referred to in this paragraph. The information on estimated costs may be expressed in terms of time, products, volume, weight or service depending on the circumstances of storage and the nature of the goods.

(c) Right of holder of the decision to seek compensation

7.224 Recital (24) to the Customs Regulation points out that although the applicant for customs action should bear the costs incurred by customs authorities in taking action, nevertheless this should not preclude the holder of the decision from seeking compensation from the infringer or other persons that might be considered liable under the legislation of the Member State where the goods were found. Such persons might include intermediaries, where applicable. Costs and damages incurred by persons other than customs authorities as a result of a customs action, where the release of goods is suspended or the goods are detained on the basis of a claim of a third party based on intellectual property, should be governed by the specific legislation applicable in each particular case.

7.225 Article 29(2) provides that this Article shall be without prejudice to the right of the holder of the decision to seek compensation from the infringer or other persons in accordance with the legislation applicable.

(d) Costs of translation

Article 29(3) provides that the holder of a decision granting a Union **7.226** application shall provide and pay for any translation required by the competent customs department or customs authorities which are to take action concerning the goods suspected of infringing an IPR.

4. Penalties

Article 30 provides that the Member States shall ensure that the holders of **7.227** decisions comply with the obligations set out in this Regulation, including, where appropriate, by laying down provisions establishing penalties. The penalties provided for shall be effective, proportionate and dissuasive.

The Member States shall notify those provisions and any subsequent amend- **7.228** ment affecting them to the Commission without delay.

The TRIPS Agreement does not refer to the effectiveness of penalties, nor to **7.229** the requirement that penalties be proportionate and dissuasive. However, Art 61 of the TRIPS Agreement states that the criminal remedies available shall 'include imprisonment and/or monetary fines sufficient to provide a deterrent, consistently with the level of penalties applied for crimes of a corresponding gravity'. Article 61 then goes on to speak of 'appropriate cases' in which the remedies available shall also include 'the seizure, forfeiture and destruction of the infringing goods and of any materials and implements the predominant use of which has been in the commission of the offence'. Article 61 was addressed in the WTO's Dispute Panel determination in relation to the US complaint about copyright enforcement in China.[125] Australia argued that Art 61 created an obligation of result, namely to put in place penalties that are sufficient to actively discourage others from engaging in such acts and that the question whether punishments were sufficient to provide such a deterrent was to be assessed in light of the circumstances in a Member's territory.[126] This submission was not assessed by the Panel, which decided the question on other grounds.

The issue of deterrence is also mentioned in Art 41.1 of TRIPS, which **7.230** requires that enforcement procedures specified in the Agreement are 'available' so as to permit 'effective action' against any act of infringement of the IPRs covered by the Agreement, including 'remedies which constitute a deterrent to

---

125 *China – Measures Affecting the Protection and Enforcement of Intellectual Property Rights*, WT/DS362, 26 January 2009, paras 7.670ff.
126 Ibid., at para 7.672.

further infringements'. The Dispute Panel's determination in relation to the US complaint about copyright enforcement in China suggested that enforcement procedures under Art 41 permitted effective action if they were 'available'.[127] Article 46 of TRIPS, which refers to 'other remedies', provides that in order to 'create an effective deterrent to infringement', the judicial authorities 'shall have the authority to order that goods that they have found to be infringing be, without compensation of any sort, disposed of outside the channels of commerce in such a manner as to avoid any harm caused to the right holder'. Thus confiscation of infringing goods seems to be a category of deterrent remedy.

H. EXCHANGE OF INFORMATION

7.231 Recital (27) to the Customs Regulation explains that the exchange of information relating to decisions on applications and to customs actions should be made via a central electronic database. The entity which will control and manage that database and the entities in charge of ensuring the security of the processing of the data contained in the database should be defined. Introducing any type of possible interoperability or exchange should first and foremost comply with the purpose limitation principle, namely that data should be used for the purpose for which the database has been established, and no further exchange or interconnection should be allowed other than for that purpose.

7.232 Chapter V of the Customs Regulation deals with the exchange of information between the Commission and competent customs authorities.

1. Exchange of data on decisions relating to applications and detentions between the Member States and the Commission

(a) *Notification of decisions by customs department to the Commission*

7.233 Article 31(1) provides that the competent customs departments shall notify without delay the Commission of the following:

(a) decisions granting applications, including the application and its attachments;
(b) decisions extending the period during which the customs authorities are to take action or decisions revoking the decision granting the application or amending it;
(c) the suspension of a decision granting the application.

---

127   Ibid., at paras 7.177–7.181.

(b) Detail of information to be communicated

7.234 Article 31(2) provides that without prejudice to point (g) of Art 24 of Regulation (EC) No 515/97,[128] where the release of the goods is suspended or the goods are detained, the customs authorities shall transmit to the Commission any relevant information, except personal data, including information on the quantity and type of the goods, value, IPRs, customs procedures, countries of provenance, origin and destination, and transport routes and means.

(c) Central database

7.235 Article 32 provides for the establishment of a central database to be operational as soon as possible and not later than 1 January 2015.

7.236 Article 31(3) provides that the transmission of the information referred to in Art 31(1) and (2) and all exchanges of data on decisions concerning applications as referred to in Art 14 between customs authorities of the Member States shall be made via a central database of the Commission. The information and data shall be stored in that database.

7.237 Article 31(4) provides that for the purposes of ensuring processing of the information referred to in Art 31(1)–(3), the central database referred to in Art 31(3) shall be established in an electronic form. The central database shall contain the information, including personal data, referred to in Art 6(3), Art 14 and this Article.

(d) Access to information in the central database

7.238 Article 31(5) provides that the customs authorities of the Member States and the Commission shall have access to the information contained in the central database as appropriate for the fulfilment of their legal responsibilities in applying this Regulation. The access to information marked for restricted handling in accordance with Art 6(3) is restricted to the customs authorities of the Member States where action is requested. Upon justified request by the Commission, the customs authorities of the Member States may give access to the Commission to such information where it is strictly necessary for the application of this Regulation.

---

128 Council Regulation (EC) No 515/97 of 13 March 1997 on mutual assistance between the administrative authorities of the Member States and cooperation between the latter and the Commission to ensure the correct application of the law on customs and agricultural matters, OJ L 082, 22.03.1997 pp. 1–16. Regulation 515/97 is the legal base for the establishment of the Customs Information System (CIS). Art 24 provides that the CIS shall consist of a central database facility and it shall be accessible via terminals in each Member State and at the Commission. It shall comprise data including '(g) goods detained, seized or confiscated'.

(e) Introduction of information to the central database

7.239 Article 31(6) provides that the customs authorities shall introduce into the central database information related to the applications submitted to the competent customs department. The customs authorities which have introduced information into the central database shall, where necessary, amend, supplement, correct or delete such information. Each customs authority that has introduced information in the central database shall be responsible for the accuracy, adequacy and relevancy of this information.

(f) Technical and organisational arrangements

7.240 Article 31(7) provides that the Commission shall establish and maintain adequate technical and organisational arrangements for the reliable and secure operation of the central database. The customs authorities of each Member State shall establish and maintain adequate technical and organisational arrangements to ensure the confidentiality and security of processing with respect to the processing operations carried out by their customs authorities and with respect to terminals of the central database located on the territory of that Member State.

2. Data protection provisions

7.241 Article 33(1) provides that the processing of personal data in the central database of the Commission shall be carried out in accordance with Regulation (EC) No 45/2001[129] and under the supervision of the European Data Protection Supervisor.

7.242 Article 33(2) provides that the processing of personal data by the competent authorities in the Member States shall be carried out in accordance with Directive 95/46/EC[130] and under the supervision of the public independent authority of the Member State referred to in Art 28 of that Directive.

7.243 Article 33(3) provides that personal data shall be collected and used solely for the purposes of this Regulation. Personal data so collected shall be accurate and shall be kept up to date.

---

129 Regulation (EC) No 45/2001 of the European Parliament and of the Council of 18 December 2000 on the protection of individuals with regard to the processing of personal data by the Community institutions and bodies and on the free movement of such data, OJ L 8, 12.1.2001, pp. 1–22.

130 Directive 95/46/EC of the European Parliament and of the Council of 24 October 1995 on the protection of individuals with regard to the processing of personal data and on the free movement of such data, OJ L 281, 23.11.1995, pp. 31–50.

Article 33(4) provides that each customs authority that has introduced **7.244** personal data into the central database shall be the controller with respect to the processing of this data.

Article 33(5) provides that a data subject shall have a right of access to the **7.245** personal data relating to him or her that are processed through the central database and, where appropriate, the right to the rectification, erasure or blocking of personal data in accordance with Regulation (EC) No 45/2001[131] or the national laws implementing Directive 95/46/EC.

Article 33(6) provides that all requests for the exercise of the right of access, **7.246** rectification, erasure or blocking shall be submitted to and processed by the customs authorities. Where a data subject has submitted a request for the exercise of that right to the Commission, the Commission shall forward such request to the customs authorities concerned.

Article 33(7) provides that personal data shall not be kept longer than six **7.247** months from the date the relevant decision granting the application has been revoked or the relevant period during which the customs authorities are to take action has expired.

Article 33(8) provides that where the holder of the decision has initiated **7.248** proceedings in accordance with Art 23(3) or Art 26(9) and has notified the customs authorities of the initiation of such proceedings, personal data shall be kept for six months after proceedings have determined in a final way whether an IPR has been infringed.

I. MISCELLANEOUS PROVISIONS

1. Repeal

Article 38 provides for the repeal of Regulation (EC) No 1383/2003[132] with **7.249** effect from 1 January 2014.

---

131 Regulation (EC) No 45/2001 of the European Parliament and of the Council of 18 December 2000 on the protection of individuals with regard to the processing of personal data by the Community institutions and bodies and on the free movement of such data, OJ L 8, 12.1.2001, pp. 1–22.

132 Council Regulation (EC) No 1383/2003 of 22 July 2003 concerning customs action against goods suspected of infringing certain intellectual property rights and the measures to be taken against goods found to have infringed such rights, OJ L 196, 2.8.2003, pp. 7–14.

2. Transitional provisions

7.250 Article 39 provides that applications granted in accordance with Regulation (EC) No 1383/2003 shall remain valid for the period specified in the decision granting the application during which the customs authorities are to take action and shall not be extended.

3. Entry into force and application

7.251 Article 40(2) provides that the Customs Regulation shall apply from 1 January 2014, with the exception of:

(a)   Art 6, Art 12(7) and Art 22(3), which shall apply from 19 July 2013;
(b)   Art 31(1) and (3) to (7) and Art 33, which shall apply from the date on which the central database referred to in Art 32 is in place.

8

THE PROTECTION OF EU GEOGRAPHICAL INDICATIONS OUTSIDE EUROPE AND THE PROTECTION OF FOREIGN GEOGRAPHICAL INDICATIONS IN THE EU

A. INTRODUCTION

Prior to specific agreements with overseas countries concerning the protection **8.01** of GIs, European producers sought to protect their GIs through the passing off and consumer protection laws of foreign jurisdictions. This proved to be quite challenging, as it was difficult to prove that foreign consumers were aware of the quality/geography relationship of products sourced from European countries. An example of these difficulties is the results of cases brought by European wine producers against Australian wine producers in the early 1980s. In a 1981 case, which concerned the importation and sale of 'Spanish Champagne',[1] the Federal Court in declining to find a breach of the Australian consumer protection law[2] was influenced by the evidence of consumers 'that they regarded 'champagne' as a bubbly drink particularly appropriate for

---

1   *Re Comite Interprofessionel Du Vin De Champagne and Charles Barker Australia Pty Ltd v N L Burton Pty Ltd T/As Freixenet Spanish Champagne Distributors and Garland Farwagi & Partners Pty Ltd* [1981] FCA 196; (1981) 57 FLR 434

2   Trade Practices Act 1974, s 52.

festive occasions'. A similar case concerned a 1983 fight between an importer and a distributer of Lambrusco wine in Australia.[3] The judge in that case referred to the earlier Champagne case 'as an illustration of the reluctance of the courts to find misleading or deceptive conduct in respect of the use of a name descriptive of a particular type of wine'.

8.02 Cases such as these precipitated the negotiation of an Agreement between the European Community and Australia on trade in wine, which came into effect on 1 March 1994.[4]

8.03 This Wine Agreement was the first of a number of bilateral agreements seeking to protect GIs registered in the EU outside the EU through bilateral agreements with other countries and also through the intellectual property chapters of free trade agreements (FTAs). Examples of the latter are the EU-Vietnam FTA and the EU-Singapore FTAs, concluded in 2017 and 2018 respectively.

8.04 Reciprocally, the EU also recognises non-EU GIs which are registered in their home countries.

B. BILATERAL AND FREE TRADE AGREEMENTS

1. Agreements on GIs in relation to wines

(a) Australia

8.05 The Agreement between the European Community and Australia on trade in wine provided that in exchange for the European Community reducing the technical barriers for Australian wines exports, Australia agreed to phase out the use of European GIs and other geographical names listed in Schedule 2 to the agreement. Article 8 of the Agreement provided a number of transitional periods after which Australia had to discontinue its use of European names designated These were:

  (a) transitional period ending on 31 December 1993: Beaujolais, Cava, Frascati, Sancerre, Saint-Emilion/St Emilion, Vinho Verde/Vino Verde, White Bordeaux;

---

3 *Re Gavioli Luigi & Figli SNC and European Foods Wholesalers Pty Ltd v GJ Coles & Co Pty Ltd and Orifici Holdings Pty Ltd* [1983] FCA 353; (1983) 74 FLR 250.
4 See Blakeney, 2012b.

(b) transitional period ending on 31 December 1997: Chianti, Frontignan, Hock, Madeira and Malaga.

Article 9 of the Agreement provided for the negotiation by 31 December 1997 of transitional periods for: Burgundy, Chablis, Champagne, Claret, Graves, Marsala, Moselle, Port, Sauternes, Sherry and White Burgundy. A transitional period for 'Beaujolais' was to be subject to an agreement between the Australian producers and the competent French authorities representing the producers of 'Beaujolais'.

The Wine Agreement and the 1993 amendments to the Australian Wine and **8.06** Brandy Corporation Act 1980 sought to preserve existing commercial agreements. Thus for example, although 'Bereich Kaiserstuhl', a sub-region of Baden, was listed as a Federal Republic of Germany Geographical Indication in Annex II of the Agreement, that the provisions of the commercial agreement reached between Zentralkellerei Badisher Winzergenossenschaften e.G. and Barossa Co-operative Winery Ltd regarding the use of Kaiser Stuhl continued to apply.[5]

It was subsequently decided that the matters still to be negotiated would be **8.07** included in an updated wine agreement and on 23 October 2000, the Council of Europe authorised the European Commission to negotiate a new agreement and a new agreement between the European Community and Australia on trade in wine[6] was initialled by both Parties on 5 June 2007 and signed in Brussels on 1 December 2008, coming into force on 1 September 2010.[7]

The Agreement inserted the phase-out dates, which were not agreed in the **8.08** 1994 Agreement, for some GIs. Thus, a 12-month termination date was agreed to prohibit use of: Burgundy, Chablis, Champagne, Graves, Manzanilla, Marsala, Moselle, Port, Sauterne, Sherry and White Burgundy and Port.

Article 12 of the 2009 Agreement, in relation to the wines of Members of the **8.09** EU, provides for: (i) the protection of GIs for wines listed in Annex II, Part A; (ii) references to the Member State in which the wine originates or other names used to indicate the Member State; and (iii) the traditional expressions

---

5 Notice of this determination was published by the Chairperson of the Australian Wine and Brandy Corporation in the Commonwealth of Australia, Government Notices Gazette No. GN 50 of the 21st December 1994.http://www.wineaustralia.com/australia/Default.aspx?tabid=1075.

6 Dated 30 January 2009, http://eur-lex.europa.eu/LexUriServ/LexUriServ.do?uri=OJ:L:2009: 028:0003: 0087:EN :PDF.

7 http://europa.eu/rapid/pressReleasesAction.do?reference=IP/10/1078.

listed in Annex III. Annex II, Part 8 contains 78 pages of European GIs to be protected in Australia.

8.10 Following the negotiation of the Australia – United States Free Trade Agreement (AUSFTA) which came into effect on 1 January 2005, a number of changes were required to the system for protection of wine GIs in Australia which were implemented by amendments to the Australian Wine and Brandy Corporation Act 1980 which permitted cancellation procedures for wine GIs and the ability for a trade mark and GI to co-exist.

(b) South Africa

8.11 The EC and the Republic of South Africa Agreement on trade in wine came into force on 28 January 2002.[8] Article 7.1 of that Agreement required each Contracting Party to provide the appropriate legal means to ensure effective protection for the reciprocal protection of the names referred to in Art 8, used for the identification of wines originating in the territories of the Contracting Parties.

8.12 Article 8 provided that without prejudice to Art 9 and the Protocol the following names are protected with regard to wines originating in the EC: (i) references to the name of the Member State in which the wines originates, and (ii) the GIs referred to in Annex II. In the case of wines originating in South Africa: (i) the name 'South Africa' or other names used to indicate this country, (ii) the GIs referred to in Annex II.

8.13 Transitional provisions regarding port and sherry and related trade marks, were contained in Art 9, whereby the Contracting Parties agreed to implement the provisions regarding Port and Sherry referred to in Annex X to the TDC Agreement.

8.14 Article 10 provided that without prejudice to Art 9, the Contracting Parties should take the measures necessary to ensure that, in cases where wines originating in the Contracting Parties are exported and marketed outside their territories, the protected names of one Contracting Party referred to in Art 8 are not used to describe and present a wine originating in the other Contracting Party.

8.15 Article 12.1, dealing with enforcement, required that if the appropriate competent body became aware that the description or presentation of a wine,

---

8   OJ L 28, 30.1.2002, pp. 4–111.

particularly on labels or in official or commercial documents or in advertising, was in breach of this Agreement, the Contracting Parties should apply the necessary administrative measures and/or initiate legal proceedings as appropriate in order to combat unfair competition or to prevent in any other way the improper use of a protected name.

Article 12.2 provided that these measures and proceedings should be taken **8.16** in particular where the translation of descriptions provided for by EC or South African legislation into the language or languages of the other Contracting Party results in the appearance of a word which is liable to be misleading as to the origin, nature or quality of the wine thus described or presented or where packaging or descriptions, trade marks, names, inscriptions or illustrations which directly or indirectly give false or misleading information as to the provenance, origin, nature, vine variety or material qualities of the wine appear on containers or packaging, in advertising, or in official or commercial documents relating to wines whose names are protected under this Agreement.

(c) Switzerland

An Agreement between the European Community and the Swiss Confeder- **8.17** ation on trade in agricultural products[9] contained a Joint Declaration on the protection of geographical indications and designations of origin of agricultural products and foodstuffs. In this Joint Declaration the Parties agreed that the mutual protection of designations of origin (PDOs) and geographical indications (PGIs) was essential for the liberalisation of trade in agricultural products and foodstuffs between the Parties and that mutual protection would be agreed for the protection of the names of wines, spirit drinks and aromatised wine-based drinks.

Annex 7 to the Agreement dealt with the trade in wine sector products. **8.18**

Article 2 provided that the Annex applied only to wine-sector products as **8.19** defined: for the EC in Council Regulation (EEC) No 822/87(1), as last amended by Regulation (EC) No 1627/98(2) and for Switzerland in Chapter 36 of the Ordinance of 1 March 1995 on foodstuffs.

Article 3(a) provided that for the purposes of this Annex 'wine-sector product **8.20** originating in' followed by the name of one of the Parties meant a product

---

9   OJ L 114, 30.4.2002, pp. 132–368.

within the meaning of Art 2, produced in the territory of the said Party from grapes entirely harvested in its territory in accordance with this Annex.

8.21 Article 5.1 obliged the Parties to take all necessary steps to ensure mutual protection of the names referred to in Art 6 and used for the description and presentation of wine-sector products originating in the territory of the Parties. 'Wine sector products' were defined in and to introduce the appropriate legal means to ensure effective protection and prevent GIs and traditional expressions from being used to describe wine-sector products not covered by the indications or descriptions concerned.

8.22 Article 3(b) defined 'geographical indication' as any indication, including designations of origin, within the meaning of Art 22 of the TRIPS Agreement, that is recognised by the laws or regulations of one Party for purposes of describing and presenting a wine-based product within the meaning of Art 2 and originating in its territory; Art 3(c) defined 'traditional expression' as a traditionally used name referring in particular to the method of production or the quality, colour or type of wine-sector products within the meaning of Art 2 that is recognised by the laws and regulations of a Party for the purpose of describing and presenting a product originating in the territory of that Party; Art 5.2 provided that the protected names of the Parties shall be reserved exclusively for the products originating in the Party to which they apply and may be used only under the conditions laid down in the laws and regulations of that Party.

8.23 Article 5.3 provided that the protection as referred to in paras 1 and 2 shall exclude in particular any use of protected names for wine-sector products within the meaning of Art 2 which do not originate in the geographical area in question, even if:

- the actual origin of the product is shown,
- the geographical indication in question is used in translation,
- the name is accompanied by terms such as 'kind', 'type', 'style', 'imitation', 'method' or other expressions of the sort.

8.24 In the case of homonymous geographical indications, Art 5.4 provided that where two indications protected under the Annex were homonymous, protection shall be granted to both of them, provided the consumer is not misled as to the actual origin of the wine-sector products. Also where an indication protected under the Annex was homonymous with the name of a geographical area outside the territory of the Parties, Art 5.4 permitted the latter name to be used to describe and present a wine-sector product in the geographical area to which the name referred, provided it was traditionally and consistently used, its use for that purpose is regulated by the country of origin and consumers are not misled into believing that the wine originated in the territory of the Party concerned.

Article 5.5 provided the same rules for homonymous traditional expressions: **8.25**

Article 5.7 provided that the Parties waived their right to invoke Art 24.4–7 of **8.26**
the TRIPs Agreement in order to refuse to grant protection to a name from the other Party.

Article 5.8 provided that the exclusive protection provided for in Art 5.1–3 **8.27**
would apply to the name 'Champagne', but that for a transitional period of two years from the entry into force of this Annex, such exclusive protection should not prevent the word 'Champagne' from being used to describe and present certain wines originating in the Swiss canton of Vaud, provided that such wines are not marketed in Community territory and that the consumer was not misled as to the real origin of the wine.

Article 6 provided that the names for wine-sector products originating in the **8.28**
EC should be protected:

(a) referring to the Member State in which the product originated;
(b) the specific Community terms appearing in Appendix 2; and
(c) the GIs and traditional expressions appearing in Appendix 2.

As regards wine-sector products originating in Switzerland, Art 6 provided that the following should be protected: (a) the terms 'Suisse', 'Schweiz', 'Svizzera', 'Svizra' and any other name designating that country; (b) the specific Swiss terms appearing in Appendix 2; and (c) the GIs and traditional expressions appearing in Appendix 2.

Appendix 2 provided that protected names for wine-sector products originat- **8.29**
ing in the EC included:

1. Specific EC traditional terms referred to in Article 1 of Council Regulation (EEC) No 823/87(1) of 16 March 1987:[10]

---

10 Laying down provisions relating to quality wines produced in specified regions, as last amended by Regulation (EC) No 1426/96(2).

(i)   the terms 'quality wines produced in specified regions', 'quality wines psr' and the equivalent terms and abbreviations in the other Community languages;

(ii) the terms 'quality sparkling wines produced in specified regions', 'quality sparkling wines psr' and the equivalent terms and abbreviations in the other Community languages, and the terms 'Sekt bestimmter Anbaugebiete' or 'Sekt b.A.';

(iii) the terms 'quality semi-sparkling wines produced in specified regions', 'quality semi-sparkling wines psr' and the equivalent terms and abbreviations in the other Community languages;

(iv) the terms 'quality liqueur wines produced in specified regions', 'quality liqueur wines psr' and the equivalent terms and abbreviations in the other Community languages.

2. The following terms referred to in Council Regulation (EEC) No 4252/88(3) of 21 December 1988:
- 'οίνος φυσικός γλυκύς' ('vin doux naturel')
- 'vino generoso'
- 'vino generoso de licor'
- 'vinho generoso'
- 'vino dulce natural'
- 'vino dolce naturale'
- 'vinho doce natural'
- 'vin doux naturel'.

The term 'Crémant.'

3. A list of GIs and traditional expressions by Member State.

8.30 Article 7.1 provided that the registration of a brand name for a wine-sector product within the meaning of Art 2 which contained or consisted of a GI or a traditional expression protected under this Annex should be refused or, at the request of the Party concerned, invalidated if the product in question did not originate in the place to which the GI referred, or the place where the traditional expression was used.

8.31 Article 8 required the Parties to take all steps necessary to ensure that, where wine-sector products within the meaning of Art 2 originating in the Parties were exported and marketed outside their territory, the names of one Party protected under this Annex were not used to describe and present such products originating in the other Party.

8.32 Article 9 provided that in so far as the relevant legislation of the Parties permitted, the protection afforded by this Annex extended to natural and legal persons, federations, associations and organisations of producers, traders and consumers whose head offices were located in the territory of the other Party.

Where the description or presentation of a wine-sector product on the **8.33** labelling, in official or commercial documents or in advertising, affected the rights arising from this Annex, Art 10.1 required the Parties to apply the necessary administrative measures or the initiation of legal proceedings with a view to combating unfair competition or preventing the wrongful use of the protected name by any other means. Article 10.2 required these measures and proceedings to be taken in the following cases:

(a) where the translation of descriptions sanctioned under Community or Swiss legislation into one of the languages of the other Party gives rise to a word which is liable to be misleading as to the origin of the wine-sector product thus described or presented;

(b) where indications, trade marks, names, references or illustrations which directly or indirectly give false or misleading information as to the provenance, origin, type or material characteristics of the product appear on containers or packaging, in advertising or in official or commercial documents relating to a product whose name is protected under this Annex; and

(c) where the containers or packaging used are misleading as to the origin of the product.

(d) USA

On 23 March 2006, the European Community and the USA entered into an **8.34** agreement on trade in wine.[11] The objectives of the agreement included laying the foundation for a broad agreement on trade in wine between the Parties and providing a framework for continued negotiations in the wine sector.[12]

Article 6.1 provided that with respect to wine that was sold in the territory of **8.35** the USA, the USA would seek to change the legal status of the terms in Annex II to restrict the use of the terms on wine labels solely to wine originating in the Community and that the labels for such wines may use the terms in Annex II in a manner consistent with the US wine labelling regulations in force as of 14 September 2005. Annex II referred to: Burgundy, Chablis, Champagne, Chianti, Claret, Haut Sauterne, Hock, Madeira, Malaga, Marsala, Moselle, Port, Retsina, Rhine, Sauterne, Sherry and Tokay. Article 6.2 excluded wines not originating in the EC. Article 6.4 obliged the USA to take measures to ensure that any wine not labelled in conformity with this Article was not placed on or was to be withdrawn from the market until it was labelled in conformity with this Article.

---

11   L. 87/2 OJ, 24.3.2006.
12   Art 1.

8.36   Article 7.1 required the USA to provide that the names of the wine-producing districts of the Member States of the EC listed in Annex IV, Part A could only be used for wines coming from those places.

8.37   Article 7.2 required the EC to provide that the names of viticultural significance in the USA listed in Annex V could be used as names of origin for wine only to designate wines of the origin indicated by such name.

8.38   Article 7.3 required the competent authorities of both Parties to take measures to ensure that any wine not labelled in conformity with this Article was not placed on or was withdrawn from the market until it is labelled in conformity with this Article.

8.39   Article 7.4 required that in addition to the obligations of paras 1 and 3, the USA was required to continue to recognise as non-generic, the EC wine names of geographical significance listed in Annex IV, Part C.

8.40   Article 8.1 required each Party to provide that labels of wine sold in its territory shall not contain false or misleading information in particular as to character, composition or origin.

2.   Agreements on GIs for spirits

(a)   Mexico

8.41   On 11 June 1996 the EU and Mexico entered into an agreement for the mutual recognition and protection of designations for spirit drinks.[13] Article 4 provides that protected EC names may not be used in Mexico otherwise than under the conditions laid down in EC laws and regulations in return for the recognition of protected Mexican names in the EC. Article 3 defines as protected designations those listed in Annex I regarding spirit drinks originating in the EC and concerning Mexico those listed in Annex II (which lists the Agave spirit drinks, TEQUILA and MEZCAL).

8.42   By exchanges of letters dated 30 April 2004 and 23 November 2004, Annex I to the agreement was amended to take account of the enlargement of the EU.

---

13   https://eur-lex.europa.eu/resource.html?uri=cellar:30da3b97-660b-4c8f-8822-4e0c3cda302c.0004.02/DOC _2&format=PDF, accessed 22 Jan. 2019.

(b)   South Africa

An agreement between the EC and South Africa on the trade in spirits came **8.43** into force on 28 January 2002.[14] Article 5 of the agreement required the parties to provide the appropriate legal means to ensure the effective reciprocal protection of the names referred to in Art 6 used for the identification of spirits originating in the territories of the Contracting Parties.

Article 6.1 provided that the following EC names were protected with regard **8.44** to spirits:

(i)   references to the name of the Member State in which the spirits originated;
(ii)   the GIs referred to in the Annex;
(iii) the specific denominations: Grappa, Ouzo/Oýæï, Korn, Kornbrand, Jägertee, Jagertee, Jagatee and Pacharan.

Article 6 provided that the following South African names were protected with regard to spirits (i) the name .South Africa. or other names used to indicate this country and (ii) the geographical indications referred to in the Annex.

Article 5.2 provided that the protected EC names were exclusively reserved in **8.45** South Africa to the spirits originating in the EC to which they apply, and should not be used otherwise than under the conditions laid down in the laws and regulations of the EC. Similar rules applied *mutatis mutandis* with regard to South African names:

Article 5.3 provided that the protection provided for in this Agreement **8.46** prohibited any use of indications protected by virtue of this Agreement for spirits not originating in the geographical area indicated, even when:

(a)   the true origin of the spirits is indicated;
(b)   the geographical indication is used in translation; and
(c)   the indications are accompanied by expressions such as: kind, type, style, imitation, method or the like.

In the case of homonymous GIs, Art 5.4 provided that: **8.47**

(a)   where such indications protected by virtue of this Agreement are homonymous, protection shall be granted to each indication, provided it has been used traditionally and consistently and the consumer is not misled as to the true origin of the spirits;

---

14   OJ L 28/113, 30.1.2002.

(b) where such indications protected by virtue of this Agreement are homonymous with the name of a geographical area outside the territory of the Parties, the latter name may be used to describe and present spirits produced in the geographical area to which the name refers, provided the name is traditionally and consistently used, its use for that purpose is regulated by the country of origin and consumers are not misled into believing that the spirit originates in the territory of the Party concerned.

8.48 Article 5.5 permitted the Contracting Parties to determine the practical conditions of use under which the homonymous names referred to in para 4 will be differentiated from each other, taking into account the need to ensure equitable treatment of the producers concerned and that consumers are not misled.

8.49 Article 5.6 preserved the right of any person to use, in the course of trade, their name or the name of their predecessor in business, except where such name is used in such a manner as to mislead consumers.

8.50 Article 5.7 provided that nothing in the Agreement obliged a Contracting Party to protect a name of the other Contracting Party which was not or ceased to be protected in its country of origin or which had fallen into disuse in that country.

8.51 Article 8 require the Contracting Parties to take the measures necessary to ensure that, in cases where spirits originating in the Contracting Parties are exported and marketed outside of their territories, the protected names of one Contracting Party referred to in Art 6 are not used to describe and present spirits originating in the other Contracting Party.

(c) Switzerland

8.52 The Agreement between the European Community and the Swiss Confederation on trade in agricultural products[15] in Annex VIII provided for the mutual recognition and protection of names of spirit drinks and aromatised wine-based drinks. Article 2 defines the scope of the Annex as applying to:

(a) spirit drinks as defined: in EC Regulation No 1576/89 and for Switzerland, in Chapter 39 of the Ordinance on foodstuffs, as last amended on 7 December 1998;[16]

---

15   OJ L 114, 30.4.2002, pp. 132–368.
16   RO 1999 303.

(b) aromatised wines, aromatised wine-based drinks and aromatised wine-product cocktails (hereinafter called 'aromatised drinks'), as defined: in EC Regulation No 1601/91 and for Switzerland, in Chapter 36 of the Ordinance on foodstuffs.

The names to be protected under the Agreement were defined in Art 4.1: **8.53**

(i) as regards spirit drinks originating in the EC, the names listed in Appendix 1;
(ii) as regards aromatised drinks originating in the EC, the designations listed in Appendix 3; (iii) as regards the names for protected names for spirit drinks originating in the Switzerland, the designations listed in Appendix 2; and
(iv) for aromatised drinks originating in the Switzerland, the designations listed in Appendix 4.

Article 4.2 provided that under EC Regulation , the names 'marc' and 'grape **8.54** marc spirit' could be replaced by the name 'grappa' for spirit drinks produced in the Italian-speaking parts of Switzerland from grapes from those regions and listed in Appendix 2. Article 5.1 and 5.2 provided that the protected names of each party should be reserved exclusively for the spirit drinks and aromatised drinks originating in their country.

Article 5.3 provided that without prejudice to Arts 22 and 23 of the TRIPS **8.55** Agreement the Parties should take all the necessary measures, in accordance with this Annex, to ensure reciprocal protection of the names referred to in Art 4 and that each Party should provide interested persons with the legal means of preventing the uses of a designation to designate spirit drinks or aromatised drinks not originating in the place indicated by the designation in question or in the place where the designation in question is traditionally used. Article 5.4 required that the Parties not deny the protection provided for by this Article in the circumstances specified in Articles 24.4, 24.5, 24.6 and 24.7 of the TRIPS Agreement.

Article 6 provided that the protection afforded by Art 5 should also apply **8.56** where the actual origin of the spirit drink or aromatised drink was indicated or where the name was used in translation or is accompanied by terms such as 'kind', 'type', 'style', 'way', 'imitation', 'method' or other analogous expressions, including graphic symbols, which might lead to confusion.

In cases of homonymy concerning names of spirit drinks and aromatised **8.57** drinks, Art 7 provided that protection be accorded to each name. This Article permitted the Parties to lay down the practical conditions under which the homonymous names in question were to be differentiated from each other, taking into account the need to treat the producers concerned fairly and to avoid misleading the consumer.

8.58 Article 8 provided that this Annex in no way prejudiced the right of any person to use, for trade purposes, their own name or the name of the person whose business they have taken over, provided that such names were not used in a way that misleads consumers.

8.59 Where a name was not protected or ceased to be protected in its country of origin or which had fallen into disuse in that country, Art 9 provided that nothing in this Annex oblige a Party to protect such name.

8.60 Article 10 required the Parties to take all measures necessary to ensure that, in cases where spirit drinks or aromatised drinks originating in the territory of the Parties were exported and marketed outside their territory, the names of one Party protected under this Annex were not used to designate and present spirit drinks or aromatised drinks originating in the other Party.

8.61 Article 11 extended the protection afforded by the Annex to cover natural and legal persons and federations, associations and organisations of producers, traders and consumers whose head offices were located in the territory of the other Party.

8.62 Article 12 required the Parties to shall apply the necessary administrative measures or to initiate suitable legal proceedings with a view to combating unfair competition or preventing the wrongful use of the protected name in any other way, if the description or presentation of a spirit drink or aromatised drink appeared, in particular on the labelling, in official or commercial documents or in advertising.

8.63 Article 13 exclude from the application of the Annex spirit drinks and aromatised drinks which:

(a) pass in transit through the territory of one of the Parties; or
(b) originate in the territory of one of the Parties and are consigned from one Party to the other in small quantities in the following ways:
   (aa) as part of the personal effects of travellers for their own private consumption;
   (bb) as consignments from one private individual to another for personal consumption;
   (cc) as part of the household effects of individuals moving house or in the event of inheritance;
   (dd) as imports of up to one hectolitre with a view to scientific and technical experiments;

(ee) as imports forming part of the duty-free allowances of diplomatic missions, consular posts and assimilated bodies;

(ff) as part of the supplies carried on board international means of transport.

(d) USA

By an agreement in force since 25 March 1994, the European Community **8.64** (EC) and the USA agreed to the reciprocal recognition of names relating to distilled spirits and spirit drinks.[17] The USA agreed to restrict, within its regulatory framework, the use of the product designations: 'Scotch whisky', 'Irish whiskey'/'Irish whisky', 'Cognac', 'Armagnac', 'Calvados' and 'Brandy de Jerez' to distilled spirits/spirit drinks products of the Member States of the EC, produced in compliance with Council Regulation (EEC) No 1576/89 and with the laws of the Member States in which those products originate.

The EC agreed to restrict, within its regulatory framework (Council Regu- **8.65** lation (EEC) No 1576/89, Article 11 or an equivalent successor regulation), the use of the product designations: 'Tennessee whisky'/'Tennessee whiskey', 'Bourbon whisky'/'Bourbon whiskey' and 'Bourbon' as a designation for Bourbon whisk(e)y to distilled spirits/spirit drinks products of the USA produced in compliance with the laws and regulations of the USA.

The USA and the EC agreed to meet at a mutually convenient time in the **8.66** future to discuss the possibilities of extending restrictive recognition to additional distilled spirits/spirit drinks products which either Party may propose for such consideration.

3. Agreements on GIs in relation to wines and spirits

(a) Albania

On 12 June 2006 the EU concluded an Interim Agreement on trade and **8.67** trade-related matters with Albania, which entered into force on 1 April 2009.[18] Protocol 3 to the Agreement provided for the reciprocal recognition, protection and control of wine, spirit drinks and aromatised wine names and Annex II to Protocol 3 is an agreement to this effect. Articles 4 and 6 of the Agreement provided for the protection of the names of wines, spirit drinks, or aromatised wines originating in the EC, referring to the name of a Member

---

17 Available at https://www.ttb.gov/itd/pdf/us-ec-spirits-agreement.pdf, accessed 3 February 2019.
18 Council Decision 2006/580/EC, available at https://eur-lex.europa.eu/legal-content/en/TXT/?uri=uriserv:OJ.L_.2006.239.01.0001.01.ENG#L_2006239EN.01010601, accessed 22 Jan. 2019.

State and listed in Part A to Appendix 1 to the Agreement. Part A lists several hundred names, arranged by Member State.

8.68 As regards these products originating in Albania, names referring to Albania and listed in Part B to Appendix 1 are to be protected.

8.69 Article 7.1 to this Agreement provided that Albania could not use traditional Community expressions listed in Appendix 2 to this agreement and in Art 7.2 that 'Albania shall provide appropriate legal means to ensure an effective protection and prevent traditional expressions from being used to describe wine not entitled to those traditional expressions, even where the traditional expressions used are accompanied by expressions such as 'kind', 'type', 'style', 'imitation', 'method' or the like.'

8.70 The traditional expressions listed in Appendix 2 include:

Austria: Qualitätswein, Spätlese/Spätlesewein , Strohwein , Heuriger , Schilcher;

France: Appellation d'origine contrôlée, Vin doux naturel, Vin de pays, Château, Claret, Clos, Cru Artisan, Cru Bourgeois, Grand Cru, Premier Cru, Villages;

Germany: quality wines Qualitätswein, Auslese, Eiswein, Spätlese, Affentaler, Hock, Liebfrau(en)milch, Moseltaler, Winzersekt;

Hungary: bikavér, siller;

Italy: Denominazione di Origine Controllata/D.O.C., Inticazione geografica tipica (IGT), Vino Dolce Naturale, Amarone, Brunello, Classico, Falerno, Fior d'Arancio, Lacryma Christi, Morellino, Riserva, Rubino, Vecchio, Vino Fiore, Vino Nobile, Vino Novello or Novello, Vin santo/Vino Santo/Vinsanto;

Portugal: Denominação de origem (DO) Vinho generoso, Colheita Seleccionada, Ruby, Tawny;

Slovakia: mášláš, samorodné, výberová esencia;

Slovenia: Penina, izbor Cviček;

Spain: wines and liquors: Denominacion de origen (DO), Vino dulce natural, Vino generoso, Amontillado, Añejo, Clásico, Fino, Gran Reserva, Noble, Oloroso, Reserva, Sobremadre, Solera.

8.71 These traditional expressions, where they are in the language of the country concerned, could be characterised as indirect GIs.

8.72 Article 8 of the Agreement concerns trade marks and in para 1 requires that the responsible national and regional offices of the Contracting Parties shall refuse the registration of a trade mark for a wine, spirit drink or aromatised wine which is identical with, or similar to, or contains or consists of a reference to a GI protected under Art 4 of the Agreement. Article 2 provides for the refusal of the registration of a trade mark for a wine which contains or consists of a traditional expression protected under this Agreement if the wine in question is not one to which the traditional expression is reserved as indicated in Appendix 2. Finally, Art 8.3 required Albania to adopt the necessary measures to amend the trade marks: Amantia (Grappa) and Gjergj Kastrioti Skenderbeu Konjak so as to fully remove, by 31 December 2007, all reference to Community GIs protected under Art 4 of the Agreement.

(b) Bosnia-Herzegovina

Protocol 6 to an Interim Agreement on Trade and Trade-Related Matters **8.73** between the European Community and Bosnia-Herzegovina, dated 1 July 2008, required wines, spirits and aromatised drinks to be produced in accordance with European Community law.[19] Annex II to Protocol 6 is an Agreement between the EC and Bosnia-Herzegovina on the Reciprocal Recognition, Protection and Control of Wine, Spirit Drinks and Aromatised Wine Names. This provided for the protection of the GIs of the EC in the same terms as the EC-Albania Agreement described above. Article 8 of the Agreement also required Bosnia-Herzegovina to refuse the registration of a trade mark for a wine, spirit drink or aromatised wine which is identical with, or similar to, or contained or consisted of a reference to a GI or traditional expression.

Appendix I to the Agreement listed the names which are protected in both **8.74** countries and Appendix II lists the traditional expressions used in the EC, both Appendices were similar to those in the Agreement with Albania.

(c) Canada

On 6 February 2004, the Community and Canada entered into an Agreement **8.75** on Trade in Wines and Spirit Drinks.[20] Article 10 of the Agreement dealt with the protection of geographical wine names. It provided in Art 10.1 that the names listed in Annex III(a), which identified a wine as originating in the territory of the Community where a quality, reputation or other characteristic of the wine was essentially attributable to its geographical origin 'and was officially recognised and protected as a geographical indication within the meaning of Article 22(1) of the TRIPs Agreement by the applicable laws in the Community, were eligible for registration as protected geographical indications for wine in Canada'. Annex III(a) listed several hundred of European wine GIs arranged according to Member State.

---

19 See https://eur-lex.europa.eu/LexUriServ/LexUriServ.do?uri=OJ:L:2008:169:0013:0807:en:PDF, accessed 22 January 2019.
20 OJ L 35, 6.2.2004, pp. 3–99.

8.76 Article 10.2 provided that a protected GI may not be used to describe or present a wine not originating in the place indicated by the GI in question, 'including translations, whether or not accompanied by expressions such as 'kind', 'type', 'style', 'imitation' or the like', and whether or not the protected GI is accompanied by a reference to the true place of origin.

8.77 Article 10.3 required Canada to take the necessary steps to have the names listed in Annex III(a) to be entered on the list of protected GIs in Canada 'after an application for registration had been made in good and due form'.

8.78 Reciprocally Art 11 provided that the names listed in Annex III(b), which identified a wine as originating in the territory of Canada where a quality, reputation or other characteristic of the wine is essentially attributable to its geographical origin and is officially recognised as a GI within the meaning of Art 22.1 of the TRIPs Agreement by the applicable laws in Canada, are eligible for protection as GIs in the EC.

8.79 Annex III(b) listed: Fraser Valley, Lake Erie North Shore, Niagara Peninsula, Okanagan Valley, Pelee Island, Similkameen Valley and Vancouver Island.

8.80 Article 11.3 provided that after receiving 'an official application by diplomatic note from Canada justifying that the names in paragraph 1 are geographical indications', the EC would take the necessary steps to have the names listed in Annex III(b) protected by the competent authorities responsible for enforcement so that any wines incorrectly presented or described with a protected Canadian GI are not placed on, or are withdrawn from, the market.

8.81 Article 14 dealt with GIs for spirits and provides in Art 14.1 that the names listed in Annex IV(a), which identify a spirit drink as originating in the territory of the EC where a quality, reputation or other characteristic of the spirit drink is essentially attributable to its geographical origin and is officially recognised as a protected GI within the meaning of Art 22.1 of the TRIPS Agreement by the applicable laws in the Community, were eligible for registration as protected GIs for spirit drinks in Canada. Annex IV(a) listed 192 GIs for spirits in 16 categories.

8.82 Article 10.3 requires Canada to take the necessary steps to have the names listed in Annex IV(a) entered on the list of protected GIs in Canada after an application for registration has been made in good and due form.

8.83 Article 15 provides for the protection of GIs for Canadian spirits listed in Annex IV(b) in the same way that Canadian wine GIs were to be protected.

Canadian Rye Whisky and Canadian Whisky were the only spirit GIs listed in Annex IV(b). Article 22 proposed some interim measures until the Agreement was fully implemented.

(d) Chile

An Agreement establishing an association between the EC and Chile came **8.84** into force on 30 December 2002.[21] Article 90 referred to The Agreement on Trade in Wine and the Agreement on Trade in Spirit Drinks and Aromatised Drinks which were attached as Annex V and VI, respectively. Articles 5 and 6 of Annex V provided for the mutual protection of GIs in relation to wines. Article VI defined those GIs, as being listed in Appendix 1 for the EC and Appendix 2 for Chile. Appendix 1 listed the various geographical regions of EC Member States. Appendix 2 listed as the GIs of Chile: Vino Pajarete, Vino Asoleado and the wines of the subregions, zones and areas of the following Viticole Regions Atacama, Coquimbo, Aconcagua and the Regions: Valle Central and Del Sur.

Article 7.1 of the Agreement prohibited the registration of a trade mark for **8.85** wine which was identical with, or similar to, or contained a geographical indication protected under Article 5 and Art 7.2 required the trade marks listed in Appendix VI to be cancelled within 12 years for use on the internal market and five years for use for export from the date of entry into force of the Agreement. These trade marks were: ALGARVES, ALSACIA, ASTI, BADEN, BORGOÑO, BURDEOS, CARMEN, MARGAUX, CARMEN RHIN, CAVA DEL REYNO, CAVA VERGARA, CAVANEGRA, CHAMPAGNE GRANDIER, CHAMPAÑA RABAT, CHAMPAGNE RABAT, CHAMPAÑA GRANDIER, CHAMPAÑA VALDIVIESO, CHAMPENOISE GRANDIER, CHAMPENOISE RABAT, ERRAZ-URIZ PANQUEHUE CORTON, NUEVA, EXTREMADURA, JEREZ R. RABAT, LA RIOJA, MOSELLE, ORO DEL RHIN, PORTOFINO, PORTO FRANCO, PROVENCE, R OPORTO RABAT, RIBEIRO, SAVOIA MARCHETTI, TORO, UVITA DE PLATA BORGOÑA, VIÑA CARMEN MARGAUX, VIÑA MANQUEHUE JEREZ, VIÑA MANQUEHUE OPORTO, VIÑA SAN PEDRO GRAN VINO BURDEOS.

Article 8 requires the Parties to take all necessary steps to ensure the mutual **8.86** protection of the traditional expressions or complementary quality mentions referred to in Art 9 in relation to wine. Article 9 Appendix III List A and List

---

21 http://ec.europa.eu/world/agreements/downloadFile.do?fullText=yes&treatyTransId=879, accessed 22 December 2019.

B identifies the traditional expressions or complementary quality mentions, which are reserved to the EC and Appendix IV List A and List B identifies the traditional expressions and complementary quality mentions as regards wine originating in Chile.

8.87 Article 10 provides that the registration of a trade mark for a wine in a Party which is identical with, or similar to, or contains a traditional expression or a complementary quality mention contained in List A of Appendix III or IV shall be refused.

8.88 Annex VI to the Association Agreement is an Agreement on Trade in Spirit Drinks and Aromatised Drinks. It provides in Art 5 for the mutual recognition of the names referred to in Art 6 and used for describing and presenting spirit drinks and aromatised drinks. Article 6 provides that those names for both the EC and Chile are those listed in Appendix I. Article 7 prohibits the use of those names for trade marks.

8.89 Annex IV to the 2002 Association Agreement was updated by an exchange of letters on 24 April 2006.[22]

(e) Serbia

8.90 The Stabilisation and Association Agreement (SAA) between the EU and Serbia entered into force on 1 September 2013.[23] Article 28 provides that arrangements applicable to the wine and spirit drinks products referred to in Protocol 2 are laid down in that Protocol, Annex II to which is an agreement dealing, inter alia, with the reciprocal recognition, protection and control of wine, spirit drinks and aromatised wine names. Article 4 of this Agreement provides for the protection in Serbia of the EU GIs listed in Appendix 1, Part A and the EU traditional expressions listed in Appendix 2, Part A. It also provides for the protection in the EU of the GIs of wines, spirit drinks or aromatised wines originating in Serbia listed in Appendix 1, Part B and the Serbian the traditional expressions listed in Appendix 2, Part B.

8.91 Article 5 provides for the equivalent reciprocal protection for the GIs and traditional expressions for wines, spirit drinks or aromatised wines of the EU Member States and Serbia and Art 6 requires them to be used in accordance with the rules of the respective parties.

---

22   https://eur-lex.europa.eu/legal-content/EN/TXT/PDF/?uri=CELEX:22006A0224(01)&from=en,   accessed 22 Jan. 2019.
23   OJ L 278, 18.10.2013, pp. 14–471.

Article 6.6 provides that if GIs listed in Appendix 1 are homonymous, **8.92** protection shall be granted to each indication provided that it has been used in good faith. The Parties shall mutually decide the practical conditions of use under which the homonymous GIs will be differentiated from each other, taking into account the need to ensure equitable treatment of the producers concerned and that consumers are not misled.

Article 6.7 provides that if a geographical indication listed in Appendix 1 is **8.93** homonymous with a geographical indication for a third country, Art 23.3 of the TRIPS Agreement applies.

Article 6.8 provides that the provisions of the Agreement in the Annex shall in **8.94** no way prejudice the right of any person to use, in the course of trade, that person's name or the name of that person's predecessor in business, except where such name is used in such a manner as to mislead consumers.

Where a GI of the other Party listed in Appendix 1 which is not or ceases to **8.95** be protected in its country of origin or which has fallen into disuse in that country, Art 6.9 exempts its protection.

On the entry into force of this Agreement, Art 10 provides that the Parties **8.96** shall no longer deem that the protected GIs listed in Appendix 1 are customary in the common language of the Parties as a common name for wines, spirit drinks and aromatised wines as foreseen in Art 24.6 of the TRIPS Agreement.

Article 7 provides the same scheme of protection for the traditional expres- **8.97** sions of both parties listed in Appendix 2.

Article 8 required the responsible offices of the Parties to refuse the registra- **8.98** tion of a trade mark for a wine, spirit drink or aromatised wine which is identical with, or similar to, or contains or consists of a reference to a GI or which contains or consists of a traditional expression protected under the Agreement.

Article 9 required the Parties to take all steps necessary to ensure that, where **8.99** wines, spirit drinks and aromatised wines originating in a Party are exported to a third country, the protected GIs and traditional expressions of the Parties are not used to describe and present products originating in the other Party.

4. GIs for agricultural products and foodstuffs

(a) Iceland

8.100 By an agreement dated 23 March 2017 and which came into effect on 1 May 2018 between the EU and Iceland on the protection of GIs for agricultural products and foodstuffs,[24] the Parties agreed to the reciprocal recognition of their GIs for these products.

8.101 Article 2.1 recited that the EU having examined the legislation of Iceland listed in Part A of Annex I, namely, the Act on the protection of product names as designation of origin, geographical indications or traditional speciality (No 130, 22 December 2014) it concluded that that legislation meets the elements laid down in Part B of Annex I as an appropriate GIs statute. Similarly Art 2.2 provided that Iceland having examined the legislation of the EU listed in Part A of Annex I, namely, Regulation (EU) No 1151/2012 on quality schemes for agricultural products and foodstuffs; Commission Delegated Regulation (EU) No 664/2014 of 18 December 2013 supplementing Regulation (EU) No 1151/2012 and Commission Implementing Regulation (EU) No 668/2014 of 13 June 2014 laying down rules for the application of Regulation (EU) No 1151/2012 of the European Parliament and of the Council on quality schemes for agricultural products and foodstuffs, Iceland concluded that that legislation also met the elements laid down in Part B of Annex I.

8.102 Article 2.3 and 2.4 required both Parties after having completed an opposition procedure in accordance with Part C of Annex I to protect those GIs according to the level of protection laid down in this Agreement.

8.103 Article 3.1 recited the agreement of both Parties to the possibility of adding new GIs, but Art 3.2 provided that a Party shall not be required to protect as a GI a name that conflicts with the name of a plant variety or an animal breed and as a result is likely to mislead consumers as to the true origin of the product.

8.104 The scope of protection of the GIs listed in Annex II, including those added pursuant to Art 3.1, were required by Art 4 to be protected against:

> (a) any direct or indirect commercial use of a protected name for comparable products not compliant with the product specification of the protected name, or if such use exploits the reputation of a GI;

---

24 OJ L 274/3, 24.10.2017.

(b) any misuse, imitation or evocation, even if the true origin of the product is indicated or if the protected name is translated, transcribed, transliterated or accompanied by an expression such as 'style', 'type', 'method', 'as produced in', 'imitation', 'flavour', 'like' or similar;

(c) any other false or misleading indication as to the provenance, origin, nature or essential qualities of the product, on the inner or outer packaging, advertising material or documents relating to the product concerned, and the packing of the product in a container liable to convey a false impression as to its origin;

(d) any other practice liable to mislead the consumer as to the true origin of the product.

Article 4.2 provided that protected GIs shall not become generic in the territories of the Parties. **8.105**

Where GIs are wholly or partly homonymous, Art 4.3 provided that protection shall be granted to each indication if it has been used in good faith and with due regard for local and traditional usage and the actual risk of confusion. The Parties shall mutually decide the practical conditions of use under which the homonymous GIs will be differentiated from each other, taking into account the need to ensure equitable treatment of the producers concerned and that consumers are not misled. A homonymous name which misleads the consumer into believing that products come from another territory shall not be registered even if the name is accurate as far as the actual territory, region or place of origin of the product in question is concerned. **8.106**

Where a Party, in the context of negotiations with a third country, proposes to protect a GI of that third country, and the name is homonymous with a GI of the other Party, Art 4.4 requires that the latter shall be informed and be given the opportunity to comment before the name is protected. **8.107**

Article 4.5 provided that a Party was not obliged to protect a GI of the other Party which is not or ceases to be protected in its country of origin and that the Parties shall notify each other if a GI ceases to be protected in its country of origin. **8.108**

Article 4.6 provided that nothing in this Agreement shall prejudice the right of any person to use, in the course of trade, that person's name or the name of that person's predecessor in business, except where such name is used in such a manner as to mislead the consumers. **8.109**

Article 5.1 provided that a name protected under this Agreement may be used by any operator marketing agricultural products and foodstuffs conforming to the corresponding specification and Art 5.2 provided that once a GI was **8.110** protected under this Agreement, the use of the protected name should not be subject to any registration of users or further charges.

8.111   In relation to trade marks Art 6.1 required the Parties to refuse to register or should invalidate, *ex officio* or at the request of any interested party in conformity with the legislation of each Party, a trade mark that corresponds to any of the situations referred to in Art 4(1) in relation to a protected GI for like products, provided the application to register the trade mark has been submitted after the date of application for registration of the GI in the territory concerned.

8.112   Article 6.2 provided that for GIs referred to in Art 2, the date of application for registration shall be the date of entry into force of this Agreement. Article 6.3 provided that for GIs referred to in Art 3, the date of application for registration shall be the date of the transmission of a request to the other Party to protect a GI.

8.113   Article 6.4 provided that the Parties shall have no obligation to protect a GI pursuant to Art 3 where, in the light of a reputed or well-known trade mark, protection is liable to mislead consumers as to the true identity of the product.

8.114   Where a prior trade mark exists, Art 6.5 provided that it may continue to be used and renewed irrespective of the protection of the GI, provided that no grounds for the trade mark's invalidity or revocation exist in the trade marks legislation of the Parties.

8.115   Article 7 required the authorities of the Parties to appropriately enforce the protection provided for in Arts 4–6 in order to prevent and, where appropriate, stop any unlawful use of the protected GI and that they shall also enforce this protection at the request of an interested party.

(b)   Serbia

8.116   The SAA between the EU and Serbia entered into force on 1 September 2013.[25] Article 33.1 of the SAA obliged Serbia to provide protection for the GIs of the Community registered in the Community under Council Regulation (EC) No 10/2006 of 20 March 2006 on the protection of geographical indications and designations of origin for agricultural products and foodstuffs (although of course this regulation had been replaced by Regulation (EU) No

---

25   OJ L 278, 18.10.2013, pp. 14–471.

1151/2012 on quality schemes for agricultural products and foodstuffs).[26] Article 33.1 also permitted the GIs of Serbia to be eligible for registration in the Community under the conditions set out in that Regulation.

Article 33.2 required Serbia to prohibit any use in its territory of the names **8.117** protected in the Community for comparable products not complying with the GI's specification, even where the true GI of the good was indicated, the GI was used in translation, or the name was accompanied by terms such as 'kind', 'type', 'style', 'imitation', 'method' or other expressions of the sort.

Article 33.3 require Serbia to refuse the registration of a trade mark the use **8.118** of which corresponds to the situations referred to in para 2 and such trade marks which have been registered in Serbia or established by use, were required by Art 33.4 not to be used five years after the entry into force of this Agreement. However, this did not apply to trade marks registered in Serbia and trade marks established by use which are owned by nationals of third countries, provided they were not of such a nature as to deceive in any way the public as to the quality, the specification and the geographical origin of the goods.

Article 33.5 provided that any use of GIs protected in accordance with **8.119** Art.33.1 as terms customary in common language as the common name for such goods in Serbia had to cease at the latest five years after the entry into force of this Agreement. Article 33.6 required that Serbia should ensure that goods exported from its territory five years after the entry into force of this Agreement did not infringe the provisions of this Article. Serbia had to ensure the protection referred to in paragraphs 1 to 6 on its own initiative as well as at the request of an interested party.

5. GIs for wines, spirits and foodstuffs

(a) Armenia

The EU-Armenia Comprehensive and Enhanced Partnership Agreement **8.120** (CEPA) was signed on 24 November 2017 and came into force provisionally in June 2018.

---

26 Ibid.

8.121 Article 230 limited the application of the GIs chapter of the CEPA to GIs originating in the territories of the Parties and were to be protected by the other Party, if they were covered by the scope of the legislation referred to in Art 231.

8.122 Article 231.1 recited that having examined the legislation of the Republic of Armenia listed in Part A of Annex IX,[27] the EU concluded that that legislation met the elements for registration, control and protection of GIs laid down in Part B of that Annex. Reciprocally, Art 231.2 recited that after examination, Armenia concluded that the EU GIs legislation[28] met the elements laid down in Part B of that Annex.

8.123 Article 231.3 and 231.4 reported that the Parties having completed an objection procedure and examined the GIs of each other and listed in Annexes IX and X were to be protected in accordance with the level of protection laid down in this Agreement.

8.124 Article 232.1 permitted the Parties in accordance with the procedure set out in Art 240.3 to add new GIs to the list of protected GIs set out in Annex X, after the objection procedure has been completed and the new GIs have been examined to the satisfaction of each Party, in accordance with Art 231.3 and 231.4.

8.125 Article 232.2 provided that Parties had no obligation to add a new GI to the list referred to in the previous paragraph where:

    (a)   it would conflict with the name of a plant variety or an animal breed and as a result would be likely to mislead consumers as to the true origin of the product;

    (b)   in the light of a reputed or well-known trade mark, protection of that GI would be likely to mislead consumers as to the true identity of the product; or

    (c)   the name of the term is generic.

---

27   Law of RA on 'Geographical Indications', HO-60-N adopted on 29.04.2010, entered into force on 01.07.2010; Civil Code of RA, arts 11-791183; Rules on 'Filling out, filing and processing an application of Geographical indications, Designation of origin and Guaranteed traditional products', confirmed by decision 310 –N of the Government of RA on 10.03.2011.

28   (1)   Regulation (EU) No 1151/2012 of the European Parliament and of the Council of 21 November 2012 on quality schemes for agricultural products and foodstuffs, with its implementing rules;

     (2)   Regulation (EC) No 110/2008 of the European Parliament and of the Council of 15 January 2008 on the definition, description, presentation, labelling and the protection of geographical indications of spirit drinks and repealing Council Regulation (EEC) No 1576/89, with its implementing rules;

     (3)   Regulation (EU) No 1308/2013 of the European Parliament and of the Council of 17 December 2013 establishing a common organisation of the markets in agricultural products;

     (4)   Regulation (EU) No 251/2014 of the European Parliament and of the Council of 26 February 2014 on the definition, description, presentation, labelling and the protection of geographical indications of aromatised wine products and repealing Council Regulation (EEC) No 1601/91.

The scope of protection of GIs was set out in Art 233. Paragraph 1 provided **8.126** that the GIs listed in Annex X should be protected by each Party against:

(a) any direct or indirect commercial use of a protected name for comparable products not compliant with the product specification of the protected name, or in so far as such use exploits the reputation of a geographical indication;

(b) any misuse, imitation or evocation, even if the true origin of the product is indicated or if the protected name is translated, transcribed, transliterated or accompanied by an expression such as 'style', 'type', 'method', 'as produced in', 'imitation', 'flavour', 'like' or similar;

(c) any other false or misleading indication as to the provenance, origin, nature or essential qualities of the product which is likely to convey a false impression as to its origin, placed on the inner or outer packaging, in advertising material or documents relating to the product concerned, or on the packing of the product in a container; and

(d) any other practice likely to mislead the consumer as to the true origin of the product.

Article 233.2 provided that protected GIs shall not become generic in the territories of the Parties.

Where GIs are wholly or partially homonymous, Art 233.3 provided that **8.127** protection shall be granted to each such GI, provided that it has been used in good faith and with due regard for local and traditional usage as well as for the actual risk of confusion. Article 233.3 provided that without prejudice to Art 23 of the TRIPS Agreement, the Parties shall mutually decide the practical conditions of use under which homonymous GIs will be differentiated from each other, taking into account the need to ensure equitable treatment of the producers concerned and that consumers are not misled. Finally, Art 233.3 provided that a homonymous name which misleads consumers into believing that a product comes from another territory shall not be registered even if the name is accurate as far as the actual territory, region or place of origin of the product in question is concerned.

Where a Party, in the context of negotiations with a third country, proposes to **8.128** protect a GI of a third country which is homonymous with a GI of the other Party Art 233.4 provided that the latter shall be informed and be given an opportunity to comment before the third party's GI becomes protected.

Article 233.5 provided that neither Party was obliged to protect a GI of the **8.129** other Party which is not, or ceases to be, protected in its country of origin and that each Party shall notify the other Party if a GI ceases to be protected in its country of origin.

8.130 Article 233.6 provided that nothing in this Agreement shall prejudice the right of any person to use, in the course of trade, that person's name or the name of that person's predecessor in business, except where such name is used in such a manner as to mislead consumers.

8.131 The right of use of GIs was conferred by Art 234.1 upon any operator marketing agriculture products, foodstuffs, wines, aromatised wines or spirit drinks conforming to the corresponding specification. Article 234.2 provided that once a GI was protected under this subsection, the use of such protected name shall not be subject to any registration of users, or further charges.

8.132 Article 235.1 provided that a Party shall refuse to register or shall invalidate a trade mark that corresponds to any of the situations referred to in Art 233.1 in relation to a protected GI for like products, provided that an application to register that trade mark is submitted after the date of application for protection of the GI in the territory concerned.

8.133 Article 235.2 provided that for GIs referred to in Art 231, the date of application for protection shall be the date of entry into force of this Agreement, but for GIs referred to in Art 232, the date of application for protection was provided by Art 235.3 to be the date of the transmission to the other Party of a request to protect a GI.

8.134 Article 235.4 required each Party to protect the GIs listed in Annex X where a prior trade mark existed. By way of derogation from this paragraph, Art 235.5 provided that prior trade marks of the Republic of Armenia which consisted of or contained the EU GIs 'Cognac' or 'Champagne', including in transcription or translation, registered for like products and not complying with the relevant specification, be invalidated, revoked or modified in order to eliminate that name as an element of the whole trade mark, at the latest within 14 years for 'Cognac' and two years for 'Champagne', following the entry into force of this Agreement.

8.135 Article 236 required each Party to enforce the protection of GIs in accordance with Arts 233–235 through appropriate administrative action by its public authorities and that each Party should also enforce such protection at the request of an interested person.

8.136 Article 237.1 permitted goods which were produced and labelled in conformity with domestic law before the entry into force of this Agreement, but which do not comply with its requirements, to continue to be sold after the entry into force of the Agreement until their stocks run out.

Article 237.2 provided that for a transitional period of 24 years to count as of **8.137**
one year after the entry into force of this Agreement for 'Cognac' and for a
transitional period of three years after the entry into force of this Agreement
for 'Champagne', the protection pursuant to this Agreement of those GIs
should not preclude those names from being used on products originating in
the Republic of Armenia and exported to third countries, where the laws and
regulations of the third country concerned so permit, in order to designate and
present certain comparable products originating in the Republic of Armenia,
provided that:

(a)   the name is labelled exclusively in non-Latin characters;
(b)   the true origin of the product is clearly labelled in the same field of vision; and
(c)   nothing in the presentation is likely to mislead the public as to the true origin of
       the product.

Article 237.3 provide that for a transitional period of 13 years to count as of **8.138**
one year after the entry into force of this Agreement for 'Cognac', and for a
transitional period of two years after the entry into force of this Agreement for
'Champagne', the protection pursuant to this Agreement of those GIs shall
not preclude those names from being used in the Republic of Armenia on the
same proviso as the previous paragraph.

Article 237.4 provided that for the purposes of facilitating the smooth and **8.139**
effective termination of the use of the GI 'Cognac' for products originating in
the Republic of Armenia, as well as assisting the industry of the Republic of
Armenia in maintaining its competitive position in export markets, the EU
would provide to the Republic of Armenia technical and financial assistance,
including actions for developing a new name and promoting, advertising and
marketing the new name in domestic and traditional export markets. Article
237.7 provided that this financial and technical assistance should be provided
not later than eight years after the date of the entry into force of this
Agreement.

(b)   Columbia and Peru

A Trade Agreement between the EU and Colombia and Peru[29] came into **8.140**
force in Peru on 12 March 2013 and in Colombia on 1 August 2013. Article
207(c) of the Agreement required each Party to protect geographical
indications for agricultural and foodstuff products, wines, spirit drinks and
aromatised wines listed in Appendix 1 of Annex XIII.[30] Article 207(d)

---

29   http://trade.ec.europa eu/doclib/docs/2011/march/tradoc_147704.pdf, accessed 22 Jan 2019.
30   See http://trade.ec.europa.eu/doclib/docs/2011/march/tradoc_147725.pdf, accessed 22 Jan 2019.

provided for the protection of GIs for GUACAMAYAS for Handicrafts and CHULUCANAS for Pottery listed in Appendix 1 of Annex XIII.

8.141 Article 208 provided for the mutual recognition of those GIs and Art 209 provided for the addition of new GIs. Article 210 required the parties to protect the GIs listed in Appendix 1 of Annex XIII against unauthorised use. Article 211 prohibited the registration of protected GIs as trade marks.

(c) Georgia

8.142 On 12 March 2013 an Agreement between the EU and Georgia on the mutual protection of GIs of agricultural products and foodstuffs[31] came into force. On 27 June 2014 the European Union and Georgia signed an Association Agreement (AA), including a Deep and Comprehensive Free Trade Area (DCFTA).[32] Following the completion of the ratification process, the AA entered into force on 1 July 2016 after being applied on a provisional basis since 1 September 2014.[33] Since the provisional application of the DCFTA, updates have been introduced in the AA annexes containing: List of EU agricultural products and foodstuffs other than wine and spirits to be protected in Georgia (Annex XVII-C) and List of spirit drinks of the EU to be protected in Georgia (part B of Annex XVII-D).[34]

(d) Moldova

8.143 On 27 June 2014 the EU and the Republic of Moldova signed an AA with a DCFTA as an integral part.[35] The AA entered into force on 1 July 2016.[36] Article 297 to the Agreement provides for the reciprocal protection in the EU and Moldova of the GIs for agricultural products and foodstuffs listed in Annex XXX-C and the GIs for wines, aromatised wines and spirit drinks

---

31 https://eur-lex.europa.eu/legal-content/en/TXT/?uri=uriserv:OJ.L_.2012.093.01.0001.01.ENG#L_2012093 EN.01000301, accessed 22 Jan. 2019.

32 The EU-Georgia Association Agreement was published in OJ L 261, 30.08.2014, available at. http://eur-lex.europa.eu/legal-content/EN/TXT/PDF/?uri=OJ:L:2014:261:FULL&from=EN, accessed 3 Feb 2019.

33 The European Commission has noted that the application of the DCFTA to the breakaway regions Abkhazia and South-Ossetia, will require *de facto* government control over those territories which is not the case at present. European Commission, Country reports and info sheets on implementation of EU Free Trade Agreements, SWD(2017) 364 final, available at https://eur-lex.europa.eu/legal-content/EN/TXT/PDF/?uri= CELEX:52017SC0364&from=MT, accessed 3 Feb 2019 at n.2.

34 OJ L 335, 9.12.2016.

35 Published in OJ L 260, 30.08.2014. http://eur-lex.europa.eu/legal-content/EN/TXT/PDF/?uri=OJ:L: 2014:260:FULL&from=EN, accessed 3 Feb 2019.

36 In November 2015, Moldova announced that the conditions had been fulfilled for DCFTA application on the entirety of its internationally recognised territory, on this basis allowing to keep the EU market open to goods from the breakaway region Transnistria. European Commission, Country reports and info sheets on implementation of EU Free Trade Agreements, SWD(2017) 364 final, available at https://eur-lex.europa.eu/legal-content/EN/TXT/PDF/?uri= CELEX:52017SC0364&from=MT, accessed 3 Feb 2019 at 14.

listed in Annex XXX-D. Article 298 provided for the addition of new GIs. Article 299.1 detailed the scope of protection of the GIs as prohibiting any direct or indirect commercial use of a protected name, or any misuse, imitation or evocation, 'even if the true origin of the product is indicated or if the protected name is translated, transcribed, transliterated or accompanied by an expression such as 'style', 'type', 'method', 'as produced in', 'imitation', 'flavour', 'like' or similar', or any false or misleading indication as to the provenance, origin, nature or essential qualities of a product, or any other practice liable to convey a false impression as to the origin of a product. Article 299.2 required the refusal of the registration as a trade mark a homonymous name which misleads the consumer into believing that products come from another territory, even if the name is accurate as far as the actual territory, region or place of origin of the product in question is concerned.

Annexes XXX-C and XXX-D were supplemented in September 2014.[37] **8.144** Further amendments to these two annexes were made by the Third Geographical Indications (GIs) Sub-Committee, which met on 18 October 2016. Also, at that meeting it was agreed that the Moldovan authorities should undertake necessary actions in order to ensure the protection of the EU wine GI *Prosseco*.[38]

(e) Montenegro

A Stabilisation and Association Agreement (SSA) between the EC and **8.145** Montenegro, dated 29 March 2010, provided in Art 33 1 that Montenegro should provide protection for the GIs of the EC 'registered in the Community under Council Regulation (EC) No 510/2006 of 20 March 2006 on the protection of geographical indications and designations of origin for agricultural products and foodstuffs'. It also provided that the GIs of Montenegro 'shall be eligible for registration in the Community under the conditions set out in that Regulation'. It should be noted that Regulation 510/2006 was repealed by Art 58 of Regulation 1151/2012, but Art 58.2 provided that references to the repealed Regulation should be construed as references to Regulation 1151/20122.

The SSA provided in Art 33.2 that Montenegro should prohibit any use in its **8.146** territory of the names protected in the EC for comparable products not

---

37 Decision No 1/2016 of the EU-Republic of Moldova Geographical Indications Sub-Committee amending Annexes XXX-C and XXX-D to the AA, OJ L 335, 9.12.2016.

38 European Commission, Country reports and info sheets on implementation of EU Free Trade Agreements, SWD(2017) 364 final, available at https://eur-lex.europa.eu/legal-content/EN/TXT/PDF/?uri=CELEX: 52017SC0364&from=MT, accessed 3 Feb 2019 at 26.

complying with the GI's specification, even where the true geographical origin of the good is indicated. Articles 33.3 and 33.4 required the refusal of the registration and use of trade marks in situations described by Art 33.2.

8.147 Article 33.6 required Montenegro to ensure that goods exported from its territory after 1 January 2009 did not infringe the provisions of this Article.

8.148 Annex II to the SSA was an *Agreement between the EC and Montenegro on the reciprocal recognition, protection and control of wine, spirit drinks and aromatised wine names*,[39] Arts 4 and 6 of that Agreement provided for the protection of EC names listed in Appendix 1 Part A and traditional expressions listed in Appendix 1 Part B. As regards wines, spirit drinks or aromatised wines originating in Montenegro, Art 4 provided for the protection of names which referred to Montenegro and the GIs listed in Appendix I Part B. Article 5 provided for the reciprocal protection of the names for wines, spirit drinks or aromatised wines in Montenegro and the EC.

8.149 In the case of homonymous GIs listed in Appendix 1, Art 6 permitted their use if in good faith.

8.150 Article 6.8 provided that the provisions of this Agreement did not prejudice the right of any person to use, in the course of trade, that person's name or the name of that person's predecessor in business, except where such name was used in such a manner as to mislead consumers.

8.151 Article 6.9 provided that nothing in this Agreement would oblige a Party to protect a GI of the other Party listed in Appendix 1 which ceased to be protected in its country of origin or which had fallen into disuse in that country.

8.152 Article 6.10 provided that on the entry into force of this Agreement, the Parties shall no longer deem that the protected GIs listed in Appendix 1 were customary in the common language of the Parties as a common name for wines, spirit drinks and aromatised wines as foreseen in Art 24.6 of the TRIPS Agreement.

8.153 Article 7 forbade the use in Montenegro, the traditional expressions for the EC listed in Appendix 2 and that Montenegro had to provide appropriate

---

39 Available at https://eur-lex.europa.eu/legal-content/en/TXT/?uri=uriserv:OJ.L_.2010.108.01.0001.01.ENG #L_2010108EN.01000301, accessed 2 Feb 2019.

legal means to ensure an effective protection and prevent traditional expressions from being used to describe wine not entitled to those traditional expressions, even where the traditional expressions used are accompanied by expressions such as 'kind', 'type', 'style', 'imitation', 'method' or the like.

Article 8 required the responsible offices of the Parties to refuse the registration of a trade mark for a wine, spirit drink or aromatised wine which was identical with, or similar to, or contains or consists of a reference to a GI protected under Art 4 of this Agreement not having this origin and of a trade mark for a wine which contains or consists of a traditional expression protected under this Agreement if the wine in question is not one to which the traditional expression is reserved as indicated in Appendix 2. **8.154**

Article 8.3 required Montenegro to remove all reference to EC GIs protected under Art 4 in registered trade marks before 31 December 2008. **8.155**

(f) Ukraine

An AA was signed between the EU and its Member States and Ukraine[40] on 25 May 2014, but its ratification remains pending. On 1 January 2016 both Parties have started to implement a DCFTA on a provisional basis, as the main economic pillar of the AA. Chapter 9 of the AA dealt with intellectual property. Article 202 recited that the Ukrainian and EU legislation listed in Annex XXII-A Part A to the Agreement, met the reciprocal obligations of the parties to recognise and protect the GIs of each other and that Ukraine would protect the EU GIs for the agricultural products and foodstuffs listed in Annex XXII-C and the EU GIs for wines, aromatised wines and spirit drinks listed in Annex XXII-D to this Agreement. The EU agreed that it would protect the GIs for the wines, aromatised wines and spirit drinks of Ukraine listed in Annex XXII-D. In the case of both parties this recognition was subject to any oppositions raised under the procedure set out in Annex XXII-B. **8.156**

The addition of new GIs was provided for by Article 203.1. **8.157**

Article 203.2 provided that a Party shall not be required to protect as a GI a name that conflicts with the name of a plant variety or an animal breed and as a result is likely to mislead the consumer as to the true origin of the product. **8.158**

---

40   OJ L 161, 29.5.2014, pp. 3–2137.

8.159 The scope of protection of geographical indications was set out in Art 204, providing that the GIs listed in Annexes XXII-C and XXII-D, including those added pursuant to Art 203, shall be protected against:

(a) any direct or indirect commercial use of a protected name for comparable products not compliant with the product specification of the protected name, or in so far as such use exploits the reputation of a geographical indication;

(b) 'any misuse, imitation or evocation, even if the true origin of the product is indicated or if the protected name is translated, transcripted, transliterated or accompanied by an expression such as 'style', 'type', 'method', 'as produced in', 'imitation', 'flavour', 'like', or similar';

(c) any other false or misleading indication as to the provenance, origin, nature or essential qualities of the product, on the inner or outer packaging, in advertising material or documents relating to the product concerned, and on the packing of the product in a container liable to convey a false impression as to its origin; or

(d) any other practice liable to mislead a consumer as to the true origin of the product.

8.160 Article 204.3 provides that if GIs are wholly or partially homonymous, protection shall be granted to each indication provided that it has been used in good faith and with due regard for local and traditional usage and the actual risk of confusion, without prejudice to Art 23 of the TRIPS Agreement, Art 204.3 provided that the Parties shall mutually decide the practical conditions of use under which the homonymous GIs will be differentiated from each other, taking into account the need to ensure equitable treatment of the producers concerned and that consumers are not misled. A homonymous name which misleads the consumer into believing that products come from another territory shall not be registered even if the name is accurate as far as the actual territory, region or place of origin of the product in question is concerned.

8.161 Article 204.4 provided that where a Party, in the context of negotiations with a third country, proposes to protect a GI of the third country, and the name is homonymous with a GI of the other Party the latter shall be informed and be given the opportunity to comment before the name is protected.

8.162 Article 204.5 provided that the Parties were not obliged to protect a GI of the other Party which is not or ceases to be protected in its country of origin and that in accordance with Art 211.3, the Parties shall notify each other if a GI ceases to be protected in its country of origin.

8.163 Finally, Art 204.6 provided that nothing in this Agreement shall prejudice the right of any person to use, in the course of trade, that person's name or the name of that person's predecessor in business, except where such name is used in such a manner as to mislead the public.

The right of use of GIs was set out in in Art 211(3), which provide that the **8.164** commercial use of a name protected under this Agreement for agricultural products, foodstuffs, wines, aromatised wines or spirit drinks conforming to the corresponding specification was open to any entity and that once a GI was protected under this Agreement, the use of such protected name shall not be subject to any registration of users or further charges.

Article 206 dealt with the relationship between GIs and trade marks. Article **8.165** 206.1 provided that the Parties shall refuse to register or shall invalidate a trade mark that corresponds to any of the situations referred to in Art 204(1) in relation to a protected GI, for like products, provided an application to register the trade mark is submitted after the date of application for registration of the GI in the territory concerned.

For GIs referred to in Art 202, Art 206.2 provided that the date of application **8.166** for registration shall be the date of entry into force of this Agreement and for GIs referred to in Art 203.3 provided that the date of application for registration shall be the date of the transmission of a request to the other Party to protect a GI.

Article 206.4 provided that the Parties had no obligation to protect a GI **8.167** pursuant to Art 203 where in the light of a reputed or well-known trade mark, protection is liable to mislead consumers as to the true identity of the product.

Article 206.5 provided that without prejudice to Art 206.4, the Parties shall **8.168** protect GIs also where a prior trade mark exists, ie which has been applied for, registered or established by use, if that possibility is provided for by the legislation concerned, in the territory of one of the Parties before the date on which the application for protection of the GI is submitted by the other Party under this Agreement. Such a trade mark may continue to be used and renewed notwithstanding the protection of the GI, provided that no grounds for the trade mark's invalidity or revocation exist in the legislation on trade marks of the Parties.

Border protection of GIs, pursuant to Arts 204–206, was provided for by Art 207.

The run out of stocks of products which were produced and labelled in **8.169** conformity with national law before this Agreement entered into force but which did not comply with the requirements of this Agreement was permitted by Art 208.1.

8.170 Article 208.3 provided that for a transitional period of ten years from the entry into force of this Agreement, the protection pursuant to this Agreement of the following EU GIs should not preclude their use to designate and present certain comparable products originating in Ukraine: Champagne, Cognac, Madeira, Porto, Jerez/Xérès/Sherry, Calvados, Grappa, Anis Português, Armagnac, Marsala, Malaga, Tokaj.

8.171 Article 208.4 provided that for a transitional period of seven years from the entry into force of this Agreement, the following GIs could be used in order to designate and present certain comparable products originating in Ukraine: Parmigiano Reggiano, Roquefort, Feta.

8.172 Article 209.3 provided that the registration of GIs protected under this Agreement could only be cancelled by the Party in which the product originated.

8.173 Article 211 provided for the establishment of a Sub-Committee on Geographical Indications among its functions was the amendment or modification of the Annexes to the Agreement.

8.174 The first meeting of the Sub-Committee on Geographical Indications (GIs) took place on 18 May 2017 in Kyiv at which both sides exchanged lists of new GIs for the purpose of considering their protection under the Agreement.

C. FREE TRADE AGREEMENTS

1. Africa

8.175 The EU-Morocco Association Agreement was signed in February 1996 and entered into force in March 2000. The two sides subsequently negotiated an additional protocol setting up a dispute settlement mechanism, which entered into force in November 2012, and an agreement on further liberalisation of trade in agricultural products which entered into force in October 2012.

2. Asia

8.176 In 2016 the EU and China negotiators reached clear conclusions on an ambitious and comprehensive scope for an EU-China investment agreement and established a joint negotiating text. The 18th round of negotiations took place in Brussels from 12 to 13 July 2018.

Negotiations between the EU and a number of ASEAN Member States **8.177** commenced in June 2007. To date Singapore[41] and Vietnam[42] have agreed to recognise EU GIs, reciprocally with their own. Each FTA has annexed a list of the GIs of both signatories to be protected.

The EU commenced trade and investment negotiations with Malaysia, **8.178** prefatory to an FTA, in September 2010. After seven rounds, these negotiations were put on hold in April 2012 at the request of Malaysia. In 2016, a stocktaking exercise was initiated to assess the prospect to resume negotiations. In February 2013 negotiations on an FTA with Thailand commenced in February 2013. However, these have been stalled by the military takeover in Thailand in May 2014 and no further FTA rounds have been scheduled. Negotiations for an FTA with Indonesia commenced in September 2016. The latest round of negotiations took place during the week of 15 October in Indonesia. Trade and investment negotiations with the Philippines were launched in December 2015. Technical discussions were held during 2016 and 2017 and are set to resume.

3. Latin America

(a) Mercosur

Negotiations rounds were resumed in 2016 after an exchange of market access **8.179** offers took place in May 2016. A first round was held in Brussels in October 2016, followed by rounds alternatively in Mercosur and Brussels.

(b) Mexico

The EU and Mexico met in Brussels in June 2016 to start the negotiation **8.180** process for the modernisation of the EU-Mexico Global Agreement. The third negotiating round, which took place in Brussels in April 2017, was preceded by the exchange of textual proposals in almost every chapter. The last round of negotiations took place in Mexico City from 12 to 16 February 2018.

---

41 EU-Singapore FTA, 29 June 2015. Discussed in Leong, 2017, 235–56.
42 EU-Vietnam FTA, 20 January 2016.

(c) Chile

8.181 The first round of negotiations took place on 16 November 2017 in Brussels. The second one in Santiago de Chile on in January 2018. The last round took place in Brussels in May 2018.

D. FOREIGN GIS REGISTERED IN THE EU

1. Foodstuffs

8.182 The EU GIs regulations provide for the recognition of non-EU GIs in Europe. Thus, for example, Recital (27) of Regulation 1151/2012 on quality schemes for agricultural products and foodstuffs states that:

> The Union negotiates international agreements, including those concerning the protection of designations of origin and geographical indications, with its trade partners. In order to facilitate the provision to the public of information about the names so protected, and in particular to ensure protection and control of the use to which those names are put, the names may be entered in the register of protected designations of origin and protected geographical indications. Unless specifically identified as designations of origin in such international agreements, the names should be entered in the register as protected geographical indications.

8.183 Article 11 of Regulation 1151/2012, which establishes a Register of protected designations of origin and protected geographical indications, provides in para 2 that:

> Geographical indications pertaining to products of third countries that are protected in the Union under an international agreement to which the Union is a contracting party may be entered in the register. Unless specifically identified in the said agreement as protected designations of origin under this Regulation, such names shall be entered in the register as protected geographical indications.

8.184 Foodstuffs of third countries for which registrations have been obtained or applied for in the EU are set out in Tables 8.1–8.4 below.

Table 8.1   Protected geographical indications

No	Country	Indication	Product	Status
KH/PGI/0005/0215	Cambodia	*Skor Thnot Kampong Speu*	Palm sugar	Published
ID/PGI/0005/02115	Indonesia	Kopi Arabika Gayo	Coffee	Registered

No	Country	Indication	Product	Status
TR/PGI/0005/2310	Turkey	Kayseri Mantısı	Ravioli	Applied
TR/PGI/0005/2311	Turkey	Kayseri Pastırması	Bacon	Applied
TR/PGI/0005/2312	Turkey	Kayseri Sucuğu	Sausage	Applied
LK/PGI/0005/02298	Sri Lanka	Ceylon cinnamon	Cinnamon	Applied
TH/PGI/0005/01115	Thailand	Khao Sangyod Muang Phatthalung	Rice	Registered
MN/PGI/0005/02143	Mongolia	Uvs Seabuckthorn	Berry	Applied
KH/PGI/0005/01263	Cambodia	(Mrech Kampot) 'Poivre de Kampot'	Pepper	Registered
TH/PGI/0005/00814	Thailand	Kafae Doi Tung	Coffee	Registered
TH/PGI/0005/00815	Thailand	Kafae Doi Chaang	Coffee	Registered
TR/PGI/0005/01260	Turkey	İnegöl Köfte	Coffee	Applied
TR/PGI/0005/0781	Turkey	Antep Baklavası/ Gaziantep Baklavası	Pastry	Registered
TH/PGI/0005/00729	Thailand	Khao Hom Mali Thung Kula Rong-Hai	Rice	Registered
CN/PGI/0005/0624	China	Dongshan Bai Lu Sun	Asparagus	Registered
CN/PGI/0005/0625	China	Yancheng Long Xia	Lobster	Registered
TR/PGI/0005/01029	Turkey	Afyon Sucuğu	Sausage	Applied
TR/PGI/0005/01030	Turkey	Afyon Pastırması	Cured Meat	Applied
CN/PGI/0005/0630	China	Zhenjiang Xiang Cu	Vinegar	Registered
CN/PGI/0005/0622	China	Jinxiang Da Suan	Garlic	Registered
IN/PGI/0005/0659	India	Darjeeling	Tea	Registered
MA/PGI/0005/00906	Morocco	Argane	Oil	Applied
CN/PGI/0005/0627	China	Lixian Ma Shan Yao	Sweet Potato	Registered
IN/PGI/0005/0672	India	Kangra Tea	Tea	Applied
CO/PGI/0005/0467	Colombia	Café de Colombia	Coffee	Registered
TT/PGI/0005/02442	Trinidad and Tobago	Trinidad Montserrat Hills Cocoa	Cocoa	Applied
TR/PGI/0005/02404	Turkey	Antep Lahmacunu	Pizza	Applied
IN/PGI/0005/2425	India	Basmati	Rice	Applied
TR/PGI/0005/02451	Turkey	Antakya Künefesi	Pastry	Applied

Source: http://ec.europa.eu/agriculture/quality/door/list.html?&recordStart=256, accessed 12 April 2018.

Table 8.2   Protected designations of origin

No	Country	Indication	Product	Status
TR/PDO//0005/02379	Turkey	Milas Zeytinyaği	Olive Oil	Applied
TR/PDO/0005/01221	Turkey	Malatya Kayısısı	Apricots	Registered
TR/PDO/0005/02217	Turkey	Taşköprü Sarımsağı	Garlic	Applied
DO/PDO/0005/01197	Dominican Republic	Café de Valdesia	Coffee	Registered
TR/PDO/0005/01116	Turkey	Aydın İnciri	Figs	Registered
TR/PDO/0005/01362	Turkey	Aydın Kestanesi	Chestnuts	Applied
CN/PDO/0005/0628	China	Pinggu Da Tao	Peach	Registered
VN/PDO/0005/0788	Viet Nam	Phú Quốc	Fish Sauce	Registered
BR/PDO/0005/00991	Brazil	Camarão da Costa Negra	Shrimps	Applied
CN/PDO/0005/0621	China	Longjing cha	Tea	Registered
CN/PDO/0005/0626	China	Guanxi Mi You	Pomelo	Registered
CN/PDO/0005/0629	China	Shaanxi ping guo	Apples	Registered
ZA/PDO/0005/02427	South Africa	Rooibos-Redbush	Tea	Applied
TR/PDO/0005/02398	Turkey	Edremit Körfezi Yeşil Çizik Zeytini	Olives	Applied
TR/PDO/0005/02391	Turkey	Bayramiç Beyazı	Nectarine	Applied
AM/PDO/0005/02164	Armenia	Sevani Ishkhan/ Sevan Trout	Fish	Applied
TR/PDO/0005/02419	Turkey	Giresun Tombul Fındığı	Hazelnut	Applied
TR/PDO/0005/02318	Turkey	Antepfıstığı/ Antep fıstığı	Pistachio	Applied

Source: http://ec.europa.eu/agriculture/quality/door/list.html?&recordStart=256, accessed 12 April 2018.

2. Wines

Table 8.3   Geographical indications registered pursuant to bilateral agreements

Australia

Adelaide Hills Piccadilly Valley	Great Southern-Frankland River	Mudgee	Swan Hill
Adelaide Hills Lenswood		Great Southern-Mount Barker	Tumbarumba
Adelaide Plains	Great Southern-Mount Barker	Murray Darling	Upper Goulburn

Alpine Valleys	Great Southern-Porongorup	Orange	Wrattonbully
Barossa Valley	Gundagai	Padthaway	Yarra Valley
Beechworth	Hastings River	Peel	New South Wales-Northern Slopes
Bendigo	Heathcote	Pemberton	New South Wales – Western Plains
Blackwood Valley	Henty	Perricoota	South Australia – Adelaide
Canberra District	Hilltops	Perth Hills	South Eastern Australia
Clare Valley	Hunter	Pyrenees	South Australia – The Peninsulas
Coonawarra	Kangaroo Island	Riverina	Tasmania Victoria – Gippsland
Cowra	King Valley	Riverland	Northern Territory
Currency Creek	Langhorne Creek	Robe	Western Australia – Central Western Australia
Eden Valley High Eden	Macedon Ranges	Rutherglen	Western Australia – Eastern Plains, Inland and North of Western Australia
Geelong	Manjimup	Shoalhaven Coast	Western Australia – West Australian South East Coastal
Geographe	Margaret River	South Burnett	Australian Capital Territory
Glenrowan	McLaren Vale	Southern Fleurieu	Tumbarumba
Goulburn Valley	Mornington Peninsula	Southern Flinders Ranges	Upper Goulburn
Grampians	Mount Benson	Southern Highland	Wrattonbully
Granite Belt	Great Southern-Frankland River	Strathbogie Ranges	Yarra Valley
Great Southern-Denmark	Great Southern-Mount Barker	Swan District	New South Wales-Northern Slopes
			New South Wales – Western Plains

Albania

Berat	Gramsh	Kurbin	Pogradec
Bulqizë	Has	Lezhë	Pukë
Delvinë	Kavajë	Librazhd	Sarandë
Devoll	Kolonjë	Lushnjë	Shkodër
Dibër	Koplik	Mallakastër	Skrapar

541

Table 8.3 (continued)

Durrës	Korçë	Mat	Tepelenë
Elbasan	Krujë	Mirdite	Tiranë
Fier	Kuçovë	Peqin	Tropojë
Gjirokastër	Kukës	Përmet	Vlorë

Bosnia and Herzegovina

Kozara	Trebisnjica Mostar
Majevica	Trebisnjica Listica
Rama Jablanica	Ukrina
Srednja Neretva	

Brazil

Vale dos Vinhedos

Canada

Fraser Valley	Pelee Island
Lake Erie North Shore	Similkameen Valley
Niagara Peninsula	Vancouver Island
Okanagan Valley	

Chile

Aconcagua	Valle de Curicó *whether or not followed by* Valle del Teno
Atacama	Valle de Curicó *whether or not followed by* Valle del Teno
Coquimbo	Valle de Curicó *whether or not followed by* Valle del Lontué
Sur	Valle de Curicó *whether or not followed by* Valle del Lontué
Valle Central	Valle de San Antonio *whether or not followed by* Valle de Leyda
Valle de Aconcagua *whether or not followed by* Panquehue	Valle de San Antonio *whether or not followed by* Valle de Leyda
Valle de Casablanca	Valle del Bío-Bío *whether or not followed by* Yumbel
Valle de Copiapó	

Georgia

Akhasheni	Kvareli
Atenuri	Manavi
Gurjaani	Mukuzani
Kakheti (Kakhuri)	Napareuli
Kardenakhi	Sviri
Khvanchkara	Teliani
Kindzmarauli	Tibaani
Kotekhi	

Montenegro

Crnogorski basen Skadarskog jezera Podgorički *whether or not followed by the name of wine-growing commune and/or the name of a vineyard estate*

Crnogorski basen Skadarskog jezera Bjelopavlićki

Crnogorski basen Skadarskog jezera Riječki

Crnogorski basen Skadarskog jezera Crmnički

Crnogorski basen Skadarskog jezera Katunski

Crnogorsko primorje Grahovsko-nudoski

Crnogorsko primorje Ulcinjski

Crnogorsko primorje Budvansko-barski

Crnogorsko primorje Boko-kotorski

Republic of Moldova

Ciumai/Чумай	Ştefan Vodă
Codru	Valul lui Traian
Romăneşti	

Republic of Serbia

Алексиначки	Крушевачки	Опленачки	Тимочки
Банатски	Књажевачки	Поцерски	Поцерски
Београдски	Лесковачки	Поцерски	Чачански
Врањски	Млавски	Северни[43]	Јужнобанатски
Западноморавски	Нишавски	Севернобанатски	Јужни[44]
Косовско-метохијски[45]	Нишавско-јужноморавски	Сремски	Јужнобанатски
Крајински	Нишки	Суботичко-хоргошка пешчара	

South Africa

Boberg	Welgemeend	Papegaaiberg	Kloofzicht
Breede River Valley	Upland	Overgaauw	Twee Jonge Gezellen
Calitzdorp	Robertson *whether or not followed by* Agterkliphoogte	Avontuur	De Heuvel
Cape Point	Ardein	Bellevue	Theuniskraal
Coastal Region *whether or not followed by* Groot Constantia	Boesmans River	Bonfoi	Tygerberg *whether or not followed by* Bloemendal
Constantia	Courage	Bottelary v	Diemersdal

---

43 This designation is without prejudice to positions on status, and is in line with UNSCR 1244/1999 and the ICJ Opinion on the Kosovo declaration of independence.

44 This designation is without prejudice to positions on status, and is in line with UNSCR 1244/1999 and the ICJ Opinion on the Kosovo declaration of independence.

45 This designation is without prejudice to positions on status, and is in line with UNSCR 1244/1999 and the ICJ Opinion on the Kosovo declaration of independence.

Table 8.3 (continued)

Klein Constantia	Bonnievale	Devon Valley	Meerendal
Darling *whether or not followed by* Ormonde	Dewetshof	Devonvale	Altydgedacht
Groenekloof	Eilandia	Elsenburg	Durbanville
Douglas	Excelsior	Fort Simon	Worcester *whether or not followed by* Du Preez
Klein Karoo *whether or not followed by* Montagu	Goedverwacht	Goede Hoep	Goudini
Klein Karoo	Hoops River	Grand Provence	Leopard Hill
Mons Ruber	Klaasvoogds	Hartenberg	Nuy
Tradouw	Le Chasseur	Jacobsdal	Opstal
Lutzville Valley *whether or not followed by* Koekenaap	Le Grand Chasseur	Jonkershoek Valley	Scherpenheuvel
Olifants River *whether or not followed by* Bamboo Bay / Bamboesbaai	McGregor	Kaapzicht	Slanghoek
Olifants River *whether or not followed by* Vredendal	Mon Don	Kanonkop	Aan-de-Doorns
Piekenierskloof	Mont Blois	Klawervlei	Bergsig
Spruitdrift	Nicholaas L Jonker	Klein Gustouw	Deetlefs
Paarl *whether or not followed by* Rhebokskloof	Rietvallei	Koopmanskloof	Cederberg
Ruitersvlei	Springfield	L'Avenir	Ceres
Oude Wellington	Van Zylshof	Le Bonheur	Elim
Onverwacht	Vink River	Lievland	Goudveld
Nelson's Creek	Weltevrede	Lushof	Hartswater
Mischa	Wonderfontein	Meerlust	Herbertsdale
Paarl *whether or not followed by* L'Ormarins	Zandvliet	Middelvlei	Loopspruit
Akkerdal	Stellenbosch *whether or not followed by* Alto	Monterosso	Lower Orange

Backsberg	Asara	Mooiplaas	Overberg *whether or not followed by* Elgin
Cabriere	Zevenwacht	Morgenhof	Goedvertrouw
De Zoete Inval	Warwick	Morgenster	Hamilton Russel Vinyards
Franschhoek Valley	Vergenoegd	Mount Rozier	Paul Cluver
Hildenbrand	Vera Cruz	Muratie	Wildekrans
Jacaranda	Uitkyk	Neethlingshof	Prince Albert Valley
Johann Graue	Uiterwyk	Oude Nektar	Riet River, FS
Landskroon	Slaley	Swartland *whether or not followed by* Allesverloren	Ruiterbosch
Laborie	Simonsig	Malmesbury	Swartberg
Seidelberg	Simonsberg-Stellenbosch	Riebeekberg	
Simonsberg-Paarl	Rust-en-Vrede	Swellendam *whether or not followed by* Buffeljags	
Wellington	Remhoogte	Tulbagh *whether or not followed by* Lemberg	

Switzerland

Aargau *whether or not followed by the name of a smaller geographical unit*	Jura	Ticino *whether or not followed by* Mendrisio	Vaud *whether or not followed by* Nord vaudois
Appenzell Ausserrhoden	Luzern	Ticino whether or not followed by Lugano	Vaud *whether or not followed by* Vully
Appenzell Innerrhoden	Neuchâtel	Ticino *whether or not followed by* Locarno	Zürich *whether or not followed by* Limmattal
Basel-Land	Nidwalden	Ticino *whether or not followed by* Leventina	
Basel-Stadt	Schaffhausen	Ticino *whether or not followed by* Blenio	Zürich *whether or not followed by* Züricher Unterland
Bern / Berne	Schwyz	Ticino *whether or not followed by* Bellinzona	Zürich *whether or not followed by* Zürichsee

Table 8.3 (continued)

Fribourg / Freiburg	Solothurn	Uri *whether or not followed by the name of a smaller geographical unit*	Zürich *whether or not followed by* Weinland
Geneva	Thurgau	Vallais / Wallis	
Glarus	Ticino *whether or not followed by* Riviera	Vaud *whether or not followed by* Lausanne	
Graubünden	Ticino *whether or not followed by* Valle Maggia	Vaud *whether or not followed by* Côtes-de-l'Orbe	

Ukraine

Новий Світ / Novyj Svit (Novy Svet)	Сонячна Долина / Soniachna Dolyna (Soniachna Dolina)

USA (697 Records in the data base)

Source: http://ec.europa.eu/agriculture/markets/wine/e-bacchus/indexcfm?event=resultsPThirdgis &language=EN, accessed 14 April 2019.

3. Spirits

Table 8.4   Registered geographical indications for spirits

Guatemala

Ron de Guatemala

Mexico

Tequila

Source

Pisco

Source: https://ec.europa.eu/info/news/commission-approves-protected-geographical-indication-mexico-2019-mar-20_en, accessed 14 April 2019.

9

THE IMPACT OF BREXIT ON GEOGRAPHICAL INDICATIONS PROTECTION

A. PROTECTED BRITISH GIS

The UK has registered and applied for EU registrations of GIs in relation to **9.01** agricultural products and food, wines and spirits. The status of these registrations is indicated in Tables 9.1–9.3 below. As they are a significant feature of the UK's export trade, particularly to the EU, their status after Brexit will be of some economic significance to the UK.

Table 9.1   Agricultural products and food

PGI

Registration No	Indication	Status
GB/PGI/0005/02108	Vale of Evesham Asparagus	Registered
GB/PGI/0005/01229	Carmarthen Ham	Registered
UK/PGI/0005/02198	Broighter Gold Rapeseed Oil	Applied
UK/PGI/0205/02133	Welsh lamb	Applied
UK/PGI/0005/00889	Traditional Ayrshire Dunlop	Registered
UK/PGI/0005/0667	West Country Lamb	Registered
UK/PGI/0005/0668	West Country Beef	Registered
UK/PGI/0005/0652	Yorkshire Wensleydale	Registered

Table 9.1 (continued)

PGI

Registration No	Indication	Status
GB/PGI/0005/01087	Pembrokeshire Earlies / Pembrokeshire Early Potatoes	Registered
GB/PGI/0005/00908	Orkney Scottish Island Cheddar	Registered
UK/PGI/0005/00887	Fenland Celery	Registered
GB/PGI/0005/00876	Stornoway Black Pudding	Registered
GB/PGI/0005/00863	Scottish Wild Salmon	Registered
UK/PGI/0005/00882	Newmarket Sausage	Registered
UK/PGI/0005/0792	Armagh Bramley Apples	Registered
GB/PGI/0005/00807	New Season Comber Potatoes / Comber Earlies	Registered
UK/PGI/0005/0796	Lough Neagh Eel	Registered
UK/PGI/0005/0727	Cornish Pasty	Registered
UK/PGI/0005/0715	Traditional Cumberland Sausage	Registered
UK/PGI/0005/0589	Cornish Sardines	Registered
UK/PGI/0005/0132	Traditional Grimsby Smoked Fish	Registered
UK/PGI/0005/0335	Melton Mowbray Pork Pie	Registered
UK/PGI/0105/0141	Scottish Farmed Salmon	Registered
UK/PGI/0117/0275	Scotch Lamb	Registered
UK/PGI/0117/0274	Scotch Beef	Registered
UK/PGI/0005/0227	Arbroath Smokies	Registered
UK/PGI/0005/0081	Welsh Lamb	Registered
UK/PGI/0005/0057	Welsh Beef	Registered
UK/PGI/0005/0001	Exmoor Blue Cheese	Registered
UK/PGI/0005/0002	Dorset Blue Cheese	Registered
UK/PGI/0017/0285	Teviotdale Cheese	Registered
UK/PGI/0017/0371	Whitstable Oysters	Registered
UK/PGI/0017/0290	Gloucestershire Cider/Perry	Registered
UK/PGI/0017/0291	Worcestershire cider/perry	Registered
UK/PGI/0017/0292	Herefordshire Cider/Perry	Registered
UK/PGI/0017/0296	Kentish Ale and Kentish Strong Ale	Registered
UK/PGI/0017/0373	Rutland Bitter	Registered
UK/PGI/0005/02448	Scottish Wild Venison	Applied
UK/PGI/0105/0667	West Country Lamb	Applied
UK/PGI/0105/0668	West Country Beef	Applied
UK/PGI/0005/02090	Traditional Welsh Caerphilly/ Traditional Welsh Caerffili	Registered
GB/PGI/0005/01250	Traditional Welsh Perry	Registered
GB/PGI/0005/01251	Traditional Welsh Cider	Registered

PGI

Registration No	Indication	Status
UK/PGI/0005/01350	London Cure Smoked Salmon	Registered
GB/PGI/0005/01180	West Wales Coracle Caught Sewin	Registered
GB/PGI/0005/02297	Forfar Bridie	Applied
GB/PGI/0005/01179	West Wales Coracle Caught Salmon	Registered
GB/PGI/0005/02286	Ayrshire New Potatoes/ Ayrshire Earlies	Applied

PDO

Registration No	Designation	Status
UK/PDO/0005/01304	Conwy Mussels	Registered
GB/PDO/0005/01068	Anglesey Sea Salt / Halen Môn	Registered
UK/PDO/0005/0885	Fal Oyster	Registered
UK/PDO/0005/0951	East Kent Goldings	Registered
UK/PDO/0005/00891	Lakeland Herdwick	Registered
UK/PDO/0005/00855	Isle of Man Queenies	Registered
UK/PDO/0005/0737	Native Shetland Wool	Registered
UK/PDO/0005/0633	Yorkshire Forced Rhubarb	Registered
UK/PDO/0005/0340	Isle of Man Manx Loaghtan Lamb	Registered
UK/PDO/0005/0354	Staffordshire Cheese	Registered
UK/PDO/0005/0014	Cornish Clotted Cream	Registered
UK/PDO/0017/0276	Shetland Lamb	Registered
UK/PDO/0017/0027	Jersey Royal Potatoes	Registered
UK/PDO/0017/0272	Orkney Beef	Registered
UK/PDO/0017/0273	Orkney Lamb	Registered
UK/PDO/0017/0277	White Stilton Cheese / Blue Stilton Cheese	Registered
UK/PDO/0017/0279	West Country farmhouse Cheddar Cheese	Registered
UK/PDO/0017/0280	Beacon Fell traditional Lancashire Cheese	Registered
UK/PDO/0017/0281	Single Gloucester	Registered
UK/PDO/0017/0282	Swaledale Cheese	Registered
UK/PDO/0017/0283	Swaledale Ewes' Cheese	Registered
UK/PDO/0017/0284	Bonchester Cheese	Registered
UK/PDO/0017/0287	Buxton Blue	Registered
UK/PDO/0017/0300	Dovedale Cheese	Registered
GB/PDO/0005/02287	The Vale of Clwyd Denbigh Plum	Registered
UK/PDO/0005/02159	Lough Neagh Pollan	Registered
GB/PDO/0005/01188	Welsh Laverbread	Registered
GB/PDO/0005/02285	Cambrian Mountains Lamb	Applied

Table 9.1 (continued)

TSG

Registration No	Designation	Status
UK/TSG/0007/0057	Traditional Bramley Apple Pie Filling	Registered
UK/TSG/0107/0004	Traditional Farmfresh Turkey	Applied
UK/TSG/0007/0062	Watercress	Applied
UK/TSG/0007/0024	Traditionally Farmed Gloucestershire Old Spots Pork	Registered

Source: http://ec.europa.eu/agriculture/quality/door/list.html?&recordStart=256, accessed 17 April 2019.

Table 9.2 Wines

PDO

Registration No	Designation	Status
PDO-GB-N1636	Darnibole	Registered
PDO-GB-A1585	English	Registered
PDO-GB-A1587	Welsh	Registered
PGI		
PGI-GB-A1589	English Regional	Registered
PGI-GB-A1590	Welsh Regional	Registered

Table 9.3 Spirits

Reference No	Designation	Category	Status
2	Irish Whiskey/Uisce Beatha Eireannach/Irish Whisky	Whisky or Whiskey	Registered
2	Scotch Whisky	Whisky or Whiskey	Registered
9	Somerset Cider Brandy	Cider spirit and perry spirit	Registered
32	Irish Cream	Liqueur	Registered
99	Irish Poteen/Irish Poitín	Other	Registered

Source: http://ec.europa.eu/agriculture/spirits/index.cfm?event=searchIndication, accessed 17 April 2019.

B. BREXIT

By a referendum held on 23 June 2016, a 51.9 per cent majority of British **9.02** electors voted to leave the EU. On 26 January 2017, the European Union (Notification of Withdrawal) Bill 2017 received its first reading. This Bill sought to confer power on the Prime Minister to notify, under Art 50(2) of the Treaty of Lisbon, the UK's intention to withdraw from the EU. Following the discussion of proposed amendments, the Bill passed through both Houses of Parliament on 13 March 2017. The Act came into effect when Royal Assent was signified on 16 March 2017. On 29 March 2017, Prime Minister Theresa May wrote to Donald Tusk, the President of the European Council, informing him of Britain's intention to withdraw from the EU.[1] This was delivered in accordance with the Treaty of Lisbon.[2] A two-year negotiating phase commenced, during which Art 50(2) envisaged the administrative arrangements for withdrawal would be settled, and a framework for the future relationship between Britain and the EU.

On 20 June 2018 the European Union (Withdrawal) Act 2018 passed through **9.03** both Houses of Parliament and became law by Royal Assent on 26 June 2018. The Withdrawal Act in s 1 repeals the European Communities Act 1972 on the day which the UK exits the EU. Sections 2 and 3 convert EU law as it stands at the moment of exit into domestic law before the UK leaves the EU and preserves laws made in the UK to implement EU obligations. Thus should the UK leave without any agreement with the EU, the GIs legislation will remain part of UK law. However, as UK law, after Brexit, it can amended or repealed at any time by the UK Parliament.

On 25 November 2018 a Withdrawal Agreement was agreed by the leaders of **9.04** the EU and the European Atomic Energy Community at a Special Meeting of the European Council.[3]

At the time of writing the Withdrawal Agreement has not been accepted by **9.05** the UK Parliament.

---

1 http://uk.reuters.com/article/uk-britain-eu-letter-text/text-ofpm-mays-letter-to-eus-tusk-triggering-brexit-process-idUKKBN1701JH., accessed 14 April 2019.

2 Treaty of Lisbon amending the Treaty on European Union and the Treaty establishing the European Community, 2007 O.J. C 306/1.

3 Available at https://assets.publishing.service.gov.uk/government/uploads/system/uploads/attachment_data/file/759019/25_November_Agreement_on_the_withdrawal_of_the_United_Kingdom_of_Great_Britain_and_Northern_Ireland_from_the_European_Union_and_the_European_Atomic_Energy_Community.pdf, accessed 16 April 2019.

9.06 When an agreement is finally struck, or if Britain crashes out of the EU without an agreement, the intellectual property arrangements between Britain and the EU will have to be negotiated. The options range from a 'hard Brexit' in which British IP rights will have to be disentangled from those of the EU, to a 'soft Brexit', in which the continuing IP arrangements will not be dissimilar to the pre-Brexit arrangements.

C. UK GI ARRANGEMENTS POST-BREXIT

9.07 On 5 February 2019 the Department for Environment Food and Rural Affairs (Defra) published a guide: 'Protecting food and drink names if there's no Brexit deal'.[4] It stated that if the UK leaves the EU without a deal, the UK will set up its own GI schemes, which will mirror the EU schemes and fulfil the UK's WTO obligations. This will be managed by Defra, which will maintain a register of protected products and process new applications.

9.08 The Defra guide indicates that the new UK schemes use the same classes as the current EU GI schemes: Protected Designation of Origin (PDO), Protected Geographical Indication (PGI) and Traditional Specialities Guaranteed (TSG). Local authority trading standards bodies will be responsible for enforcement.

9.09 All existing UK products registered under EU GI schemes will automatically get UK GI status and will remain protected in the UK.

9.10 Food and drink producers seeking protection for new products will be able to apply to the relevant UK scheme, which will be open to UK, EU and non-EU country producers.[5]

9.11 New UK logos will represent three classes of GI product.

9.12 For UK food and agricultural GI products – including beer, cider and perry – sold in the UK, traders will have to use the relevant UK GI logo on packaging, observing rules for use such as size and placement.

9.13 Non-UK producers of food and agricultural products recognised under the UK scheme can use the UK GI logo.

---

4 https://www.gov.uk/guidance/protecting-food-and-drink-names-if-theres-no-brexit-deal, accessed 15 March 2019.

5 Defra will publish guidance on how to apply to the UK GI schemes in October 2019. See ibid.

The UK GI logo can be used by producers of a registered wine, spirit drink, **9.14** aromatised (fortified flavoured) wine.

The Defra advice explained that producers will have three years from the **9.15** launch of the UK schemes to adopt the relevant UK logo on food and agricultural product packaging.

The Defra advice is uncertain whether UK GIs will continue to be protected **9.16** in the EU, but that UK GI status will assist in new applications to the EU. Reciprocally, producers of existing EU GIs may need to apply to the relevant UK scheme to secure UK GI status.

Defra states that when the UK leaves the EU, the UK government expects UK **9.17** GI protection to continue for products currently named in non-EU countries' free trade agreements with the EU.[6]

The advice states that 'Irish whiskey, Irish cream and Irish poteen produced **9.18** anywhere on the island of Ireland will have EU and UK GI protection and no action is required.'

D. EU ARRANGEMENTS CONCERNING UK GIS POST-BREXIT

The Withdrawal Agreement of 25 November 2019[7] provides in Art 126 for a **9.19** transition or implementation period, to start on the date of entry into force of the Agreement and ending on 31 December 2020. Article 4(5) provides that in the interpretation and application of the Agreement, the UK's judicial and administrative authorities 'shall have due regard to relevant case law of the Court of Justice of the European Union handed down after the end of the transition period'.

1. Continued protection in the UK of EU GIs

Article 54 of the Agreement deals with IP arrangements post Brexit. It deals **9.20** specifically with GIs in Art 54(2), which provides that:

> Where a geographical indication, designation of origin or traditional speciality guaranteed within the meaning of Regulation (EU) No 1151/2012 of the European

---

6 See Chapter 8.
7 See n 3 *supra.*

Parliament and of the Council,[8] a geographical indication, designation of origin or traditional term for wine within the meaning of Regulation (EU) No 1308/2013 of the European Parliament and of the Council,[9] a geographical indication within the meaning of Regulation (EC) No 110/2008 of the European Parliament and of the Council[10] or a geographical indication within the meaning of Regulation (EU) No 251/2014 of the European Parliament and of the Council,[11] is protected in the Union on the last day of the transition period by virtue of those Regulations, those persons who are entitled to use the geographical indication, the designation of origin, the traditional speciality guaranteed or the traditional term for wine concerned shall be entitled, as from the end of the transition period, without any re-examination, to use the geographical indication, the designation of origin, the traditional speciality guaranteed or the traditional term for wine concerned in the United Kingdom, which shall be granted at least the same level of protection under the law of the United Kingdom as under the following provisions of Union law:

(a) Points (i), (j) and (k) of Article 4(1) of Directive (EU) 2015/2436 ... [Trade Marks Directive];[12] and

(b) in view of the geographical indication, designation of origin, traditional speciality guaranteed or traditional term for wine concerned, Article 13, Article 14(1), Article 24, Article 36(3), Articles 38 and 44 and point (b) of Article 45(1) of Regulation (EU) No 1151/2012; Article 90(1) of Regulation (EU) No 1306/2013 ... [Common Agricultural Policy Regulation];[13] Article 100(3), Article 102(1), Articles 103 and 113, and point (c)(x) of Article 157(1) of Regulation (EU) No 1308/2013; Article 62(3) and (4) of Commission Regulation (EC) No 607/2009 [Wine Regulation];[14] the first subparagraph of Article 15(3), Article 16 and Article 23(1) of Regulation (EC) No 110/2008 [Spirits Regulation]and, in so far as to the extent related to compliance with those provisions of that Regulation, Article 24(1) of that Regulation; or Article 19(1) and Article 20 of Regulation (EU) No 251/2014 [Aromatised Wine Products Regulation].

---

8 Regulation (EU) No 1151/2012 of the European Parliament and of the Council of 21 November 2012 on quality schemes for agricultural products and foodstuffs, OJ L 343, 14.12.2012, p. 1.

9 Regulation (EU) No 1308/2013 of the European Parliament and of the Council of 17 December 2013 establishing a common organisation of the markets in agricultural products ... , OJ L 347, 20.12.2013, p. 671.

10 Regulation (EC) No 110/2008 of the European Parliament and of the Council of 15 January 2008 on the definition, description, presentation, labelling and the protection of geographical indications of spirit drinks and repealing Council Regulation (EEC) No 1576/89, OJ L 39, 13.2.2008, p. 16.

11 Regulation (EU) No 251/2014 of the European Parliament and of the Council of 26 February 2014 on the definition, description, presentation, labelling and the protection of geographical indications of aromatised wine products and repealing Council Regulation (EEC) No 1601/91, OJ L 84, 20.3.2014, p. 14.

12 Directive (EU) 2015/2436 of the European Parliament and of the Council of 16 December 2015 to approximate the laws of the Member States relating to trade marks, OJ L 336, 23.12.2015, p. 1.

13 Regulation (EU) No 1306/2013 of the European Parliament and of the Council of 17 December 2013 on the financing, management and monitoring of the common agricultural policy, OJ L 347, 20.12.2013, p. 549.

14 Commission Regulation (EC) No 607/2009 of 14 July 2009 laying down certain detailed rules for the implementation of Council Regulation (EC) No 479/2008 as regards protected designations of origin and geographical indications, traditional terms, labelling and presentation of certain wine sector products, OJ L 193, 24.7.2009, p. 60.

Where a GI, designation of origin, traditional speciality guaranteed or **9.21** traditional term for wine referred to in the first subparagraph ceases to be protected in the Union after the end of the transition period, Art 54(2) provides that the first subparagraph shall cease to apply in respect of that GI, designation of origin, traditional speciality guaranteed or traditional term for wine.

Article 54(2) also provides that the first subparagraph shall not apply where **9.22** protection in the EU is derived from international agreements to which the EU is a party. A final agreement between the UK and the EU is envisaged in s 184 of the Withdrawal Agreement and Art 54(2) provides that it shall apply unless and until an agreement as referred to in Art 184 enters into force or becomes applicable.

2. Registration procedure

Article 55(1) of the Withdrawal Agreement provides that the registration, **9.23** grant or protection pursuant to Art 54(2) shall be carried out free of charge by the relevant entities in the UK, using the data available in the registries of the European Union Intellectual Property Office, and the European Commission. Annex III to Regulation (EC) No 110/2008 (concerning GIs for spirit drinks) shall be considered a registry for the purpose of this Article.

Article 55(2) provides that for the purposes of Art 55(1) 'those persons who **9.24** are entitled to use a geographical indication, designation of origin, traditional speciality guaranteed or traditional term for wine referred to in Article 54(2) shall not be required to introduce an application or to undertake any particular administrative procedure'.

Article 55(3) provides that the European Union Intellectual Property Office **9.25** and the European Commission shall provide to the relevant entities in the UK the information necessary for the registration, grant or protection in the UK pursuant to Art 54(2).

Article 55(4) provides that this Article shall be without prejudice to renewal **9.26** fees that may apply at the time of renewal of the rights, or the possibility for the holders concerned to surrender their IP rights in the UK in accordance with the relevant procedure under the law of the UK.

3. Exhaustion of rights

9.27 Article 61 of the Withdrawal Agreement provides that IP rights which were exhausted both in the EU and in the UK before the end of the transition period under the conditions provided for by EU law shall remain exhausted both in the EU and in the UK.

E. FUTURE UK OBLIGATIONS IN RELATION TO GIS

9.28 The Withdrawal Agreement was accompanied by a *Political Declaration Setting Out the Framework for the Future Relationship Between the European Union and the United Kingdom*.[15] Section VII of this Political Declaration dealt with IP rights and in clause 45, noting the protection afforded to existing GIs in the Withdrawal Agreement, committed the Parties to 'seek to put in place arrangements to provide appropriate protection for their geographical indications'.

F. CONCLUDING COMMENTS

9.29 The EU is currently considering the extension of GI protection to handicrafts and artisanal production. A European Parliament resolution of 6 October 2015 commended the possible extension of GI protection to non-agricultural products.[16]

9.30 In anticipation of this extension some Member States have begun to grant GIs of this type. For example, the French National Institute of Intellectual property (INPI) has approved three GIs for non-agricultural products under the *loi de la consommation* (Consumer Act) of March 2014: 'Savon de Marseille' (soap), 'Espadrilles de Mauléon' (shoes) and 'Granit de Bretagne' (Brittany Granite).[17] Two UK trade associations, responsible for non-agricultural products for which GIs are proposed, are: The Savile Row Bespoke Association and the Harris Tweed Authority, which in March 2016

---

15 Available at https://assets.publishing.service.gov.uk/government/uploads/system/uploads/attachment_data/file/759021/25_November_Political_Declaration_setting_out_the_framework_for_the_future_relationship_between_the_European_Union_and_the_United_Kingdom__.pdf, accessed 16 April 2019.

16 http://www.europarl.europa.eu/sides/getDoc.do?pubRef=-//EP//TEXT+TA+P8-TA-2015-0331+0+DOC+XML+V0//EN, accessed 16 April 2019.

17 INPI's GI database is available at https://base-indications-geographiques.inpi.fr/, accessed 16 April 2019.

became members of The Organization for an International Geographical Indications Network (oriGIn).[18]

The Withdrawal Agreement makes no mention of non-agricultural GIs, which will mean that this is a subject for further negotiations between the EU and the UK.   **9.31**

A paper prepared for the Scottish Parliament suggests that the reluctance of the UK to accept reciprocal protection of EU GIs might be linked to its aspirations for agreeing new trade deals after Brexit with countries like Australia and the USA, which protect GIs only through their certification and collective marks systems.[19]   **9.32**

---

18 See https://www.origin-gi.com/medias/press-releases/archive/view/listid-6/mailid-303-press-release-two-prestigious-uk-non-agricultural-geographical-indications-savile-row-bespoke-and-harris-tweed-join-origin.html, accessed 16 April 2019.

19 Iain McIver, *Geographical Indications and Brexit*, Edinburgh, The Scottish Parliament, 2018, 16, available at https://digitalpublications.parliament.scot/ResearchBriefings/Report/2018/8/23/Geographical-Indications-and-Brexit, accessed 16 April 2019.

BIBLIOGRAPHY

Addor, F. and A. Grazioli (2002). 'Geographical Indications beyond Wines and Spirits – A Roadmap for a Better Protection for Geographical Indications in the WTO TRIPS Agreement' *Journal of World Intellectual Property* 5(6): 865–97.

Agarwal, S. and M. Barone (2005). *Emerging Issues for Geographical Indication Branding Strategies*, Iowa, Iowa State University, MATRIC.

Agdomar, M. (2008). 'Removing the Greek from Feta and Adding Korbel to Champagne: the Paradox of Geographical Indications in International Law' *Fordham Intellectual Property, Media and Entertainment Law Journal* 18(2): 542–607.

Albayrak, M. and E. Gunes (2010). 'Implementations of Geographical Indications at Brand Management of Traditional Foods in the European Union' *African Journal of Business Management* 4(6): 1059–68.

Almeida, A. F. R. de (2005). 'The TRIPS Agreement, the Bilateral Agreements Concerning Geographical Indications and the Philosophy of the WTO' *European Intellectual Property Review* 27(4): 150–53.

Armistead, J. (2000). 'Whose Cheese Is It Anyway? Correctly Slicing the European Regulation Concerning Protections for Geographic Indications' *Transnat'l L. & Contemp. Probs.* 10(1): 303–24.

Auer, A. (2008). 'Legal Implications of Accession to the European Union on Geographical Indications and Designations of Origin for Agricultural Products and Foodstuffs', *Croatian Yearbook of European Law and Policy.* 2:137– 72.

Babcock, B. A. (2003). 'Geographical Indications, Property Rights, and Value-Added Agriculture' *Iowa Ag Review* 9(4) available at http://www. card. iastate.edu/iowa_ag_review/fall_03/article1.aspx.

Banerjee, R. and M. Majumdar (2011). 'In the Mood to Compromise? Extended Protection of Geographical Indications under TRIPS Article 23' *Journal of Intellectual Property Law & Practice* 6(9): 657–63.

Banks, J. and T. K. Marsden (2000). 'Integrating Agri-Environment Policy, Farming Systems and Rural Development: Tir Cymen in Wales' *Sociologia Ruralis* 40(4): 466–80.

Barham, E. and B. Sylvander (eds) (2011). *Labels of Origin for Food. Local Development, Global Recognition*, Wallingford, Oxford, CAB International.

Barjolle, D., B. Sylvander and E. Thévenod-Mottet (2011). 'Public Policies and Geographical Indications' in Barham and Sylvander (2011), 92–105.

Beier, F-K. and R. Knaak (1994). 'The Protection of Direct and Indirect Geographical Indications of Source in Germany and the European Community' *IIC* 25(1): 1–84.

Belletti, G. and A. Marescotti (2002). 'Link between Origin-Labeled Products and Rural Development, WP Report 3. Development of Origin-Labeled Products': Humanity, Innovations, and Sustainability (DOLPHINS) project, Le Mans.

Belletti, G. and A. Marescotti (2011). 'Origin Products, Geographical Indications and Rural Development' in Barham and Sylvander (2011) 75–91.

Belson, J. (2002). 'Certification Marks, Guarantees and Trust' *EIPR* 24(7): 340–52.

Bendekgey, L. and C. H. Mead (1992). 'International Protection of Appellations of Origin and Other Geographic Indications' *Trademark Reporter* 82: 765–92.

Bently, L. and B. Sherman (2006). 'The Impact of European Geographical Indications on National Rights in Member States' *TMR* 96(4): 850–905.

Beresford, L. (2007). 'Geographical Indications: the Current Landscape' *Fordham Intellectual Property & Entertainment Law Jnl* 17(4): 979–97.

Blakeney, M. (2000). 'Geographical Indications in Trade' *International Trade Law & Regulation* 4: 48–55.

Blakeney, M. (2001). 'Proposals for the International Regulation of Geographical Indications' *Journal of World Intellectual Property* 4(5): 629–52.

Blakeney, M. (2006). 'Geographical Indications and TRIPS' in M. Pugatch (ed.), *The Intellectual Property Debate. Perspectives from Law, Economics and Political Economy*, Cheltenham, UK, Edward Elgar, 293–304.

Blakeney, M. (2009). *Intellectual Property Rights and Food Security*, Wallingford, CAB International.

Blakeney, M. (2012a). *Intellectual Property Enforcement. A Commentary on the Anti-Counterfeiting Trade Agreement (ACTA)*, Cheltenham, UK, Edward Elgar.

Blakeney, M. (2012b). 'Geographical Indications and the International Trade in Australian Wines' *International Trade Law & Regulation* 18(1): 70.

Blakeney, M. and M. Lightbourne (2005). 'Geographical Indications, Traditional Knowledge and Basmati Rice' in B. O'Connor (ed.), *Agriculture in WTO Law*, London, Cameron May, 349–76.

Blakeney, M. and G. Mengistie (2011). 'Intellectual Property and Economic Development in Sub-Saharan Africa' *The Journal of World Intellectual Property* 14(3): 238–64.

Blakeney, M., T. Coulet, G. Mengistie and M. T. Mahop (eds) (2012). *Extending the Protection of Geographical Indications. Case Studies in the Protection of Agricultural Products in Africa*, London, Earthscan.

Bornkamm, J. (2007). 'E-Commerce Directive vs. IP Rights Enforcement – Legal Balance Achieved' Paper presented at a conference in Brussels on 6 March 2007, published in English at [2007] *GRUR Int* 642. 431.

Botis, D. (2013) Deputy Director for Legal Affairs at OHIM, '*Collective and Certification Marks in the EU*' www.worldipreview.com/news/ecta-2013-explaining-the-mysterious-collective-ctm.

Bramley, C. and E. Bienabe (2012). 'Developments and Considerations Around Geographical Indications in the Developing World' *Queen Mary Journal of Intellectual Property* 2(1): 14–37.

Bronckers, M. C. E. J. (1998). 'The Exhaustion of Patent Rights under World Trade Organization Law' *J. World Tr. L.* 32(5): 137–59.

Caenegem, W. van (2003). 'Registered Geographical Indications' *Journal of World Intellectual Property* 6(5): 699–719.

Caenegem, W. van (2004). 'Registered GIs: Intellectual Property, Agricultural Policy and International Trade' *European Intellectual Property Review* 26(4): 170–81.

Calboli, I. (2006). 'Expanding the Protection of Geographical Indications of Origin under TRIPS: "Old" Debate or "New" Opportunity?' *Marquette Intellectual Property Law Review* 10(2): 181–203.

Charlier, C. and M.-A. Ngo (2007). 'An Analysis of the European Communities: Protection of Trademarks and Geographical Indications for Agricultural Products and Foodstuffs Dispute' *Journal of World Intellectual Property* 10(3–4): 171–86.

Charlier, C. and M.-A. Ngo (2012). 'Geographical Indications Outside the European Regulation on PGIs, and the Rule of the Free Movement of Goods: Lessons from Cases Judged by the Court of Justice of the European Communities' *European Journal of Law and Economics* 34(1): 17–30.

Chever, T., C. Renault, S. Renault and V. Romieu (2012). *Value of Production of Agricultural Products and Foodstuffs, Wines, Aromatised Wines and Spirits Protected by a Geographical Indication (GI)*, Final Report for European Commission, available at http://ec.europa.eu/agriculture/external-studies/2012/ value-gi/final-report_en.pdf

Conrad, A. (1996). 'The Protection of Geographical Indications on the TRIPs Agreement' *TMR* 86: 11–46.

Corte-Real, A. (2005). 'The Conflict Between Trade Marks and Geographical Indications – The Budweiser Case in Portugal' in C. Heath and A. Kamperman Sanders (eds), *New Frontiers of Intellectual Property Law: IP and Cultural Heritage, Geographical Indicators, Enforcement, Overprotection*, Oxford, Hart, 149–60.

Cottier, T. and P. Véron (eds) (2011). *Concise International and European IP Law, TRIPS, Paris Convention, European Enforcement and Transfer of Technology*, 2nd edn, Alphen aan den Rijn, Wolters Kluwer.

Creditt, E. C. (2008). 'Terroir vs. Trademarks: the Debate over Geographical Indications and Expansions to the TRIPS Agreement' *Vanderbilt J Ent & Tech L.* 11(2): 425–59.

Dawson, N. (2000). 'Locating Geographical Indications: Perspectives from English Law' *Trademark Reporter* 90: 590–614.

Doster, I. (2006). 'A Cheese by Any Other Name: A Palatable Compromise to the Conflict over Geographical Indications' *Vanderbilt L. Rev.* 59:3: 874–903.

Echols, M. A. (2008). *Geographical Indications for Food Products: International Legal and Regulatory Perspectives*, Austin, Kluwer Law International.

Ermert, M. (2013). 'Governments Disagree on GI Protection at TLD Level' *Intellectual Property Watch* 1 August, available at http://www.ip-watch.org/2013/08/01/governments-disagree-on-geographical-indication-protection-at-tld-level/

Evans, G. E. (2008). 'The Multilateral Register for Geographical Indications and The Doha Mandate': *Anuario Andino De Derechos Intelectuales* [*Andean Yearbook of Intellectual Property Rights*], Palestra, Lima, 397–419.

Evans, G. E. (2009). 'Substantive Trademark Law Harmonization: On the Emerging Coherence between the Jurisprudence of the WTO Appellate Body and the European Court of Justice' in G. Dinwoodie and M. Janis (eds), *Trademark Law and Theory: A Handbook of Contemporary Research*, Cheltenham, UK and Northampton, MA, Edward Elgar, 177–203.

Evans, G. E. (2010). 'The Comparative Advantages of Geographical Indications and Community Trade Marks for the Marketing of Agricultural Products in the European Union' *International Review of Intellectual Property and Competition Law (IIC)* 41(6): 645–674.

Evans, G. E. (2012). 'The Simplification of European Legislation for the Protection of Geographical Indications: the Proposed Regulation on Agricultural Product Quality Schemes' *European Intellectual Property Review* 34(11): 33–49.

Evans, G. E. (2013). 'The Protection of Geographical Indications in the European Union and the United States under Sui Generis and Trade Mark Systems: Signs of Harmonisation?' *IPQ* 1: 18–29.

Evans, G. and M. Blakeney (2006). 'The Protection of Geographical Indications after Doha: Quo Vadis?' *Journal of International Economic Law* 9(3): 573–614.

Evans, G. and M. Blakeney (2007). 'The International Protection of Geographical Indications Yesterday, Today and Tomorrow' in G. Weskamp (ed.), *Emerging Issues in Intellectual Property*. Queen Mary Studies in Intellectual Property, Cheltenham, UK and Northampton, MA, Edward Elgar, 359–441.

561

Evans, P. (2006). 'Geographic Indications, Trade and the Functioning of Markets' in M. Pugatch (ed.), *The Intellectual Property Debate: Perspectives from Law, Economics and Political Economy*, Cheltenham, Edward Elgar, 345–360.

Forrest, H. A. (2013). *Protection of Geographic Names in International Law and Domain Name System Policy*, Alphen aan der Rijn, Kluwer.

Frayssignes, J. (2011). 'Roquefort Cheese (France)' in Barham and Sylvander (eds) (2011), 177–83.

Fusco, S. (2008). 'Geographical Indications: A Discussion of the TRIPS Regulation after the Ministerial Conference of Hong Kong' *Marquette Intellectual Property Law Review* 12(2): 197–262.

Gangjee, D. (2006). 'Melton Mowbray and the GI Pie in the Sky: Exploring Cartographies of Protection' *Intellectual Property Quarterly* 3: 291–309.

Gangjee, D. (2007). 'Say Cheese! A Sharper Image of Generic Use Through the Lens of Feta' *European Intellectual Property Review* 29(5): 172–179.

Gangjee, D. (2007). 'Quibbling Siblings: Conflicts between Trademarks and Geographical Indications' *Chicago-Kent Law Review* 82(3): 1253–1291.

Gangjee, D. (2012). *Relocating the Law of Geographical Indications*, Cambridge, Cambridge University Press.

Gervais, D. J. (2010). 'Reinventing Lisbon: the Case for a Protocol to the Lisbon Agreement (Geographical Indications)' *Chicago Journal of International Law* 11(1): 67–126.

Gerz, A. and F. Dupont (2006). 'Comté Cheese in France: Impact of a Geographical Indicationon Rural Development' in P. van de Kop, D. Sautier, and A. Gerz (eds), *Origin-Based Products: Lessons for Pro-Poor Market Development*, Amsterdam, KIT Publishers, 75–87.

Geuze, M. (2009). 'The Provisions on Geographical Indications in the TRIPS Agreement' *The Estey Centre Journal of International Law and Trade Policy* 10(1): 50–64.

Gevers, F. (1990). 'Geographical Names and Signs Used as Trade Marks' *European International Property Review* 8: 285–286.

Goebbel, B. (2003). 'Geographical Indications and Trademarks the Road from Doha' *Trademark Reporter* 93(4): 964–995.

Goldberg, S. D. (2001). 'Who Will Raise the White Flag? The Battle between the United States and the European Union Over the Protection of Geographical Indications' *University of Pennsylvania Journal of International Economic Law* 22(1): 107–51.

González, M. A. M. (2012). 'Collective, Guarantee and Certification Marks and GIs: Connections and Dissimilarities' *Journal of Intellectual Property Law & Practice* 7(4): 251–63.

Gragnani, M. (2012). 'The Law of Geographical Indications in the EU' *Journal of Intellectual Property Law & Practice* 7(4): 271–82.

Günzel, O. (2012). 'Opposing Third Parties' Applications for Geographical Indications under Regulation 510/2006' *Journal of Intellectual Property Law & Practice* 7(4): 244–50.

Gutierrez, E. (2005). 'Geographical Indicators: A Unique European Perspective on Intellectual Property' *Hastings Int'l & Comp L Rev.* 29: 29–50.

Haight, F. C. (2000). 'Conflicts Between U.S. Law and International Treaties Concerning Geographical Indications' *Whittier Law Review* 22(1): 73–88.

Handler, M. (2006). 'The WTO Geographical Indications Dispute' *The Modern Law Review* 69(1): 70–91.

Handler, M. and R. Burrell (2011). 'GI Blues: the Global Disagreement Over Geographical Indications' in K. Bowrey, M. Handler and D. Nicol (eds), *Emerging Challenges in Intellectual Property* Victoria, Oxford University Press, 126–44.

Heald, P. J. (1996). 'Trademarks and Geographical Indications: Exploring the Contours of the TRIPS Agreement' *V and J Transnat'l L.* 29: 635–60.

Heath, C. (2005). 'Geographical Indications: International, Bilateral and Regional Agreements' in C. Heath and A. Kamperman Sanders (eds), *New Frontiers of Intellectual Property Law: IP and Cultural Heritage, Geographical Indicators, Enforcement, Overprotection*, Oxford, Hart, 97–132.

Hughes, J. (2006). 'Champagne, Feta, and Bourbon: the Spirited Debate about Geographical Indications' *Hastings L.J.* 58: 299–373.

Ilbery, B. and M. Kneafsey (2000a). 'Registering Regional Speciality Food and Drink Products in the United Kingdom: the Case of PDOs and PGIs' *Area* 32(3): 317–25.

Ilbery, B. and M. Kneafsey (2000b). 'Producer Constructions of Quality in Regional Specialty Food Production: a Case Study from Southwest England' *Journal of Rural Studies* 16(2): 217–30.

Insight Consulting (2013). *Study on Geographical Indications Protection for Non-agricultural Products in the Internal Market* available at http://ec.europa.eu/internal_market/indprop/docs/geo-indications/130322_geo-indications-non-agri-study_en.pdf.

Ittersum, K. van, M. J. J. M. Candel and M. T. G. Meulenberg (2003). 'The Influence of the Image of a Product's Region of Origin on Product Evaluation' *Journal of Business Research* 56: 215–26.

Jennings, J. (2011). *Revolution and the Republic: A History of Political Thought in France Since the Eighteenth Century*, Oxford, Oxford University Press.

Josel, K. H. (1994). 'New Wine in Old Bottles: the Protection of France's Wine Classification System beyond Its Borders' *Boston University International Law Journal* 12: 471–92.

Josling, T. (2006). 'The War on *Terroir*: Geographical Indications as a Transatlantic Trade Conflict' *Journal of Agricultural Economics* 57(3): 337–63.

Kazmi, H. (2001). 'Trademarks in the International Arena: International Conventions and Agreements: Does It Make a Difference Where That Chablis Comes From? Geographic Indications in TRIPs and NAFTA' *J. Contemp. Legal Issues* 12: 470–474.

Kemp, D. J. and L. M. Forsythe (2006). 'Trademarks and Geographical Indications: a Case of California Champagne' *Chapman L. Rev.* 10: 257–98.

Kireeva, I. (2009). 'European Case Law and the WTO Ruling on Conflicts Between Geographical Indications and Trademarks' *ERA Forum* 10: 199–214.

Kireeva, I and B. O'Connor (2010). 'Geographical Indications and the TRIPS Agreement: What Protection is Provided to Geographical Indications in WTO Members?' *Journal of World Intellectual Property* 13(2): 275–303.

Knaak, R. (1996). 'The Protection of Geographical Indications According to the TRIPS Agreement' in F.-K. Beier and G. Schricker (eds), *From GATT to TRIPS – Agreement on Trade-Related Aspects of Intellectual Property Rights*, IIC Studies, vol. 18. New York, Weinheim, 117–32.

Kur, A. and S. Cocks (2007). 'Nothing but a GI Thing: Geographical Indications under EU Law' *Fordham Intellectual Property, Media and Entertainment Law Journal* 17(4) 999–1016.

Lang, A. C. (2006). 'On the Need to Expand Article 23 of the TRIPS Agreement' *Duke Journal of Contemporary and International Law* 16(2): 487–510.

Lenzen, L. C. (1968). 'Baccus in the Hinterlands: A Study of Denominations of Origin in French and American Wine-Labeling Laws' *Trademark Reporter* 58: 145–88.

Leong, S. H. S. (2017). 'European Union-Singapore Free Trade Agreement: A New Chapter for Geographical Indications in Singapore' in I. Caboli and N. W. Loon, *Geographical Indications at the Crossroads of Trade, Development and Culture*, Cambridge, Cambridge University Press.

Lindquist, L. A. (1999). 'Champagne or Champagne? An Examination of U.S. Failure to Comply with the Geographical Provisions of the Trips Agreement' *Georgia J. of International and Comparative L.* 27: 309–44.

Lucatelli, S. (2000). 'Appellations of Origin and Geographical Indications in OECD Member Countries: Economic and Legal Implications'. OECD, Directorate for Food, Agriculture and Fisheries, Trade Directorate. COM/AGR/APM/TD/WP(2000)15/FINAL. 57–65.

Marette, S. (2005). 'The Collective-Quality Promotion in the Agribusiness Sector: An Overview', Working paper 05-WP406 Centre for Agricultural and Rural Development, Iowa State University.

Marie-Vivien, D. (2010). 'The Role of the State in the Protection of Geographical Indications: From Disengagement in France/Europe to Significant Involvement in India' *Journal of World Intellectual Property* 13(2): 121–47.

Marsden, T., J. Banks and G. Bristow (2000). 'Food Supply Chain Approaches: Exploring their Role in Rural Development' *Sociologia Ruralis* 40(4): 424–38.

Martin, J. M. C. (2004). 'TRIPS Agreement: Towards a Better Protection for Geographical Indications?' *Brooklyn Journal of International La*w 30(1): 117–84.

McCarthy, J. T. and V. C. Devitt (1979). 'Protection of Geographical Indications: Domestic and International' *Trademark Reporter* 69: 199–213.

McIver, I. *Geographical Indications and Brexit*, Edinburgh, The Scottish Parliament, 2018, 16, available at https://digitalpublications.parliament. scot/ResearchBriefings/Report/2018/8/23/Geographical-Indications-and-Brexit, accessed 16 April 2019.

Mendelson, R. and Z. Wood (2013). *Geographical Indications in the United States: Developing a Preliminary List of Qualifying Product Names*, oriGIn paper, Geneva, OriGIn.

Mengistie, G. (2010). 'Intellectual Property as a Tool for Development: the Ethiopian Fine Coffee Designations and Trade Marking and Licensing Experience' *Int. TL & R* 16(1): 1–25.

Montén, L. (2006). 'Geographical Indications of Origin: Should They Be Protected and Why? An Analysis of the Issue from the U.S. and EU Perspectives' *Santa Clara Computer & High Technology Law Journal* 22(2): 315–49.

Monteverde, P. (2012). 'Enforcement of Geographical Indications' *Journal of Intellectual Property Law & Practice* 7(4): 291–7.

Morgan, K., T. K. Marsden and J. Banks (2006). *Worlds of Food: Place, Power, and Provenance in the Food Chain*, Oxford, Oxford University Press.

Munzinger, P. (2012). 'Blue Jeans and Other GIs: An Overview of Protection Systems for Geographical Indications' *Journal of Intellectual Property Law & Practice* 7(4): 283–90.

Murphy, K. M. (2003). 'Conflict, Confusion, and Bias under TRIPs Articles 22–24' *American University International Law Review* 19(5): 1181–230.

O'Connor, B. (2004). *The Law of Geographical Indications*, London, Cameron May.

O'Connor, B. and I. Kireeva (2003). 'What's in a Name? The "Feta" Cheese Saga' *International Trade Law and Regulation* 9(4): 110–21.

O'Connor, B. and I. Kireeva (2004). 'Overview of the EC Case Law Protecting Geographical Indications. The Slicing of Parma Ham and the

Grating of Grana Padano Cheese' *European Intellectual Property Review* 26(7): 312–22.

O'Connor & Co. (2005). 'Geographical Indications and the Challenges for ACP Countries', Agritrade, CTA, Paper available at http://agritrade.cta.int/

O'Connor & Co. (2007). 'Geographical Indications and TRIPS: 10 Years Later … Part II – Protection of Geographical Indications in 160 Countries around the World' (Report Commissioned for European Commission, DG Trade, available at http://trade.ec.europa.eu/doclib/docs/2007/june/tradoc_135089.pdf

Olszak, N. (2001). *Droit des appellations d'origine et indications de provenence*, Paris, Tec & Doc.

Pacciani, A., G. Beletti, A. Marescotti and S. Scaramuzzi (2001). 'The Role of Typical Products in Fostering Rural Development and the Effects of Regulation (EEC) 2081/92'. 73rd Seminar of the European Association of Agricultural Economists, Ancona 28–30 June.

Parry, B. (2008). 'Geographical Indications: Not all Champagne and Roses', in L. Bently, J. C. Ginsburgh and J. Davis (eds), *Trade Marks and Brands: An Interdisciplinary Critique*, Cambridge, Cambridge University Press, 361–80.

Pflüger, M. (2011). 'Article 10' in T. Cottier and P. Véron (eds), *Concise International and European IP Law TRIPS, Paris Convention, European Enforcement and Transfer of Technology*, Alphen aan den Rijn, Wolters Kluwer, 274.

Profeta, A., R. Balling, V. Schoene and A. Wirsig (2009). 'The Protection of Origins for Agricultural Products and Foods in Europe: Status Quo, Problems and Policy Recommendations for the Green Book' *The Journal of World Intellectual Property* 12(6): 622–48.

Rangnekar, D. (2004). 'The Socio-Economics of Geographical Indications: A Review of Empirical Evidence from Europe', UNCTAD/ICTSD Capacity building project on intellectual property rights and sustainable development, Geneva.

Raustiala, K. and S. R. Munzer (2007). 'The Global Struggle over Geographic Indications' *The European Journal of International Law* 18(2): 337–365.

Ray, C. (1998). 'Culture, Intellectual Property and Territorial Rural Development' *Sociologia Ruralis* 38(1): 3.

Renaud, J. R. (2001). 'Can't Get There from Here: How NAFTA and GATT Have Reduced Protection for Geographical Trademarks' *Brooklyn Journal of International Law* 26(3): 1097–123.

Resinek, N. (2007). 'Geographical Indications and Trade Marks: Coexistence or "First in Time, First in Right" Principle' *European Intellectual Property Review* 29(11): 446–55.

Réviron, S. and M. Paus (2006). *Special Report: Impact Analysis Methods. WP2 Social and Economic Issues. SINER-GI Project.* European Commission – Sixth framework program, February 2006.

Réviron, S., E. Thevenod-Mottet and N. El Benni (2009). 'Geographical Indications: Creation and Distribution of Economic Value in Developing Countries' NCCR Working Paper no 14.

Ricolfi, M. (2009). 'Is the European GIs Policy in Need of Rethinking' *IIC* 40(2): 123–124.

Ruse–Khan, H. G. (2011). 'A Trade Agreement Creating Barriers to International Trade?: ACTA Border Measures and Goods in Transit' *Am. U. Int'l L. Rev.* 26(1): 645–726.

Saez, C. (2013). 'GI Proponents Seek Recognition in New Internet Domains Programme at ICANN', *Intellectual Property Watch* 11 July available at http://www.ip-watch.org /2013/07/11/ gi-proponents-seek-recognition-in-new-internet-domains-programme-at-icann/.

Sanders, A. K. (2005). 'Future Solutions for Protecting Geographical Indications Worldwide' in C. Heath and A. Kamperman Sanders (eds), *New Frontiers of Intellectual Property Law: IP and Cultural Heritage, Geographical Indicators, Enforcement, Overprotection*, Oxford, Hart, 133–45.

Schricker, G. (1983). 'Protection of Indications of Source, Appellations of Origin and Other Geographic Designations in the Federal Republic of Germany' *IIC* 14(3): 307–28.

Shimura, K. (2010). 'How to Cut the Cheese: Homonymous Names of Registered Geographic Indicators of Foodstuffs in Regulation 510/2006' *Boston College International and Comparative Law Jnl.* 33(1): 129–52.

Snyder, D. (2008). 'Enhanced Protections for Geographical Indications Under TRIPs: Potential Conflicts Under the U.S. Constitutional and Statutory Regimes' *Fordham Intellectual Property, Media & Entertainment Law Journal* 18(5): 1297–323.

Stanziani, A. (2004). 'Wine Reputation and Quality Controls: the Origin of the AOCs in 19th Century France' *European Journal of Law and Economics* 18(2): 149–67.

Stanziani, A. (2009). 'Information, Quality and Legal Rules: Wine Adulteration in Nineteenth Century France' *Business History* 51(2): 268–91.

Stasi, A., G. Nardone, R. Viscecchia and A. Seccia (2011). 'Italian Wine Demand and Differentiation Effect of Geographical Indications' *International Journal of Wine Business Research* 23(1): 49–61.

Staten, T. L. (2005). 'Geographical Indications under the TRIPS Agreement: Uniformity Not Extension' *Journal of the Patent & Trade Mark Office Society* 87(3): 221–45.

Stenrücken, T. and S. Jaenichen (2007). 'The Fair Trade Idea: Toward an Economics of Social Labels' *Journal of Consumer Policy* 30: 201–217.

Stern, S. (2001). 'The Overlap Between Geographical Indications and Trade Marks in Australia' *Melbourne Journal of International Law* 2: 224–41.

Sylvander, B. (2004). 'Development of Origin Labelled Products: Humanity, Innovation and Sustainability', Dolphins WP7 Report, January.

Teil, G. (2010). 'The French Wine "Appellations d'Origine Contrôlée" and the Virtues of Suspicion' *The Journal of World Intellectual Property* 13(2): 253–74.

Teuber, R. (2010). 'Geographical Indications of Origin as a Tool of Product Differentiation: the Case of Coffee' *Journal of International Food & Agribusiness Marketing* 22: 277–98.

Teuber, R. (2011). 'Consumers' and Producers' Expectations Towards Geographical Indications: Empirical Evidence for a German Case Study' *British Food Journal* 113(7): 900–918.

Torsen, M. (2005). 'Apples and Oranges: French and American Models of Geographical Indication Policy Demonstrate an International Lack of Consensus' 95 *TMR* 1415.

Treagar, A. (2003). 'From Stilton to Vimto: Using Food History to Re-think Typical Products in Rural Development' *Sociologia Ruralis* 43(2): 92, 439

Tregear, A., F. Arfini, G. Belletti and A. Marescotti (2007). 'Regional Foods and Rural Development: the Role of Product Qualification' *Journal of Rural Studies* 23: 12–22.

Treagar, A. and G. Giraud (2011). 'Geographical Indications, Consumers and Citizens' in Barham and Sylvander (eds) (2011), 63–74.

United Nations Industrial Development Organization (UNIDO) (2010). *Adding Value to Traditional Products of Regional Origin. A Guide to Creating a Quality Consortium*, Vienna, UNIDO.

Vandecandelaere, E., F. Arfini, G. Belletti and A. Marescotti (2009). *Linking People, Places and Products: A Guide for Promoting Quality Linked to Geographical Origin and Sustainable Geographical Indications* Rome, Food and Agriculture Organization of the United Nations (FAO) and SINER-GI.

Vincent, M. (2007). 'Extending Protection at the WTO to Products Other Than Wines and Spirits: Who Will Benefit?' *Estey Centre Journal of International Law and Trade Policy* 8(1): 57–68.

Vittori, M. (2010). 'The International Debate on Geographical Indications (GIs): the Point of View of the Global Coalition of GI Producers – oriGIn' *The Journal of World Intellectual Property* 13(2): 304–14.

Vivas-Egui, D. and C. Spennemann (2006). 'The Treatment of Geographical Indications in Recent Regional and Bilateral Free Trade Agreements' in M. P. Pugatch (ed.), *The Intellectual Property Debate: Perspectives from Law, Economics and Political Economy*, Cheltenham, UK, Edward Elgar, 305–40.

Vroom-Cramer, B. M. (1997). 'PDOs and PGIs: Geographical Denominations Protected' *European Food Law Review* 3: 336–375.

Wilkof, N. and S. Uzrad (2008). 'PDO/GI: In the Matter of the Appellation of Origin for "JAFFA"' *Journal of Intellectual Property Law & Practice* 3(1): 17–20.

Williams, R. M. (2007). 'Do Geographical Indications Promote Sustainable Rural Development: Two UK Case Studies and Implications for New Zealand Rural Development Policy' Lincoln University, available at http://researcharchive.lincoln.ac.nz/dspace/bitstream/10182/585/1/williams_mnr mee.pdf

WIPO (n.d.). *Geographical Indications. An Introduction*, Geneva, WIPO. Wongprawmas, R., M. Canavari, R. Haas and D. Asioli (2012). 'Gatekeepers' Perceptions of Thai Geographical Indication Products in Europe' *Journal of International Food & Agribusiness Marketing* 24(3): 185–200.

Yu, P. (2011). 'Six Secret (and Now Open) Fears of ACTA' *SMU L. R.* 64: 101–249.

Zacher, F. G. (2005). 'Pass the Parmesan: Geographic Indications in the United States and the European Union – Can There Be Compromise?' *Emory int'l L. Rev.* 19: 427–42.

Zanzig, L. (2013). 'The Perfect Pairing: Protecting U.S. Geographical Indications with a Sino-American Wine Registry' *Washington Law Review* 88: 723–57.

Zou, J. (2005). 'Rice and Cheese, Anyone? The Fight over TRIPS Geographical Indications Continues' *Brooklyn Journal of International Law* 30(3): 1141–174.

Zylberg, P. (2002). 'Geographical Indications v. Trademarks: The Lisbon Agreement: A Violation of TRIPS?' *U. Baltimore Intell. Prop. L. J.* 11: 1–69.

INDEX